WATERLOO
The Campaign of 1815

Volume 2

Winner of the Templer Medal for British Army History
of the Society for Army Historical Research

Winner of the Duke of Wellington Medal for Military History
of the Royal United Services Institute

21730

Altesse Royale, en but aux factions qui divisent
mon pays et à l'inimitié des plus grandes
puissances de l'Europe, j'ai terminé ma carrière
politique et je viens comme Themistocle m'asseoir
sur le foyer du peuple Britannique. je me
mets sous la protection de ses lois que je
reclame de votre altesse Royale comme au
plus puissant, au plus constant et au plus
généreux de mes ennemis.

Rochefort 13 Juillet 1815

Napoleon

WATERLOO
The Campaign of 1815

Volume 2

FROM WATERLOO TO THE RESTORATION OF PEACE IN EUROPE

John Hussey

Foreword by

Major General Mungo Melvin

Greenhill Books

Waterloo, The Campaign of 1815
This paperback edition published in 2019
by Greenhill Books

First published in 2017 by
Greenhill Books,
c/o Pen & Sword Books Ltd,
47 Church Street, Barnsley,
S. Yorkshire, S70 2AS

www.greenhillbooks.com
contact@greenhillbooks.com

ISBN: 978–1–78438–538–5

CIP data records for this title are available from the British Library

Designed and typeset by Donald Sommerville
Maps by Peter Wilkinson

Printed and bound in the UK by TJ International Ltd, Padstow

Typeset in 11/13.7 pt Arno Pro Small Text & Arno Pro Light Display

---

Frontispiece: Napoleon's letter from Rochefort, dated 13 July 1815,
surrendering to the Prince Regent. *(Royal Collection)*

The lyf so short, the craft so long to lerne,
Thassay so hard, so sharp the conquering.

Geoffrey Chaucer, *The Parlement of Fowles*

If I have seen further it is by standing on the shoulders of Giants.

Isaac Newton to Robert Hooke, 1676

Contents

APPENDICES

ORDERS OF BATTLE

Plates and Illustrations

Plates

Plates and Illustrations

Maps, Diagrams and Tables

Maps

Charts and Diagrams

Tables

Foreword

by Major General (ret'd) Mungo Melvin, CB, OBE

EDWARD CREASY'S CLASSIC WORK of military history, *The Fifteen Decisive Battles of the World,* was first published in 1851, the year of the Great Exhibition. With this demonstration of British industrial prowess in mind, Creasy triumphantly concluded his account of Waterloo, his fifteenth battle, by claiming that 'no battlefield':

> ever witnessed a victory more noble, than that, which England, under her Sovereign Lady and her Royal Prince, is now teaching the peoples of the earth to achieve over selfish prejudices and international feuds, in the great cause of the general promotion of the industry and welfare of mankind.

Although such patriotic bombast reads oddly today, it must be remembered that Creasy penned his words at nearly the midpoint of Britain's long peace following the Napoleonic Wars. The brief interruption of the Crimean War had yet to break the heady national optimism of the times.

While Napoleon had certainly lost the Battle of Waterloo on 18 June 1815, Wellington only had secured victory over the French with the assistance of Blücher's Prussians. Yet overall Britain won the resultant peace. This second volume of John Hussey's magisterial account of the Waterloo campaign helps explain why. Wellington, as commander-in-chief of the Anglo-Allied army, not only fought Napoleon's proud army to a standstill on the low ridge of Mont St Jean, thus garnering much military prestige and glory in the process, but also exercised a moderating influence in the Allied cause thereafter. Rather than seeking a destructive vengeance on the French, as the Prussians were bent on, Wellington's diplomatic skills as a political general helped shape the capitulation of Paris on 3 July 1815, which effectively terminated both the Waterloo campaign, and the Napoleonic Wars as a whole, without further recourse to costly battle.

Waterloo, famously, had been a close-run affair of hard pounding, coming two days after the preliminary actions at Ligny and Quatre Bras on 16 June

1815, both described in detail in Volume 1. In terms of intensity of casualties in both short time and confined space, Waterloo was probably the hardest and closest-fought battle of the Napoleonic era. The explanation is quite simple: there was little to distinguish between the armies concerned in either quality or quantity. Therefore it is entirely apt in my view for John Hussey to quote from Field Marshal Sir Douglas Haig's final despatch following the end of the First World War:

> In every stage of the wearing-out struggle losses will necessarily be heavy on both sides, for in it the price of victory is paid. If the opposing forces are approximately equal in numbers, in courage, in morale and in equipment, there is no way of avoiding payment of the price or of eliminating this phase of the struggle.

Such truths historians, politicians and soldiers ignore at their peril for seldom are there cheaply won shortcuts to success and victory. And so it had proved at Waterloo. Whereas in the case of the campaign of 1815 the 'wearing out' stage only took a few days, the continuous engagement on the Western Front of the First World War, the opening and closing stages of which took place over much the same piece of terrain, lasted over four years.

While battlefield tactics and weapon technologies steadily evolve, much of land combat has an enduring nature. Thus it is still possible to draw valuable lessons for today from the Battle of Waterloo some two centuries and more ago. The senior commanders concerned – the 'giants' – had to make a series of difficult decisions in the heat of battle; to inspire and lead their troops throughout; and to attempt to make good wherever possible their own miscalculations or mistakes (or those of their subordinates), of which there were several. In this respect, John Hussey spares none of Napoleon, Wellington or Blücher in his meticulous but fair-minded analysis, bringing the actions of the last's chief of staff, August Graf Neithardt von Gneisenau, into particularly sharp relief.

Carl von Clausewitz, who served as the chief of staff in Thielemann's III Corps that fought Marshal Grouchy in the parallel fight at Wavre on 18–19 June 1815, reminds us of the ever-present elements of friction and chance in war. The Battle of Waterloo proved no exception to the general rule that no plan survives first contact with the enemy (Moltke the Elder's dictum): even the apparently simple task can turn out far less straightforward and take far longer than originally envisaged. The much-delayed, but ultimately vital, Prussian march from Wavre to the Waterloo battlefield on 18 June 1815 surely serves as a case in point. Yet it is tempting for retired armchair generals, academic historians and battlefield guides alike to re-run or war game the battle far away from the contemporary realities – the real fear and fog of war. John Hussey, however, avoids such temptations. He tells the story of Waterloo strictly 'as it was', and not as it *might* have been, carefully distinguishing between cause and effect, scrupulously dissecting order and counter-order, and painstakingly comparing at times quite contradictory accounts of particular engagements, battles and campaign.

Furthermore, as masterfully as Hussey narrates the events of 17 and 18 June 1815, what makes this volume stand out is his equally compelling examination of Waterloo's immediate aftermath – the Allies' march to Paris, the abdication of Napoleon and the forging of the peace – and his sage reflections on the main battle. Throughout, readers will be engaged not only by his vivid descriptions of decisions and combat, but also by his compassion in documenting the terrible human price of conflict. I therefore warmly commend this second volume as Hew Strachan did so eloquently for the first: John Hussey has taken the historical field of Waterloo by storm. He richly deserves to hold it for a very long time to come.

JOHN HUSSEY is a Cambridge graduate who spent thirty years working for BP around the world. He has been writing articles for journals on British military history for many years and served as a member of the International Historical Committee for the Restoration of the Waterloo Battlefield. He is the author of *Marlborough: Hero of Blenheim* as well as numerous articles on aspects of the 1815 campaign, the campaigns of the First World War and the role of Sir Douglas Haig. He is a Fellow of the Royal Historical Society.

Preface

THIS VOLUME CONCLUDES my study of the 1815 campaign and in all likelihood the historical researches that began in 1988 when, following my retirement from globe-trotting after thirty years' service with BP, I first met that great historian the late John Terraine. The book was conceived long after his death in 2003, but a mutual friend – Captain Christopher Page, RN (rtd), a hands-on engineer officer, an historian of the magnificent Royal Naval Division of 1914–1918, and latterly head of the Naval Historical Branch – on reaching the end of my first Waterloo volume touched me deeply in writing 'John would have been proud of you.' Those words have more than repaid the weary months when it seemed almost impossible that I could shape my researches into something coherent, let alone convincing.

During many of these last thirty years I worked as an historical 'powder monkey', researching and writing up topics, often in great detail, and producing some result that could be delivered to the 'master gunner' for his use; the small article that would in its way help an author of some future great book. That skill in detail, in explaining the specific incident, and the reshaping of some event, has a value; and to be a footnote in some masterpiece of the next Gibbon or a new Macaulay or a future Maitland brings its own reward.

So it required something seismic to enlarge my perspectives and to switch my line of investigation, to decide to write a large book; just as, once that had actually happened, it needed the quiet persistent encouragement from friends and those dear to me to help me write what has proved to be a *very* large book. Their names graced my first Preface, and if I now pick out for mention in this second Preface one friend only it is because without Lionel Leventhal the project would have foundered totally in the near shipwreck of my life in 2014.

Readers of this second instalment may find it less full of fresh or surprising matter than the first. For after all the great battle is familiar, and not many histories devote much time to events much before or after *the great four days*. Moreover, in the telling of 18 June I have sought to retain some sense of scale between that one day and the inception, events, and aftermath of the Hundred Days' adventure: as Sir Hew Strachan pointed out in his Foreword to Volume 1, Clausewitz spoke of a battle as a phase in 'the purposes *of the war*'. In a story a thousand pages long I think rather more than two hundred devoted to 18 June is not unreasonable.

Due to the size of Volume 1, Orders of Battle could not be included there, and we judged that as the second and shorter volume would appear within months, their absence would not be an irritant for very long. They now take their due place at the end of this volume, but I suspect that specialists may find them a happy hunting ground for error, just as they may for the statistics appearing in various places. In part this is because standard authorities disagree between themselves, because the original compilers of returns sometimes made mistakes, because fresh error can creep in during successive transcriptions – and in my own case because at 83 and with cataracts, proofing has been a troublesome tiring business. What I warned my late friend Paddy Griffith about when discussing Sir Charles Oman's pages of statistics (see Chapter 36, Section V) is sadly as true as ever in my own case.

History being an endless debate, Volume 1 had no sooner gone to the printers than my comment that new material 'is indeed still surfacing', proved almost embarrassingly accurate. A most important document emerged thanks to an American researcher, Stephen Beckett's, enthusiastic quest. This letter, dictated by Napoleon to the trusted General Bertrand on 10 June 1815, materially affected the story told in my Chapter 19 of French planning for the campaign; but although concerning an important point of detail, it has a further significance as touching on the Emperor's method of command. The result is a fifteen-page Appendix 4 to my second volume.

So the old story changes, but that does not diminish my admiration and respect for the earlier writers, many, like the great Prussian historian Pflugk-Harttung, working over a hundred years ago. The reader will note from my 'Sources Consulted' that a fair number of modern works have been used, but that probably the older ones predominate. For when scrutinised closely and then copied by hand a word at a time, I found that they often yielded information and valuable insights not apparent on a first reading. Pure scholarship is a fine thing in itself and among such scholars I admire the great Latinist A. E. Housman, who in his Cambridge Inaugural Lecture as Kennedy Professor in 1911 made a telling plea for our predecessors, and one that I support:

> If a man, fifty or a hundred years after his death, is still remembered and accounted a great man, there is a presumption in his favour which no living man can claim ... It is the dead and not the living who have most advanced our learning and science; and though their knowledge may have been superseded, there is no supersession of reason and intelligence. Clear wits and right thinking are essentially neither of today nor yesterday, but historically [i.e. in the span of human history] they are rather of yesterday than of today... If our concepts of scholarship and our methods of procedure are at variance with theirs, it is not indeed a certainty or a necessity that we are wrong, but it is a good working hypothesis... Do not let us disregard our contemporaries, but let us regard our predecessors more.

*

It is a pleasure once more to thank my dedicated production team of Michael Leventhal, Peter Wilkinson my cartographer who took my changes of mind and late instructions with splendid equanimity, and above all the endlessly patient, minutely careful, and ever agreeable Donald Sommerville, my copy-editor. Together they have worked so hard to ensure that the book should be worthy of its great subject and that the two volumes should stand side by side as a most handsome set.

As Sir Hew was to my first volume, so Major-General Mungo Melvin stands godfather with his very generous Foreword to Volume 2. I had long since been struck by the incisiveness and masterly treatment of his study *Manstein: Hitler's Greatest General,* and when some years later I met Mungo at a conference, I found to my delight not only a man of strong but considered views, but a genial one as well, who had gone to my Cambridge college, Downing, twenty-three years after me. I thank him not only for what he has written but also for his probing questions as he read my text, forcing me into further and useful reflection.

*

Now it is time to bid my account farewell and wish it a fair wind. But I hope that it may be said of my two volumes what was said about the greatest of modern English historians, Frederic William Maitland (1850–1906), when unveiling his memorial in Westminster Abbey: '*he sought to open a subject up, not also close it down*'.

*

Illustration Acknowledgements

I thank The Royal Collection and Her Majesty Queen Elizabeth II, for her gracious permission to reproduce Napoleon's letter to the Prince Regent dated Rochefort, 13 July 1815, as the frontispiece. For supplying the illustrations reproduced in the plates I also thank the curators and staff of the Anne S. K. Brown Military Collection; the Fitzwilliam Museum, Cambridge; the Historic England Archive; the Musée Wellington at Waterloo; National Museums Scotland; and the Victoria and Albert Museum.

Editorial Conventions

As the corps system was used to a greater or lesser extent by all three armies in the 1815 campaign, I have adopted Roman numerals for the Allies and Arabic numerals and italics for the French, so as to make the difference plainer for the reader. Thus: British II Corps, Prussian II Corps, but French *2e Corps*. The same non-italic and italic rule applies to smaller units in the respective armies: 1/52nd Foot, 13th Infantry Regiment, *13e Ligne*.

Prologue

The first volume of *Waterloo, The Campaign of 1815*, told of Europe's defeat of Napoleon in 1814, of the problems that arose thereafter in France and in central Europe, of the stresses between the victorious powers and how, in early 1815, Napoleon judged that he might once again become ruler of France (and a France larger than its post-1814 borders). It described his sudden return, the collapse of opposition to him in France, and how a fresh European coalition determined to defeat him once and for all.

The coalition's primary intention was totally clear, but the many secondary questions – the future of France, the establishment of a coalition strategy, the commanding, manning, payment and feeding of grouped allied armies took an unconscionable time to agree. I considered these matters essential to an understanding of how the campaign came to be fought, and my book bulked large as a result.

Such problems produced an unforeseen situation. The eastern front beyond the Rhine, so integral a part of the allied plan for the invasion of France, was still awaiting a final agreed plan in mid-June because of bickering monarchs and a weak high commander. Meanwhile in Belgium the two allied armies under Blücher and Wellington, by now in reasonable though not perfect shape for the impending task, were marking time, necessarily dispersed, and had increasingly taken the view that Napoleon would most probably (though not certainly) conduct a defensive campaign behind river-lines in France. Together Blücher and Wellington judged that, united, they had a 2:1 numerical superiority over Napoleon. Wellington's army was an assemblage of contingents and the Prussians had doubts over its cohesion; some of Prussia's forces were relatively raw. But provided they held together they were confident of riding Napoleon's blows: numbers would tell. By contrast Napoleon's smaller but veteran army was fanatically devoted to him, though there were difficult relationships among the higher commanders. The continuing delays beyond the Rhine gave Napoleon his chance. He snatched the initative and attacked the allies in Belgium, trusting to defeat decisively each in turn, to capture Brussels within three days and Antwerp within seven. He would re-annexe Belgium and the Rhineland and then settle matters with the defeated powers whose will he would have broken.

It had been the Emperor's intention to attack on a favourite anniversary, 14 June. Confused orders forced a delay of one day, but it seemed the allies were not aware of the impending offensive. He would first attack the Prussians, one of whose four army corps was exposed very close to the frontier around Charleroi. He would thrust them back north-east and away from the easternmost Brussels highway, take on the rest of the Prussian army as it hastened up from the far rear, and smash it decisively. One wing of Napoleon's army would meanwhile thrust up that Brussels highway as far as possible. The thrust would sever communication between Blücher and Wellington and, once the Prussians were smashed, the French could pivot north and march on Brussels and a now isolated Wellington.

Blücher and Wellington were both surprised; they were still widely dispersed. The Prussians at least knew at once that they were being battered by Napoleon, but their messages to the Duke were inadequate to the occasion. He, by contrast, could not be sure that this first attack was not a feint and that the main attack might yet come in his sector, which contained three great highways to Brussels and one to Ghent and Antwerp. His concentration had to be rushed and still without certainty as to Napoleon's real intention, but unlike the Prussians Wellington had planned his concentration far back from the frontier so that contact with the enemy could not occur on Day 1, whereas by Day 2 Napoleon's plans would be clearer. Thus in Wellington's mind any major battle would be on Day 3, by which time both allies would be concentrated and assembled close to each other. The Prussians on the other hand were intent on a major battle well forward and on Day 2, irrespective of whether Wellington was present or not.

The first day, 15 June, went generally very well for Napoleon. He tumbled the isolated Prussian troops, took Charleroi and moved north-east to Fleurus. By nightfall much, but not all, of his army, was in its intended positions north of the River Sambre at Charleroi and his right wing and centre were well placed for a further advance on the 16th. His left wing had made good progress up the Brussels highway but, having marched 25 miles, and fought several combats, it just failed to take the Quatre Bras crossroads that the two allies depended upon for communication. Nevertheless the crossroads could easily be taken at first light on the morrow, and the timetable that the

Emperor had set himself was not badly adrift. However, it did require the most perfect understanding between imperial headquarters and the semi-independent commanders of the two wings, and already on this first day confusion and changes of orders had been too noticeable in the French high command.

Napoleon expected his cavalry to drive the Prussians back north-eastwards on 16 June but it soon became clear that Blücher was standing firm just north of Fleurus and intending to give battle. Napoleon marshalled his central forces but had to wait until about 1 p.m. for his most rearward corps to join the battle line. Two Prussian corps held a line of quickly fortified villages along an S-shaped brook, in the central stretch of which was Ligny, all the villages being backed by more infantry and artillery up the slopes to the crest line, along which ran the high road from Namur to Quatre Bras. On this crest road and to the east stood the small III Corps awaiting the arrival of the most easterly IV Corps hastening from beyond Namur. But belatedly it was learned that IV Corps could not arrive that day, so that support from Wellington had now to be sought.

Wellington's army on 15 June had received orders to shift away from a western defence to one more protective of the southern approaches to Brussels and Nivelles. Only at midnight did the Duke learn of a French presence at Quatre Bras and the unexplained abandonment of that highroad by the Prussians. His army now had to scramble from the west and from Brussels to block the French, and he himself went forward, reaching the crossroads in mid-morning of the 16th and finding it still held by some of his own Netherlands units. Everything appeared quiet. There was no sign of the French nor of the Prussians. He rode 5 miles to Blücher's command post, saw the Prussians and French massed in battle array, and discussed possible actions with Blücher. He would support the Prussians if he was not himself attacked by the French.

Napoleon meanwhile discovered that Ney, commanding his left wing, was wasting the morning. He sent him imperative orders to take Quatre Bras and then swing round east against the Prussians to produce an annihilating success. Ney launched his attack on the crossroads at 2 p.m., but just before the thin screen of defenders gave way the first of Wellington's reinforcements came up. From a situation of overwhelming superiority at 2 p.m. Ney found the balance steadily moving against him. Each successive thrust he made during the afternoon found the Duke's reinforcements arriving just in time. Finally in late evening he was forced to retire south onto his previous camping place. At no time had he found himself free to turn against the Prussian flank.

Soon after opening his attack on Ligny Napoleon had realised that he needed more support. The Prussian resistance was tough and unyielding and Napoleon's numbers were insufficient. He had left a small corps in the rear, available for himself or for Ney. He called that forward. But he also summarily called upon one of Ney's two large army corps to leave Ney's force and come to his own left flank. What then followed was one of the great command muddles of all time. D'Erlon, the corps commander, received the order as he was moving up to support Ney. He turned east to march to the Emperor. Ney, desperate for troops, overrode the order and called d'Erlon back. The latter, though nearing the battlefield of Ligny, left part of his force there, stationary, and took the rest back to Ney, arriving after dark with the battle of Quatre Bras ended. Due to confusion in orders and weak leadership, d'Erlon's 20,000 men served neither at Ligny nor at Quatre Bras, when their intervention on either field might have been decisive.

Nor was that all. By late afternoon in stifling sultry weather and with villages ablaze there was near stalemate along the Ligny stream. Casualties were very heavy and still the Prussians were holding out. Yet when d'Erlon's urgently awaited force was perceived in the distance, Napoleon ordered his left flank to cease attacking and be ready lest that body should be a foe. The uncertainty took some time to resolve, by which time half d'Erlon's force had retired and the rest simply stood still. Vital, irrecoverable time lost played to the Prussians' advantage. At 7 p.m. Napoleon launched a final attack with his exhausted troops, in a great thunderstorm. He backed it with his elite *Garde*, and the Prussians finally gave way. In a last rally Blücher was unhorsed and hurt but was carried from the field, and his chief of staff accepted that the battle was lost. The two Prussian corps most heavily engaged dispersed and went north over the crest and into the night, the third corps fell back north-east.

But although the casualties on both sides were heavy, and some 11,000 Prussians had fled, it was not the annihilating victory Napoleon needed. He could not long afford to incur such casualties when the outcome was not decisive. His troops launched no pursuit. In the Napoleonic timetable 'Brussels by 17 June' was now infeasible: a day had been lost. And meanwhile the Prussians, or some of them, were still 'in being' and Wellington was certainly undefeated. As I said at the end of Volume 1:

> The first two days of this campaign have now passed. Opinions and plans have had to undergo sudden and great changes. Misunderstandings and mistakes have occurred – and on both sides. The fighting has seen increasingly savage action in an attempt to secure a decisive victory on

the second day, and the outcome has fallen short of that. The balance of advantage as it stood on the morning of Thursday 15 June has been shifting, first one way, but now another. Despite mistakes and setbacks each of the three greatest commanders of their time is bringing his mind and will to bear so that decisive victory shall indeed shortly be achieved for his side. What Saturday 17 June 1815 will bring we shall see at the start of Volume 2.

Chapter 31

The Allies

Dawn to Midday, 17 June

I

THE FIGHTING AT LIGNY AND QUATRE BRAS had died down with the onset of darkness around 9 p.m., and overnight there were no messages exchanged between the two allies. From 2.30 p.m. on the 16th the fighting on both fronts had been intense and by 5.30 p.m. it was understood by both Allied commanders that no decision had been reached at Ligny although the balance of advantage at Quatre Bras that the French had originally enjoyed was moving to equilibrium. During the afternoon Müffling had sent several messages to Ligny about the struggle, and although a Prussian messenger from Ligny, Major von Winterfeldt, was shot down at Thyle, about a mile and a half from Quatre Bras, and was unable to deliver a message,[1] he was followed by Lieutenant von Wussow, who told Wellington at between 5 and 6 p.m. that the Prussians thought they could hold the Ligne brook till nightfall, but being without Bülow's support they would need Wellington's help if they were to secure victory. Wussow saw for himself how matters stood at Quatre Bras and was told by the Duke that his immediate intention to pass to the counter-attack was the best help that he could offer. Wussow reported this to Gneisenau at a time when Ligny was still held by the Prussians (therefore before 8 p.m. at the latest). Müffling said that another messenger reached Quatre Bras at about 8.30 p.m. reporting that Blücher was still at his command post and hoping to retain Ligny, while the injured Hardinge sent his brother to Wellington with a message that arrived after dark, that the Prussians were 'still holding their position' despite confusion and some desertions. Certainly the Prince of Orange and FitzRoy Somerset believed that night that the Prussians had retained the field or even gained the advantage. Blücher's final attempt to snatch victory, his fall, Gneisenau's assumption of command, and the successful French attack all occurred between 7.30 and 8 p.m. in the final hour of daylight, at a time when both headquarters seem to have felt that

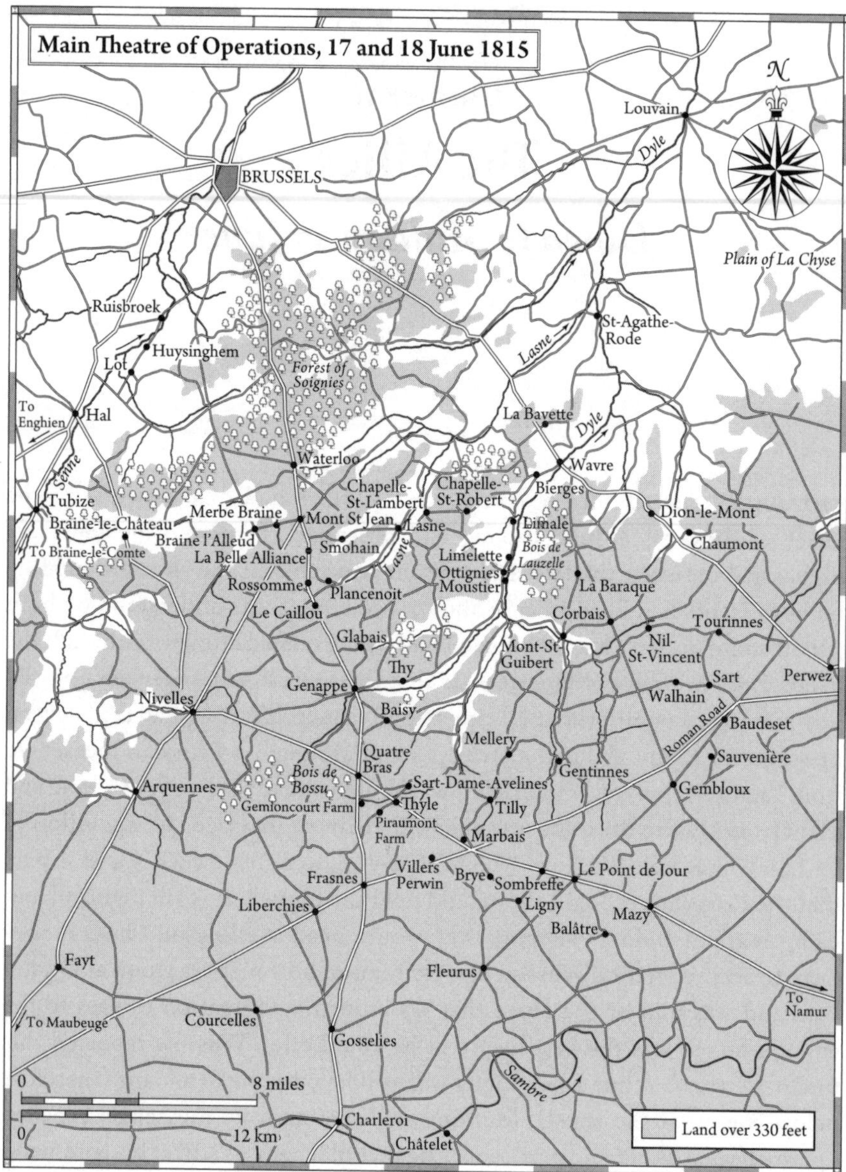

sending couriers across a battlefield on a moonless night would have been too difficult.[2]

The night of 16/17 June was not trouble-free at Quatre Bras and, as shadows moved, peering sentries fired occasional shots. At one time this turned into a prolonged musketry exchange between French and Hanoverian pickets as a result of which, for the day of 17 June, the Bremen battalion reported 4 killed, 39 wounded, and 18 missing, out of the entire 1st Hanoverian Brigade's casualty figure of 121.[3] The firing was actually heard by Thielemann as far away as Gembloux. But by full morning the situation seemed calm enough, and on waking at Genappe Wellington's thoughts were on renewing the action and pushing Ney back.

As neither army sent out messengers overnight, on rising Wellington rode from Genappe to Quatre Bras while ordering one of his ADCs, Lieutenant-Colonel Sir Alexander Gordon, to take a patrol and ride east to establish the facts. Around 3 a.m. Gordon left with Captain Grey and some troopers of the 10th Hussars, and somewhere near Tilly he encountered men of the second brigade of the Prussian II Corps cavalry and possibly their commander Sohr, and thus learned that they were the rearguard of the retreat from Ligny. Enemy scouts were also seen. Gordon returned and reached Wellington between 7.30 and 8 a.m.[4]

The previous day's assessments from Lieutenant Wussow, possibly from a second Prussian officer, and even from Captain Hardinge now appeared to have been far too optimistic. Müffling says that the Duke looked 'as if he wished to ask whether I had known the thing and concealed it from him on good grounds. But on my saying quite naturally, "This is probably the account which the officer, who was shot down, was bringing me," and adding, "but now you cannot remain here, my Lord," he immediately entered with me as usual on the measures to be taken . . . We knew nothing farther of the Prussian army but the direction of their retreat . . .'[5] FitzRoy Somerset wrote that they were surprised at Müffling's saying that the Prussian destination was Wavre, the Duke remarking, '*Ma foi, c'est bien loin*' ('Faith! That's a very long way'). Müffling then sent off one of his own ADCs, Lieutenant Wucherer, to find Blücher and tell him that *if* the Prussians returned to the attack Wellington would *still advance* from Quatre Bras that day.[6]

Shortly after Gordon's return there arrived Lieutenant von Massow, with word from Gneisenau, the acting C-in-C. His arrival is usually given as around 8 a.m. on 17 June, and certainly cannot have been much later than 9;[7] this implies that he may have started out from Mellery a little after daybreak. His message was that the Prussians needed to eat and to replenish their ammunition but, after that, they were prepared to return to the attack if Wellington did likewise. The reply was immediately given, and can be seen in a letter of Gneisenau written at noon on this day. With Wucherer's and Massow's reports fresh in the mind, he wrote of a message from Wellington early that morning ('*heute früh*') in which the Duke had said that he would 'offer battle at Waterloo in front of the forest of Soignies', if the Prussians sent two corps (*zwei Korps geben wollen*').[8]

II

Wellington now had to disengage his forces from their over-exposed position. Several eye-witnesses recorded seeing him from early to mid-morning, and there are the usual occasional discrepancies in their recollections. Four are particularly vivid, and cannot be omitted, even if they do not exactly agree, and all demonstrate the extraordinary calm that he evinced as he recast his plans.[9]

Captain Bowles of the Coldstream Guards, the Duke of Richmond's close assistant and friend, met Wellington, who conversed with him for some time until a staff officer came up and said something to the Duke. Wellington had said to Bowles that he was surprised to have heard nothing from Blücher; now he turned and said, 'Old Blücher has had a good licking and gone back to Wavre, eighteen miles. As he has gone back, we must go too. I suppose in England they will say we have been licked. I can't help it; as they have gone back, we must go too.' He stood there and issued the orders within five minutes.

Lieutenant James Hope of the 92nd Foot saw Wellington ride up to Quatre Bras (this must have been at around 4 a.m.), and as the morning was cold the Duke called, 'Ninety-Second, I will be obliged to you for a little fire.' The men rushed to find materials and built a fire in front of a bivouac of tree branches, and it was here that he received the news of the Prussian retreat. He remained inside the shelter for a while, met there all his senior commanders including Lord Hill, and issued the orders for the retreat, then,

> for an hour walked alone in front of it. Now and then his meditations were interrupted by a courier with a note, who, the moment he had delivered it, retired some distance to wait his Grace's will. The Field Marshal had a small switch in his right hand, the one end of which he frequently put to his mouth, apparently unconscious that he was doing so. His left hand was thrown carelessly behind his back.

Constant Rebecque noted in his journal that the Duke,

> seated in a hut of foliage behind Quatre Bras farm dictates his marching orders to Colonel De Lancey. According to these orders the army must start moving at 10 a.m. in order to take up the position in front of Waterloo, where the Duke will have his headquarters.

Sir Hussey Vivian commanded the cavalry on the left wing along the Namur road and it was one of his regiments from which Grey's patrol had been selected. Vivian rode up to the Duke. His timing differs slightly from the others (he was writing in 1839), and he suggests that it was after the day had warmed up. He recounts that:

> The Duke received some despatches from England, and shortly after that I think he gave orders for the retreat ... He then lay himself down on the ground, covered his head with one of the newspapers he had been reading, and appeared to fall asleep, and in this way he remained some time; when he again rose and mounted his horse and rode down the field in front of Quatre Bras a little distance, and looked about through his glass ... expressing his astonishment at the perfect quiet of the enemy.

III

The first task was to evacuate the wounded. From first light Wellington's army had been searching in the corn for wounded survivors of the previous day's battle. Then at around 10 a.m. the assembly was called and soon after the contingents began their retreat. So early an hour was made necessary by the impossibility of moving at speed. A sad procession of men, horses, and ambulances trailed north among and between the marching regiments. Several observers recorded the scene. Sir A. S. Frazer claimed that 'on our side we left the enemy nothing but his own wounded, and the dead on both sides. Our own wounded we brought off on cavalry horses, except such as could not be found in the standing corn.' Clark Kennedy's squadron of the Royal Dragoons was employed 'in conveying as many of the wounded men to the rear as were able to bear the motion of the horse, and a considerable number were removed in this manner to the rear of the position of Waterloo, though several that were severely wounded were necessarily left behind'. Basil Jackson remarked that Picton first knew that he would have to abandon the Quatre Bras position from the Duke's order 'to gather in the wounded'. He added:

> the first sign of the army being about to retire was the gathering in of the wounded, troopers were sent out to the front, who placed such disabled men as could sit in a saddle on their horses, they themselves walking by their side, lending them support with one hand while with the other they led the docile animals. Sometimes a poor fellow might be seen toppling from side to side, requiring two men to keep him in his seat, the horses moving gently, as if conscious that the motion was torture to their suffering riders. Some required to be carried in a blanket, but, one way or another, every man that could be found with life in him was brought in and sent to the rear. I think it was near mid-day ere this duty was completed.

A Nassauer noted that 'on the road were ambulances carrying the wounded and an endless wagon train'.[10]

Lord FitzRoy Somerset wrote that Lord Hill had ridden to Quatre Bras ahead of his marching forces and was there in the morning (as Lieutenant Hope had also noted). Thus Wellington was able to set out his intentions to his three senior subordinates, the Prince of Orange, Lord Uxbridge and Lord Hill, and these were embodied in orders timed '9 a.m.', itemising each division's duties for the day. They indicated several destinations for the different units or columns. For instance, the 4th Division, marching from Braine-le-Comte, was now ordered to remain there; the baggage on the road from Braine to Nivelles was ordered back to Braine and thence to Hal and Brussels; three divisions were ordered to march 'to Waterloo'; the spare musket ammunition and the reserve artillery were to be taken north of Genappe, while the reserve artillery wagons were 'to be parked in the Forest of Soignies'.[11]

The infantry and foot artillery formed up, and the retirement began with the Belgians, Nassauers and Dutch, followed by the Brunswickers, Hanoverians and British. Some of Alten's men marched on the right of the high road to keep it unencumbered, probably to assist the movement of the wounded. FitzRoy Somerset suggests that the retirement was even 'leisurely'.[12]

IV

The Prussian retreat during the night of 16/17 June had been preceded by a sizeable mass of 11,000 fugitives and deserters. Blücher had disappeared and was perhaps dead, and Gneisenau had initially thought to re-group at Tilly, but later changed this to Mellery. But the lack of any pursuit enabled a degree of control to re-emerge, and by daybreak much of I and II Corps (minus their deserters) were resting between Tilly, Mellery and Gentinnes, Grolman commanding the rearguard. Grolman indeed seems to have been the leading spirit at this time, for it was he who had sent Wussow along the roads and gradually given direction to the retreat,[13] with Wavre as the rallying point in the north. It was Grolman, as QMG, who prescribed the sites for the army to bivouac, close to Wavre: two on each side of the River Dyle: I Corps at Bierges (1 mile west of Wavre), II at St Anne (now in Wavre), III at la Bavette (on a hill north of Wavre), IV at Dion-le-Mont (2 miles south-east of Wavre), and any artillery needing repair going to Maastricht.

As the headquarters staff sought shelter for the night in Mellery, they came across Nostitz and the battered and bruised Commander-in-Chief sheltering there, laid on straw and only partly conscious. Nostitz recorded that the old man slept well and was even able to mount a horse in the morning. His personal servants were nowhere to be found, and his beautiful horse was dead, so he went on with the horse that Under-Officer Schneider had found for him. As he swayed along the way to Wavre the troops cheered him, and the effect on both Prince and the men must have been electrifying, for when Nostitz spoke of the troops' rising morale – and desire to resume fighting – Blücher replied 'That is my firm intention [*fester Wille*]'. Napoleon's admiring words to Neil Campbell return to mind: 'That old devil, if he was beaten, then the next moment he would rise again ready for battle.' But the ride exhausted him and on reaching Wavre he was put to bed there and slept for much of the day, having returned the horse to Schneider with a gift of 20 gold Fredericks: *noblesse oblige*.[14]

Towards noon Lieutenant Massow arrived from Quatre Bras, bearing Wellington's message of being ready to fight at Mont St Jean if provided with Prussian assistance. However, at this time the high command faced a serious ammunition shortage, and was not certain when III and IV Corps could be expected at Wavre. Colonel Röhl, temporarily commanding the Prussian artillery during the later hours of 16 June, had sent the artillery parks of I and II Corps back to Gembloux; these he later ordered to continue to Wavre. Orders had gone to Liège to send the siege artillery back as far as Maastricht and, if necessary, even to destroy the cannon foundry. This had to be countermanded, and so messengers were sent to Maastricht to bring ammunition in carts and wagons of any description if the normal ammunition wagons were insufficient. Similar orders went to Cologne, Wesel and Münster.[15]

Contact had been lost with III and IV Corps. What had happened was this. The last orders sent to Lieutenant-General Thielemann told him that if he could not join the western units of the army he was to fall back about 3 miles north-eastwards on Gembloux, seek General Bülow, and await further orders. III Corps had begun to move at 2 a.m., with its 9th Brigade and cavalry forming the rearguard on the Namur road. Most of the corps was at Gembloux by 6 a.m. or a little after. Patrols went out and found Bülow at Baudeset (3 miles north of Gembloux), and handed him a letter from Thielemann. Thielemann reported the defeat and scattering of the army, but said that III Corps still had 18,000 men, and that Jagow of 3rd Brigade, I Corps, had joined him with five battalions and two regiments of cavalry:

> I have had no orders from Prince Blücher but imagine [*vermute*] that he is going to St Trond [another 30 miles to the north-east]. Early this morning there was fighting on my right flank, probably with Wellington. The enemy

> is not pursuing us. I will move towards your Excellency at 1 p.m,, but I should wish to receive your intentions before I march.[16]

Thielemann at Gembloux, 3 miles from the battlefield, was about 10 miles south-southeast of Wavre but, as this letter clearly shows, had no knowledge of any intention to re-group there, further proof of how casually Wavre was chosen. Yet for him to suggest to Bülow that they should retreat some 25 miles further to the north-east to St Trond (on the way to the Rhine) was surely unjustified. He had heard firing at Quatre Bras (possibly the noisy flare up between the Bremen battalion and the French), although it was somewhat misleading to say it was on his 'right flank' when it was all of 10 miles away. The firing must mean that over there, at least, resistance was continuing, while on this front the French were quiescent. To commit to St Trond in such circumstances was a grave decision, and a premature one. However, that was the message Thielemann sent to Bülow.

Bülow instantly and rightly rejected the idea that Blücher could think of retiring on St Trond, and, although Bülow's message has not survived, Thielemann's extant reply to him shows that the latter dropped the St Trond idea and adopted Bülow's requirement that the march should be towards Wavre, and issued orders accordingly.[17]

In the meantime Thielemann had sent Major Weyrach, one of Blücher's ADCs, separated from his master in the battle, to find the *Feldmarschall* and get new instructions. Weyrach found him at Wavre, and on riding back encountered Bülow at Baudeset, at some time after 10 a.m. Based upon Weyrach's report, Bülow wrote to Thielemann at 10.30. This extant message is his second instruction to III Corps' commander:

> I have just received the order to move to Dion-le-Mont, near Wavre. I imagine that by the time this reaches you, your Excellency will have received the same order. The direction of march sent to you previously [in the non-extant message] is not amended by this. I will deploy my rearguard at Mont-St-Guibert, with its support at Vieux Sart [half way between Mont-St-Guibert and Dion-le-Mont]. I shall march at once, and leave to you the choice of time of your departure, but it would not be good to become caught in any serious rearguard action, as it would be better to save our strength until we are together. The cavalry and artillery which, according to your report, is on your left flank, could be Colonel v. Borcke, coming from Namur, according to the Field Marshal's staff officer.

As Lettow-Vorbeck pointed out, the force seen by Thielemann could not have been Borcke's Neumark Dragoons (1st Brigade of II Corps Reserve

Cavalry), but may have been some of Exelmans's French dragoons which were closing upon Gembloux at 9 o'clock. Since the ADC was coming south from Wavre, his suggestion that the troops in question could be Borcke coming north-west from Namur must have been based on assumptions spoken of at headquarters rather than on any direct knowledge – a good instance of the dangers of imagination. But for our immediate purpose it is sufficient to note that army headquarters could hope that once Weyrach had delivered his message (probably before noon), the two missing corps would begin to march on Wavre.

In some respects the high command was indeed better informed about the French than about the eastern segments of its army. This was because Count Gröben had been posted on a hill near Tilly to watch Napoleon's movements, and his excellent reports (the first was signed at 7 a.m.) told of French inactivity at Sombreffe and Brye and even of a reduction in their numbers, although units were moving about; and he even reported a battalion marching on the Roman road, apparently in a *south-westerly* direction. (His further reports were not received at Wavre until the afternoon, and so will be mentioned later.)

Royal headquarters at Heidelberg had been warned by both Blücher and Gneisenau on the evening of 15 June that battle was impending, that the entire army of four corps would be assembled in a chosen position against a French army of perhaps 120,000 men. Virtually nothing had been said about Wellington's situation, but Gneisenau had suggested that the French might have advanced so far that communications with Nivelles might be cut.[18] Now, by noon on the 17th, enough information from his various commanders had reached Gneisenau for a report to be written. Explaining a defeat is never easy, and it must surely have been complicated by an inner consciousness that concentration and marching orders had been handled very belatedly (but he may not have realised that his wording of the midnight order to Bülow was open to misunderstanding), and that Müffling had been left poorly informed. Additionally, Bülow was well regarded at royal headquarters whereas he himself had critics there and even enemies.

What Gneisenau knew by now was that Ziethen's I Corps was approaching Bierges, and II Corps was not far behind, while III and IV had been traced and given orders to move on Wavre. The army was still in being, and the report from Gröben assured him that the French were not in pursuit so far. Blücher was now with the army, though it was not yet possible to judge if he would be fit enough to take command in the next day or so. Gneisenau had also received a series of reports the previous day from Müffling as to the fight at Quatre Bras and even if he discounted Müffling's capacity he had additionally received an informative account from his own man Wussow. Today, Massow had reported his morning interview with Wellington, so that Gneisenau knew that a considerable body of the French had been engaged at Quatre Bras and had been checked and repulsed, and that Wellington had wished to press forward to maintain the advantage.

The full text of the report written on 17 June can be read in the appendix to this chapter.[19] In essence, Gneisenau explained that the Prussian army at Ligny had suffered a setback. It had fought hard and long against greatly superior numbers (80,000 Prussians to 120,000 French, *including the corps of d'Erlon and Reille*) and forced a standstill, expecting further help. For it had engaged in battle on the basis of orders to IV Corps and because of a 'written guarantee' of support from Wellington, who undertook to strike at the enemy rear if the Prussians should be attacked (just as they had promised to assist him in return, if needed). Assistance from either of these formations would have produced a glorious victory. Bülow's IV Corps had been warned at noon on 14 June to be ready to march from Liège and orders had been given before midnight for it to do so, and on all reasonable calculations it was expected to reach the battlefield 'by noon' on 16 June. Why this had not happened was as yet unknown. And there was more: 'on the morning of 16 June, the Duke of Wellington promised to be at 10 a.m. with 20,000 men at Quatre Bras, his cavalry at Nivelles'.

Hence, the report stated, the decision taken to give battle at Ligny had been 'based upon' receiving these reinforcements. This was not a correct statement of the matter. We know that at noon and again on the evening of 15 June Blücher was determined that the next day would be the 'decisive' one; that by late morning on the 16th the high command knew from Feldjäger Rothe that it would not be joined that day by IV Corps; and that Wellington did not reach Brye for his meeting with Blücher until around 1 p.m., by which time (as J. C. Ropes pointed out) Blücher had *already* firmly decided on battle that afternoon, certainly without IV Corps and irrespective of what Wellington might do.[20]

Gneisenau's account of the fighting was fairly factual, amounting to about a quarter of his whole report. He emphasised that the position was excellent for the Prussian artillery and that the infantry fought well, although a considerable number of guns were eventually lost. But Gneisenau had almost nothing good to say of the cavalry. This seems unduly sweeping, for the cavalry arm was known to be the weakest element in the army in terms of numbers, organisation and training, and the position chosen limited their actions to short counter-attacks ordered by Blücher and the high command. Of Prussian battle tactics and the premature commitment of valuable reserves there was, understandably, no mention. Gneisenau made no effort to minimise the losses of cannon, but he did indicate that, although the Prussians had been obliged to retire by divergent routes, the enemy had taken such a pummeling that there was no active pursuit.

One should allow for the fact that Gneisenau had been through a couple of days of strain by the time he penned his report. It does not seem to have struck him that the Prussian officers' accounts of the struggle at Quatre Bras meant that *not all* of Napoleon's army could at Ligny. And his memory may have become fogged concerning those messages received the previous day. This was apparent from his remark that Wellington had given a 'written promise' to have '20,000 men at Quatre Bras by 10 a.m., the cavalry at Nivelles' and to 'attack the enemy's rear'. Müffling had written of an assembly at Nivelles during the 16th and Wellington at Frasnes had written that the Reserve could be at Genappe by noon, but both forecasts had a clear qualification: there should be a meeting with Blücher before deciding on any commitment to action. Gneisenau either forgot or ignored the qualification. As to attacking the enemy's rear, a possibility raised in Müffling's letter of the 15th, it had certainly been discussed at the Brye meeting but had actually been *strongly opposed* by Gneisenau.[21] And the Brye discussions were obviously conditional on whether or not the French took action against the Prussians only, or also struck at Quatre Bras. All this suggests that Gneisenau was still confused and was snatching at recollection. For instance, one such item may have come from Brunneck's report of Orange's views at Quatre Bras at 6.30 a.m. on the morning of the 16th that much of the army could be at Nivelles within three hours and seventeen battalions were coming from Brussels to support his Netherlands forces already or soon to be at Quatre Bras: hence Gneisenau's '20,000 men at Quatre Bras by 10 a.m.'

But if we put down to mis-recollection and stress these quite serious mistakes of record, it is more difficult to excuse Gneisenau's overall treatment of his ally's performance in this report. In explaining the Prussian setback, the essence of Tacitus' warning must have been loud in his ears: 'the crowning injustice of war: all claim credit for success, while defeat is laid to the account of one'.[22] The responsibility for the Ligny defeat needed shifting. Thus Wellington's concentration was belated (one might ask: *whose was not*?) and only 'a part of his Reserve' reached Quatre Bras, and four hours late at that. There they had to fight, winning glory '*for the British*', but then retreated for reasons not explained. Yet by the time that he wrote Gneisenau certainly knew from the reports of Müffling and Wussow on the 16th, of Massow and Wucherer before he wrote, how the fighting developed at Quatre Bras. It was only after Massow had told Wellington of the *Prussian retreat* that Wellington had dropped plans for a morning offensive and had felt obliged to order a retirement to Mont St Jean, and from Gneisenau's own letter we can see that Massow had already told his chief of that interview and the Duke's reply. Gneisenau's depiction of a tardy, selfish, and un-cooperative 'ally' insistent on retreat, when added to his earlier suspicions, became his *idée fixe* from this time on.[23] Certainly he convinced himself. Did he set out to convince others? One can guess at its effect on the minds of distant recipients hoping to read good news, and indeed it became an article of faith for some Prussian historians thereafter.

This unfortunate way of presenting matters was not totally redeemed by the statement that 'the Duke of Wellington's left wing was apparently attacked early this morning, from the sounds heard, but this has not been confirmed. He will accept battle at Waterloo at the entrance to Soignies forest if we will give him two corps.' That would depend upon fresh munitions reaching the Prussians. 'If this can be found then we will agree the Duke's request, send Bülow's corps to him, with the remaining full-strength battalions from the other corps, and with the rest we will stage a feint.'

Limiting about half the Prussian army to 'staging a feint' or demonstration, was Gneisenau's own intention as acting C-in-C. Had the old man not recovered, that would have been the policy on 18 June.

I have gone into this much detail over Gneisenau's report of 17 June because it discloses his personality and his views as acting Commander-in-Chief, shedding a revealing light on his handling of facts, and his presentation of his ally in a major report to his government. It did not augur well for easy Allied co-operation on 18 June. However, to his innermost confidante he did add one thing privately: whereas nine days earlier Wellington's army had been somewhat arrogantly dismissed as 'completely useless', now after the defeat at Ligny the Prussian army must not risk standing alone but instead seek safety with the British. If they did that, then they could risk battle.

*

Appendix: Gneisenau's Letters to Knesebeck and to his Wife, 17 June 1815

Here is the full text of Gneisenau's report on the events of 16 June, addressed to royal headquarters, where General Knesebeck was the King's ADC. It is taken from Lettow-Vorbeck, Anlage 11, pp. 526–8.

Wavre, one staging-post distant from Brussels, 17 June 1815, midday.

The Prussian army has been forced back to this place after a bitter infantry battle.

On 15 June I Army Corps had survived a long action, we received written assurances [*schriftliche Zusicherung*] from the Duke of Wellington that, if the enemy were to attack us, he would attack the enemy's rear; he expected such assurances from us if he were to be attacked.

At midday on the 14th concentration orders were given [*erteilen*] to IV Corps cantoned between Hannut and Liège, to be ready to centre on Hannut in a single march. Before midnight that same day we gave the order for all units and the headquarters itself to move to Hannut. From Hannut to Sombreffe is 7–8 [German, or about 28–32 British] miles and so the corps had eight hours to march to reach the battleground, so if it marched at 4 a.m. one could expect it at noon.

On the morning of 16 June, the Duke of Wellington promised to be at 10 a.m. with 20,000 men at Quatre Bras (the crossroads where the Namur–Nivelles road crosses that from Charleroi to Brussels), his cavalry at Nivelles.

Based on these arrangements [and promises – *added in another hand*] we undertook battle, which began only at 3 p.m. that day. The position was very concentrated, and very advantageous for artillery fire. The right flank occupied the village of Brye, on the left flank Ligny, with St Amand in front. The III Corps stood at the position of the Point du Jour.

St Amand was attacked first by large masses and defended with determination, then lost, then retaken by us and also by the enemy, and thus the battle raged for several hours around this point under heavy artillery fire. St Amand the Little and La Haye, a village connected to St Amand, remained in our possession the whole time.

Around 5 p.m. large masses of troops were sent against the village of Ligny. Here the battle was even more murderous. The village lies on the Ligne brook. The enemy had his artillery on the heights on his side and we had placed ours on those on our side. The village remained in the possession of both sides despite alternating attempts to seize all of it, and the fighting lasted for four hours with unusual intensity. The fighting here had come to a standstill, and if our corps had received help from anywhere, then a difficult but glorious victory would have been the reward for so much effort.

But this help did not appear! Due to misunderstandings that have not yet been explained, General v. Bülow was still in Liège yesterday afternoon and his corps still around and behind Hannut. The concentration of Wellington's army did not take place within the promised time. Four hours later than promised, a part of the Reserve from Brussels reached Quatre Bras but then had to fight a battle itself, the result of which was glorious for the British army but nonetheless resulted in the Duke of Wellington retreating [*den Rückzug des Herzogs Wellington*].

Why IV Corps did not reach the battle and why the Duke of Wellington's concentration happened so late and in such small numbers remains to be clarified by both sides.

As a result we had to fight with around 80,000 men against the *1er* and *2e* [*sic*], and *3e* and *4e* French corps and the *Reserve* corps of General Mouton [Comte Lobau's family name], and against the *Garde* and against numerous cavalry formations: altogether around 120,000 men, as we were informed by a high-ranking French officer who came over to our side, and an aide of Napoleon who was taken prisoner.[24] Whether or not National Guard units were also present is not known with any certainty.

Towards evening General Thielemann's III Corps was attacked.

In this manner the battle lasted until 9 p.m., when a squadron of French cavalry came through an opening that had been made in the village of Ligny and attacked our cavalry, throwing it into disorder.

No assembling, no speaking to them helped. They were led against the enemy several times but would not stand up to them and fell back, at times even riding over our infantry that had been standing fast. The Field Marshal himself put himself at their head and they promised to follow him but did not keep their word. Officers of his staff made great efforts to restore order in the cavalry, but in vain! The infantry was left to its fate, but not a single unit was overrun. However, some guns were lost. Because the corps are not united here, reports on this vary. There is talk of 12 to 20 pieces lost. One battery supposedly went towards Gembloux.

The cavalry units that performed so badly were partly from I Corps and two regiments from II Corps and stood on the left wing on the heights by Ligny village. The cavalry on the right wing performed better. The cavalry of III Corps also let its [horse artillery] battery be taken.

For battle we lack ten batteries, including four of 12-pounders. They were not yet attached to their horses and in part not yet equipped and repaired.

The retirement of the troops was directed towards the village of Tilly, on the road starting at the Brussels highway and leading towards Wavre. The rear guard remained at Tilly, the other troops stand at Gentinnes. General v. Thielemann went with III Corps and part of General v. Jagow's Brigade towards Gembloux.

IV Corps has now been ordered here and will probably first arrive tomorrow morning. The rest of the army stands here behind the Dyle, one corps on the right bank of this river, and tomorrow IV Corps is supposed to push its advance guard forward to Mont-St-Guibert, where currently Colonel Sohr is positioned with two cavalry regiments and half a horse-artillery battery.

The Duke of Wellington's left wing was apparently attacked early this morning, from the sounds heard, but this has not been confirmed. He will accept battle at Waterloo at the entrance to Soignies forest if we will give him two corps. This we would like to do if we had the ammunition. But we have no news about the munitions for two of the corps. If this can be found then we will agree the Duke's request, send Bülow's corps to him, with the remaining full-strength [*vollzähligen*] battalions from the other corps, and with the rest we will stage a feint [*und mit den übrigen figurieren*].

As the enemy pursued us for only half an hour we may conclude that he is exhausted also. He has not yet followed us further and even the battlefield is held only by vedettes.

General Kleist [North German Federal Army Corps, in Luxembourg], General Dobschütz [GOC Rhenish Prussia] and the commandants of Luxemburg and Jülich have been sent the necessary instructions. General Kleist is supposed to occupy and defend Cologne in the unlikely event that this becomes necessary.

As for what the enemy may do, he might take Liège [*sic*] in order to go up the Rhine and attack the Russian columns in the flank and thereby threaten the operations of Prince Schwarzenberg. The route through the Argonne forest is now doubly precarious.[25]

The fact that Bonaparte was allowed to concentrate so much strength in front of us is the result of the inexplicable delays in the march of various armies and the lack of secrecy about the proposed [Allied] actions.

But all is not lost, if rapidity and determination are brought to operations. If we lose many such hard-fought actions like that of yesterday then the numerical relationship between the Allied armies and his will be altered even more to his disadvantage. All we must do is hold on and remain tough, and we will attain our goal.

Wavre, sealed at 2 p.m. on 17 June: GR[AF] N. v. GNEISENAU.

[P.S.] The infantry generally fought in an exemplary fashion. The Field Marshal greatly exposed himself to danger and personally led a battalion into the village of St Amand. In the cavalry attack his horse was shot through and through. It finally fell, and he came under it and was almost taken prisoner. The fall deeply hurt his shoulder and thigh. Your Excellency should provide a copy of this letter to the War Minister. General Holzendorf was wounded by a spent cannon-ball, and General Jürgass by a musket shot. Colonel Thümen was shot dead. We cannot yet say anything about the number of dead and wounded.

To his wife, Gneisenau wrote:

> Yesterday we fought a battle against heavy odds, that is to say about 80,000 men against a force of 120,000 that Bonaparte had brought against us, and did so until 9 p.m. with great honour to our brave infantry. But because promised help did not come and misunderstandings had occurred, we were forced to retreat in order to draw nearer and unite [*sic*] with the army of the Duke of Wellington. We went back one and a half German miles, and through today's short march have drawn closer to the British army, and want to seek a new battle.[26]

Chapter 32
Napoleon
Morning, 17 June

I

NAPOLEON WAS IN NO DOUBT that he had failed in his main objective. Certainly he had defeated the Prussians, but he had expected to annihilate them. Nevertheless, at 8.30 p.m. on the 16th he had sent a short buoyant message by express courier to his brother Joseph in Paris:

> The Emperor has gained a complete victory over the Prussian and English armies united under the orders of Lord Wellington and Marshal Blücher. At this moment our army is moving through the village of Ligny in front of Fleurus to pursue the enemy. I hasten to announce this happy news to Your Imperial Highness.[1]

In fact the French army was in no state to pursue the Prussians at this time. Rest was imperative after so grim and punishing a battle. As to Quatre Bras, overnight 16/17 June (if not earlier, for several couriers had been moving back and forth) reports of the fighting there had reached the Emperor. Colonel Baudus claimed that, having been detained by Ney for staff duties, he left once the fighting was over and reached Fleurus at 2 a.m. (4–5 hours for a 7-mile night journey). Flahaut said that he himself dined with Ney and then left at 1 a.m., reaching Fleurus at 6–7 a.m. (which seems extraordinarily slow given the growing light). Ney had written his brief report timed 10 p.m. and that must have been at headquarters by early morning (perhaps Baudus carried it?). None of these could have left any doubt of the setback to French plans.

One of the greatest tests of generalship after a victorious but hard-won attack is to inspire and then maintain a pursuit that transforms a defeated army's retreat into the scattered flight of broken men. The instinct of the victorious soldier is to slake his thirst, clean weapons, eat, replenish stores, maybe savour the moment, and sleep. Starting off once more – into the night, perhaps into an ambush, to struggle across miles of unfamiliar ground – goes against a tired man's instincts and wishes. And where the enemy has fought with such stubbornness, given ground so reluctantly, and pulled back under cover of a tough rearguard as dusk comes down over the countryside, the wish to let well alone is not far below the surface. It requires a great general to insist on a relentless chase far beyond the field of battle in order to reap the full reward: Marlborough at Ramillies in May 1706 drove his pursuit of the French into the night and for several days on end, so that entire provinces fell to him with scarcely a shot fired.

For a man undertaking such a gigantic task as Napoleon did in June 1815, 'a battle of annihilation' that had ended without shredding the enemy beyond recovery made an instant pursuit a necessity. It did not require him to stay up all night or to lead the squadrons, but it did require him to issue the appropriate orders at once, and to infuse his dominant will and determination into the cavalryman Grouchy (not exhaustively employed that day) to launch the pursuit. There was to hand also Lobau's corps, which had done no fighting, only a little marching. Did it necessarily have to remain in reserve overnight? (We see one of its divisions allocated to the pursuit during the morning of the 17th.) Less certainly, there were the tired commanders Vandamme and Gérard: had they been given instant promotion for their endeavours at Ligny (a baton, a higher rank of nobility), might they have responded to fresh stimulus and pushed their men? But that brings us back to Napoleon's basic problem – he had attempted too large a task for the means available. His *3e* and *4e Corps* desperately needed rest and food before starting another long trek.

The fact remains that Napoleon did nothing during the final hours of Friday 16 June, and for that he alone was responsible.

It was the Emperor's habit to sleep for a few hours, then rise at about 1 a.m., receive reports issue orders, and work on papers before snatching more rest and waking again with the dawn.[2] Certain orders were then issued, but as so often in this campaign there is confusion and contradiction over the matter: Napoleon, Grouchy, and thus many historians, being at variance.

We begin with the Emperor. In writing of the success of Ligny, Napoleon in his memoirs, having listed the guns and colours captured and the trophies taken, added: 'Marshal Grouchy, and Generals Pajol and Exelmans were remarked on for their intrepidity.' But that refers to the past. Having said this, his next sentence ran: 'During the night Lieutenant-General Monthyon was ordered to pursue the Prussian left wing,' a statement that the strategist and historian Jomini later refined into 'searching for the enemy towards Tilly and Mont-St-Guibert'. However, as Houssaye remarked, the Prussian observer

Gröben, watching from a hill *near Tilly*, did not report any French patrols moving in his direction that morning, and there is nothing recorded from Monthyon.[3]

But Napoleon's account would seem to mean that no overnight orders were addressed to Grouchy and his principal cavalry subordinates. The orders issued overnight for a cavalry pursuit, nominated not a line commander but a staff officer, Monthyon, to carry them out. And Bailly de Monthyon, as Soult's most senior staff officer, was presumably much needed at headquarters, and had no recent command of any cavalry. Such an account raises more problems than it solves.

To confuse matters further, Grouchy seems to have made contradictory statements. Houssaye summarised from two pamphlets Grouchy issued in 1819 and 1840 in this manner: 'First, Grouchy saw the Emperor at Fleurus at 11 p.m. on the 16th; secondly, the Emperor enjoined him to pursue the enemy with the cavalry this same night or tomorrow at first light.' But in Grouchy's later memoirs (which are supposed to be based on the earlier pamphlets and fresh documents) the matter is presented quite otherwise:

> During the night of 16/17 Marshal Grouchy, although without orders from the Emperor or the Chief of Staff, thought it necessary to send officers to commanders of his light cavalry, enjoining them to push reconnaissances in different directions and gather news of the enemy. Thus between 2 and 3 a.m. Exelmans went north towards Gembloux, Pajol eastwards on the Namur road with Teste's division [*21e Division, 6e Corps*] detached under his command. At daybreak Comte Grouchy mounted and went to imperial headquarters, where the Emperor was still sleeping but suffering greatly. The Chief of Staff, despite the requests of the commander of the right wing, refused to waken Napoleon from his troubled sleep, and declared that he could not take upon himself to issue orders. Grouchy waited in the antechamber till 8 a.m.[4]

Yet somebody *did* issue orders shortly after midnight to 1 a.m., for Pajol at Balâtre (4 miles from Fleurus) sent an ADC to Soult at 3 a.m. saying that he was preparing to march in pursuit of the enemy. The fact that he wrote to *Soult* and not to Grouchy suggests that, despite what Grouchy said in the passage just quoted, the orders had indeed come from imperial headquarters. Exelmans seems also to have received direct orders from headquarters, for he wrote to his superior, Grouchy, from Gembloux at midday that 'I informed you [*sic*] this morning of the movement I made on Gembloux in pursuit of the enemy who is massed there . . .' There is a further place where Grouchy's memoirs seems adrift on this matter: Teste's division was not placed under

Pajol by Grouchy's overnight orders, but (as we shall see) by imperial headquarters later in the morning.[5]

These memoirs are thus unsafe in their claims, but we may trace a possible course of events. Grouchy neither received nor issued orders overnight. The failure to give him orders was remedied by headquarters either sending Monthyon on a mission with cavalry that (somehow) was not recorded by any French cavalrymen or any regiment (or by Prussian observers) – all of which seems improbable; or alternatively (and more probably) telling Monthyon to send (or even sending Monthyon to bear) orders directly to Pajol and Exelmans for them to take horse and execute the search. Grouchy learned this only at dawn or on reaching headquarters.

II

At some time in the morning Soult at Fleurus wrote to Ney at Frasnes, unhelpfully dating his letter '15 [*sic*] June'. As if to emphasise this carelessness, he half-admitted his own thoughtlessness in not keeping Ney informed of the battle at Ligny. He certainly left Ney in no doubt how dissatisfied the Emperor had been with the conduct of the Quatre Bras battle and he summarised for Ney the Emperor's analysis of his operational blunders, some of which we can see were fully justified. Soult spelled out the Emperor's basic principles of war (perhaps with some relish, since he disliked Ney so much). It must have been galling for Ney to read such a lecture about his mistakes, to be given orders for the day in minute and insulting detail, and to find himself entirely to blame for the d'Erlon *affaire* and thus for denying Napoleon overwhelming victory. These little touches cannot have smoothed the relations between imperial headquarters and the commander of the left wing, nor between the brother marshals Ney and Soult, upon whom so much depended. The letter reads as follows:

> Fleurus, 15 June 1815:
>
> Marshal, General Flahaut who has just arrived [after 6 a.m. according to Flahaut, years later], says that you are uncertain about yesterday's results. I believe however that you have been advised of the victory the Emperor has gained. The Prussian army has been put to flight, and General Pajol is pursuing them on the roads to Namur and Liège. We have already taken several thousand prisoners and 30 cannon. Our troops behaved very well; a charge of six battalions of the *Garde*, some service squadrons, and General Delort's cavalry division pierced the enemy line, created the greatest disorder in their ranks and carried the position.

The Emperor is going to the windmill of Bry by which passes the great road from Namur to Quatre Bras; it is thus not possible for the English army to act against you; if it should, the Emperor will march against it directly by the Quatre Bras road while you attack it from the front with your divisions, which must at present be collected together, and that army will be instantly destroyed. Consequently inform the Emperor of the exact position of divisions and of all that is passing in front of you.

The Emperor was pained to see that you did not unite the divisions yesterday; they acted in isolation, and thus you suffered losses.

If the corps of Comtes d'Erlon and Reille had been together, not one Englishmen in the force that attacked you would have escaped. If Comte d'Erlon had carried out the movement on St Amand that the Emperor ordered, the Prussian army would have been totally destroyed and we might have taken perhaps 30,000 prisoners.

The corps of Generals Gérard, Vandamme and the *Garde Impériale* were always united; one risks setbacks when detachments are endangered.

The Emperor hopes and wishes that your seven infantry divisions and the cavalry are well assembled and formed up, and together do not occupy more than a league of ground, so that they are well under your hand for use as necessary.

His Majesty's intention is that you take position at Quatre Bras in accordance with the orders you have been given; but if for any reason that is impossible, immediately report with details, and the Emperor will come to you, as I have said; if on the other hand there is only a rearguard, attack it and take the position.

It is necessary to finish this operation in the day, today, to complete the re-munitioning, and to bring in the isolated men and the detachments. Give orders accordingly, and ensure that the wounded are treated and transported to the rear; there are complaints that the ambulances have not carried out their duties.

The famous partisan Lützow, who has been taken, said that the Prussian army was lost and that Blücher has for a second time put in danger the Prussian monarchy.[6]

We can see from the activity thus far how poorly headquarters had operated. When going to bed on the 16th Napoleon had not issued any orders for the following day. Then at some time before dawn Napoleon sensed that he had let matters slip. In haste, bypassing Grouchy, he had Soult issue direct orders to Pajol and Exelmans to begin the search for the Prussians. Quite soon after rising Napoleon knew definitely that Ney had been foiled at Quatre

Bras. But Ney had not been told anything about the outcome at Ligny until Flahaut pointed this out.

Writing to Ney with new orders Soult emphasised that it should be possible to defeat the British today (the 17th), and with Napoleon's assistance as well they could scarcely hope to escape. But in outlining Napoleon's intentions Soult passed over in silence two important matters: the condition of the victorious army that lay at Ligny–Sombreffe overnight, for it would have been wise to warn that the force at Ligny was scarcely ready for another major engagement on the 17th; and secondly, by omitting mention of Exelmans's sector of search, Gembloux or Mont-St-Guibert or Wavre, Soult showed fairly clearly that all attention at headquarters relative to the Prussians was already turning towards Pajol's mission towards Namur. When writing to Ney that the Emperor 'would march directly by the Quatre Bras road' in his support, what seems to have been in mind was a new attack on an immobile British army 'in position' at Quatre Bras, for the previous morning's idea of a thrust towards Genappe and Brussels was nowhere mentioned, and indeed would have conflicted with the order to re-munition and re-group the scattered soldiers in Ney's sector.

III

We have just seen that at Fleurus around 6 a.m. attention was becoming drawn towards Pajol's mission. And as it happened, at about that same hour Pajol's cavalry came up with some Prussian troops near Mazy on the road to Namur. As Aerts put it:

> Sometimes the smallest occurrences have an incalculable effect: towards the end of the battle the horse battery Nr. 14 of II Corps, having exhausted its ammunition, retired on Sombreffe but could not find the ammunition parks. Despite Thielemann's order to fall back on Gembloux or rally with III Corps, the battery wasted time in marching back and forth until it took the direction of Namur in the morning, mingling with some supply wagons and joined by the third squadron of the 7th Uhlans (III Corps) which had been stationed at Onoz at the battle's commencement, and left there by oversight.[7]

Most of the soldiers escaped, but the French captured the wagons and six of the cannon,[8] and sent the guns back to imperial headquarters, thus increasing Napoleon's attention to the eastern road. *Namur* – perhaps Maastricht and Germany – might well be the destination of the Prussian army. Nothing this day had so great an effect on the campaign.

In the first half of the morning Napoleon left Fleurus by coach – times differ, from after 8 a.m. to about 11 a.m. – then took to horseback and inspected the Ligny battlefield and the troops. As usual he received thunderous acclamations, heard by a Prussian observer on a hill near Tilly who saw the French troops assembled at '9 a.m.' It would seem that the Emperor spent valuable time talking to his entourage about the fighting, but also about Parisian politics and the irritants of having to listen to views from the Chambre. Some of his hearers were disturbed that such ruminations ran on and that there were no fresh orders. Indeed Soult and the staff had been left at Fleurus and did not re-join Napoleon until midday, when he was stationed in Blücher's former eyrie, the Brye windmill

Nevertheless, during the morning Napoleon did decide on further action. After a while he spoke again to Grouchy and gave him verbal orders, upon which the Marshal departed: this may have been around 10.30–11 a.m. Then other orders were issued: Lobau's *6e Corps* (*19e* and *20e Divisions* only, less Teste's *21e Division* now detached) was ordered to march west to Marbais, half-way to Quatre Bras, and the *Garde* was given similar instructions shortly after. But Napoleon continued to mull over prospects and means, and next came to feel that cavalry support was necessary. As Soult was not yet come, he used General Bertrand as his secretary. He ordered Grouchy to detach three cavalry divisions from his command and send them to Marbais.[9] On further reflection Napoleon decided to modify his instructions yet again. As a result, he ordered Bertrand to write a second letter, stating his new requirements in a series of somewhat disconnected thoughts:

> Repair to Gembloux with General Pajol's [*1er*] *Cavalry Corps*, the light cavalry of the *4e Corps* [Maurin's *7e*], General Exelmans's [*2e*] *Cavalry Corps*, General Teste's [*21e*] division – of which you should take special care as it is detached from its corps, and the infantry of *3e* and *4e Corps*.[10] You will explore in the direction of Namur and Maastricht and you will pursue the enemy. Find out his direction of march and inform me of his manoeuvres in order that I can discover what he intends to do. I am moving my headquarters to Quatre Bras, where the English still were this morning. Our communication will then be directly by the paved road of Namur. If the enemy have evacuated Namur, write to the general commanding the second military division [district] at Charlemont to occupy Namur with several national guard battalions and some artillery batteries from Charlemont. He should put it under a brigadier-general.
>
> It is important to penetrate the enemy's intentions: whether he is separating from the English or is still intending to join them, to cover

> Brussels and [*sic*!] Liège, in seeking the fate of a new battle. In all circumstances keep your two infantry corps together within one league's extent, and every night [*tous les soirs*] hold a good military position, with several different paths of retreat. Place intermediate cavalry detachments for communicating with headquarters. Ligny, 17 June (In the absence of the Chief of Staff, dictated by the Emperor to Grand-Marshal [of the Palace] Bertrand).[11]

The Emperor was rapping out thoughts in his usual staccato way, with topics appearing and reappearing as they come to mind, in no particular order.[12] When read carefully, the letter is quite definite on one point: that Grouchy must persistently pursue the enemy wherever he goes, but without risking a defeat through actual combat. This pursuit is seen as likely to take several days (hence *tous les soirs*) and take Grouchy far from the main force's immediate protection, for, if the enemy turns, Grouchy must be able to retreat in several directions. Above all it is information that Napoleon seeks, not Grouchy fighting a detached battle. He is at a loss as to the enemy's intentions (and so can give no guidance to Grouchy). He has no idea of where the Prussians are, so that Grouchy should search eastwards, principally north-east to Maastricht and south-east to Namur. Napoleon is still uncertain whether Blücher is abandoning the British or trying to join them again to cover Brussels (to the north) and Liège (to the east).[13]

And there is another unhelpful confusion in Napoleon's mind about united Allies, and it goes beyond a mere slip of the pen (whether he meant 'or' instead of 'and' when speaking of the assembled Allies covering Brussels *and* Liège). For if the two Allies *unite* to the *north* they can certainly cover Brussels. But as to an *eastern* junction, since the British are at Quatre Bras (to the west), how is Wellington to get to Liège in the east, even if Blücher can? The Prussians may possibly cover Liège, but the *two* allies cannot. Did the French high command think some British forces to be somewhere in the north-east? Confused thought and impractical instructions will not assist Grouchy in deciding on his task.[14] One further point: the force selected by Napoleon for Grouchy amounts to some 6,800 cavalry, 27,000 infantry (and if all units keep their guns with them, some 110 guns).[15] This force is likely to meet at least that many, and very probably more, Prussians, and in consequence Napoleon insists that it should not be caught up in a battle. It is thus too small to face an army by itself, and yet too large for a reconnaissance force.

That this last point was recognised is plain from a remark by Pétiet of the French staff: 'word spread at headquarters that the Chief of Staff had represented to Napoleon the danger of reducing forces aimed at beating the English army; that the detachment for Grouchy was too large. But the Emperor, used to the passive obedience of Berthier, would not listen.'[16]

At noon Soult 'in front of Ligny' sent Ney a message informing him that an infantry corps and the *Garde* were taking position in front of Marbais and that Napoleon required Ney to attack and take Quatre Bras, that the Marbais force would support him, and that Napoleon was going to Marbais and impatiently expected reports.[17]

So at midday the French army divided once more, with Napoleon moving towards Ney, while Grouchy departed eastwards. Their activities for the rest of the day are best treated separately.

Chapter 33
Napoleon Pursues Wellington
Afternoon to Nightfall, 17 June

I

THE EMPEROR HAD TURNED HIS ATTENTION away from the Prussians and towards Wellington, leaving one task unfinished in order to attempt another. He would not use the troops who had fought the day before; he would use only a part of his reserve in support of Ney. He turned his back on the task of smashing the Prussians and undertook the destruction this day of a general who yet again had bested Ney, and who was known among the French as extremely skilful in retreat. It all turned upon the British general being taken unawares at Quatre Bras between two converging and vengeful French attacks by Ney and Napoleon, Ney's men somewhat worn and disappointed, the Emperor's force fresh but only a detachment from the main army

Napoleon reached Marbais, only 4 miles from the Quatre Bras crossroads by about 1 p.m., but could hear no firing from Ney's front. He had intended to second Ney's attack, but in the absence of any signs of activity or any reports, he sent out a patrol towards him. The patrol sighted scarlet-coated lancers and fired upon them, until it was found they were Colbert's *Lanciers*.[1] Napoleon meanwhile took the lead himself, hastening forward with his light and heavy cavalry and their horse artillery in an attempt to trap and destroy Wellington. As he rode forward 'a captured English *vivandière*' was brought to him who told of the movement in retreat of the British army.[2] Next, he encountered d'Erlon, whose corps had formed up close to Villers Perwin. There followed a brief exchange on the mishaps of the previous day and an order to d'Erlon to march immediately behind the cavalry along the road to Brussels.[3] Then, it would seem, Ney arrived.

The account of their meeting given in Napoleon's memoirs is short but pointed: the Emperor upbraided Ney for the morning's dithering and delay, 'so that he had cost him three very precious hours,' and the marshal excused himself by saying that he thought he faced Wellington's entire army.

When we recall that Ney had been defeated once again by his old opponent Wellington, who seemed always to produce fresh troops when least expected (just as Reille had warned) and that Napoleon had snatched away Ney's main reserve at the critical moment, it is perhaps fair to suggest that Ney was suffering from a sense of repeated ill-usage at Napoleon's hands and a crisis of confidence to the point of paralysis of will. But there may have been a second possibility.

French sources are silent on this, so we have to turn to British accounts: Lord Uxbridge and his ADC, watching the front with Captain Mercer of the Royal Horse Artillery (RHA), noticed smoke rising from the French positions and judged that they were cooking and would not attack until they had eaten. Taylor of the 10th Hussars also remarked on the cooking fires. This may have been Ney's reason for inaction – that, as Foy had emphasised the previous night, the troops had no rations left, and therefore as usual spent the morning foraging for anything they could find. This vicious system of seizure, living off the land, had been fatal to the French in the Peninsula, and was to impede their operations both on this day and on the morning of 18 June.[4]

As midday passed to an airless and sultry afternoon Napoleon deployed his forces, with himself at the head: the artillery at the front, with the cavalry on both flanks, and the troops of Reille, Lobau and the *Garde* following.[5] The *cuirassiers* had earlier been observed by Wellington because the sun caught their accoutrements as they rode from Marbais to Quatre Bras. Once formed up, the *lancier* regiments rode forward with the *cuirassiers* immediately behind them. By this time almost all Wellington's infantry were safely beyond Genappe, and only the reserve cavalry held the front as rearguard, a piquet of the 10th Hussars being the most forward unit.

Wellington had been at the front for much of the morning, and at one point seems to have wondered at the silence and asked himself whether the enemy were retreating. At midday, while his infantry steadily moved back, he questioned whether to stand and risk fighting with cavalry, until dissuaded by Uxbridge. The conclusion must be that, as the mass of fresh enemy troops began to appear from Marbais, a cavalry encounter would be too rash, unsupported by infantry. Having got his cavalry united with the rest of his army only late on the evening of 16 June, Wellington was not disposed to risk it unnecessarily on the 17th. Thus there was agreement between the two men that the withdrawal should continue and the cavalry screen should bring in the rear. One of Wellington's ADC's, Lord Arthur Hill, said to a gunner officer that 'Lord Uxbridge had positive orders not to have an affair of cavalry.'[6]

Wellington was aware from bitter experience of the cavalry's proclivity to treat warfare as a fox hunt rather than as a considered and disciplined military operation. He had decided to retreat and required the cavalry to do no more than serve as an effective rearguard, but in leaving Uxbridge in overall command he was trusting to the self-control of a *beau sabreur*, whose relationship with him was delicate. Uxbridge and he had finally come to terms, following tension due to the former's seduction of Wellington's sister-in-law (Henry Wellesley's wife) in 1809, and, as we saw, the Duke had not objected when in April 1815 the Horse Guards proposed Uxbridge for command of Wellington's cavalry, even though Uxbridge had seen no action since Corunna and Walcheren in 1808–9. Uxbridge had been slightly senior to Wellesley as major-general and lieutenant-general but he had been unemployed since 1809, while Wellington's career prospered. Wellington seems for both family and former grounds of military precedence to have decided to leave Uxbridge great latitude in his present command, despite his not having commanded in action for over five years. That latitude almost certainly resulted in the cavalry rearguard staying in position unduly long.[7]

Captain Mercer of the RHA had been posted with his troop to support the final rearguard, with minimal ammunition in his limbers, the ammunition wagons having withdrawn by order. This made quite plain the absolute importance of avoiding a serious engagement. Uxbridge came up, and seeing some cavalry to the south-east, declared '"By the Lord, they are Prussians!", jumped on his horse, and, followed by his two aides, dashed off like a whirlwind to meet them.' With the general acting like a cornet of horse and forgetting to tell Mercer anything, the latter feared that the commander of all the cavalry would be cut off and taken, leaving the rearguard entirely without any orders, but Uxbridge realised his mistake in time and galloped back, and ordered a salvo to check the French advance and then a retirement at full speed.[8] So much for a timely and coordinated withdrawal.

It was now 2 o'clock. The French advanced rapidly and in great force and swiftly reached the Quatre Bras crossroads. The outlying pickets dashed back and the British cavalry brigades quickly moved off, falling back in three roughly parallel columns.

II

Almost at the moment that the French cannons opened fire the lowering heat brought on a tremendous thunderstorm. The effect of this rain cannot be over-stated; it made all operations for the next eighteen hours a misery and it sapped morale, although it may have diminished the enthusiasm of the pursuers more than it affected the weary determination of the pursued:

> The first gun that was fired seemed to burst the clouds overhead, for its report was instantly followed by an awful clap of thunder, and lightning that almost blinded us, whilst the rain came down as if a waterspout had broken over us. The sublimity of the scene was inconceivable. Flash succeeded flash, and the peals of thunder were long and tremendous; whilst, as if in mockery of the elements, the French guns still sent forth their feebler glare and now scarcely audible reports – their cavalry dashing on at a headlong pace, adding their shouts to the uproar.[9]

The effect was to turn the ground into a quagmire, and the intensity of the rain to slow the movement of mounted men in both armies, soaking them to the skin, and limiting vision to very short distances. This phenomenon was mentioned by almost every man who left any records of this day, but its effect on the afternoon's fighting is not always recognised by historians.

Uxbridge meanwhile had found himself dangerously exposed as a result of his own thoughtlessness. His circumstances were well described by Mercer, his involuntary companion, who had correctly guessed that as Blücher was known to have retired last night, any cavalry coming from Marbais were more likely to be French than Prussian. Instantly limbering up the guns:

> we galloped for our lives through the storm, striving to gain the enclosures about the houses of the hamlets, Lord Uxbridge urging us on, crying, 'Make haste! – make haste! For God's sake, gallop, or you will be taken!' We did make haste, and succeeded in getting among the houses and gardens, but with the French advance close on our heels. Here, however, observing the *chaussée* full of [British] hussars, they pulled up. Had they continued their charge we were gone, for these hussars were scattered about the road in the utmost confusion, some in little squads, others singly, and, moreover, so crowded together that we had no room whatever to act with any effect – either they or us.[10]

Uxbridge gathered the hussars and got Mercer to swing two guns into position and fire a salvo.

> The whole transaction appears to me so confused and wild ... the general-in-chief of the cavalry exposing himself amongst the skirmishers of his rearguard, and literally doing the duty of a cornet! 'By God! We are all prisoners' (or some such words), exclaimed Lord Uxbridge, dashing his horse at one of the garden-banks, which he cleared, and away he went, leaving us to get out of the scrape as best we could.

Then 'away we went, helter-skelter – guns, gun-detachments, and hussars, all mixed *pêle-mêle*, going like mad, and covering each other with mud,' while the rain was so heavy that 'it extinguished every slow-match in the brigade'. Perhaps unsurprisingly, the pursuers slowed up, and the British rearguard reached the bridge at Genappe as the thunder ceased, leaving only the rain to torment the soldiers.

Turning for the moment from the cavalry commander's troubles, we must see how the columns fared. The central column kept to the paved road. It comprised the bulk of the artillery and the two brigades of heavy cavalry, plus the 23rd Light Dragoons and the 7th Hussars bringing up the rear. The left column of Vandeleur's and Vivian's light cavalry retired through the fields, while the right, made up of Grant's light brigade and Dörnberg's force (now reduced to 2nd Light Dragoons, King's German Legion [KGL], and the Cumberland Hussars, since the 23rd Light Dragoons was detached) likewise kept to the fields. One of Vandeleur's ADCs wrote that they 'retired quietly'.[11] Vivian's force had been the closest to the French, had come under fire very early on, and it seemed possible that it could be charged. He retreated, following in the tracks of Vandeleur's brigade until they reached a little bridge over the Thy stream (a tributary of the Dyle) near Genappe. It then experienced a difficulty with Sir John Vandeleur. Vivian had expected Vandeleur's troops to follow Peninsular practice: to stand, open ranks, and let Vivian's men pass through – and he did remark later that he understood that Uxbridge had explained the point to Vandeleur. Vandeleur refused, apparently on the basis of his understanding of the orders received, and passed his brigade over, leaving Vivian to continue to skirmish for some while yet.[12] It was another instance of the difficulties that can arise when the commanding general is not available to watch against and settle such matters.

III

The rain turned the fields into quagmires, and the borders of streams into marshes. Ingleby of the RHA was with Vivian's men, and his remarks bear significantly upon the story of that afternoon. For he noted that the rain and mud made it

> impracticable for the French cavalry to press our column in any force. In fact, out of the road in the track of our own cavalry, the ground was poached into a complete puddle. Seeing this, and having lost the shoe from off a Gun horse, I halted and had it put on in spite of some skirmishers who began to

> press on us, but were kept at bay by our own skirmishers forming as if to charge them. This will show how impracticable it was for them to press us on this cross road.[13]

After a retirement of 3 miles, the centre column crossed the River Dyle by the narrow bridge at Genappe, a bridge wide enough only for two horses and a travelling carriage or farm cart. O'Grady of the 7th Hussars was writing by 1837 of cavalry passing it 'in file'.[14] The flanking columns found ways over the stream both upstream and downstream of Genappe, and, once across, some files dismounted and unslung carbines to defend the crossings. It is scarcely surprising that the pursuers had abandoned the trampled and spongy field paths to concentrate on the better going along the high road, and thus Genappe became the scene of fighting. Uxbridge was now back in command. Where the road mounts on the northern exit of the town he stationed his own regiment, the 7th Hussars, also the 23rd Light Dragoons and, several hundred yards further back, the 1st Life Guards.[15] The French cavalry, led by the *2e Lanciers* (*Chevaux légers*) under Colonel Sourd, massed in the single street of the town, the advance guard at the halt with lances levelled, but the rear units continuing to press forward until the street was choked.

Uxbridge ordered his own regiment to charge. It dashed forward but its sabres could make no impression on the *lanciers*, and it was enfiladed from the flank by some French guns. It pulled back, having lost quite heavily, suffering 11 per cent casualties. It was more a sacrifice than an achievement, splendid though the effort was; O'Grady remarked at the time that 'success was not even possible' and in retrospect that 'of course our charge could make no impression', adding that Dörnberg was against charging against an enemy whose flanks were not open to attack. The French now surged forward along the narrow road, hampered in deployment by the flooded ditches and the soaked ground. Uxbridge found the Light Dragoons somewhat unwilling to challenge them, and so ordered the Life Guards to charge.[16] They rode into and severely mauled the *lanciers* who, driven back into the choked and narrow street, could scarcely swing their long weapons.

From this moment the rearguard was able to resume its withdrawal. The French continued to follow them but there was little more fighting, though the gunners still sent the occasional shot at their opponents when they could manhandle their pieces into position on (or rather in) the sodden ground. The horses sank ever deeper into the mud, wheels were up to the axle in filth. Everyone was soaked to the skin. By early evening the British cavalry had re-joined the infantry and were filing into the positions allocated for them back at Mont St Jean, still in pouring rain.

IV

The afternoon retreat and the *affaire* at Genappe have been treated very differently by the French and British. There is a fine painting, *The Eve of Waterloo, 17 June*, in the Musée de l'Armée in Paris, by Henri Chartier, showing the British in disorderly flight, the sun bright on their tunics and their shadows clear on the dry earth track, with Napoleon and his squadrons racing after them across the baking fields. It was not quite like that, and the detail is much less simple, less dramatic and less satisfying for nationalist pride on either side.[17]

The essence of a good rearguard action is to keep the main body safe, to delay the enemy as much as possible without actually getting cut off, and – where cavalry and guns are involved – for the rearguard to give their guns' safety the higher priority. It is always a matter for fine judgement: Ney was at his best in such situations, and his successive withdrawals from Pombal, Redinha and Condeixa in March 1811 were much praised, though in the last instance he inadvertently placed the main army in real danger.[18] Here in Belgium, on 17 June, the main army and its guns went off in total safety, though some wagons and material were abandoned along the way, possibly pushed aside by the more rearward units delayed by the narrowness of the highway at some points (bridges).[19] Likewise, Uxbridge's three columns managed to retire without disorder, and although they had to move with rapidity, the instance of a horse being re-shod without any effective enemy molestation indicates that the pursuit was not headlong. Of course it was different with the little group directly under Uxbridge's orders: Mercer's vivid account makes plain that his guns (and the commanding general) did have to make a precipitate retreat at full speed, because they had been retained at the very front beyond the point of prudence. But the story of Mercer cannot fairly be extended to comprise the entire cavalry force.[20]

The ten regiments of British cavalry suffered a total of 91 casualties. The heaviest loss was in the two regiments that fought at Genappe: the 7th Hussars had 45 casualties: 3 officers (1 each, k, w, m) and 42 men (6k, 21 w, 15 m); the 1st Life Guards suffered 18 (1 officer w, 8 men k and 9 w), in both cases losses of 11 per cent. The seven other regiments had 28 casualties.[21]

When we turn to the French side (for which other rank casualty statistics are lacking) we find that only two regiments recorded any officer casualties on 17 June. The *1er Lanciers* reported one officer wounded. Unsurprisingly, given their position in the advance, the *2e Lanciers*, which went into battle with about 37 officers and 375 men (morning state, 10 June), suffered 14 officers wounded, including their heroic Colonel Sourd, a 38 per cent rate among officers.[22] It seems reasonable to conclude from all this that, apart from the bloody encounter in Genappe, the fighting on this afternoon was not intense, and most of the (very few) injuries were such as the occasional bullet might inflict in weather when movement and visibility were so bad.[23]

Uxbridge considered that it all resembled manoeuvres, 'the prettiest field-day'. It may be so. But as to the cavalry general's performance and guidance of the 8,000 men who looked to him for command, it is hard to see a great deal to admire. The reliable and experienced Tomkinson's view was that Uxbridge thought like a cavalry colonel intent on putting his own regiment (the 7th Hussars) in the way of glory, pushing it in preference to other regiments, and in circumstances that were ill-judged. The experienced Dörnberg thought it wrong to set the 7th Hussars at the *lanciers* while the latter were protected by houses and without open flanks. The regiment lost many men without gaining much credit. Uxbridge was judged as not *thinking* as an independent commander of ten regiments. 'I think the result to the Duke must be, that Lord Uxbridge is too young a soldier to be much relied on with a separate command, from a feeling that he will risk too much in a desire to do something.'[24] It is difficult to disagree, on the evidence of this day.

V

On leaving Lord Uxbridge, Wellington and his staff had ridden to join the DQMG, whom they met on the Mont St Jean ridge.[25] Constant Rebecque said that they found De Lancey 'seated on the ground with a large sketch map of the position before him. He did not know that he would be killed the next day at this same place. He informed me of the order of battle designated by the Duke on the position, and asked me to place the troops of the Low Countries.'

De Lancey was then called upon to issue two instructions, both dated 17 June. The first was sent in the afternoon, as it directed Prince Frederik of the Netherlands 'to move from Enghien this evening' to take position in front of Hal, with two battalions in the château there, and for Estorff's cavalry brigade to fall back from the south-western frontier to place itself under Frederik's orders at Hal. The second was addressed to Major-General Sir Charles Colville, commanding the 4th Division:

> The army retired this day from its position at Quatre Bras to its present position in front of Waterloo. The brigades of the 4th Division at Braine-le-Comte are to retire at daylight tomorrow morning upon Hal.
>
> Major-General Colville must be guided by the intelligence he receives of the enemy's movements in his march upon Hal, whether he moves by the

direct route or by Enghien. Prince Frederick of Orange is to occupy with his corps the position between Hal and Enghien, and is to defend it as long as possible.

The army will probably continue in its position in front of Waterloo tomorrow.

Lieutenant-Colonel Torrens will inform Major-General Sir Charles Colville of the position and situation of the armies.[26]

We see the clear concern that the river valleys of the Senne and Senette that join at Tubize, just south of Hal, should be firmly blocked, stopping any western approach to Brussels through Hal, but also rendering it more dangerous for a French force to move against Braine l'Alleud and Merbe Braine on Wellington's western flank. That Wellington considered that Napoleon could plan such a flanking attack was emphasised by his warning to Colville that he might have to make a detour via Enghien, which is some 8 miles north-west of Braine-le-Comte

The soaked and weary troops trudged up the rise towards the Mont St Jean ridge. The ground had softened further under the downpour and the mud and discomfort was extreme. Fires were hard to light, and once lit they smoked heavily – unless the bonfire was so large, piled with doors or furniture scavenged from the Belgian cottages, that it blazed like an inferno despite the rain. The rations could not be found. The rain continued hour after hour. There was little or no shelter and many found it impossible to sleep. The assistant surgeon of the 12th Light Dragoons finally found a ditch for shelter, threw in a bundle of straw and lay down on it in his cloak: but rainwater filled the ditch, rose through the straw and so he was wetter below than above. A soldier of the Royal Dragoons called it 'a real Wellington night', with thunder and rain made more trying because of a very high wind. The experienced Kincaid of the 95th slept reasonably well, but was unaccountably remiss in looking to his weapons, for during a bad moment the next day he found his sword stuck rusted inside the scabbard by the rain. The commissariat was roundly cursed for failing to provide nourishment, although judging by the recollections of Assistant Commissary-General Tupper Carey, a commissary who had Peninsular experience, this concentration on the main position 'was attended with confusion' due to camp followers having wreaked havoc to baggage wagons and food wagons during the retirement of the afternoon, so that the supply trains had been diverted, or pillaged, or overturned in Soignies Forest.[27]

The infantry had moved to the reverse side of the summit on either side of the Genappe to Brussels highway. The artillery batteries and horse artillery troops were stationed a little in front of them, with pickets, like the 33rd Foot, posted to keep watch. The cavalry came up the slope, passed through the infantry and settled for the night behind the infantry divisions.

VI

The advancing French were drenched, hungry, and disappointed of their prey. It made no difference whether a man was French or British, belonging to the new levies or the *Garde*: the weather was equally terrible.

Napoleon – soaked to the skin in his grey riding-coat and with the fastenings of his cocked hat detached by the weight of water so that the flaps hung down – was anxious to learn whether the British would halt or fall back on Brussels. He ordered four light batteries to fire at the high ground of Mont St Jean. The guns of Lloyd and Cleeves replied, until Wellington angrily ordered them to cease. They had, however, given Napoleon his answer.[28]

The Emperor could now fix his plans, and his formations were ordered to find places to rest overnight. To speak of 'finding their positions' would be to misuse words. Most of d'Erlon's corps was indeed beyond the crest, with its cavalry division (Jacquinot) watching the enemy. The troops lay down between the village of Plancenoit and the farm called Monplaisir. Behind them at Rossomme on the crest were Milhaud's *cuirassier* divisions, Domon and Subervie's cavalry divisions, and the *Garde* cavalry. But the rest of the army was far behind. Reille's troops and those of Lobau and the heavy cavalry of Kellermann, were all hunched around Genappe. The infantry of the *Garde* had, perhaps unwisely, sought to bypass the columns that were moving painfully slowly along the road. The *grognards* sank into the mud and struggled through a featureless country till they halted towards midnight at Glabais, two miles north of Genappe. Sergeant de Mauduit of the *2e Bataillon, 1er Grenadiers à Pied*, veteran of many campaigns, said that the rough going across the fields, through hedges, losing shoes in the bog, made everyone grumble and curse and even mutter 'Treason!', until they found their bivouac at midnight. If that was the state of the *Garde*, what must it have been like for less disciplined troops? In short, Napoleon's forces were stretched on or near the road for miles back and they would take several valuable hours to join him in the morning. Houssaye adds two depressing details, both of significance for the action next day:

> After piqueting their horses, a number of horsemen *got back into the saddle* and slept, leaning over their horses' necks, wrapped in their great cloaks. All

> the four days' rations of bread carried in each knapsack had been consumed. *Men were famished.* In most of the regiments, the distributions were made only in the middle of the night *and even in the morning.*

Such appalling horsemastership must have tortured, worn down, and weakened the burdened horses immeasurably. And the lack of provisions (felt by both sides that night) had the consequence that, left without food for up to 24 hours (maybe longer in some cases), French soldiers who should have been assembling as early as possible in order to march to the battlefield, spent instead the first hours of the day of battle scavenging everywhere for food, and far from their regiments.[29]

*

Appendix: Where Did Wellington Intend to Stand? Genappe, La Belle Alliance, Mont St Jean

This matter of where Wellington intended to fight is something of a curiosity, because several well-regarded officers seemed to disagree: either that the spot was above Genappe, and so nearly 5 miles south of Mont St Jean; or that it was 3½ miles north of Genappe, on the Le Caillou/Belle Alliance ridge; or that it really was at Mont St Jean that the Duke intended to fight.

The answer seems to me to be indeed the Mont St Jean ridge. This is not simply because the balance of evidence looks conclusive, but also for more general considerations. However, since some of my best friends and fine authorities have adopted the Belle Alliance thesis, I set out the matter in detail here.

Genappe

General Vivian, who retained a consuming interest in the Waterloo campaign to the very end of his life, recorded in 1839 a frequently repeated claim by the late Sir Frederick Ponsonby (1783–1837), of the 12th Light Dragoons. Vivian remembered it in these words:

> He [Ponsonby] knew it to be a fact that the Duke had himself halted some regiments in position on the Brussels side of Genappe, meaning to have halted his army there, having that town and the small river that runs through it in his front, but that De Lancey, his Quartermaster-General, who had been sent to the rear, came to him and described the position of Waterloo, and that the Duke determined to retire from that on which he was then halted to take up that on which the battle was fought.[30]

Genappe lies in the valley of the River Dyle. To its north the road rises gently for a mile: today the interchange of the N 5 and N 25 roads is at this point at the top of the slope. Then the road sinks slightly to the small dip in which Glabais lies (just off the road), then passes over another gentle rise and on to Le Caillou (just under 2 miles north of the interchange). De Lacy Evans called the slope out of Genappe 'open high ground' but made it clear that on 17 June it was to be where the cavalry rearguard was to check the French advance.[31] Genappe's single street and tiny bridge certainly created a bottleneck that could complicate an attacker's means of reinforcement and re-supply, but the Dyle was everywhere fordable, as the British cavalry proved. The concept of fighting the main French army there seems highly improbable, especially as even in this recollection of Ponsonby's story it would appear that Wellington's own eye had selected this high ground and that he was only dissuaded from standing there by a last minute word of advice from De Lancey, that it would be better to fight 'at Waterloo', in other words in front of the Forest of Soignies.

Let it be granted that Wellington had a good opinion of De Lancey though he had in the past called him 'the idlest fellow'.[32] But Wellington's eye for a battlefield was famously good and if he had himself selected Genappe heights as suitable, would he really have instantly accepted a snap judgement from De Lancey on so important a matter? I think not. Incidentally this account, for the little it is worth, dismisses the Belle Alliance ridge theory.

The Belle Alliance Position

FitzRoy Somerset's account, given his position as Wellington's Military Secretary, carries more weight than the Vivian/Ponsonby recollection. The difficulty is that he provided somewhat conflicting statements. As they came up to the crest upon which stands the inn La Belle Alliance, Wellington:

> thought it was the position the QMG would have taken up, being the most commanding ground, but [De Lancey] had found it too extended to be occupied by our troops so had proceeded further on and marked out a position: this was to the right near Braine l'Alleud thence to the left [east] across the high road which joined on the rear near Mont St Jean. About four o'clock the Duke found the troops on that spot [i.e. MSJ]. On looking at the position, finding the ground between Braine l'Alleud and Hougoumont broken, he ordered the right to be thrown back, the angle or elbow in the rear of Hougoumont, and the extreme right on Merbe Braine, intending that Braine l'Alleud should be occupied by a battery.[33]

Yet in the same account, writing of the retirement from Quatre Bras on the 17th he wrote that Wellington: 'despatched De Lancey, the QMG, to mark out a position in front of the Forest of Soignies, which the Duke proposed to take up with his army'.

It is scarcely reasonable to claim that the inn at La Belle Alliance is 'in front of the Forest of Soignies', given that Waterloo barrier at the outskirts of the forest is a full 3 miles from the inn. Moreover, in one version De Lancey was expected to mark out the Belle Alliance ridge as a fighting position, but in the other he had been sent straight past that place to mark out a position close to the Forest of Soignies. I see no way of reconciling Somerset's two statements, but for reasons that will become plain I accept the latter one.

Mont St Jean

Constant Rebecque's journal is clear. In the first place, Constant writes in his journal of Wellington's morning orders of 17 June to De Lancey: 'According to these orders the army must start moving at 10 a.m. in order to take up the position in front of Waterloo.' Then, later, as recorded in my main text, Constant found De Lancey sitting near the place where he was mortally wounded the next day – that is, on the Mont St Jean ridge – sorting out the placement of troops on that position, which again is in front of Waterloo.[34] A passing comment was made by Augustus Simon Frazer in a letter dated 'Waterloo, June 18, 3 a.m.', about retiring 'to a position previously selected, and we shall now make a stand; our right towards Braine l'Alleud, our left towards Limalle . . . the forest of Soignies . . . in our rear'.[35] All that testimony goes against any position other than Mont St Jean.

There is the statement of Sir Henry Clinton of 2nd Division, written on 23 June 1815 about the Mont St Jean position that he and his division had occupied on the 18th, which 'is a good one and had been noticed by the Duke of Wellington in the excursion he had made last August, I copied the remarks which he then briefly made'.[36]

But most valuable of all, there is the account of Major Oldfield, RE, written in July 1815. His account has always been recognised as of real authority, and he states that just prior to the opening of the campaign Colonel Carmichael Smyth (who had carried out the 1814 survey) had asked Oldfield:

> for the plan of the position of Waterloo [*sic*], which had been previously reconnoitred. The several sketches of the officers had been put together and one fair copy made for the Prince of Orange. A second had been commenced in the drawing room for the Duke, but was not in a state to send, I therefore forwarded the original sketches of the officers.

Oldfield times the forwarding as on the 16th, and says that he rode forward and joined Wellington and Smyth at Quatre Bras on the morning of the 17th. Smyth asked Oldfield to take possession again of the plan that the latter had forwarded. This he did. Upon news of the Prussians retreating:

> the Duke . . . called Colonel Smyth and asked him for his plan of the position of Waterloo, which I immediately handed to him (or in his sabretache attached to the saddle, I forget which). The Duke then gave directions to Sir William Delancey to put the army in position at Waterloo, forming them across the Nivelles and Charleroi *chaussées* which coming from Brussels divided at this point [*sic*], we were consequently in a line with the Prussians at a distance of about eight miles [from them] and eight miles [*sic*, a very fair estimate] in rear of Quatre Bras. The Duke at the same time ordered Colonel Smyth to give directions for Braine l'Alleud to be entrenched and made defensible . . .[37]

Such are the witnesses' various statements. It is a fact that in the summer of 1814 Wellington had required surveys to be made of several positions for the defence of Belgium and one had been made of Mont St Jean, the actual site of the battle of 1815. Clinton was correct in his remarks. In 1815 itself staff officers had ridden again all over Belgium studying sites and would have amassed quite a store of sketches and plans, and may well have made notes of the Belle Alliance position (we do not know one way or the other). There is a map, found in De Lancey's tunic, preserved, and several times printed: it covers the ground from south of la Belle Alliance to well north of Mont St Jean, but a map of that extent of ground does not answer our question.[38]

It is unlikely that Wellington had time to visit all these positions himself in the summer months of 1815, and in general he spent many of his visiting days in Hill's western sector, checking on defences between the coast and the Tournai, Ath, Hal area, the sector where he most expected attack. Further east he was concerned to establish strong defences at and between Soignies and Nivelles, trusting to halt any attack at those points, so that a place to their north would really be designed as a precautionary back-stop. Perhaps that is why Orange as sector commander was given the first fair copy of Oldfield's map? And so on the 16th Wellington would rely upon Carmichael Smyth and his staff for that map before giving his orders to De Lancey.

Oldfield's detailed testimony seems decisive here, for he links Wellington's orders for the Mont St Jean position by reference to the road junction, and to an order to entrench Braine l'Alleud which place was a vital component of his thinking in terms of the Mont St Jean position. There is no such road fork on

La Belle Alliance ridge, and Braine is not relevant in terms of an immediate defensive entrenchment on the southern ridge.

There are some other references to the Duke's opinion on the position in June 1815. In 1816 Colonel J. F. Burgoyne, RE, wrote: 'The Duke did not wish to have any ground entrenched beforehand which might give any clue to his intentions, but would have been glad to have had anything which could be thrown up at the time.'[39] While this is not of direct help it does conform with some of Oldfield's other remarks and thus endorse his general account.

Moreover, we have to remember that the 9 a.m. orders of 17 June required various units and columns to move to Waterloo, and for some wagons to continue into the forest beyond it. And these orders show that Constant's journal is an accurate one. Furthermore, early that morning Wellington had told the Prussian Massow that he would fall back to 'the camp at Mont St Jean' and fight there. Gneisenau (at noon on the 17th) had recorded his understanding of those words as 'offering battle at Waterloo in front of the forest of Soignies', subject always to being promised Prussian assistance. That assistance needed to have a firm directional objective, and so from Wellington's words would be predicated on marching to Mont St Jean in front of the forest of Soignies.[40]

The Belle Alliance position would have had a definite disadvantage for Wellington, judged by the numbers he could field, for it might be perhaps a third wider than Mont St Jean, and did not appear to have any forward

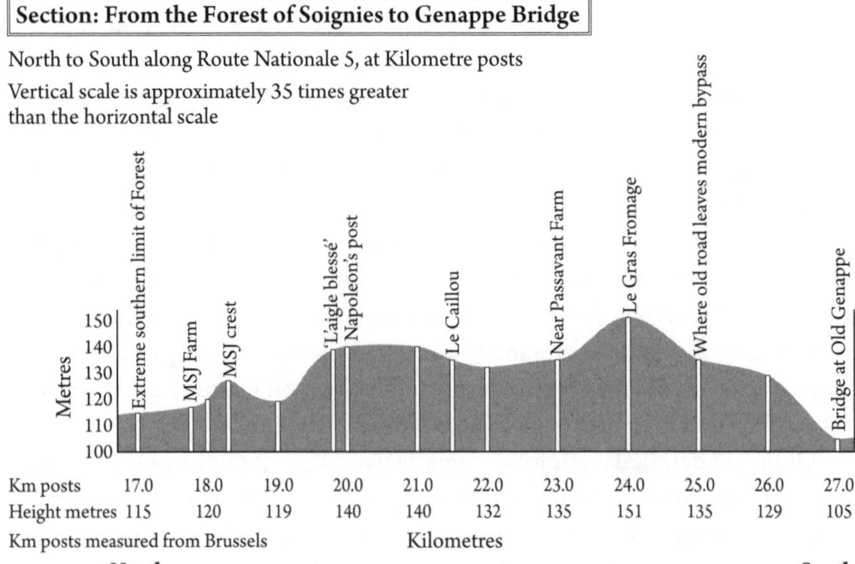

bastions such as Hougoumont, La Haye Sainte, and Papelotte. But perhaps just as importantly (as anyone can *see* when looking north from Le Caillou, slightly north of La Belle Alliance), an army forced to retreat northwards under fire from this summit would be exposed to attack as it struggled back a full mile through the broad and extensive valley and on up the slope until it could find cover on the Mont St Jean crest: it could face massacre from artillery and cavalry. By contrast an army defeated at Mont St Jean could hope to make a fighting retreat through the open forest of Soignies, the forest similarly making a rapid advance difficult for pursuers.

Taking all these statements and indications I think that Wellington's considered intention was to stand on the Mont St Jean ridge, with a wing at Braine l'Alleud to the right. He did not plan to fight a decisive battle at La Belle Alliance, and definitely not at Ponsonby's imagined Genappe.

Chapter 34

Grouchy and the Prussians

Afternoon to Evening, 17 June

I

NAPOLEON HAD LET SLIP THE FIRST HALF of 17 June. The Prussians had had some fifteen hours to regroup and retire beyond his grasp. Grouchy meanwhile had been obliged to kick his heels until given Napoleon's verbal orders at about 10.30–11 a.m. but these had been amended by two successive written orders that he must have received around noon: the first removing three cavalry divisions from him to serve instead with the Emperor; the second allocating him certain other units to make a force of 27,000 infantry and 6,000 cavalry, with Vandamme, Gérard, Pajol and Exelmans as his main subordinates.[1] The two cavalry subordinates had been ordered to fan out, Pajol eastwards along the route to Namur and Exelmans north-east towards Gembloux. Grouchy himself was now to go to Gembloux and undertake a prolonged search for the Prussians wherever they might be, paying special attention to Namur and Maastricht, but avoiding serious engagement. As Napoleon was moving from Ligny to Quatre Bras all communication should be by the Namur road. That line of communication tells us how little attention headquarters gave to any activities further to the northwards.[2]

The Marshal sent orders to General Vandamme, whose corps was resting between St Amand and La Haye, and rode to Ligny to speak personally to General Gérard, outlining his intentions to each. Neither general liked or respected Grouchy; each felt himself worthier of the marshal's baton for earlier services and again for their exertions on 16 June. It was with very poor grace that they obeyed. They were to march their infantry via Le Point du Jour to Gembloux, but in this respect Grouchy's decision to place *3e Corps* in the lead entailed further delay, for it had to move past Ligny and *4e Corps* to get there, whereas time could have been saved by placing Gérard's force in the van, with Vandamme following. As it was, Vandamme did not begin his march until 2 p.m., by which time the rain was pelting down; Gérard started an hour later.[3]

Meanwhile, the cavalry under Pajol and Exelmans had spent the morning scouting east and north, and the results of their patrols were reported to Grouchy as he began the afternoon.

Pajol, as we know, had captured six Prussian cannons (of Battery Nr. 14) on the road going east towards Mazy, and he then went on for a further mile or so but could discover no traces of the enemy. From local gossip he then gathered that the Prussians might have changed direction and so he moved at midday in a northward direction towards Perwez and Louvain. He was joined in the search by Teste's division. Pajol's force at midday was about 6 miles east of Le Point du Jour and the same distance south-east of Gembloux.

Exelmans had intended going north-eastwards, but one of his dragoon brigades under Berton had for some reason followed the Namur road and not that to Gembloux. Eventually being told that the Prussians were much further north, Berton halted, sought new orders and then moved to Gembloux, from where the Prussians could definitely be seen. Then Exelmans came up with his other troops, studied the enemy's dispositions, concluded that they numbered about 20,000 men, and so contented himself with watching them for some sign of movement. It is a surprise to find that he did not immediately inform his colleague Pajol or his superior Grouchy of the presence of the Prussians – this omission he remedied after noon, with a report to Grouchy, but three hours late.

Grouchy was at Le Point du Jour when, belatedly, he learned of this sighting close to Gembloux – coincidentally at the moment when Thielemann was beginning his march from Gembloux to Wavre. Exelmans entered Gembloux at 3 p.m. and then continued to Sauvenière (2 miles further north), where he bivouacked. The rain and the twelve hours of activity may have accounted for this decision to halt. But at least he did not cease altogether to look for the Prussians, because from Sauvenière he sent out one regiment north-east to Perwez and a full brigade north to Tourinnes. His men saw at Tourinnes the last vestiges of the Prussian rearguard. But it was late and the cavalry fell back to quarters west of Sauvenière; the detached regiment reported rumours that Wavre was the Prussian destination. At 6 p.m. Grouchy had heard from Pajol his belief that the Prussians were retiring on Louvain, and after nightfall Exelmans had reported on the fresh news on his front about Wavre being the Prussian destination.

So these reports all pointed generally north – or perhaps somewhat to the north-east. 'The paved road of Namur' was thus irrelevant as a route for direct communication. But Grouchy was puzzled by other wisps of information that led him to wonder about Namur and Liège as possible refuges for the Prussians, as we shall see. He even wondered if they might be hastening to join with Wellington to the west. There can be little doubt that if Grouchy had ridden forward in the early afternoon he might have re-activated Exelmans's pursuit, obliging him to cling to the tail of the retreating column. Although his cavalry could not hope to engage the Prussians with any chance of success, they could at least have established in which direction a large component of the Prussian army was headed. Instead they were allowed to slip away and Grouchy continued to believe that some elements were fleeing east.

For the infantry of Grouchy's force there could be no hope of overtaking the retreating enemy. Again, the different psychologies of retreat and pursuit come into play. Had the French been in a state to launch a real pursuit immediately after the last struggles of the evening and when the Prussians were reeling back, they might have turned retreat into rout and collapse. But they were not in that state, and the Prussians were granted time to recover a degree of control, and to restore order and discipline – becoming once again a formed body of troops. To avoid being overtaken, the Prussians would march until they dropped: the extra ounce of energy was still in reserve, and if the conditions were vile, they were vile equally for the pursuers. For the French infantry, barely restored by a short night's rest, it was mere slogging with no enemy in sight: just more misery; the pace would drag, morale would sink.[4]

Why then the cavalryman Grouchy remained with Vandamme's infantry is not clear. The infantry did not reach Gembloux until 7 p.m., with Gérard arriving even later, as night drew on.[5] Thus it was after dark by the time Grouchy himself had all the information from Pajol and Exelmans, and that meant that it would be 18 June before he could direct his contingent towards the Prussians. At 10 p.m. Grouchy therefore wrote:

> Sire, I have the honour to report that I am occupying Gembloux, with my cavalry at Sauvenières. The enemy, about 30,000 strong is continuing his retreat; we took 400 head of horned cattle, supplies and baggage.
>
> From all the reports reaching Sauvenières, the Prussians seem to be divided into two columns, one taking the route to Wavre, passing by Sart-à-Walhain, the other column apparently going towards Perwez.
>
> One can possibly infer that one portion will join Wellington, and that the centre, which is Blücher's army, is retiring on Liège. As another column with the artillery has retreated on Namur, General Exelmans has orders to press six squadrons on Sart-à-Walhain [north-west], and three squadrons towards Perwez [east]. Depending upon their reports, if the mass of the Prussians is retiring on Wavre I shall follow them in that direction, so that they cannot reach Brussels, and to separate them from Wellington.

> If on the contrary, my information proves that the principal Prussian force is marching on Perwez, I shall move by that town in pursuit of the enemy.
>
> Generals Thielmann and Borstell were part of the army that Your Majesty beat yesterday; they were still here at 10 a.m. and gave out that 20,000 of their men had been made *hors de combat*. They enquired distances to Wavre, Perwez and Hannut. Blücher was slightly wounded in the arm, which did not stop him commanding after the wound was dressed. He certainly has not passed by Gembloux. I am etc.[6]

Having written this despatch, at 10 p.m. Grouchy issued his orders for the following morning. The cavalry of Exelmans were to go north to Sart-à-Walhain in the general direction of Nil-St-Vincent and Tourinnes. The infantry of Vandamme were to follow them, starting at 6 a.m. with *4e Corps* infantry following them from 8 a.m. Pajol's cavalry, and the cavalry of *4e Corps,* were to move on Grand Leez, 3 miles north-east of Gembloux because 'the enemy is retiring on Perwez'.

As Houssaye remarked, having told Napoleon that he was aware of the need to check on Wavre, the actual morning orders made much greater stress on Perwez (in a quite different direction) as the point of attention. 'Wavre' as such was comparatively neglected.[7]

II

Grouchy has been much criticised for his interpretation of the orders given him and for his appreciation of the situation in the field. But the orders in the second Bertrand letter were themselves far from perfect. For they required Grouchy to find the enemy wherever he might be, but they repeatedly directed his attention eastwards: towards Maastricht (once), towards Liège (once) and up to and into Namur (the town was mentioned at least three times), and furthermore the orders required communication to pass by the *Namur* to Quatre Bras *chaussée*. On the other hand, Napoleon admitted that he had no idea of what the Prussians planned to do, and he did worry that they might join Wellington and together cover Brussels and Liège – an Allied disposition that is difficult to fathom.[8] What was clear was that Grouchy was to search hard while not involving his force in serious fighting.[9]

It cannot be said that Grouchy or his subordinates had performed their tasks very well. Vandamme and Gérard had moved with agonising slowness, and although Pajol had learned enough to swing away from the Namur road and turn north, Exelmans had been both supine in activity and remiss in his reporting. It was impossible for Grouchy to be with both Pajol and Exelmans, but had he ridden forward with either force he could have obtained better information on each sector very much sooner – had he gone to Exelmans he might have learned enough to grasp where 'the mass' of Prussians was tending. After all, Wavre was in the direction of Brussels, and on that point Napoleon's concerns were totally clear. Indeed Grouchy himself had just told Napoleon that 'if the mass of the Prussians is retiring on Wavre I shall follow them in that direction, so that they cannot reach Brussels, and to separate them from Wellington'.

Here again we see the poverty of Grouchy's thinking. In the first place, he knew that he was at least 5 miles (three or more hours in this weather) behind the rear files of the Prussians as they went towards Wavre. How could he possibly so manoeuvre his force as to get *beyond* them 'so that they cannot reach Brussels'? Secondly, why should any commander think that the Prussians would continue to fragment into smaller groups moving in separate directions, when every precept was that strength lay in unity: why some to Wavre and some to Perwez? Why some to join in covering Brussels with Wellington (whom Napoleon stated to be at Quatre Bras) and some to Liège? Lastly, and most importantly in the circumstances, if he was to keep the forces at Wavre from joining Wellington (as he stated), his one hope was to cross the River Dyle to its western (left) bank, and place himself athwart the roads leading towards Mont St Jean from Wavre. This he failed to do.[10]

All that Napoleon knew was that the whereabouts of the Prussians were still unclear and they were still out of reach. He could only guess whether they might seek to join Wellington. But at least Grouchy at Gembloux had promised to search in the morning towards Wavre, or Perwez, places 9 and 14 miles distant from imperial headquarters.

III

The Prussian situation was still difficult, but it was slowly improving. By the middle of the day Massow's report, coming after the news that Müffling and Wussow had provided late on the 16th, gave a fairly clear idea of what had happened at Quatre Bras and what Wellington now wished to do. Consequently, at 3 p.m. Gneisenau had instructed Ziethen to alter his current orders and to watch the entire left bank of the Dyle 'and maintain communications with Lord Wellington [*und die Kommunikation mit dem Lord Wellington unterhalten wird*]'.[11]

By about 5 p.m. there arrived at Wavre the long-awaited column of wagons from Maastricht with the desperately needed ammunition for two corps.

This undoubtedly changed Prussian thinking; the half of the army that was already at Wavre was no longer a collection of beaten men, it was an armed force once more. When the less battered III Corps and the fully equipped IV Corps came in, the Prussian Army of the Lower Rhine could fight again.

Gröben's reports from his eyrie near Tilly had continued: at 11.30 a.m. he sent his second message of the day: there had been minor movements among the French at Marbisou near Tilly, though nothing at Sombreffe, but the firing from Wellington's direction had almost died away. It is nowhere indicated at what time any of Gröben's reports were received at headquarters, but it seems reasonable to think that those sent before noon had come by late afternoon.

There were two afternoon messages from Gröben, comprising several intermediate up-dates, and it may be simplest to summarise them all at this point. The first was signed and sent 'at 5 p.m.' and was followed by a final one (Lettow-Vorbeck terms it the 'fourth' of the day) at no stated time. At 12.30 p.m. Gröben registered that strong French patrols were close to Tilly, possibly with infantry following them, that one of Sohr's patrols had found that British posts to the right had been slightly withdrawn. Then at 1 p.m. he noted that French cavalry had deployed near Tilly and infantry were on the move from Brye, and he thought that they might be moving against Wellington. At 2 p.m. he saw that all the troops were moving past Tilly towards Genappe. At 5 p.m. he confirmed the retirement of Sohr's rearguard past Mont-St-Guibert, of the comparative inactivity of the French against it, of the arrival of Lieutenant-Colonel Ledebur's detached force, forming part of IV Corps rearguard, and of French moves along the River Dyle and to the west of Mellery. His final message was that he had heard cannon-fire commence in Wellington's sector around 4 p.m. and he feared that the French might move between the Prussian observation posts and Wellington's eastern flank. As he closed, he warned that the cannonade against Wellington now seemed to be at Genappe.

Meanwhile the march of III and IV Corps was under way. Once Thielemann had received Bülow's orders at the end of the morning, he gave his III Corps the necessary instructions to march from north of Gembloux to Wavre, a distance of about 10 miles. The march began at 2 p.m. in drenching rain and the head of the column reached the bridge at Wavre at about 8 p.m., crossed it and continued to a site to the north of the town. The rearguard came in at around midnight and von der Marwitz's cavalry re-joined, having served on the western wing in the previous day's battle. IV Corps had detached a force under Ledebur to replace Sohr's rearguard, and this detachment, comprising Ledebur's own cavalry regiment, two light infantry battalions and two guns from a horse-artillery battery, took position in the deep and wooded valley at Mont-St-Guibert, an almost perfect defensive position. It remained there for the next twenty-four hours. The remainder of IV Corps trudged slowly along the routes northwards, some on paved roads, some on tracks that were deep in mud and water, reaching the village of Dion-le-Mont, south-east of Wavre, at times between early evening and midnight. Bülow himself wrote to headquarters from Dion-le-Mont at 10 p.m. announcing that most of his corps had arrived except for the rearmost 13th Brigade that, because of the forced marches, had been obliged to rest. Outposts had been placed to watch against enemy movements but apart from some *cuirassiers* seen near Baudeset there was no sign of the French. Having posted his brigades one behind the other on the road he stated that the corps 'can move in any direction. I now request Your Highness to inform me where the other corps are situated and how I can make contact with them.' Meanwhile his brigades bivouacked around the road they had trudged with cavalry patrols watching the Namur–Louvain road lest the French should appear.[12]

Apart from some scattered units, the army was reunited. But the troops were wet, tired, and most of them very hungry, and the high command had work planned for them. It is probable that by the time that headquarters went to rest, all these highly informative reports had been received and read, although the deluge in the afternoon must have delayed progress for the couriers with the later messages.[13]

Let us summarise the emerging prospects. Even without the two later Gröben messages, we can still see that by the late afternoon of 17 June the Prussian high command at Wavre was fairly well informed about I and II Corps, could reckon that even after some 18,000 casualties, they retained about 47,000 men, and would be re-supplied with ammunition over-night. They could reasonably expect III and IV Corps that evening because, after Weyrach had reported their whereabouts and condition in the morning, they had sent Bülow clear orders calling on him to march both formations on Wavre. Sufficient intelligence had come from Gröben to know that the French were inactive on the Ligny battlefield even in full morning, so that, from his and Weyrach's reports, it was unlikely that Thielemann and Bülow would be heavily attacked. The high command knew that Wellington had inflicted a setback on the French at Quatre Bras and recovered the position that initially appeared lost; indeed he had been so successful that he had thought of going onto the offensive with Prussian support. Even now Wellington was proposing to give battle at Mont St Jean, if supported.

That was encouraging, but for the anxious generals at Wavre that night there were doubts as well. First of all, Wellington's army was not an elite homogeneous force, and while it had done well at Quatre Bras it had not been fighting Napoleon and the main army. It might be defeated, and in that case the two Prussian corps that had been requested would share in the disaster. Gneisenau had been haunted by fears of Britain abandoning the Continent. Were Wellington to be defeated, captured or killed such a fear could become a certainty. The rest of the Prussian army would then have to make for Antwerp or the Rhine, pursued by Napoleon, and its chances of escape would be slim to non-existent. But that was only the first danger. If there should be a defeat in front of the forest of Soignies, would Schwarzenberg and the Tsar and the Austrian Emperor rally, or look to their own safety and seek for peace? Whereas Britain, however greatly humiliated, could continue to hold out behind the Royal Navy, the loss of Blücher's army could spell the end of the Prussian monarchy – and of Prussia itself, perhaps divided between France and Russia and Austria in a new 'settlement of Europe'. In short, what the Prussian high command faced that evening was a stark choice between terrible risk and certain doom. They would run a risk in joining with Wellington's 'useless army' – possibly gaining a victory thereby, and ensuring Prussia a strong role in the new Europe – but they might face a second great defeat, which could spell disaster. Yet if they did not join him, he would fall back and they would certainly be left to their isolated fate, which inevitably meant disaster.[14]

At this point the old warrior prince began to take control again. Carried to Wavre in the morning, he found the energy to rise from his litter and assert himself. There is a story that Müffling had sent his own ADC, Lieutenant Wucherer, from Quatre Bras in the early morning to learn what had happened to the Prussians on the 16th. The historian Hofmann (relying on Müffling, presumably) wrote that Wucherer met Nostitz at Wavre, that Nostitz at first refused to let him wake Blücher, then relented. The Field Marshal listened to Müffling's messenger, then replied, 'Tell the Duke that I cannot advance today, but tomorrow I will come with the fresh corps, and with the others.'[15]

Reported remarks of Colonel Hardinge add some details to the story of the debate, but they are Lord Mahon's (Stanhope's) record of a conversation and may not be quite what Hardinge actually said. Stanhope's recollection places the event in the night of 16/17 at Wavre, which is plainly a mistake, for it must have been at the end of the night of 17/18 at Wavre. Hardinge said that:

> Next morning Blücher sent for me in, calling me *Lieber Freund*, etc., and embracing me. He said to me *Ich stinke etwas*, that he had been obliged to take medicine, having been twice rode over by cavalry, but that he should be quite satisfied if in conjunction with the Duke of Wellington he was

> able now to defeat his old enemy. I was told that there had been a great discussion that night in his rooms, and that Blücher and Grolman carried the day for remaining in communication with the English army, but that Gneisenau had great doubts as to whether they ought not to fall back to Liège and secure their own communication with Luxembourg. They thought that if the English should be defeated they themselves would be utterly destroyed.[16]

There is a second story in print. This was published by Colonel J. F. Maurice in 1890, who had ascertained that:

> The present Lord Hardinge [1822–94] has often heard his father mention the circumstances of which I am about to speak. Colonel Hardinge had been wounded on the 16th, and, he records, that as he was on the 17th lying on his bed Blücher burst into his room, triumphantly announcing: 'Gneisenau has given way. We are to march to join Wellington.'[17]

Hardinge's recollection of Blücher's words seems to match the old man's character. Whether he was quite fair to Gneisenau is less certain. We saw that Gneisenau in mid-afternoon was ordering contact to be maintained with Wellington, as offering a degree of mutual security. If he voiced his concerns over the Prussian dilemma that I have just outlined, surely that was his right as a thinking chief of staff, ensuring that Blücher was aware of the situation before making a decision. On the other hand, in linking Blücher and the ever-positive Grolman in opposition to Gneisenau, Hardinge may have been very close to the truth, sensing Gneisenau's general gloom and sense of mistrust. There is just one further piece of evidence to quote. Blücher wrote to his wife from Wavre on this 17 June: 'Today I have moved closer to Lord Wellington, and in a few days there probably will be another battle. Everyone is full of courage and if Napoleon still wants to deliver such a battle he and his army will be finished.'[18]

It would seem that at around 11.30 p.m. a letter came from Müffling telling of the Duke's overnight positions in preparation for battle. It thus obliged the Prussians to come to a final decision. Lettow-Vorbeck inclined to the view that Blücher's reply was signed and sent about midnight, and it is certain (as we shall see) that Wellington had read it before 3 a.m. Blücher's letter, addressed to Müffling, ran as follows:

> Headquarters, Wavre, 17 June 1815: I beg to inform your Excellency that in consequence of your report to me that the Duke of Wellington will accept battle in the position from Braine l'Alleud to La Haye, my troops will be set in motion as follows: Bülow's corps will advance at daybreak from Dion-le-

> Mont, via Wavre to St-Lambert, and attack the enemy's right flank; II Corps will follow immediately after, and I and III Corps will hold themselves in readiness to follow in that direction. The exhaustion of the troops some of whom have not yet arrived, makes it impossible to start earlier. I request your Excellency to inform me in good time when and how the Duke may be attacked, so that I can take measures accordingly.[19]

And so, at midnight, orders were written for Bülow to march on Chapelle (St-Lambert), to take position there if the French were not attacking Wellington in force, but in the event that Napoleon was delivering full-scale attacks, then IV Corps was to hasten to attack the French right flank. The appropriate orders went to the other corps; II Corps would follow immediately, the others would assemble, cook and make ready to move accordingly. Baggage, train, and impedimenta were to be sent to Louvain.[20]

Dawn would break on this dark wet morning by 3.30 at latest. From Dion to Wavre was 2 miles, and from Wavre to Chapelle-St-Lambert another 5. Once there, Ohain was 1 mile away, and Frischermont about 2 miles. Wellington's patrols on his eastern flank could now be warned to watch for them. On such a timetable, with nine hours for the march, IV Corps might be in the battle line not too long after midday. Such at least was the hope.

*

Appendix 1: The Texts of Grouchy's Letter of 10 p.m., 17 June

Ropes and Pollio have both pointed out variations between the published texts of this letter, and I have followed their preferred version, that of 1830. The letter was published by General Gérard in 1830, accompanied by an authentication from Gourgaud: 'certified as identical with the original given me by the Emperor Napoleon, and which is in my hands' (see Siborne, *History*, 3rd edn., p. 186 fn.). Grouchy published his version in 1843, and his son re-published it in 1874 in the *Mémoires*, volume iv, p. 58 and again p. 263, stating that he took the text 'from the original under my eyes'.

> *Gérard, 1830:* Sire, I have the honour to report that I am occupying Gembloux with my cavalry at Sauvenières.

> *Memoirs of 1874:* Sire, I have the honour to report that I am occupying Gembloux, where *4e Corps* is just arriving; *3e* is in front of this town; and a part of my cavalry at Sauvenières.

> *Gérard, 1830:* From all the reports reaching Sauvenières, the Prussians seem to be divided into two columns, one taking the route to Wavre, passing

by Sart-à-Walhain, the other column apparently going towards Perwez. One can possibly infer that one portion will join Wellington, and that the centre, which is Blücher's army, is retiring on Liège.

Memoirs of 1874: From some reports, it seems that on arriving at Sauvenières, a part of the Prussian army divided: one column going to Perwez-le-Marché, another having taken the route to Wavre, passing by Sart-à-Walhain. One can possibly infer that some Prussian forces will join Wellington, and the others will retire on Liège.

Gérard, 1830: Depending upon their reports, if the mass of the Prussians is retiring on Wavre I shall follow them in that direction, so that they cannot reach Brussels, and to separate them from Wellington. If on the contrary, my information proves that the principal Prussian force is marching on Perwez, I shall move by that town in pursuit of the enemy.

Memoirs of 1874: If I learn from the reports that I hope to receive overnight, that large masses of Prussians are moving on Wavre, I shall follow them in that direction and attack them as soon as I shall have come up with them.

Whatever the copy in Grouchy's out-letter register said, there seems no doubt about the text the Emperor received.

Appendix 2: 'The Decisive Moment of the Century'

The phrase '*Es war der entscheidende Augenblick des Sätulums*' first got into general circulation in 1897, although it had been written on 24 June 1815. The German book in which it appeared made no very marked impression, but this phrase in it was noted by the great French historian of the 1815 campaign, Henry Houssaye who quoted it: '*Ce fut le moment décisif du siècle.*' As all Europe read Houssaye's masterpiece it passed into the general currency.[21]

Houssaye was praising Gneisenau's decision to retreat on Wavre and he linked the phrase to that event. But he misread his source, and he mistakenly thought that Wellington had said it. 'Wellington wrote emphatically to the King of the Netherlands "It was the decisive moment of the century",' and he cited the Duke's despatch to the King dated 19 June 1815, 'of which a copy was made and sent to the King of Württemberg on 24 June'. He duly acknowledged the German book of 1897, written by the Württemberg General Pfister.[22]

But the phrase is nowhere in any letter from the Duke to the Netherlands King, and it is not in the despatch of 19 June (the Waterloo Despatch), copied and adapted into Dutch.[23]

What Pfister wrote was that the Württemberg envoy at The Hague copied the 19 June despatch from Dutch into German and sent it to his monarch in Stuttgart. Pfister went on to say that the envoy *then added a comment of his own*, of 24 June, and it was this:

> on the evening of 16 June Blücher was not beaten, insofar as his army was sufficiently together to choose freely its road of retreat. The path it chose was not the one expected by the enemy, who did not find it for two whole days, and it finally led to the ruin of the enemy. It was the decisive moment of the century.

Whether or not the envoy was correct in his belief is a matter that we do not need to discuss here. It is a pity that we have not been given the envoy's name, for it is a striking phrase, even a portentous one: was he an ancestor of Oswald Spengler, who specialised in *Welthistorische* theory? When spoken aloud it sounds extremely fine in German. But it was never said by the Duke, and indeed it is very unlike his style, which tended to understatement and the avoidance of anything like gush. He was against talk of world events or speaking in terms of centuries. What the Duke thought, he said very plainly in his Waterloo Despatch. It was fair to Blücher, it was complimentary, it did praise his friend suitably. That was enough. I think we can leave it there.

Chapter 35

Wellington and the Battleground

Overnight, 17/18 June

I

ON THE EVENING OF SATURDAY 17 JUNE the Duke of Wellington rode back to the village of Waterloo, accompanied by his staff and the Allied commissioners attached to his headquarters. At this moment the one essential commissioner was General Müffling. In the morning he had spoken with Gneisenau's emissary Massow, and later had sent his own ADC Wucherer to find Blücher and update him on Wellington's situation and views; Wucherer had duly returned from Wavre with a verbal promise that Blücher would come on the 18th 'with the fresh corps, and with the others'. All that had been in the earlier part of the day, and now with evening coming on and as the Anglo-Allied army under torrential rain reached the chosen ridge north of La Belle Alliance, Müffling had written a confirmatory note and sent it to his high command, restating Wellington's firm intention to fight there, provided that the verbal promise of assistance by two Prussian corps still held good. Darkness, rain and increasingly muddy roads all affected the two armies' communications, and the final assurance would take a considerable time to come from Wavre. Wellington went to bed in the inn called *À Jean de Nivelles*, ordering his staff to wake him whenever news came in.

At some time after 2 a.m. Blücher's letter was read out to the Duke (see the text in Chapter 34, Section III), so that now he knew for certain that the whole Prussian army would move to his support, two corps leading the way at daybreak. The 10-mile march from Wavre should bring the heads of column within sight of Wellington's army by the middle of the day, or very shortly after.

The Duke immediately wrote three longish letters, all timed 'Waterloo, 18 June, 3 a.m.' To the governor of Antwerp he ordered the city to be placed in a state of siege, but to admit the exiled French royal family, if they should arrive, and also the British and other civilians who were leaving Brussels.

The second letter was to the Bourbon duc de Berri, summarising for him the events of the 16th and 17th, and confirming that the armies of the two allies were assembled and able to fight. However, he added some precautionary advice. 'It could be that the enemy will turn us at Hal, although the weather is terrible and the roads detestable, and despite my placing Prince Frederik's corps in position between Hal and Enghien.' If that should happen, then the exiled royal family should retire to Antwerp, and meanwhile they should send there all but essential stocks and stores.

> I hope, and more, have every reason to believe, that all will be well, but one must allow for everything; and one does not want to make large losses. That is why I pray that Your Royal Highness do what is written in this letter; and that His Majesty [Louis XVIII] should leave for Antwerp, not on false rumours, but upon definite information that the enemy has (despite myself) entered Brussels by turning [my position] at Hal. His Majesty will always have time to go via northern Flanders.

The third letter was to Sir Charles Stuart, ambassador to the Dutch court and the Bourbons, enclosing the first two letters for instant on-forwarding. Given the weather and the pre-dawn darkness, his summary was calm, even cheerful, and his prediction one that few would have dared to write at such a moment:

> You will see in the letter to the Duc de Berri the real state of our case and the only risk we run. The Prussians will be ready again in the morning for anything. Pray keep the English quiet if you can. Let them all prepare to move, but neither be in a hurry or a fright, as all will yet turn out well.

He added that the use of post horses had been embargoed in his name so as to avoid people running off with them, but Stuart could release them to anyone he thought deserved one, and he remarked in passing on the trials of dealing with King Willem's officials. The imminence of battle did not stop him covering many points in very few words.[1]

Closer to his heart was a fourth letter, also timed 3 a.m., to his current *petite amie*, Lady Frances Wedderburn Webster, advising her and her family to make preparations to go to Antwerp 'in case such a measure should be necessary' but that there was no immediate danger: 'at present I know of none'. He mentioned the varied fortunes of the Prussians and the British on 16 June, and went on: 'the course of the operations may oblige me to uncover Bruxelles for a moment, and may expose that town to the enemy'.[2]

This may be circumlocution to warn her that Napoleon might march into and take Brussels. But it may also help explain his 'western strategy', which we shall discuss in due course.

II

The topography of Waterloo has been described in every book on the battle, sometimes in great detail, and so what will be offered here is a very summary account of the main features, sufficient to explain the siting of the opposing forces. Individual features will be noted in their appropriate places.[3]

The full extent of the battlefield was within a quadrilateral extending about 2½ miles west to east, and somewhat less north to south. In the west the little town of Braine l'Alleud marked one limit, while Smohain hamlet and Frischermont château defined the eastern boundary. The northern limit of the battlefield comprised the ridge of Mont St Jean, which was slightly curved so that its extremities were somewhat forward of the ground in the central sector. The southern limit to the field was the somewhat higher ridge of La Belle Alliance and nearby Rossomme; and between the two ridges was a shallow undulating valley draining east. It was a much smaller area than the battleground of Ligny and was much more densely held.

Three roads were of primary importance within this quadrilateral. The first was the *chaussée* from Charleroi running due north through the centre, that I shall call the Charleroi or great road, which continued to Mont St Jean hamlet, thence to Waterloo and to Brussels. It divided the battlefield into equal parts, west and east. A second paved road ran diagonally across the western segment, from Nivelles (beyond the south-western corner) to Mont St Jean hamlet, where it met the Charleroi road (again beyond the northern edge of the battlefield). This junction we have noted in earlier chapters as the Mont St Jean fork. There was a third road, of lesser quality, running east to west from Wavre through Ohain to Braine l'Alleud, and it ran for the most part along the Mont St Jean ridge: this was the road along which Wellington expected the Prussians to come. From the air these three roads would have resembled two large legs of a capital A with the cross-bar high up and extending far beyond each leg. Where the minor Wavre to Braine l'Alleud road (the cross-bar) crossed the Charleroi road (the right leg) Wellington set up his command post at an easily recognisable solitary tree. There was one other minor road, running from Wavre to Chapelle-St-Lambert and thence south-west, up the Lasne brook, to Plancenoit and the Rossomme sector, but it did not form part of any Wellingtonian plan, and in Napoleon's scheme was judged as a road requiring only a precautionary guard. Apart from these two paved *chaussées* and two minor roads, all other paths across the field were what we today would consider mere tracks. What this road layout meant was that an army attacking the Mont St Jean ridge would have to make a *frontal* attack on a concave position from which converging fire would come, whereas the defender on the ridge could use the *lateral* minor road either as a front position or for movement and communication.

The Mont St Jean ridge had a fairly definite forward (southern) slope down to the valley,[4] and a gentle and broad reverse slope that fell away sufficiently to conceal mounted men stationed behind the summit. This ridge extended for about a mile west of the crossroads, and much of this western sector was around the 440-foot contour, with the valley at about 390 feet. East of the crossroads the ridge continued for about 2 miles until it sank into featureless open ground; this eastern sector was at a slightly lower level than the western, save for a knoll about 800 yards east of the crossroads which touched 430 feet, and then the ridge continued eastwards sinking gradually towards 400 feet. The valley floor below the eastern ridge was at 360–330 feet, also sinking eastwards.[5] Thus the forward slope of the ridge was not too steep for cavalry to fight over, although exertion in the soft and wet soil conditions of 18 June soon blew the horses. However, these slopes were not broad and were clearly segmented, since below the slope sat several separate habitations, all quickly fortified by Wellington's troops: the estate of Hougoumont in the west, then half a mile to the east the small farm La Haye Sainte on the Charleroi road, then almost a mile further east Papelotte farm, and then La Haye and Smohain hamlets and Frischermont house furthest east – these last three sitting in more broken country different in nature from the open slopes to the west. Mark Adkin aptly calls this section of the front '*bocage* country'.[6]

The battlefield was covered with summer crops, the corn and rye standing 5–6 feet tall and doubtless concealing the little folds in the ground.[7] In the valley there were no hedges and very few trees other than in the estates and farm gardens.

The opposing or French ridge was fairly regular, standing at Rossomme at about 460 feet, but at La Belle Alliance at about 430 feet. The slope to the valley floor was longer and easier than on Wellington's ridge. These southern heights had one special feature, a subsidiary ridge extending north-west, generally about the 400 feet height, passing west of the low-lying château of Hougoumont and ending close to Braine l'Alleud. In its turn this secondary ridge threw out spurs tending north-east that passed north of La Belle Alliance and across the Charleroi road: one of these was to become the site of Napoleon's Grand Battery of artillery.[8]

To the west of Rossomme stood a timber three-stage observation tower about 50–60 feet tall, and this provided a clear view over the intervening ground, although apparently it did not enable viewers to see behind the Mont St Jean ridge. This tower was reportedly used by Napoleon during the day.[9]

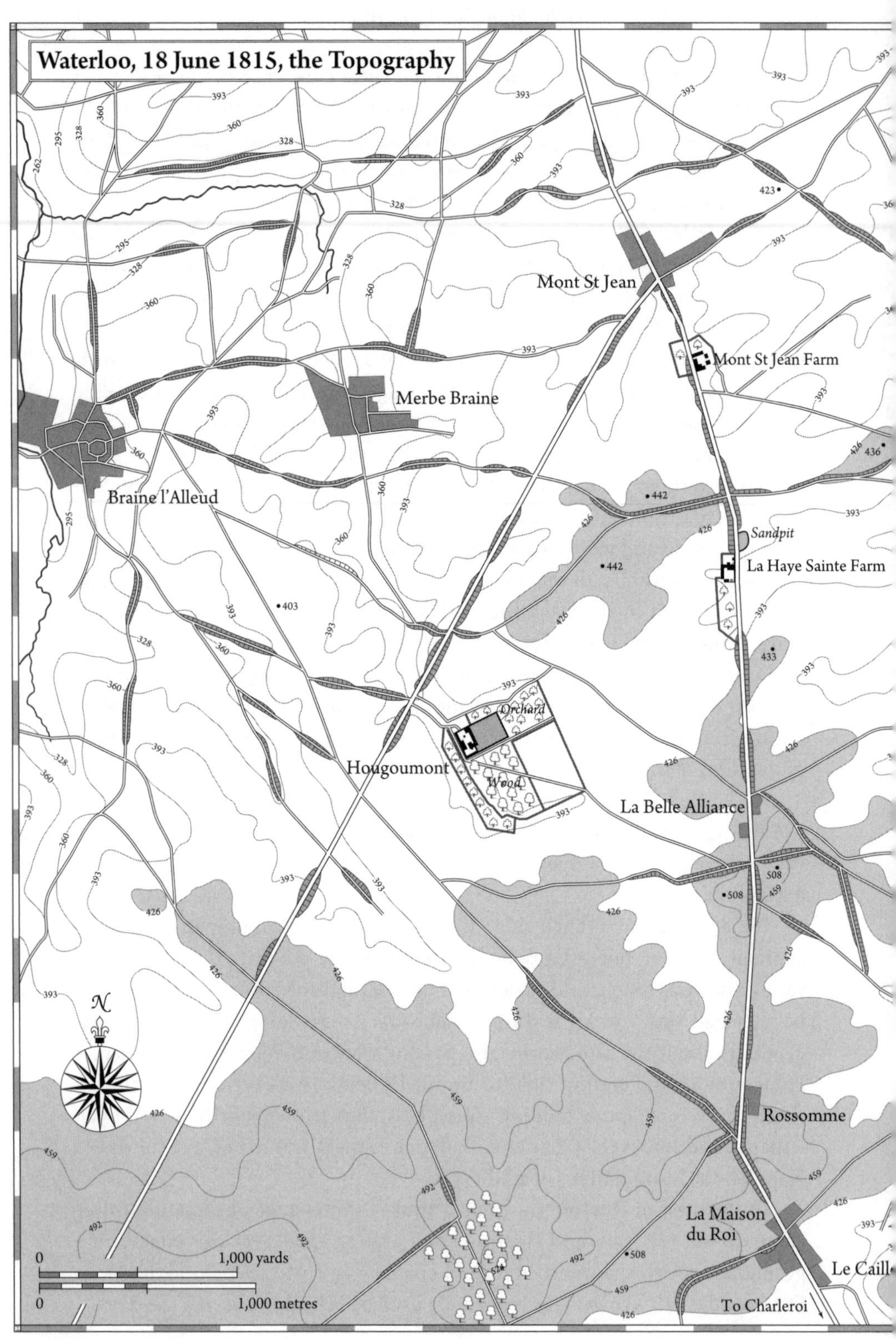

Waterloo, 18 June 1815, the Topography
Mont St Jean
Mont St Jean Farm
Merbe Braine
Braine l'Alleud
Sandpit
La Haye Sainte Farm
Orchard
Hougoumont
Wood
La Belle Alliance
Rossomme
La Maison
du Roi
To Charleroi
N
0
1,000 yards
0
1,000 metres

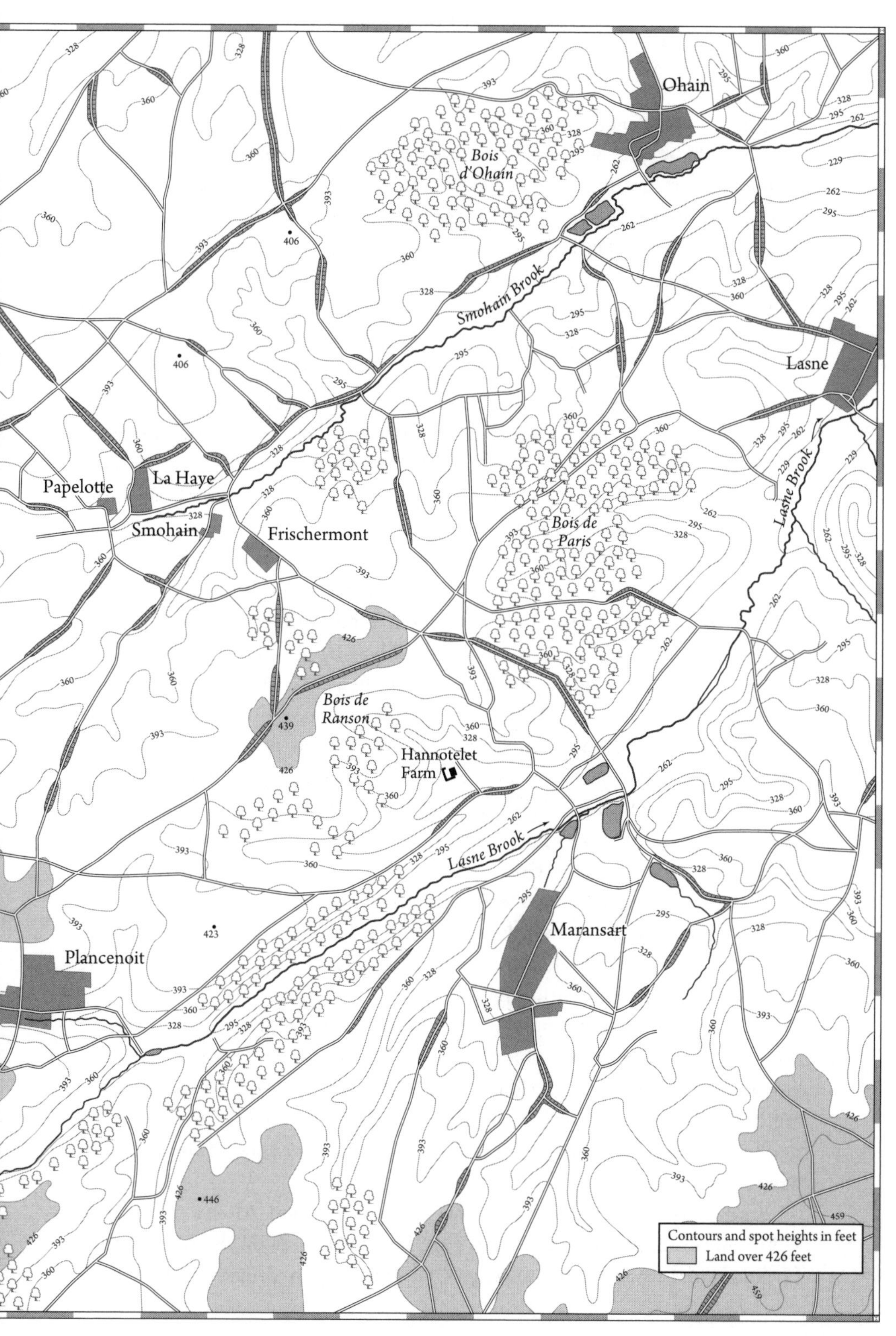
Ohain
Bois d'Ohain
Smohain Brook
Lasne
Lasne Brook
Papelotte
La Haye
Smohain
Frischermont
Bois de Paris
Bois de Ranson
Hannotelet Farm
Lasne Brook
Maransart
Plancenoit
Contours and spot heights in feet
Land over 426 feet

III

Wellington positioned much of his army in the sector west of the Charleroi road, and the way in which weaker and stronger units were placed and intermingled is instructive. At the extreme west, in the town of Braine l'Alleud, and watching the bridges on the north-flowing River Hain, he posted Chassé's 3rd Netherlands Division of 12 battalions, 7,000 men, and 16 guns. This flanking force could be further supported by (or if necessary could fall back upon) the contingent made up of the 1st Netherlands Division and Anthing's Indian brigade, plus Estorff's cavalry (in all a further 16 battalions, over 10,000 men, plus cavalry, and 16 guns), stationed 6 miles further south between Saintes and Tubize, and guarding the Senne and Senette river crossings. In addition there were the 6th British and 6th Hanoverian brigades of 4th Division, and 6 guns. This force blocked any flanking threat via Hal, and could defend river crossings against attacks directed from either bank, from the west or the east – as Wellington remarked to Croker in 1825 (see Section VI below). Young Prince Frederik was the nominal commander but the sector was really under the Duke's most trusted subordinate Lord Hill.

East of Braine l'Alleud and across the Hain valley stood the heights of Merbe Braine, held by Clinton's 2nd British Division, made up of Hugh Halkett's 3rd Hanoverian Brigade (4 battalions), with Du Plat's 1st Brigade KGL (4 battalions) to Halkett's left and Adam's 3rd British Brigade (4 battalions and some companies) slightly to the rear. The Brunswick contingent (8 battalions) was behind on the reverse slope. This meant that the whole Merbe Braine height was a mini bastion of its own. The next high ground was where Cooke's 1st British Division (4 strong battalions of Guards) overlooked Hougoumont. Cooke also provided much of the garrison for that estate, forming an advanced bastion lower down the slope, the Guards garrison in Hougoumont being supported by Hanoverian and Nassau troops. (A squadron of the 15th Hussars covered the intervening space between the château and the main position.)

The Merbe Braine and Hougoumont positions thus made up an interlocking re-entrant of high ground and formed a very strong barrier to any attack on Wellington's right flank. When we note that in addition the Netherlanders further west, in Braine l'Alleud, could counter-attack the left flank of any French thrust at the re-entrant, we can see how strong this mini bastion was.

From above Hougoumont to the crossroads stood Alten's 3rd British Division, containing Colin Halkett's 5th British Brigade on the right or west (4 battalions), then Kielmannsegge's 1st Hanoverian Brigade (5 battalions and some companies), and finally Ompteda's 2nd KGL Brigade (4 battalions) touching the Charleroi road and with a KGL garrison inside La Haye Sainte. Kruse's Nassauers (3 battalions) were in second line. Thus all across this part of the front British and KGL were placed between Hanoverians, with the Brunswickers and Nassauers slightly further back.

By the start of the battle the artillery west of the crossoads was deployed as follows. On the Merbe Braine redoubt were three batteries, Sympher (KGL), Bolton, and Webber-Smith (RHA), making 18 guns; from Hougoumont to the Charleroi road were 42 guns: Ramsay and Beane (both RHA), Kühlmann (KGL), Sandham, Lloyd, Cleeves (KGL), and on the road Ross (RHA). Behind these were the Brunswickers (16 guns), the artillery of the Netherlands cavalry (8 guns), and Bull, Mercer, and Whinyates (all RHA, 18 guns, plus rockets).[10]

Wellington had intended to keep a reserve comprising the RHA Troops of Ross and Beane, plus Sinclair's newly arrived foot battery from Lambert's force, but both Ross and Beane were called forward almost at once. The remainder of the RHA had been attached to Uxbridge's cavalry, but Uxbridge released them to Sir A. S. Frazer, who left Gardiner's Troop on the flank with Vivian, Whinyates' rockets behind the centre, and deployed the remainder in or just behind the line from Hougoumont to the Charleroi road. My tabulation of Wellington's artillery is given in Appendix 2 to this chapter.

The cavalry in the western sector comprised Grant's, Dörnberg's and Arendschildt's 5th, 3rd, and 7th Light Cavalry Brigades. Close to the Charleroi road and slightly back stood the 'Heavies' of Lord Edward Somerset's 1st Cavalry Brigade. Thus west of or on the Charleroi road were 24 light squadrons and 9 heavy squadrons. Well behind Somerset's brigade, and spreading east of this road, were 23 squadrons of the Netherlands Cavalry Division under Collaert (the only Allied cavalry formation to fight as a division and not in brigades).[11] Brunswick and Hanoverian cavalry were in deep reserve.

Placed either on the flat of the broad summit or on the reverse slope, none of this considerable force of infantry, cavalry and artillery was much – if at all – visible to the French, apart from the skirmishers on the forward slopes. The lateral minor road assisted in this respect. As one of Wellington's ADCs, George Cathcart, explained, looking west from the crossroads, the lateral road:

> for a hundred yards or less it was very hollow ... 10 or even 15 feet deep ... an obstacle of considerable extent, or some of us [mounted men] would have crossed it ... but at about three or four hundred yards, and [or] perhaps less

distance from the main road, it was little or no obstacle, and was frequently passed by cavalry.[12]

But as the minor road came to the western end of the plateau and began to descend towards Braine l'Alleud it again passed into several short cuttings – and the same was true in places of the Nivelles *chaussée* when descending the slope behind Hougoumont. The effect of these further cuttings was to create a form of dry ditch protecting the knoll of high ground at Merbe Braine, useful for its defence. So much for the western sector.

IV

East of the Charleroi road the position was more lightly held: 24 battalions, 29 squadrons and 28 guns were in the line. From the road eastwards stood Kempt's 8th British Brigade (4 battalions) of Picton's 5th British Division. Bylandt's Brigade (5 battalions) of Perponcher's 2nd Netherlands Division came next, standing slightly forward of its British comrades.[13] Ponsonby's heavy cavalry of the Union Brigade (9 squadrons) lay in reserve behind Kempt and Bylandt. East of Bylandt and slightly more to the rear stood Pack's 9th British Brigade (4 battalions) of the 5th Division. To Pack's east and on the 430 foot knoll, the highest part of the ground, stood Best's 4th Hanoverian Brigade (4 battalions), with Vincke's 5th Hanoverian Brigade (4 battalions) beyond. From that point the line forked: slightly thrown back were two light cavalry brigades: Vandeleur's 4th Cavalry (9 squadrons) and still further east Vivian's 6th Cavalry (10 Squadrons), keeping open the road to Ohain along which the Prussians were expected. But from Best's eastern flank and angled slightly forward, through Papelotte, the hamlet of Smohain and to Frischermont, there were detachments of Saxe-Weimar's 2nd Brigade (5 battalions) of Perponcher's 2nd Netherlands Division. A patrol of the 10th Hussars was watching their furthest flank and also waiting for sight of the Prussians. More than three artillery batteries were within half a mile of the Charleroi road: first was Rogers's, then a part (only) of Byleveldt's Netherlands battery, then two Hanoverian batteries, Braun and Rettberg; the other part of Byleveldt's battery was further east covering Papelotte. Lastly, Gardiner's E Troop, RHA, was held back almost on a extreme wing, on Vivian's flank. Whinyates's rockets were in second line near the crossroads. Again, skirmishers were out in force to the front.

Wellington's eastern wing was thus much less solidly held than his west and centre, but the broken ground and *bocage* were more an obstacle for the attackers, and the stream that rose west of Papelotte and flowed east past

Smohain, though minor, had swelled from the rain that had pelted down over the past eighteen hours and would present difficulties for those trying to move artillery forward. Moreover it was thought that by midday the leading Prussians would be arriving.

V

The dispositions resemble a fine piece of marquetry, fitting different elements of varying strengths into a whole. But as with marquetry there were potential weaknesses everywhere. The army was polyglot, trained in systems that were not uniform, and holding various allegiances; and they were facing troops of a single nation, well trained and devoted to their cause. Wellington's most trusted troops were undoubtedly his British and KGL infantry, but they represented under 40 per cent of his infantry strength, and a number of British battalions were fairly raw. Of the other contingents it is probably not unfair to estimate at least a quarter as raw units whose training was rudimentary: some had only reached the army in June. The cavalry mix was more favourable, permitting the weaker contingents to stay in reserve. As for the British cavalry, the horses were in fine condition (as Blücher and even Gneisenau had remarked less than three weeks earlier), and the men well trained; the light horse were nearly all with long experience from the Peninsula, but of the seven regiments in the two heavy brigades, only the Royal Dragoons had much Peninsular experience, the 1st and 2nd Life Guards and the Blues very little, and the King's Dragoon Guards, Scots Greys and Inniskillings none.[14] In such circumstances of relative inexperience it was the 'fox hunting' headlong mentality that was really the greatest weakness in Wellington's heavy cavalry: charging was easy, but it made the need for obedience to recall and to rally all the more important. Thus strong self-disciplined leadership of the cavalry arm was vital, and if controlled it could make a significant contribution to final victory. As to artillery, the Duke was insistent that it should be employed against the vulnerable masses of men and horses and not wasted in counter-battery fire, gun versus gun.

In the later stages of the Peninsular War Wellington had begun to adopt a corps system, and had again set one up in Belgium in the spring of 1815. But this structure, established a few weeks earlier, does not seem to have applied at Waterloo, or perhaps it would be more true to say it operated spasmodically. Wellington handled each of his three corps commanders differently. Hill enjoyed his total confidence based upon years of close co-operation, but that was because Hill was unlikely to go beyond the Duke's general instructions, or if he did act independently his prudence was such that Wellington had no real cause to worry. Moreover Hill was an ideal man to have in overall charge of the western sector.

Uxbridge was by character and upbringing much more self-confident, at ease with the royal dukes and sure of himself: perhaps that is why he had been put in his place when he asked about Wellington's battle plans on the evening of 17 June. He had proved himself a dashing if over-bold leader of light cavalry at Sahagun and Benevente in 1808, but he had been on the shelf for over five years. Wellington had given him virtually unfettered authority over the cavalry, and left him great freedom of action during the fighting.[15] But on his first fighting day Uxbridge had not shown mature judgement in command during the retreat from Quatre Bras. And this morning his responsibilities increased. Whereas the Prince of Orange, by his own special request, had until now retained direct authority over the Netherlands cavalry, on the morning of 18 June Orange had a change of mind and told Wellington that it would be better for Uxbridge to command his cavalry. This seriously unsettled the established organisation. Uxbridge did not know much of the Netherlands cavalry commander, Collaert, or his subordinates, and they knew little or nothing about him, as Uxbridge pointed out.[16]

It was the third corps commander who was seen as the real danger. It had been the Duke's original intention (as he had told Richmond early in April) that the Prince of Orange would not command in a senior capacity. But he was a crown prince to whom his father had committed large forces; in addition as a British full general he outranked Uxbridge and Hill, and Britain had invested him with the command in Belgium in 1814. It had taken little time to see that his ideas as a strategist were of minimal value, and in his first day as a battle tactician at Quatre Bras he had shown himself brave but inept, and even dangerous. There was not much that Wellington could do, but what he could do he did. Perponcher's 2nd and Chassé's 3rd Netherlands Divisions were so placed and so dispersed that the Prince had little chance to interfere, and, with the 1st British Division of Orange's corps behind Hougoumont, only Alten's 3rd British Division was left under Orange's immediate command in the centre: the Duke trusted to Alten's restraining influence and to his own opportunities to correct misjudgements whenever passing that sector.[17]

Hence for the encounter with Napoleon the Duke was determined to keep the tightest hold over his infantry and artillery resources and direct them exactly as he saw best. There were no clear orders on what commanders might be free to do in his absence. On this day Wellington was usually able to see where matters needed re-direction and personally make the changes in time, and the number of occasions when he did this was remarkable; but it was placing upon himself a burden of prevision that no man could be sure of meeting on *every* occasion. That was the danger of Wellington's system. As one of his best battalion commanders remarked, they had no fear of the outcome *so long as the Duke was there*: but what if he fell, or was in another part of the field? And what if he had so concentrated his mind on one possibility that he had overlooked weakness elsewhere – as would be the case over La Haye Sainte? In the result one really horrifying crisis blew up that was saved by Picton and Uxbridge not only acting entirely without orders but also without any guidance from the Commander-in-Chief.

VI

Less than 2 miles behind Wellington's front was the village of Waterloo marking the southern edge of the great Forest of Soignies that stretched north-west almost to Brussels and was at that time some 7 miles broad (from La Hulpe almost to Hal). As Capitaine's map of 1796 shows very clearly, in addition to the *chaussée* running north from Waterloo, the forest had many country paths through it in different directions: it was an open forest and in many places without dense undergrowth.

Napoleon in his *apologia* for the defeat at Waterloo argued that everything the British general did was wrong. The Emperor did recognise that the Forest of Soignies was 'too formidable an obstacle for a French army to risk advancing through it' if there were a strong defensive army waiting on the northern skirts, but he argued that Wellington was wrong to position himself on the south side, as 'he had behind him the tracks through Soignies forest; if he was beaten, no retreat was possible'. But this does in fact suggest that formed bodies of men (such as his French army) *could* find their way through the forest *if* the opposition was light. There *were* forest paths and if bodies of men could advance along them, how much more easily could bodies of men retreat along them as well.[18]

The state of the forest and its roads on that morning was well described by the artilleryman Colonel Frazer: 'Four *pavés* run through it. The wood is open and practicable for infantry or cavalry. The trees are high, the roads and the whole wood very dark, and except in the paved part of the road, the ground is very deep. When I came this way last night the road was crowded and choked with carriages of every kind, many of them overturned.' He had this problem reported to the Adjutant-General and 'in consequence, baggage has been removed, and the waggons which had broken down have been burnt'.[19]

It may be objected that Frazer made no remark about moving artillery through the forest, but we do know that ways back through the trees were examined by various commanders. On the night of 17/18 June another artillery officer, Lieutenant Ingleby of Gardiner's troop:

> received instructions to set out by times in the morning to find a practicable road which should lead parallel to the main road, and through the wood of Soignies and by the left of Brussels, so that in case of further retreat Sir Hussey's brigade might retire covering the left flank of the army. I left the bivouac just at dawn and succeeded in making myself acquainted with a road practical for light guns (six-pounders) and cavalry.[20]

From this it would seem that a fighting retreat through the forest was thought practicable – not easy, not without cost, but feasible – by officers under Wellington's command. Moreover, there are two judgements by experienced military writers of the epoch that may be helpful in this matter. Jomini examined Napoleon's argument, asking: 'Would an army with its rear resting upon a forest, and with a good road behind the centre and each wing, have its retreat compromised, as Napoleon imagined, if it should lose the battle? My own opinion is that such a position would be more favourable for a retreat than an entirely open field.' Jomini argued that although some artillery might be lost, infantry and cavalry (and even some artillery) could make an orderly retreat more easily through the trees than across a plain, provided that no outflanking movement had been made earlier to trap the retreat at the exit from the forest.[21]

The historian of the Peninsular War, William Napier, then a lieutenant-colonel, arrived too late for the battle but had ridden through the forest three days after the action, and judged (in common, so he said, with experienced staff officers who had seen it on the day) that it was practicable for infantry, and in parts for cavalry, that there was no encumbrance of undergrowth, and that considerable numbers of soldiers and civilians went along the roads even on the day of the 18th, and despite the weather conditions.[22]

As I have quoted Napoleon's view, I shall also give two opinions by the Duke. The first was recorded by E. J. Littleton on 8 December 1825. Croker had pointed out that French writers blamed Wellington for fighting without a practicable retreat. He replied:

> They failed in their attempt to put it to the test. The road to Brussels, however, was every yard of it practicable for such a purpose. I knew every yard of the plain beyond the forest and the road through it. The forest on each side the *chaussée* was open enough for infantry, cavalry, and even for

> artillery, and very defensible. Had I retreated through it, could they have followed me? The Prussians were on their flank – and would have been in their rear. The co-operation of the Prussians in the operations I undertook was part of my plan, and I was not deceived.
>
> But I never contemplated a retreat on Brussels. Had I been forced from my position I should have retreated to my right, towards the coast, the shipping, and my resources. I had placed Hill where he could have lent me important assistance in many contingencies. That might have been one – and again, I ask, if I had retreated on my right, could Napoleon have ventured to follow me? The Prussians, already on his flank could have been in his rear. But my plan was to keep my ground till the Prussians appeared, and then to attack the French position – and I executed my plans![23]

It may be objected that although the logic of the argument is sound, and the condition upon which Wellington accepted battle is a fact, this was a record made ten years after the event, and not a document of 1815. So I turn to my second reference, the letter to Lady Frances Wedderburn Webster, written just *before* the battle, indicating which way Wellington thought he might be obliged to move: 'the course of the operations may oblige me to uncover Bruxelles for a moment, and may expose that town to the enemy'. So it confirms the 1825 statement that, if forced back, he would not retreat on Brussels, but instead 'retreat to the right'. I think it conclusive.[24]

VII

This inevitably brings us to the Duke's concern for his western flank. It had dominated his thinking all through the year, as we have seen earlier. He was determined to keep shut the western road to Brussels and to guard his lines of communication with Ostend and Antwerp.

Wellington's assessment was recorded by Lieutenant-Colonel the Hon. James Stanhope some time in the third quarter of 1815, when at Paris:

> I will relate the opinions of the Duke of Wellington as I heard him express them on these points for I believe them to be the truth. At a dinner at Grassini's at Paris, a Frenchman asked if he might speak frankly to the Duke about the battle, who answered yes, and in answer to several questions [the first question was Grouchy's difficulties, and then] was asked what he should have done if he had been Bonaparte. He said 'I think I should have respected the English infantry more after what I must have heard of them in Spain and that I should not have taken the bull by the horns; I should have turned a flank, the right flank [Hal]. I should have kept the English army occupied

> by a demonstration to attack or perhaps by slight attacks, whilst I was in fact moving the main body by Hal on Brussels; but if I had determined to attack as Bonaparte did, *nobody could do more* [italics in original].[25]

On his own front Wellington had the bastion formed by Hougoumont–Merbe Braine–Braine l'Alleud, and he had placed a strong force on the next great *chaussée* to the west at Tubize and Hal, blocking the Senne and Sennette river valleys: a blocking force of about 17,000 Netherlands, British and Hanoverian troops, with 22 guns. It should be noted that downstream north of Hal the river could be crossed at three places in the next five miles, at Huysinghem, Lot and Ruisbroek, so that Hal covered several escape routes for a force retreating westward.[26] Prince Frederik was nominally in command, but with Colville as the foremost British officer, and there can be no doubt that Lord Hill would have joined them and taken command if the main attack had indeed developed there.

Wellington, with regular input from the expert duc de Feltre, had studied the composition of Napoleon's army with care and had a good idea of its strength and organisation. In the Waterloo Despatch written early on 19 June 1815 he defined the force assembled between Rossomme and La Belle Alliance: 'The enemy collected his army, with the exception of the 3rd Corps, which had been sent to observe Marshal Blücher.' In other words Wellington thought Napoleon had under his direct command perhaps 100,000 troops, after detaching *3e Corps'* 16,000 men. We know that this estimate of Grouchy's detachment was too little: Grouchy had the infantry of two corps and the light cavalry corps of Pajol and Exelmans, or up to 34,000 men in total. But in Wellington's calculation the numbers he had estimated could allow a significant force to operate against his right wing, a real threat, because it still allowed a force of a strength sufficient to pin him down and hold him on the Mont St Jean front. This calculation of Wellington is seldom given its due weight and is judged a major error because Napoleon's plan took a different turn. As we have seen it was based upon a very clear and sensible appreciation.[27]

Nor was that appreciation a total misreading of Napoleon's mind. There are several indications that he thought of a western attack, though none that he did anything about implementing his ideas. In his memoirs he wrote that during the night of 17/18 June 'a corps of 2,000 cavalry was sent towards Hal, threatening to turn the right of the Forest of Soignies and move on Brussels' and that this caused Wellington to send (and leave) the 4th Division there, whereupon the French cavalry slipped back to camp. It is difficult to evaluate this claim, and it is not in Gourgaud's dictated *Campaign of 1815*.[28] The force would have had to make a very long detour from Genappe and in appalling weather, and then retire by night, something like a 30-mile round trip. No units are specified although it is virtually equal to a whole corps of cavalry. Such a large force could scarcely have made such a journey without it being seen and reported, and there is not the least suggestion that anyone in the Tubize–Hal force saw or heard anything of it on the night, or later. If it did occur, then it did not impinge on the Allied forces' consciousness, and it wore out the cavalry to no purpose. At St Helena, on 4 or 5 December 1815, Napoleon spoke at dinner about Waterloo:

> If he had followed the idea of turning the enemy right flank he would have succeeded easily; but he had chosen to pierce the centre and separate the two armies. But everything about this affair was fatal and turned into absurdity, and yet he ought to have won the victory. None of his battles had been less in doubt; it was still impossible to conceive how it had all happened.

So 'the idea' that Napoleon here implied was possibly the better one and certain of 'easy success' – though not finally adopted – was to turn the flank furthest from the Prussians, the Hal position. And that was precisely where Wellington was awaiting him. Success might not have been so easy.[29]

Those were fairly general statements, but another with rather more precision emerges again in Gourgaud's *Campaign of 1815* (but not in the memoirs). It is timed just as the guns had opened up against the Mont St Jean position, and at the moment when Napoleon first realised that Bülow was advancing against him:

> [Napoleon] remained fixed in his determination to give battle, but he hesitated a few moments whether or not he should change his line of operations, in order to place it on the Nivelles road, by outflanking the left [west] of the English army instead of the right, and marching on Mont St Jean by the Nivelles road, after having taken possession of Braine-la-Leud.

But, wrote Gourgaud, although this would have moved Napoleon's line of retreat further from the Prussians, it would have left Grouchy unsupported if he attacked Bülow when at that time Napoleon was not close enough to him to join the attack on the Prussians, and it would have facilitated the junction of the allies.[30]

We can choose at our leisure which concept was more likely of success, knowing that we can cite Napoleon's words in support of whichever we prefer. On the day the Duke had to take account of both.

VIII

All through the night a great deal of work had been undertaken to strengthen Hougoumont, to loophole its walls and build firing steps, while ammunition was sent there in considerable quantities. For reasons that are now unfathomable no such attention was paid to La Haye Sainte in the centre, and this must be deemed one of Wellington's most dangerous mistakes.[31] Nor were any field fortifications dug, a point that Colonel Burgoyne criticised on first seeing the site in 1816 (as we saw in Chapter 34). However, that is not to say that there was no field cover. The Wavre–Braine minor road and its cuttings in the western sector has already been mentioned, and east of the crossroads this road likewise had shallow scoops in places, and the track was bordered by a double hedge of straggly bushes for some 600 yards; and although the hedges did not form a solid barrier like a wall, yet hedges remain a real obstacle to a man on foot and give some shelter – even if morally rather than physically – and serve as a tactical rallying point in a fairly nondescript landscape.[32]

This inoffensive gentle ridge, almost devoid of visible troops, was what the French army was about to attack.

*

Appendix 1: A Wellington *Hors de Combat*

One of the great and unanswerable questions that always arises in discussion of Waterloo is: what would have happened if Wellington had been badly injured or killed during the battle? It was a miracle that he emerged unscathed from those hours when all around him were being hit by that tempest of fire; and he himself wrote on the morning of 19 June 'The finger of providence was upon me, and I escaped unhurt.'

There can be no answer because to make one factor variable while forcing all other factors to remain fixed, is to reduce history to a spurious form of mathematics.[33] Yet if the question does not earn itself a place in my narrative, it may still be of interest to put some thoughts into an appendix.

The British Cabinet and the Commander-in-Chief at the Horse Guards were apparently content that Wellington should exercise sole diplomatic and military authority in Belgium in 1815, and in Volume 1 I remarked on the consequences of this, particularly in Chapters 8 and 18. What I then said was:

> On the eve of Waterloo itself the Duke answered the question posed by his senior subordinate Lord Uxbridge as to how he would fight the battle, by another question: 'Who will attack the first tomorrow – I or Buonaparte?' –

> *'Buonaparte'* – 'Well, Buonaparte has not given me any idea of his projects; and as my plans depend upon his, how can you expect me to tell you what mine are?' It was the ultimate in a supremely self-confident pragmatism.
>
> Generally speaking, Wellington did not relish his corps commanders to act independently: the experienced Hill seldom did, and the impetuous Orange must not. (We find Blücher insisting on the same point in his orders of 5 May 1815.) In the Peninsula his fine QMG, Murray, was rarely encouraged to proffer independent advice. It was the Duke's system, and had worked well in Iberia. But in 1815 – indeed in the later months of the Peninsular campaign – the size of his forces stretched his capacity to see to everything. In this campaign his force was more heterogeneous than ever, and his QMG (first Lowe and then De Lancey) did not measure up to Murray's standard. Was it really sufficient to answer Uxbridge, as Wellington did, with the mantra 'whatever happens you and I will do our duty'? And if the Duke were killed or rendered *hors de combat* who could take over and save the army from possible disaster?

And later in the volume:

> If a senior Cabinet minister, and one sympathetic to the Duke, had been posted to Brussels to lighten the (political) burden, it might have proved advantageous. Castlereagh had a double portfolio of Foreign Office and Leader of the Commons and could not be spared, but there surely must have been someone who could have helped bear the burden. The Duke of Richmond, living in Belgium to recoup the cost of his long tenure as Ireland's viceroy and not greatly occupied, could not serve with the army – as a full general who had no experience of command in battle he insisted on ruling himself out – but as a great noble with political experience, and a long-time personal friend of Wellington, might he have been usefully employed to take off a little of the burden? And one word of such a request from Wellington would surely have led to sympathetic consideration and perhaps agreement by the Cabinet. He never raised the matter. He preferred to act alone.

The question thus demands consideration both military and political.

Let us start with the *Army List.* Taking the latest one of March 1815 and leaving aside the Regent's four royal brothers who were field marshals, we find among the better known full generals Moira (governing in India), Cathcart (of the 1805 Hanover and 1807 Copenhagen expeditions, now a commissioner with the Russian army), Chatham (of Walcheren notoriety), and in the promotion of 1814, Richmond, Cradock (a man by then soured by misfortunes not of his own making), David Baird (who had somewhat disappointed in his final field command in the Corunna campaign), and the Prince of Orange. Below them stand Niddry (John Hope, twentieth in the lieutenant-generals and dating from 1808, successor to Graham and judged by government as worthy to rank above all other commanders in Wellington's Peninsular army), Uxbridge (22nd) and the Duke of Brunswick (30th), Lynedoch (old Thomas Graham), Edward Paget, Brent Spencer (quite a sound divisional commander till replaced in 1811); from 1812 Combermere (Stapleton Cotton), Rowland Hill (94th), John Murray (of Tarragona!) and Beresford; from 1813 Dalhousie (108th), Picton, Lowry Cole; and from 1814 Nightingall, Henry Clinton, and Charles Stewart (now posted to Vienna). Some of these were Peninsular-trained, but taken as a whole there were rather too many who had demonstrated considerable limitations in active commands, or who had little battle experience, or who could not be spared from other duties, or who were too elderly. (That criticism of age could certainly not be levelled at the one British and Netherlands full general serving in Wellington's army, the Netherlands crown prince.) But measured against any terms of reference one may choose for the post of potential C-in-C of British forces in Belgium – let alone of the Netherlands and German contingents that the Duke commanded – there was no one but Wellington who fitted the bill.

If the Allied plan had been implemented, if Wellington and Blücher and Schwarzenberg had all marched with half a million troops into northern and eastern France and fought a hopelessly outnumbered Napoleon on the Aisne or Marne or upper Seine, the Duke's death in battle could have been no more than a setback which his army might brush aside, for in such circumstances military genius was no longer of such importance for the success of the campaign: a sensible tactician and good administrator could fill much of the role.

But we are now talking of the campaign as it was actually fought, and thus – although the question is always raised over Waterloo – we need to think also of Quatre Bras. Certainly on 16 June 1815 the loss of Wellington would have had a serious effect. His foresight and skill in detecting weak points and positioning units as they came up to Quatre Bras crossroads certainly made the difference between defeat and success. But there was more: his reputation made even the boldest French commanders uneasy, and this produced an intangible but real advantage for the defenders. Consider, then, Quatre Bras with the Duke dead or disabled. Orange lacked ability; it is difficult to detect in the Duke of Brunswick (even had he lived) the coordinating gifts that were required on that day; Picton and Alten and Cooke had no authority over Netherlands or Brunswick forces; Uxbridge and Hill were still far distant.

And then suppose that the French saw and reported the Duke's wounding or death; what a lift to spirits and courage and daring that would have given them. Indeed, would there have been Waterloo?

On 18 June the situation was somewhat different. Wellington was in a defensive position of his own choosing. It was of no very great length, and his intention was simply to hold it until the promised Prussian assistance should come by the mid-afternoon. Perhaps that is why he made his laconic reply to Uxbridge. He would watch and wait on Napoleon's moves and then make the necessary riposte. Given that the overnight rain had ensured a late start to the battle, the hours of attritional combat need not be many. Then, once the Prussians were in action, it would be possible to go onto the offensive, and once again, numbers would tell. But in the first phase he could rely with total confidence upon men trained in his methods – like Hill, Picton, Kempt, Pack, Alten, the two Halketts, Maitland, Adam, Barnard, Colborne, and Macdonell.[34]

Uxbridge, who had last led cavalry in the combats of the Corunna campaign, had shown erratic judgement on 17 June and was again to act impulsively (if to a large degree successfully) at Waterloo. It is that impulsiveness that might have made his troops doubt him had he taken over in the crisis of the Duke's removal. On the other hand, Orange, his social and military superior, had suddenly made over to him command of the Netherlands cavalry on the very morning of the battle, so that it is just possible that the young Prince was beginning to recognise his own limitations, and might have accepted that he, Orange, could not claim to succeed the Duke. The question remains open.

There is an interesting comment by Tomkinson of the 16th Light Dragoons after Uxbridge's scamper from Quatre Bras and the minor affair at Genappe on 17 June, that he was 'too young a soldier [i.e. without sufficient campaign experience] to be much relied on with a separate command, from a feeling that he will risk too much in a desire to do something'. By contrast,

> the conduct of Lord Hill (when Sir Rowland) was quite the reverse [when commanding a detached force] ... His orders were to watch the enemy's force opposed to him; he never engaged but when obliged, and lost so many chances of bringing on petty affairs that the men called his division the Observing Division.[35]

That, it may be thought, is something of a double-edged reassurance.

So how did Wellington judge Hill? When considering names for the chief command in the American war in 1814, Wellington recommended John Hope, Lord Niddry, as best.

> Hill is an excellent fellow, but I should say he wants [needs] a commander. He likes to have his troops in order but he is too good natured to exert himself about it, and he would require some assistance in that way. He has talents and God knows experience enough for any situation and he might command in chief as well as anybody else; but I should be inclined to doubt it; and to have him fail as well as our troops would be terrible.[36]

But in the present situation these objections may be put aside. They may be valid for a long and extensive campaign, but we are now examining an afternoon or evening crisis. The army trusted Daddy Hill, he knew the Duke's general intentions, and he had been specially selected for command of the western wing of the army and the routes and river crossings to the west: 'I had placed Hill where he could have lent me important assistance in many contingencies,' as we have just noted the Duke saying. Hill, it is true, was thrown and stunned in the evening 'crisis', but that was soon shaken off and I see no reason to see why he could not have held the army together that evening and to have established control over-night. For we have yet to consider one further factor, the British regimental officers and their men.

Just after Waterloo an unnamed observer questioned 'officers of nearly every regiment of British that was in the battle, as to their own private opinions on the point of expected defeat so loudly assumed by our own and foreign writers'. He found:

> Many told him that at particular moments they expected to have been beaten. He put the enquiry, 'Did you expect your own regiment to give way?' 'Oh, no, certainly not my own corps, but I thought some other would.' Such was the universal answer … Our regiments, accustomed to act and live alone, are not taught to dread the failures of adjoining corps in combined operations; they cannot yield readily to the belief that the defeat of a corps in their neighbourhood can license themselves to flee: penetrate an English line, you have gained but a point; cut into a continental line, even a French one, and the morale of everything in view, and vicinity, is gone. The English regiment will not give way, because the English regiment of the same brigade has done so, but will mock the fugitive, and in all likelihood redouble its own exertions to restore the fight – a true bull-dog courage against all odds – if well led.[37]

There may be an over-patriotic tinge to this opinion, but it rings true in the main, and a reading of the many regimental recollections and memoirs does lead to a generally similar conclusion. The British Army could certainly be deemed an army, but it was primarily a congerie of regiments, and in that weakness lay also its strength.[38] Under a trusted general such as Hill, the remnants would have sought to keep some coherence. An exhausted French army was in no condition to launch a pursuit (let alone one as persistent as Blücher's on that night). Indeed it still would have had to turn back to protect its eastern flank and rear. Dawn for the Anglo-Allied forces on 19 June, even without Wellington, might have found them imbued with a fierce dogged determination.

There is one last consideration that I proffer, and here I anticipate my later chapters. The sagacity and moderation that Wellington displayed in the days that led to the surrender of Paris and the restoration of Louis XVIII, added to his new prestige for Waterloo, and his 'alpha male' qualities, made his influence of enormous value to Castlereagh in the summer and autumn peace settlement. Had Wellington not been there the balance would have been different and Castlereagh's task all the harder. We owe a great deal to that 'finger of Providence'.[39]

Appendix 2: Wellington's Field and Horse Artillery, 1815

The subject of artillery in 1815 can be confusing, especially when discussing numbers and roles of artillerymen, horse teams (a 6-pounder required six horses to draw it; a 9-pounder two more horses), equipment, limbers, caissons and wagons. British artillery drivers were a further complication, not forming part of the Royal Regiment of Artillery. This appendix sets out some of my own findings, but I have been unable to establish details of stocks of ammunition, powder, and other supplies as at 15 June 1815, although Duncan in his regimental *History* recorded the expenditure of 10,400 rounds in the fighting (ii, p. 416). Lipscombe, *Wellington's Guns*, p. 386, reports 9,044 rounds fired at Mont St Jean.

Nor does this appendix extend to Wellington's battering train that was deployed as an indispensable part of his Prussian ally's summer sieges.

All the British divisions had foot artillery companies with five 9-pounder guns and one howitzer each, except for Braun's Hanoverian company (5th British Division – 5 BD) that had five 6-pounders and one howitzer. In four of the RHA's troops (Ross, Beane, Mercer and Ramsay) the standard 6-pounder was replaced by a 9-pounder. Bull's RHA troop had six howitzers and no cannon. The Netherlands and Brunswick batteries each had 6-pounders and a howitzer.

The units of Wellington's intended artillery reserve are underlined in the table.

British/KGL/Hanoverian/Brunswick				
Formation	*Gun+How (Establishment)*	*Mont St Jean*	*Braine l'Alleud*	*Elsewhere*
1 BD: Sandham; Kuhlmann KGL	10+2	12		
3 BD: Lloyd; Cleeves KGL	10+2	12		
2 BD: Bolton; Sympher KGL	10+2	12		
4 BD: Rettberg (Han.);[a] Brome[b]	10+2	6		6 Hal
5 BD: Rogers; Braun (Han.)	10+2	12		
6 BD: Sinclair;[c] Unett[d]	10+2	6		6 somewhere on march
RHA: Ross, Gardiner, Webber-Smith, Mercer, Ramsay, Bull, Whinyates,[e] Beane	35+13 + rockets	48 + rockets		
18-pdr (Hutcheson, Morrison, Ilbert)	12+0			12, re-equipping Ostend/Vilvorde
Brunswick: Heinemann, Moll	16+0	16[f]		
Sub-total	148	124[f]		24
Netherlands				
1 D: Wijnand	6+2			8 Hal
Indian Bde: Riesz	6+2			8 Hal
2 D: Byleveldt; Stevenart [k, QB]	8+2 [4+2 lost QB]	10 [2 ex-Stevenart]		
3 D: Kramer; Lux	12+4		16 [to Mont St J. 4 p.m.]	
Cav D: ½ Petter; ½ Gey	6+2	8		
Netherlands sub-total	56 [less 6]	18	16	16
Total	204 [less 6]	158		40
By nature of weapon:	6-pdr = 84; 9-pdr = 75; how = 33; 18-pdr = 12; total 204			

a Rettberg's Hanoverian Battery of 4 BD served with 5 BD under Picton at Quatre Bras, and perhaps switched to Picton's command at the same time as Best's 4th Hanoverian Brigade of 6 BD. It did not return to 4 BD but remained under Picton with Best at Waterloo. Despite thereby confusing lovers of 'orders of battle', all turned out well on both days.

b Brome (whom Laws, *Battery Records*, p. 163, shows in Belgium from April) is generally stated as being at Hal. Also there were the batteries of 1st Netherlands Division and the Indian Brigade (16 guns). However, Dalton's *Waterloo Roll Call* confusingly states him being both at Hal and with 6 BD, which was moving to Waterloo from Ostend, Lambert's men having just arrived from America.

c Sinclair's company was in Belgium in May, as Captain Ilbert in Brussels saw him as he 'rode in from his brigade [company]' on 1 June (*WA*, iii, no. 118). It is generally deemed to have marched with Lambert's 10th Brigade of 6 BD, which had just landed from America. Sinclair initially formed part of Wellington's artillery reserve (with Ross and Beane's RHA Troops), posted just north of Mont St Jean village, but was called forward almost at once. Confusingly, Laws, p. 163, records Sinclair's company only reaching Ostend from Canada on 21 July.

d Unett's company had been near Ghent from April, and was still there on 1 June; there seems to be no more information about it until it was recorded (together with Webber-Smith and Brome) at the capture of Cambrai by 4 BD (see Colville's report to Wellington, 25 June, in *WD*, 503/164). If reporting to 6 BD on 18 June it may have been marching to join Lambert, or perhaps was marching on Hal, but it seems still to have been somewhere on the road on 18 June and neither at Waterloo nor Hal. Gen. Marshall-Cornwall's 'The Royal Regiment in the Waterloo Campaign' (in *Royal Artillery Journal*, vol. 92, March 1965, pp. 1–21), written to flesh out Fortescue's account, is not without error (the date of Napoleon crossing the Sambre is given as the day of Ligny) and he allocates Unett to Hal (p. 4) but without giving any evidence. 'Waterloo Artillery' (*Smoothbore Ordnance Journal*, S. Summerfield (ed.), no. 5, 2012), p. 34, states that Unett had 'four 18-pounders' but was not at Waterloo, whereas on p. 9 the 18-pounders were 'not engaged despite being in Mont St Jean'. These statements seem doubtful, as from the ordnance returns (WP 1/467/30) we know that eighteen 18-pounders were sent from England on 10, 16 and 24 May, and Ilbert's letters in *WA* iii show that the first three companies (12 pieces) were being set up as Waterloo was being fought, with Unett not named as one of the three. The 18-pounders were to form part of the siege train under the command of Sir A. Dickson; he was with Sir G. Wood at Waterloo but was without his force and thus served as a general assistant.

e Whinyates had five 6-pounders, one howitzer, plus rockets, according to Sir George Wood's letter of 8 May, stating that the Duke permitted Whinyates to 'take into the field eight hundred rounds of rockets with his six guns, which makes him very complete'; also Wood's return of 2 June 1815 (Duncan, ii, pp. 417–18). Siborne, *History*, p. 220, wrote of Whinyates having '6 guns, and provided with rockets', but Warde (serving in Ross's Troop adjacent to Whinyates's Troop) thought his neighbour had 'five light 6-pdrs' wihout mentioning a howitzer (*WL*, no. 86). Wood's further artillery return of 8 June 1815 (*WSD*, x, 744), again showed at that date all RHA Troops (excluding Bull's all-howitzers Troop) had one howitzer apiece. Mark Adkin, p. 283, considered that Whinyates had no howitzer, and he is supported by Waterloo Artillery (*Smoothbore Ordnance Journal*, no. 5, 2012), p. 34, and Lipscombe, p. 358. This may account for some authorities giving Wellington only 157 guns at Waterloo, whereas I find a total of 158.

f See Sir A. S. Frazer's letter, 3 a.m. 19 June 1815, stating, 'we had 108 British and 16 Belgic Guns in play' (*JSAHR*, vol. 42, 1964, p. 114; now in *WA*, iv, no. 50). If Frazer meant Brunswick instead of Belgic, his figures seem correct. In also writing that Ramsay's Troop had '1 Gun disabled, not with the Troop, 1 Waggon ditto' Frazer leaves us uncertain whether he meant Ramsay's field strength before the battle (which would falsify his 108), or during, or after, the battle.

Chapter 36
Napoleon Plans his Battle
First Light to 11.30 a.m., Sunday 18 June 1815

I

NAPOLEON SPENT THE NIGHT OF 17/18 JUNE in the little farmhouse called Le Caillou. Taking it over at the last minute, the Emperor's staff had to sort out rooms and bedding, bring food and firewood, while he rested on a bundle of straw close to a bivouac fire. There is indirect evidence that Napoleon drew up an initial battle directive during the evening, aiming for an advance at 5 a.m.[1] Once in bed he supped and managed a little sleep, while the staff continued to work. Soult and the staff slept in a room above, on straw, Ney in the nearby farm of Chantelet.

Then came Grouchy's letter from Gembloux, reporting the situation at nightfall (Chapter 34, Section 1). It gave little or no help to Napoleon in divining what the Prussians might be doing: but it indicated that Grouchy would move from Gembloux, perhaps north towards Wavre, or east towards Perwez. Grouchy's several references to Perwez may have had their effect on the minds of both writer and reader. From the directions that Grouchy mentioned and in view of the deluge of the past twelve hours, Napoleon could be fairly certain that on the 18th the detached force would be between a half and a full day's march from the main army.[2]

In his memoirs Napoleon says that he and Bertrand made an inspection of the pickets a little after midnight, saw the sky in the north ablaze with camp fires, and thus knew that Wellington was not retiring. Later his staff were sent to study Wellington's position to see if field works were being dug, others were sent to examine the ground and report on its practicability for horses and artillery, and they apparently reported that twelve hours of drying weather were needed. (By 9 a.m., however, they seem to have said that the guns could move in one hour, albeit still with some difficulty.)[3]

At some time between dawn and 5 a.m. Soult wrote the following order, incidentally updating the directive of the previous evening and amending it by delaying the 5 a.m. start of operations by four hours:

> Imperial headquarters, 18 June: To the Marshal Prince of the Moskova – The Emperor orders that the army shall be ready to attack the enemy at 9 a.m.; corps commanders will assemble their men, get their arms in readiness and let the troops cook soup; they will also feed the soldiers; so that at 9 a.m. precisely everything will be ready for battle, with artillery and ambulances, on the battle position that the Emperor indicated in his order of yesterday evening [*sic*].
>
> The lieutenant-generals commanding the infantry and cavalry corps will at once send officers to the Chief of Staff to report their positions and take orders.[4]

II

The memoirs set out Napoleon's remembrance of his morning discussions and, if it is not easy to reconcile his account with the recollections of others, they fully convey the confidence that filled him. At 8 a.m., the Emperor was breakfasting among his generals. Ney entered the room just as Napoleon was saying, 'The enemy army is greater than ours by almost a quarter; we have not less than 90 per cent chances in our favour and less than ten against.' Ney is supposed to have remarked that this would doubtless be the case if Wellington were so foolish as to stand, but 'I have to inform you that his forces are in full retreat, disappearing into the forest.' This Napoleon dismissed: 'You have observed badly; he has no time left. He is exposed to certain defeat; he has thrown the dice and they declare for us!'

On the main point Ney was wrong, but not entirely so. Although Wellington was standing firm and was not in retreat, his troops *had disappeared*, they were invisible. If we accept that Napoleon had gone forward during the pitch black night to satisfy himself that Wellington was there, his conclusion can only have been based upon the light of fires along the ridge and perhaps some sounds of musketry – for the 2nd Netherlands Division had an alarm at about 2 a.m. and loosed off a lot of shots.[5] He can have seen nothing of Wellington's dispositions and his estimate of the Duke's battle strength was of his own imagining. Yet once more he was painting pictures in his mind.

Napoleon's valet Marchand claimed that in the morning the Emperor breakfasted with Jerome, Reille and several other generals, and finished by remarking, 'If my orders are well executed, we will sleep in Brussels this evening.'[6]

This remark fits very well with a number of others in emphasising Napoleon's confidence, but it also shows his concern to begin at once, since he was concerned to limit the slippage of time. He had already prepared and printed a proclamation 'to the Belgians and the occupants of the left bank of the Rhine' and dated it from 'the Imperial château of Laeken, 17 June 1815', and he was by his own dating therefore at least one day late; to sleep at Brussels in the evening required a victory during the morning.[7]

Then there are the two statements of Maximilien Foy, which are based on his journal, but plainly with subsequent revisions.[8] He noted in his journal for 18 June that Napoleon had already dismissed the idea of an Allied stand before Brussels, and when Foy marched forward on that Sunday morning, he was half inclined to believe him:

> The Emperor has said on the contrary that the English will be at Antwerp before the 21st ... It is 5.30 a.m. ... my division marches the last of the whole army. Either Wellington will accept battle or he will lose many people in retiring.

Foy's second statement was dated 23 June 1815. He had passed to Prince Jerome some remarks that a waiter in an inn at Genappe said he had heard Wellington's staff let drop in the dining room, suggesting what the Allied plans might be:

> On the morning of the 18th, Jerome being with his brother at Le Caillou farm, told him of the Genappe waiter's words. The Emperor replied, 'The junction of the Prussians and the English is impossible in less than two days, after a battle such as that at Fleurus [Ligny] and being followed as they are, by a considerable corps of troops.' His Majesty added, 'We are only too happy that the English want to stand. The forthcoming battle will save France and will be celebrated in the world's annals. I shall play on them with my numerous artillery, I shall charge with my cavalry to force the enemy to show themselves, and when I am certain of the point occupied by the English nationals, I shall march straight at them with my *Vieille Garde*.'

If Foy's note is not infected with hindsight after the disastrous way in which a whole series of disjointed attacks wrecked the French army, then it tells us that the sequence of partial attacks was not an aberration of Ney's but something that the Emperor already envisaged. It also indicates how poorly Napoleon had judged Wellington's skills and his troops' endurance.

Unsurprisingly, Soult was not quite at ease with all this, according to his ADC Baudus. On the previous evening it seems he had suggested calling back at least some of the troops given to Grouchy, and he is now supposed to have repeated this. But once again this is Soult at his most ineffective (and, for Napoleon, annoying) for whether the idea had been floated at 8 p.m. or at 8 a.m. the effect of it could have had little impact on operations at Mont St Jean in the morning or mid-period of the 18th. As Soult knew perfectly well, Grouchy was simply too far away; he might have arrived to cover a retreat in the evening of 18 June, but not even Soult at this moment envisaged such a disastrous setback.[9] It is not altogether surprising that Baudus records that Napoleon was irritated and so made a crushing retort. However, the snub was not about Grouchy, time, and distance, but about something that Soult really did know all about. Napoleon turned on him with the words: 'Because you have been beaten by Wellington you regard him as a great general. And I, I tell you that Wellington is a bad general, that the English are bad troops, and it will be only an affair of a breakfast', a matter of a few hours. Soult could only reply 'I hope so.'[10]

Reille, when asked what he thought of the British, is supposed to have made a similar warning:

> Well posted as Wellington knows how to, and attacked frontally, I regard the English infantry as *inexpugnable* because of their calm tenacity, and their superior firepower. Before attacking them with the bayonet one should wait until half the enemy is beaten. But the English army is less agile, less supple, less manoeuvrable than ours. If one cannot beat it by a direct attack, one can do so by manoeuvring.

Napoleon broke off the discussion with an exclamation of incredulity. However, this anecdote of Ségur, who had it from Reille, is qualified by another of Reille's friends who reported a slightly different version. According to Aumale, Reille did not speak to Napoleon but to d'Erlon, and when the latter told Reille that he ought to give this opinion to the Emperor, he answered, 'To what purpose? He will not listen to us!'[11]

Given the miserable record of some of these generals, the Emperor may perhaps be forgiven for mistaking wise advice for defeatism, but he should have recalled that they had all risked their futures in re-joining him in 1815: their advice was genuinely meant to help him, and it was in their own interests that he should beat Wellington. He was too used to berating his generals all the time, for what they did wrong – and even for what they did right if it conflicted with his advice.[12] But his system had raised quite ordinary men to positions beyond their capacities, or had condemned men of ability for using their own judgement and initiative. The events of the past ten years had demonstrated that the imperial structure had come to depend on the whim of a single man whose will could only be implemented blindly by nonentities or the very young and junior. He would not listen. If a general said the British were good he would say the contrary, whatever his real opinions. He had his own ideas, of Wellington, the battlefield, and the Prussians, and he would go his own way.

III

At 10 a.m., as Napoleon made his mind up on the way he would fight the battle, he had Soult write to Grouchy in reply to the latter's 10 p.m. report:

> The Emperor has received your last report dated from Gembloux; you speak only of two Prussian columns that passed by Sauvenière and are at Walhain. However, reports speak of a fairly strong third column having passed by Géry and Gentinnes, moving on Wavre. The Emperor commands me to warn you that at this moment His Majesty is about to attack the English army which has taken position at Waterloo, close to the Forest of Soignies; thus His Majesty desires that you should move on Wavre in order to come closer to us, put yourself in touch with the operations, and link communications, pushing before you the corps [*les corps*, plural] of the Prussian army that have taken that direction and should have arrived at Wavre, and which you must reach as soon as possible.
>
> You will send some light forces to follow the enemy columns that have gone to your right, so as to observe their movements and take their stragglers.
>
> Let me know immediately of your dispositions and of your march, as well as all news you have of the enemy, and do not neglect to keep in contact with us; the Emperor wants to have very frequent reports from you.[13]

From the map in Chapter 31 it can be seen that the information now in Napoleon's possession did suggest that there could be a general Prussian concentration on Wavre, since the force that Grouchy had identified as leaving Sauvenière (north-east of Gembloux) for Walhain (due north) was certainly moving in the general direction of Wavre and Brussels, and another force (Napoleon's 'third column') had passed Gentinnes, apparently also going to Wavre. Moreover, Gentinnes was west of Gembloux, where Grouchy lay overnight, and thus there was an enemy force reportedly moving between Grouchy and the main French army. But obviously all this was less clear to Grouchy who, when he wrote his report, was unsure of the direction in which the mass of Prussians were moving. Gembloux was at least 12 miles from Le Caillou as the crow flies, perhaps a three-hour ride, and Grouchy was leaving it at dawn and going off in one direction or the other, towards an uncertain location. If the Marshal was not to pass beyond Napoleon's control it was important, therefore, to re-focus Grouchy's attention and to give him the most precise orders for the day.

According to the new 10 a.m. orders Grouchy was definitely to march at once on Wavre, but thereafter Napoleon seemed unclear on precisely what was required: moving on Wavre in order to 'come closer to us, put yourself in touch with the operations' (presumably at Mont St Jean, but possibly further north) and 'link communications', suggested possible co-operation; but 'pushing the Prussians before you' (and using a small force to follow those moving east, 'right') could be read to mean that pursuing the Prussians continued to be Grouchy's primary task. Indeed, the phraseology tends to suggest that Grouchy was driving sheep that could be easily sent on the path of his choice, and yet in fact it must have been clear that by now Grouchy was so far to the south of the Prussians that he could scarcely hope to overtake them, or head them off from Brussels or from Ohain. Battle was imminent, and, if Grouchy's support was needed, could he in the time available even regain touch with the main army, from wherever he was when the order reached him?

There was a curious aftermath to the writing of this despatch, and it was provoked by the arguments about whose fault it was that Waterloo was a defeat. A Polish orderly officer, Comte Zenowicz, blamed for the late delivery of an order, accused Soult of a scandalous ninety-minute delay in writing the order, and Zenowicz's account was used (somewhat inaccurately) by the historian Thiers. What the Pole wrote suggests that if Soult had been recommending overnight that Grouchy should be called in to assist the coming attack on Mont St Jean, he scarcely injected this sense of concern into the message that he now dictated. Zenowicz's account is vivid, clearly sincere, but problematical. I give it in Appendix 2 to this chapter.

IV

From about 9 a.m. the French army was drawing together, some food was eaten, brandy was served out, sometimes extra brandy where there was no food, and the divisions and corps shook themselves and formed battle order.[14] In his memoirs Napoleon spoke of the formation in eleven great columns in a first, second, and reserve line, formed to the east and west of the Charleroi road and tapering back to the reserve line. He estimated that the entire force was in place by 10.30 a.m., but that in fact was not entirely right, for General Petit of the *Garde* stated that they arrived at Rossomme after the fighting had already begun, and Durutte's *4e Division* was not on the field until noon or later.

Napoleon's battle line was set out as follows. Looking from west to east, the first line had Piré's *2e Division de Cavalerie* of Reille's corps on the extreme west, on the Nivelles road. Facing Hougoumont were Reille's three divisions: Jerome's *6e*, Foy's *9e* and Bachelu's *5e Division*. To their front were four batteries totalling thirty guns (6-pounder guns, with howitzers). Behind Reille stood Kellermann's heavy cavalry of *3e Corps de Cavalerie* (*11e* and *12e Divisions de Cavalerie*). To the east of the road was d'Erlon's *1er Corps*: Quiot's *1re Division*, Donzelot's *2e*, Marcognet's *3e*, later to be joined by Durutte's *4e Division* on the right. With them were five batteries, totalling thirty-eight guns (6-pounders and howitzers). On the eastern flank was d'Erlon's corps cavalry: Jacquinot's *1re Division de Cavalerie*. Behind d'Erlon stood Milhaud's heavy *4e Corps de Cavalerie* (*13e* and *14e Divisions de Cavalerie*). As it came up, the reserve comprised Lobau's small *6e Corps* (*19e* and *20e Divisions d'Infanterie*, *3e* and *5e Divisions de Cavalerie*) with forty-two guns, drawn up just west or east of the road, and the *Garde* (separately organised: infantry, cavalry, artillery, engineers, numbering 20,000 men and ninety-six guns). A reserve of twenty-four guns (12-pounders and howitzers) stood along the road from Rossomme northwards.

As to the command structure it was as follows: Ney had been given command of *1er* and *2e Corps*, thus including the light cavalry of Jacquinot and Piré. Napoleon told d'Erlon's artillery chief de Salle to command the Grand Battery. He kept under his own hand *6e Corps*, the light cavalry of Domon and Subervie, Kellermann's *3e Corps de Cavalerie* (dragoons, carabiniers, and *cuirassiers*), and Milhaud's *4e Corps de Cavalerie* (*cuirassiers*), and the *Garde* infantry, artillery and cavalry (light and heavy).

There is some uncertainty over where Lobau's force was placed, and for what purpose. And because the matter is of some importance for an understanding of the battle, and because it encapsulates some of the difficulties placed in the way of that understanding, it merits a comment. In most *Histories* and their maps, *6e Corps* appears west of the great road, and thus behind Reille's *2e Corps*. That is where Napoleon described it in his memoir. His *Bulletin* written at Laon on 20 June 1815 says otherwise, but for a particular reason. For on the 20th Napoleon said that Lobau and Domon were 'destined to stand behind our right, so as to oppose a Prussian corps that seemed to have escaped Marshal Grouchy and that intended to fall on our right flank, an intention that we knew of from our reports and from a Prussian general's letter, carrying an instruction taken by our scouts'.[15] As there is solid evidence to show that at this time Napoleon totally discounted any Prussian appearance, the reason for this disposition cannot be right; what he may have been seeking particularly to persuade the French public was that he had taken all possible precautions, and thus moved the receipt of news about the Prussian general's letter from the afternoon to the morning.

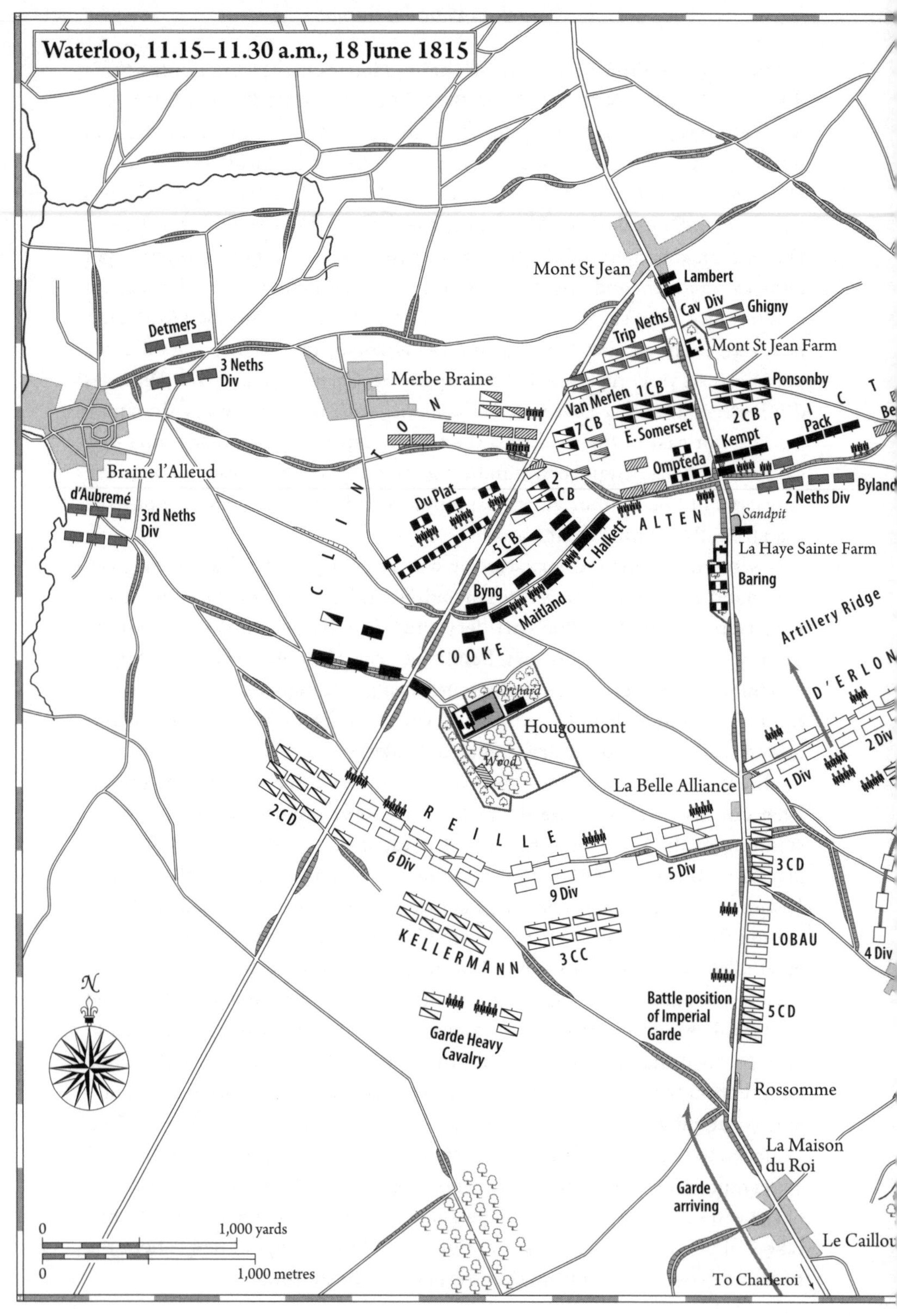

Waterloo, 11.15–11.30 a.m., 18 June 1815
Mont St Jean
Lambert
Trip Neths Cav Div
Ghigny
Mont St Jean Farm
Detmers
3 Neths Div
Merbe Braine
Ponsonby
Van Merlen
1 CB
7 CB
E. Somerset
2 CB
Kempt
Pack
Braine l'Alleud
Ompteda
2 CB
Du Plat
d'Aubremé
3rd Neths Div
2 Neths Div
Bylandt
Sandpit
ALTEN
C. Halkett
5 CB
La Haye Sainte Farm
Baring
CLINTON
PICTON
Byng
Maitland
Artillery Ridge
COOKE
D'ERLON
Orchard
Hougoumont
Wood
2 Div
1 Div
La Belle Alliance
2 CD
REILLE
6 Div
9 Div
5 Div
3 CD
LOBAU
KELLERMANN
3 CC
4 Div
Battle position of Imperial Garde
5 CD
Garde Heavy Cavalry
N
Rossomme
La Maison du Roi
Garde arriving
0
1,000 yards
0
1,000 metres
Le Caillou
To Charleroi

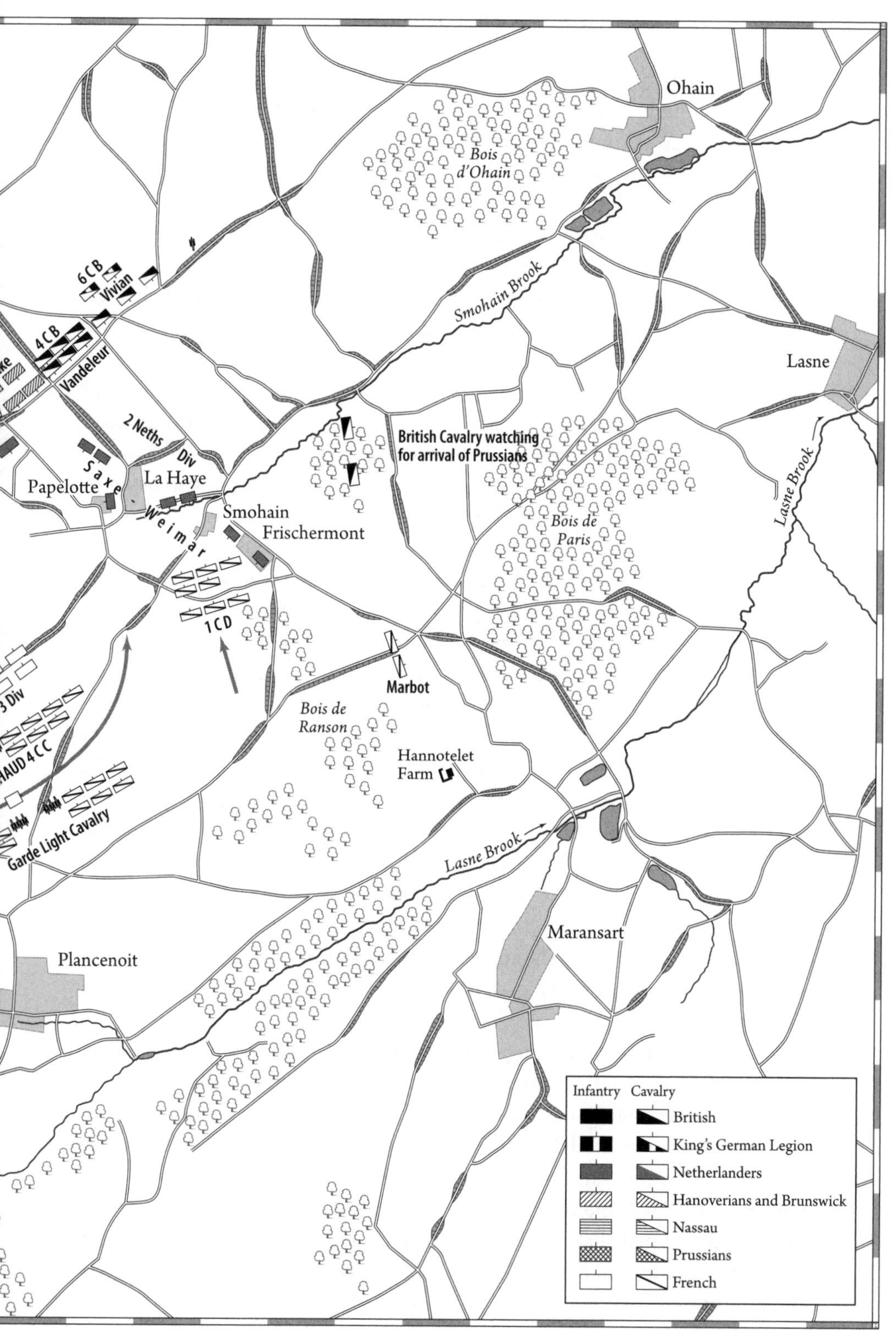

Ohain
Bois d'Ohain
6 C B
Vivian
4 C B
Vandeleur
Smohain Brook
Lasne
2 Neths Div
British Cavalry watching for arrival of Prussians
Saxe Weimar
Papelotte
La Haye
Smohain
Frischermont
Lasne Brook
Bois de Paris
1 C D
3 Div
Marbot
Bois de Ranson
Hannotelet Farm
Garde Light Cavalry
Lasne Brook
Maransart
Plancenoit
Infantry
Cavalry
British
King's German Legion
Netherlanders
Hanoverians and Brunswick
Nassau
Prussians
French

Then, a year or two after the *Bulletin* account, we find in Gourgaud's *Campaign of 1815*, published in Britain in 1818, that Lobau's *6e Corps* is 'formed in close column on the right of the Charleroi road: by this means it was in reserve behind the left of *1er Corps*, and *en potence* behind the centre of the first line'. As battle began, the Prussians were observed and Domon and Subervie were ordered to seize and hold all approaches, while Lobau followed them: 'thus the destination of this corps was changed'.[16] In this version the intention was to support d'Erlon in his great attack and help take the vital crossroads, and only the news of the Prussians changed it.

Finally, in 1820 the memoirs altered Lobau's initial position by 10.30 a.m. to '50 *toises* [around 100 yards] behind *2e Corps* second line' and 'along and to the left of the Charleroi road, his artillery on his left flank' while Domon and Subervie had their 'left' touching the Charleroi road. These forces would still be well placed to assist the great thrust on La Haye Sainte and beyond. This is the disposition accepted by most historians. However, Napoleon then says that his initial intention had been 'to turn the enemy left rather than his right, so as to cut him off from the Prussians who were at Wavre'. The problem is that he was not really certain where the Prussians were or where they were going, and if he wanted to break through with his *right* wing, surely Lobau should have been on that side and not behind Reille? So confusion continues. Then, according to the memoir, the Prussians were seen and the cavalry despatched eastwards; the Prussian prisoner arrived and the captured letter was read. 'Shortly after,' Lobau was ordered 'to cross the Charleroi road by a change of direction to the right by division and to go to the support of the light cavalry around St-Lambert; to choose a good intermediate position, where, with 10,000 men he could hold back 30,000, should that become necessary.' The 1820 account says that 'it was of the highest importance that Comte Lobau's movement should take place without delay'; and the next section of the narrative begins, 'It was midday and the skirmishers were busy all along the line'. But the timing is all wrong.[17]

Thus we have a whole range of conflicting accounts from Napoleon, with changes of intention, placement, and timing. Coppens and Courcelle, who have given particular attention to these various versions, consider that Napoleon sought deliberately to obscure matters, conceal the truth and shift any blame onto other shoulders. But there could also be another explanation: that Napoleon was so uncertain as to what best to do as the morning developed that his dispositions changed in his mind almost from minute to minute, and remained somewhat confused when he came to write his accounts.

Coppens and Courcelle produce some other sources about the original placement of Lobau. They cite the little-studied account by Durutte of *4e Division* on the far right of d'Erlon's line. He said to someone (unspecified) that as he could see enemy troops on his flank at Smohain, it would be wise in mounting d'Erlon's great attack to place some formation *en potence* to guard against an enemy attack in his flank, but that he received the reply that nothing could be changed. Durutte then claimed that Lobau's small *6e Corps* was placed behind *4e Division* in direct support (facing north), and not *en potence* (which would mean facing east). And apparently Janin, on Lobau's staff, wrote: '*6e Corps* went forward to support the attack on the centre.' If that is correct, then at 2 p.m. Lobau's force was committed to assist in d'Erlon's great attack, and was not already deployed against the Prussians.[18] We shall return to that possibility in Chapter 43.

V

Napoleon made an inspection of his troops, and was everywhere greeted with cheers and acclamations. The rain was ceasing and, with victory promised, the troops responded just as Napoleon wished.[19] He has been criticised for wasting time with a showy display, but it was essential to whip up his own soldiers' enthusiasm, and the sheer size and number of his columns, and the noise and cheering were intended to weaken the morale of his opponents. This may have succeeded with some of the weaker Allied contingents, and there were numerous British observers who remarked on the magnificence of the sight spread before them.[20]

Napoleon then rode to the mound near Rossomme and made final preparations for the battle. A small table was set up, upon which his maps were spread, held down by stones. As staff came and went with information and orders, he stood, leaning over the maps and studying the battleground with his telescope, his face set in an expression of total calm. Andrew Field has printed the opinions of some observers who wrote of Napoleon's 'apathy' or 'extreme depression' but he dissents from these views, arguing that some are coloured by hindsight, and that, if he *was* glum, the Emperor was more likely to be discontented and impatient at the time it was taking to get to battle stations, or perhaps frustrated at the limitations to how much he could see.[21] Like him, I do not see Napoleon as in any way 'depressed'. His marble-like impassiveness was based upon supreme confidence in himself and his troops, a calm willingness to incur heavy casualties to achieve his personal ends. Moreover there was that absorption in calculating, and the stimulus of decision-taking, that almost subconsciously imposed self-restraint by cutting out all other emotions. If the wet weather was annoyingly delaying the start of battle, he seems to have been convinced that the ground was drying faster than many had expected a few hours earlier.

The question of the wet ground and its drying qualities is one that will for ever be debated. There was universal agreement that the month of June in Belgium had been wet rather than otherwise, and also that the deluge of 17/18 June was of tropical power and intensity. The mud and wet of the previous eighteen hours made cleaning and attention to weaponry an essential prelude to any moves on 18 June. The conditions in the early part of the day certainly must have impeded operations, yet during the afternoon the French *cuirassiers* and the British heavy cavalry could operate across the ground for several successive hours, and guns weighing one and even two tons were manhandled across it, albeit with extreme difficulty.[22] Indeed the going must have deteriorated under such operations as the afternoon wore on, so that by (say) 5 p.m. it was more cut up and difficult than at 2 p.m.

It is a matter of opinion, but I suspect that the wet ground was less of an obstacle to an early start to the battle than was the delay caused by the continuing indiscipline among the scattered groups of soldiers lost to view as they scavenged early in the day.[23] That delay factor must indeed have been infuriating for the Emperor.

One last possibility is that the train carrying artillery ammunition was so far behind on its journey that it enforced a delay on the start. Unfortunately, there is almost nothing recorded about this part of the French army, and we can only surmise.

At mid-morning Wellington's army was settled in position, but Napoleon's was not quite ready. As to comparative strength, the leading authorities produce differing figures. Houssaye estimated that Wellington had 67,000 men to Napoleon's 74,000, while Siborne, Digby Smith, Adkin and Haythornthwaite do not agree in all respects, especially as Siborne's figures comprise in most cases 'rank & file' so that an eighth needs adding to them for officers bandsmen and others.[24]

I give below my own tentative estimate of the balance of forces at the start of the battle, recognising that for some readers the figures will be open to challenge on this or that detail. Use of figures is essential, and I shall deploy them at various points in my story. But long immersion in morning states and casualty returns has made me cautious as to the solidity of numbers; and I recall my friend the late Paddy Griffith's rueful and half-amused surprise when I pointed out the many arithmetical mistakes in the statistical appendices in even so fine a work as Oman's *Peninsular War*, where lines and columns did not add up, although whether the individual figures were wrong or just the totals, whether clerks or the transcribing historian or even the printer had made the errors, it was quite impossible to tell: *caveat emptor.*[25]

Balance of Forces at Waterloo

*All ranks**	*Wellington†*	*Napoleon*	*Force ratio*
Infantry	46,840 (73 battalions)	49,624 (105 battalions)	1.00:1.07
Cavalry	13,828 (93 sqdn.)	15,224 (113 sqdn.)	1.00:1.10
Artillery/Others	4,550	8,000	1.00:1.76
Total	65,218	72,848	1.00:1.17
Guns	142 + rockets	246	1.00:1.73

* Excluding Wellington's force at Hal/Tubize, and Grouchy's force. In the totals of battalions and squadrons allowance also needs to be made for units smaller than a full battalion or cavalry regiment, like 3/95th, and the *Gendarmes d'Elite.*

† I have excluded from these figures the detached 3rd Netherlands Division posted at Braine l'Alleud, nearly a mile beyond the Merbe Braine western bastion, because this division (although close to hand) was placed to meet a different threat and moved to the Mont St Jean position only in mid-afternoon. I estimate it at 6,700 all ranks, plus 450 gunners and train and 16 guns. If included in the figures for the start of battle, this division would increase Wellington's infantry to 53,510, his artillerymen etc. to 5,650 and his guns to 158, giving a grand total of 72,368. This would consequently change the force ratios for infantry to 1.07:1; for gunners etc. 1:1.41; for guns 1:1.52; total, for every 1 soldier of Wellington's there were 1.12 Frenchmen.

These numbers show that Napoleon enjoyed a significant advantage in cavalry, but that his greatest advantage was in the number and weight of his artillery. In addition his army was entirely French and comprised many veterans, whereas Wellington's was a combination of British, Belgians, Dutch and Germans, many fairly newly raised. While we cannot allocate a factor for this, we need to remember the qualitative advantage that Napoleon could count upon. In artillery Napoleon disposed of 142 six-pounders and 36 twelve-pounders, plus 68 howitzers, compared to Wellington's 62 six-pounders (16 of which, however, were detached at Braine l'Alleud), 65 nine-pounders, and 31 howitzers. Overall this gave Napoleon one artillery piece for every 296 soldiers, whereas Wellington had one for every 459. Napoleon decided to concentrate a large number of twelve-pounder guns in a 'Grand Battery' intended to blast an irreparable hole in the defensive line as a part of his central attack. Wellington for his part deployed all the RHA troops (except Gardiner's Troop that remained with Vivian's cavalry on the eastern flank), placing them among the foot companies, so that west of the crossroads he had a 'semi-grand' battery.

Sir A.S. Frazer had succeeded in replacing ten of the RHA 6-pounders with 9-pounders by 15 June, which considerably raised Wellington's hitting power, but delays in England deprived the army of three brigades (total twelve pieces) of 18-pounder guns. Three brigades were assembling the weapons which by 18 June had left Ostend and were at Vilvorde and Brussels. This meant that three brigades (whether with the new heavy 18-pounders or with lighter guns) were sadly missing from the line on a day when maximum artillery power was desperately needed.[26]

If Wellington's infantry could be worn down fast enough by Napoleon's artillery superiority, and/or held down or otherwise detained in parts of the field remote from Napoleon's intended break-in point, then the tiny, potentially inadequate, numerical superiority in French infantry would not matter, and the Emperor's cavalry numbers should ensure break-out and victory. But time was limited, and setbacks to the plan could wreak havoc with the timetable.

VI

The Emperor now confirmed the indications that, according to Foy, he had previously given to his brother Jerome. With a maximum of ten hours of daylight left, there was no question of fancy manoeuvring to turn wings. Such alternatives were in any case fraught with problems at so late a stage.[27] The simple, brutal, central frontal attack was the quickest way to break through Wellington's line:

> To the commander of each army corps, 18 June 1815, 11 a.m.: Once the entire army is assembled for battle, at around 1 p.m., at the moment the Emperor gives the order to Marshal Ney, the attack will open to take the village of Mont St Jean, where are the crossroads. To this end the 12-pounder battery of *2e Corps* and that of the *6e* will join that of *1er Corps*. These twenty-four cannon will fire on the troops on Mont St Jean, and Comte d'Erlon will mount the attack, leading with his left division and supporting it as circumstances may require with the divisions of *1er Corps*.
>
> *2e Corps* will advance so as to guard the flank of Comte d'Erlon.
>
> The companies of sappers of *1er* Corps will be ready to barricade themselves at once at Mont St Jean.[28]

D'Erlon should lead it with his left flank on the Charleroi road and La Haye Sainte, his centre taking the ridge (where Picton stood), with the 12-pounders of *1er*, *2e* and *6e Corps*, all now released to d'Erlon's artillery commander De Salle to provide a crushing weight of cannon fire from eighteen guns, the effective range of which was about 800 yards.[29] Once on the ridge he could blast away the Allied remnants. Reille on the left wing would support this central attack.

A line of communication with Grouchy was necessary, and this task was given to Colonel Marbot of the *7e Hussards* in Jacquinot's mounted division. In 1830 he made a long statement about this. Towards 11 o'clock the Emperor's ADC La Bédoyère rode to the extreme right wing and briefed Marbot with Napoleon's special instructions: to go with his regiment, three guns and an infantry battalion to a point within sight of the battlefield, place some skirmishers in Frischermont wood, a squadron in Lasne village with scouts out to St-Lambert further down the Lasne stream, and another squadron with scouts at places on the River Dyle, including the bridges at Moustier (Mousty) and Ottignies (5 miles from Wavre to the north-east and Corbais to the east, both places being mentioned in Grouchy's morning report as possible destinations), also to the south at Couture. Marbot's duty was to watch for Grouchy and send the news to Napoleon with the utmost speed. This was the counterpart of the 10 a.m. order to Grouchy that he 'should move on Wavre in order to come closer to us, put yourself in touch with the operations'. Both the stream and the river were natural lines of communication with the marshal. Nothing was said of any Prussian threat.[30]

What occurred in the result was also described in the 1830 statement; however, it does not fit happily with what Marbot had written on 26 June 1815, and Marbot's notorious facility in embroidering his recollections means that once again we are left doubtful as to what really happened. All this will be explained in Chapter 41.

VII

At some time in mid-morning imperial headquarters received a message from Grouchy, written from Gembloux at 6 a.m.:

> Sire, all my information and reports confirm that the enemy is retiring on Brussels, to concentrate there or give battle after joining with Wellington. The I and II Corps of Blücher's army seem moving thus: I on Corbais and II on Chaumont. They must have left Tourinnes at 8.30 p.m. last night and marched through the night; luckily the night was so bad that they cannot have made much progress. I am leaving this instant for Sart-à-Walhain from where I shall continue on Corbais and Wavre.[31]

In sum, the Prussians had started from Tourinnes, 5 miles north of Gembloux, some nine hours before this note was written, with one column going north-west to Corbais and Wavre, the other northwards to Chaumont (now Chaumont-Gistoux). Even if the roads were detestable and the difficulties of night-marching all the greater in consequence, the advantage that the Prussians had gained was clear, for the conditions must also affect the pursuers to a large degree. (In reality the Prussians had all reached the vicinity of Wavre by midnight, so that the situation was worse than the French high command thought, but here we are dealing only with what intelligence showed.)

As the commentator Colonel Grouard noted, Grouchy's assumption of a retirement on Brussels was not unreasonable, given that he had not been told about Wellington's movements, but it must have been clear to Napoleon, knowing that Wellington was standing on the Mont St Jean ridge, that there was a possibility of the Prussians marching there and not to Brussels and that it would be wise to take that into account.[32] It was for Napoleon now to inform Grouchy of the true situation; for Napoleon to reassess his battle plan to take account of a fresh risk, to calculate march-times and distances between the Prussians and Wellington, between Grouchy and the Prussians, and between Grouchy and himself; and then to tell Grouchy in unmistakeable terms what he wished him to do.

Grouchy's message came at mid-morning, but no reply was sent until 1 p.m.

VIII

Having made up his mind between 10 and 11 in the morning, Napoleon now had further thoughts, and called for a change of plan. Ney consequently added to the formal 11 a.m. order a pencil note: 'Comte d'Erlon will understand that the battle will commence by the left instead of the right. Communicate this new disposition to Comte Reille.'[33]

By this change the great attack planned for 1 p.m. would open not on La Haye Sainte, the crossroads and the ridge, but on Hougoumont down in the valley. Napoleon's memoirs are uninformative on why he changed the initial leading role from d'Erlon to Reille. All that he wrote was that he had given the necessary orders for the attack on La Haye Sainte and La Haye, and that:

> While everything was in preparation for this decisive attack, Prince Jerome's division, on the left, opened a fusillade on the woods of Goumont;

> this soon became very lively. The enemy having unmasked around 40 pieces of artillery, General Reille pushed forward the artillery battery of his *2e Division* [this must mean Piré's horse artillery battery], and the Emperor ordered General Kellermann to send forward his 12 pieces of light artillery. The cannonade soon became extremely heavy. Prince Jerome several times took Goumont wood, and was repulsed several times: it was defended by the English Guards division, the enemy's finest troops, whom one saw with pleasure on the right, which facilitated the great attack on the left.[34]

Strangely, the phrase 'the great attack on the left' did not feature in Napoleon's first St Helena account of his plan, dictated to Gourgaud. There it was 'to penetrate the centre of the English army', which is exactly what the 11 a.m. order said, 'the Mont St Jean crossroads'.[35]

The order for the attack on Hougoumont was probably never written down, and we can only infer the way it was passed on. Ney never referred to the matter, and Reille merely remarked that the 11 a.m. orders were for the attack to begin by the right (d'Erlon), with *2e Corps* 'supporting this movement by covering the left of the wood of Hougoumont. Prince Jerome, commanding the *9e Division* [read: *6e*], was directed on that point' with the infantry and cavalry of Reille's force in support; Reille said nothing of the fresh order.[36] Even what he did write helps very little, for 'support' and 'covering' are precisely the opposite of what the final order specified. Nor is Jerome very consistent. He had been with the Emperor early in the morning, but exactly what happened later is somewhat confused. In Jerome's memoirs he said that at '11.30 a.m.' he was ordered to take Hougoumont with his 1st Brigade (Bauduin), but also that he received the order to attack at '12.15 p.m.'[37]

The second element in the change of plan concerned the heavy artillery. The divisional artillery (6-pounders, small howitzers) was moving with the divisions, but the heavy 12-pounders were further back and still straining forward. At 11 a.m. Napoleon had dedicated 'twenty-four' 12-pounders (the batteries of *1er, 2e, 6e Corps,* making only eighteen) to the pulverisation of the defenders on the ridge. Now he added one of the three *Garde* 12-pounder batteries to the task, although that could further delay the opening of d'Erlon's attack.

Thus even after he had dictated the 11 a.m. order Napoleon's intentions remained open to significant modification, although the reasons for further change were never explained. At St Helena he thought on occasion that he planned to attack the centre, and then that he intended to attack the left or eastern flank, and again that he half intended to attack the right or western flank. As I have previously noted, two days earlier, on the morning of Ligny/ Quatre Bras, his letter to Ney contained contradictory ideas, and his later orders set out changes of plan very difficult to execute smoothly.[38] This seems to have been another such instance. It may have been no more than the cascading forth of constant new or revised ideas, almost in a stream of consciousness; or it may indicate a simple delight or obsession in gambling. In the matter of Hougoumont it can have been either a late recognition of its importance to Wellington, a means of pulling the Duke off-balance and leaving his centre weak; or to stop the defenders of Hougoumont being free to enfilade d'Erlon's advance up the road some 800 yards east of the little estate; or merely that d'Erlon needed more time if he was to get his artillery forward over the soft ground. As to strengthening the artillery, little in the enemy's dispositions can have changed since daybreak but with the day drawing on some additional batteries would speed up the pulverising. Either way, changes at this late stage cannot have helped the ordering of the units and formations, or the task of explaining tactical intentions and timings to the companies and platoons.

The most likely explanation would seem to be that Napoleon only gradually received sufficient information about Wellington's hitherto undisclosed Mont St Jean position. There are several slight traces that together point to this. Napoleon sent Captain Coignet to examine the western sector of Wellington's line; Coignet says that he went through the rye crop towards some cavalry, did a little 'swaggering' and came under fire from a gun, after which he reported back with his estimate of the strength of that part of the Allied line. A British officer, Lieutenant Riddock of the 44th, noted that at 9 o'clock some French officers rode from west to east a hundred paces from the front, until fired upon by troops in Best's 4th Brigade, when they were forced to abandon the examination before reaching the end of the line. Perhaps in consequence, a separate investigation was made later of the furthest sector, for Lieutenant Bacon, 10th Hussars in Vivian's brigade, stated that 'about an hour and a half before the battle commenced ... a French lancer rode up to the left squadron of our line to within 20 yards of our men, turned his horse leisurely to the left and rode down the whole line till he came to Vandeleur's brigade, when he turned off towards the French position'. Having made an assessment of the ground and a quick estimate of the troops there, the lancer possessed the first real intelligence of the strengths and weaknesses of Wellington's left wing, but his report would have been received at imperial headquarters only after the 11 a.m. order had been issued. Although nobody else in the 10th Hussars recorded this incident, it certainly occurred; and therefore it is probable that expert riders went along other sectors of the line and sent in their reports during the morning.[39]

In that way and at that time was the Hougoumont assault decided.

*

Appendix 1: The Sommelier of Genappe

One of the minor puzzles about the immediate prelude to Waterloo concerns a waiter at the inn of Genappe and the information he gathered and passed to the French. It seems to be mentioned only by General Foy (1775–1825), but with considerable detail.[40] The first reference is in his journal for the morning of 18 June:

> An officer of Wellington's staff said here [Genappe] yesterday that Blücher was retiring on Wavre to join the English before Brussels and to try another throw at arms. The Emperor has said on the contrary that the English will be at Antwerp before the 21st... I supped yesterday with Prince Jerome at *Le Roi d'Espagne.*

He reverted to this topic in an entry dated 23 June. In recalling his supper with Jerome on the night of the 17th he wrote that a *Kellner* (waiter) who served at table said that:

> Lord Wellington had eaten the night before at the inn, and that one of his ADCs said at table that the English army would await the French at the entrance to the forest of Soignies and that it would be joined by the Prussian army, which was moving on Wavre. This report was illuminating for Guilleminot [Jerome's chief of Staff] and me. On the morning of the 18th, Jerome, being with his brother at Le Caillou farm, told him of the Genappe *sommelier*'s [wine-waiter's] words.

But the Emperor totally dismissed the information as impossible.

The difficulty lies in the British officer's remarks made at Wellington's table. For, as we saw, when the Duke dined at the Genappe inn in the late evening of Friday 16 June after the success at Quatre Bras, he and his staff were under the impression that Blücher had either won the day or at least had held his own. If the officer was Captain Hardinge who came from Ligny, he was still without certain information, and we know that the consensus around the table was (but perhaps only silently) against his depressing news. Indeed, Wellington was that evening still ordering forward various units, and planned an offensive in the morning. He was not planning a battle in front of the forest. Moreover, no Prussian commander at that time at Brye or at

Tilly had decided on Wavre or any particular place as an objective, and so the British group at Genappe cannot have known it.

It seems reasonable to accept that the waiter heard something. But whatever he heard cannot have been much more than general speculation or perhaps British relief at an outcome for the day more satisfactory than had at one time seemed likely (for instance, might the general chat run somewhat like: 'Praise be, we didn't find Ney already at Genappe, or we should have had to fight close to the forest'?). With Wellington and De Lancey and Somerset working on orders for the next day's advance, probably alongside the Prussians, any talk among the better-informed could not have resembled what Foy said the waiter reported. And 'Wavre' was unthought-of.

Can we trace in a Napoleonic source any such remark as the waiter recounted, about Blücher retiring on Wavre to join Wellington in front of Brussels? The *Correspondance* volume on the campaign (xxviii) tells nothing. Gourgaud's *Campaign of 1815* (1818) explains Napoleon's views rather differently, for it describes him judging overnight on 17/18 June that the Prussians might move on Liège or on Brussels or stay in Wavre, which is fairly vague. However, we do find a probable source in Napoleon's memoirs, first published in 1820. There the phrase appears: 'it was probable that the Duke of Wellington and Marshal Blücher would use this night [17/18] to pass through the Forest of Soignies and unite in front of Brussels'. [41]

It therefore seems likely that Foy, on reading the St Helena memoirs, added some touches to his own original account, dated 18 June and again 23 June 1815, to make a vivid story. But really we shall never know.

Appendix 2: The Zenowicz Story

We saw that Soult wrote to Grouchy at 10 a.m. giving general approval to the latter's intentions, but adding comments from the Emperor. A Polish officer, Comte Georges Constantin Zenowicz (1780–1854), said that it was he who was handed the despatch and charged with its urgent delivery. In 1820 (revised 1848) he wrote:

> On 18 June 1815, the day of the battle of Waterloo, I served as senior officer at imperial headquarters, and I was ordered never to quit Napoleon for an instant.
>
> Towards nine o'clock in the morning the Emperor mounted his horse, and I followed him. Moving to the right of the army's line, having spoken to Comte d'Erlon for some moments, he left his entourage behind him and accompanied only by the Chief of Staff he climbed a small mound from

which could easily be seen the various positions of the two armies. Having studied [them] for some time with his glass, without changing place, he addressed some words to the Chief of Staff; then, at the moment the latter went away, the Emperor signed to me to come up to him. I obeyed. He then spoke these words:

'*There is Comte d'Erlon, our right,*' showing me that general's corps; then, after making a circle with his hand towards the right of the line, he continued, '*Grouchy marches in that direction; go to him at once, go by Gembloux following his tracks; the Chief of Staff will give you a written order.*' I wanted to tell the Emperor that the route he had specified was too long; but without giving me time to finish, he said to me, '*All the same, you will be captured in taking the shortest route,*' and pointing at the extreme right flank of our line, he went on, '*You will come back to me here when Grouchy debouches on the line. I am anxious* [il me tarde] *that he should be in direct communication and in the battle-line with us. Go, go.*'

As soon as I received this order I ran after the Chief of Staff who was then walking to the farm of Le Caillou, where the imperial headquarters had spent the night. We got there at 10 a.m.; the Chief of Staff went to his room and called for his secretary. The first thing one does in beginning to write an order is to write the date and hour; it is plain that this hour cannot be the hour of the despatch's departure, for before the departure one needs time to write it, and it must also be inscribed in the Chief of Staff's order register. All that demands quite a time; on ordinary duty where hours and minutes are of no account, this remark is without importance, but in a special case, when hours and minutes count, when one makes a wrong allegation against the bearer, it is necessary to set out the facts as they happened.

I repeat, the order that I was to carry was dated 10 a.m.; I withdrew to the orderly room. After waiting half an hour I went back to the Chief of Staff. Nothing more than the date had been written; the Chief of Staff was looking at the map, and his secretary amusing himself in cutting a quill pen. I went back to the orderly room where I found M. Regnault, chief commissary of *1er Corps* who, learning that I had not found anything to eat for 24 hours because I was always travelling [on service], was so good as to send to his wagon for a morsel of bread and brandy. After my meal, I again went to the Chief of Staff; he was busy dictating the order I awaited; so once more I went back to the orderly room. After half an hour I was called; Marshal Soult, in giving me his written order, repeated to me roughly what the Emperor had said. I left at once.

All these details that I have just given show super-abundantly that the observations on my mission made by writers are inexact. Some of these

> writers have the excuse that they could not know these particulars; on the basis of published orders they have judged me according to the incorrect hour for my departure; as to others who have sacrificed truth for political hatred I shall not bother with their partial and unfounded criticisms.
>
> I had galloped scarcely more than a few minutes when the cannonade and fusillade broke out; from this fact it is clear that I left the Chief of Staff towards noon, the hour at which battle commenced. To be precise as to the minute is difficult; to concern oneself with the hour when in such a situation requires powerful motives; on the battlefield the soldier forgets hours as when with a beautiful woman, and does not think of time. The first halt I made was to ask the route to Gembloux, and later, at Gembloux, to ask for information on the direction taken by Grouchy's corps, but I could get no satisfactory reply to this last question. I therefore went in accordance with the advice of the Emperor and in the direction that he himself had indicated. I was fortunate: between 3 and 4 o'clock I reached a division of the rearguard that formed part of the body to which I had been sent; a quarter of an hour later I met the Comte de Grouchy; he was with General Gérard in a little room where an ambulance [*sic*] had been established. I presented my despatches to the Marshal and told him personally what I had been charged to tell him.[42]

(What Grouchy did next belongs to a later chapter.)

Such was Zenowicz's account. It is full of circumstantial detail and seems sincere. We have already seen that at Fleurus on 16 June Napoleon and Soult, when sending an emissary with a despatch, repeated the gist of it and told the courier to repeat it to the recipient. That seems to bear out Zenowicz. But now we encounter two difficulties.

The first difficulty is that between 9 and 10 a.m. Napoleon was not concerned to bring Grouchy to him – that desire arose after 1 p.m. At this time in the morning he was not anxious that Grouchy should 'debouch' on his right wing. Secondly, the terms of the 10 a.m. despatch do not fit the message that Zenowicz thought he was carrying. He does not claim to have read it, merely to have been given a verbal summary by Soult of what Napoleon wanted Grouchy to do. And he makes no mention of the Emperor being present at or joining in that final briefing.

We have seen enough of Soult's ways as Chief of Staff to accept that he did not always perform his duties very adequately or accurately. In mid-morning, with battle imminent across the valley, Napoleon and his staff had many matters to attend to as units came up and were directed to their battle stations – and a message to Grouchy, important though it would have been, may not have been given top priority. Zenowicz implies that Soult was thinking of other matters, although he leaves us with an impression of slackness, emphasised by the secretary's idleness. But even if Soult was preoccupied with the Mont St Jean sector, ninety or so minutes does seem an exceptionally long delay.

Furnished with the message that must have been that of 10 a.m. (see this chapter, section III), Zenowicz set off. Almost at once. Almost at once he heard gunfire, and from his rough estimate of time this would coincide with the attack on Hougoumont, a little before noon.

An hour later (as we shall see in due course in Chapter 38), at 1 p.m., Soult wrote another despatch to Grouchy, on this second occasion half suggesting that he should 'manoeuvre in our direction' and 'join our right'. But before it could be sent there came further and disturbing news about Bülow appearing and moving against Napoleon's right flank. A staccato postscript was added and signed by Napoleon himself: 'Therefore lose not an instant in drawing near and joining us, in order to crush Bülow, whom you will take *en flagrant délit*.' This takes us to 1.30 p.m.

The contents of this message and postscript do fit with Zenowicz's story in almost every material point but one. The nature of the message fits. The noise of guns could be the Grand Battery's commencement. The departure time would fit with any of Grouchy's claimed times of receipt. But whoever was the courier for this message *could have been in no doubt of the palpable sense of alarm at headquarters and of Napoleon's presence*, even if (which itself is unlikely) he left the verbal briefing to Soult.

Grouchy, writing from Dinant on 20 June, assured the Emperor that he did receive Soult's message about marching to St-Lambert and attacking Bülow, but only 'towards 7 p.m.'[43] That would mean a courier taking something close to 5½ hours to reach him, which would of course excuse Grouchy for not breaking off battle and not marching in the last hour of daylight to save Napoleon. But that makes the journey suspiciously long. Still Grouchy repeats that in his memoirs. He quotes Soult's 1 p.m. message (though with one word carefully altered), he accepts the 1 p.m. time on the message, and again states that he received it 'towards 7 p.m.' (iv, p. 82). But then, being Grouchy at his most confusing, elsewhere in the memoirs he times the receipt 'towards 5 p.m.' (iv, p. 42).

My belief is that Zenowicz carried the second or 1 p.m. message, not the first of 10 a.m. Either his memory played him up, or he chose to pass over in silence Napoleon's part in sending the belated call, instead blaming it on Soult. But after two hundred years of confusion, who really can say?

Chapter 37

Battle Commences

The Attack on Hougoumont

I

GENERAL SIR JAMES SHAW KENNEDY by common consent established for all time the most convenient method to discuss the battle at Mont St Jean. It was, he said, a battle of five separate attacks, 'four of which were isolated attacks, and one only, that is the last, was general on the whole Anglo-Allied line: those five attacks were distinct and clearly separated from each other by periods of suspension of any close attacks . . . a great drama in five acts, with distinct and well-defined intervals; those intervals being marked simply by the firing of batteries, without that fire being accompanied by any other action of the troops.'[1] There was however a parallel drama that was playing from the approaches to St-Lambert and up the Lasne stream, first noticed by Napoleon just as he launched his battle. This drama culminated at Plancenoit and Frischermont, and was the Prussian contribution to this Allied struggle. It was part of the compact sealed overnight and in the morning between the Duke and Blücher.

Provided that we keep this parallel drama in mind, then we can accept Shaw Kennedy's generalisation, for it will help to make sense out of the intense yet confusing recollections of dozens of thousands of men. The first act concerns the fight for Hougoumont.

At approximately 11.30 a.m. the French infantry on the left began to move forward, and at once the British guns above Hougoumont opened fire on them. Upon this a French general bombardment began against the long Anglo-Allied front, although the rearmost formations marching from Genappe were still not in place. Prince Jerome's large *6e Division* closed on the southern border of the little estate of Hougoumont. The fighting was to continue for the next eight hours, and it became a battle within the battle.[2]

II

Hougoumont was a modest, steep-roofed brick château, in a small estate with a working farm, set in a compact rectangle of land low down in front of the Allied slope. Its boundaries were about 550 yards long on each side, and it lay some 250 yards south of the Nivelles road. In addition to the carriageway from that road, there was a sunken track running along the northern face of the property and winding north-eastwards up the slope to the Allied position. The estate's southern edge was in the lowest part of the dip and along the lie of the shallow dip in the land. The rectangle may be thought of as comprising four unequal segments: in the north-west stood the house and buildings; in the north-east was a formal garden extending east from the wall of the house, with a narrow strip of orchard along its north side, and with a great orchard

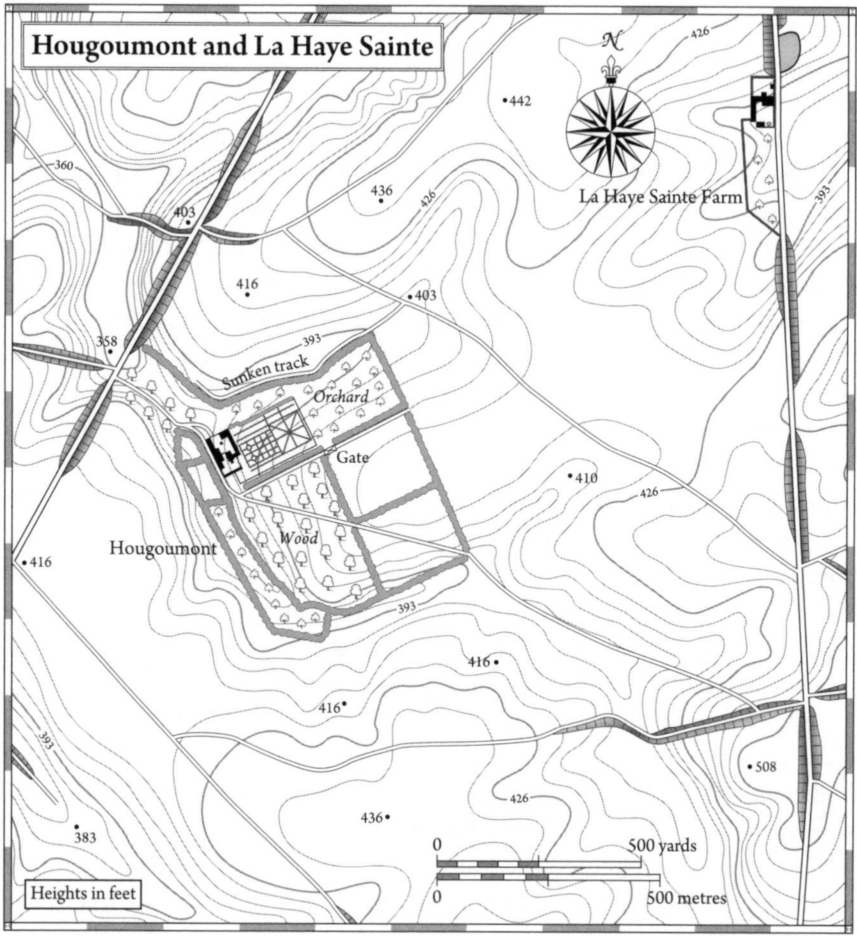

east of the formal garden and filling most of the north-east segment. To the south-east were two grass paddocks, with a gate (by now barricaded) into the great orchard; the south-west segment was mainly woodland. The exterior boundary was mainly hedge, hawthorn and stunted beech,[3] but inside the estate there was a brick wall some 7 feet high running from the south front of the buildings round the south and east sides of the formal garden; the wall was proof against musket bullets, and fortunately was sheltered by woodland trees to the south and the orchard to the east, else it could not have withstood cannon balls. In front of and along the south front of the brick wall was a glade or strip of open ground, thirty paces broad, laid down to vegetables: an attacker coming up through the southern woodland trees would find this open strip a death trap. The wood and orchard in summer leaf concealed from the French much of the configuration of buildings, walls, and open glades, as well as the tracks into the estate. Cannon-fire would lose much of its effectiveness, although high-angle howitzer fire could do considerable damage.

The Hougoumont complex of buildings in the north-west segment comprised an outer set of contiguous inward-facing barns, the farmer's and servants' quarters, stables, sheds, and offices, together making up about 80 per cent of the external frontages, with exterior walls accounting for the rest. These outbuildings formed something akin to two hollow squares, the northern part being the farmyard with a well in its centre; the southern part containing the château and chapel. The château was joined to buildings on the eastern side, and had a curtain wall (with a doorway in it) linking it to the outbuildings on the western perimeter. The curtain wall and door thus separated the farmyard from the courtyard.

There were only only four entrances into the Hougoumont buildings complex. On the east side a garden gate opened from the south courtyard into the formal garden; on the west side was a small external door out of a store building; on the south side was a wagon-way out through a tunnel in a building, with doors at both inside and outside ends of the tunnel; and on the north front was a two-door great gate that was left open by the defenders for wagons to bring in ammunition and supplies via the carriageway, and that was of course visible to the Allied troops back on the slope.

Everything favoured the defence against an attack from the south and east: woods and wall and buildings provided successive lines of defence, and required a relatively small garrison compared to the attackers' force. Overnight a great deal of work had been done to improve the defences, with fire-steps built behind the walls, loopholes cut, stores and ammunition accumulated. During the night the light companies of the two battalions of the 1st Guards (Lord Saltoun commanding) had stood to arms as scouts from

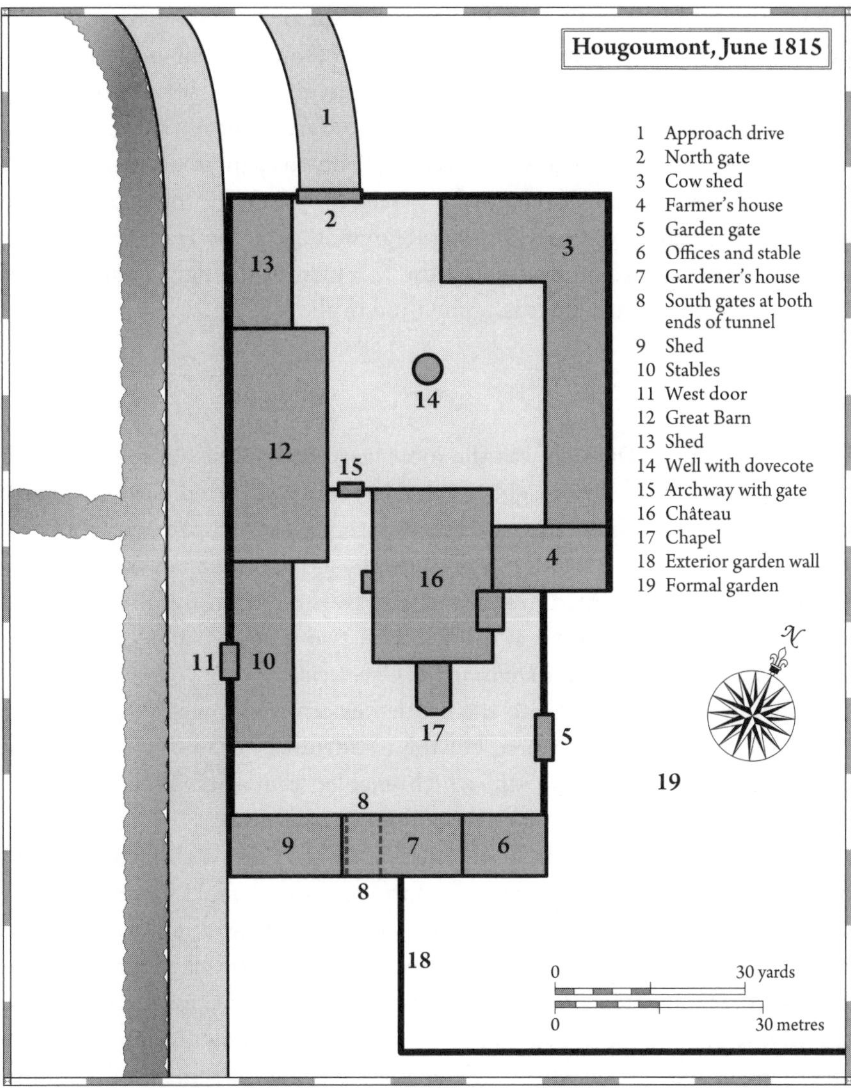

the French lines were thought to be probing the position, but if the French really were investigating, nothing had come of this.

Wellington had visited the post between 5 and 6 a.m. and had ordered Lieutenant-Colonel Macdonell of the Coldstream Guards to hold the position at all costs. Macdonell commanded the light companies of his battalion and that of the 3rd Guards, placed in the grounds of the property.[4] The Duke then decided to call in reinforcements, and at 9 a.m. the 1st Battalion of the Nassau Regiment Nr. 2 was brought from Wellington's eastern flank at Papelotte and filed down by a sunken track to the north-eastern boundary of the estate and thence along to the north gate, into the château and formal garden. At this point Saltoun's companies were ordered out of Hougoumont and back to rejoin their battalions on the summit; who ordered this is not entirely clear. On making a second visit, Wellington encountered Saltoun's force moving up the slope, and immediately ordered it back down again to occupy the great orchard. Before Saltoun's return the garrison by mid-morning on 18 June comprised 900 men of the 1st/Nassau Regiment Nr. 2, 100 Hanoverian Jäger and 100 Hanoverian Landwehr, and the 200 men of the light companies of the Coldstream and 3rd Guards, some 1,300 in all.

III

Prince Jerome's *6e Division* was the most westerly of Reille's three infantry divisions, with only Piré's light cavalry beyond it. It faced the south-west corner of the estate, some 300 yards away. Jerome sent forward his right-hand or *1re Brigade* (General Bauduin), preceded by a thick screen of skirmishers,[5] while five batteries opened fire on the woods: three from Reille's divisional artillery (from Piré, Jerome and Foy); plus two which Napoleon had sent forward from the *11e* and *12e Divisions de Cavalerie.*

Bauduin led his troops into the south-western wood, where he was shot dead by Hanoverian marksmen, but the tree-trunks were not thick and the trees were free of undergrowth, which enabled the 4,000 French to push the severely outnumbered Hanoverian and Nassau troops out of the wood and even across the great orchard. The Nassau garrison within the fortified buildings could do little to check any of this. Bauduin's replacement, Colonel Cubières (himself injured at Quatre Bras), led the *1re Brigade* up to open space beneath the garden's south wall, but at this point the Guards launched a double counter-attack. Lieutenant-Colonel Macdonell brought the light companies of the Coldstream and 3rd Guards out of the buildings, down their west front and round into the wood, checking Cubières; at about the same time Saltoun's light companies of the 1st Guards came south across the sunken track to which the Hanoverians and Nassauers had fallen back, fired into the great orchard, and charged. They retook the great orchard, being joined there by some of the Germans.[6] Jerome's first assault had been repulsed.

We have seen Reille's colourless and unhelpful account of the orders he received, and his instructions to Jerome. It comes, therefore, as something of a surprise to read the remarks of another officer of Soye's *2e Brigade*:

> Comte Reille, who commanded *2e Corps*, came to give us the order to take the position held by the English and to take the farm as a *point d'appui* and

> to maintain ourselves in this position during the battle, without losing or seizing terrain.[7]

Unless this officer was totally mistaken, which seems highly unlikely, the attack by Soye's brigade was decided well above Jerome's level of command. Yet Reille in this campaign never gave the impression of a commander keen to decide matters on his own initiative: his feeble performance on the morning of 16 June had shown that. The order must surely have come from Napoleon in person.[8] The battle within a battle was maintained by the deliberate choice of Napoleon, from beginning to end. It was never called off, despite the wasteful effort and the casualties. And never once did Napoleon – so quick to blame others when matters went awry – declare that it was a mistake or that he had wanted it to be called off.

IV

Soye's *2e Brigade* went up through the wood and into the northern part of the paddock, to the right of Cubières' *1re Brigade*, which was working its way leftwards to attack the western wall of the buildings. Thus Soye was close up to the 7-foot-high garden wall and the hedge at the edge of the orchard, facing the Nassauers and the Guards' light companies. Wellington had personally ordered up Bull's howitzers (I Troop, RHA) from the rear to join the field guns, telling him to direct plunging fire upon the wood, which he did to considerable effect. But the British batteries up on the summit could not drive off the attackers, who made a massive frontal assault against the château complex and garden wall. An officer of the *1re Ligne* (of Soye's brigade) recalled that after their initial attack, the resultant 'debris' of the *1er bataillon* was joined with the *2e* for a fresh assault. That having failed, 'the remains' of these two battalions advanced with the *3e Bataillon* under 'murderous' fire for a final unsuccessful attempt,[9] although in the great orchard Saltoun's force was thrust back to the sunken track. If Soye's efforts fell short of success, at least he distracted the garrison and helped Cubières in his left flanking move. He drove in Macdonell's light companies on the western front, forcing them to take shelter inside the complex via the big north gateway. French skirmishers even crossed the access road to the north-west and opened fire on the British batteries up the slope, while a storming party of about thirty men under Sous-Lieutenant Legros, the man famed as '*l'enfonceur*', dashed at the north gateway, which Macdonell's men had just pushed closed but had not yet barred. The French seemed on the brink of capturing the buildings.

It has so often been the tragic fate of many brave and brilliant local successes that they fail because they had not been foreseen or allowed for by commanders, and so they end in useless deaths: on a large scale one thinks of the 36th (Ulster) Division's extraordinary achievements on 1 July 1916 at the Somme, that finally came to nothing. And so it was with Legros and his men. By point-blank shooting through the doors, through main strength and axe blows, the men under Legros forced open the gates. The north face was gaping open. Had Cubières – who was wounded in leading the attack on the west wall – deployed a company more closely in support, and had Legros held the gateway, kept up a steady fire but not gone inside, the defenders might well have been overcome and the position lost. But he and a couple of dozen others plunged into the north courtyard; and the defenders, who had taken shelter in the buildings round the yard, shot them down.

Just too late, support for Legros came rushing towards the gateway, as Macdonell and nine officers and men heaved and swung the gates shut in the face of the enemy, and dropped the cross-bar. Even then, the French sought to scale the north wall, but without success. Providentially for the garrison, help came from the summit behind them, as Colonel Woodford of 2nd Coldstream Guards with three of his companies cleared the north front of enemy troops and brought down four more companies to reinforce the garrison by another 700 men.

V

Jerome's second attack was clearly seen as unsuccessful by those under his command. Indeed General Guilleminot, acting as second-in-command and adviser to Jerome, later said that after the first assault he advised against the subsequent ones. With *6e Division* shaken, someone ordered Foy's *9e Division* into the attack. Here we need to be cautious: British historians generally claim that the whole division was eventually committed to the assault on Hougoumont, but Foy, who was an honest witness, described it somewhat differently. He wrote of his division (or some of it) attacking the eastern side in support of Jerome, but he defined that support in fairly restrictive terms: 'at various times I furnished battalions to the wood, to support or replace those of Jerome'.[10] He wrote 'battalions', not 'my division', which suggests something of a piecemeal approach, feeding rather than augmenting the attack.

Either way, it is certain that between 1 and 2 p.m. Foy's *1re Brigade*, commanded by Tissot (the senior regimental commander, as Gauthier had been seriously wounded at Quatre Bras), went into the paddock, although suffering from the British shelling from the ridge. At the end of the paddock Tissot was checked at the hedge protecting the orchard, and was subjected to intense musketry fire; unable to break through the hedge, the attackers were shot down in large numbers. But there was a gate between the paddock and the orchard, and the French seized this and pushed into the orchard, forcing the defenders back across it right to the northern hedge by the sunken track. A group of French soldiers dragged one of their howitzers forward into the paddock, and this soon proved an intolerable nuisance to the defenders crouched at the edge of the orchard; in consequence Saltoun led an attack against it, but was driven back. Although some French soldiers thought that they 'remained masters of the wood and orchards' this was perhaps an overstatement, for their thrusts northwards through the orchard were hampered by musketry fire from the loopholed eastern wall of the formal garden that overlooked the fruit trees. The garrison had Nassauers and Coldstreamers posted there to good effect. The second great assault came to a halt.

VI

If we look beyond Hougoumont and examine the battle as a whole and ask what had been risked and what had been achieved this far, the answer can be framed in different ways.

It is a fact that only at Hougoumont had there been any serious fighting, and the small garrison, which had risen from 800 Nassauers, 200 Hanoverians and 200 Guards, to about 1,100 Guards and the 800 Nassauers, had resisted two major attacks by Jerome's division and part of Foy's, amounting to about 10,000 men. The wood, paddocks and orchards had been taken by the French, so that in the grounds of the estate only the sunken track was still in Allied hands. But the buildings were still safely held, and attempts to break in had been foiled

Holding Hougoumont was an essential part of Wellington's plan, and thus far he had succeeded. What must have made this the more necessary was the Duke's belief that he faced some 10,000–15,000 more men than was actually the case, for he thought that only Vandamme had been sent against the Prussians.[11] He dared not weaken the Braine l'Alleud–Merbe Braine–Hougoumont sector. He also had to watch the crest from there east to the crossroads and beyond against a main attack. The crest was strongly held by both brigades of the Guards Division, all three brigades of the 2nd Division, Mitchell's brigade of 4th Division, and Colin Halkett's brigade of 3rd Division a little to the east, plus Brunswick forces further back in reserve, three batteries of artillery behind Hougoumont, with Cleeves's battery to the east also giving support, and Grant's cavalry brigade.[12] But the reason why they were so strongly massed (especially when compared with the force deployed east of the crossroads) was that Hougoumont acted as a magnet, potentially disturbing the balance of the defensive line. It made more vulnerable the line east of the crossroads should the French launch a mass attack there.

Napoleon's plan was quite different from Wellington's. He wanted to take, or at the very least neutralise, Hougoumont. And he wanted to mass his Grand Battery and launch d'Erlon's assault on the centre without it being counter-attacked from west of the crossroads by Wellington's best troops. A weak feint against Hougoumont would not deceive Wellington, so that Reille had to make a serious assault, take Hougoumont, and provoke severe Allied retaliation in attempts to recapture it. That is the meaning of Reille's remark that it would be for the French 'a *point d'appui*' to be 'held during the battle, without losing or seizing terrain'. Hougoumont was to serve as a continual distraction for Wellington's men, who in their turn would be wasted and shot down in trying to re-take it. It would tie down a significant percentage of the Duke's best troops while the battle was won elsewhere. This meant that until the Grand Battery and *1er Corps*' assault were both ready, Reille's infantry would have to be thrown time and again against Hougoumont, regardless of casualties (a consideration anyway that never greatly disturbed Napoleon). And they were.

At this point in the Hougoumont story Shaw Kennedy's *First Act* really came to an end, for the next *Act* concerned d'Erlon's great attack on the ridge, to which we must turn next. We shall revert to Hougoumont in Chapter 39, but while looking elsewhere meanwhile let us remember that the heroic men of both sides at Hougoumont continued to fight on for the next two hours and went on even beyond that until the evening.

Chapter 38

The Second Act

d'Erlon's Great Attack and its Defeat

I

NAPOLEON HAD SOUGHT TO DRAW Wellington's attention to the fight for Hougoumont while he and Ney prepared the main attack on the centre. For this the Grand Battery was essential, but hauling guns weighing up to two tons each over the uneven and soft ground took an agonisingly long time. Slowly and very painfully 'the Emperor's beautiful daughters' came up the paved road and were then dragged to the chosen position, well forward of the Belle Alliance ridge.

The deployment and position and even size of the Grand Battery have been matters of serious disagreement between historians, and this will doubtless continue long into the future, for such evidence as there is can be read in different ways, and tactical matters also complicate the arguments.

From the main French ridge the slopes ran down to the valley broad bottom, but there was a definite ridge extending north-west as far as the west of Hougoumont and from this ridge subsidiary fingers of high ground tended in an east-northeast direction. Had the Grand Battery been placed immediately north of the main ridge, (say) somewhere near the track that runs from La Belle Alliance to Papelotte and Smohain, then it would have been well protected by d'Erlon's formations and by skirmishers in front; but it would have stood some 1,200 yards from the Mont St Jean crossroads and thus at the very limit of its range. It would, in other words, have been sited mainly for its moral effect, shaking the nerves of Wellington's troops rather than pulverising his men and horses and cannon. I find it hard to believe that so limited a use for massed artillery was to Napoleon's taste. He fully intended to shake nerves, but given that he now had relatively few hours left to him that day if he was to dine in Brussels, he would want to destroy Wellington's men, horses and guns as soon as possible and thus add to the certainty of d'Erlon's attack succeeding.

If it was also his intention that the Grand Battery should mount the Mont St Jean ridge to continue the pulverisation once d'Erlon had taken it, then it would take a considerable time to move it three-quarters of a mile of shot-over ground trampled by some 20,000 men, and then reposition it. This argument also applies to moving individual batteries from position to position, for they would cease to blast at the enemy for perhaps half an hour or so, though remaining under fire, while they were dragged through the mud and carnage of the slopes, a material reduction in Grand Battery firepower at a time when the maximum weight of fire was sought.[1]

There is a finger of high ground further to the north of the Belle Alliance ridge extending for a quarter of a mile east of the Charleroi road (which Mark Adkin terms the Battery ridge). This faced the west-centre of Wellington's slightly concave line only some 600–900 yards away. Placed here the Grand Battery would be unprotected by the main body of d'Erlon's force and would depend for its safety on the thick swarms of skirmishers out in front. Wellington's strength (or weakness) could not easily be judged, but would he risk launching an attack across the open at massed guns and certain to suffer significant losses in the attempt? He had stayed mute and almost invisible all morning, and Ney had suspected that he was not thinking offensively but was trying to slip away.[2] D'Erlon's troops would have to thread their way through the Grand Battery as they marched to the attack, but if it was then to be hauled up to the crest the distance would be less and the delay shorter. Moreover the punishment that the Grand Battery should wreak on Wellington's position was expected to be immeasurably greater at such close range.[3]

No two contemporary accounts correctly calculate the Grand Battery totals, or explain how Napoleon came to his 'twenty-four' 12-pounders, and all subsequent writers rely to some degree upon surmise.[4]

De Salle, who wrote that he received the order from the Emperor's ADC La Bédoyère, claimed that he was to command 'a battery of eighty pieces' made up of 'twenty-four 12-pounders' – which supports the Emperor's figure – the other guns being 6-pounders. Since his calculation came to a stated if confusing total of 'fifty-four' (not eighty), if we deduct the Emperor's 24 then we are seeking thirty 6-pounders, which is the equivalent of the thirty 6-pounders of the four infantry and one cavalry divisions of *1er Corps*. What then of the total 'eighty'? As Napoleon definitely ordered the deployment of 'twenty-four 12-pounders' his orders must have been obeyed, so I think the Grand Battery comprised eighteen 12-pounders from the *1er*, *2e* and *6e Corps*, plus six 12-pounders from the *Garde*. Allowing for sixteen howitzers, that leaves forty 6-pounders to find to make the 'eighty'; I tentatively suggest that the forty came by selecting elements from among the 110 guns that supported the *Garde*'s infantry (total, 24 × 6-pounders) and cavalry (16), the infantry of *1er*, *2e* and *6e Corps* (54 in total) and their cavalry (16).

As to the position, De Salle stated that it was, in command terms, 'one battery of all these pieces in the position we held, half-way on the slope, in one single line', but he then indicated that it was moved or was moving to a ridge further north and closer to the enemy.[5] That I take to be the Grand Battery ridge and that it was in fact occupied before the bombardment started, since it was close enough to the enemy to come under howitzer or mortar fire. Behind the shallow summit and on the south side of the ridge were hundreds of caissons and wagons, and some 800 men and around 1,400 horses required to haul and service the guns. These at least were somewhat sheltered from any counter-battery fire. Mark Adkin reckons that the ammunition stocked with and just behind the guns amounted to over 22,000 rounds, of which they expended just over half during the battle.

The decision to assemble this mass battery was not finally made until 11 a.m., and whether that was due to the reports made between 8 and 11 a.m. on the improvement in ground quality and/or the tardy movement of French forces from Genappe, or to a slowly growing recognition of the strength of Wellington's position, we cannot be sure. What the French high command did *not* recognise at this point was the importance of the La Haye Sainte buildings, nestling a quarter of a mile away on the open slope, for the instructions to the gunners did not call for their destruction: it would not have taken many minutes to have wrecked them and wiped out the garrison.

For the moment those at imperial headquarters could only wait till the battery should begin firing, and it was now that Soult wrote a second despatch to Grouchy, just before 1 p.m. The 10 a.m. orders sent to Grouchy had been far from specific. Further directions were advisable, because (as we can see in the first part of Soult's new 1 p.m. letter) Napoleon was not quite at ease concerning what the Prussians might do. What kept Soult from writing somewhat sooner is not known, for from the information that had been received at mid-morning from Grouchy it appeared that he had so far been unable to approach the Prussians or hamper their plans for the day. The Prussians were thus an unknown quantity complicating any plan for battle, but that did not seem to be a major concern at this time when the defence of Hougoumont was drawing in Wellington's troops and the Grand Battery was starting to pound the crest to 'soften up' the Anglo-Allied defence. The battle could progress over the crest and northwards, hence the distant Grouchy could be given only very general guidance 'for manoeuvring in our direction':

> Marshal: you wrote to the Emperor at 6 a.m. this morning that you would march on Sart-à-Walhain; and your plan then was to march to Corbaix and to Wavre. This movement conforms to His Majesty's dispositions that have been communicated to you. However, the Emperor orders me to tell you that you must always manoeuvre in our direction so that no Prussian force can get between us. I do not give you the direction to take; it is for you to see the point where we are and to act accordingly, and to link our communications, also to be always capable of falling on any of the enemy's troops that may seek to annoy our right, and to destroy them.
>
> At this moment battle is engaged [*est engagée*] on the Waterloo line in front of the forest of Soignies; the enemy's centre is at Mont St Jean; [the next words are squeezed in immediately above the date and signature, but in the same clerk's hand] therefore manoeuvre to join our right.
>
> 18th at 1 p.m. (sgd) THE MARSHAL DUKE OF DALMATIA.

Then, before the letter could be handed to a messenger, came more troubling information. A Prussian courier had been captured and brought to headquarters, bearing a letter for Wellington from Bülow, saying that the latter was either preparing to advance, or was advancing, and seeking directions and advice from the Duke (the letter has never been quoted and seems no longer to exist). The messenger gave some verbal details, but exactly what is uncertain. The Prussian letter must have been written at some time in mid-morning by which time the leading files of IV Corps were approaching the descent to the Lasne brook or had reached the stream. This information alerted imperial headquarters to a new potential problem just at the time when the Grand Battery was in the midst of pummelling the Mont St Jean crest prior to d'Erlon's great attack.

In his memoirs the Emperor claimed that he observed through the haze a cloud on the eastern heights, that nobody could agree on what it was, and that Soult thought it might be 5,000–6000 of Grouchy's men. Napoleon maintained that this was before he authorised Ney to launch the battle, and that without further delay he sent Domon's and Subervie's cavalry to investigate whether these were friends or foes and act accordingly. He then told Soult, 'This morning the chances were 90 per cent in our favour, Bülow's appearance costs us 30 points but we still have 60 against 40.' In all this I find that last remark totally believable. He was assessing the chances of an early and rapid destruction of Wellington's line, judged against a much later problem somewhere down in the Lasne valley; he had to judge when to adapt his plan, when or if to detach troops from his northward attack or from his own reserve and send them past Plancenoit. But for the rest I do not accept this version; and moreover his next phrase (ostensibly to Soult) misrepresented the orders sent to Grouchy only a few hours earlier and used a timetable that he must have known was infeasible: 'and if Grouchy repairs the terrible fault he committed yesterday in wasting time at Gembloux and sends his force rapidly, our victory will be decisive for Bülow's force will be totally destroyed'.[6]

At headquarters a postscript to the letter for Grouchy was dictated, written at the bottom of the page and carried onto the reverse side:

> P.S. A letter that has just been intercepted says that General Bülow is to attack our flank. We believe we see this corps on the heights of St-Lambert [5 miles away]; therefore lose not an instant in drawing near and joining us, in order to crush Bülow, whom you will take *en flagrant délit.* [signature: a squiggle in a hand different from that of Soult or the clerk].[7]

Doubts have been raised about this letter and postscript, some alleged inconsistencies, the document's authenticity or later fabrication and so forth. I examine these matters in Appendix 1 to this chapter. I deal with what happened thereafter in later chapters.

II

Marshal Ney duly sent the order to the Grand Battery, and at some time around 1 p.m. (or a little later) the French guns fired their shatteringly loud and powerful first salvo. This continued for some thirty minutes, the lighter guns probably managing two rounds per minute and the 12-pounders half that rate, their target extending about three-quarters of a mile along the top of the slope and into the rear zone behind. That meant some 3,000 iron shot and shell smashing into the crest at a rate of about 100 per minute for half an hour, but over half the shots hit the forward slope, and even where they landed on the crest or behind, the soft ground absorbed them, checked the skid or bounce effect, and did far less physical damage to Wellington's troops than Napoleon probably thought. Yet even if the destruction was less than expected, the noise was frightful and must have tested nerves very severely; the din making thinking difficult and the smoke, drifting thickly across the front, obscuring the view. Nor was the work easy for the French artillerymen. The recoil pushed back the guns and dug them deep into the soil, necessitating frequent re-positioning. Luckily for them, Wellington's ban on British counter-battery fire left the French gunners relatively unmolested.[8]

As the pounding continued, so d'Erlon's 20,000 troops formed up and threaded their way forward, between and around the limbers, wagons and caissons and then up over battery ridge. As they advanced through the guns, the cannons had to cease firing. The advance to the attack took about thirty minutes and nobody watching from the ridge could doubt the severity and direction of the impending onset. D'Erlon's task was to complete what the bombardment had begun, the capture of the forward bastions of La Haye Sainte, the crest itself, where only a straggling hedge sheltered the road along it, and the La Haye and Papelotte complex. Once this vital tactical position had been taken, the infantry might be able to move down the reverse slope, or could dominate it with musketry volleys, while the cavalry came up to exploit the success. Just conceivably the artillery could have been hauled up from battery ridge to the crest to assist in the massacre, although this would have taken a considerable time to effect and much longer than it would take the cavalry to deploy. But once Wellington's centre had gone, annihilation was foreseeable.

As a plan it was simple, brutal, and likely to prove sufficient: by 3 p.m. Wellington's army should be broken and disintegrating. The decisive battle vainly hoped for on 16 June would have been won, this time against Wellington, with his Anglo-Allied army wrecked beyond recovery. And not that only, for the Prussian force seen to the east (Bülow's leading units) would be isolated and destroyed between the two wings of the French army. This double shock would paralyse the enemies' will. Brussels would welcome Napoleon and all the immense political consequences for France and Europe would follow. Napoleon rated his chances at 60/40, and the operation against the ridge might indeed have succeeded, though whether the larger consequences would follow must remain open to question.

III

Leaving the French advancing across the valley, it is time to study the Allied centre, and to see how the bastion of La Haye Sainte compared with Hougoumont. This small farm formed a hollow square of buildings, barn, stables and a barricaded main gate, on the west side of the Charleroi road, a couple of hundred yards south of the crossroads. On its north face was a small cottage garden, to the south a long narrow hedged orchard. There were two large gates: the firmly shut main gate and a gateway in the south barn, but unfortunately the barn door had been torn off and burnt as fuel during the wet night. There were several small gates through the boundary walls, or doors out of the buildings to the cultivated zones, and there was a pond and a well inside the property. The buildings had very few windows on the outside.

The road up to the crossroads at the top of the slope went through a cutting where, on the east side of the Charleroi road just opposite the north-eastern

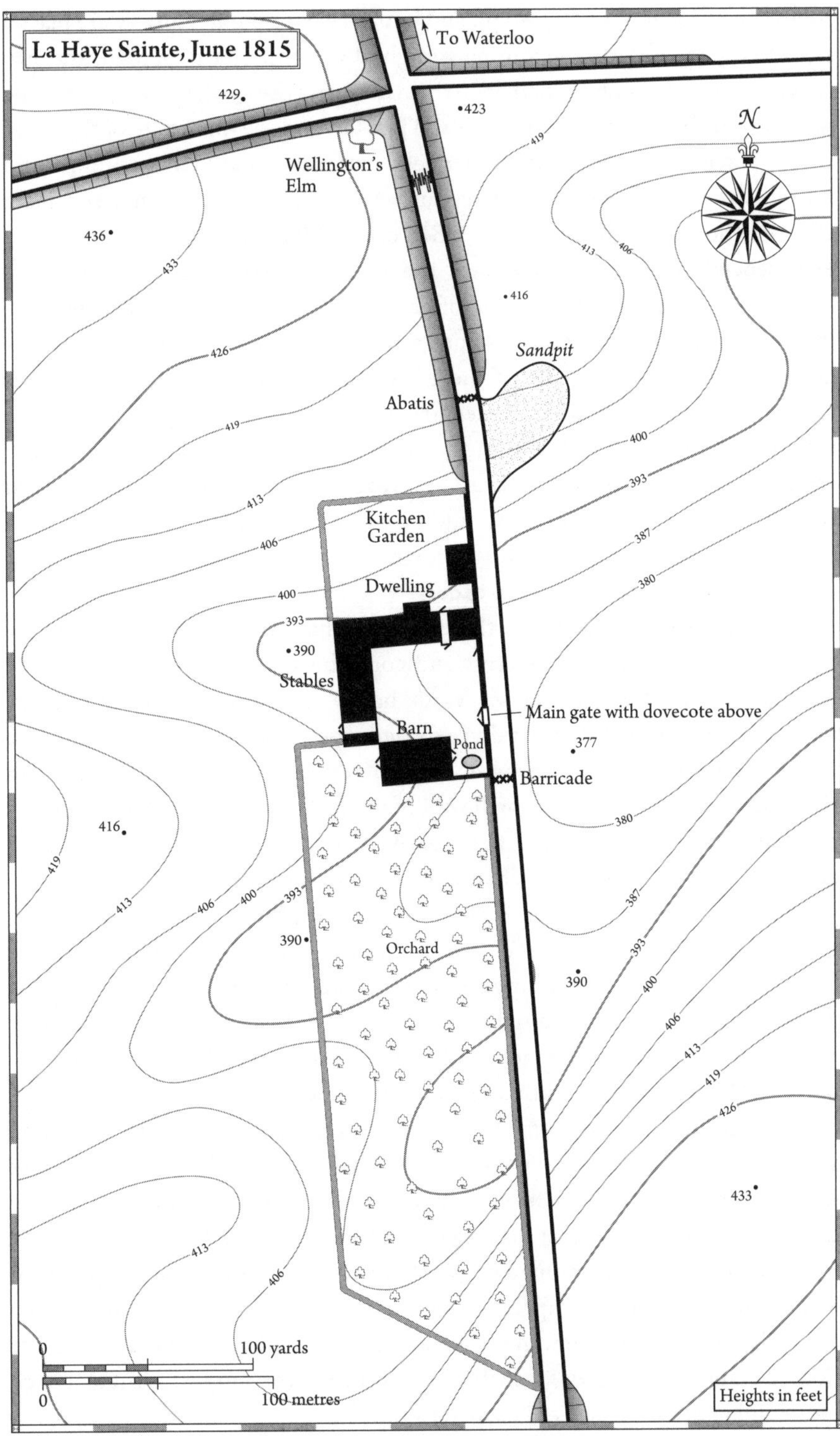
La Haye Sainte, June 1815
To Waterloo
Wellington's Elm
Sandpit
Abatis
Kitchen Garden
Dwelling
Stables
Barn
Pond
Main gate with dovecote above
Barricade
Orchard
0
100 yards
0
100 metres
Heights in feet
N

edge of the property, was a sandpit and knoll. Two 9-pounder guns were placed close to the crossroads and aiming straight down the Charleroi road, and two rough barricades or *abatis* had been thrown across the road, one just above the sandpit and the other further down and just beyond the main gate of the farm.

La Haye Sainte was altogether less extensive than Hougoumont and it required a much smaller garrison: it was initially held by some 400 men, all from the 2nd Light Battalion, KGL, under Major George Baring, a most experienced officer. By its nature the battalion would use the standard Baker rifle so that only one type of cartridge was needed; the average rate of fire would be about two shots per minute, and the ammunition pouches held 60 rounds each, so that if the entire garrison had been in continuous action re-supply would be necessary in half an hour or when 24,000 rounds had been fired. But from the shape of the buildings and the lack of windows it was unlikely that everyone would be firing all the time, and so the ammunition consumption should take much longer, but it would be good sense before battle started to bring down into the buildings a replenishment of ammunition plentiful even to excess.[9]

For the main problem of the site was that while it was covered by Wellington's artillery on the crest and could be supported by troops in the nearby sandpit, it was about 250 yards below the summit, and all support would have to cross that totally exposed open zone before reaching the nearest range of buildings, where was situated the one sheltered door from the kitchen garden into the north wall of the farmhouse. French skirmishers and cannon-fire would make that journey dangerous, doubly so if French cavalry were close enough to charge the reinforcing parties.

What is extraordinary is that during the night so little attention was given to strengthening the defences, building fire-steps, loopholing the blank outer walls, and massing reserves of rifle ammunition to permit the defence to continue for many hours. All those measures had been taken at Hougoumont, so why not here? Who was responsible for this dangerous oversight? Wellington, so alive to the requirements at Hougoumont, seems to have ignored the problem. In the centre Orange was shifting guns and artillery ammunition from one part of the line to another but seemed to have said nothing as to this bastion. Alten, the divisional commander holding this section of the line, and his brigade commander Ompteda, seem to have issued no orders or summoned extra labour to do anything about it. General Shaw Kennedy, who as Captain Shaw was on Alten's staff at the time as an AQMG, made no comment in his *Notes* on the lack of defensive works, other than to state that there was a northern entrance to the property. There will be more said later on this lack of preparation.

The part of Wellington's line that awaited the great attack comprised Alten's 3rd Division west of the crossroads, and Picton's 5th Division to its east (perhaps the most battered of all the formations that had fought at Quatre Bras). Stretched between Kempt's and Pack's brigades of Picton's division, and supported by them, was Bylandt's brigade of Netherlanders, officially part of Perponcher's division. Next came Best's 4th Hanoverian brigade, beyond Pack, and finally the other brigade of Perponcher's division, Saxe-Weimar's Nassauers in the collection of buildings in the Papelotte sector. Apart from Vandeleur and Vivian on the extreme eastern flank the cavalry was well back behind the infantry and thus below the skyline. Six batteries were on or close behind the summit, but one of them (Gardiner) was far distant on the Ohain road well to the east, and Whinyates's mixed gun and rocket troop was back in reserve. The other four batteries were Rogers in front of Kempt's brigade, Braun and Rettberg in front of Best's brigade and to Rogers's east, and the Netherlands battery of Byleveldt partly near Rogers and partly behind Saxe-Weimar's brigade at Papelotte. The front line (excluding Gardiner and Whinyates) thus had only 28 pieces (ten 9-pounders, thirteen 6-pounders and five howitzers) concentrated against d'Erlon's force. Again we note that Wellington's conception of a major threat to his western wing and his expectation of Prussian reinforcement during the early afternoon left his centre and eastern wing very lightly protected.

IV

The Grand Battery had punished the Allied front for about thirty minutes and for its part had escaped molestation, because by Wellington's express orders the Allied artillery was prohibited from counter-battery fire, instead reserving all its ammunition for the expected infantry and cavalry attacks. Napoleon's confidence was such that he had nothing but a skirmishing screen to protect the guns, but it gave sufficient cover so long as the Allied line remained passive. Now came the order for the great thrust for the crest – and victory. While individual brigades on the wings attacked the strong-points of La Haye Sainte and La Haye/Papelotte, the centre would roll forward, blazing its way over the summit with musketry, then try to bring up artillery and blast to shreds the remains of Wellington's centre, while the cavalry took up the pursuit.

So at about 1.30 p.m. Quiot's *1re Division* moved through the guns and began the attack, one brigade (Charlet) to the west of the Charleroi road closing on the long orchard of La Haye Sainte, while its other brigade (Bourgeois) marched towards the sandpit below the crossroads. In succession to its right and slightly back in echelon came the other divisions of d'Erlon's corps,

Donzelot (*2e*) and then Marcognet (*3e*), with Pégot's Brigade of Durutte's *4e Division,* the furthest back. All were marching against the line held by Picton and Best. On the right Durutte's second brigade (Brue) swung away towards Saxe-Weimar's position at La Haye and Papelotte. Thus, leaving aside the flankers, the central frontage was the equivalent to three divisions, spread over nearly two-thirds of a mile: each end formed as a brigade front (Bourgeois and Pégot, four battalions deep) and between them two broader divisional fronts. The divisions were not all of the same strength, but as a generalisation each had a frontage of about 125 yards (one battalion ranged in three ranks deep; capable of instant fire from its broad first and second ranks, say 250 shots) with battalions massed one behind the other, creating a dense column. Where the division was of four regiments (eight battalions) this made a column depth of twenty-four ranks, a mass judged of almost unstoppable momentum.

There has never been any consensus on who ordered this formation, and one can argue for or against the decision being the Emperor's, or Ney's, or d'Erlon's, or even Soult's: there is no means of knowing. The mass column was cannon-fodder, relying on the pressure from the rear to keep the momentum going (Macdonald's great column at Wagram in 1809 had similarly served Napoleon's purpose, at terrible cost, and had been formed at the Emperor's insistence). The thin columns in the Peninsula were much more flexible and suited to the ground, but their weakness was the time it took to deploy from column into musketry line at the moment of closing on the enemy, and the British line in defence had the advantage in instantly opening fire on a column-head or a semi-deployed spread. The formation adopted for d'Erlon's attack maintained the impetus of the column but with fully deployed musketry along its entire front: Wellington's Peninsular advantage in musketry ratios compared to manpower strengths would no longer apply. Once d'Erlon was on the summit his musketry superiority would be overwhelming. The problem today was that his column lacked flexibility, that its mass was difficult to control, that the men in the middle could see very little and could not react swiftly, and that it made a superb target for the Allied artillery. And as the mass came up the slope that artillery punished it mercilessly. A commander-in-chief concerned with minimising casualties might doubt the formation's suitability; one intent on gaining at any cost a ridge held by British infantry and their less stolid allies, a ridge already savagely bombarded, would appreciate its advantages.

The mass of men trudged up the slope, protected from skirmish fire by their own swarm of light infantry out in front, while the Grand Battery resumed firing over their heads. The regimental eagles were borne by each 1st battalion, the drums throbbed, the officers moved among the ranks whipping

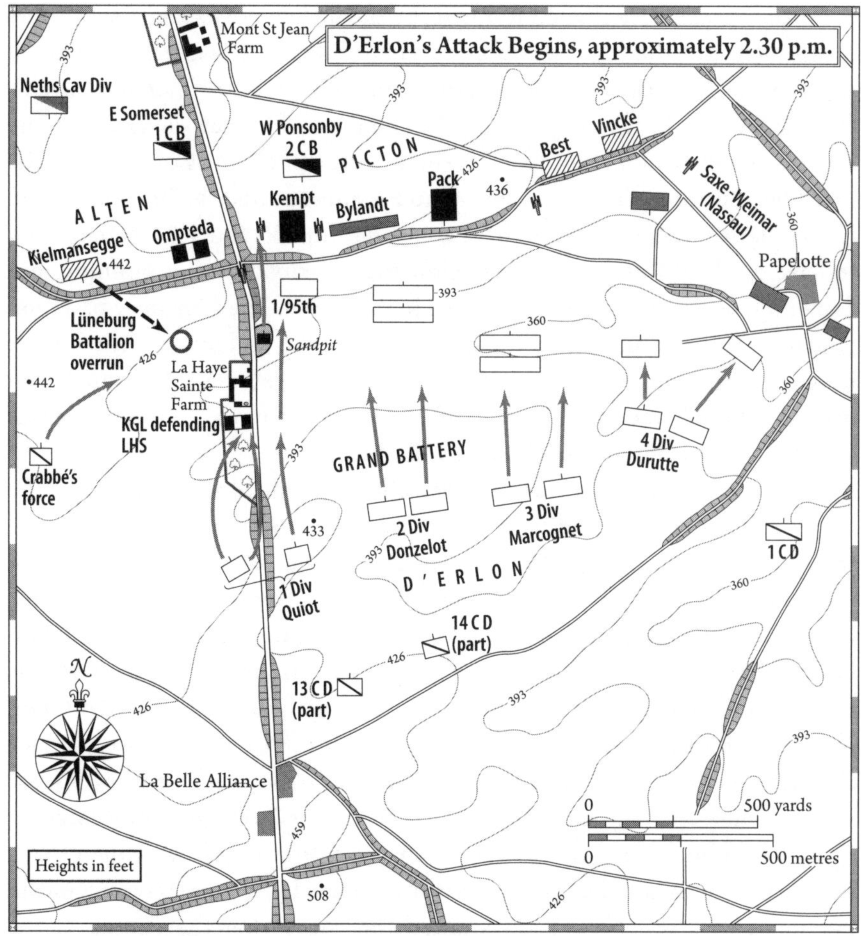

up courage and enthusiasm in the men. Ney and d'Erlon were conspicuous, leading the advance on horseback.

Charlet's Brigade closed on three sides of La Haye Sainte. The KGL light infantry garrison and some Hanoverian Jäger kept up a concentrated fire while out in the grounds, and even attempted a limited counter-attack, but weight of numbers drove them out of the orchard and back into the buildings. As noted earlier, because the barns, sheds and the house had few external apertures from which to see and fire, the defenders could do relatively little damage to the advancing French. At this point, someone on the Allied side (see Appendix 2 to this Chapter) ordered a battalion from the crest to reinforce the garrison, and the Lüneburg light battalion from Kielmansegge's Hanoverian Brigade in Alten's 3rd Division was chosen for the task. Its commander, Lieutenant-Colonel Klencke, was apparently without much command experience; he led it down the open slope, 595 strong, sent some of his men into the main position, leaving others in extended line against the French skirmishers. Near Charlet's brigade stood supporting cavalry from Milhaud's heavy corps, Crabbé's composite force of *cuirassiers*.[10] The *1er Cuirassiers* (Colonel Ordener), seeing their opportunity, dashed on the extended Lüneburgers, cut them up and scattered them before they could form square. Ordener seems to have gone on to attack some KGL squares and to have disabled Ross's two guns below the crossroads before running into firmer opposition from infantry on the high ground. The Lüneburg battalion casualties this day amounted to 205, or 30 per cent, and most of these must have been in this single charge. It was a shattering experience, leaving them useless although not annihilated. Unfortunately, the moral consequence was considerably greater and much more widespread.[11]

A couple of hundred yards away the elite 1/95th held the sandpit and the little knoll above it, providing cover for and a tenuous link with Baring and the garrison in the farm. All the accounts of the battalion's performance published before 2003 gave the impression of a strong, resolute defence against the advance of Quiot's division, and that it was because the battalion held to its position too long that its eventual retirement to the crest was slightly 'precipitate'. But in that year the publication of the battalion commander Sir Andrew Barnard's private letter of 23 June 1815 disclosed for the first time that, in his words, 'a *great* number of our men went to the rear without cause after the appearance of the cuirassiers'. He put the absentees at about a hundred men: 'Many of those that went to the rear were men that I little expected to have heard of in that situation.' He also remarked: 'Kincaid [adjutant] says very few if any quitted the corps after the charge of the cavalry,' by which he must have meant the great cavalry charge by Uxbridge, and so the disarray does not seem to apply to Ney's later cavalry onsets (the only other charges with *cuirassiers*), but instead to the earlier *cuirassier* incident with the Lüneburgers. This point was taken up by Barry Van Danzig in his 2007 tactical study, who argued that the sight of *cuirassiers* cutting up the Lüneburgers created such dismay in the 1/95th, who had never before encountered French heavy cavalry, that they turned and fled in considerable numbers. That flight affected the steadiness of Bylandt's Netherlands infantry brigade, which gave way as d'Erlon's men approached, and this in turn created a gap in Picton's line just as d'Erlon's men gained the crest. In short, Crabbé's brief attack had a significant domino effect far beyond its original purpose.[12]

Major Baring's little garrison was now isolated, but its subsequent story belongs to a later chapter. Here we are concerned with Picton's defence of the ridge and the massive assault by d'Erlon. As we have seen, the older versions of how units performed as expressed in published correspondence, such as H. T. Siborne's *Waterloo Letters* of 1891, have been refined or even changed by recent research. As part of these researches the old accounts of Bylandt's troubles and failures as d'Erlon attacked have been dissected, demolished and replaced with a less scandalous one. Whereas it was claimed that the brigade had been left on the open forward slope all day until attacked (something quite contrary to Wellingtonian tactics), that it broke *en masse* and fled at first sight of d'Erlon's advance, modern accounts place it back behind the hedge along the lane and distinguish between those of its units that fought well and those that broke. I shall not rehearse all the old arguments here, or the reasons why they fail to meet modern analysis, but treat the position and actions as though the earlier mistaken accounts had not been written.[13]

V

D'Erlon's massive broad column toiled up through the crops, slipping and stumbling in places, with the Allied cannonballs and shrapnel inflicting severe casualties. After about twenty minutes its left wing was approaching the summit, although the straggly hedge concealed the defenders and guns in many places; the column's right wing was, as I have said, much further back. The Allied skirmishers fell back through the hedge. Some way down the reverse slope Kempt's infantry brigade was formed in depth; it had Bylandt's brigade to its east, stretched out in line along the hedge (only Dutch National Militia Battalion Nr. 5 being in reserve); behind Bylandt's left shoulder stood Pack's infantry brigade, also formed in depth.[14] When the enemy were 50 paces from the hedge some of Bylandt's men prematurely opened a 'fire that was meagre and not well maintained', and then some of them broke, probably shaken by the flight of some of the 1/95th and by the looming French mass. The leading French troops could still not see over the summit but they were no longer under the fire of the Allied cannon.

Quiot's left-hand brigade (Charlet) was busy at La Haye Sainte, and his right-hand brigade (Bourgeois) had veered slightly east to avoid the sandpit, and had closed upon Donzelot's division. Together they were almost at the hedge-line, coming under rifle and musketry fire from the defenders. Then the defenders fell back and the French skirmishers tore through the southern hedge into the sunken path, sweeping past Rogers's battery of guns (only one of which had been spiked[15]). Further east Marcognet's division was closing on the hedge but had veered west into the lee of Donzelot's force, possibly due to the slope but possibly also to the effect of Rettberg's battery near Best's knoll. Thus the movements of Bourgeois and Marcognet had reduced the spacing between divisions and created virtually one mass. Further east, Durutte's division was spreading out, part in support of Marcognet, part in a slight attack on Papelotte. The leading ranks of Bourgeois, Donzelot and Marcognet were gradually coming level with each other and preparing to follow the skirmishers through the hedge.

At this moment, perhaps around 2.15 p.m., the battle was almost won and there was nothing that Wellington could do to stop the French attack. It all turned on the initiative and co-operation of subordinate commanders. It is one of the minor mysteries of this day, how Wellington could have let himself be so badly caught out. The inadequate attention to the defences of La Haye Sainte has already been mentioned. The assembling of the Grand Battery took time and must have been seen, and d'Erlon's advance was some time in coming; individually and together they indicated serious trouble for the left and centre. The evidence seems fairly clear that the Duke did not ride east of the crossroads during the afternoon, but either remained near the lone tree or rode along the front to the west. Thus Uxbridge and Picton, the most senior British commanders on the centre and left, were left to their own devices, and there is no record of them receiving any instructions from the Duke. Wellington clearly failed to realise how dangerous this situation was. He, the bold and clear thinking commander, was beholden at this crisis to the dash and courage of two men who were warriors rather than thinkers. It is very strange.[16]

Bylandt's brigade was in disarray, although its officers were trying to steady it. Its 7e Ligne (South Netherlands) Battalion held the lane and was in such close combat that one officer found the wadding of a musket ball in his wound, and British officers noted that these Belgians fought 'with great spirit' until force of numbers drove them back, and a degree of panic set in.[17] There was a definite gap in the Allied line. The brigades of Kempt and Pack rushed forward, passing on either side of Bylandt, up the reverse slope to meet the French who were reaching the sunken path and seeking to breach the northern hedge. Kempt's brigade reached the hedge first and blasted a volley through it that stopped Bourgeois's men in their tracks, then dashed forward and attacked with the bayonet. Bourgeois's force reeled back.

But Donzelot's men, who would have faced Bylandt's brigade, now faced little or no opposition as they deployed into line to bring their musketry firepower to bear. The way seemed clear. For a moment they were checked by part of Kempt's force firing from a flank. Meanwhile Marcognet's men came up, still in the original formation and mainly reliant on their bayonets to bring success. They passed the first hedge. At this moment Pack dashed forward and met them at an angle as they came out of the sunken path, firing into the French front and flank.[18] The French returned the fire and Pack's brigade momentarily staggered under it; Pack's shout tells how desperate the moment was, '92nd, everything has given way on your right and left and you must charge this column.' The battalion fired a volley at about 20 paces, but this did not throw the French into such disarray as to turn the tide. In fact, it looks as though the French musketry strength in the sunken lane and close behind might have overborne the British in a fairly short time. The British divisional commander, Sir Thomas Picton, mounted and in civilian clothes with a wide-brimmed top hat, recognised that nothing short of a desperate charge could halt the enemy, shouted out 'Charge, charge, hurrah!' while ordering an ADC 'to rally the Highlanders, who were for the instant overpowered by the masses of French infantry'. Then Picton fell from the saddle, shot through the head. Could the British infantry throw back the French?[19]

VI

Lord Uxbridge had been watching from the summit, close to the crossroads. He saw the disaster to the Lüneburg light battalion at the hands of the *cuirassiers*; he saw the battle raging round La Haye Sainte; and he could see the surge of d'Erlon's corps beyond the road. He ordered Lord Edward Somerset's heavy cavalry, just west of the Charleroi road and on the reverse slope, to prepare to charge, then raced across to Sir William Ponsonby, whose Union Brigade was about 100 yards down the reverse slope behind Kempt and Pack, and ordered him to launch the Royal Dragoons, the Scots Greys, and the Inniskilling Dragoons into a counter-attack (totalling 9 squadrons, 1,000 men). Then he rode back to join Somerset's force, the two Life Guards regiments, the Blues and the King's Dragoon Guards (9 squadrons, 1,000 men). Somerset's men topped the slope and rode down into the mass of French horsemen who were re-grouping after their recent charge. Uxbridge, *beau sabreur par excellence,* rode with the first line. The Blues were in support.

Somerset's men moved through Alten's KGL battalions and plunged down the slope west of the great road. They crashed into Crabbé's *cuirassiers* with a shock like 'two walls' meeting, as one participant said, after which the British 'rode over everything opposed to us', pouring south on both sides of La Haye Sainte. At least one French account, however, indicates that the *cuirassiers* (or some of them) were already turning and trying to reach the safety of their own lines. Some of the French horsemen were trapped in a cutting along the Charleroi road and were savagely cut up until French light infantry came to their aid.[20] The British right-hand squadrons soon came up against the

French infantry and then fell back; meanwhile the left-hand squadrons had gone across the great road and so became part of the Union Brigade's charge.

Ponsonby's Union Brigade had been well back, but now advanced to the crest with the Royal Dragoons, the Scots Greys and Inniskillings in a broad line; they passed through the infantry who wheeled back to give them passage, and found themselves at once facing the somewhat blown and disorganised French infantry struggling with the hedge and trying to get back into battle formation. There can be little doubt that even a couple more minutes would have given the French time enough, and that thereafter the balance of advantage would have been entirely theirs. But at this moment they were in no state to withstand cavalry who had been waiting for a chance to attack and were properly formed.

Ponsonby's ADC De Lacy Evans gave the signal and the charge began. Ponsonby's initial move would have been uphill, but for a short distance only, and then his entire brigade swept down, driving the French before them, riding over them, and inflicting terrible casualties. Bourgeois's and Marcognet's infantry dissolved into a broken mob in a matter of seconds, but Donzelot's men fell back in rather better order. Durutte's division had made progress on the right flank and had pushed the Nassauers out of Papelotte[21] while also seconding Marcognet's advance, but it was now attacked by the 12th Light Dragoons and forced to fall back: Durutte was bitter about the inaction of Jacquinot's *1re Division de Cavalerie,* which he claimed did little to protect him, 'due to the Emperor's refusal to place the divisional cavalry under the infantry divisional commanders'.[22] D'Erlon's battle-winning attack had totally failed at its most critical moment, and in the next moment the British cavalry had passed through the infantry and swept up to battery ridge and begun cutting down the gun teams of the Grand Battery itself, though nobody apparently halted and dismounted to spike the guns.[23]

VII

Napoleon at La Belle Alliance could only watch helplessly as his plan fell to pieces. The entire face of the battle had changed between 2 and 2.15 p.m. He had mounted and sustained a wasteful infantry attack on Hougoumont for several hours in order to keep Wellington from strengthening his centre. For nearly an hour he had expended large quantities of artillery ammunition to break down the central defences. His second large infantry force had not merely been robbed of victory just as success seemed assured, it had been tumbled into ruin. The crest had not been taken, and the pressure on La Haye Sainte and Papelotte had been reduced. Perhaps worse, the artillerymen of the Grand Battery were being slaughtered, and quite possibly the guns were being disabled. The plan had relied upon this combination of infantry attacks and bombardment to secure victory before the first effects of any Prussian advance could be felt. He still had Lobau's infantry in hand, as well as the *Garde*, but Lobau was already being deployed to face the potential threat from Bülow, and Napoleon begrudged premature deployment of his *Garde*.

The entire timetable was upset, and a fresh set of plans had to be worked out at once.

VIII

Napoleon was not alone in his moment of horror. On the opposite ridge Wellington was enduring some ghastly moments. Picton's division, already much weakened by losses at Quatre Bras, was probably not strong enough to defeat d'Erlon's masses, and disaster had been averted by the instinctive reactions of Uxbridge in launching the two heavy brigades on his own responsibility. But relief at this was of short duration. Uxbridge had all the qualities most beloved by British cavalry, and some of the defects. Riding in Somerset's first line like a subaltern, he gave up any possibility of overall control of this splendid force as it careered forward. On the far side of the road Sir William Ponsonby found that the entire Union Brigade was racing in first line, over the valley and even up towards the French infantry line, ignoring the trumpet calls to return. There was no second line, no support. Thus Wellington saw his heavy cavalry out of control, without reserves to cover the essential period of re-grouping and recall, galloping until their mounts neared exhaustion, and becoming too blown to hold out against the inevitable French riposte. This came first from Bachelu's division, watching d'Erlon's western flank, which opened a destructive fire. Then some of Milhaud's *cuirassiers* struck at Somerset's men, who wheeled and sought to regain Allied lines: here the Blues endeavoured to act as a reserve and cover the withdrawal. To the east another scene was unfolding: Durutte had complained of Jacquinot not supporting him, but the cavalry were well placed to effect a flanking counter-attack on Ponsonby, and this they did with terrible effect. The Union Brigade was attacked by Jacquinot's *3e* and *4e Lanciers*, who swept into them, spearing them and giving no quarter. Sir William Ponsonby himself was overtaken and speared to death.[24]

Wellington had that morning granted full freedom to Uxbridge on how to use the cavalry, and Vandeleur wrote that before battle was joined Uxbridge had informed Vandeleur and Vivian 'to engage the enemy whenever they could do so with advantage, without waiting for orders'.[25] Despite this, and in the absence of Uxbridge, the stolid Vandeleur appears to have doubted whether to intervene in the carnage in the valley, until at last he realised that something had to be done to stay the massacre; then he sent the 12th and 16th Light Dragoons to attack the *lanciers* and divert them from their prey.

Vital as it was in averting a catastrophic Allied defeat in the early afternoon, Uxbridge's charge came at a heavy cost. In Fortescue's words,

> Of two thousand troopers and horses that had charged, over one thousand horses and from seven to eight hundred men were killed, wounded, and missing. The 12th Light Dragoons also had lost their Colonel, Frederick Ponsonby, who was desperately wounded, and the strength of a whole squadron either hurt or slain ... The Allies had paid a heavy price for their success. The two finest brigades of the British cavalry had almost ceased to exist.[26]

Uxbridge always blamed himself for the way the charge went awry:

> I committed a great mistake in having myself led the attack. The *carrière* once begun, the leader is no better than any other man; whereas, if I had placed myself at the head of the 2nd line, there is no saying what great advantages might not have accrued from it. I am the less pardonable in having deviated from a principle I had laid down for myself, that I had already suffered from a similar error in an affair at Sahagun [1808], where my reserve, instead of steadily following as I had ordered, chose to join in the attack, and at the end of it I had no formed body to take advantage with.[27]

That was a fair verdict. It can be said in extenuation that Uxbridge had to make his decision in a split-second and that there was no time to issue and pass down through the two heavy brigades detailed orders for the conduct of the charge. Moreover there were no cavalry divisional commanders who could have helped exercise control and coordination; instead, Uxbridge had to deal with all seven brigades – and from this morning the Dutch contingent also. That a divisional organisation had not been adopted and that such basic training or re-training had been neglected does not reflect well upon the way the British Army at the Horse Guards saw its cavalry arm. Nor were matters entirely satisfactory in Belgium. The detailed and trenchant memorandum that Wellington wrote after Waterloo on cavalry tactics, could with advantage have been written much earlier, but one has to ask why senior cavalry commanders had not formulated and introduced such practice in the meantime?[28] Wellington seems to have left Uxbridge very free – possibly because of that old difficulty caused by Charlotte abandoning her husband Henry Wellesley for Uxbridge – and not to have interfered much; and Uxbridge had only six weeks in which to think about, exercise and train his force, and to instil some discipline in such tactical matters. The Duke's refusal to consider Uxbridge's request for his thoughts on a battle plan, and the delegation of all cavalry authority only on 18 June were not helpful to a cavalry commander who had to give guidance to seven subordinates.

When Uxbridge found that when sounding the Rally 'neither voice not trumpet availed' and that he was without a proper second line, he rode back up the slope. At that moment the valley seemed 'swept clean' and he later recalled that the Duke and the Allied commissioners were 'joyous', thinking the battle won. His descendant, the historian of the British cavalry, records a less glowing and probably double-edged remark by the Duke: 'Well, Paget, I hope you are satisfied with your cavalry now.'[29]

When all criticism has been said, it yet remains that d'Erlon's corps was left a spent force for several hours, the Grand Battery had been attacked and disorganised, the French heavy cavalry somewhat tumbled, pressure relieved at La Haye Sainte and Papelotte, and a pause imposed on the battle, all because of Uxbridge. If it was a flawed and costly success, it was a success nonetheless.

IX

Napoleon would have to make a totally new plan, and while he was drawing it up an order was issued that indicated some rather belated thinking on the part of the staff.[30] It was addressed to the War Minister, 180 miles away in Paris, and was timed 18 June, 1.15 p.m., but was retained for well over an hour more. It was sent just after the battle plan had collapsed, but from its contents it should have been sent at least 36 hours earlier:

> We are in action at this moment; the enemy is in position in front of Soignies forest, his centre at Waterloo.
>
> We are going to consume much ammunition; we have used a great quantity at the battle of Ligny. The Emperor orders that you send it by swiftest means to the fortified places in the north, and Avesnes. From Avesnes these munitions will be escorted by the battalions that had been designated as escorts for prisoners; the direction should be by Beaumont on to Charleroi to join the army.
>
> You will appreciate, Marshal, how important it is that the Emperor's orders should be executed promptly. Please let me know what you are doing in this regard.

> PS. It is 2.30 p.m. and the cannonade is along the whole line; the English are in the centre, the Dutch and Belgians on the right of German troops, the Prussians are on the left; the battle is general; four hundred guns are firing at this moment.

From the contents it is evident that this request should have been written and sent on the 17th at latest. That it was *not,* is a further reflection on the quality of staff-work at imperial headquarters. It was recollected during the lull before d'Erlon marched to the attack and was written out. But then came the news about Bülow. The Chief of Staff was shaken, and perhaps his master too – and the first thought was not about this message concerning ammunition re-supply since a delay of a few minutes could be of small consequence; instead it was about amending the orders to Grouchy so as to set him onto Bülow as quickly as possible. Everything was dropped while a PS was added to the missive for Grouchy. And only then was the Davout message remembered, and so a postscript was added to that, and to me that postscript does not breathe a happy confidence.

There was a second order (un-timed) that may be given here. Whether it was a reaction to the Bülow sighting or to the rising cost at Hougoumont, we cannot say, but it could not produce any benefit to the French army within the remaining hours of daylight. So severe was the need for men that even the *7e Division,* shattered at Ligny and resting there, could not be totally spared, but would have to move a step closer to the fighting, to move to the main *chaussée,* a few miles south of Genappe: 'In front of Le Caillou, 18 June [no time given]: Order to Brigadier Remond to take command of the Girard Division and to move it into position at Quatre Bras.'[31]

Having been wasteful of infantry, extravagant with gun ammunition, Napoleon now turned to his massed cavalry to break up the Allied line in the short time available.

*

Appendix 1: Soult's 1 p.m. Letter to Grouchy, and its Postscript

This letter, given in full in Section I, has been the subject of much comment, and its authenticity has been disputed. It was printed in 1870 by Prince Eduoard de la Tour d'Auvergne in his *Waterloo,* pp. 270–1, and this was seen as a corrective to a version printed many years earlier by Grouchy. In Grouchy's *Mémoires* volume iv of 1874 the letter was reprinted at p. 82. In 1892 J. C. Ropes again printed the letter, and noted that there were significant differences between la Tour d'Auvergne (whom he quoted at p. 389) and Grouchy; this left him uneasy, since Grouchy was often so unreliable with the documents that he used in his own defence. But in fact of the two versions Grouchy's (though corrupted) proved the more accurate. For at the beginning of the twentieth century Houssaye discovered the original in the War Archives and published it in facsimile in his 46th edition. It is from that facsimile that I have made my translation.

The main letter deals with the opening of the decisive battle. It was written before any setbacks had been reported, the clerk's writing is neat and the signature is undoubtedly that of the Duke of Dalmatia, as a comparison with other Soult documents demonstrates. How different is the message of the urgent postscript. The situation has changed significantly, the phrasing is urgent, staccato, imperious, and the signature is not that of Soult, but is an ill-formed wormlike squiggle. While it is unlike the sharp decided stroke of Napoleon's usual signature (see Napoleon's signature of 13 July 1815 in the frontispiece to this volume), it is in thickness of ink quite similar. The difference between the squiggle and the usual signature may be simply due to the clerk rushing to Napoleon with the letter at the end of which he had scripted the sudden additional message, and Napoleon snatching the sheet and signing it while walking about. There is no reason for treating the information as spurious.

Was the letter received by Grouchy? Yes, it was. He had no particular reason to invent this letter, any more than had Soult, and indeed Grouchy publicly stated that he received Soult's despatch, although he timed this receipt in the first instance as 'towards 5 p.m.' on 18 June (p. 42) and in the second 'towards 7 p.m.' on 18 June (p. 82). He then printed the letter and postscript in full. *Thus he publicly acknowledged the authenticity of the letter and postscript.*

There is a second proof of authenticity as to the letter and the time when it was written. Had Grouchy decided to forge a letter he would have made its contents *exactly conform* to his own line of defence, so that having forged the letter and somehow slipped it into the War Archives his defence would be smooth and perfect: see my remarks in Chapter 25, Section VII, about forgeries. But the letter was in fact *not fully satisfactory* in his defence. And so in a couple of places Grouchy had to alter the version he chose to publish.

The first change was where Soult wrote of Grouchy's overnight report having been received in the morning. Grouchy, *Mémoires*, iv, p. 82, printed it as received '*ce matin a trois heures*'. Now the first publication that I know of was in Gourgaud's *Campaign of 1815*, p. 88 in the English version of 1818, where the time of receipt was '2 a.m.', and, not having sight of the original, la Tour d'Auvergne and Ropes, also printed '2 a.m.' But Houssaye's facsimile of Soult's letter is clear and unmistakable, and it says that the report came at six in the morning: '*à 6 h*'. Had he been the forger, Grouchy would not have let that discrepancy arise.

But even more crucially, while accepting that Soult did indeed send him this message at 1 p.m., Grouchy falsified Soult's words by replacing the unmistakable and clearly written '*est engagée*' by '*est gagnée*', thus turning the phrase from 'the battle is engaged' into 'the battle is won', which of course absolved himself from blame in not at once marching to Waterloo. That is so central to the whole question that the letter cannot have been a forgery by Grouchy: he would not have gone to the trouble of writing 'engaged' in a forged document and then changing it to 'won'.

So the document is genuine, but what of the timing, that sighting of the Prussians a little after '1 p.m.'? Critics have argued that their appearance came as a total surprise *well after 3 p.m.* and so the timing is fictitious. So far as Soult is concerned there is indeed a second document that is relevant. It was written at '2.30 p.m.' as a postscript to a message to Davout in Paris, and it stated that 'the Prussians are on the left' of Wellington's battle line (see this chapter, Section IX). It does not say where, or in what numbers, but clearly they were joining or would shortly join the struggle.

Napoleon's memoirs have also been queried, and this is understandable since they deal with these events in a most unsatisfactory way. But when used to discredit the Soult 1 p.m. letter they are not really of much account. Nor are some subsidiary objections to the Soult letter particularly strong. I will take them all together. Napoleon's memoirs mentioned 'a Prussian black hussar' being brought in some fifteen minutes after the orders to Domon and Subervie. A great deal of discussion has swirled around the identity of this Prussian and the letter he carried. In addition doubts have been raised about Soult's '1 p.m.' timing, to the phrase 'the Waterloo line in front of the forest of Soignies' in the body of the letter, and to the reference to the 'heights of St-Lambert' in the postscript.

That a messenger was captured and had handed over the letter and perhaps given some information, is clear from the postscript written a little time after 1 p.m. Who he was, which regiment he belonged to and what uniform he wore we cannot say, and the anecdotes and guesses that have fed on those questions are unanswerable: Napoleon's recollection was that he was a 'black hussar', but to claim that no black uniforms were worn by Bülow's troops is to pass beyond a safe boundary. For there is evidence in abundance in this campaign of troops mistaking between tunics of dark green and dark blue and black, tints all faded and begrimed by summer fighting, and consequently of 'friendly-fire' incidents. If such fatal mistakes could happen, then to quibble over this hussar's tunic is to join in dancing on the point of a pin.

The suggestion that 'Waterloo' was not a name used until after the battle had become world-famous, so that to write it here implies a much later fabrication, may be answered thus: De Lancey wrote on 17 June 1815 that Wellington's army had retreated 'to its present position in front of Waterloo' (*WD*, 476/144); the name is in the maps of Ferraris and Capitaine; and Soult's phrase 'on the Waterloo line in front of the forest of Soignies', with the additional detail of Wellington's centre being at Mont St Jean, is a sufficient direction to a man many miles distant. It was a recognised name.

The 'heights of St-Lambert' cannot refer to the chapel of that name, down on the Lasne stream, but it may to where Chapelle-St-Robert stands, on the height a mile to the east and 130 feet higher. The place where Napoleon stood was at a height of 460 feet, and between there and Chapelle-St-Robert (395 feet) there is no higher ground for the intervening 5 miles, but only the valley of the Lasne brook in almost a straight line, dropping from 360 feet at Plancenoit to 260 feet at St-Lambert. It is not impossible, then, that a telescope might well catch the glitter of arms or the movement of men at Chapelle-St-Robert.

Appendix 2: The Order to the Lüneburg Light Battalion

In a battle such as Waterloo heavy losses are inevitable, and cannot be remarked upon at each and every occasion. But when they arise from folly or whim or thoughtlessness, it is only right to ask why. Several such occasions are recorded in the story of this campaign, and most have been examined, and a conclusion reached. One that still defies a conclusion is the subject of this appendix.

Various persons have been named as responsible for the fate of the Lüneburg light battalion of Hanoverians at La Haye Sainte, but usually on the basis of inference. In order of seniority they could be the Duke of Wellington, General the Prince of Orange, Lieutenant-General Alten, Major-General Kielmansegge, and Lieutenant-Colonel Klencke who commanded the battalion on the day. Wellington had the whole front to consider, but from Constant Rebecque's journal we know that on the morning of the battle the Prince of Orange had been virtually stripped of operational command over the Netherlands troops and the Guards Division by Wellington's decision, leaving him with nothing but Alten's 3rd Division. Alten had his three brigades to worry about, Kielmansegge six battalions, and Klencke one.

Evidence is rarely quoted in this matter, but there is some. The most important testimony is that of Captain Jacobi, a company commander in the Lüneburg battalion, because he was present and because he later sought information from Klencke and Alten on the matter. There is some subsidiary testimony. The first is from a very acute observer, Captain Shaw, AQMG in Alten's 3rd Division (later General Sir James Shaw Kennedy). Another is from a young officer of the 5th Line Battalion, KGL, Edmund Wheatley, who was very close to the action in this part of the field. Also there are two letters from a 1st Light Battalion, KGL, officer, Captain Heise. Finally, there are some passing references in the reports of Alten, just after the battle.

Jacobi's account of his experiences reads as truthful and quite accurate, and he fleshed it out with further notes using subsequent information. However, it dates in its finished form from the 1860s. He had served with Klencke from at least 1814 and knew him well; in one of his footnotes he wrote that in 1811 Klencke had left the Hanoverian forces as a junior captain but later re-joined as a senior lieutenant-colonel in charge of the battalion, then got a brigade, but in the organisational compression in early 1815 was once more commanding the battalion. Some of Klencke's colleagues were critical of him, said Jacobi, thinking him over-promoted and too inexperienced for a battalion command. Although he and his battalion performed well on 16 June, after the 18 June debacle his critics suggested that he had acted recklessly, and they claimed that:

> He had tried to outshine others in front of the army by his bold sortie, without properly considering the adverse situation. For his part the Lieutenant-Colonel [Klencke] later declared he received the order to attack from an adjutant of the Prince of Orange, the commander of our corps. General von Alten [commanding 3rd Division] later told me that he had admired the calm courage with which the battalion had advanced, but had also noted the riskiness of the undertaking; he had been unaware of any order from the Prince of Orange. A further clarification of the circumstances has never occurred.[32]

No one mentioned anything about Wellington in relation to the disaster to the Lüneburg battalion, but there is indicative evidence about his actions in the centre around this time. In 1842 Shaw Kennedy, Alten's AQMG at Waterloo, answered Siborne's queries concerning the *whereabouts of a different unit,* the 1st Light Battalion, KGL, where the Duke was in relation to it, and whether it advanced across the Charleroi road to assist Kempt's brigade in repelling d'Erlon's attack.[33]

> I have not the least idea that the Duke of Wellington was there at that moment: I stood with General Alten very near to the Lüneburg Battalion,

> and we were not aware that the Duke was there, and I do not see how he could have been without great danger of being made prisoner, unless he actually went into one of the squares [*sic*] of the division, for the whole ground was instantly covered by *cuirassiers* ... it is within the realms of possibility that the Duke of Wellington may have rode up to them [1st Light, KGL] at that time and given the orders which you mention,[34] but it is very difficult for me to suppose that such was the case. I do not know positively where the Duke was at the time, but my impression was that he then stood behind our Guards infantry, it is there I certainly would have looked for him had I been sent for orders: it is true that he was frequently in front of Alten's division and near to the left of its front, but I saw nothing of him or his staff when the charge of the *cuirassiers* took place, and I was then with Alten, on horseback, near to where the Lüneburg battalion stood.

He added that d'Erlon's attack reached the hedge before the *cuirassiers* attacked Alten's division. Of that he was 'quite certain, for Alten and I stood very quietly looking at that attack [on Picton's division]'. As Shaw Kennedy himself was beside Alten and the Lüneburgers and could not see the Duke in the vicinity, it seems fairly clear that Wellington was not involved in the Hanoverians' disaster.

Though Wellington was not with the Lüneburg battalion, Heise does repeatedly insist that he and his staff were with the KGL[35] and launched the 1st Light, KGL, to assist Kempt in smashing Bourgeois's attack: 'the Duke was behind the left wing of the battalion and called out to us, "Not yet. I will tell you when it is your time."' And shortly thereafter he said with a friendly smile, taking off his hat, "Now go my lads, hurrah!"'[36] That was the answer to Siborne's question. But the question of who sent forward Klencke's battalion is not answered by this report on the KGL.

Much later, in his *Notes on the Battle of Waterloo*, Shaw Kennedy recounted another experience. On the morning of the battle:

> General the Prince of Orange, who commanded the corps, and [Lieutenant-]General Baron Alten, who commanded the third division, discussed for some time how the division should be formed in order of battle. The Duke of Wellington, having joined them during the discussion, and being referred to, replied shortly, 'Form in the usual way,' and rode on.[37]

Alten, in his report to Wellington of 19 June 1815 did refer to this, saying 'in compliance with Your Grace's orders, and those of HRH the Prince of Orange' he had formed for attack in columns in chequerboard layout, to be capable of switching into squares, as necessary.[38] Nor should this surprise us: squares were a standard defensive formation.

Lieutenant Wheatley's diary mentions forming up in squares in the morning, the repeated French *cuirassier* attacks against KGL squares, and the bombardments from artillery when the cavalry were not present. He does mention that at some time in the afternoon (but before the Ompteda affair) there came a strange order to form in line: 'The Prince of Orange gallop'd by, screaming out like a new born infant, "Form into line! Form into line!" And we obeyed.'[39]

Colonel Frazer of the Royal Horse Artillery had been riding along the summit that morning, and found that matters were not quite right:

> Passing Sir Charles Alten, we learned that some little arrangement was necessary. Lloyd's battery, forming part of the sixteen pieces placed for the defence of that part of the position, had, by some order of the Prince of Orange, been diverted to guard the point where our line was intersected by the *pavé* from Genappe to Brussels. This weakened Alten; both points required strengthening; and by [Colonel] Wood's leave, Ross's troop was ordered from the reserve to guard the *pavé*, and I acquainted Alten that Lloyd would not be taken from him. Judge, however, of our surprise on learning that, by some misapprehension of orders, Lloyd's ammunition waggons had been sent to the rear.[40]

So Orange was involved in morning discussions with Alten over formations and square, and he was galloping about excitedly and shouting orders when Wheatley saw him in the early afternoon. Klencke privately and somewhat circumspectly 'later declared he received the order to attack from an adjutant of the Prince of Orange', which effectively means from the Prince; and he can have had no motive for falsely naming one officer as against another. Moreover Orange's grasp of tactics and formations appropriate for different circumstances was hopeless: having at Quatre Bras destroyed the 69th and seriously endangered three other battalions by his foolish instructions, he again behaved in an extraordinary way to Wheatley's mind, and later this day would send to his death the luckless Ompteda of Alten's division, with the 5th Line Battalion, KGL.

The one man who definitely was close to the Lüneburg battalion at the decisive moment was Alten. By the account he gave to Jacobi he disclaimed all knowledge of any order from Orange, and more or less said that he gave none himself. What is curious, and in fact unsatisfactory, is that he admitted that he realised the *seemingly unauthorised* movement was highly risky *yet did not interfere*. He sent no warning, nor any counter-order. He left the Lüneburg battalion to its fate. Christopher Hibbert in his commentary on Wheatley's diary, remarks that in the subsequent Ompteda affair Alten passed on the orders that Orange had given and when Ompteda pointed out the danger, Alten left it to the Prince to decide. Yet the lives of a battalion were at stake. Was he being weak here, as well?

The brigade commander, Kielmansegge, is not mentioned by any source at this moment in the day, although Jacobi did remark that, having fallen back later to re-group in rear of Mont St Jean, the remnants debated whether to return to the front, and advanced to a spot directly behind the rest of the brigade, only to be told by Kielmansegge to march back to Brussels. Jacobi attributed this *unauthorised* order to retire to his general's inexperience in war. Alten did make a brief reference in his post-battle report to Kielmansegge pulling back some troops from the front line, and this reference brought down Wellington's extreme displeasure until the unfortunate man was able to clear himself with Alten and the Duke.[41] Looking at the chain of command, if we go so far as to *reject* Klencke's private remark that the order to the Lüneburg battalion came from the Prince of Orange – knowing that Alten, as next in the chain, said that he was unaware of an order from above and himself issued none – then it is just possible that it was the brigade commander who took the rash decision to launch the Lüneburg battalion.[42] But Klencke identified Orange and not Kielmansegge, and surely he must have known.

Unfortunately the secondary authorities ascribe responsibility without giving any reason or sources. Siborne, Evelyn Wood, De Bas and T'Serclaes de Wommersom, Chandler, all plumped for Wellington. Charras and Jac Weller said that it was the Prince of Orange who gave the order. Fortescue and Hamilton-Williams thought it was Kielmansegge. Adkin (p. 377) mentions Orange and more especially Alten, but gives little detail. Fletcher expresses no opinion and nor does Glover in his *Myth and Reality*. Hofschröer, who is the author most concerned with German troops in the great battle, merely quotes Baring's report from *inside* La Haye Sainte (but Baring could see little though the small apertures) and has nothing of his own to say either on this matter or the later virtual death sentence on Ompteda.

My own view, based on what Jacobi and Shaw Kennedy recorded, is that Klencke did not act without orders, and was telling the truth in naming the Prince of Orange as the man issuing them. Alten may have been taken by surprise, let matters slide, and later sought to exculpate himself to Jacobi with a lame excuse: he does not shine in this matter. It is just conceivable that Kielmansegge took some initiative. But it does look like the work of the Prince of Orange.

Chapter 39
The Third Act
The Great Cavalry Attacks

I

TWO HOURS EARLIER, AT THE MOMENT when battle had begun, Napoleon had put the chances as still 60/40 in his favour. After the disastrous setback to d'Erlon's attack he must have re-cast the chances, but he chose to present the situation in his memoirs as almost entirely satisfactory: 'It was four o'clock; and victory would already by then have been decided had not Bülow's corps now made its powerful diversion.'[1] This is mere fantasy, and his description of subsequent events is not helpful, either.

While Napoleon reconsidered his options he was insistent that the initiative should not be lost to Wellington. Hence the artillery bombardment all along the line continued in a spasmodic way. He let Reille go on attacking Hougoumont, partly to constrain Wellington and partly because he could not give his full attention to the complications that arose from the earlier setbacks there. He also decided to launch a fresh attack on La Haye Sainte, a position that he seems to have under-rated until now. All these initiatives – and they were all piecemeal – would provide the time needed to organise his next main effort.

II

The garrison of Hougoumont had repulsed two major attacks by Reille's *2e Corps*. During the second attack a couple of companies of 3rd Guards moved down to assist Lord Saltoun's light companies near the sunken track at the northern edge of the estate. Later, after that attack had ended, Colonel Hepburn led virtually all of the rest of 2/3rd Guards down to reinforce the garrison. Saltoun, whose force had suffered heavily, was no longer able to maintain the defence, and withdrew up the slope. The defence had now an additional 700–800 fresh men.[2] Hepburn took up position in the grounds and moved forward to the south hedge of the orchard, leaving Macdonell inside the buildings. While the French infantry re-grouped, French 6-pounder guns and howitzers continued to fire at the Hougoumont buildings, and around 2–2.30 p.m. a haystack near the southern gate to the château was set alight, as were some of the buildings. At least one shot went through the southern gate, but this was barricaded before the French had time to turn this to advantage.[3] Wellington found time to send a pencil note to Macdonell:

> I see that the fire has communicated from the haystack to the roof of the château. You must however still keep your men in those parts to which the fire does not reach. Take care that no men are lost by the falling in of the roof, or floors. After they will have fallen in occupy the ruined walls inside the garden; particularly if it should be possible for the enemy to pass through the embers in the inside of the house.[4]

Despite this, numbers of wounded men could not be found and dragged out in time, and so perished horribly in the flames.

But piecemeal attacks continued sporadically. At one moment around a dozen French forced the small western door into the buildings and entered the courtyard, but were driven out with some difficulty and loss.[5] British historians maintain that Foy's *2e Brigade* was consigned to the battle early in the afternoon in support of his *1re Brigade*'s men, who were now in difficulties. Moreover, Foy's right-hand neighbour, Bachelu of *5e Division*, is reported by British gunners as having launched his *2e Brigade* against the eastern side of the grounds, only to be turned back by heavy artillery bombardment. But as Andrew Field points out, the chief of staff of *5e Division* described the afternoon in rather different terms: 'Our division and a brigade of General Foy's division still occupied the same position at 6 p.m. We had witnessed the battle without participating in it. One would have thought that we had been forgotten!'[6]

It seems impossible to reject such a statement, written by someone who could distinguish units on the south side of Hougoumont relatively clearly. On the other hand, the defenders inside the estate, peering in the gun-smoke through loopholes and between trees and with yet more smoke billowing from the fires, could sense fresh attacks but not necessarily the units involved, while those on the ridge all found the smoke of battle so dense that it called forth comment even from experienced soldiers.

The smoke may have assisted the progress of a cart of the Royal Wagon Train, brought down the slope and driven in through the north gate by Private Joseph Brewer, that provided a fresh supply of ammunition in mid-afternoon, without which the garrison might not have been able to maintain their position.[7] The French now took station on the southerly slopes of the valley and from a distance kept up a troublesome peppering of the defences, and probably inflicted quite a few casualties. But the French infantry's willingness to continue with serious and bloody assaults had gone, and the final hours were hours of little more than bickering, without any serious determination to hold on to ground. Finally, towards the end of the day, Brunswick, Hanoverian and KGL units came down the northern slope and assisted the tired garrison to push through the trees and clear the estate of French soldiers.

Casualties at Hougoumont were heavy on both sides, but difficult to quantify. There are references to ditches being full of British bodies, of the ground in front of the south wall being covered with French dead, and so on. There could be no body-count, as the priority after the battle was to find and succour the wounded, and that must have taken a great deal of time. By then the dead were so decomposed that pyres were lit to accelerate the clearance, in addition to the pits dug for the mass interment of corpses. Casualty figures vary, but different authorities put Allied casualties at 850 to 1,700 men and French anything from 5,000 up to as many as 6,500.[8]

In Wellington's Despatch, written the next morning, the defence of Hougoumont received due recognition, although only the Guards were mentioned and the contribution of the Nassauers, Hanoverians and (later) the Brunswickers and KGL was not touched upon. The command was curiously reported by the Duke. Lieutenant-Colonel Macdonell was (as the Despatch said) the post's commander during the battle, and he was apparently never superseded. He was considerably senior to Lord Saltoun and Francis Home and of course far senior to the Nassauer Captain Büsgen. Woodford, a full colonel, seems not to have tried to impose himself over Macdonell, remaining in a different part of the defences, and then Colonel Hepburn arrived but likewise without claiming the command. But it is hard to understand how Wellington thought that Home could have assumed the command later, unless he confused Home with Hepburn. Woodford is usually represented as declining the command, but in a letter dated 3 July 1815, apparently ignoring Hepburn's contribution and seniority, he remarked:

> It was your humble servant who had the command in the house latterly. I went to reinforce Macdonell, with the Coldstream, and hence [*sic* – perhaps read: *Home*? *Hepburn*?] with two companies of the 3rd [Guards] was sent to act under my orders; unluckily in the confusion of the day, this was not made clear to the Duke but I still hope it will be rectified, at least, where it is most essential.[9]

It is all very confused, but the essential point is that rank and protocol were put aside among the Guards officers in favour of the general interest.

III

For so long as both Hougoumont and La Haye Sainte held out, the approaches to the centre of the Allied line were restricted to a half-mile corridor, for although Major Baring and the 2nd Light KGL had given up the farm's orchard they had retained the buildings and the rear garden. Klencke's reinforcement had been badly cut up, but two companies of riflemen from 1st Light Battalion, KGL, had joined Baring, and as their weapons matched those of 2nd Light, they may have helped replenish ammunition stocks. Moreover the 1/95th had reoccupied the knoll and sandpit and so could provide useful covering fire.

Quiot's *1re Division* had failed in its first attack on the farm and half of it (Bourgeois's brigade) was in no condition to strike again. But Napoleon needed continued activity at the front while he prepared his next great assault, and so a fresh attack was mounted on La Haye Sainte at about 2.45–3 p.m. Ney ordered Quiot's other brigade (Charlet) to carry the position. Andrew Field points out that that only one regiment of Charlet's force seems to have taken part in the earlier attack, and so it is probable that the second assault could be quickly mounted because on this occasion it was his other regiment (say 2,000 men) that was employed. There was no great enthusiasm shown, however, and at least one general expressed concern at the prospect – leading to an eruption of wrath from Ney, who demanded that the buildings be assaulted by 'an infantry charge', when an explosive charge or a shelling might have been more sensible. In fact two companies of French engineers were close by (probably the companies of sappers held in readiness 'to barricade themselves at once at Mont St Jean' once d'Erlon's attack had succeeded), and at Ney's ADC's request, they took the initiative and went ahead as infantry. On seeing this, Charlet's men did go forward.

The attack, mounted with little enthusiasm and considerable reluctance, met with strong and determined resistance from the troops inside the walls of the farm. KGL Rifleman Lindau remarked on the tight bunching of the attackers and the relative ease with which they were beaten off, leaving considerable numbers of dead; moreover the defenders' losses on this second occasion were lighter than on the first. Apparently no French officer thought it worth directing cannon or howitzer fire on the buildings, which could have gravely affected the defenders. In short, this was an ill-planned, uncoordinated attack, using a hammer to drive in a screw, and seen as unlikely to succeed by the officers and men who were chosen for the task. It was wasteful of lives and served no real purpose.[10]

IV

Earlier in the day Napoleon had said that, having thoroughly unsettled the enemy by a heavy bombardment, he would 'charge with my cavalry' to force Wellington's men 'to show themselves', (which must mean bunched together in square) and, after he had identified where British troops stood on the crest, 'I shall march straight at them with my *Vieille Garde.*' Although he did not mention them, his own infantry of the line had a constant function in all this: to tie down Wellington's forces and make use of the bombardment to gain the ridge. Indeed, if the artillery could shake enemy cohesiveness, the line infantry might achieve enough success to leave the cavalry only the role of exploitation.

It will be remembered that from the start Ney had held command of *1er* and *2e Corps*, thus including the light cavalry of Jacquinot and Piré. Napoleon had made detachments from his reserves as the day progressed: he had sent guns from the *Garde* artillery to the Grand Battery; moreover the Emperor had also sent to Reille some of the *Garde*'s 12-pounder guns, all to assist the bombardment of the summit. Some squadrons of *cuirassiers* from Milhaud's corps had been engaged in the valley and had done severe damage to some of Alten's infantry; they, too, must have passed under Ney's command, at least temporarily. Furthermore, from early in the battle *6e Corps* and the light cavalry of Domon and Subervie had been diverted to the Plancenoit front. Allowing for these sizeable detachments, Napoleon still controlled all of Kellermann's and much of Milhaud's cavalry, and of course his own *Garde*.

Napoleon decided that it was now time to launch the cavalry, but his memoirs do not fully explain matters here and we do not have any proper record of instructions. We do not know precisely what passed between Napoleon and Ney on this, but there was some communication: Jerome Bonaparte, who spent part of the afternoon with the Emperor, tells us that much. He wrote to his wife on 15 July that Napoleon 'had ordered Marshal Ney to go against the enemy centre, to make a bludgeon stroke with a great part of the cavalry, two infantry corps, and the *Garde*'. He also claimed that the Emperor said that they were not all to be used at once, and that Ney attacked 'three-quarters of an hour too early'.[11]

These remarks contain a truth but also present a somewhat unreal impression of the situation. The 'two infantry corps' had failed, had taken heavy casualties, and were not ready for another assault on the centre, especially as Reille was still entangled in Hougoumont: it is simply misleading to say that Ney could use them, when they were in such a state. 'A great part of the cavalry' was certainly given to Ney, *and so was the Garde cavalry*, although Napoleon later denied it and said it was taken without authority. Unfortunately, the way orders were issued reflected very badly on the command structure, for some intermediate commanders found their subordinates moving unbeknown to themselves, and learnt only very tardily that Ney had been granted their use.

Milhaud was the commander of *4e Corps de Cavalerie*, comprising the *13e* and *14e Divisions de Cavalerie* (Watier and Delort). Four squadrons of Watier's *cuirassiers* had already been employed during the first attack on La Haye Sainte and had subsequently been attacked by Somerset's Heavy Brigade, but he still retained three squadrons; and Delort's two brigades of *cuirassiers* (Farine and Vial, 13 squadrons) were also still in reserve.[12] None of them was aware of the Emperor's orders, and Ney's arrival to lead them into battle took them by surprise.

Ney's temper, already much tried in previous days and not improved by the poor performance at La Haye Sainte a few minutes earlier, now brought him into a fresh *contretemps*. Ney sent a direct order to Farine to lead the cavalry attack on the Allied line, and as Farine put his two regiments in motion, Delort dashed forward to countermand the act since neither he as divisional commander nor Milhaud as corps commander had been informed. A highly irritated Ney in turn came across and 'in the name of the Emperor' insisted on taking not only both of Delort's brigades but also the rest of Watier's division. The invocation of the Emperor's name suggests – to say the least – who had issued the general order. And so Milhaud gave way and followed Ney, though he thought the attack unwise at that time. Delort said that he himself had openly expressed doubt about attacking.

Jerome told his wife that Napoleon intended Ney to use the *Garde* cavalry. But Ney had no authority whatsoever over the Emperor's *Garde* unless it was specifically delegated. And no *Garde* general would have brooked unauthorised interference. On reading in Napoleon's memoirs that the Emperor claimed that he had not authorised Ney to use the *Garde*, Lieutenant-General Guyot of the *Vieille Garde* heavy cavalry told Drouot in 1820 that Napoleon placed him under Ney's orders from 'about 2 o'clock', and he repeated this to the compilers of *Victoires et Conquêtes*, insisting that 'from 3 p.m. Napoleon had placed him [Guyot] at the disposal of the Prince of the Moskova, who had been given responsibility [*chargé*] for the great attack on the centre'. Guyot's testimony makes it more than likely that Lefebvre-Desnouettes received similar imperial orders.[13] For the *Garde* light cavalry of Lefebvre-Desnouettes joined in. The tale that he acted on a misheard or mistaken remark from Milhaud is rendered unlikely by the fact that he did not report to Milhaud but to Napoleon. Only if Ney assured him that he, Ney, really did speak in Napoleon's name would the irregularity disappear.

Houssaye argued that dips and humps in the ground stopped Napoleon seeing into the valley or noticing the movement of these several thousand horsemen until too late.[14] This is special pleading. The Emperor had stationed Milhaud and Lefebvre-Desnouettes on the east of the great road, somewhere behind d'Erlon. Yet in readying for the great cavalry charges they stood on the west of the road, in front of Kellermann's corps, and to have moved so large a body of horsemen cannot have been a matter of a few minutes, but well over a quarter of an hour (or maybe more).[15] If they were moving to the attack without Napoleon's agreement, or indeed in defiance of his express command, *what did he do*? He watched them go. Houssaye also cited Napoleon's marginal comment written in General Rogniat's book on *The Art of War* half-suggesting that he was too preoccupied with repulsing the Prussians near Plancenoit to notice or stop the premature cavalry movement.[16] But the Emperor did not leave his command post to go to Plancenoit; it was Lobau who was trying to repulse the Prussians there. And from his command post Napoleon could see his cavalry.

The decision that the heavy cavalry and the *Garde* cavalry were to be used was made at the highest level.

Jerome and Napoleon both state that on watching these spectacular charges, the Emperor said 'they are too soon', either by 45 minutes or by an hour.[17] Granted that if Wellington had been his sole opponent, another 45–60 minutes' artillery bombardment might have softened resistance to a cavalry attack. But the pressure from 'Bülow' (and indeed all the Prussians that must be following him) allowed no such delay. The *Armée du Nord* could not afford to wait for up to an hour before trying to take the ridge and break the centre. Victory was needed quickly and maximum force was essential.

V

Probably to divert Wellington's attention, Piré's *lanciers* made a demonstration close to the western flank, and drew towards themselves Grant's 13th Light Dragoons and 15th Hussars, and also Dörnberg's 2nd KGL Light Dragoons: Uxbridge noted that 'the lancers did not wait to be attacked'. Wellington further reinforced the Hougoumont sector by moving four Brunswick battalions from Merbe Braine, but as the great cavalry attack assembled in the valley he ensured that his infantry commanders maintained the chequerboard disposition for their squares. Each square thus resembled a thicket of bayonets, kneeling and standing four ranks deep, a glittering deterrent for riders with sabres, frightening for their horses, while the deliberately wide empty spaces between each square offered tempting avenues of avoidance and escape for the cavalry. What these squares were now to face, many of the men for the first time in their lives, was the most terrifying armoured mounted force and one fanatically devoted to a supreme military genius.[18]

The French heavy cavalry arm was an unforgettable sight on the battlefield: tall, heavy men, helmets and breastplates shining 'like a stormy wave of the sea when it catches the sunlight' (in Gronow's vivid phrase), mounted on great horses, horse-hair crests flowing behind them, clashing sword pommels on breastplates, determined to attain their objective no matter at what cost. The earth-shaking tramp of thousands of horses *en masse*, the menacing riders suddenly breaking into a great united shout of '*Vive l'Empereur!*' – all this had been sufficient to make many armies quail long before the leading riders had closed upon them. Napoleon used the heavy cavalry to 'determine the issue' (*créer l'événement*), whether to turn a dangerous crisis into victory as at Eylau, or to smash a key defensive position like the great redoubt at Borodino (*la Moskova*), or to shatter finally a wavering front. They were his ultimate shock-troops, in a very real sense a predecessor of the *Panzerdivision*.

Ney led this splendid array at a steady trot across the valley, through the gap between Hougoumont and La Haye Sainte towards the slope, perhaps some 2,400 of Milhaud's *cuirassiers*, over 1,900 *lanciers* and *chasseurs à cheval* of Lefebvre-Desnouettes, and 2,000 of Guyot's *grenadiers à cheval* and the Empress's Dragoons. Before long the pace slackened as they went up the muddy slope and with the tall crops dragging their flanks as they passed. As the shining force advanced so the French guns necessarily fell silent. Not so the Allied guns. The solid glittering mass was intended to overawe the infantry, but it likewise made the work of the Allied guns very easy, and round after round, and some double-shotted, ploughed through the dense ranks of horsemen, so that even in this first charge the rear formations were hampered by fallen horses and men. The gunners continued to fire until the last possible moment, then removed a wheel from each gun and took shelter in the squares. The horsemen paid little attention to the abandoned guns: possibly they were ill-equipped to disable them further. They certainly did not spike them, though in a few cases they sought unsuccessfully to drag them away. They pressed through the abandoned gun line, still sufficiently confident of their ability to frighten the infantry into breaking. But the squares had not dissolved in panic. Instead they blasted a volley into the cavalry and forced it to swerve aside and pass through the wide avenues,

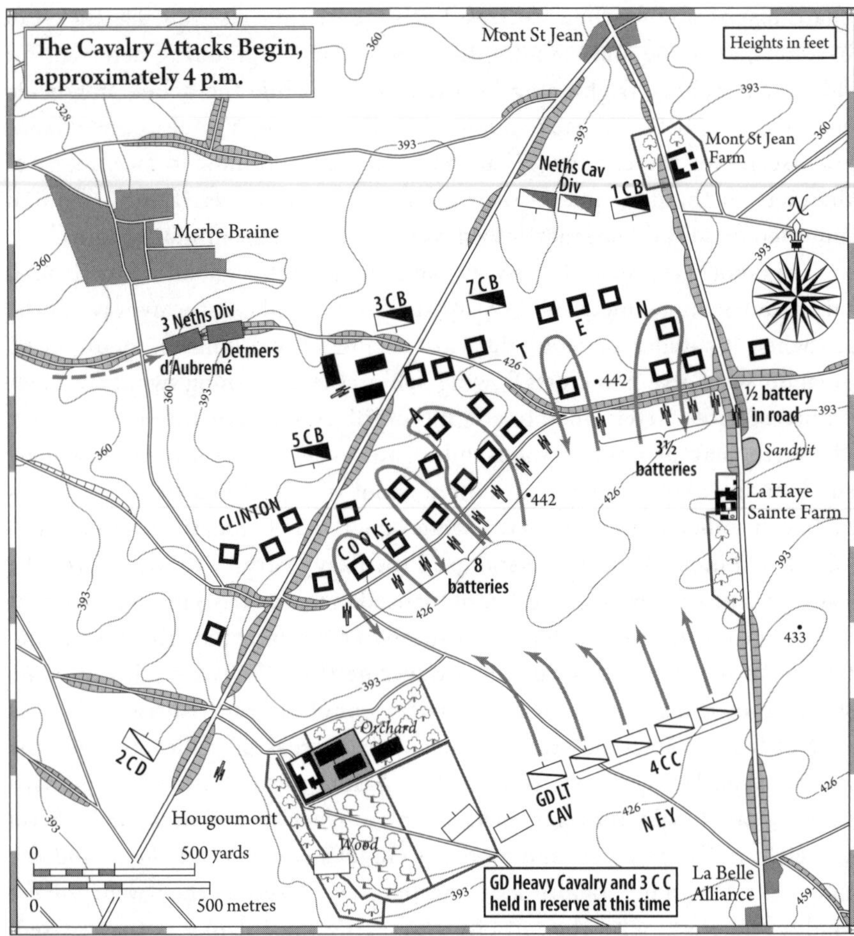

where the flanks of the squares poured in further volleys. Even when riders were prepared to throw themselves against the hedge of bayonets, the horses baulked and refused. It is difficult to say who showed the greater courage, the intrepid horsemen attacking again and again, or the infantry in the squares watching the horsemen towering over them, and 'seeing them off'.

The *cuirassier* generals had been right to doubt the wisdom of Ney's attack, for it was a repetition on a larger scale of his mistaken tactic of two days earlier. The cavalry walked round the squares and were punished for it; they might snap their pistols at the square to encourage the infantry to fire back in an unauthorised way, for it was immediately after firing that the square was weakest – but no ruse worked for the French cavalry. The attackers could not stay for long, trapped as they were between the volleys of different squares, and they turned for home. At this moment the Allied light cavalry came from the reverse slope and dashed into the retiring Frenchmen adding to their discomfiture. The gunners ran forward, set up their pieces and resumed fire. Thus ended the first charge.

VI

Wellington had already begun to alter his dispositions along the crest, drawing closer Kempt's and Pack's 8th and 9th Brigades to cover the gap left by Bylandt's withdrawal. The 6th Division's distant brigade (Lambert[19]) had by late morning reached Waterloo from Assche and was thereafter placed as support for the 5th Division. In the slack period after d'Erlon's retirement Wellington ordered Chassé's 3rd Netherlands Division from Braine l'Alleud, and it marched at 3 p.m. for Merbe Braine. This in turn enabled Wellington to call Clinton's 2nd Division to strengthen the right front, so that Adam's 3rd Brigade, Hugh Halkett's 3rd Hanoverian Brigade and Du Plat's 1st KGL Brigade were close to the Guards and reinforced the Brunswick infantry behind Hougoumont. By about 4 p.m. the artillery brigades/troops on this part of the front were Bull, Ramsay, Sympher, Webber-Smith, Mercer, Beane, Bolton, Kuhlmann, Sandham, Lloyd, Cleeves; at the crossroads or a little to the east were Ross, Whinyates and Rogers. If it could not match the French artillery in numbers and weight of cannon, these units were fully able to decimate all attacks on this front.

The gunners watched Ney launch a second charge, and again they blazed away at the dense mass of horsemen, and then took their wheels and dashed into the squares before the cavalry could catch them. Ney's cavalry pressed up the soft muddy slope, stepped over the bodies of fallen men and horses, and then circled round the squares, with the same results as before, while further down the slope French infantry from *9e Division* moved on the orchard of Hougoumont, while elements of *1re* and *2e Divisions* closed on La Haye Sainte 'in an identical manner as before', but this time with more artillery support. But the cavalry had to fall back, and the infantry with them. Uxbridge's heavy brigades having been wrecked, he had only his light cavalry to send against the *cuirassiers* and infantry, and his light horse suffered considerable loss in the result.[20]

At this point the evidence becomes confused. The horsemen that Ney had led in two charges were tired, blown and discouraged, and they had suffered terrible losses. Napoleon could see them returning down the slope and must have recognised that they had failed in their task. *He had time enough to decide what next to do* long before Ney could order another charge, or call upon cavalry hitherto unused and held well back 'behind Napoleon's left shoulder', around La Belle Alliance. Whether there would be a further charge depended entirely on Napoleon. He let this further reserve go forward.

We have seen that Napoleon had said that the assaults were premature, apparently by anything up to an hour: and thus he implied that their chance of success was much reduced. But he had not stopped them. He claimed that, once committed to the action, 'it is necessary to back up [*soutenir*] what has been done': that is, to support an action that is unlikely to succeed, to support a mistake made by Ney, to reinforce a serious failure. Such an argument is feeble to a degree; it is used by weak generals who cannot think of anything else to do. But that was not how Napoleon's mind worked. Great generals know when to break off and re-group, and when to continue. He still hoped against hope. He had looked for victory with these cavalry attacks, otherwise his cause risked doom. They had not yet brought him the expected reward, but they had to make one more great effort. For unless we are to judge Napoleon a mindless butcher or a mere puppet of Ney – and, though careless of lives, he was of outstanding intellect and a master of men – he recognised that the pressures of time and the Prussians left him no option but to smash Wellington at once. To draw back and fight another day was militarily possible, but politically fatal: all his enemies in Paris and elsewhere would rise against him.

Napoleon had held behind his left shoulder Guyot's heavy cavalry of the *Garde* and Kellermann's corps. He had let Guyot go forward, although he later denied it. Now, in his own words, he 'sent orders to Kellermann's *cuirassiers*, who throughout had been positioned on the left, to move at full trot to support the cavalry on the plateau'.[21] All the army's cavalry had now been committed to the great gamble.

*

Appendix: The Cost of the Great Cavalry Attacks

It may interest some readers to see the cost of the French heavy cavalry charges against Wellington's Mont St Jean position in the 'third act' of Waterloo. The figures are taken from the 10 June 1815 morning states and Martinien's tables of officer casualties. No allowance has been made for casualties in the early afternoon around La Haye Sainte or at the last stages of the battle. I have for this purpose arbitrarily assumed that no officer wounded on 16 June was with his regiment on 18 June, but the 16 June losses were so small that even if my assumption is wrong for some regiments, the percentage error should be insignificant. Were the percentage figures in this table to be the same for other ranks, then one would be looking at a casualty list in excess of 4,200, or three entire line cavalry divisions.

French Heavy Cavalry Casualties					
	Present 10 June Offs + ORs	*Officer casualties 16 June*	*Officers present 18 June*	*Officer casualties 18 June*	*% Officer casualties 18 June*
3e Corps de Cavalerie, 11e Division					
2e Dragons	40 + 543		40	6k, 12w	45
7e Dragons	41 + 475		41	1k, 15w	39
8e Cuirassiers	31 + 421	13w	18	4w	22
11e Cuirassiers	21 + 304	1k, 3w	17	2k, 15w	100
3e Corps de Cavalerie, 12e Division					
1e Carabiniers	30 + 403		30	8k, 13w	70
2e Carabiniers	29 + 380		29	3k, 10w	45
2e Cuirassiers	21 + 292		21	2k, 14w	76
3e Cuirassiers	37 + 427		37	2k, 11w	35
4e Corps de Cavalerie, 13e Division					
1e Cuirassiers	41 + 411		41	4k, 13w	41
4e Cuirassiers	28 + 278		28	4k, 10w	50
7e Cuirassiers	21 + 151		21	3k, 11w	67
12e Cuirassiers	22 + 226	1k, 3w	18	4k, 12w	89
4e Corps de Cavalerie, 14e Division					
5e Cuirassiers	34 + 380	1k	33	2k, 12w	42
10e Cuirassiers	26 + 309	1k, 4w	21	2k, 11w	62
6e Cuirassiers	37 + 474	2w	35	16w	46
9e Cuirassiers	32 + 327	2w	30	2k, 11w	43
Vieille Garde					
2e Chev.-Légers Lanciers	47 + 833		47	1k, 9w	21
Chasseurs à Cheval	59 + 1138		59	6k, 14w	34
Grenadiers à Cheval	44 + 732	1w (15 June)	43	2k, 16w	42
Drag. de l'Imperatrice	51 + 765	1k	50	3k, 16w	38
Total	692 + 9,269	5k, 28w	659	57k, 245w	46

Chapter 40

In Another Part of Brabant

I

THUS FAR ON 18 JUNE WE HAVE been looking across the blood-soaked valley and slopes to Mont St Jean and La Belle Alliance, trying to see into the minds of the two commanders-in-chief as they each wrestled with what they could see and what they forecast as likely to happen. Wellington had committed himself to battle on the basis of a late evening message received from Blücher before dawn on the 18th; Napoleon had framed his plans partly in light of a message sent to him by Grouchy at 10 p.m. on the 17th. Both messages were given in Chapter 34 and since then we have not concerned ourselves with Blücher and Grouchy and their subsequent thoughts and actions, away to the east in another part of Brabant. It is time to return to them.

II

It will be remembered that a steady flow of information reached Prussian headquarters at Wavre during the day and into the evening of 17 June. Before midday Massow had reported on Wellington's position at Quatre Bras and the prospects for his army, then Gröben had provided successive messages indicating that Napoleon's main force was pursuing Wellington and not the Prussians. Later he reported that fighting could be heard at Genappe, and Gneisenau had ordered Ziethen to check on this. All four Prussian corps had reached the vicinity of Wavre between the afternoon and midnight, and without molestation. Finally, towards midnight, Müffling's letter had come stating that Wellington was prepared to stand and fight at Mont St Jean in the morning, if given some Prussian support. That support was immediately promised by Blücher himself, who then sought a few hours' sleep. It was left to his staff to issue the detailed instructions for the dawn march.

The marching orders went out at about midnight, and were received by the four corps commanders within one to two hours. Wavre stands astride the River Dyle, and the Prussian forces were camped on both banks. From early afternoon on 17 June I Corps had been settling to rest near Bierges, west of Wavre, watching the Dyle and seeking contact with Wellington's eastern flank. II Corps had arrived very soon after and remained on the southern outskirts of Wavre at St Anne on the right bank. Once the munitions wagons had arrived from Maastricht in late afternoon both these corps had replenished their stocks before turning in to sleep. They had been roughly handled in the past two days, had suffered considerable losses, but it should be remembered that they did have time to clean up, feed themselves and get some rest even before dusk fell. III Corps arrived in the last hours of the evening, had crossed the Dyle downstream at Basse Wavre, and had settled by midnight, mainly at La Bavette beyond Wavre: they had not suffered as heavily as the two other corps, nor expended so much ammunition, but certainly the men were very tired. The situation of IV Corps was different; since the morning of 16 June it had marched almost continuously for about forty or more hours, covering some 50 miles. Most of the men had reached camp about 2½ miles short of Wavre, at Dion-le-Mont, by about 10 p.m. on the night of the 17th; but, though tired, IV Corps was at full strength and as yet unbattered by any fighting.

The problem for the Prussian staff was therefore whether it was better to lead with recently defeated troops who were west of the Dyle or with tired but unbloodied troops much further away and on the wrong side of the river. There was no ideal solution.

It was decided that Bülow's IV Corps should lead, with II following immediately after. Ziethen's I and Thielemann's III Corps were to stand by to march if more than two corps were needed. The Ledebur detachment from IV Corps would not be called in; it would stay at Mont-St-Guibert as an outpost covering Wavre. Bülow was informed that Wellington's battle-line stretched from Braine l'Alleud across to La Haye, that the Duke expected to be attacked in the morning, and that he had been promised Prussian support. IV Corps was to pass through Wavre itself and move to Chapelle-St-Lambert, close to the Lasne brook, 6 miles west of Wavre and 4 miles downstream from Plancenoit. Once there he was to establish whether the French were seriously engaged with the Duke: if they were, he was immediately to attack the French right flank; if the French were not actively attacking Wellington, Bülow was to remain under cover.

The wording of these instructions, and a glance at the map, show that Prussian assistance was to be independent assistance, not marching to join

Wellington's eastern flank at La Haye and Papelotte but striking at the French right rear towards Plancenoit.[1]

At some time between 7 and 8 a.m. on the 18th Count Gröben reached Wavre from his southern eyrie, and was able to confirm his earlier reports that the French pursuers had not moved from Gembloux; this confirmed Blücher in his belief that he could march with all his forces to assist the Duke, and he told Gröben so.[2]

But according to the historian General von Ollech, this news did not fully reassure the staff. Gneisenau and Grolman took Gröben into another room, studied the maps and asked him to repeat his opinion. He was unable to guarantee that the French force at Gembloux numbered no more than 15,000 men, for it might even stretch to double that number; but his own view was that the decisive place was with the British army and that one corps ought to be enough to hold Wavre. Grolman, however, judged it more pessimistically: only if the French did not attack Wavre in great numbers could I Corps – and perhaps III Corps – follow II and IV on the march to Lasne, otherwise the two corps should hold the line of the Dyle – at any rate until the main army had crossed the Lasne brook. Gneisenau agreed with Grolman.[3] This significantly modified Blücher's intention that the great mass of his army would intervene decisively close to Mont St Jean irrespective of anything that might happen on the Dyle. This new arrangement would have made *Grouchy the determinant of Prussian plans* for the coming day, hobbling up to half the Prussian army, and consequently reducing the effectiveness of the force marching to Lasne.

But then Blücher woke. He was as determined as ever that Grouchy should not steal the initiative from him and dictate Prussian strategy. He knew where the decision must be sought, and besides that nothing else mattered. In a letter timed 9.30 a.m. he dictated a great and splendid message for Müffling:

> Your Excellency is requested to say in my name to the Duke of Wellington that, ill as I am, I shall nevertheless put myself at the head of my troops to attack the right wing of the enemy as soon as Napoleon undertakes anything against the Duke. If this day should pass without the enemy attacking, it is my opinion that we should together attack the French army tomorrow.
>
> I charge Your Excellency to inform the Duke of this firm intention of mine, and that I consider this proposal to be the best and most appropriate one for our present situation.[4]

It is not clear from this whether the old man was aware that his intention for the march to start at dawn had not been implemented, but, as at 9.30 a.m. the commander-in-chief was still at Wavre and not as yet on horseback at the head of them, it did imply some delay. But he was always keen for battle

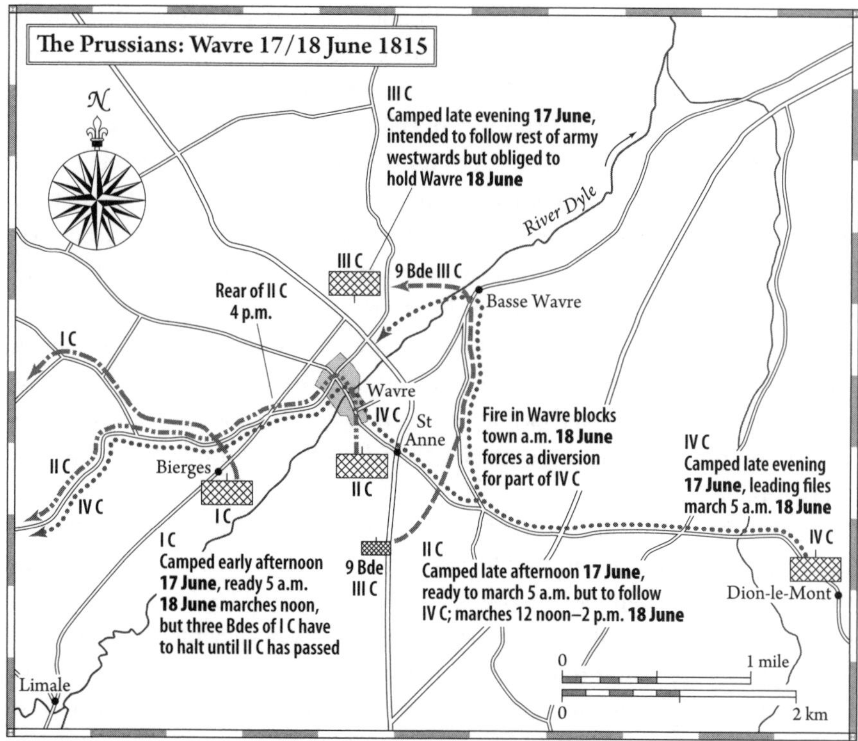

and his letter did promise growing support during this day and of course full support tomorrow. But what shines out most is that insistence that the one vital place for his army was on Napoleon's right wing. What might happen between Gembloux and Wavre was irrelevant. It contrasts with the hesitant Gneisenau/Grolman view.

Nostitz had taken down Blücher's dictated words, but Gneisenau saw the finished document and insisted that the ADC should add a significant qualification from the Army Chief of Staff. Despite all the messages of yesterday, the sounds of gunfire, and Müffling's late night assurances, there was still a doubt:

> General Gneisenau agrees/approves [*einverstanden*] the contents of this letter, but asks Your Excellency to be quite certain whether the Duke really has the firm intention to fight in his position, or whether he intends merely to demonstrate, which would be very fatal to our army.
>
> Your Excellency will be so good to let me know the Duke's intentions, because it is of the highest importance to know exactly what the Duke will do in order that we can base our movements: [sgd] Count NOSTITZ.[5]

There was a fundamental question implicit in this message, albeit never openly stated. Besides that, it suggests that Gneisenau intended it to be known that he was keeping a degree of control over the simple, trusting Prince and that he did not regard the promises of the previous night and this morning as absolute or unconditional. It is not unusual to find a Prussian chief of staff moulding and even adjusting his commander-in-chief's intentions – that was the system – and Gneisenau had done it at least once before: Müffling gives chapter and verse about another instance in February 1814, when the Chief of Staff had altered some orders in the presence of Blücher himself.[6] But the effect of this was to impose *delay*, whereas Blücher intended just the opposite. By the time a reply could be received from Müffling as to Wellington's real intentions, it would be well after noon. In the meantime the various corps already marching needed to avoid being drawn willy-nilly into a possible catastrophe.

Perhaps it may be argued that these were necessary and wise precautions to take, although they do not fit easily with Gneisenau's earlier views on the necessity to keep close to the Anglo-Allied army so as to avoid being isolated and cut up.[7] But when set against the way in which Blücher and Wellington were rising to confront their moments of fate, against what the two leaders had sought and agreed overnight, it does seem poor-spirited. In earlier months Gneisenau had more than once shown mistrust all round, had displayed somewhat contemptuous superiority in quiet times while sinking too much into carping on difficult days, for this to be excused as a chance spasm of doubt in a tired man. In this postscript, I believe, Gneisenau's limitations came through.

III

Given Blücher's intentions, even if Gneisenau and some others in the staff had qualms, there was an urgent need for proper staff coordination of the plans for the dawn assembly. They knew the size of the formations that would be marching, they knew (more or less) the sort of country they would have to traverse, they knew the weather had made paths more difficult, they knew that the Wavre bridge and narrow streets could create additional problems. The formations that were to head the advance lay on the wrong side of the Dyle. Of those two formations the furthest (IV Corps) was to be the leader, but to reach Wavre it would have to pass through the second (II Corps) before reaching the town. Once across the Dyle these two would move through Bierges, but that village was occupied by another formation (I Corps). At least I and II Corps had had half a day's rest and some sleep, and it should not have been beyond possibility to ensure that they could be so moved at dawn that they left clear the route that IV Corps was to follow – II Corps at least might have been moved through Wavre early and then halted clear of the road. But none of this was done: the worst march arrangement was left in place.

The country east of the Dyle was not particularly easy, and to the west it was hilly and wooded, with the heights rising some 200 feet above the valley bottoms, with the country tracks wriggling down steep slopes to narrow bridges. It could not be a fast route. Here is how two observers portrayed it, one in the years just after the campaign, the other at the end of the nineteenth century. General Lamarque (d. 1832) described the ground between Nil-St-Vincent and Ottignies and Moustier – that is from south of Wavre westwards to beyond the Dyle – thus: 'surprisingly high hills and deep valleys, in some places resembling the foothills of the Alps or Pyrenees, through which it would be difficult to take artillery'. The Revd H. B. George (1838–1910), a military historian, wrote of the area somewhat further west, of the winding routes from Walhain to Plancenoit: 'a fast walker, trying to show in how short a time he could cover the distance, with the ground miry from rain, but in colder weather [than June], found that he could not manage more than two and a quarter miles per hour [even though] in no way impeded by the bridges', and he contrasted this fast walker's pace with the likely progress of a column with artillery.[8]

The route to Chapelle-St-Lambert would cut diagonally across the grain of the high ground, rising from the Dyle valley and descending steeply into that of the Lasne, beyond which was another crest leading to the brook of Smohain close by Papelotte. Parts of the tracks to and from the Lasne stream were so steep that villagers had laid pegged logs across the paths as steps to assist the wayfarer. It was good defensible country, and the Prussians had reason to fear that the French could have established strongpoints in woods and on summits. But Prussian scouts soon found the country unoccupied. The Prussian advance must inevitably have been slow in such wet conditions; and nothing but praise should be given to the wretched, wet, and hungry troops who so valiantly responded to their Field Marshal's call. Nor should there be anything but praise for that magnificent old man, whose simplicity and courage called forth from the troops quite exceptional efforts through little phrases like, 'Come on, my children, one more effort! You would not have me break my word to the Duke of Wellington!' Whenever possible he granted a rest, and the exhausted men almost fell down in their ranks to recover. There was a kindly paternal strain in Blücher that none of his colleagues, allies, or enemies, possessed, and it was often given considerable rein unless discontent or mutiny (as with the Saxons), or the prospect of battle, made him into an unflinching force of steel: then no tiredness, exhaustion, or weakness was ever permitted to deflect him from his aim. Leader and led gave of their best. But that the advance to St-Lambert was *exceptionally* slow was largely due to poor Prussian staff work and decisions.

Bülow's orders had reached his various units between 2 and 4 a.m.[9] All were to be ready to assemble at the same time and march in close succession, with the wagons and impedimenta kept to the rear or sent back eastwards to Louvain. The march of Bülow's leading infantry began at 5 a.m.,[10] and had to negotiate the lines of II Corps, camped in their path. The head of 15th Brigade of IV Corps reached Wavre after a couple of hours and began filing over Wavre bridge at 7 a.m., something that was likely to take three hours for Bülow's entire formation, all being well. The second of the four brigades followed without undue difficulty, but then a fire broke out near the bridge, and a mill and two houses were ablaze, and for a time the road through the town was blocked, so that some units were diverted to the crossing at Basse Wavre. The officer commanding the corps pioneers who not only helped put out the fire but also diverted troops, maintained that the fire did not delay the march. That seems unlikely. A sudden fire in a town of narrow streets and one bridge, with munitions wagons in the streets and little room for manoeuvre, would normally lead to severe congestion if not panic; perhaps he meant that the normal delay would have been so considerable that switching some units to the north did not lengthen the stoppage. Bülow also played it down.

What this meant was that Bülow's leading units passed Chapelle-St-Robert, then descended to Chapelle-St-Lambert and halted there. This may have been at about 10 a.m. Some cavalry were sent into the Lasne valley and pressed as far upstream as Maransart (3 miles beyond Chapelle-St-Lambert and only 1 mile from Plancenoit), finding the valley empty of French troops. Until 11.30 that morning there was absolutely no sound of any gunfire to the westward, but then it began and grew steadily in intensity. Two more of Bülow's brigades had arrived by noon, although the fourth brigade joined them only at 3 p.m. The troops were on very short commons and were tired, and the mishap at Wavre could not have been foreseen, but IV Corps had taken well over ten hours to cover less than 10 miles. Plancenoit was three miles further up the Lasne valley

The commander-in-chief mounted at about 11 a.m. and rode from Wavre to Chapelle-St-Lambert. He encouraged his army as he passed it but was fully aware that the men were drawing heavily on their reserves of endurance. Two officers, Lützow and Massow, had been sent forward to advise him of the terrain. They passed beyond Lasne village and found the Bois de Paris unoccupied, and turned to report this to the Commander-in-Chief, but by chance meeting Grolman, they first informed him. Grolman had been overruled about the importance of holding Wavre but he was by nature positively minded and his chief's orders had been emphatic. He was doing all he could to carry them out. He instantly recognised the wood's importance, told Blücher, who in turn told Bülow to cross the stream and place troops in the wood and to back them with reinforcements.

So much for IV Corps. The orders for II Corps required it to *follow* the same road as IV Corps, instead of preceding it through Wavre. It had to let the long column pass, and only then start. Yet because it was ordered to assemble at the same time as IV Corps it was obliged to mark time for hours on end, instead of taking the lead. Nobody thought to suggest an alternative route for it to take. Consequently, at 11 a.m. its leading files still had not begun to march, and indeed its rear elements started only at 2 p.m., roughly at the time of d'Erlon's supposedly decisive attack on the Mont St Jean ridge, nearly 10 miles away. II Corps was through Wavre by 4 p.m.

It is true that the Prussian army was poorly supplied with bridging equipment, but there were places where the Dyle could be crossed elsewhere than Wavre. As both II and IV Corps were east of the river and the town bridge was narrow, it should not have been beyond a good staff to draw up decent arrangements to ensure that the troops were not unnecessarily held up. To insist that they should both take the same road was inevitably to threaten total immobility if anything went wrong. As if that was not bad enough, the staff arrangements for another formation, Ziethen's I Corps, were almost guaranteed to add to the confusion.

Ziethen had received orders at 2 a.m. to assemble and feed his troops, after which they should be ready to march from Bierges (west of Wavre). The next order was verbal and came at 'about midday' and required Ziethen to march due west via Froidemont and Genval to Ohain so as to approach Wellington's eastern flank. Thus in marching from Bierges in the early afternoon (instead of at say 6–8 a.m.) I Corps found itself crossing the south-western route being taken by IV and II Corps, with all the complications that such a crossing could bring. Only one of Ziethen's brigades got past this crossing before II Corps arrived, and the other three brigades had to mark time until the last of II Corps had passed in late afternoon.[11]

III Corps concentrated in Wavre and to its north. One small event may have had unintended consequences. As Bülow's corps moved away, some French cavalry scouting in front of Grouchy's columns saw IV Corps' baggage wagons on their way north. A Prussian escort covered the convoy which continued towards Louvain. Nothing more is said of this little event

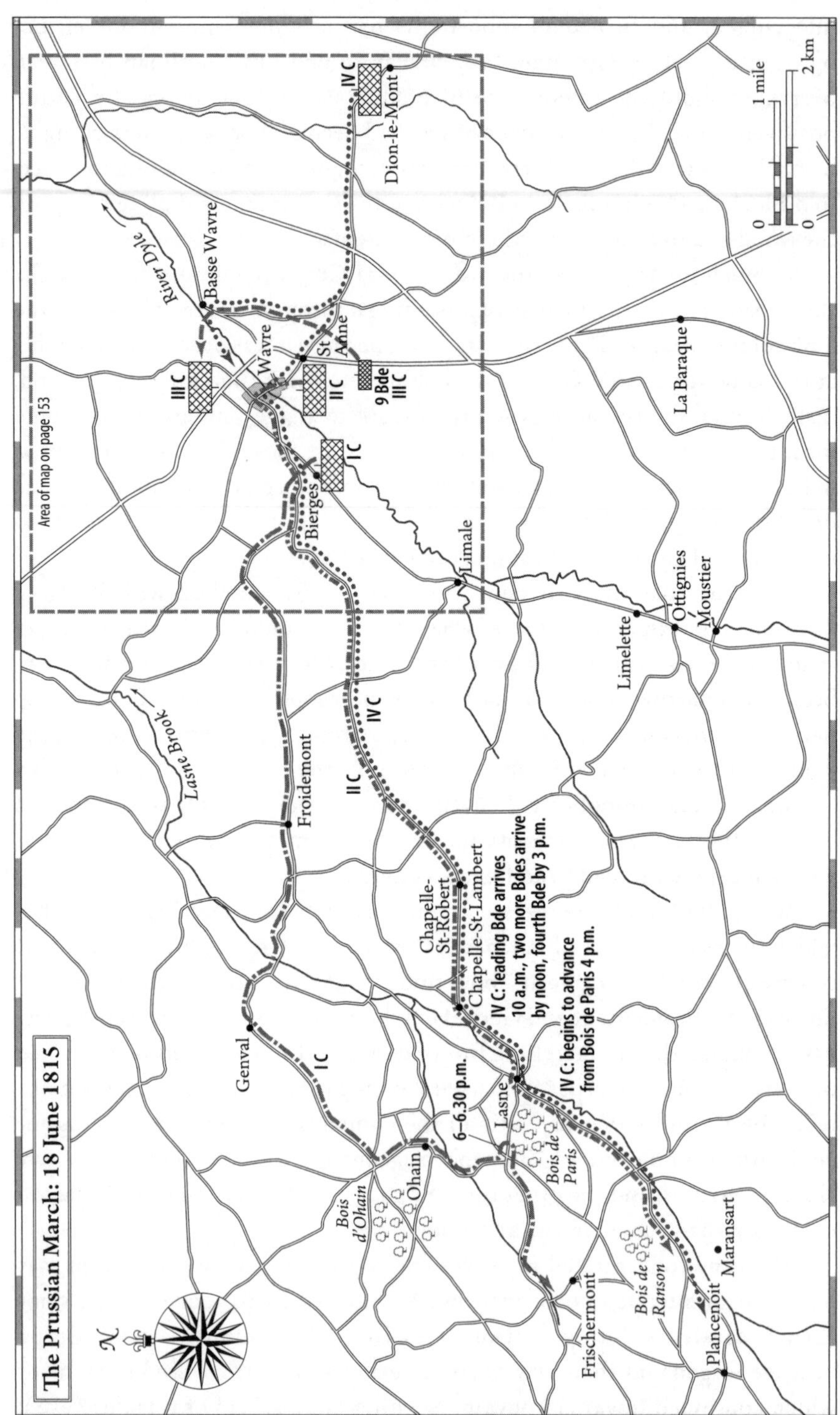
The Prussian March: 18 June 1815
N
Area of map on page 153
River Dyle
Basse Wavre
Wavre
III C
St Anne
II C
9 Bde
III C
IV C
Dion-le-Mont
I C
Bierges
Limale
La Baraque
Limelette
Ottignies
Moustier
Lasne Brook
Froidemont
IV C
II C
Chapelle-St-Robert
Chapelle-St-Lambert
IV C: leading Bde arrives 10 a.m., two more Bdes arrive by noon, fourth Bde by 3 p.m.
IV C: begins to advance from Bois de Paris 4 p.m.
Genval
I C
6–6.30 p.m.
Lasne
Bois de Paris
Bois d'Ohain
Ohain
Frischermont
Bois de Ranson
Maransart
Plancenoit
0 1 mile
0 2 km

other than that the Prussian escort could not re-join IV Corps in time for the battle. What it may also have done was strengthen Grouchy's view that the main force could be marching towards Louvain, not Plancenoit.

IV

Writing on 19 June Bülow stated that, 'in accordance with the views expressed by the Duke of Wellington, IV Corps should stay round St-Lambert until the enemy should disclose his intentions'.[12] Of course, those were the views of the Prussian high command, but what Wellington had agreed to was very slightly *different*. He himself never made any comment on all this, but there is evidence from Müffling, both in 1815 and again much later. The latter had ridden out to Papelotte and Frischermont until forced back by a French patrol, and saw three possibilities for utilising Blücher's aid: (1) if Wellington was attacked on his right flank the Prussians should march to Ohain; (2) if the Duke was attacked in his centre and left, then the Prussians should attack from St-Lambert heights; (3) if the French *turned against the Prussians* and attacked St-Lambert, then Wellington would thrust at the French flank and rear.

These ideas Müffling scribbled down and read out to the Duke: '"I quite agree," he [Wellington] called out to me,' whereupon Müffling added a note to this effect and sent it by an ADC to the Prussian Commander-in-Chief, and told the ADC to show the note to Bülow if he should encounter him.

Müffling leaves the impression in his memoirs that he stayed with the Duke. However, Peter Hofschröer (citing documentation in *Militär Wochenblatt* of 1907) found that Müffling met Bülow a little before midday and agreed all this, with Müffling noting that half of IV Corps was present by 11.30 a.m. but that its two other brigades were not expected till very much later.[13]

Müffling's three possibilities were quite obviously penned well before the French began operations, otherwise his note would not have been written in that form. But having been written, agreed to by the Duke, and sent to the Prussian high command, it is reasonable to think that Wellington (being fiercely attacked at Hougoumont from 11.30 a.m. onwards and from 1 p.m. on the crest as well) would expect the Prussians to come by Ohain and/or St-Lambert with reasonable despatch, as by midday French intentions had very unmistakably been disclosed. Indeed, if the Müffling–Bülow interview took place at St-Lambert just before noon, they must have known that the battle had started and that prompt action was called for. Müffling (writing in 1815) actually said that at 11.30 the attack opened, and 'with the utmost expedition' Bülow was informed 'that the second case was about to take place', after which 'immediately the whole Prussian army began to move'. From all this it seems evident that, in the conditions obtaining from 11.30 a.m. 'delay, or a halt', was the last thing that the Duke wanted. And indeed Bülow by this time had penned a letter intended for Wellington, announcing that he would advance; but (as already noted in Chapter 38, Section I), the messenger was captured by the French and his message seized and given to Napoleon instead.

In his 19 June report Bülow, who agreed that the battle started 'towards midday', noted that by 3 p.m. the contest was raging so that 'the moment was very favourable for acting against the enemy's right flank, as due to incomprehensible negligence they seemed to take no account of our existence'. This is scarcely an immediate response, and yet even now Bülow was not prepared to start. It took Blücher to make him. Bülow wrote: '*Disregarding* the fact that my 13th and 14th brigades had not yet reached the Lasne defile *the Field-Marshal* ordered that those troops available should move to the attack *at once*, so as to give breathing space to the English army [my emphasis].'

IV Corps did not begin its advance until 4 p.m., although the Bavarian Prince von Thurn und Taxis noted some Prussian concern lest La Haye Sainte in the centre should fall and thus make a junction of the two armies impossible; adding the significant rider: 'even if the Duke knew we were so close to each other'. This is not the timely or rapid co-operation that Blücher desired or that Wellington had been led to expect. It is not surprising that, according to de Constant Rebecque, 'the Duke at around 4 p.m. began to show disquiet at receiving no news of the Prussians'.[14]

From quite early in the day British officers had been told to watch for the arrival of the Prussians. Wellington's ADC Hervey recalled that 'Between ten and eleven o'clock in the morning the Prussian advance of cavalry was discovered about seven miles on our extreme left in the direction of Ohain, and we then hoped that they would come into play about one or two o'clock in the day, but in this expectation we were disappointed.' De Lancey gave particular directions to Vivian to watch for them, and Captain Ingilby recorded that at the very start of the battle they could see a patrol of Prussians on a hill at a considerable distance. (It may have been these Prussian patrols that Napoleon saw on 'the heights of St-Lambert'.). By mid-afternoon, said Ingilby, 'Several announcements were made by Prussian officers, sent on for the purpose, of the arrival of their army: and on the other hand two or three times officers from the Duke's staff came to ascertain if their troops had actually made their appearance.' Ingilby timed the appearance of the Prussian force 'about 5 p.m.', and this, said the Duke's ADC, Fremantle, was told to the Duke 'towards six o'clock'.[15]

But if the Allies had problems there were troubles on the French side as well.

V

Napoleon's orders to Grouchy in the second Bertrand letter (Chapter 32, Section III) came to this: while Napoleon settled Wellington's fate, Grouchy was to reconnoitre due east ('in the direction of Namur and Maastricht') and establish whether the Prussians intended to separate from the British or re-join them, 'to cover Brussels and Liège' (60 miles apart) and risk battle. Grouchy was to keep in close order and always have ways of escape: his duty was to report constantly. Historians are divided on whether Grouchy was free to attack Blücher if he found him, or whether Napoleon discouraged him from such an act, or simply gave him no useful direction. It seems to me that the terms of the second Bertrand letter are plainly that Grouchy was to reconnoitre in force, but to keep open all paths for a retreat, and thus not to venture a separate battle. But in that case cavalry should have sufficed. For mere scouting and intelligence purposes the infantry of two corps were simply a drag. Napoleon was wasting numbers by giving Grouchy the force he did.

By nightfall on 17 June Grouchy had concluded that the Prussians were falling back in two directions, north-west towards Wavre and north-east to Perwez. But here he let Napoleon's idea that the Prussians still thought of covering Brussels *and* Liège dominate his thinking: and he duly fed the idea back to his master. One portion might join Wellington, and the other, 'which is Blücher's army', could retire on Liège. But Grouchy was clear: he would follow the mass of the Prussians. Having written his despatch, at 10 p.m. Grouchy issued his orders for the following morning. The cavalry of Exelmans were to go north to Sart-à-Walhain in the general direction of Nil-St-Vincent and Tourinnes, that is to say between the two different objectives but towards neither of them. The infantry were to start quite late in the morning: those of Vandamme were to start at 6 a.m. (daybreak was around 3 a.m.), with *4e Corps* infantry following them from 8 a.m. Pajol's cavalry, and the cavalry of *4e Corps*, were to move on Grand Leez, three miles north-east of Gembloux because 'the enemy is retiring on Perwez'.[16]

And yet the morning, having begun with an inexcusable delay, brought fairly definite news that should have worried Grouchy. He now sent a detailed report to the Emperor:

> Sart-à-Walhain, 18 June, 11 a.m. Sire, I do not lose an instant in sending you the information I have gathered here; I consider the information positive and so that Your Majesty may receive it as promptly as possible I am sending it by Major La Fresnaye, your former page, who is well mounted and a good horseman.

> Blucher's I, II, and III Corps are marching in the direction of Brussels. Two of them passed by Sart-à-Walhain, or very close on the right, moving in three columns marching roughly side by side. Their passage took an uninterrupted six hours. The one within sight of Sart-à-Walhain may be estimated at 30,000 men at least, and had 50 to 60 guns.
>
> A corps coming from Liège has joined those that fought at Fleurus: attached is a [Prussian] requisition chit that proves this. Some of the Prussians in front of me are going towards the plain of La Chyse, near the Louvain road and two and a half leagues from that town [the plain is in a triangle between Wavre to the south-west, Louvain in the north-west, Tirlemont in the north-east, i.e. beyond Wavre, north-eastwards].
>
> It seems that the design is to mass together or to fight the troops who are pursuing them, or finally to join Wellington, a plan mentioned by their officers, who, with their usual boastfulness, pretend to have quit the battlefield on the 16th only in order to meet the English army at Brussels.
>
> This evening I shall be massed at Wavre and thus will be between Wellington, whom I presume is retreating before Your Majesty, and the Prussian army.
>
> I need further instructions as to what Your Majesty orders that I should do. The country between Wavre and the plain of La Chyse is difficult, cut up, and marshy.
>
> By the road to Vilvorde I can easily reach Brussels before any force that may have halted at La Chyse, if indeed the Prussians should halt there.
>
> Be pleased, Sire, to send me your orders; I can receive them before starting any move tomorrow.
>
> Most of the information enclosed with this letter has been given me by the owner of the house where I have stopped to write to Your Majesty; this officer served in the French army, is decorated, and seems entirely devoted to our interests. I enclose the information herewith.[17]

Grouchy had left Gembloux at 6 a.m., and yet by 11 o'clock had gone no further than Sart-à-Walhain, 3 miles to the north. Corbais was a further 3 miles to the north-west, about half way to Wavre and the Prussians had passed there in daylight the previous day. His information led him to think that he was pursuing three corps of the Prussian army, one corps of which had not been worn down by battle. Perhaps he thought caution necessary. Where he was led further astray was in believing intelligence that the Prussians would move to the north-east of Wavre, to the plain of La Chyse: hence his suggestion that on reaching Wavre he would have placed himself between the Prussians and Wellington (and in such circumstances he might indeed reach Brussels before them). And yet he also thought that the Allies' prime intention was to unite near Brussels. That prime intention did not fit with a move on La Chyse. He faced a contradiction that he would not resolve. He, the man closest to the enemy and yet tardy in his movements, was asking for clear military directions from a remote Emperor even less in touch with the situation on that front, and seeking guidance that in the nature of things could not be received by Grouchy before nightfall, or later. It does not inspire confidence in Grouchy's appreciation.

Houssaye blamed Grouchy for his strategic ignorance in believing that the Prussians would halt at Wavre and then continue on Brussels. His argument was eloquent and at first sight not unreasonable, and he sought to convict Grouchy out of his own mouth. 'He knew that the Emperor had forecast [*prévu*] a battle against the English before the forest of Soignies,[18] but he did not see that instead of gaining Brussels the Prussians could, from Wavre, join their allies directly by a short lateral march.' Houssaye went on to say that to stop such a junction Grouchy should not have gone via Corbais to Wavre, but should have crossed to the western bank of the Dyle at Moustier and checked any Prussian advance from Wavre, or have attacked them downstream on the left bank at Wavre (the town is mainly on the left bank, and therefore easier to attack than from the right bank), or if the Prussians had gone north to Brussels, still to march in pursuit. 'Grouchy had not the least idea of all this.' Moreover by starting so belatedly several hours after daybreak, 'under circumstances so pressing and so grave, he was guilty of an irreparable mistake . . . Unhappy man!'[19]

This may seem too dismissive, although I think that if Grouchy had crossed to the left bank of the Dyle on 17 June or at first light on the 18th he would indeed have been able to interfere and maybe check the Prussian march westward. That indeed was his worst error.

Houssaye's argument did not satisfy Colonel Grouard, an authority on Napoleonic strategy, writing under the initials 'AG, former pupil of the *Ecole polytechnique*'. AG in recognising that 'all France has read Monsieur Houssaye's book', felt that it was important to challenge some of his theories, among which was the one just mentioned. AG's reply of 1904 was cogent but just as extreme:

> The unhappy man was not Grouchy but Napoleon; or rather, if the first merits some words of commiseration it is only because for nearly a century his memory has borne an iniquitous responsibility, for that responsibility ought really to fall on Napoleon.
>
> Undoubtedly the reproach that he [Grouchy] began marching far too

> late is justified, but the fault identified is less in the delay in starting as in the direction taken.
>
> Of course with hindsight one can produce excellent reasons to show that instead of marching on Wavre, Grouchy should have marched on Mont St Jean, crossing the Dyle at Moustier. But Napoleon must have been struck by these reasons as much as Grouchy should have been. One can even say that he should have been more struck by them, for he knew almost as much as did Grouchy, whereas the latter was unaware of an important part of what Napoleon knew.
>
> He was ignorant, most notably, of the fact that on the morning of 18 June the English had stopped on Mont St Jean and that they seemed decided to give battle. By contrast Napoleon must have been more or less certain of this, from the inspection he had just made.
>
> Now, out of all the information, this was the only item that could lead one to think that the Prussians would come there, because if the English were preparing for battle, it was doubtless because they did not count on fighting alone, and if the Prussians were at Wavre, it was doubtless to join the English by the shortest route. From this, it was for Napoleon to call Grouchy to him as quickly as possible. Grouchy on the other hand, who knew no details of the English retreat, had no reason to march towards Napoleon, for if the English had continued their retreat to Brussels he would [in marching to Mont St Jean] have made a false movement.[20]

So there we have it: it was all Grouchy's fault; but no, it was primarily Napoleon's fault. Between two such distinguished Frenchmen and such decided opinions, a foreigner may reasonably feel that he need not intervene but should leave the reader to reflect and decide for himself.

So we see that on both sides, Prussian and French, decisions had been reached near Wavre that would gravely affect the combatants at Waterloo. We must now return to the battlefield.

Chapter 41
First Signs of the Prussian Advance
And Grouchy's Decisions

I

NAPOLEON AT 1 P.M. HAD TOLD SOULT that he approved Grouchy marching upon Wavre and had left his earlier instructions almost unchanged, save that he wished Grouchy to keep more in touch with the main army. Essentially he still thought that Grouchy could push away any Prussian forces. The observed presence of some troops on the heights of St-Lambert had made no real difference. It was the captured letter that changed perceptions at headquarters.

The earlier sighting had not been of some small unit ranging the distant heights. Instead it was shown to be a full corps, perhaps 30,000 men, moving westwards and seeking directions as to how and where to join Wellington. Hence the sudden change of tone in Napoleon's postscript to Grouchy. Just as two days before Napoleon had written to Ney 'the fate of France is in your hands', so here now was a similarly stacatto note of alarm, 'do not lose an instant' in returning here.[1]

The Emperor's problem was that he had already committed Reille's forces against Hougoumont, and his Grand Battery was in the process of smashing Wellington's centre prior to the great attack that d'Erlon was to make. The bombardment had to continue if *1er Corps'* attack was not to be aborted, but provided the attack was not cancelled and d'Erlon conquered the crest *before mid-afternoon*, the still remote complication of Bülow could become a mere nuisance or might even disappear. However, Napoleon either felt that he had no infantry to spare – or refused to consider releasing any – for a diversion against Bülow at this time: all were needed to ensure *1er Corps'* success whether with d'Erlon's front line or in support. Such, I believe, were Napoleon's calculations of risk, his balancing of options. Hence he made the following dispositions.

Lobau's small *6e Corps* now comprised only Simmer's and Jeannin's *19e* and *20e Divisions* totalling 6,500 men (Teste's *21e Division* had been detached to serve with Grouchy), originally with about 30 guns and howitzers, but now shorn of its 12-pounders. Hitherto it had been in reserve, but now it was ordered forward to take post behind d'Erlon's right. It was to support *1er Corps* in the great attack as double assurance that the crest should be taken. If that produced the intended victory, Lobau could be used either in consolidating the success or re-deploying eastwards. Meanwhile Napoleon detached from the forces held in his own hand the light cavalry divisions of Domon and Subervie, and these 2,000 horsemen went into the Lasne valley beyond Plancenoit to scout, though not so far eastwards as to risk being attacked while unsupported. At 1.30 p.m. there remained seven hours of daylight. By 3 p.m. the Mont St Jean crest would be in French hands, at which time any Prussians in the narrow Lasne valley would still be some way off, would probably be hampered by the French cavalry screen, and could be more firmly opposed by detaching Lobau then.

Accounts left by *6e Corps* staff officers such as Colonel Combes-Brassard and Commandant Janin both confirm that Lobau was to support d'Erlon's right wing, behind Durutte's *4e Division*.[2] The subsequent overthrow of *1er Corps* was mainly in its left and centre, and Durutte's division was rather less affected. Lobau's force remained intact. But it could not be left there to repair or reverse the damage wreaked on the Mont St Jean slopes, for the need now was to close the paths up from Chapelle-St-Lambert and Lasne. At some time after the collapse of d'Erlon's corps, maybe around 3 p.m., the order went out for Lobau to move towards the Lasne valley and Plancenoit.

Although Domon and Subervie had moved a little way downstream they had not gone as far as the Bois de Paris, and it was only when the Prussians emerged from its cover, at about 3.30 p.m. or a little later, that the first clashes took place between the opposing cavalry, clashes in which the Prussian cavalry brigade commander Count Schwerin was killed. The Prussians were within 2½ miles of Plancenoit and they faced only a screen of cavalry and the horse artillery batteries that were with the two cavalry divisions. That was the situation when Lobau's two infantry divisions hastened their skirmishers forward past Plancenoit to check and reverse the Prussian advance. Relying in part on an NCO of the *107e Ligne*, Sergeant-Major Marq, Field as usual sums it up very well. The French had 'a strong line of skirmishers. As the Prussian skirmish line engaged they were charged and driven back by the French cavalry, and the situation was only restored as more Prussian cavalry were committed. These were classic, and successful, delaying tactics.'[3] But they could only delay. It would require the full force of Lobau's *6e Corps*, and maybe more than that, to block this lane up to the Belle Alliance ridge.

II

What of the Prussians? Down in the Lasne valley, Blücher had reached 15th Brigade at the head of IV Corps between one hour and two hours after Bülow had sent his messenger to Wellington. The old Field Marshal recognised that a pause was essential, for although the leading units were halted and resting, those in rear were finding the going becoming ever more miry, and were still far back. Meanwhile patrols had reported that all was quiet east of the Dyle where Ledebur was holding Mont-St-Guibert, and that the French were doing nothing to scout or protect the Lasne valley away to the south-west. Blücher ordered two battalions and a cavalry regiment (say 1,400 infantry and 200 cavalry from the leading brigade) to be detached north-westwards as far as the Frischermont wood, to be supported in due course by the corps' rear brigades. Then the march began again.

Somewhat after 3 p.m. the leading brigade (15th, now about 5,000 strong) reached the Bois de Paris, with the second (16th) following in half an hour, then 13th Brigade at 4.30 p.m. The weak 14th Brigade came later: the cavalry and artillery had gone well ahead by then. In the meantime Blücher and his staff had reached a point from which they could see something of the great battle, and judge whether Napoleon could switch his troops to counter-attack the Prussians. Satisfied with what he saw and irrespective of the discussion around him,[4] Blücher ordered Bülow to attack with his available brigades, or even with a single brigade, without waiting the arrival of the remainder. This was in mid-afternoon.

The advance past Lasne and to the Bois de Paris had not been seen by French cavalry. The Prussians were able to occupy the wood quite peacefully and easily, and then take stock. The facts about French patrolling have been somewhat obscured by the delightful but erratic Colonel Marbot. His statement of 1830 is curious. In it he claimed that he had sent patrols as far as Frischermont, Lasne and St-Lambert, Couture, and to the River Dyle and the bridges of Moustier and Ottignies in accordance with the Emperor's orders. They found no enemy towards the Dyle, but one French patrol beyond St-Lambert encountered some Prussian hussars, took them prisoner and sent them to Napoleon for interrogation. This statement went on to say that, on going to the scene of the capture Marbot found a strong column advancing, and consequently he despatched an officer to Napoleon. Napoleon then sent a reply that it must be Grouchy driving before him scattered groups of Prussians. When Marbot then found that Napoleon's belief was wrong he made a fighting withdrawal by successive stages, and he again sent news to the Emperor, who in his next reply told Marbot to get a warning message to

Grouchy. Meanwhile one of Marbot's officers, Captain Eloy, who had been at Moustier all the afternoon, rode back at 6 p.m. and re-joined him.[5]

This account simply does not hold together. Marbot's sighting of a strong column somewhere not far from St-Lambert, must have been *east* of the Bois de Paris. His message to Napoleon had about three miles to travel and may have taken half an hour, to say nothing of the time it would take for Napoleon's reassuring reply to come back. Thus the controlled fighting withdrawal in front of Prussian troops must have been in mid- to late-afternoon, and Eloy's even later ride must have passed *through the midst* of the Prussian brigades by then massed on both sides of the valley. Yet every Prussian account insists that they occupied the Bois de Paris *unobserved and unchecked* in mid-afternoon: there were no French patrols in the wood watching the valley beyond. And in fact, in 1815 Marbot admitted that he was caught totally unprepared. In a letter dated 26 June 1815, he wrote:

> We were made to manoeuvre like pumpkins. I and my regiment were on the right flank of the army for almost the entire battle. I was assured that Marshal Grouchy would come to this point, which was guarded only by my regiment, three cannons, and a light infantry battalion, which was too weak. Instead of Marshal Grouchy it was the corps of Blücher that appeared! Judge in what manner we had been placed! We had been stuffed [*enfoncés*] and the enemy was immediately on our arses [*sur nos derrières*]! It should have been possible to put this right, but nobody gave any orders.[6]

That unvarnished account sounds very much like a total surprise and a disorderly flight. And the contrast with the 1830 version adds to the general conviction that the famous Marbot memoirs are good reading but that Oman was certainly right when he characterised Marbot's recollections as 'a set form of inaccuracy'.

It is not unreasonable to suggest that the orders given to Domon and Subervie were to check any bands of Prussians coming up the Lasne stream, but not to go so far from support as to be overwhelmed, nor to get caught up in woodland fighting for which horsemen were not well suited. How Marbot was to fit with them, if he was to fit with them, we simply do not know. Once the Prussian cavalry began to emerge from the woodland path onto open ground, then cavalry combat became possible, and it certainly took place. Meanwhile, as the horsemen rode round cutting at each other, two Prussian light infantry battalions moved out of the woodland, and the balance swung against the French, to be partially restored only when Lobau pressed down beyond Plancenoit to the little height between Frischermont and the Bois de Ranson – where he did in fact offer battle.

The Prussian guns fired a salvo, partly to inform Wellington of their arrival. The 15th and 16th Brigades pushed forward more or less side-by-side spread across about half a mile of the Lasne valley and even with a northern flank coming close to the Nassauers in the Papelotte/Frischermont area. Behind them followed the cavalry and in due course the two rear brigades (13th, 14th). The heads were now in open country, but with the woods still concealing their cavalry and rearmost units. Plancenoit was little more than a mile distant, with La Belle Alliance not much further beyond. In the distance could be heard (if not seen) the great cavalry attacks that Ney was hurling at Wellington's ridge.

It was now perhaps 4.30 p.m. Hitherto the battle had been fought on a single front, Napoleon seeking to wrest from Wellington Hougoumont, La Haye Sainte, and the Papelotte complex of buildings. Wellington's attention to La Haye Sainte had been inadequate and he had been dangerously weak in men on the sector facing d'Erlon,[7] but Napoleon's arrangements had repeatedly gone awry much more noticeably. His battle had been fought in a disjointed fashion with surprisingly little coordination between the senior commanders on the French side; d'Erlon's corps was unfit for more work at present while Reille's was getting nowhere at a ruinous cost. The additional complication of a second front required from now on a much tighter control of the battle, with only the existing reserves to offset Prussian numbers. And the only prospect for counterbalancing those increasing numbers of Prussians lay in the hope that Grouchy might realise that the plan (approved again that morning) to pursue towards Wavre was no longer appropriate by the afternoon, might guess what Napoleon really wanted him to do now, and hasten the ten difficult miles with his 33,000 men and strike the Prussians in the back. But Grouchy would only know for certain what was now needed when Soult's 1 p.m. letter arrived.

III

Marshal Grouchy's force had been slow in starting on the morning of 18 June. Pajol's cavalry moved from south of Gembloux in a wide sweep to Tourinnes, found no signs of the enemy and, in accordance with orders, then halted. Exelmans moved at 6 o'clock from Sauvenière and took the direction of Nil-St-Vincent and towards La Baraque (today on the eastern outskirts of Louvain-la-Neuve) on the route to Wavre. There he learned of a defensive post further north at the wooded defile of Lauzelle, and so he threw out reconnaissances to both flanks. Vandamme's *3e Corps* left Gembloux around 7 a.m. in the direction of Walhain, followed a little later by Gérard's *4e Corps*.

Grouchy rode up, overtook Vandamme, and they met at about 11 a.m. in the house of a notary called Hollërt at Walhain,[8] being joined there within the hour by Gérard himself, riding ahead of his men. In those four hours Vandamme's men had covered under 4 miles.

Grouchy had written to Napoleon at 11 a.m. about his intentions and had begun to eat a meal (unfortunately for his reputation it included a delicacy, a bowl of strawberries, for which France has never really forgiven him). At that time there was no noise anywhere. But when Gérard came, gunfire could be heard in the distance, and the Marshal and the General and their staffs went out to listen, after which Gérard advised that they should march to the guns. (Nobody seems to mention Vandamme, that opinionated and rebellious man; perhaps he had left the house already.) Enquiries of the local people brought confirmation that Mont St Jean was about three and a half leagues away, or up to six hours' march. This led in turn to a dispute between the staff on the practicability of the roads for a major force with nearly a hundred guns and hundreds of wagons. Gérard broke out openly in front of the twenty or so other officers, 'Marshal, your duty is to march to the cannon,' to which Grouchy retorted, 'My duty is to carry out the Emperor's orders, which require me to follow the Prussians; it would be breaking his instructions if I were to comply with your advice.'

A report came in from Exelmans whose dragoons had come up against a solid body of Prussians just south of Wavre; he thought that others had passed through the town and were marching to join the British. Gérard made a final appeal, to be allowed to take his own corps and some cavalry and march to Napoleon, leaving Grouchy with the remainder of the force east of the Dyle. This Grouchy rejected.[9]

Was Grouchy's reaction to Gérard's proposal fatal for the Bonapartist cause? Houssaye was scarcely able to conceal his contempt for Grouchy as an independent commander and distrusted him as a witness to events – and indeed Grouchy's later presentation of his evidence and silent adaptations (and even garbling) of it is as frustrating as it is depressing. Houssaye rejected Grouchy's argument. But Clausewitz was in no doubt that Gérard was wrong:

> To demand of Marshal Grouchy that he should have taken no further notice of Blücher, but instead should have marched to where another part of the army was fighting a battle against a different enemy, would have been contrary to all theory and experience. That General Gérard actually gave this advice at noon on the 18th at Sart-à-Walhain proves only that he who does not bear the responsibility for a decision should not be too emphatic in formulating it.[10]

On the larger question there is much to be said for Grouard's view that only if Grouchy had marched to join Napoleon *at 4 or 5 a.m.* might his appearance have transformed the battle. That, however, would have depended upon Napoleon issuing a positive order after receiving Grouchy's evening message of the 17th and after his own overnight reconnaissance – say, at 2 a.m. But at that time the Emperor still dismissed any danger from the Prussians. Grouard considered that by the time near noon when Gérard had proposed to march to the sound of the guns it was too late to save Napoleon from actual defeat. He then interestingly speculated that if Grouchy at noon had sent Vandamme and the cavalry after Pirch's II Corps they could have complicated the Prussians' attack. But he then continued by suggesting that Gérard could have moved to Napoleon's right flank (although Grouard did not consider the equal possibility that Gérard might have been entangled by the Prussians). With evening coming on, with Wellington's force too exhausted for a pursuit, and with Gérard's personal bravery and gifts of leadership and his *4e Corps* still unshaken, 'Gérard could have served as a rallying point for the French army in stopping Blücher's pursuit. By that action the French army could have been able to make a retreat in good order. *That is all that Grouchy could have achieved in marching to the sound of guns at midday.*'

There are rather too many suppositions in that chain of possibilities. And Grouard may have thought so himself, for he did admit that Charras thought that Grouchy's force would simply have been swept away in the rout; and in that I think, Charras, bitterly anti-Bonapartist though he was, was not unreasonable.[11]

IV

What happened thereafter on the road to Wavre is of comparatively minor interest in the sum of events on 18 June 1815. It has more importance than, say, the arrangements between battalions at Hal and Tubize on that day,[12] but the result of Grouchy's operations was small indeed. It is not that there was little bravery and devotion displayed, for manifestly there was much expended. But nothing that anyone proposed at Grouchy's headquarters that morning and nothing that anyone did or did not do south of Wavre on 18 June could affect the decisive battle being fought at Mont St Jean: the time was too late and the distance too great.[13]

In one sense, Grouchy had been given a vast and ill-defined task: to follow the Prussians wherever he found them, and drive them off further; Napoleon would see to the rest. But what he had found was nothing like what he had been led to expect, and it required from him an insight and a quality of judgement in an independent command that even the better marshals did not always possess.[14] Against him was a Prussian general who was well aware of what Blücher required: that he should hold Wavre and the River Dyle against any French attack, releasing troops to the main army when he thought it safe so to do, but ensuring that if a French attack should materialise at Wavre, he should hold out *even if* (and this point was not definite) the main force could not return to his aid. And as we shall see, this task Thielemann performed very well.

Exelmans had a not inconsiderable cavalry force and his duty was to find the retreating Prussians, hamper them, and send all information to Grouchy. This he did very poorly. During the morning he had run into a retreating Prussian force, Ledebur's detachment from IV Corps, which had just abandoned Mont-St-Guibert and was heading north for Wavre. Ledebur took post in a wood, Huzelle or Lauzelle, on hilly ground just north of La Baraque. Pirch's II Corps was a couple of miles to its north, readying itself for the march to the Dyle at Wavre. Pirch ordered his main body to continue, but sent two battalions to assist Ledebur. This knot of Prussians checked Exelmans; what is surprising is that he made no real effort to get round them or unsettle them. He merely informed Grouchy of this problem impeding his move towards Wavre.

Vandamme's *3e Corps* had halted at Walhain, and then been ordered to move about a mile forward to Nil-St-Vincent. Vandamme decided not to move in the morning, and stayed quietly 6 miles from Wavre. Grouchy came to Nil-St-Vincent at about 1 p.m. and ordered the corps to start directly for Wavre in support of Exelmans. Once Vandamme and Exelmans had combined, but hours too late, it did not take long to out-manoeuvre Ledebur; and after that Vandamme continued his advance until attaining the heights south of the town where, in accordance with Grouchy's order to him, he halted to await further orders. It was by this time well into mid-afternoon.

The Polish officer Zenowicz now found Grouchy, and handed him a letter from Soult. Unfortunately we cannot tell which letter it was. Possibly it was the letter prepared 'at 10 a.m.' (but which Zenowicz insisted was given him only as battle began); possibly it was that other letter finished at 1.30 p.m. with its shocking postscript of bad news.[15] In the first case the courier could certainly confirm that the Emperor was launching a full-scale assault on Wellington but whether any such remarks affected the written sanction by imperial headquarters to continue to Wavre must be doubted: in any case it did not call upon Grouchy to turn for Mont St Jean. Grouchy may perhaps be forgiven for thinking that the Emperor was master of all the salient facts and knew his own mind.

On the basis of Soult's 10 a.m. information Grouchy could reasonably conclude that Gérard had been wrong. Certainly, on reading the letter, Grouchy continued with his morning's plan. But what if Zenowicz carried the 1.30 p.m. letter, with its urgent and beseeching postscript? Would that not have affected impending decisions?

Pajol, who had been scouting away on the right flank, now rode up to report that the Prussians seemed not to have gone in that direction. Grouchy therefore ordered him to turn west to the French left flank, cross the Dyle, and take the village of Limale (or Limal) about 2 miles south of Wavre. This was good sense, but would have made even more sense had it been ordered at dawn. The upper reaches of the Dyle were not normally a major obstacle, but there were few bridges and those not of the best, and the recent rain had put the river in spate and softened the banks and meadows. The bridge at Limale was wooden and only wide enough to take four men at a time. Nor were there other crossings nearby, for the masonry bridge at Ottignies, 10 feet wide, was nearly 2 miles upstream from Limale, and that at Moustier a little further upstream was only 3 feet wide, made of three oak beams. Getting cannon down to the river, let alone across the bridges, was highly problematic; getting large numbers of men across in a hurry was virtually impossible.

Thus belatedly did Grouchy recognise the strategic importance of attaining the Dyle's left bank.[16] What Grouchy's new order meant was that at least some of his force would be west of the river and could menace any Prussians in Wavre, a town mainly on the west bank, and could impede any Prussians who sought to take the roads from Wavre to Mont St Jean or La Belle Alliance. The remainder of his force would threaten Wavre from the other (eastern) bank of the Dyle. That he demanded no more of his subordinates than these moves suggests that by early afternoon he was still unaware of Blücher's march westwards.

To add still further to the Marshal's woes, Vandamme, meanwhile, had once again taken matters into his own hands. Despite Grouchy's demand that he await further orders he decided to win independent glory for himself and his men by attacking the eastern suburbs of Wavre with Habert's *10e Division*, and virtually without a preliminary bombardment.

The small town (then of 5,000 inhabitants) was built mainly on the slopes above the left bank of the Dyle, but with outskirts on the flatter ground east of the river, linked by one ordinary stone bridge and one smaller one further up. Just beyond it downstream lay Basse-Wavre with a crossing; just upstream of Wavre stood Bierges village with a watermill and crossing: these two places Basse-Wavre and Bierges formed the flank defences of the town. Aerts described the position in these terms:

> A fordless river flowing through marshy meadows; two stone bridges, the larger barricaded, to be attacked under enfilading cannon-fire, two other bridges destroyed, steep slopes, roads perpendicular to the river, sharpshooters well dug in, well placed reserves: such was the Prussian position at Wavre.[17]

As we saw earlier, Blücher's intention was that Thielemann's III Corps should stay in position until it was clear that the French were not approaching in force; then to follow the three other corps to the Lasne valley. By mid-afternoon Thielemann had begun to move, leaving two battalions deployed in defence of the eastern suburb, while the remainder of the corps began to march. Then Vandamme's troops came in sight on the eastern heights, very probably intending to seize the town. Thielemann sent a warning to Blücher that he might not be able to check the French, but meanwhile the greatest part of III Corps was ordered back to the defence: the artillery on the heights, the cavalry well back, sharpshooters lining the entire river bank, the 11th and 12th Brigades between Bierges and the lower town, and the 10th in rear. The bridges were barricaded as far as possible with the means available, and the smaller ones damaged. Thielemann's 9th Brigade (Borcke) had dropped two battalions (and then a third) and some cavalry to hold the central sector (the infantry were II and III/30th and III/1st Kurmark Landwehr, all under Colonel Zeppelin[18]), but for some reason Borcke continued with the remainder of his force to Chapelle-St-Lambert, possibly because of confusion or non-receipt of orders. In all, 17,000 men held the town, with 34 guns. And fortunately a detachment from I Corps (1,200 men under Colonel Stengel) had not yet left the Dyle, did not follow the rest of Ziethen's force, and took post upstream from Wavre at Limale. It is not clear whether, or to what degree, authority over Stengel's detachment was vested in Thielemann.

Vandamme at Wavre cannot have had any real conception of the position he was about to attack. The attackers charged into the eastern suburb but were totally checked when they tried to rush the main bridge. The divisional commander Habert himself was wounded and also lost some 600 men in a few minutes, but their ability to withdraw was hampered by the raking fire of Prussian cannon, so that the French found themselves almost trapped in the streets. Those who wrote of this afternoon's action were all fairly critical of the generalship, and for that Vandamme must bear the largest share of blame. But it placed Grouchy in a further difficulty: unless he was to abandon Habert's force to its fate, he had been committed by Vandamme's action to a full-scale battle for the town. Grouchy therefore decided on a pincer movement on Wavre: he sent troops of another of Vandamme's formations, *8e Division*, to cross the river upstream at Bierges and threaten Wavre from the west, while the cavalry of Exelmans was to do the same downstream of the town from the east bank.

This messy and muddled battle had fettered Grouchy just at the moment that Soult's letter of 1 p.m. and its urgent postscript came into his hands.[19]

At midday Grouchy had rejected Gérard's proposal to divide his little army. Now he did just that. Although he still ordered Vandamme and Exelmans to use their entire strength to take Wavre, he aimed to cross to the left bank of the Dyle with the rest. He sent to Pajol to speed his march from Tourinnes (6 miles from the river) to Limale. He rode to Gérard, at La Baraque (Louvain-la-Neuve) well south of Wavre, where the *12e* and *13e Divisions* still were (Hulot's *14e* was already almost at Wavre), and ordered his corps to Limale likewise. His right and left wings would be fighting for the river crossings at Limale and at Wavre (and nearby Bierges), 2 miles apart from each other. For reasons that are as inexplicable as the evidence is contradictory, the two rear divisions continued to Wavre. Matters were going ill at the Bierges crossing, and the leading generals were in open disagreement on the best solution. Grouchy and Gérard arrived to stimulate the troops to another effort at turning the Prussian defence, when Gérard was hit in the

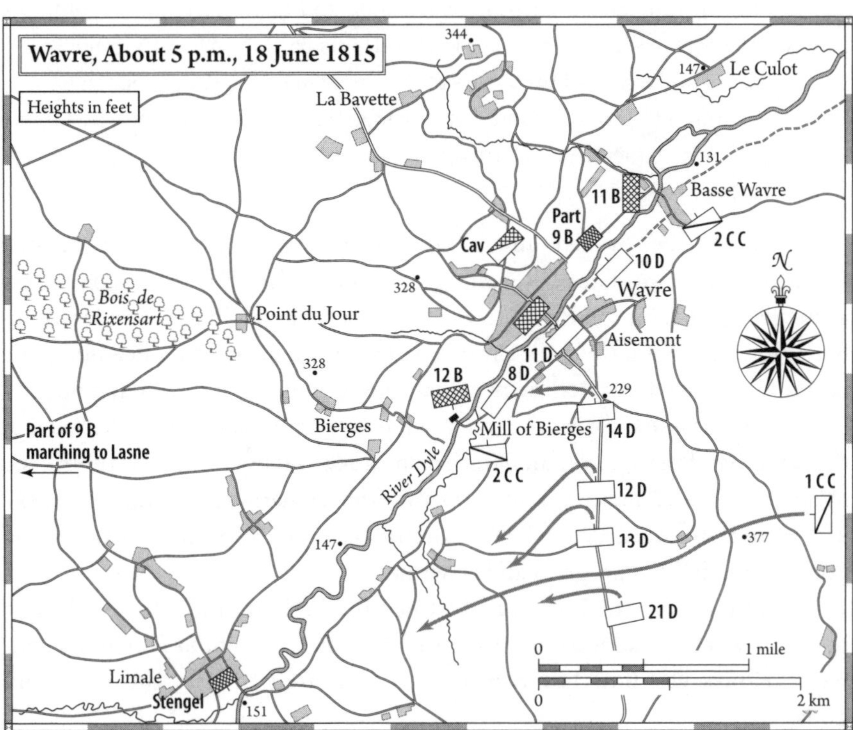

chest and borne away for treatment, and his replacement openly rejected Grouchy's plan of attack.

The Marshal then burst out, whether in rage or agony nobody can say, 'If a man cannot make himself obeyed, then it only remains to get himself killed!' It is a telling sign when tough and experienced leaders reach the point of challenging and then defying their commander's intentions, for it means either a dangerous mood of insubordination, a breakdown of trust, proof that the general's plan has become unrealistic, or sheer hopeless desperation on the commander's part.[20]

Grouchy now took the two rear divisions of *4e Corps* and led them to Limale.

V

By the time night had fallen the situation was this. Vandamme had continued to throw troops at the Wavre defences, but in vain. The suburb repeatedly changed hands as one attack went in after another. When the fighting died down the Prussians still held the town after a battle that had lasted as long as Ligny. As Aerts wrote in praise of Zeppelin's force:

> In the 1815 campaign the names of Waterloo and Ligny have thrown into shadow that of Wavre. Yet it was a long and bitter battle, and this seven-hour battle is not the least of the glories of the Prussian infantry. It is enough to cite among all these forces four young battalions, the II and III/30th, I/4th Kurmark and the III/1st Kurmark, commanded respectively by Majors Beaufort, Sprenger, Grolman and Bornstädt.[21]

Upstream the French attack on the narrow bridge at Limale had succeeded. This was Grouchy's only real success of the day, and in one sense a surprising one, for the Prussian commander Colonel Stengel had left it unbarricaded and intact. Pajol's cavalry had won the bridge by a headlong and amazingly bold charge, following which they cut up the infantry defenders.[22] The attackers were soon reinforced by infantry, led by Teste's *21e Division*, but the remains of the 1,200-man detachment under Stengel was now reinforced by part of Thielemann's 12th Brigade (the remainder holding Bierges). The Prussians counter-attacked in the dusk, found the unfamiliar ground difficult, made little progress and so withdrew.

Thus by 11 p.m. the French had gained the high ground and could listen in the darkness for sounds to westward. 'The road to Mont St Jean was open,' wrote Houssaye, 'but they had long since ceased to hear the Emperor's guns.'[23]

Chapter 42

The Fourth Act

La Haye Sainte Falls, The Centre Begins to Crumble

I

NEY'S CAVALRY ATTACKS WERE SPECTACULAR but did not make the infantry collapse. What they did achieve was the bunching of infantry in squares that Napoleon's artillery could scythe through as soon as the cavalry drew back. Had the French really attended to the coordination of all three arms an advantage might have been gained, for while the cavalry swung around the Allied squares the British guns stood silent and unprotected, and thus any advancing French infantry would have been spared. Yet the infantry seemed forgotten. Two of Reille's divisions were exhausted, but there remained unemployed one brigade of Foy's *9e Division* and both brigades of Bachelu's *5e Division,* standing quietly close to the great road. They chafed at being forgotten. Then Ney, enraged at another repulse, sent them up the slope to do what his horsemen had failed to do.

But time had been wasted. Wellington had looked to Clinton's 2nd Division on his western wing, and had called eastwards both Du Plat's 1st KGL Brigade and Adam's 3rd British Brigade. They took over the front line hitherto held by the Brunswickers, who were now showing symptoms of uncertainty. He also brought up two more 9-pounder batteries, Sinclair's from 6th Division and Mercer's G Troop from the centre rear. Thus when the French infantry, perhaps 5,000 strong came up in columns the Allied line had been strengthened. Foy, writing five days later, described the shattering outcome:

> While the French cavalry undertook this long and terrible charge, the fire of our artillery was already slackening and our infantry remained still. When the cavalry had come back and the English artillery, which had been silent for half an hour, had recommenced firing, orders were given to the divisions

> of Bachelu and Foy to scale the plateau in the face of the squares that had moved forward during the cavalry charge and had not fallen back. The attack was mounted in column by echelons of regiments, Bachelu forming the more advanced echelons, I holding to the hedge to my left, with a battalion of skirmishers to my front. When close to the English we received a very intense fire of musketry and canister-shot. It was a hail of death. The enemy squares' first ranks were kneeling and presented a hedge of bayonets. The columns of the *1re* [*sic,* read *5e*] *Division* were the first to take flight and this spread to my columns. At this moment I was wounded: my right upper humerus was crossed by a ball from above to below, but the bone was untouched. On being hit, I thought it was only a contusion and I remained on the field. Everyone was fleeing. I rallied the debris of my division in the hollow adjacent to Hougoumont wood. We were not followed; our cavalry continued to hold the plateau and the enemy cavalry dared not move. The enemy fire was so intense and so hard that it hit our soldiers even down in the hollows.[1]

So conclusive a summing up of the attack speaks for itself. The casualties of the three brigades were between 1,000 and 1,500 men, a ruinous outcome at a time when infantry shortages were really critical. But there is one small point in Foy's statement that is relevant to the complex argument over which formation the *Moyenne Garde* adopted when attacking the Mont St Jean ridge as the day waned (Chapter 44). For Foy wrote of the attack being 'mounted in column by echelons of regiments', and Bachelu's chief staff officer likewise wrote that they were 'formed in divisional column'. The ground conditions at this time were roughly as they would be an hour or so later, the troops were fresh, the commanders competent. And that was the formation Foy and Bachelu adopted.[2]

British cavalry were not very effective in trying to drive the French cavalry off the slopes. The remnants of Lord Edward Somerset's Household Brigade made little impression, and the conflicts swung back and forth. Seeing the difficulties Uxbridge called on the relatively intact Netherlands Heavy Brigade to assist. There is general acceptance that Trip's Netherlands carabiniers would not fight, but disagreement on *why* they would not. Certainly, instead of helping, these troops rode back through the KGL cavalry, unsettling them in the process, and then stayed in reserve.[3] What is not in dispute is that when Uxbridge turned to the Cumberland Hussars, a regiment of gentlemen volunteers from Hanover, they could not stand the fire and fled, upsetting those in their path, and continuing on to Brussels. The senior cavalry commanders thus had to exercise all their powers of leadership in holding their men and stopping the contagion of fear from spreading: indeed, when advised to draw back, Lord Edward refused on the grounds that if he moved his own men the Dutch cavalry now in reserve would immediately disappear. Thus had matters gone just west of the Mont St Jean crossroads.

Meanwhile the French high command had somewhat belatedly recognised the vital importance of the farm of La Haye Sainte to the security of Wellington's position.

II

During the afternoon the farm garrison had been reinforced by two companies of riflemen from the 1st Light Battalion, KGL, and these 170 or so men were deployed to the defence of the garden on the north side, while Baring's original garrison held the farm buildings. Away towards their left shoulder the 1/95th again held the sandpit, the two positions being mutually supporting. Then a company of the 1st Line Battalion, KGL, was sent to the farm, and subsequently two flank companies of the Nassau Regiment Nr. 1, both units with muskets and not rifles, so that henceforth two sorts of ammunition were required. But by now the reserves of ammunition were seriously depleted and the reinforcements (170 riflemen and 100 musketeers) brought in only 60 rounds per man for themselves.

Mark Adkin is the author who has given most thought to the problem, and he concludes that as the ammunition lasted until about 6 p.m. the garrison rate of fire must have averaged under 150 shots per minute by a force comprising around 500 men. Given the weight of attack throughout the afternoon that is quite a low rate of fire. He argues that the lack of defensive preparation must have played a part, for had there been more loopholes and fire-steps the rate would have been much higher, the ammunition would have run out sooner, and the farm could therefore have fallen sooner than it did. But this is a secondary factor. Adkin emphasises that 'What Baring needed was not a few soldiers with stuffed pouches but full casks, which in turn meant an ammunition wagon such as the one delivered to Hougoumont.' For an explanation he turns to Shaw Kennedy, AQMG to the 3rd Division (of which Baring's men of course formed a part).[4]

> Much has been said of Baring's having sent repeatedly for ammunition, and that none was sent to him. This matter had certainly been grossly mismanaged. The arrangement for the brigades getting their spare ammunition was, that each brigade should communicate with the guard

> over the ammunition, and order forward what was wanted. How the brigade [Ompteda's 2nd KGL Brigade] failed to do this has not been explained, as so many of its superior officers fell in the action. Baring could not account for it, which I know from our having slept together on the ground close to the Wellington Tree on the night after the action, when he mentioned his having sent more than once for a supply of ammunition and his having received no answer. The unexplained want of ammunition by Baring's battalion is placed in an extraordinary view when it is considered that the battle of Waterloo lasted eight hours and a half, and that all three brigades [C. Halkett, Ompteda, Kielmansegge] of the division got the ammunition they required, with the exception of this one battalion. The simple fact of Baring's application for spare ammunition having been made by him late in the day, when, owing to the enemy's position, there could be no certainty of its being got into the place, proves an extraordinary oversight. The spare ammunition should have been sent for early in the morning. What were 60 rounds per man for the defence of such a post?[5]

Shaw Kennedy might have put it even more strongly. La Haye Sainte was an outpost far beyond and below the main position. Once battle began, enemy fire was bound to make communication difficult and movement of carts and wagons almost impossible. The upper slope was totally open. If the post was to be held at all costs and for all the hours till darkness would permit re-supply, then a massive stock of ammunition should have been delivered before battle commenced: after that it would be too late. This was not done.

From Baring's own account[6] it is plain that it was not until the first great attack had been beaten off – and the garrison had been joined by Klencke's Hanoverians and the men from the 1st Light KGL – that he realised that *more than half his ammunition* had been expended. He immediately sent an officer for new ammunition, 'which was promised'. An hour later he sent another officer as nothing had arrived. Once the 5th Line Battalion, KGL, had come, he sent a third officer on the same quest. Then the Nassauers came. Further fighting reduced the stocks of cartridges: 'there was not more than three to four each', so a fourth officer was sent, equally without result. No request for rifle ammunition seems to have been made to the 1/95th in the sandpit nearby, although they used the same rifle as the KGL light infantry.

Either Baring had over-estimated his initial stocks or he had not ordered sufficient before action began, but what is also extraordinary is that none of Ompteda's or Alten's staff visited Baring's post during the afternoon and that nobody up on the summit thought that he might be in need of re-supply. The four messengers must have seen someone in authority, but it would seem that they left the impression that reinforcements of men with pouches would be sufficient to ensure the garrison's safety. It may be that an ammunition wagon was overturned in the flight of the Cumberland Hussars, but then why was no replacement ordered up? But it does look as though the intensity of enemy fire would have made any approach by horse and wagon almost impossible, and the existence of the upper *abatis* blocking the higher part of the road near the sandpit would have been a further obstacle. The responsibility for this dangerous state of affairs must rest primarily with Baring, but his immediate superior Ompteda and 3rd Division's staff (including Shaw) have their share as well.[7]

From late afternoon, therefore, the plight of La Haye Sainte had become desperate, the defence relying on bayonet and physical blows rather than rifle- and musket-fire to stop the French breaking in. Unfortunately, the great door of the barn had been smashed and burnt by the soaked and chilled garrison during the previous night – something that Baring either had not noticed in time or had failed to stop. Only a breastwork of French corpses and some bits of farm equipment now checked entry there. The other doors were either gone or terribly damaged, and parts of the buildings had been set on fire, adding to the confusion. Baring's initiative in using camp kettles to throw water on the flames proved successful, but any fresh and determined attack could scarcely fail.

Ney had hitherto thrown waves of infantry against the position without success, relying on what units he could muster from Reille's and d'Erlon's corps, whereas a concentrated blasting from artillery might have been more effective in smashing the defence. There came a few minutes of relief when the great cavalry charges began and for a while the little post seemed almost forgotten as the horsemen passed up and down the long slope. Then, towards 6 o'clock, the final infantry assault formed up, Ney deploying an entire elite light infantry regiment from Donzelot's *2e Division* as well as a brigade from Durutte's *4e Division*, drawn from the eastern flank, with the engineer company crouched along the road tasked to blast away the last defences.

This force of some 2,000 men encircled three sides of the defences, fired in through the open doorways, scrambled up onto the roofs and poured down a fire on the virtually ammunition-less KGL inside the courtyard; the engineers got past the lower *abatis* and blew in the gate to the road. Baring pulled his men back through the house and into the northern garden.

The Prince of Orange on the crest had seen French skirmishers working their way up the western edge of the farm as though trying to enter the northern garden. He ordered into line two battalions of Ompteda's KGL Brigade, the 5th Line on the right and the 8th Line on the left, to attack with the bayonet and drive the French away. They charged forward in line, the 8th somewhat in advance, but at that moment a force of *cuirassiers* swept down on their flank and the 8th was mercilessly rolled up and its right companies virtually cut to pieces, its colonel killed, and its King's colour lost to the enemy (though retrieved later in the day). The 5th Line was more fortunate, as the French horsemen were distracted by a charge of Edward Somerset's heavies that drove them away, allowing time for the battalion to form square, apparently with Ompteda in the square with them. The two battalions, one of them a mere remnant, then went back and took position behind the crest. It was an instance of the Prince's precipitancy and rashness that was not lost on their brigadier, Colonel Ompteda.

The French now had taken the farm, but it had taken many hours, and the little garrison had not been exterminated during its long and gallant defence. The captors were so preoccupied with clearing the buildings of defenders that they seem not to have bothered with the retreating little group of Baring's men as they made their way back to the rest of Alten's division. That morning the 2nd Light Battalion, KGL, had mustered 33 officers and 398 other ranks; their casualties on 18 June were 16 officers and 195 other ranks killed, wounded, and missing (including men like Wheatley, who was made captive but then escaped, and re-joined some days later). We do not have casualty figures for the men of the other units that served with him, as they went back to their parent units and their figures were merged in the whole. But Gareth Glover after considerable research concludes that of 871 soldiers who during the day comprised the garrison, up to 323 men became casualties, or nearly 37 per cent, which serves to correct the catastrophic impression left by Baring's remark that of his own battalion 'only 42 remained effective' by the battle's end.[8]

This was the first great success won by the French army on this day, and it posed a terrible threat to the centre of Wellington's position. But it had come late and at enormous cost through poor leadership. Coordinated tactics employing in a flexible combination the artillery, infantry, and cavalry might have attained this result much earlier and at a lesser cost. By this time Napoleon's gunners were beginning to worry about ammunition stocks; the infantry of both *1er* and *2e Corps* had been horribly mauled on both sides of the Charleroi road, so that Reille's men were tired and dispirited and d'Erlon's scarcely fit to launch a second great attack; and the magnificent cavalry had been decimated in heroic but ineffective sacrifice. Houssaye described the scene in a brilliant few sentences, listing the cavalry commanders hit:

> The atmosphere was heavy; one could scarcely breathe: 'the air resembling that issuing from an oven' [*Mercer's phrase*]. General Donop was wounded,

> General Delort was wounded, General Lhéritier was wounded, General Guyot was wounded, General Roussel d'Hurbal was wounded. Edouard de Colbert charged arm in sling. Likewise wounded were Generals Blancard, Dubois, Farine, Guiton, Picquet, Travers, Watier. Marshal Ney, his third horse killed under him, was on his feet, alone, near an abandoned battery, furiously beating with the flat of his sword the bronze muzzle of an English cannon. The entire battlefield was strewn with non-combatants, dismounted *cuirassiers* trudging heavily under the weight of their armour towards the valley floor, the wounded crawling out of the piles of dead, riderless horses galloping madly under the lash of bullets whistling about their ears.[9]

The comments of those who had ridden in these brave and desperate charges varied from disbelief at the folly of it, to a growing sense of despair as much of this magnificent arm was shattered. We shall never know whether the great mass could have recovered its *élan* sufficiently to launch a really killing pursuit if the *Garde* had captured the ridge in the early evening: a harrying pursuit as the final stage in rendering Wellington's army incapable of fighting on the morrow. I suspect that its effectiveness had been too badly damaged. Some units however, still retained their spirit, as we shall soon see.

III

Ney now sought to improve on success in the centre. Earlier, Ney had said to de Salle, commanding *1er Corps* artillery, 'Have you ever seen a battle like this? What a slaughter!' but still had invited the gunner to dine in Brussels that evening. It was probably at this moment that he sent a message to Napoleon calling for more troops, only to receive the famous reply: 'Where do you expect me to find them? Do you expect me to make them?' Heymès said that this was spoken in front of Jerome and Drouot, and was repeated in those precise words to the Marshal. The penalty for the late start, the wasteful misuse of troops and the lack of combination was being exacted.[10]

And so the combat continued in a scrappy and poorly coordinated way. On the Allied side retaining the crossroads had become ever more essential. When Lambert's brigade engaged in the afternoon (see Chapter 39, Section VI) the 1/27th Foot (Inniskillings), 750 all ranks, had been placed in square blocking the way. It shared to the full the fate of Wellington's squares that day, condemned to endure the blast of artillery: at 7 p.m. Kincaid saw that 'the twenty-seventh regiment were lying literally dead, in square'; the historian

Fortescue added that, 'pent up in square by the crossroads above La Haye Sainte, [it] was cruelly punished without an opportunity of firing a shot in reply'. Of the officers, 71 per cent fell dead or wounded, and of the other ranks 63 per cent were casualties.[11]

Close by, an officer of the Rocket Troop dashed forward from the crossroads to fire his rockets down the road against the French pushing past the east front of the farm. He was hit, but his sergeant coolly fixed the rocket staves in the bushes on the roadside and fired them along the ground to the surprise and horror of the enemy.[12]

Meanwhile French sharpshooters in the farm's north garden were firing on the British riflemen at the sandpit and at Kempt's men further up the slope. Ney had ordered forward a horse battery to drive away the 1/95th from the sandpit and knoll as a prelude to a further thrust at the crest. Although the gunners were quickly picked off, more French guns came up and soon won the fire-fight, so that Kempt's brigade was subject to a galling and costly bombardment. A French column moved forward against the sector to the west of the crossroads: the wedge inserted into Wellington's front was going deeper and might soon create a sufficient gap.

Alten decided to meet this attack and at the same time try to retake the farm. He sent an order to Colonel Ompteda to lead his 5th Line KGL down the slope. Ompteda could see some *cuirassiers* not far off, and pointed out the danger of being yet again caught by them in the open; he asked Alten to reconsider. This was, of course, a situation not unlike that facing Klencke a few hours earlier, when Alten had under-performed as a senior commander. Orange intervened, claiming that the horsemen were Dutch. When he was shown to be wrong, he displayed again that tactical incompetence blended with royal self-importance that had twice already cost his troops so dear. This young man – who less than two years earlier had been a not very diligent ADC – ignored the dithering Alten and gave a direct order to advance in line: 'I must still repeat my order to attack in line with the bayonet, and I will listen to no further arguments.'

Ompteda mounted, asked someone to protect his two nephews who were with the battalion, and rode in front of his men, as they marched in line towards La Haye Sainte. The French infantry stood immobile in astonishment and without firing as Ompteda rode up to them, and only when he tried to push into their ranks did they fire point-blank and kill him. The *cuirassiers* immediately charged and cut up the battalion: 12 officers, 12 sergeants, 1 drummer and 128 men fell, and the battalion's King's colour was one of the *cuirassiers'* trophies. What Alten said in congratulation to the Prince, and the Prince to him, is not known.[13] The situation could not be righted now, though

Dörnberg's 1st and 2nd Light Dragoons, KGL, dashed forward and drove away the French horsemen.

The indefatigable French sharpshooters continued their harassment; the French artillery continued to tear gaps in the squares. There was no sign of the Prussians. All Wellington could physically do was to bring in units from the flanks and rear, to encourage the men to stand firm, to direct a counter-attack at an opportune moment. And he did one thing more: he gave to officers and men alike the impression of unyielding calm control, while he waited – and waited. For the men, the situation was dire.

'The French artillerymen had now brought us so completely within range that if we had continued much longer in this exposed situation I should probably not have lived to tell my tale,' said Ensign Keppel of the 14th Foot. Kincaid of the 1/95th wrote: 'I had never yet heard of a battle in which everybody was killed; but this seemed likely to be an exception, as all were going by turns.' Sergeant Lawrence of the 40th remembered that 'the men in their tired state were beginning to despair, but the officers cheered them on continually throughout the day with the cry of "Keep your ground, my men!" It is a mystery to me how it was accomplished, for at last so few were left that there were scarcely enough to form square.' The officers certainly earned this praise: Ensign Leeke of the 1/52nd saw four men in square smashed by a cannonball: 'the rear man made a considerable outcry on being wounded, but on one of the officers saying kindly to him, "O man, don't make a noise," he instantly recollected himself, and was quiet.' The devotion to duty of the men was exceeded only by that of the NCOs and officers.[14]

IV

Sir Andrew Barnard of the 1/95th was once asked if he had had any fear of the outcome, and his reply said it all: 'Oh no, except for the Duke. We had a notion that while he was there nothing could go wrong.'[15]

Wellington spent the hours continually riding up and down his line, ignoring the tempest of bullets and shells, but always seeming to be at the critical place at the moment of danger. His silent and apparently imperturb-able presence, his short decided orders delivered in a cool clear tone, gave courage to the desperately tried soldiers. Walter Scott, who arrived in Paris on 14 August 1815 and met many officers and men, wrote of their testimony: 'There was scarcely a square but he visited in person, encouraging the men by his presence, and the officers by his direction. Many of his short phrases are repeated by them as if they were possessed of talismanic effect.' Ensign Macready of the 30th Foot recalled that Wellington was:

> coolness personified. As he crossed the rear face of our square a shell fell among our grenadiers, and he checked his horse to see its effect. Some men were blown to pieces by the explosion, and he merely stirred the reins of his charger, apparently as little concerned at their fate as at his own danger. No leader ever possessed so fully the confidence of his soldiery, 'but none did love him' – whenever he appeared, a murmur of 'Silence, stand to your front, here's the Duke' was heard through the column and then all was steady as on parade.

Macready added that late in the evening Colin Halkett asked for some reinforcement, and Wellington replied simply, 'It is impossible, Halkett,' whereupon Halkett replied 'If so, sir, you may depend on the brigade to a man!' Words were sparing, 'Hard pounding, this, gentlemen; let's see who will pound longest!' was a long speech for him. Ensign Gronow, thought him 'perfectly composed, but looked very thoughtful and pale'. That he now expected the Prussians was evident, for as Ney's horsemen roved among the squares, Gronow noted that the Duke,

> sat unmoved, mounted on his favourite charger. I recollect his asking Colonel [James] Stanhope what o'clock it was, upon which Stanhope took out his watch, and said it was twenty minutes past four. The Duke replied, 'The battle is mine; and if the Prussians arrive soon, there will be an end of the war.'

But the Prussians did not appear and the battle was still not won.[16]

On Wellington's left wing the Nassauers under Saxe-Weimar had been gradually winkled from their farm buildings at Smohain and La Haye by Durutte's men, but had not been expelled as yet from Papelotte or from all of Frischermont. East of the crossroads the line held despite the constant bombardment; on the right wing Hougoumont held out, and was backed by Du Plat's and Hugh Halkett's brigades, while at about 4 p.m. there arrived from Braine l'Alleud the resolute Chassé (*Général Baïonnette*) and his 3rd Netherlands Division, whom Captain Mercer remembered as two dense columns 'pushing forward at a quick pace, crossing the fields, shouting, yelling, and singing'.[17] They were placed by Wellington in support of Maitland's brigade of the 1st Guards. In the centre he stretched his Household Brigade as a thin line in support of Kielmansegge's battered Hanoverians and the relics of Ompteda's men.

Kincaid had noted with 'anxiety' that by the end of the afternoon, 'our division, which had stood upwards of five thousand men at the commencement of the battle, had gradually dwindled down into a solitary line of skirmishers'. This was when he noted the 27th dead in square. Shaw Kennedy did not exaggerate when he described the crumbling centre in a classic passage:

> La Haye Sainte was in the hands of the enemy; also the knoll on the opposite side of the road; also the garden and ground on the Anglo-Allied side of it; Ompteda's brigade was nearly annihilated, and Kielmansegge's so thinned that these two brigades could not hold their position. That part of the field of battle, therefore, which was between [Colin] Halkett's left and Kempt's right, was unprotected; and being the very centre of the Duke's line of battle, was consequently that point above all others which the enemy wished to gain. The danger was imminent; and at no other period of the action was the result so precarious as at this moment. Most fortunately Napoleon did not support the advantage his troops had gained at this point, by bringing forward his reserve; proving that he did not exert that activity and personal energy in superintending and conforming to the progress of the action, which he ought to have done.
>
> The Duke of Wellington stood at this moment on the left of the Nivelles road, behind the left of Maitland's brigade of Guards. The Prince of Orange, Count Alten, and so many officers of the 3rd Division, had, before this event happened, been killed, or wounded and obliged to leave the field, that I did not then know, nor do I now know, who was, at the moment I allude to, senior officer of the division on the field. I therefore, as the staff officer present, galloped direct to the Duke and informed him that his line was open for the whole space between Halkett's and Kempt's brigades. This very startling information he received with a degree of coolness, and replied to in an instant with such precision and energy, as to prove the most complete self-possession; and left on my mind the impressions that his Grace's mind remained perfectly calm during every phase, however serious, of the action; that he felt confident of his own powers of being able to guide the storm which raged around him; and from the determined manner in which he then spoke, it was evident that he had resolved to defend to the last extremity every inch of the position which he then held. His Grace's answer to my representation was in the following words, or very nearly so: 'I shall order the Brunswick troops to the spot, and other troops besides; go you and get all the German troops of the Division to the spot that you can, and all the guns you can find.'
>
> Of such gravity did Wellington consider this great gap in the very centre of his line of battle, that he not only ordered the Brunswick troops there, but put himself at their head; and it was even then with the greatest difficulty

> that the ground could be held. But Count Kielmansegge soon led back his gallant Germans to the spot; the Brunswickers held their ground supported by part of the Nassau force; and ultimately Vivian's brigade of cavalry supported these troops; and the artillery officers responded to the utmost of their available means in strengthening this most vulnerable and dangerous part of the position.[18]

V

Shaw Kennedy's reference to Vivian's 6th Cavalry Brigade brings the story to another great moment of decision. Who inspired it, and who decided on that movement from the eastern wing to the centre, has been disputed, for both Müffling and Vivian claimed the credit, although there are yet other possibilities.

Hitherto the cavalry of Vandeleur and Vivian had stood watching the eastern slopes and the route to Ohain. Uxbridge had been given full control over all the cavalry, and his ADC Thornhill had been sent in the morning to all the cavalry brigade commanders authorising them verbally that, under certain limitations, they could act according to their discretion.[19] Vivian certainly used this discretion when the Union Brigade was in difficulties, and even Vandeleur eventually did so once he saw the massacre of the heavy cavalry taking place. So that it is odd that Müffling later claimed that he asked them to act in the Union Brigade crisis and that they had refused, as Wellington insisted on absolute obedience to his instructions (which in this case would have prescribed their standing firm on the left wing): and Müffling added that when later he mentioned this to the Duke, the Duke replied that the two generals were perfectly correct, that even a successful intervention, if unauthorised, would have brought them to a court-martial.[20] Given Uxbridge's and Thornhill's evidence and Vivian's actions, it seems on balance that Müffling's memory was not quite accurate on that occasion. And this conflict of evidence arises again in the next crisis in the late afternoon.

Just as La Haye Sainte fell, British officers saw in the distance signs of the Prussian advance. But they could also see Durutte's *4e Division* making yet another determined attempt to capture Papelotte and thereby cut off any Prussian approach routes to Wellington's eastern wing. The French attack was under way and there could be no expectation of physical intervention by Blücher's forces for perhaps another hour or so; if Durutte succeeded, another wedge would be in place to keep the Allies apart. Was it better for Wellington's cavalry on the eastern ridge to assist in the defence of Papelotte, or to turn west and shore up the centre? It was a choice between two dangers, and the decision could not wait. Whether or not Saxe-Weimar could hold on, whether the Prussians could exert pressure and distract the French on the eastern flank, the crisis in the centre was so great and so immediate that the British cavalry moved to the Charleroi road to close the gap.[21]

Who took this decision? In recounting this crisis and the decision, Müffling's account seems in contradiction to what he had previously said concerning the earlier occasion. For at this later crisis he 'begged' Vandeleur and Vivian to march to the distressed centre as the Prussians would henceforth cover the left wing, and *in accordance with the Prussian liaison officer's suggestion* 'these regiments marched off'. Müffling seems to imply that in sending him to the left wing, the Duke expected and authorised him to do more than observe and liaise, that Wellington also delegated to him some command function, that Müffling's *plea* somehow 'authorised' the move.[22]

What should one make of this? 'Begging' is surely the significant word. Wellington had delegated command of all the cavalry to Lieutenant-General Lord Uxbridge who was actively riding along the line throughout the day. *Ad hoc* 'authority' suddenly given to a Prussian major-general would have caused confusion since Müffling had no command status in a British army. I do not think it was Müffling who inspired the move.

Vivian's account is clear enough. He repeated it several times. On 19 June 1815 he wrote that 'towards the end of the battle, the whole of the cavalry on the right being almost annihilated, I heard that they were in want of us, and the Prussians arriving on my left, I trotted along the rear of our line to the right and formed in the rear of our infantry where there was the most tremendous fire of round, grape and musketry that I ever experienced.' On 23 June he wrote to another person, 'about 6 o'clock I learnt that the cavalry in the centre had suffered dreadfully, and the Prussians about that time having formed to my left, I took upon myself to move off from our left, and halted directly to the centre of our line,' adding (to his wife), 'I arrived in the rear of the infantry just at the time that several small squares of foreign troops were giving way . . . halted two of them and gave them confidence.' Much later, in 1839, he told Siborne that when

> there could be no longer any apprehension of our left being turned, and hearing from Colonel Delancey Barclay [1st Guards and an AAG under General Barnes] that cavalry were wanted in the centre, I proposed to Sir O Vandeleur to move with his brigade and mine – he was the senior officer [much senior, by three years' promotion and 208 places], although we acted separately – towards the centre where we might be of service. Sir

> O V objected to moving without orders and I then put my own brigade in motion and passed along the rear of Sir O V's Brigade, and soon after having commenced my march I met Lord Anglesey who was much pleased at what I had done and, sending orders to Vandeleur to follow, proceeded to accompany my brigade towards the centre.[23]

This evidence seems convincing enough: one of Barnes's officers had alerted Vivian to the need for action. However, it is qualified, perhaps challenged, by two other witnesses from Lord Uxbridge's own staff, and by a ducal note. Lord Greenock, Uxbridge's AQMG, said that it was his chief, aware of the French successes, who 'gave orders for the better concentration of his corps by removing brigades [*note the plural*] from the left of La Haye Sainte towards the right of the position, as soon as their presence in that quarter became no longer necessary in consequence of the arrival of the Prussians on that flank', adding that Vivian was the best guide for what happened 'subsequently'. Without mentioning Vandeleur's brigade, Uxbridge's ADC Seymour (whose later exploit in Paris was immortalised by 'Captain Trevanion of the 43rd Foot' in Charles Lever's *Harry Lorrequer*) wrote that 'when delivering the order for Sir Hussey Vivian's Brigade to move towards the centre, we saw the advance of the Prussians'. Thus the claim for Uxbridge.[24]

But there is more. There exists a pencil note on a strip of prepared skin written by Wellington that must have been sent to Uxbridge at some time in mid-afternoon. It proposed the movement of cavalry from the left wing to the centre. It made no reference to Saxe-Weimar, and it made no reference to the Prussians; they were not part of the consideration. The Duke was intent upon the weak point reported to him by Shaw. Whether it was the spur to which Uxbridge reacted, or whether Uxbridge acted without it we shall never know, but it does show that several commanders superior to Vivian were intending that most of the light cavalry should move west. It reads:

> We ought to have more of the Cavalry between the two high Roads. That is to say, three Brigades at least, besides the Brigade in observation on the Right & besides the Belgian Cavalry & the D of Cumberland's Hussars. One heavy & one light brigade might remain on the left.[25]

Whether the Adjutant-General's man or the cavalry commander's man reached Vivian first we cannot say, but (if we choose to consider the Duke's note as a recommendation and not an order) it seems clear that Uxbridge saw the need and issued orders, certainly to Vivian and possibly to Vandeleur. Whether Vivian acted before receiving the orders will probably always remain in question, and Uxbridge's pleasure at what Vivian had done could well be no more than approval at an instant performance of his orders. On the other hand, why did nobody query Vandeleur remaining stationary if he, too, had received a general order? It could be that, before Uxbridge's ADC arrived, Vivian had taken the decision, and for that he – and Uxbridge – are entitled to their full measure of praise, 'sufficient for the glory of many' to adapt Wellington's phrase of 1842 – as indeed Vivian for his part left nobody in any doubt. For the moment the centre had been shored up.

*

Appendix: Trip's Heavy Brigade of Netherlands Cavalry

In the forty-second paragraph of his Waterloo Despatch the Duke of Wellington wrote: 'General Kruse of the Nassau Service likewise conducted himself much to my satisfaction as did General [*name left blank*] com[mandin]g a Brigade of Infantry of the King of the Netherlands'. On second thoughts he went back and inserted after 'as did' the words, 'General Trip commanding the Heavy Brigade of Cavalry and'. That is how General Trip came into international prominence.

Sir Charles Oman remarked that 'History does not record Lord Uxbridge's feelings on reading Wellington's honourable mention of Trip in the Waterloo Despatch'. Of course on 19 June the future Marquess of Anglesey was in no condition to give Wellington a full appraisal of the cavalry's performance, but long after, in a memorandum of 1839 Anglesey remarked that 'I have the strongest reason to be excessively dissatisfied with the General commanding a Brigade of Dutch Heavy Cavalry.'[26] His remark should not be seen as a national bias: in his correspondence with Siborne he was equally ready to comment on his own failings and those of a British regiment like the 23rd Light Dragoons at Genappe. But how did he come to his view?

Major-General A. D. Trip's Heavy Brigade formed part of Collaert's Cavalry Division, the two other brigades being light cavalry. The Heavy Brigade on 18 June comprised three regiments of Carabiniers, the 1st under Lt.-Colonel Coenegracht, the 2nd under Lt.-Colonel de Bruijn, and the 3rd under Lt.-Colonel Lechleitner.[27] The official casualty returns list officers by name, but lump men into unhelpful categories of 'killed plus missing', and 'wounded', as a result of which there has always been a suspicion that the first category conceals the numbers of those who simply fled.[28] These figures (see table overleaf) cover three different phases of the afternoon. Trip's own battle report states that he was initially placed by his divisional commander Collaert behind the British infantry. Other reports place Trip's brigade on the reverse slope behind Somerset's Household Brigade, remaining there for the first hours of battle, suffering from the cannon-shot coming over the crest. We do not know how much damage these shots inflicted, other than that at about 2.30 p.m. Lt.-Colonel Coenegracht was mortally wounded by a cannon-shot and that half an hour later so was Lt.-Colonel Lechleitner, so that two regiments had lost their commanding officers *while still in waiting behind the slope*: so in looking at deaths in *combat* they must be excluded from the regimental totals. Doubtless some rank and file also were hit in this way.

Dutch–Belgian Heavy Cavalry Casualties

Carabinier Regiment	*Officer strength*	*Officers killed/dow*	*Officers wounded*	*Casualties*		
1st – Dutch	24	3*	8†	46%		** incl C.O.*
2nd – Belgian	22	1	3	23%		*† incl 2 i/c*
3rd – Dutch	21	2‡	1	9%		*‡ incl C.O.*
	O/R strength	*O/R killed+msg*	*O/R wounded*	*Casualties*	*Oman formula killed*[29]	*Oman formula missing*
1st	422	25	66	22%	19	6
2nd	377	87	64	40%	18	69
3rd	371	32	29	16%	9	23

Uxbridge had told his British and KGL commanders to be ready to use their initiative in favourable circumstances, and this message was also passed to Collaert, for in Trip's words, 'towards half past one I received the order from Lieutenant-General Collaert to seize on every opportunity whenever there was a chance of advantageously making a charge with my brigade'.[30] We may think, but cannot be sure, that Collaert would have passed on to Trip the news that Uxbridge was now the supreme cavalry commander.

Trip said that it was at 'about 3 p.m.' when a senior British officer told him of an enemy attack coming up the main road. This must have been after the great charge of Somerset and Ponsonby; but Trip does not refer to any cavalry combat having taken place. He 'at once' placed his troops in readiness: two squadrons of the 3rd Carabiniers in column on the road, the 1st at an oblique angle, the 2nd in reserve. 'The charge of the enemy having failed, I considered the presence of my brigade was no longer of use at that part' and so he moved to 'cover the English infantry'. It was then that he saw the *cuirassiers* preparing to mount the slopes near La Haye Sainte. He went forward with the 1st Carabiniers against the *cuirassiers* who were menacing the Hanoverian infantry (Bremen and Verden), and they charged into the French, followed by two squadrons from the 2nd. The 3rd moved forward, possibly as a reserve, but accounts differ as to whether it, too, joined in this *mêlée*: Trip said so, but Captain Marbotter, a Carabinier officer, thought not. Opinion was that the Dutch weapons were inadequate and their lack of armour a disadvantage against the heavy Frenchmen; the 1st Carabiniers 'had 6 or 7 officers wounded, including Major Bisdom [acting C.O.]'. Trip's force retired to its previous position.[31]

This was a creditable performance, and *if* it was seen by Wellington it would have left a favourable impression in his mind. It must also represent a considerable part of the 1st Carabiniers' casualties, and maybe those of the 2nd as well.

After this, said Trip, the brigade was 'chiefly engaged in guarding that position, or were led by me to any spot where they seemed most needed', and he found nothing more to report until the Prince of Orange ordered him at about 5.30 p.m. 'to take up my position behind some squares of English and Nassau troops'. There he remained until at 7 p.m. Uxbridge ordered him to join the British cavalry. Collaert was wounded by then, and as van Merlen the next senior commander was dying, Trip took command of the division. Thereafter, said Trip, he received no further orders of any kind. He was replaced as commander of the heavy brigade by the Belgian officer commanding the 2nd Carabiniers, Lt.-Colonel de Bruijn. When the infantry advanced Trip said that he followed them and regulated his movements by those of the British cavalry. The report gives the impression that nothing much happened after the principal clash in mid-afternoon, and that they saw no more opportunities for action, although Ney's great cavalry charges continued, La Haye Sainte fell, and the *Garde* made its supreme attack. Perhaps being behind the crest affected all this.[32]

It was towards the moment of final crisis at La Haye Sainte that Uxbridge had to take personal charge of the cavalry in this sector. The evidence of the British officers is unanimous in criticising the inaction of Trip's brigade at this time. Anglesey said in the memorandum already quoted:

> Seeing a [French] corps formed for attack and advancing, I brought forward a brigade of Dutch Heavy Cavalry, and they promised to follow me. I left them beyond the ridge of the hill, a little to the left of Hougoumont. There they halted, and finding the impossibility of making them charge, I left them and retired.

His former ADC Sir Horace Seymour added:

> As to the conduct of the Dutch Brigade of Heavy Cavalry, the impression still on my mind is that they did show a lamentable want of spirit, and

> that Lord Anglesey tried all in his power to lead them on, and while *he* was advancing, I believe I called his attention to the fact of his not being followed. The Household Brigade at this time were very much reduced…
>
> I was desired by my General to recommend to Lord Edward Somerset to withdraw his Brigade (who were extended in single file to make a show) from the heavy fire that was kept on them by the enemy's artillery. Lord Edward's remark was that should he move, the Dutch Cavalry, who were in support, would move off immediately. The Household Brigade retained their position until the end of the action.[33]

Gawler of the 52nd wrote of a time after 4 p.m.: 'Dutch Heavy cavalry, wearing high feathers perpendicular to the tops of their helmets, were seen retiring in confusion' across the Nivelles road behind Hougoumont, and Shaw Kennedy noted in relation to Ney's great cavalry attacks in late afternoon,

> the extraordinary fact that the large bodies of Dutch–Belgian cavalry, and the Cumberland Hussars, that stood in reserve behind the 1st and 3rd divisions of infantry, took no part in the action; the only cavalry which did act being the small remains of Lord Edward Somerset's brigade, the 3rd Hussars of the King's German Legion, and part of Grant's brigade.[34]

Much of this is not in dispute. But some years ago a Dutch historian, Dr F. Snappers, added some interesting comments, touching upon the continuing role of the Prince of Orange, on the possible breakdown in communication due to language limitations, and on the person to whom Uxbridge spoke.[35]

He notes particularly that it was the Prince who ordered Trip to move behind the British and Nassau squares although Orange had ceded the cavalry command to Uxbridge. Here we see the confusion between Orange as Crown Prince and future monarch, and Orange as line commander. Maybe it was an irregularity justified by need, but the circumstances that might justify that are not visible in Trip's report.

The Dutch historian De Bas had noted a further intervention by the Prince, and he timed this as taking place about 7 p.m., just after Collaert had been wounded and Trip had taken command of the division.[36] Orange, in this version, saw the brigade preparing to charge some French cavalry, went to the 2nd Carabiniers, praised them in French, and told them not to charge but to 'retake your positions, you have done enough today [*vous en avez assez fait aujourd'hui*]'. Dr Snappers follows De Bas in this.

But the timing must be wrong. For at 7 p.m. the situation was desperate and it called for every man to strain every nerve to resist and defeat the rising surge of the great attack that was coming. It was not a time for working to rule.

If this timing were correct it would display the Prince in a most appalling light. And how could the Prince say such a thing when he himself was about to join Kruse and his Nassauers in charging the French infantry – there was no 'we have done enough for the day' in that reaction. The Prince's own actions go quite counter to any such speech. However, the incident and the speech could fit the moments after Trip's successful charge in mid-afternoon, and that is where I believe it belongs.[37]

Dr Snappers suggests that when Uxbridge rode up to the Heavy Brigade, Trip (no longer the brigade but the divisional commander) was not present and that the senior regimental colonel, a Belgian, had taken command. Certainly, if we look back at the various complaints and remarks made by the British cavalry officers we see the post mentioned, but without a name. He follows another Dutch historian in suggesting that the Belgian saw an excited officer speaking in an unknown language, waving his arms, pointing, and then riding forward. The Belgian did not know that this was his commander or what he was talking about. (Anglesey, however, thought that 'they promised to follow me', which implies no language problem, probably no dispute over his right to command them, a response from some, but some countermand after he turned to the front.) The suggestion is that Trip was ready enough to charge, but he had just received at 7 p.m. the Prince's order not to charge because the heavy cavalry had 'done enough for the day'. Therefore he let the officer (Uxbridge) ride forward alone, and would not order the brigade to do anything. If my reading of the revisionist case is correct, then that is its essence.

Uxbridge as a young man had spent two years on the Grand Tour, with many months in Lausanne, and his descendant and biographer wrote that in consequence 'he had acquired fluency in French'.[38] Living among French-speakers in Belgium in 1815 for a couple of months would have removed any rustiness. It is difficult to believe that he could not make himself understood in French on 18 June 1815; additionally the general situation and Uxbridge's gestures would have been explanatory enough to most people. He was quite obviously a senior commander, and with a most pressing need. That is when generals like Trip have to justify the salutes, the gold braid and their pay, by following a lead (or even giving one), and not in raising pettifogging objections.

In the days of horsed cavalry in warfare much fun was made of 'The Cavalry Spirit' and its 'we'll do it: what is it?' habit, but it is hard to see that spirit in the brigade in the revisionist version of events. Nelson wrote in his great memorandum before Trafalgar a simple and essential truth that *mutatis mutandis* can apply to land as well as sea: 'Something must be left to chance

... no captain can do very wrong if he places his ship alongside that of an enemy.'

So, between the angry British and the explanatory Netherlanders, what is the likely solution? I accept that Trip's brigade did not leave the field in the early evening, but stood its ground behind the crest; but that after losing two commanding officers early in the day and then fighting well in a severe mid-afternoon clash with the *cuirassiers*, it had by late afternoon lost the will to immolate itself again in the general carnage,[39] unless there was some particularly bold leadership on its commander's part. Uxbridge, undoubtedly a brave and bold leader of cavalry, personally called on the brigade commander (whether Trip or the Belgian colonel) to give a lead to his men, and (to adapt Nelson's words) to place himself alongside the enemy; and the brigade commander did not do so. To shelter behind some words of the Prince of Orange spoken in mid-afternoon would be invidious. Alternatively to suggest that Trip had heard of Uxbridge's rashness on 17 June and thought him unfit to give orders was scarcely good enough when success or defeat were plainly in the balance.

As to the Duke's praise in the Despatch, first we must remember that Uxbridge was under the surgeons elsewhere and in no condition to give an account of the actions of his numerous brigades; and Wellington had to rely on what he had seen in passing. Possibly he had seen Trip's brigade at its best, when it did charge in mid-afternoon.

Against that, Wellington's record in commending senior officers in his despatches, *whether or not they merited it*, is well known. Colborne remarked that 'the Duke was occasionally not above writing in his despatches to please the aristocracy ... I don't mean to say this was peculiar to the Duke; it used to be a common thing with general officers.' Taking two examples (the first indeed instanced by Colborne himself): in his Oporto despatch of 12 May 1809 Wellesley praised Castlereagh's half-brother, Brigadier-General the Hon. Charles Stewart, for directing a charge by Felton Hervey of the 14th Light Dragoons. It was a brilliant exploit, but due to Hervey alone, for his superior, Stewart, merely cheered him on. Again, Oman remarked that in the middle of the Peninsular years Sir William Erskine was a pet aversion, unstable and generally less than competent, and yet politically so well supported that Wellington's despatches regularly commended him. Oman noted that in general, even 'when grave mistakes had been committed, he still stuck the names of the misdemeanants in the list, among those of men who had really done the work ... [making it] little more than a formal recital in order of the senior officers present'.[40] And again, James Stanhope heard that after Waterloo Orange was concerned lest some Netherlands' actions should be remarked on, and had been reassured that the Duke 'would praise generally and not in detail'.[41]

Trip may possibly have been noticed by the Duke during his finest moments in mid-afternoon, but it is equally possible that Trip got his mention by virtue of his military rank and as an obligatory general genuflection to the Netherlands alliance.

Chapter 43

The Prussian Intervention

Bülow, Ziethen, Müffling

I

AT SOME TIME AFTER 4 p.m. when Wellington was telling Colonel Stanhope that the war was won if the Prussians now appeared, old Prince Blücher was pushing General Bülow to move out of the peaceful shelter of the Bois de Paris and set forth for Plancenoit, two miles further up the Lasne valley. From the tone of Bülow's post-battle report, he was unwilling to do this of his own volition before he had grouped his entire corps around him, but the Prince would brook no delay.[1]

It is important to recognise the extent of Blücher's thinking as he entered the battle. His main aim was the capture of Plancenoit as prelude to severing the French line of communication along the Charleroi road, and for this he was using his one fresh formation, as IV Corps was the only corps that had so far not been bruised by fighting, much though it had tested in the incessant marching of the last two days. If he could take Plancenoit and then seize La Belle Alliance, he would cripple Napoleon and bring relief to Wellington. But the plan went far beyond that. Wellington was the anvil upon which Napoleon would be flattened by the Prussian sledgehammer. Once the Prussians had smashed Napoleon's eastern wing and reached the great road and the French rear, they would have cut off Napoleon's retreat and so could capture the entire French army. That is why IV Corps was striking so far south of Mont St Jean, and that is why I Corps' task of linking with Wellington's left wing was so much less important. The battle plan should give the Prussians their own victory in revenge for Ligny; it would be the Prussian contribution, perhaps the decisive contribution, and not a subsidiary or an auxiliary effort under the command of his ally.

We saw in Chapter 41 how the Prussian cavalry moved forward,[2] and almost at once engaged with Domon's and Subervie's cavalry to the west of the Bois de Paris. Some lively skirmishes sent the French back up the valley.

To secure his flanks General Bülow pushed out troops to the higher ground on each side of the valley, and the tale of those flanks can be briefly dealt with here before we turn to the fight for Plancenoit.

On the right flank Losthin's 15th Brigade sent three battalions (two from the 18th Infantry Regiment and one from the 3rd Silesian Landwehr) in the direction of Smohain; they made momentary contact with the Nassauers. But it was not full support, for Saxe-Weimar's Netherlands brigade continued to fight alone for some hours and was almost driven out of its positions as evening began.[3] When Saxe-Weimar's men saw assistance coming, the support was not from Bülow's IV Corps but from Ziethen's I Corps. Even then it came at a price.

On the left flank in the Lasne valley two Fusilier battalions (from 15th Infantry Regiment and 1st Silesian Landwehr) under Major von Keller covered the southern flank of Hiller's 16th Brigade and encountered no opposition. We shall see more of Keller's little force much later, in the final moments of the French defence of Plancenoit.

Meanwhile, on the French side Lobau had placed Simmer's *19e Division* (3,700 bayonets) upon a knoll dominating the little road that came straight to it, spreading the infantry on both sides and up to woods that gave some protection to both flanks. Jeanin's rather smaller *20e Division* (2,900 bayonets) was drawn up along the road, but further back. Together with the cavalry of Domon and Subervie, Lobau's force thus presented a defensive mass of 15 battalions, 20 squadrons, and 16 guns to resist Bülow's attacking force of 18 battalions (including the five flanking battalions), 12 squadrons and 32 guns. Bülow's cavalry were under the command of the King of Prussia's younger son Wilhelm, then aged eighteen (he became King in 1861; and is mainly remembered for becoming in 1871 the first German *Kaiser*, a title he disliked). Just as the fighting started Wilhelm received a valuable reinforcement of four more regiments (16 squadrons).

Lobau saw at once that he had to disrupt the Prussian advance before more enemy reinforcements should come. He ordered his guns to open fire, while his infantry dashed to the attack. They fought hard with 15th Brigade and the cannon-fire disabled three of Losthin's 6-pounder guns. But Prussian reinforcements were coming up the valley, and Blücher decided on a wide outflanking movement to the left. These reinforcements, IV Corps' 13th (Hake) and 14th (Ryssel) Brigades, and the cavalry, and twelve more 6-pounders, gave Bülow more confidence. While Losthin's 15th Brigade remained on his right wing, the 13th moved up behind it and also covered the centre, while Hiller's 16th, backed by the 14th, moved in a swing along the wooded left bank of the Lasne brook. Houssaye notes that the Prussian guns (now 59 in number) were pounding Lobau hard, with the over-shots even falling among the *Garde* close to the Charleroi road.[4]

Under such pressure Lobau was unable to hold the little ridge, but from there the ground fell away until it reached Plancenoit, without a good rallying point. It was the village that presented itself as his next tactical position. He therefore very sensibly let his right wing come back, placing Bellair's brigade of *19e Division* in the village of Plancenoit, while his left brigade (Jamin) still reached out towards Durutte's division close to Papelotte. But he had ceded well over a mile of ground, and was now under a mile from the vital great road. Plancenoit comprised about a hundred houses at most, one part on the slopes of a spur on the south side of the village, the other part being grouped along the lane from the bottom towards Le Caillou, with a big church and spire standing prominently on a large mound. A circular cemetery surrounded the church and was bounded by a wall. The main street was narrow and with many side alleys, the houses were solidly built, and the whole lay in the narrowing confines of the valley head.[5] The village formed a bastion that had to be held at all costs.

II

The first Prussian assault went in between 5 and 6 p.m., ten battalions strong and Lobau's force was not able to resist it, despite using cannon at point-blank ranges, Bellair's brigade taking heavy casualties and losing Colonel Roussille of the *5e Ligne*.[6] The Prussians stormed the walled churchyard, took the church, and part (possibly all) of the lower village.

But Napoleon was by now concentrating more and more attention on this front, and was quick to realise that Lobau needed more support. He sent Duhesme with the *Jeune Garde* (4 battalions of *voltigeurs* and 4 of *tirailleurs*, in total over 4,000 elite troops) to strengthen Lobau's right wing. While from 5 p.m. onwards the Prussian 13th Brigade was moving towards Frischermont, the 15th could perhaps have found it more useful as a support in front of Plancenoit. For the 15th Brigade was unable to move, apparently due in part to the skirmishers having 'used up all their ammunition'.[7] It had lost momentum just when a further push was needed. In consequence Losthin's 15th Brigade had to be helped out by the support of a battalion from Hiller's 16th Brigade. But it was at this moment that the *Jeune Garde* made its presence felt, snatching back the initiative, dashing forward in two columns, the left coming alongside Jamin, the right plunging into the streets and buildings, retaking the churchyard and clearing the houses.

Blücher promptly ordered Bülow to renew the attack, and the 16th Brigade went forward in three columns, with further support on the left from two battalions from Ryssel's 14th Brigade. This battering ram of 9,000 men was blasted by the fire of the *Jeune Garde* and by artillery, but still it came on, wrested the cemetery from the French, captured the guns and reached the further and upper end of the village. Some of the *Jeune Garde* continued to hold out in the houses, from which they poured heavy and accurate fire upon the Prussians in the streets, but Duhesme himself was mortally wounded. A cavalry charge by Subervie's lancers came to nothing because of intense cannon-fire. The 16th Brigade's I/2nd Silesian Landwehr was joined by three battalions of Pomeranian Landwehr from two of 14th Brigade's regiments; by dint of sheer determination, and at a heavy cost, the Landwehr forced the *Jeune Garde* towards the margins of the village. With this last effort the Prussians reached near exhaustion.

There was no prospect of imminent reinforcement: II Corps was still toiling from Chapelle-St-Lambert to Lasne;[8] III Corps – depending on local circumstances – was thought to be somewhere between Wavre and the road to St-Lambert; I Corps was strung out along the road towards Ohain.

Such a situation may not have shaken, though it must have frustrated, the brave and ever impatient Blücher. But it must have concerned the positively minded Grolman, who was at his side, and been thoroughly unsettling for the less optimistic Gneisenau. And now further bad news reached them, for Lieutenant Wussow brought a message from Thielemann that the French were attacking the Dyle crossings and that he feared being overborne unless supported. Nobody has ever described how each of these three men in the hollows near Plancenoit absorbed the news and its implications, though Gneisenau's 20 June official report provides a partial indication, for he wrote that the Field Marshal refused to be disturbed (*'nicht erschüttern'*) by it. Every authority on the campaign agrees that Gneisenau dictated a reply for Wussow to take. Some historians have given Gneisenau the credit for the reply, but it seems inconceivable that it was not the supreme commander who took the decision, given Gneisenau's own comment and indeed the entire character of the old hero. The crisis both before and behind him required an instant reaction. It was a decision that Blücher was not only peculiarly well suited to take, but one that he would never have abandoned to the option of a staff officer. He heard, decided, rapped out a few words, and turned back to mastering the problem of Plancenoit, leaving to Gneisenau the task of briefing the messenger. Gneisenau dictated the reply to Wussow: 'He is to dispute with all his might every step forward that the enemy takes, for the greatest losses to his corps would be more than outweighed by victory over Napoleon.'[9] It was a magnificent reply – and it was quintessential Blücher.[10]

III

While IV Corps had in its second attack made progress in the village, it was not secure there, and in addition to the possibility of a counter-attack from Lobau's small *6e Corps*, the light cavalry, and the somewhat shaken *Jeune Garde*, it was soon to face yet another challenge. But meanwhile it is time to turn to the fortunes of Ziethen's I Corps.

Steinmetz's 1st Brigade, approached along its own road from Froidemont to the vicinity of Lasne. Then it halted to wait for the 2nd Brigade. Ziethen's chief staff officer, Colonel Reiche was sent to see what was happening on the Mont St Jean battlefield, while the corps commander rode back down the line to urge his rear units forward. Müffling, who was on the watch, encountered Reiche and left him in no doubt of Wellington's urgent need for Ziethen's introduction to the battle. As a consequence Reiche then, rightly and on his own responsibility, ordered the advance-guard to resume its march, only to see one of Blücher's staff, Major von Scharnhorst, ride up and countermand the order. Instead, Scharnhorst brought an order to turn south to reinforce the much-tried IV Corps in its assaults on Plancenoit. Here again we see that Blücher unhesitatingly gave priority to Plancenoit over Papelotte: the linkage with Wellington, and smashing Durutte in the right-angle in the French line was of secondary consideration only. Reiche sought to convince Scharnhorst of the better course to take:

> I pointed out to him what had been arranged with Müffling, that Wellington was relying implicitly on our arrival. But Scharnhorst would not listen, and said that this was Blücher's order and he would hold me responsible for the consequences if it was not carried out … I was nearly in despair [at this impasse] all the more so as the head of the advance-guard was just arriving and wanted to know where to march next. General Ziethen himself was not in sight, and General Steinmetz, who commanded the advance-guard, came up to the halted troops at this very moment, stormed at me in his usual violent manner, and insisted upon an advance [in accordance with Scharnhorst's message]. He was scarcely willing to listen to how things stood. My embarrassment increased not a little when General Steinmetz let the head of the column resume its march and himself went past the point where the road to Frischermont branches off… As this took place in view of the Nassau troops, it had never crossed my mind that this apparent withdrawal could be misunderstood and could make a bad impression, as was in fact the case for a minute or two. Fortunately General Ziethen came up at this critical very moment. I hurried over to him and when I had given my report, he issued orders for the march to be directed without fail towards the English army.[11]

It is far from certain how Ziethen came to his final decision. In Müffling's words, Ziethen had been intending to advance on Papelotte, but the advance-guard 'suddenly turned round, and disappeared from the height just as the enemy took possession of Papelotte'. 'An inexperienced young man' whom Ziethen had sent forward to report on the progress of the battle, had returned to say that the British right wing was 'in full retreat' – with its implication for a Prussian move on Wellington's eastern wing. Müffling's account of his own part in the great dispute then continues:

> On my assuring General von Ziethen of the contrary, and undertaking to bring the corps to the appointed place, and since in any movement downwards from Papelotte he would not only find difficulties, but also lose the time for co-operation, he instantly turned round and followed me, and continued to advance until it grew dark, driving the enemy before him.[12]

Aerts notes that Steinmetz's second-in-command, Colonel Hofmann, stated that the delay in coming to a final decision 'seemed very long to us, given the urgency of the situation, but it was certainly not for half an hour,'[13] but even a few minutes at such a stage in the battle was bad enough. The only good thing about it was that the rearward units were gradually coming closer. So we are left wondering whether Reiche or Müffling convinced Ziethen, or whether it was the effect of both arguing in the same sense. But we need to remember that it was Ziethen who would be accountable to his commander-in-chief for his decision, particularly if it proved unfortunate. Ziethen's decision was the right decision, and it was a brave one.

Nobody speaks of any times, but it may be suggested that this delay and discussion took place after 6 p.m. The second effort to take Plancenoit began at about 6 (perhaps a little earlier, perhaps slightly later) and as Ziethen's help was needed because it was not going well, we might time Ziethen's eventual rejection of that call as coming at something like 6.30 p.m.

Of course Müffling had not been the only officer looking for signs of the Prussians. Uxbridge's ADC Seymour, in delivering the order to Vivian to move to the centre, 'saw the advance of the Prussians', went to check and then rode back to Wellington and Uxbridge with the news. Wellington sent him back to ask Bülow for some Prussian infantry to fill the gaps in his line of battle, but Seymour's horse was killed and it was the Duke's own ADC, Fremantle, who took the message. For his part Fremantle said he went to ask for 3,000 men, met Ziethen and Bülow, and heard their assurance 'that the whole army was coming up, and that they could not make a detachment'. He told them that he would give that answer to the Duke, and left. There is no Prussian comment on this, so far as I know.[14]

It is plain that the operational decisions were taken in a situation of great confusion, that the decisions themselves were understood and recorded quite differently. Blücher had planned to operate as an independent ally, and it does look as though the two Prussian generals (whoever they were) who spoke to Fremantle understood perfectly well that putting a Prussian 'detachment' under a foreign commander was totally unacceptable.

So the question was, how would they co-operate? The French were surging forward into Smohain and the château of Frischermont. This, if successful, would drive a wedge between the two Allied armies, and Vivian 'was surprised to see the tremendous fire the French were able to direct against the Prussians' even at this late hour.[15]

IV

Ziethen's men pressed on towards Smohain, closing on the flank of the French who were savagely attacking the Nassauers. The latter were gradually becoming somewhat fragmented and now fell back in some confusion. Then there occurred one of those small but painful misfortunes of war, an instance of 'friendly fire', and indeed the worst in the campaign. In Reiche's words:

> As the Nassauers were dressed in the French style of that time, our men took them to be the enemy and fired at them. Their commander Prince Bernard of [Saxe-]Weimar rushed up to General Ziethen to clarify the misunderstanding, which he did in no uncertain terms. The General, not knowing the Prince, made no excuses and calmly replied, 'My friend, it is not my fault that your men look like French.'[16]

Saxe-Weimar's superior General Perponcher had just come to this part of his division and quickly intervened. He ordered the Nassauers to withdraw while he righted the matter (he had served as Netherlands ambassador to Berlin, 1814–15). He later lent a company of Nassauers to assist the Prussians, which shows a certain magnanimity.

The ever-active Reiche left Papelotte and took forward two batteries of 6-pounder artillery to the heights beyond, where, to the east of Best's Hanoverian infantry, Captain Rettberg's 9-pounder battery stood silent, out of ammunition. The smoke drifting over the field was often dense and there was a continuing risk of 'friendly fire'. Fremantle, returning from his meeting with the Prussian commanders, certainly feared so, for he 'found a Prussian battery of eight guns firing between our first and second lines, and desired the officers to cease firing . . . and begged the generals to send orders for the battery to cease fire'.[17] The firing then turned against the left flank of Lobau, while Ziethen led forward his cavalry units, some to the left of Best's infantry, some behind them, and the 1st Silesian Hussars close to where the Ohain road met the track from Papelotte. This would have been at about 7 p.m. or perhaps even later. The Belgian historian Winand Aerts remarked, 'This regiment was at first the only one in line. It had to serve as liaison between the English army and Steinmetz's brigade which received the order to speed up its march.'[18]

At this moment the struggle for Plancenoit still was undecided, as Napoleon sent more elite troops to restore the position and Bülow was awaiting the support of II Corps' leading brigade. Blücher's position was unenviable: he knew that he faced problems both in front and far away at Wavre. If Wellington could not hold out any longer then the Prussians might be in the gravest danger. The role of I Corps in the battle was a subsidiary one; it did not match in significance that of IV Corps at Plancenoit. Nevertheless I Corps had its part to play, so before we examine that next phase at Plancenoit it may be simplest to complete the story of the achievements of Ziethen's corps.

The sequence of events around the eastern buildings at La Haye and Papelotte, Frischermont and Smohain is far from easy to disentangle. We know that Durutte was fighting in this area when he

> saw some cavalry units to the right, though one could not at first see what they were. Some time later one heard a cannonade begin on that side, and there was no longer any uncertainty but that it was the Prussians who were behind our right. All the cavalry that was near the Durutte division, as well as the *Garde* artillery, received the order to march to that point.[19]

Troops of the 24th Infantry Regiment cleared Durutte's troops from Smohain and then pressed on, with the Nassauers alongside them. Beier's West Prussian Uhlans of Prince William's IV Corps Reserve Cavalry maintained contact between Ziethen's and Bülow's forces. Jacquinot and Durutte continued to resist, but to no great purpose.

The advance guard of Ziethen's I Corps could claim that it had paid off the scores resulting from 15 and 16 June. Its casualties on this day amounted to 34 killed, 172 wounded and 111 missing. Of this corps total of 317 no fewer than 293 were infantry (188 or 60 per cent in the 24th Regiment; 63 or 20 per cent in the 12th Regiment, mainly in its Fusilier Battalion; 42 in other regiments). If we accept the figures of Aerts, then 1st Brigade sent into action 7,300 men and 16 guns, of which 6,200 were infantrymen (9½ battalions), so that the losses overall came to less than 5 per cent.[20] In terms of Waterloo losses this casualty list tells us that the fighting on I Corps front was not heavy. Heavy casualties are no part of a general's glory, but the slight losses in I Corps do imply that, by the time they came to grips, the French were at least on the point of exhaustion so that they did not resist very long.

It is impossible to give a figure for the casualties the Prussians inflicted on Durutte's division, for that formation had been fighting previously in attacks against the ridge or in assaults on the cluster of buildings around Papelotte and vicinity. Durutte had entered the battle with about 4,000 troops, and his recorded officer casualties for the whole six to seven hours were 9 killed and 61 wounded, which according to Oman's method of calculation could mean about 1,450 French casualties overall, so that during the Prussian period the losses may have been roughly equal on each side. But we do not know.[21]

Such was the contribution of I Corps. The main Prussian contribution to victory, however, was due to the troops fighting so desperately at Plancenoit.[22] That story, Napoleon's further strengthening of the position, and the eventual triumph of the Prussians in taking Plancenoit must await a later chapter.

Chapter 44

The Fifth Act

Climax and Decision

I

NAPOLEON HAD TO WREST PLANCENOIT from the enemy, come what may. As Lobau had been unable to contain the Prussians or even to hold the village, then the *Jeune Garde* would have to do so. But they, too, had failed in this, so that out of the 32 battalions of troops of the Line and the *Garde* that Napoleon held under his own hand at midday, he had already had to detach 17, only to find that number insufficient.[1] The Prussians were almost within sight of La Belle Alliance, the French army's jugular vein. Napoleon ordered two battalions of the *Vieille Garde* instantly to restore the situation (one each of *grenadiers* and *chasseurs*).

This magnificent and terrifying fighting force advanced rapidly but without losing step, one thousand veterans to sweep away something like ten times their number. They had orders not to fire but dash forward with the bayonet. Even the sight of their bearskin helmets looming up was enough to strike fear, and as the Prussians fell back at bayonet-point towards the gun batteries, the gunners who might have fired and checked the attack, simply abandoned their guns. And so, instead of being mown down, the attackers pressed on even beyond the batteries. The situation was transformed, and the *Jeune Garde* and Lobau's men were able to reoccupy lost ground. Within a few minutes the *grognards* had undone much of Bülow's and Blücher's costly achievement. The best of all the accounts of the worsening crisis for the French inside the village and for this sudden recovery, is that of General Pelet of the *Garde* but, fine though it is, it is too long to quote in detail and too intricate to summarise satisfactorily.[2] Another general of the *Garde* made a short summary of the results, which may suffice. General Petit wrote:

> The enemy was immediately driven off with great loss. We pursued them with the bayonet all across the higher ground. The *chasseurs* and *grenadiers*

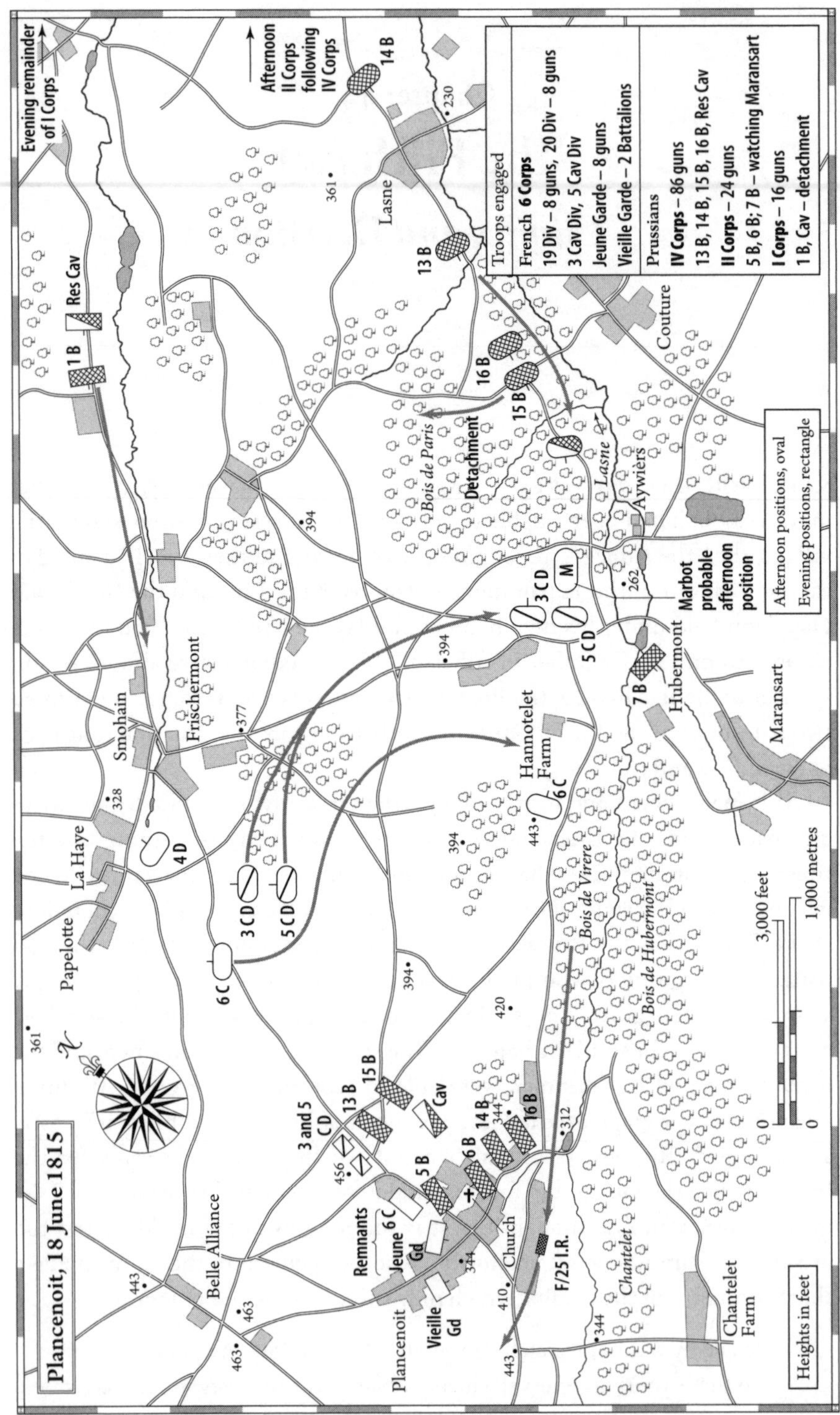
Plancenoit, 18 June 1815
Troops engaged
French 6 Corps
19 Div – 8 guns, 20 Div – 8 guns
3 Cav Div, 5 Cav Div
Jeune Garde – 8 guns
Vieille Garde – 2 Battalions
Prussians
IV Corps – 86 guns
13 B, 14 B, 15 B, 16 B, Res Cav
II Corps – 24 guns
5 B, 6 B; 7 B – watching Maransart
I Corps – 16 guns
1 B, Cav – detachment
Afternoon positions, oval
Evening positions, rectangle
Heights in feet
Evening remainder of I Corps
Afternoon II Corps following IV Corps
Marbot probable afternoon position
Remnants 6 C
Jeune Gd
Vieille Gd
F/25 I.R.
Plancenoit
Belle Alliance
Papelotte
La Haye
Smohain
Frischermont
Hannotelet Farm
Hubermont
Maransart
Aywiers
Couture
Lasne
Chantelet Farm
Church
Bois de Paris
Bois de Virere
Bois de Hubermont
Chantelet
Detachment
0 3,000 feet
0 1,000 metres

> marched straight up to the Prussian batteries, which were abandoned in a moment. This was at about 6 o'clock. While this was taking place the *1er Régiment* of *Grenadiers* formed into two squares, a battalion to each, one on the right of the *chaussée* (facing the enemy), on the summit of the position dominating the little road out of Plancenoit which leads to the main road. *Tirailleurs* were thrown out to the extreme right of this village to watch the enemy, who were found in force. Several were taken with an *adjutant-major* who had gone too far. The other square was to the left of the road, on the mound where the Emperor had been at first. It was joined by a battery of six 8-pounders [*sic*: *6 pièces de 8*; but this must mean 6-pounders as there were no obsolete 8-pounders present] and by companies of sappers and marines of the *Garde*.[3]

Inside the village the situation was frightful, the houses ablaze from the shelling, and perhaps set alight as a means of checking the other side's attacks, and around the main formations came swirls of cavalry seeking opportunities to surprise the infantry.

Napoleon had won for himself both ground and time on this front. Against any other Prussian general he might have felt safe from further immediate danger, but he was dealing with 'that old devil' and so, as Petit said, he had to keep these battalions of *grognards* in square (and with gunners and ancillary troops of the *Garde*) to support the tired soldiers in Plancenoit. He was reduced to juggling with his reserves, and meanwhile Ney's recent impetus near the crest of Mont St Jean was simply dying away for want of fresh troops. If he was not facing immediate defeat, decisive victory was almost beyond hope, and, with commanders like Wellington and Blücher facing him, the situation was not one where stalemate might be a likely outcome. Through the day several officers had thought that an early retirement to a fresh position where the fight might be renewed tomorrow would be a sensible move to make,[4] but Napoleon did not and could not trust the political leaders in Paris. They might snatch the occasion to force through changes that would hobble him as a ruler. So he fought on.

II

Bülow's IV Corps had been checked for the time being, and I Corps' leading units were still waiting on the outcome of the arguments between Reiche and Scharnhorst, and then between Müffling and Ziethen, when at last were seen Tippelskirch's 5th and Krafft's 6th Brigades of II Corps, together with the corps cavalry. This addition of fresh troops enabled Blücher to prepare a new assault on the ruined village. This time the 5th Brigade would make the attack on the left, aiming at the sector from the church northwards, while fresh Prussian artillery, now mustered in place, punished the defenders, and also sought by counter-battery fire to divert the French gunners from cannonading the attacking columns. Units from the 14th and 16th Brigades would move in behind. Bülow's right-hand force would be the 13th and 15th Brigades, with a strong cavalry presence on their outer flank. In sum, five fresh battalions would lead on the left and the remains of fourteen on the right. The main cavalry of II and IV Corps were massed to follow through. Rearward units of II Corps were ordered to support this thrust as and when they arrived. This should secure the Plancenoit position, for Lobau could not count on more than 25 battalions (all worn), 20 squadrons (also tired) and about 50 guns with which to repulse 47 battalions, some 50 squadrons and over 100 guns. But in addition Blücher planned a southern flanking movement to bypass the French on their right and aim for the great *chaussée*. This was undertaken by Major Witzleben of the 25th Regiment (5th Brigade), which moved through the woods along the Lasne stream aiming at the high ground near Le Caillou; to them was added the two-battalion force that had already been sent to that flank under Major Keller at the beginning of the operation.

Surely this plan must succeed. But it could not be ignored that as yet no decision had been reached. In the words of Gneisenau, 'It was 7.30 p.m. and still the battle was continuing.'[5]

III

It would be wrong to speak of a total lull in the fighting along the slopes of Mont St Jean, for the sound of musketry and cannon-fire never really died away and the Allied line continued to suffer heavy casualties. But Ney was short of the men he needed, and once again Wellington had time to find more reserves and to distribute them to the weakest points of his front. Vivian's and Vandeleur's cavalry were now behind the centre, serving as a second line and also as a barrier to any infantry seeking to depart for Brussels.[6] Wellington personally encouraged and led forward the young Brunswickers to reinforce the shattered Hanoverians of Kielmansegge. During the morning Sir John Lambert's brigade had reached the field and had moved behind Kempt and Pack, and in mid-afternoon *Baïonnette* Chassé's 3rd Netherlands Division arrived and stood in reserve west of the road. Lambert and Chassé thus constituted Wellington's last infantry reserve.

The smoke of battle remained dense, drifting slowly in the slight westerly breeze, but the light was beginning to change as 6.30 approached. Men saw the Duke, composed but pale, his entire attention seeming concentrated on the enemy movements and the state of his own line. But underneath, as Thomas Hardy's *Spirit of the Pities* says, 'the hour is shaking him, unshakable as he may seem!' He had hoped to see the Prussians approach at 2 o'clock, certainly expected them by 4, and yet, even now, reports of their coming suggested that they were still struggling along the roads and not committed in full strength. No wonder that he kept looking at his watch![7] But as he was no simple *bon général ordinaire* he was not caught up merely in the present: he was thinking of the next phase also, when darkness would fall, what further action was still possible, or whether the whole line would have to stand and perhaps die where it stood. What his innermost thought was that evening we shall never know, for in those recollections that listeners recorded in the months and years after the battle his memory must have been affected subconsciously by the fact of victory. The nearest we can get is his own admission of how wafer-thin he judged the margin, one in a remark made to Constant Rebecque that same evening, and one in a letter to his brother the next morning: 'By God, I *saved the battle* four times myself' and 'It was the most desperate business I ever was in; I never took so much trouble about any battle; and *never* was so near being *beat*.'[8]

For the moment there was little movement in the valley. Then a *cuirassier* galloped away from the enemy line and came up the slope shouting '*Vive le Roi*.' Reaching where Colborne's 1/52nd (Adam's Brigade of 2nd Division) were waiting behind the crest, he warned that Napoleon was about to launch the *Garde* in a fresh attack, and pointed out the intended route.[9] The battalion formed on the reverse slope near the crossroads at 'nearly 7 o'clock', Colborne looking at his watch and remarking 'the wounded had better be left where they are, the action must be over in half an hour'.[10]

IV

Napoleon must have had a fairly clear impression of the balance of forces at 7 o'clock. He knew that very considerable Prussian forces were pressing on his right flank, perhaps 30,000, and with more massing behind. Looking north, although Wellington had been repeatedly battered and his ammunition must be running low, he still kept an unbroken line even though his casualties might amount to 10,000 men or more. Nor were the Emperor's own forces, spread across both fronts, in better state.

In the short two-hour span of remaining daylight he had to win decisive success, if not on both fronts, at least on one. He decided to order a general assault against Mont St Jean all along the line, supported by the Grand Battery that was now in a more forward position following the recent success in the centre. This general assault and bombardment would tie down the defenders and stop any reserves moving from one part of the crest to another. It would coincide with a final deadly thrust by his elite force of the *Garde* at a point in the line just west of La Haye Sainte, leading to breakthrough and victory.

On the right d'Erlon's re-formed divisions, those of Marcognet and Donzelot, and Pégot's brigade from Durutte's, were ordered up the slope behind a thick scattering of sharpshooters. The other half of Durutte's force was entangled in the fighting at Papelotte and holding in check Ziethen's Prussians, and could not be spared for the main attack. So d'Erlon's men were led forward, bloody and exhausted though they were. Despite the almost incredible bravery of their officers in trying to lead them to the assault, some slowed, stopped to let off their muskets at the crest, went to ground, or fell back.[11] Some of d'Erlon's units seem to have advanced with the greatest determination and one officer in Marcognet's division actually thought that as the *Garde* attack went in, 'the divisions of Marcognet and [a brigade of] Durutte crowned the plateau'.[12] The impression given by many British observers was that Donzelot's men came in force and with determination until hit by a devastating volley at quite short range.

To the west of the great Charleroi road Reille's corps showed less enthusiasm, for it had been decimated either at Hougoumont or in seconding the great cavalry attacks. Reille commented that to have had any chance of success Ney's cavalry attacks 'should have been assisted by the entire *Garde*, and now when this [*Garde*] reserve did go forward, the cavalry and infantry of the first line had suffered for so long, and part of the plateau had been abandoned, so that they could not second this attack with much vigour'.[13] Much of the cavalry was too shaken to do much more than watch, but what is curious is that Piré's cavalry, stationed almost motionless to the west of Hougoumont for much of the afternoon and very lightly used, remained virtually inactive at the crisis.

Many guns in the Allied line were disabled, others had sunk deep into the ground from repeated recoils; moving them was difficult, due in part to the losses among their horse-teams, losses that also affected the limbers and caissons and thus the smooth re-supply of ammunition. But there was just sufficient ammunition and manpower for the artillery still to make a further and merciless effort if an attack should come on. The infantry had been so worn by sharpshooters, musketry and artillery fire that it was nearing exhaustion, with some units approaching the limits of morale. But there were 'bitter-enders' as well: Kincaid wished for the chance to make 'a last thrust' and remarked that 'However desperate our affairs were, we still had the satisfaction of seeing that theirs were worse.'[14] The cavalry were holding on, and watching against any rearward defections from the ranks on the crest.

Wellington's line, looked at along the three-quarters of a mile from the crossroads to behind Hougoumont, comprised the following brigades (although by now that term scarcely describes the skeletons of battalions in most of them). The wrecks of Ompteda's KGL battalions had to their right Kielmansegge's battered Hanoverians, Kruse's Nassau contingent and the Brunswickers. Next came Colin Halkett's British brigade, beyond which were Maitland's Guards. Then came Adam's British brigade, while behind Hougoumont and its undefeated garrison were Hugh Halkett's and the KGL brigade that Du Plat, until his death, had led. The seven British/KGL cavalry brigades stood behind the line of infantry, with Chassé's 3rd Netherlands Division placed as reinforcement for any part of the line that required it. Almost all of Wellington's British/KGL and Hanoverian batteries were along the front, but by now ammunition was in short supply and some batteries like Lloyd's and Cleeves's were out of ammunition.

While formed in square the infantry had been forced to endure the artillery fire. Now there was a partial change. The cavalry behind the slope still had to remain in their saddles, for their task was to corral the infantry and also be ready to charge at a moment's notice; hence they had to continue 'to bear it', but the battalions (or at least some of them) were told to lie down to avoid additional casualties. Then, when the *Garde* was seen moving up the slope the infantry brigades were told to form behind the summit, in line, four deep.

V

Napoleon went to launch his final reserve into attack, while his command post remained guarded by the *1/1er Chasseurs à Pied* under the Dutch Major Duuring. After deducting that unit the *Garde* under his hand now comprised only eleven battalions: of the *Vieille Garde* there were three battalions of *Grenadiers à Pied* and two of *Chasseurs à Pied* (excluding Duuring's *1/1er Chasseurs*). There was in addition the *Moyenne Garde*: three battalions of *Grenadiers* and three of *Chasseurs* (one a combined battalion due to the *Chasseur* casualties at Ligny). From what General Petit (commanding the *1er Grenadiers*) wrote it would seem that the *Garde* had been formed in square along the high road, and it was in this cumbrous formation that Napoleon personally led the entire *Moyenne Garde* down into the valley, where they formed up for the great assault. There he stood, and spoke to Ney as he handed to him the last resource of the Empire.

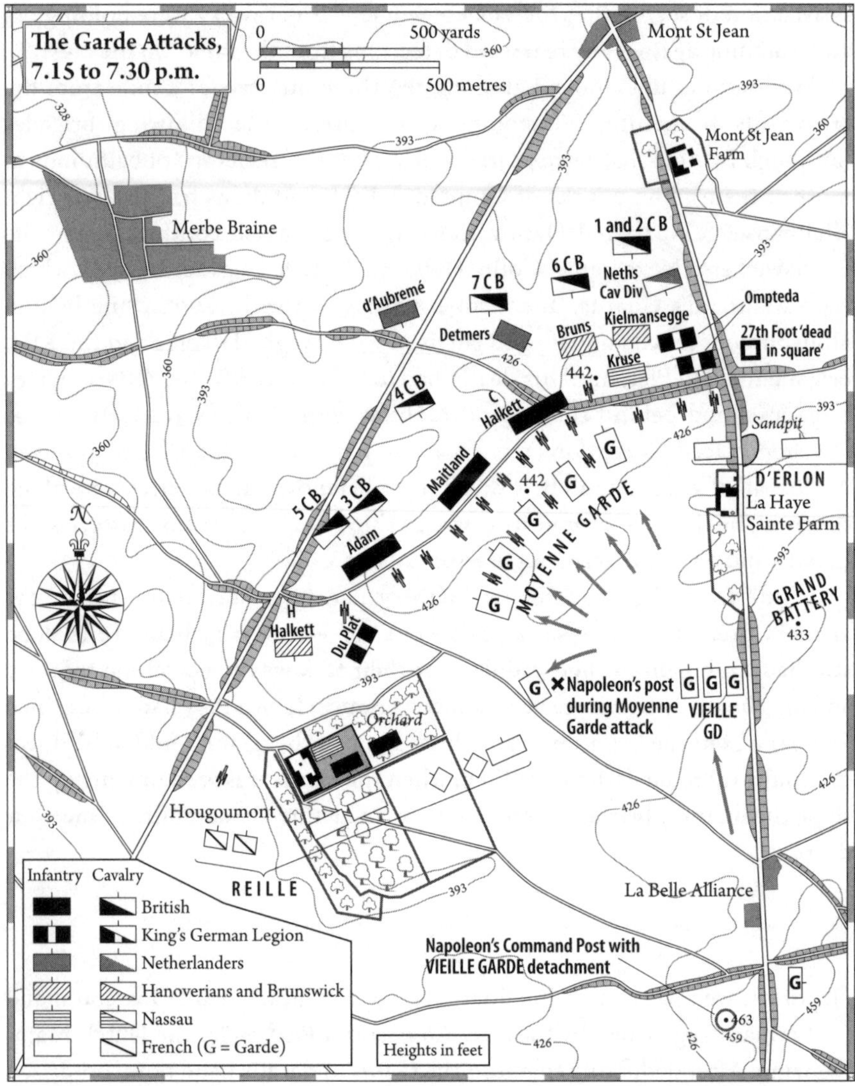

The question of the formation in which the *Garde* finally advanced has never been settled in a definite fashion: put very simply, did it advance in squares or did it advance in column, and in how many squares or columns, and at what feature did it aim? I set out the problem and the evidence that has gone to form my own conclusion in Appendix 2 to this chapter.[15]

It is agreed generally that the force handed to Ney was grouped in a six-fold formation that some call a column, and others call square. Four columns were each made up of a battalion of the *Moyenne Garde*'s third regiments of *grenadiers* and *chasseurs,* and two columns came from from the two small fourth regiments of *grenadiers* and *chasseurs*. But then the formation comprising the *2/3e Grenadiers* was diverted by being ordered to move 'a cannon-shot distance to the west to watch against any Allied threat' from behind Hougoumont, and it was with this unit and from that position that Napoleon watched the start of the advance. Thus it seems agreed that this further detachment to the west reduced the attack to *five columns*. Some sources place Napoleon here; others suggest that he returned to his earlier command point.

The *Garde* formed up close to the orchard of La Haye Sainte. Before it could get to grips with its enemy it had to cross almost half a mile of ground that was swept by cannon fire, and that would take perhaps fifteen minutes. It was an elite force, but it would instinctively want to cross the open ground as quickly as possible, and it needed to keep formation. The *Garde* moved, certainly in the later stages of the advance, at the *pas de charge*, and since the slope, though gentle, was nothing like a bowling green and was covered with debris from the battle, and much cut up by shot and hooves, this would add to the problems had it been in a square formation. The five columns were led by experienced generals, with Ney among them, with the right-hand column in advance and the others in echelon westwards.

The bias of the slope insensibly led to the advance veering several degrees off the original line of advance. There were no skirmishers out in front and the five columns had to guess where the enemy were, for apart from the artillerymen serving the British guns there were few men to be seen. The Allied guns were low on ammunition and short of men and horses, but in accordance with Wellington's orders, the British artillery concentrated again on the French infantry, firing double-shotted. Between the advancing French columns were light 6-pounder guns from Duchand's *Garde* horse artillery batteries, that had been sent to multiply the effectiveness of the *Garde*'s musketry once they had reached the summit and deployed into line for the musketry fire-fight.[16]

The summit seemed bare. On the *Garde*'s right flank Donzelot's men were moving past La Haye Sainte, but there was little sign of support from Reille's men to the left, and Hougoumont represented a continuing flanking threat, a threat offset mainly by the *2/3e Grenadiers* motionless further back. The Grand Battery's shot, flying overhead and striking the ridge, was the best comfort the attackers could hope for.

The Allied infantry were under orders to hold their fire till within lethal range, and the men who would face the assault were under orders to lie down in shelter while they could. One after another the columns came up, with the leading one facing the western edge of Colin Halkett's sector with the others to the left generally coming against the front held by British Guards. The impression made on the defenders was enormous, as a dozen accounts testify: the Emperor's finest soldiers, never defeated in battle, marching with ported arms, their great bearskin helmets adding to their height, led by most intrepid regimental officers, with ten generals including their senior commanders Friant (*Grenadiers*) and Michel (*Chasseurs*) encouraging them, and Ney himself among them.

Down in the valley bottom, short of La Haye Sainte, Napoleon could see the *Moyenne Garde* moving away to the decisive attack; turning the other way he saw, halted at the ready, three senior battalions from the *Vieille Garde* (*2/2e Grenadiers* and both battalions of *2e Chasseurs*) under Roguet. Roguet's force would turn the first wave's break-through into full-scale break-out.[17]

VI

It was 7 in the evening. The Nassauers and Brunswickers seemed shaken by the sight of d'Erlon's left wing coming at them. But Wellington came up and steadied them and they did not break. According to General Kruse, the Prince of Orange ordered a bayonet charge, which he and Kruse personally led with the two Nassau battalions. The Prince was wounded and the Nassau regiment recorded that the attack was 'largely unsuccessful'; Kruse even wrote of their 'confusion and retreat ... leaving on the plateau only small bodies of brave men'. Its role in the fighting now ended.[18]

The French covering cannonade ceased as the *Garde* neared the crest, and the columns had to endure murderous double-shotted cannon-fire from the British, fired at '200 yards' or even less. Everywhere there was smoke, sometimes dense, so that men could almost blunder on each other quite unexpectedly, to the surprise and discomfiture of both sides at different moments.

The leading column of the *Garde* came up and was faced by Colin Halkett's 5th Brigade behind the ammunition-less batteries. At this point Chassé sent forward Major van der Smissen's horse battery under Captain Kramer and this immediately proved its value in blasting the French at short range, while Halkett's 2/30th, 2/73rd, 33rd and 2/69th sought to stem the advance. Virtually all the men of the 2/30th who later recorded their memories are insistent that they fired and charged, and that the *Garde* fell back. But there is evidence of a loss of nerve among Halkett's men at some point, and (as the *Garde* did not break through) this may have been at first encounter, with a subsequent recovery thrusting back the French.[19] My impression is that the *3e* and *4e Grenadiers à Pied* came up, exchanged fire with Halkett's men, who gave way, that van der Smissen blasted the French at point-blank range and shook them so severely that the re-steadied British infantry could fire, charge and drive them off.

What role, then, did Chassé's division play in this repulse? For there were many claims, particularly in the first years of the twentieth century, that the 3rd Netherlands Division played a large part in repulsing the *Garde*. De Bas and T'Serclaes de Wommersom wrote that 'the enemy vanished before the bayonets of Detmers's brigade, led by General Chassé', and that seeing Halkett's brigade hesitate and fall back, Chassé 'lifted his sword and ordered, as he had done on so many battlefields, "Forward, with the bayonet!" ... ordering the drums to beat the charge.' They also quoted the divisional narrative: 'Shouting "*Orange boven, Vive le Roi!*" the brigade rushed forward despite the very heavy musketry fire and although threatened on the flank by an attack of cavalry, when suddenly the French *Garde*, against whom our attack was directed, left its position and disappeared before us.'[20] Detmers's 3,300-strong brigade certainly suffered 399 casualties (of whom 184 were wounded – so that killed may have been about 70) which would mean about 11 per cent (or 7 per cent if a deduction is made for missing) and all these in the last part of the action. So it may be that such losses match the intense French musketry fire from adversaries such as the *Garde*. British accounts may be too critical, but there is a telling observation by Macready, about which he is unlikely to have been mistaken. After his battalion had suffered its last casualties, 'a heavy column of Dutch infantry (the first we had seen) passed, drumming and shouting like mad, *with their chakos on top of their bayonets*, near enough to our right for us to see and laugh at them, and after this the noise went rapidly away from us. Soon after we piled arms, chatted, and lay down to rest.'[21] Who would advance to battle through heavy enemy fire from an elite unit with shakos on their bayonets? Is it not more likely to be the mode when following up a disappearing or broken enemy?

Wellington was now behind Maitland's 2nd and 3rd Battalions of the 1st Guards, watching as the two battalions of the *3e Chasseurs à Pied* came up. The Guardsmen were invisible to the *Garde* who could see only an empty summit. Wellington called out, 'Now, Maitland! Now's your time!' At a word of command the Guards Brigade rose, in line four deep, making a scarlet barrier some 600 feet long (about 250 men) with muskets at the ready. This sudden apparition only thirty paces away was immediately followed by a devastating British volley into the body of the French column whose regimental colonel and both battalion commanders went down, as did some 20 per cent of the rank and file, already sore and reduced in numbers from the cannonade they had endured on the approach. Ney's horse had gone down (the fifth that day) so that Ney was leading his men on foot, almost blackened with smoke and powder and mud. The *Garde* had already seen General Friant retiring wounded, and now General Michel fell shot dead. Ney's ADC Crabbé recorded that 'calmly, the regiment formed into square [*sic*] and retired in order'.[22]

How orderly that retirement was is doubtful. For British practice, as shown many times in the Peninsular years, was for the volley to be followed by an immediate bayonet charge. The two battalions of the 1st Guards dashed forward, and the psychology of cold steel did the rest: the *3e Chasseurs* started to break apart and scatter as they fell back. But the *3e Chasseurs* were fortunate in that the *4e Chasseurs* were coming up on their left.

Maitland saw the danger and ordered the Guards to halt before they passed beyond command. His words were misheard, and while his left-hand battalion formed square on the forward slope the other turned back, or it may be that those flanking men who should have formed the sides of squares went on back up to the summit. Anyway, there was disorder and a confused dash back, so that the brigade only re-formed and came together on its original station as the *4e Chasseurs* continued to advance. Thus the threat was far from over, since the Guards needed a moment or two to settle again and the *4e Chasseurs* might not grant them the time. Fortunately Adam's Brigade (2/95th, a detachment of 3/95th, the large 1/52nd and the 71st) stood only a little further west.

VII

Three men saw the danger and independently reached the same decision. Wellington himself sent word to Colonel Sir John Colborne to intervene with his 52nd. The second was Wellington's ever-trustworthy Rowland Hill, for Clinton of the 2nd Division states that Adam's brigade of that division 'acted under Lord Hill's immediate direction' at this moment, which implies that Hill was personally involved.[23] But before any order could reach him Colborne had acted on his own initiative, saying to Adam, his brigade commander, 'I'm going to make that column feel our fire.' It was one more indication of that instinctive harmony that years of fighting collaboration had instilled into Wellington's best subordinates, and of those other words of trusting faith that Nelson enunciated to his 'band of brothers' in his great memorandum on how Trafalgar should be fought: 'Captains are to look to their particular Line as their rallying point. But, in case signals can neither be seen or perfectly understood, no Captain can do very wrong if he places his ship alongside that of an enemy.'

Every student of Waterloo will have a personal selection of the truly great decisions, but among the first half dozen, nearly everyone will include Colborne's action: in old age, Field Marshal Sir William Gomm thought that those words of Colborne's 'sealed the fate of the battle'.[24] Sir John, so skilled in outpost fighting and so brilliant in the quick decisions that go with it, wheeled back his left wing by 45 degrees and wheeled forward the rest of his battalion in 'two lines, not four deep' so that it could 'move on the left flank of the Imperial column, and fire into the column to retard the movement'. The effect on the column's flank was instant and terrible. The attention of the attackers was fixed upon the disarray among the Guards immediately in front of them, Adam's men being back behind the crest; so that the movement of the 52nd took the *Garde* totally by surprise. One account says that 'it was not until the 52nd's skirmishers fired into them that the Imperial Guard halted, then as many files as possible, on the left of each company of their leading column, faced outwards and returned the fire';[25] the British skirmishers slipped away to the sides as Colborne's battalion closed and fired without halting, the ranks leap-frogging while the leaders reloaded, so that the musketry never ceased for an instant. For a few moments the French kept order and fired back, inflicting heavy casualties (Colborne put his casualties at 150 men in a battalion of about 1,000 rank and file), but the impact of Colborne's surprising wheel, his volleys, and then his order to charge with the bayonet destroyed the spirit of the raked and ravaged column, and it gave way. The Guards, now back under discipline and ready for the next assault, heard Lord Saltoun shout to his men, 'Now's the time, my boys!' and the entire brigade of Guards took up the word and dashed forward to complete the counter-attack.[26]

Colborne, for his part, was quite aware that his right or outer flank was open, since the 71st (which would have to make a much wider wheel) had not caught up. Just as the 2/95th and the 71st came forward, a body of horsemen was seen nearby and Sir John was preparing to halt and re-form, lest they should be French.[27] Wellington, who had personally ordered the 2/95th in support of the 52nd, was riding to join him, and could see that the horsemen were the 23rd Light Dragoons, and so called out to him, 'Well, never mind, go on, go on!' During these minutes Hill's horse was brought down and he himself was ridden over, but he soon recovered and found a fresh horse; Adam was with the Duke as he went forward, but at some point was incapacitated by a shot in the leg. The 52nd went down the slope, observing away to the left the stationary presence of 2,000–3,000 *Gardes* (perhaps the *Vieille* battalions); and then Colborne began to step out towards the further ridge beyond the dip. The 2/95th and the 71st gradually caught up with the 52nd in the advance.

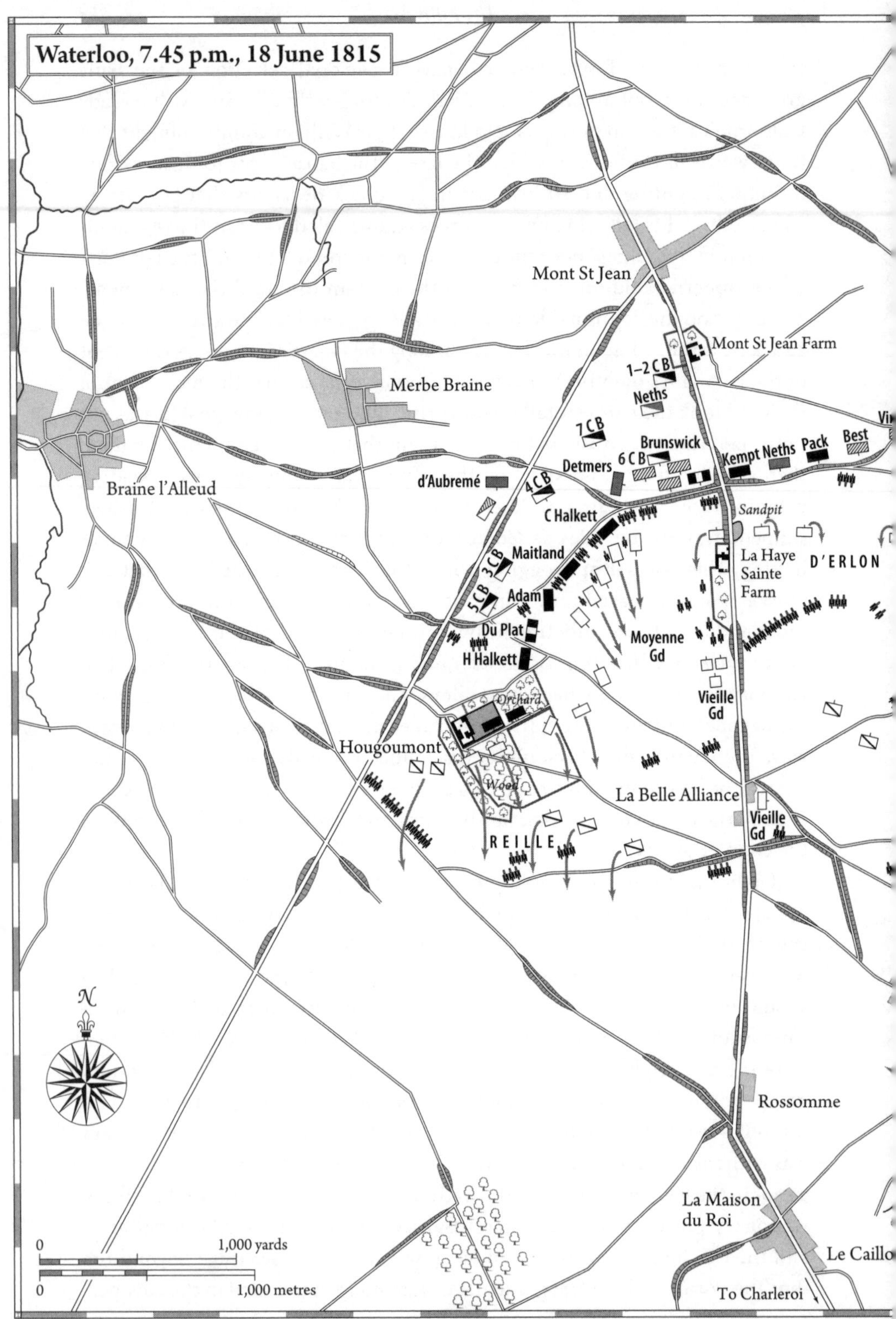
Waterloo, 7.45 p.m., 18 June 1815
Mont St Jean
Mont St Jean Farm
1–2 C B
Neths
Merbe Braine
7 C B
Brunswick
6 C B
Detmers
Kempt
Neths
Pack
Best
d'Aubremé
4 C B
Braine l'Alleud
C Halkett
Sandpit
Maitland
3 C B
La Haye Sainte Farm
D'ERLON
Adam
5 C B
Du Plat
Moyenne Gd
H Halkett
Vieille Gd
Orchard
Hougoumont
Wood
La Belle Alliance
Vieille Gd
REILLE
N
Rossomme
La Maison du Roi
0
1,000 yards
0
1,000 metres
Le Caillo
To Charleroi

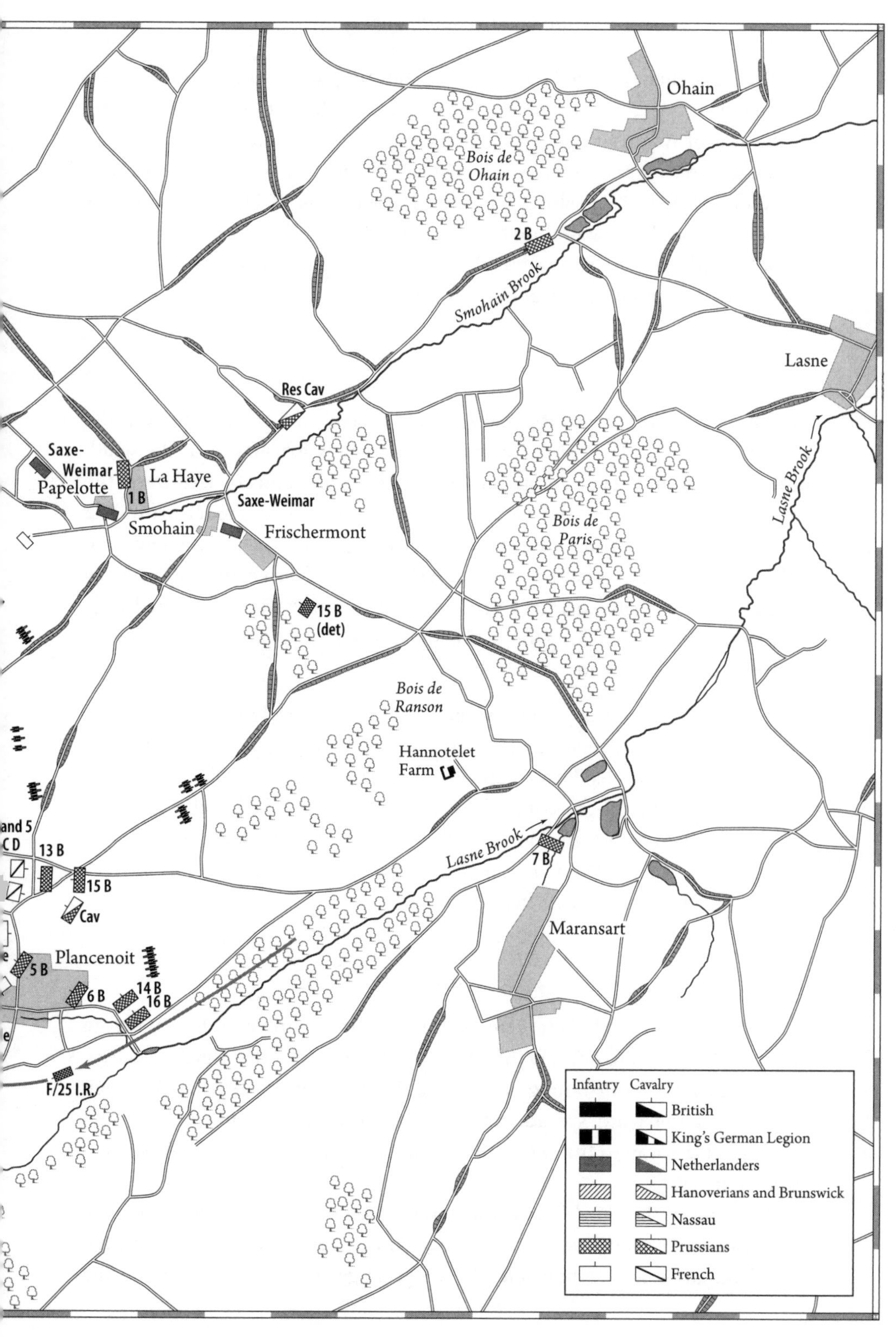
Ohain
Bois de Ohain
2 B
Smohain Brook
Lasne
Res Cav
Saxe-Weimar
La Haye
Papelotte
1 B
Saxe-Weimar
Smohain
Frischermont
Bois de Paris
Lasne Brook
15 B (det)
Bois de Ranson
Hannotelet Farm
and 5 C D
13 B
15 B
Cav
Lasne Brook
7 B
Maransart
Plancenoit
5 B
6 B
14 B
16 B
F/25 I.R.
Infantry
Cavalry
British
King's German Legion
Netherlanders
Hanoverians and Brunswick
Nassau
Prussians
French

The Duke then reached Hugh Halkett, standing on the summit and beyond Adam's position. Clinton meanwhile had ordered Halkett forward in support of the rest of Adam's brigade that was advancing and catching up with the 52nd. Halkett sent his Bremenvörde, Quackenbrück and Salzgitter Landwehr battalions to help in pushing back the French around Hougoumont. His Osnabrück Landwehr battalion he led personally to follow the 71st and cover its right flank, and it was Hugh Halkett who during the general advance was to capture the famous General Cambronne, as we shall soon see.[28]

VIII

Wellington now turned the cavalry of Vivian and Vandeleur on the retreating French. East of the crossroads Sergeant Robertson of the 92nd, now commanding two companies since the only officers left were the commanding officer and the adjutant, saw confusion in the French army. The adjutant wondered if the French were mutinying, and ordered the battalion to be ready to march forward. Then an ADC galloped past shouting, 'The day is our own, the Prussians have arrived,' and the men were restrained only with difficulty from dashing forwards. There was a pause of several minutes.[29]

Robertson continued:

> The Duke was standing in his stirrups with his hat elevated above his head. Every eye was fixed upon him, and all were waiting with impatience to make a finish to such a hard day's work. At last he gave three waves with his hat and the loud three cheers that followed the signal were the heartiest that had been given that day. On seeing this, we leapt over the hedge that had been such a protection to us during the engagement and in a few minutes we were among the French lines.[30]

IX

Adam's brigade and Halkett were pushing a mass of French infantry before them, and these were not line infantry only, but many of the *Moyenne Garde*. The sight of the *Garde* falling back broke the nerve of the exhausted French troops, and the word spread, rippling out from this vicinity further and further, all the way to the very ends of the line: '*La Garde recule!*' And then, '*Sauve qui peut!*'

The sight of the *Garde*'s defeat was in itself enough to engender this sense of despair, but it may have been worsened by the feeling of betrayal for which Napoleon alone was responsible. As the great general attack began and the firing at Plancenoit behind the right wing grew louder, the Emperor had sent his ADCs galloping from unit to unit shouting 'Grouchy is arriving!' as an encouragement for the supreme effort in front. Ney, a week after the battle, summed it up in a way that can scarcely be bettered:

> About seven o'clock in the evening, after the most frightful carnage that I have ever witnessed, General La Bédoyère came to me with a message from the Emperor, that Marshal Grouchy had arrived on our right, and attacked the left of the English and Prussians united. This general officer, in riding along the lines, spread this intelligence among the soldiers, whose courage and devotion remained unshaken, and who gave new proofs of them at that moment, in spite of the fatigue which they experienced. Immediately after, what was my astonishment – I should rather say, indignation – when I learned that so far from Marshal Grouchy having arrived to support us, as the whole army had been assured, between 40 and 50,000 Prussians attacked our extreme right, and forced it to retire! Whether the Emperor was deceived with regard to the time when the Marshal could support him, or whether the march of the Marshal was retarded ... the fact is that at the moment when his arrival was announced to us, he was only at Wavre.[31]

It had been a desperate improvisation, and only success could have excused it. Failure exposed the Grouchy story as a lie, and a lie told to the most loyal and trusting men in the French Empire. Ney spoke for many. It was as well that for several years nobody guessed the truth about the actual messages between Napoleon and Grouchy.

But in other respects Ney may have confused matters, for his remarks seem to suggest that it was a mythical 'stab in the back' that broke the final attack (what Ludendorff and his friends a century later would call '*der Dolchstoss von hinten*', and with no better justification). For in 1815 (as in 1918) the army broke from the front, defeated in a straight fight. Shaken and discouraged at the repeated setbacks they had suffered, they were utterly dismayed at the ultimate throw for victory. The *Garde*'s failure broke their hearts, and the deception over Grouchy's 'arrival' when instead it was the Prussians who came, proved the final straw. The *Garde*'s defeat left Ney standing, furiously calling on the troops to rally. Morale had gone with that shock defeat. The lie merely added to the despair.

Foy's men broke and fled, Reille saw *2e Corps* disintegrate, d'Erlon's force streamed back, and on the right wing the morale of Durutte's soldiers evaporated and they turned for the south and the road to France. It was now between 7.30. and 7.45 p.m Sir A. S. Frazer wrote: 'The enemy was forced to give way. I have seen nothing like that moment, the sky literally darkened with smoke, the sun just going down, and which till then had not for some hours broken through the gloom of a dull day.' De Lacy Evans, further to the left, noted that 'the firing now died away. The smoke gradually dispersed. At this moment the setting sun, hitherto darkened by clouds and mists, burst forth with unusual majesty, disclosing to our transported view all the triumphant scene.'[32] It was an historic sunset, since a whole century would elapse before the next sunset on a battlefield in a war in which every major power in Europe would be joined.

X

Ney's angry words of 26 June and mention of Durutte lead us back to flame-ravaged Plancenoit and the street fighting that won it for the Prussians, with all the costs that such tactics impose. It is grim enough in its own right and yet it is dwarfed by the greater tragedy that was already befalling the French army and its finest troops on the slopes of Mont St Jean.

The end of the fight for Plancenoit can be told very quickly, for once the F/25th Infantry Regiment had got through the woods and begun to emerge above and behind the French right flank in the village, the defenders could no longer hold on. The *2e Chasseurs* under General Pelet formed the rearguard, but had to abandon cannon, ammunition and wagons. Pelet famously shouted, 'To me, *Chasseurs*, save the eagle or die round it!'; and the call was heard by the Prussians and recorded in the 25th Infantry Regiment's *History*.[33]

This brought the fighting to an end on this front. A glance at the map gives an idea of the progress of the advance since 4.30 p.m., or, to put it the other way, the firmness of the defence. Blücher had continually reinforced his attack, so that it is probable that around 25,000 men of IV and II Corps had been involved in driving back a French force that is not likely to have exceeded 10,000 at any point in the fighting. The casualties are known for the Prussian side: just under 6,700 men killed wounded and missing; French officer casualties are known,[34] and by making an estimate for the lower ranks we may come to a figure of between 5,000 and 6,000 other-rank casualties. What this means is that, while the smaller French contingent suffered proportionately much more than the Prussians, their desperate defence had bought valuable time for Napoleon, time that he had squandered. Had Napoleon captured the ridge at Mont St Jean, then (to adapt the Blücher/Gneisenau message to Thielemann) he might plausibly in typical *Bulletin* fashion have justified the French suffering at Plancenoit as not mattering because of the greater good in victory over Wellington. Instead, it added to the ruin.

XI

And so the ruined village of Plancenoit finally was lost despite a remarkable and sustained effort by the French. Hofschröer writes: 'By 8.30 p.m. the Prussians were masters of the key to the French rear,'[35] which suggests that the lock could now be opened. But timing is everything. The key had been won too late, as the judgement by the great Prussian historian Pflugk-Harttung made plain: 'If Bülow had captured Plancenoit an hour earlier, he would have achieved the decisive results in the flank and rear, which Wellington now won at the front.'[36]

*

Appendix 1: A French Military Thinker on Waterloo

One of the most insightful military thinkers of the mid-nineteenth century was Colonel Charles Ardant du Picq, who served in the Crimea, in Syria and North Africa, and who died of wounds in the Franco-Prussian War, on 19 August 1870, aged forty-eight. His testament is his *Etudes sur le Combat*, which was reprinted from the 1903 complete edition as recently as 1942, and was praised as an outstanding examination of the psychology of war by my late friend Dr Paddy Griffith in his *Modern Studies of the War in Spain and Portugal, 1808–1814* (1999), which was a review and critique of Sir Charles Oman's masterpiece.[37]

Ardant du Picq was not an historian in the sense that Oman was, but his perception was acute and his judgements remarkably free from nationalist prejudice. Here is his summary assessment of Waterloo:

> But who can speak of Waterloo – about which one has over and over spoken passionately – and speak impartially without shame? Waterloo gained would scarcely have advanced our affairs; Napoleon attempted the impossible, and against the impossible genius itself can do nothing. We had not made serious inroads during the terrible fight against English solidity and tenacity during the period before the Prussians arrived. Then the Prussians appeared (and had the wit to do so just at the right time for our self-esteem) and we faced to the flank against them. The rout began, however, not among the troops engaged against the Prussians, but among those facing the English. We were tired perhaps but no more than they were. Expecting succour from our right but instead coming under attack there, morale collapsed. Our right flank followed the [central rearward] movement, and what a movement!!![38]

Appendix 2: The *Garde* on the Slopes of Mont St Jean

There are two main problems for historians concerning the *Moyenne Garde*'s attack: the casualties and the attack formation. There is no certainty about the one and strong and continuing disagreement about the other. For what it is worth, I set down my own reasoning upon which I have based my text, but I cannot claim anything definite for it.

Casualties

In writing this account of Waterloo I have relied very heavily on various statistical tables in standard histories such as De Bas and T'Serclaes de Wommersom (DBTS), and Sir Charles Oman's articles in the *English Historical Review* (*EHR*) of October 1904 and January 1906. In 1904 Oman produced a statistical analysis of officer casualties based on a morning state of 10 June 1815 printed by Couderc de St Chamant (1902) and Martinien's tables of officer casualties (1899). But Couderc's 10 June morning state excluded the *Garde*. Subsequently Commandant Balagny found a return for the *Garde*, signed by General Dériot, Chief of Staff of the *Garde* and dated 16 June 1815, and passed it to Oman who published it in the *EHR* of 1906. In 1908 DBTS, vol. iii, pp. 168–9, provided a complete morning state of the *Garde* at 16 June 1815, but its officer numbers differed slightly from those of Dériot. Both Dériot and DBTS used morning figures before Ligny, where five officers were wounded (but whether or not they remained active, we do not know).[39]

Garde Infantry Casualties				
	Officers present 16 June	*Other ranks present 16 June*	*Officers killed and wounded, 18 June*	*Other ranks losses pro-rata to officers*
1er & 2e Gren. à Pied, VG	78 [64]	2,069	28 (36.4%)	745
1er & 2e Chass. à Pied, VG	68	2,402	18 (26.5%)	637
3e & 4e Gren. à Pied, MG	61 [59]	1,649	33 (57.9%)	955
3e & 4e Chass. à Pied, MG	64, inc. 4 wounded at Ligny	2,069	40 (62.5%)	1,293
Jeune Garde	117, inc. 1 wounded at Ligny	4,166	34 (29.3%)	1,221

The table summarises the *Garde* figures, which may be seen more fully in the sources cited. It gives Dériot's numbers for officers present [with the DBTS figures in square brackets where there is a difference]; DBTS numbers for other ranks present; the numbers for officer casualties and percentage from Oman; and *my own extrapolated figure for other ranks casualties* derived by using the *same* percentage as for officers. Naturally these extrapolated figures are merely indicative.

Some of the *Vieille Garde* fought at Plancenoit, and some on the Mont St Jean front – in the aftermath of the defeat of the *Moyenne Garde*. The *Vieille Garde* figures cannot be broken out between fronts, but as the *Jeune Garde* served only at Plancenoit, their casualty rate may help indicate the possible heaviness of the *Vieille* battalions' casualties there.

The *Moyenne Garde* fought only at Mont St Jean and the figures show clearly how terrible were its casualties. It is probably a fair generalisation to say that the more senior a *Garde* unit the more likely it was for other ranks to stay with the colours and fight to the end. Nevertheless, in comparing the official morning states immediately before the battle and those of 26 June 1815, the *Vieille Garde* reported a 59 per cent loss, the *Moyenne* 82 per cent and the *Jeune Garde* 86 per cent.[40] This does suggest that numbers of men, and possibly considerable numbers, had gone their own ways after the defeat and had not yet returned.

The Attack Formation

The second problem is the formation adopted by the *Moyenne Garde* for its attack, for some have written of an attack in columns and others of an attack in squares. Who is right it is impossible to say with certainty, although I believe Napoleon's words are fairly conclusive. There is no doubt whatever that before the Mont St Jean attack the *Vieille* and *Moyenne Garde* had been posted in squares as a reserve against a breakthrough at Plancenoit, and that after the failure of that attack and then in the evening as the French army fled, the remnants of the *Garde* resisted in squares (or when short of men, in a triangle). But both these occasions were defensive, and for that the square was well suited.

The attack was across a stretch of ground between Hougoumont and La Haye Sainte, rising from the valley floor (*le ravin*) to a featureless summit – ground that in later wars would be called 'no man's land', an open area about half a mile wide and slightly under half a mile in depth. It was not exactly easy going: the ground was somewhat irregular with little hollows and bumps, slippery with crushed stalks of rye, by now littered with dying men and horses, ploughed up and poached by hooves and shells. Indeed one infantryman who crossed from one side of the field to the other, wrote of 'the heavy state of the ground in the valley, into which, trampled and retrampled as it had been by twenty thousand horsemen, the sturdy rear-rank men sunk at times knee deep'.[41] This would present even more difficulties for a battalion of tall, heavy men. A walker today, if he did not want to turn his ankle, would take a good ten to fifteen minutes to cross it in poor conditions.

Whatever defenders there might be were more or less invisible in the dense gun-smoke, but the British artillery were wreaking havoc with double-shotted fire on the attackers as they crossed the open ground. The *Garde* had no skirmishers out to swarm round and neutralise the British guns, and cover their advance; all they had during the approach march was cover from the Grand Battery, which was blasting at the 'empty' summit.

There is one other feature to note. There was a spur of slightly higher land leading from the northern ridge well west of the crossroads, and towards the valley floor not far from the La Haye Sainte orchard. Part of the attack went up this spur and is most clearly marked on Craan's map of 1816, running from 'V' to 'v' according to his markings. But on both sides of it there were downward outer slopes, so that those to the west of the spur were subject to a leftward sideways pull.

In these conditions, and under such fire, what was required was a formation that combined speed and coordinated movement, one that was familiar and was easy to maintain. The column of attack did have these advantages, whereas the moving square was much more complicated. On a smooth level parade ground, highly trained men can certainly perform such manoeuvres, continually dressing by the right and left to maintain neat ranks, but on poached or ploughed-up ground, under fire, it is better simply to concentrate on the knapsack of the man immediately in front of you and trudge behind him, making the best possible speed to limit the damage from the cannons, than to have continually to look right and left to check your dressing, while worrying about turning your ankle.

If we had sight of the orders given to the *Garde*, that would naturally settle the question, but nobody has ever mentioned any, and so we have to rely on those who were at La Belle Alliance and saw it leave, those who were with the *Moyenne Garde* during the advance and retreat, and those who saw it approach out of the smoke. There is one witness to the start of the movement, and on that particular point he cannot be doubted. What he said thereafter is less safe as first-hand evidence. There are numerous French accounts of the advance that are non-specific, and some French ones that support the advance in column, for the battalions advanced at the *pas de charge*, which is quick step (and not slow or parade time, that would be more suitable for a movement up the encumbered slope in a square formation). Some of these French accounts state that once the *Garde* had been checked, it then formed square and retired as best it could.[42] Every British eye-witness watching the *Garde*'s approach stated that it was made in columns.

For the departure we have the evidence of General Petit, commanding the *1er Grenadiers à Pied* of the *Vieille Garde*.[43] He claimed that the actual attack was made in squares by battalion (in other words two squares to a regiment), except for the two *4e Régiments* (each of only one battalion of *Grenadiers* and one of *Chasseurs*) which formed one each, and that 'it was in this formation that they went forward', the squares gradually bunching closer to each other. Since he was very close to the starting point he must be believed when he states that they *left* the reserve position at La Belle Alliance 'in square of battalions [*en carrés sur bataillons*]' down to the valley floor. But he remained behind, watching against a threat from Plancenoit; he states that his '*1er Régiment de Grenadiers* formed into two squares . . . on the summit of the position dominating the little road out of Plancenoit,' where it remained, and so his view of what took place in the valley must have been somewhat limited, and what occurred near Mont St Jean even more so.[44]

Once down in the valley Napoleon re-formed the attack, for he diverted the *2/3e Grenadiers* from the other battalions to a holding position further west, then handed over command to Ney, and himself went to stand with the diverted unit. He had several times during this campaign complained of Ney's performance. This was a moment even more critical, and he was giving the Marshal part of his cherished *Garde*: did he really not ensure that Ney understood perfectly *this time* what his master wanted him to do? Moreover, he saw the formation in which the attack was to be made. If it was not to his liking he had only to order Ney to conform.

Taking French accounts of the attack, we should note the number that speak of 'column', 'deployment', 'forming square', and ask ourselves what the troops deployed from or what was the formation before they formed square.

Ney's ADC Levavasseur said that the force advanced 'by platoons', which implies individual half-companies. When Crabbé, one of Napoleon's ADCs, was sent with fresh instructions for Ney he came up with the attackers advancing (understandably) at 'the *pas de charge*', not an easy pace in hollow square, but normal in a column. The contributors to *Victoires et Conquêtes* wrote that pressing up the slope and passing a first line and a disabled battery, 'The French column [*la colonne française*] . . . came upon a second enemy line posted with artillery in the sunken way or behind various obstacles . . . while the French battalions deployed [*les bataillons françaises se deployaient*] at pistol distance, fresh artillery and musketry fire swept away the head of this column [*la tête de cette colonne*] and ravaged the masses in its interior.'[45] On closing with the enemy, said one battalion commander, Guillemin, 'we opened fire in two ranks', but when the British replied with a volley and artillery fire a Captain Prax recalled that 'all our heads of columns were put *hors de combat*'. General Pelet remarked on 'the ravage this fire made in the depth of the column; it attempted to deploy' into line. The attack had been stopped.

Although Napoleon's comments are scattered ones, there is a letter to Bertrand of 27 March 1813 that sets out his general views at that time, two years before Waterloo,[46] but more importantly there is a comment that Bertrand recorded at St Helena on 23 October 1817: 'Ideas are not fixed today on the means of attack. A general never knows if he should attack in line or in column . . . If you attack in column you lack firepower. At Waterloo the *Garde* did not have time to deploy, did not open fire, and that led to the *déroute*.'[47] This is supported by a passing reference in Gourgaud's *Journal*, where on the 20th of the same month in a tête-à-tête with him Napoleon remarked 'at Waterloo the *Garde* was unable to deploy', and which in Gourgaud's *Campaign of 1815* became: 'The Emperor was then forming his guard into columns for the projected attack . . . without waiting until all the columns should be formed . . . he marched with the four first battalions to the left of La Haye Sainte,' and handed them to Ney who went forward to the heights.

> A quarter of an hour after, the other eight battalions arrived on the brink of the ravine: the Emperor formed them in the following order: one battalion in order of battle, having two in close column on its flanks, a formation which united the advantages of the narrow and the deep order. Two of these brigades thus ranged and marching at battalion distance, formed a first line, behind which the third brigade was posted in reserve . . . Meanwhile the four battalions of the middle guard were engaged with the enemy; they repulsed all before them [so that] upon the arrival of the old guard we should be masters of the whole field of battle.

The story then recounts the cries of treachery that ruined matters, and the retreat of the four battalions after several hours on the height. Plainly Gourgaud's story is problematical, but it would seem that he believed that the *Moyenne Garde*'s projected attack was in column, and that the second wave was differently organised.[48]

Thus there is considerable French evidence (and Napoleon's in particular) that supports the unanimous evidence of the British who saw the advance as nearing them in 'columns', 'in column as if marching on parade', 'the leading column', 'in an echelon or line (and not in a mass) of columns', that is, in a formation noticeably distinguishable as not in square. The dense smoke on the summit meant that an individual might see a formation coming straight at him, but could be only vaguely aware of formations approaching other parts of the front, and it was this that must have led so many to speak of two *Garde* columns approaching. There seems good reason to think that there were five, in echelon.

This brings us to the retirement. When the attackers gave way and retreated, the Allied infantry and cavalry were ordered forward. Against cavalry a square is essential. Crabbé remarked, 'the regiment formed into square and retired in order'. At some stage in the retirement (for the words by their very nature cannot be placed earlier) Guillemin saw Ney 'come into my square' and declare that there was nothing left but to die there. Prax, who earlier had seen the heads of his *Garde* column put *hors de combat*, also recounted the closing stages, and wrote that he saw 'the centre of the army' with 'columns that were fleeing', which again suggests that columns were pretty general in this attack.

Two accounts speak of squares, but in various respects they are not entirely reliable. One old soldier called Salle, a farrier in the *1/2e Chasseurs* spoke of the attack phase: immediately forming in square and marching on [*'on forma de suite le carré et nous fûmes dirigés sur'*] the village of Waterloo, but the account is full of mistakes and the village where his battalion was engaged was actually Plancenoit. Yet another, Franquin of the *3e Grenadiers* in the *Moyenne Garde*, wrote of a late stage in the contest, well after the failure of the attack: 'The English blazed at us. We had formed square [*nous avions formé le carré*] and replied as best we could to the fire that made great gaps in our ranks. Several times an English general called on the *Garde* to surrender, and each time I heard General Cambronne reply: "The *Garde* dies and does not surrender"': this would seem to place the account not on the slopes but back in the valley or even close to La Belle Alliance, for Cambronne was not with the *Moyenne Garde* but commanded a battalion of the *Vieille Garde*.[49]

Exactly how column was formed we cannot say, but it may be that each battalion (of four companies) was possibly in *colonne d'attaque par division* by companies, that is two companies abreast, each three ranks deep, followed by two more two companies abreast (also each of three ranks), thus with a frontage of about 50 yards (say 60 men) and a depth of six ranks (about 35 yards deep), which permitted the rear companies to change front to form square or to swing out into line on either side of the leading companies when deploying for the musketry battle.[50] There is at least one source (Guillemin) who said that the deployed depth was reduced from groups of three ranks, to two ranks: that would increase the frontage and initial fire-power.

The two main arguments for the square are width of objective, and danger from cavalry. Taking the first, it is argued that the French attacked a front stretching from Colin Halkett's position to Maitland's: that is on a front a quarter mile (440 yards) long, and that if there were only two columns they could not have extended across so long a front.[51] The argument is perhaps weakened (a) if the frontage of each column were broad (two ranks instead of three) and (b) if *five* such columns came up in echelon: the protagonists of squares maintain that there were five of them.[52] As to the Allied cavalry, it had been fairly inactive in the later phases of the day and, if it had been judged a real threat, *why was Piré*'s little used and comparatively fresh cavalry division not deployed to protect the *Garde*? This seems to suggest that Allied cavalry were not deemed a serious threat before and during the *Garde* attack.

All but one of the British eye-witnesses on the crest, watching the *Garde* come up out of the smoke, moving as much as possible at the *pas de charge* (not in a ceremonial and cumbrous slow formation), and coming to within pistol shot of them – all these eye-witnesses said that they were in column.[53] British soldiers knew the difference between a square and a column, and the *Garde* was visible, coming closer, not far off. Why would they say they were in column if they were in square? One observer might be mistaken, but surely not virtually every individual, when all independently said the same. Given the *unanimity* of British accounts, given *the number* of French accounts that speak of a *colonne* in the *attacking* phase, and *afterwards* of a *carré* being formed in defeat, how much credence should we give Petit at Plancenoit, peering through smoke and the best part of a mile away?

The Pull of the Slope

There is a minor matter in addition: did the attack go off course, and if so, did it matter? The *Moyenne Garde* was drawn up quite close to the ruins of La Haye Sainte, and there Ney took over the command. As they went up the spur of higher ground, the pull of the side slope made the attackers drift slightly to the left and brought them towards Maitland's sector.[54] It is said that Napoleon burst out that Ney had once again ruined his plans by attacking obliquely instead of in the centre; but the problem is that nobody then or later can say where, in this context, 'the centre' was. The crossroads was behind La Haye Sainte and the wrecked buildings would be an impediment for any attack aiming at the crossroads; *and in fact that sector was left to Donzelot,* whose attack was merely to support the flank of the main attack and hold the Allies down. Someone had ordered the Grand Battery to bombard west of the crossroads, which implied that the attack was aimed at an area from the crossroads towards where the Lion Mound now stands. Anyone who stands on the rise, or looks at Mark Adkin's remarkable photograph (pp. 394–5) of the ridge seen from below (and blanks out the Lion Mound, built 1824–7) will see how featureless the area is. So the attack was aimed at somewhat to the left of the crossroads, and did go off further leftwards, but as Hougoumont was held by Wellington, the area where the column arrived, well to the east of Hougoumont, was still a vital part of the line. Did it matter in the end? Yes, because it brought the *Garde* up against the British Guards and close to Colborne's 52nd, rather than against less cohesive forces like those of Halkett and Kruse. But did Napoleon or Ney know that or guess that beforehand? I suspect not.

As I have said, these are my personal views, and I am aware that good authorities, including Mark Adkin and Andrew Field, have adopted the square as the formation. They may be right. Whatever we all argue, it is really a matter for the reader.

Chapter 45

The Victory

The Reckoning

I

THE SIGHT OF WELLINGTON, standing in his stirrups with his hat held high, is one of the iconic moments of this desperate day. The French were breaking, and the Anglo-Allied army was on the brink of victory amid the carnage of the Mont St Jean ridge; but if it advanced in an uncoordinated way it might still meet with a serious check. Wellington's principal concerns at this point were to maintain momentum and retain control.

Adam's Brigade was advancing down the slope, led by the 52nd; 2/ and 3/95th and the 71st were slightly behind them; Hugh Halkett was leading the Osnabrück Landwehr from above Hougoumont; Chassé's Netherlanders were pressing forward in the centre. By the time they reached the valley bottom their ranks were becoming disorganised, and if any resolute French cavalry should turn on them they might be in trouble. Wellington had already ordered his most lightly used cavalry brigade (Vivian) to close on the retreating French and force them into flight, but not to engage unless reasonably certain of success. Vandeleur was ordered to second him. Vivian led his men down the slope, noted that squares of the *Vieille Garde* were holding a mound, and that *Garde* cavalry were active nearby. Adam's men had by now passed La Haye Sainte's orchard and Vivian feared that they could be a target for the enemy horse, and decided to attack. There was a short cavalry combat and the French horsemen gave way.

In later years Vivian tended to magnify his actions in the pursuit and to link them perhaps a little too directly with the climax on the summit: the unshowy and level-headed Tomkinson of Vandeleur's brigade remarked that 'Sir Hussey told me he had *turned* the fate of the day by charging with his brigade. The place he charged at was two miles out of the position and half an hour after the enemy retired.'[1] To which the only comment must be 'Ouch!' Those who wish to venture into the claims and counter-claims and further ripostes on who 'turned' the fate of the day at the climax, are respectfully advised to turn to the substantial articles and piles of correspondence – penned with the same self-belief, dogged determination and lust for victory as in the great battle – to be found in Colburn's *United Service Journal* (later *Magazine*) and in the Siborne collection of letters.

Vandeleur's cavalry came alongside Vivian, and they all attacked the mounted Grenadiers and Chasseurs. The infantry paused in the valley, got second wind, and restored their formations. How long this pause lasted is not clear: Siborne says 'a few moments', others that it may have lasted for up to ten or more minutes, but the pause was a noticeable one. It could not last long, lest it give the enemy chance to recover breath.[2] The Duke scrutinised the French troops and told Adam, 'They won't stand, better attack them.' Adam's men again went forward, exchanged fire with the *Garde* squares, and forced them to give way. To Adam's right Halkett and his Osnabrückers saw two battalions of *chasseurs à pied* whose general was vainly trying to rally them: in the result Halkett took the officer prisoner. He was Cambronne.[3] At this point a fresh enemy force was seen, and had it been actively deployed it might have gained time and helped cover the French retreat. Piré's light cavalry division was moving along the crest, but it ignored any opportunities down on the slopes and made its way beyond Rossomme. Further to Wellington's right the remnants of French infantry in the thickets round Hougoumont were winkled out. The entire right wing and centre of his line were now in full pursuit of the defeated enemy.

II

The effects of Wellington's advance started to reach the French right wing. D'Erlon's men feared that they would be cut off and they disintegrated and fled, d'Erlon going with them, despite Ney's cry, 'D'Erlon, if we survive this you and I will be hanged!'[4] On the far right Brue's brigade of Durutte's division was still holding out quite well, though Durutte had been grievously wounded and disfigured by two sabre cuts and could no longer command. Ney rushed to Brue and tried to use his men to check the disintegration, but they, too, were infected by the general panic and broke in turn, afraid of being cut off if they remained where they were.[5]

Thus far Wellington's advancing troops had driven off infantry and cavalry. Now they seized the most desired objective in any battle – the enemy's final gun line. The guns either had not been hitched up, or their traces had been cut and the horses purloined, or they were stuck in the soft ground. 'Saving the guns' often serves military historians and history-painters as a way of off-setting what would otherwise be an unmitigated defeat: Maiwand and Colenso are notable instances in British annals. There was no such attempt here. There would be no saving French guns; tomorrow there would be no French cannon to blast away Allied men and horses in further fighting. Wellington's men passed through the guns, merely chalking their regimental numbers on them as claim for possession on the morrow. Whatever the French might do in future, they would do it without this magnificent arsenal; *in a very real sense taking the gun line was the decisive moment of victory.*[6]

Tired as they were, still the troops did not halt. They reached La Belle Alliance and passed beyond it. Only then did Adam's brigade halt, having covered 2 miles of broken ground since their strike against the *Garde*. But they encountered a new problem: more friendly fire. Müffling in his 1815 *History* summed it up quite briefly: 'The cannon-shot of Bülow's artillery [near Plancenoit], directed against the enemy's troops near La Belle Alliance, by recoiling [i.e. ricochet], already reached the British army, which advancing through the hollow could not be perceived by General Bülow's artillery.' Wellington sent the Sardinian commissioner de Sales to Bülow to warn him.[7] Bülow for his part was to note in his battle report:

> The Duke of Wellington had warned us that he was about to attack [*dass er im Begriff sei einem Sturm Angriff*] the position of La Belle Alliance and we duly suspended our artillery fire, and our right wing therefore advanced as rapidly as possible without the aid of cannons; and our cavalry reserves from all the army corps passed through our infantry and pushed rapidly as far as the Brussels *chaussée*, where they found the enemy in full flight. Night and the blockages on the road from abandoned enemy guns put an end to our pursuit.[8]

That report ignores a minor incident on this sector that may be timed immediately after Bülow's ceasing fire but before his right wing reached the summit and advanced without cannon support. Lobau had been endeavouring to hold off the Prussians at Plancenoit, but was also becoming fearful for his rear. He sent a column of artillery and infantry up the hollow track to La Belle Alliance and this reached the summit just after a *Vieille Garde* square had retreated past the junction. The column found itself not back among Frenchmen but almost face to face with the 52nd: the French infantry fired and tried to escape, the artillery ran into the bank beside the track and the artillery horses were brought down. Men fled or surrendered, and the guns were seized by the 52nd.[9]

Though the French line regiments were breaking, the *Vieille Garde* was retiring in magnificent order, beating off a charge by the 10th and 18th

Hussars, but suffering all the time from the converging fire of the advancing victors. Men fell in ones and twos, often more, with every onset. It had not only the enemy to face, it had also to struggle through the mob of soldiers that poured past its sides and on down the road. Still the *Vieille Garde* kept its ranks, the last relic of the last army of France. It had more than fulfilled its oath to the Emperor.

Napoleon, with Soult, Lobau, Bertrand and Drouot, rode away to the southern summit, and joined the *1er Bataillon* of the *1er Chasseurs à Pied*, stationed to secure the treasury wagons and the imperial carriages. Most of the vehicles had already departed, but it would seem that the carriage of the Secretary of State (Maret, Duc de Bassano[10]) broke down and he had to flee on foot, leaving the vehicle full of papers and personal effects that were seized by the Prussians. There was nothing for Napoleon to do but ride into the night and seek to return to France.

One commander, abandoned by his colleagues and his men, still stood on the slopes below La Belle Alliance. Michel Ney, without hat, without horse, 'looking less like a man than a wild beast', was shouting, 'Come, see how a Marshal of France dies!' but the men streamed past him, and the bullets that he sought all passed him by. He found one square of the *Garde* still holding out, but as darkness fell the square received Napoleon's direct order to retreat, and Ney was left to trudge and stagger exhausted along the high road, until supported by a corporal. At last he encountered Lefebvre-Desnouettes, and by him was given a spare horse.[11] Ney went into the night, his great career ending in ruin. Only once more in his life was he to confront musketry.

III

All observers spoke of the intensity of the musketry and cannon-fire, and of the heaps of fallen men, and yet in this tempest of fire Wellington – like the salamander Ney – somehow miraculously escaped: 'his person, as usual, seemed invulnerable, although his sword was struck'.[12] Officers and men were astounded at his survival, for so many of his colleagues fell, and continued to fall until the very last shots fired.

The Earl of Uxbridge was at the Duke's side during the final advance, and expressed concern lest the advance went too far and suffered a setback, but Wellington simply replied, 'Oh damn it! In for a penny, in for a pound is my maxim and if the troops advance they shall go as far as they can.'[13] Uxbridge decided to ride ahead, join the light cavalry, and keep up their momentum, but at that moment was hit by a cannon shot that shattered his right knee, upon which the famous exchange is supposed to have occurred 'By God, sir,

I've lost my leg!' – 'By God, sir, so you have!' He was supported in the saddle by the Duke, and then carried back by his aides to Waterloo village where the leg was amputated. That day eight horses had been killed under him, and he was riding his ninth, a borrowed animal. Vandeleur took over from Uxbridge.

By this stage the Duke's companions were few indeed: the Sardinian Comte de Sales was almost the only commissioner left, for Müffling was absent near Papelotte, the Austrian Vincent had been wounded, the Russian Pozzo and the Spanish Alava had been hit or badly bruised. Lord FitzRoy Somerset, Wellington's Military Secretary, had been hit in the right arm at 6 p.m. and was about to have it amputated; General Barnes, Adjutant-General, was wounded, as was his deputy Elley; De Lancey, DQMG, was mortally wounded; of the Duke's five ADCs, Canning and Gordon were dead or dying. As a result the help of two unofficial aides was of the greatest value: the Duke of Richmond came to watch the fighting as a civilian 'in plain clothes', cheering on the Inniskillings in the great Union Brigade charge, and performing small errands. His partially blind younger son Lord William Pitt Lennox did what he could to help, as well. Also, Lord Bathurst's eldest son, Lord Apsley, though in the diplomatic service, 'in a plain blue coat and round hat . . . conveyed orders for the Duke to different parts of the field'. These deeds are worth remembrance.[14]

Of the three corps commanders, Uxbridge had just been seriously wounded, Orange had been hit in the shoulder, and Hill had been knocked over but was back again on his feet; among divisional commanders, Picton was dead, and Cooke and Alten wounded. Among the cavalry brigade commanders, Ponsonby had been killed, Dörnberg and Grant wounded, while the Netherlands cavalry commanders Collaert and van Merlen were mortally wounded; in the infantry, Du Plat was dead, Kempt, Pack and Colin Halkett were all wounded. The burden that these casualties threw upon the Duke and his remaining staff in administering the army in the coming days cannot be overstated.

IV

One who joined Wellington as the evening drew on was the able and intelligent de Constant Rebecque, who, once he had seen the injured Prince of Orange taken from the field, went to find the Duke. As well as providing information and assistance, he recorded their snatches of conversation.

> A battery was on the plateau on the right of a village in our rear and taking us for the enemy, directed all its fire on us. At the Duke's request I sent

several officers, among others, General Chassé's ADC Mr Omphal, to General Bülow to warn him and cease his fire on us. We were then close to the farm of Rossomme. In riding forward the Duke speaking of the battle asked me [these next exchanges are in English in the journal]: *'Well, what do you think of it?'* and I replied *'I think, sir, it is the most beautiful thing you have done as yet.'* He added *'By God, I saved the battle four times myself!'* I then said [these exchanges are in French]: 'I suppose the battle will be named Mont St Jean!'; he replied 'No, Waterloo'. At Rossomme[15] we reached the *chaussée* which was littered with enemy cannon and we had difficulty in getting through the hamlet of la Maison du Roi, because of the abandoned guns found there, so we took to the right by the fields, and as it was 10 p.m. and full night, the Duke ordered the troops to halt and I took this order to Colonel Detmers's brigade, which bivouacked between La Maison du Roi and Caillou wood. We then returned with the Duke by the *chaussée* and between Caillou farm and La Maison du Roi encountered Field Marshal Blücher, General Bülow, and their staff. We congratulated each other, and agreed that the Prussians should continue the pursuit.

This account is so early and so detailed that it must be judged reliable, and it shows that the famous meeting took place about a mile south of La Belle Alliance and over 3 miles from Genappe. Yet both high commands placed it wrongly. Gneisenau in his victory despatch of 20 June 1815 was the first to misplace it:

All the Prussian columns had been marching towards this farm [La Belle Alliance], visible from all sides, where Napoleon stood during the battle, whence he sent his orders, where he flattered himself with hopes of victory, and where his ruin was decided. By happy chance it was there also that Marshal Blücher and Lord Wellington met in the dark and saluted each other as victors [Constant Rebecque wrote on his copy: 'They met further away, between Le Caillou farm and La Maison du Roi.'].[16]

Wellington, irritated by repeated questions from admirers and would-be historians about where the meeting took place, further complicated matters. Within one year he had somehow convinced himself that the meeting was at Genappe and he derided the claim that it was at La Belle Alliance.[17]

As darkness fell, Sergeant Robertson of the 92nd Gordons recorded that, 'We were ordered to halt for the night, while the Prussians marched past us. The place where we bivouacked was immediately at the end of the house where Napoleon had stood all day, which was by this time filled with the wounded.' As the Highlanders halted beyond the abandoned guns, 'The

Prussian cavalry advanced along the Brussels road, saluted as they passed, their bands playing "God save the King" and took up the pursuit.'[18]

It was the next phase that concerned Blücher and Wellington, not the details of what had passed, or the whys and wherefores of the day, or the name for the battle. It was quite sufficient for the fine old hero to burst out: '*Mein lieber Kamerad! Quelle affaire!*' It can have taken no more than a few minutes to agree that the Prussians would continue the pursuit, even though it must be with only a very small force. Those troops that were not picked for the pursuit bivouacked between La Belle Alliance and La Maison du Roi. Three battalions of light infantry were designated for the pursuit, two of them emerging from the ruins of Plancenoit: the F/25th Infantry Regiment (5th Brigade, II Corps) and the more heavily used F/18th Infantry (15th Brigade, IV Corps). The third was Witzleben's F/15th Infantry (16th Brigade, IV Corps) that had served on the left flank, working through the woods to bypass the French defences; this unit was far less knocked about. The light infantry went forward with General Gneisenau, and met no real opposition even when they reached Genappe, 4 miles away.[19]

V

The fleeing French choked the one street through Genappe, fighting each other with sword and bayonet to reach the bridge. Here the imperial travelling carriage still stood, on the wrong side of the bridge. Napoleon having reached the town was endeavouring to instil some order, but to no purpose. Then the Prussians were seen in the moonlight, and Napoleon had to abandon his carriage and take to horseback. Apparently the F/15th seized the carriage and its contents, including the famous 'proclamation from Laeken', uncut diamonds, gold worth 900,000 francs that had been stitched by his sister the beautiful Princess Pauline Borghese into the lining of a cloak, and Napoleon's dressing-case, uniform, telescope and sword; the jewels were sent to the Prussian king and became part of the regalia, and Blücher received the hat and effects. It was at Genappe that Lobau was captured; the famous and outstanding surgeon Larrey, now slightly injured, also fell into the hands of the pursuers,[20] and there Duhesme died in the arms of his ADC from the wounds suffered at Plancenoit. When Prince Blücher arrived a little before midnight he was lodged in the much frequented inn *Le Roi d'Espagne*: on this occasion what the *sommelier* heard is of no great concern for historians, although what he poured for his latest distinguished guest – and in what quantities – might be worth knowing.

The Prussian cavalry selected for the pursuit were units of I Corps, for they had mainly been in rear of the fighting infantry during the afternoon and evening. About 900 men were selected to lead the mounted force, the Brandenburg Dragoons Nr. 5 and the Brandenburg Uhlans Nr. 3, while the Kurmark (the old electoral Brandenburg) Landwehr Cavalry Nr. 2 (about 200 strong) were to follow. By the time that they reached Genappe the infantry were already in possession. The cavalry continued south under Gneisenau's personal command, passed through Quatre Bras, and continued for some while with a drummer-boy mounted on a carriage-horse and beating a relentless tattoo to frighten the enemy fugitives. They pulled up to rest between Liberchies, Frasnes and Mellet, about 7 miles beyond Genappe. It is said that the Kurmark unit passed on and even reached Charleroi; if so it was a bold excursion for so weak a force, and they were fortunate that no elements of French cavalry had re-formed.

As for Wellington, he rode north to his quarters in the village of Waterloo where, upon his dismounting, his charger Copenhagen kicked out and narrowly missed him. He went in, where his mess table was spread, but with many empty seats round it. Every time the door opened he looked up in hope that it would be one of his suite entering. But the places were not filled by the time he went to bed, and in the other rooms lay some of his wounded staff. There at midnight we shall leave him, meditating that 'Next to a battle lost, the greatest misery is a battle gained.'[21] For what happened on the Allied side in the early hours of Monday 19 June belongs to the next chapter.

VI

Had they found time for meditation, the French soldiery would have had nothing to mitigate the knowledge that 'the greatest misery is a battle lost'. All that splendid devotion, all the sacrifice, all the bullet-wounds and sabre cuts, the mutilation and disembowelling by cannon-shot had achieved nothing. Napoleon would not ride in triumph into Brussels, there would not be a fresh name to add to the many victories on the colours, the Empire would not strike terror into its neighbours, and the frontiers would not expand across Europe. Napoleon might raise another half-million men to hurl against the great coalition, but that would depend upon the mood in France, and it was no longer clear to the people of France (though Houssaye was reluctant to admit this) that 'France' meant nothing but 'the Emperor', that his views (enforced by his faithful soldiers) must be their views.

That at the highest level of argument the defeat of Napoleon was good for the peace of Europe surely needs no justification. It was perhaps a necessary evil that the Empire should founder so bloodily that never again could it represent the same threat to the nations around it. But as I pass in review all the events of these four days it is the tragedy of the French soldiers and their dream that haunts me: fed on promises and fed on little else, and condemned to die in their thousands for the satisfaction of one man's ambition. And for one soldier in particular I feel true sorrow. He was a man of a single talent and simple ideals who chose to throw in his lot with genius. The genius in these final months promised him much and then treated him badly, called him up belatedly, left him only half-informed, and sought to blame him for several of the mistakes that were not really all his fault. Many and great though his own faults were in 1815, I find Michel Ney the saddest victim of the last Napoleonic adventure and the future Napoleonic myth.

As a prelude to establishing the cost of victory and defeat, I shall begin with some of the accounts of the final hours of the drama written by senior officers, and starting with the Commander-in-Chief. Napoleon wrote three accounts, the first on 20 June 1815, next in 1817–18, and finally in 1819–20, and they differ so much in the way events are presented (or passed over) that it is difficult to draw up a synoptic account with the same events presented side by side in the three versions. Here I shall take some of the later paragraphs from the account written at Laon on 20 June 1815 and published in the next day's *Moniteur* (and for interest I shall add in square brackets and italics a few marginal comments de Constant Rebecque made on reading the document, the only ones known to me).[22]

At the point where my extract starts it is nearly 7 p.m. Having reinforced his right flank and shaken Wellington's troops by the use of the *cuirassiers*, as evening neared, Napoleon felt reasonably optimistic:

> As things stood, the battle was won. We occupied all the positions that the enemy held at the start of the action [*false*]; our cavalry having been employed too soon and badly we could no longer hope for a decisive success. But Marshal Grouchy, having learned of the movement of a Prussian corps, marched on the rear of that corps, thus assuring us of a striking success during the next day. After eight hours of firing and charges by infantry and cavalry, all the army saw with satisfaction that the battle was gained and the battlefield in our power.
>
> Around 8.30 p.m. the four battalions of the *Moyenne Garde*, which had been sent to the plateau beyond Mont St Jean [*error*] to support the *cuirassiers*, being irritated by the enemy cannon-fire, marched with the bayonet against the enemy to take his batteries. The day was ending; a charge on their flank by several English squadrons threw them into disorder; the fleeing men

came back across the valley; the neighbouring regiments, seeing some troops belonging to the *Garde* in flight, thought they were the *Vieille Garde*, and gave way; cries of 'All is lost, the *Garde* has been repulsed!' were heard; some soldiers even say that malevolents stationed at various points cried '*Sauve qui peut!*' However that may be, a terrified panic spread all at once across the entire battlefield; men dashed in the greatest disorder on the line of communications; soldiers, gunners, caissons fought to reach it; the *Vieille Garde* that was in reserve was assailed and itself borne away.

In an instant the army was nothing but a confused mass, all arms were mixed up, it was impossible to re-form a corps. The enemy who saw this astonishing confusion, launched cavalry columns; the disorder grew, the confusion of night made it impossible to rally the troops and show them their error.

Thus a battle concluded, a day finished, the false measures put right, the greatest success assured for the next day, all was lost by a moment of panic terror. Even the service squadrons, drawn up beside the Emperor, were overthrown and disorganised by these tumultuous waves, and there was nothing to do but follow the torrent. The reserve parcs, the baggage that had not been sent beyond the Sambre and everything still on the battlefield remained in the enemy's power. There was no means of waiting for the troops of our right. That was the fate of the bravest army in the world, when disordered and when its organisation no longer exists.

The Emperor passed the Sambre at Charleroi at 5 a.m. on the 19th. Philippeville and Avesnes have been given as assembly points. Prince Jerome, General Morand and the other generals have already rallied a part of the army [*false*]. Marshal Grouchy with the corps of the right is operating on the lower Sambre.

The enemy's loss must have been very great to judge from the colours we have taken from him [*false*] and by the retrograde movements he made. Ours cannot be calculated until the troops have rallied. Before the disorder broke out we had already suffered considerable losses, especially in our cavalry, so fatally and yet so bravely engaged. Despite these losses this valiant cavalry constantly guarded the position it had taken from the English, and only abandoned it when the tumult and disorder of the battlefield forced it to. In the middle of the night and with obstacles encumbering the road, it could not, however, maintain its organisation.

The artillery as usual covered itself with glory.

The carriages of the imperial staff stayed in their ordinary position, no retrograde movement being judged necessary. In the course of the night they fell into the hands of the enemy.

Such was the issue of the battle of Mont St Jean, glorious for the French armies and yet so fatal.

In every account of a battle there must be selection, and for some of Napoleon's remarks the obscurity of a dull day and thick smoke may be the reason, but it is scarcely a satisfactory relation of what happened and there is degree of wishful thinking that clouds matters. But that was what Napoleon was prepared to say to the people of France immediately after the battle. His revised opinions at St Helena were formed without access to statistics and documents, but it is not certain that he had no access to the books published in Europe after the battle. His later accounts are unsatisfactory, although they do disclose small points occasionally (as Gourgaud's version did for 16 June). Anyone who needs proof of the degree to which myth was carefully worked up should compare the above account with the final version that I print in Appendix 3 to this volume.

Ney's account was short, and bitter:

> I saw four regiments of the *Moyenne Garde* arriving, conducted by the Emperor. With these troops he wished to renew the attack and to penetrate the enemy's centre. He ordered me to lead them on; generals, officers, and soldiers all displayed the greatest intrepidity; but this body of troops was too weak to resist for long the forces the enemy opposed to it, and it was soon necessary to renounce the hope which for a few moments this attack had inspired. At my side General Friant had been struck by a ball, and I myself had my horse killed, and fell under it. The brave men who will return from this terrible battle will, I hope, do me the justice to say that they saw me on foot with sword in hand during the whole of the evening, and that I only quitted the scene of carnage among the last, and at the moment when retreat could no longer be prevented. At the same time the Prussians continued their offensive movements, and our right sensibly retired; the English advanced in their turn. There still remained to us four squares of the *Vieille Garde* to protect the retreat. These brave *grenadiers*, the chosen of the army, forced successively to retire, yielded ground foot by foot, till overwhelmed by numbers they were almost entirely annihilated. From that moment a retrograde movement was declared, and the army formed nothing but a confused mass. There was not, however, a total rout, nor the cry '*Sauve qui peut!*' as has been calumniously [*sic*] stated in the Bulletin.[23]

General Drouot of the *Garde*, speaking in the Chambre des Pairs on 23 June 1815, described in stark terms the French collapse. Having mentioned the *Garde*'s approach to the summit and the deadly volleys fired into it, he went on:

> The great number of wounded who broke away led to the belief that the *Garde* was falling back. Terrified panic spread to the neighbouring corps who fled precipitately. The enemy cavalry, perceiving this disorder, was let loose in the plain but was contained for some time by the twelve battalions of the *Vieille Garde* that had not yet given way, and that, themselves drawn along by this inexplicable movement, but still in good order, followed the path of those fleeing. All the artillery wagons rushed to the great road, and soon were so many that they could not move; for the most part they were abandoned on the road and unharnessed by the soldiers, who took the horses. Everyone rushed for the bridges at Charleroi and Marchiennes, from where the wreckage of the army [*les débris*] was directed on Philippeville and Avesnes.[24]

Jerome, light-weight and somewhat shaky on details and times, wrote to his wife in July 1815 that,

> All went well until Friant was wounded, and by what fatality I know not, the *Garde*'s attack failed and it fell back. It was necessary to retreat, but there was no time; the Emperor wanted to kill himself; we were in the midst of bullets and the enemy. Wellington had some fresh cavalry that he launched into the plain at 8 p.m.; at 9 p.m. a panicky terror took hold of the army; at 10 p.m. it was a rout.[25]

The artilleryman De Salle's recollections include this passage:

> I continued my fire. I can still see the *Garde* settle in columns [*en colonnes*], go down into the valley and climb to attack the famous English square. There was no hesitation or wavering. But it was received with calm, and a Belgian battery assisted the terrible fire of the English files. The *Garde* was astonished at such resistance, hesitated, began to waver right and left, resisted for a few more minutes, after which it was shaken and forced to retreat. Finally it spun into disorder and in its flight, dragged faster and faster all behind it who still held out, right up to the heights where our guns had first stood. I had not left the advanced position from which I had supported this attack. I still wished to stay, for the victor is he who remains last on the field. When General Delcambre, sent by Comte d'Erlon, came looking for me, he pointed to all the enemy troops closing on us. My 12-pounders, though well harnessed, could only go slowly up the slope, so that by the time we reached the summit the enemy cavalry were on us and I had only time to throw myself inside the last square of the *Garde*. The *Grenadiers* with bayonets fixed called me in, and it was then that I found my commanding general and his chief of staff in the midst of the most awful brawl that I have seen in all my military career. No

> sooner was the enemy charge driven off than I joined my general and his chief of staff, surrounded by their ADCs. As for me I was absolutely alone, without even an orderly: everyone had abandoned me and joined the rout. I do not complain of that, for the position I had held all day was scarcely agreeable. When we retreated, the Comte d'Erlon and the others, we made attempts twenty times over to create a feeble nucleus with which to march. The effort was useless! Terror was on every visage. Incessant panic gave legs for these unhappy soldiers to flee, but their heads were gone.[26]

So much for the impressions of those who faced their defeat. Their remarks lead us to the cost of the battle.

VIII

There is an unforgettable watercolour by Turner, showing a white road stretching from Belle Alliance ridge and passing La Haye Sainte in the near foreground. Lightning flashes in a threatening distant sky. There is not a living soul in sight. And the near ground is almost invisible, for it is covered with broken muskets, cuirasses, abandoned and shattered artillery pieces, and bodies, bodies, bodies everywhere. That is the price of victory and the cost of defeat.

Waterloo was an outstanding victory and a costly one. But perspective is needed here. A century later Field Marshal Sir Douglas Haig, in his Final Despatch, placed the greatest victories that any British armies have ever won – the Hundred Days of Victory from 8 August to 11 November 1918 – in the context of that entire four years of war. And he stated a grim truth. He explained why in wars between great, powerful and determined nations 'in the stage of the wearing-out battle losses will necessarily be heavy on both sides, *for in it the price of victory is paid*. If the opposing forces are approximately equal in numbers, in courage, in morale and in equipment, there is no way of avoiding payment of the price.'[27] All the chief commanders in Belgium in 1815 understood and accepted this truth. Indeed, as it is a truth, how could they not?

And so we must look at each group of armies in turn.

IX

The casualties on this day in Wellington's army may have been some 12,500 men of all ranks and all nations, but as usual the figures vary from one authority to the next. In a number of places I have followed Philip Haythornthwaite's careful analysis in the appendices to his *Waterloo Armies*; also the Adjutant General's final return of 1816 for the British and KGL for the campaign, but allowing for known casualties on 16 and 17 June, and assuming that some of those wounded on the earlier days remained with the colours on the 18th – men 'hit' and men 'wounded, unfit for duty' may differ. However, for the Netherlands Army, whose returns are almost intended to baffle the enquirer, I have had to make such use as I could with the figures served up by De Bas and T'Serclaes de Wommersom (and some estimates made by Oman).[28]

This would seem to result in Wellington's forces suffering a grim 10,567 killed and wounded, plus a further 1,758 missing.

Wellington's Casualties

	Officers killed	*Other ranks killed*	*Officers wounded*	*Other ranks wounded*	*Officers missing*	*Other ranks missing*
British/KGL*	69	1,303	325	4,128	4	290
Hanoverians	19	300	79	1,228	3	207**
Brunswickers	8	140	27	430	–	50
Nassauers	5	249	19	370	–	–
Netherlands Army	21	334	61	1,452	1	1,200
Total	122	2,326	511	7,608	8	1,747

* I have used the revised British and KGL regimental and artillery non-officer figures issued from the Adjutant General's office in April 1816. Officer casualties for British/KGL infantry and cavalry are from Haythornthwaite, but artillery officers (taken from Duncan) have been added.[29] Whereas Siborne estimated the non-officer 'missing, presumed dead' as 799, the AG's return shows that many in fact returned to their units.

** The Hanoverian 'missing' may well be the Cumberland Hussars.

Casualties are a tragedy; they are not to be gloried in, nor should anyone boast of them. No sane commander would wish to lose a single man if he could avoid it; but he has to carry this burden if he is to perform his duty. What casualties do tell is the intensity of the fighting, the bravery and endurance of the men (like the 27th Foot), although possibly they may be mitigated a little where good commanders act with intelligence. And certainly casualties tell of the cost of mistakes (such as over the Lüneburgers). They may teach lessons but, irrespective of that, they certainly stand as a memorial to the sacrifices made.

The punishment that Wellington's British and KGL infantry had taken from musketry and artillery, and sometimes from cavalry (if caught in the open), had been dreadful. Taking other-rank casualties as the yardstick, the 2/73rd suffered 69 per cent casualties; the luckless 1/27th, 63 per cent; Baring's 2nd Light KGL, 45 per cent; 3/1st Guards, 40 per cent (having had a 24 per cent loss at Quatre Bras); 1/79th, 39 per cent (having lost 41 per cent at Quatre Bras); 1/95th, 36 per cent (after 13 per cent at Quatre Bras); while the 2/95th, 2/30th, 1/32nd, 1st Light KGL, 5th Line KGL, 3/1st, and 1/28th all suffered between 36 and 30 per cent. As to the seven cavalry brigades, the five light brigades averaged between 22 per cent and 14 per cent losses (the 7th Hussars in Grant's Brigade suffering 43 per cent); but the two heavy brigades were more unlucky at 44 per cent and 46 per cent average: in Somerset's Brigade the 2nd Life Guards lost 70 per cent and the King's Dragoon Guards, 48 per cent; in Ponsonby's the Inniskilling Dragoons lost 49 per cent, and the Royals and Scots Greys each 44 per cent. The wrecking of the Heavies in their famous charge left Wellington grievously hampered for the rest of the day.

By comparison, and despite Mercer's vivid account that seems full of grievous casualties, the artillery suffered less seriously. Figures compiled by Frazer on 19 June for his branch and by Wood a few days later do not differ significantly for the RHA and may be accepted as authentic for the other branches. The impression that officer casualties were very high may stem from the fame of Norman Ramsay's troop, in which, of its five officers, two were killed and two wounded, but the entire RHA lost only 3 officers killed and 14 wounded, and all the officers in Mercer's troop emerged uninjured. Taking the men (for comparison to the infantry and cavalry figures just quoted), we find that a casualty rate of 10–11 per cent was incurred for RHA and KGL and perhaps 3–4 per cent for foot batteries.[30]

The Hanoverian contingent at Waterloo suffered one shameful setback, the flight of the volunteer Cumberland Hussars, which must account for quite a high proportion of its 'disappeared' or missing. Taking the contingent as a whole and including these scapegraces, then other rank casualties came to 15 per cent killed, wounded and missing; or slightly less if only infantry are considered. Kielmansegge's battalions in his 1st Infantry Brigade (average 28 per cent) bore losses of between 39 per cent and 16 per cent;[31] Hugh Halkett's 3rd Brigade averaged 9 per cent, with the Osnabrück battalion taking 85 casualties (14 per cent).

The Brunswickers had been battered at Quatre Bras and were shaken by their Duke's death there. They were to some extent lightly employed at Waterloo, so that their other rank casualties were 577 or just over 9 per cent.[32]

The Netherlands army and the Nassauers (part of whom were in that army, and part not) present real problems, as the Netherlands way of compiling casualties conceals an undisclosed number of missing among the killed. The totals are therefore 'overall' ones. Perponcher's 2nd Division (which included the Nassau Infantry Regiment Nr. 2 and Orange-Nassau Nr. 28) seems to have suffered 12 per cent other rank casualties (having endured 16 per cent losses on 15–16 June), while Chassé's 3rd Division took casualties of 11 per cent, and the Cavalry Division 35 per cent. The Nassau Infantry Regiment Nr. 1 (not in the Netherlands Army but in Kruse's contingent) lost in killed and wounded 17 per cent, but if missing are added this rises to 31 per cent.[33]

To summarise: the British and KGL bore the brunt of the fighting with 26 per cent infantry casualties, while the Hanoverians bore 14 per cent, Brunswickers 9 per cent, and the Netherlanders around 12 per cent. The cavalry losses were British/KGL, 29 per cent, and the Netherlanders (a suspect) 35 per cent. The heaviest infantry casualties must have been due to artillery fire, to the cost of defending La Haye Sainte and Hougoumont, and to mishaps when attacked in line by cavalry; those of the cavalry were principally due to the loss of control in Uxbridge's vital charge.

These losses came two days after a fairly stiff engagement at Quatre Bras, where British/KGL losses were 22 per cent, Netherlands 16 per cent, Brunswick 13 per cent, and Hanover 7 per cent.

No two battles are the same, but if we glance at Ligny we find Prussian casualties there came to 23 per cent including missing, of which 14 per cent were killed and wounded.

X

This consideration leads naturally to the Prussian effort and losses on 18 June. At Ligny the Prussians were essentially on the defensive; at Plancenoit and Smohain they were in attack; and on both days they were involved in street fighting in villages well suited for defence.

A glance at the map gives an idea of the progress of the Prussian advance from the time battle began close to the Bois de Paris around 4 p.m.; or, put another way, the firmness of the French defence. After four hours the French had been evicted from Plancenoit and the great *chaussée* was the next objective: 2 miles had been won, foot by foot. Each contested step had imposed casualties. Starting with the Prussians, we know that IV Corps' casualties amounted to 1,154 killed, 4,020 wounded, 1,178 missing (most of them probably dead under the ruins), giving a total of 6,352, or about 21 per cent of the men of IV Corps engaged in the battle. Twenty-one per cent is a grim statistic, but in terms of 18 June 1815 one has to say that it is not unusually heavy. Its supporting force, II Corps, suffered 37 killed, 195 wounded, 97 missing, or a total 329 (just over 1 per cent), an insignificant total – and Ziethen's 317 (under 5 per cent) at Frischermont and Papelotte cannot be thought punitive.

The opposing forces at Plancenoit were vastly different in numbers; although they varied from hour to hour it may not be unreasonable to put them at 25,000 Prussians against about 10,000 French. Using Oman's figures for the French (based on itemised officer morning states and lists of casualties) it would seem that Lobau's corps suffered 40 per cent officer casualties, the *Jeune Garde* 29 per cent, Domon's cavalry over 37 per cent and Subervie's over 27 per cent (the *Vieille Garde* figures cannot be segregated from those for the Mont St Jean action). Extending the officer figures and percentages (which are not in doubt), to estimate the casualties for the other ranks produces an overall French casualty figure of 5,500–6,000 at Plancenoit.[34]

XI

So what were the French casualties on Wellington's front? Looking back at the day that grim comment of Wellington comes repeatedly to mind: 'There is nothing more mournful than a battle won, except a battle lost.' The French had given everything for their Emperor, and it had not sufficed; ruin faced him, it probably faced them, and possibly it faced France as well. The scale of the ruin for the *Armée du Nord* can be seen corps by corps. We may start with d'Erlon's *1er Corps*, and with a detachment that generally escaped the worst that befell the other divisions. He had to detach one of Durutte's two brigades and Jacquinot's cavalry division to deal with the Papelotte and Smohain sector, and this detached force fought against not only Saxe-Weimar's brigade (a part of Wellington's army) but in the later hours of the battle also against Ziethen. Durutte's division fielded 160 officers, 71 of whom became casualties (35 per cent), and Jacquinot's cavalry suffered the same percentage. D'Erlon's other three infantry divisions suffered the following casualties among officers present: *1re Division* 52 per cent, *2e Division* 49 per cent, and *3e Division* 64 per cent. Two regiments lost eagles in the great Uxbridge charge and their officer casualties were 79 per cent in the *105e Ligne*, and 72 per cent in the *45e Ligne*; such catastrophic losses affected leadership and morale.[35] Of the sixteen regiments in the four divisions, three suffered over 70 per cent losses, six more over 50 per cent and only one had less than 40 per cent (in Durutte's division, the *29e Ligne*).

Reille's corps had slightly lighter losses among its officers, despite the slaughter at Hougoumont, but then it had already suffered the experience of Quatre Bras that had cost some good leaders. On 18 June Jerome's *6e Division* unsurprisingly had the heaviest toll, 46 per cent, while Bachelu's had 32 per cent and Foy's 33 per cent, and Piré's cavalry 34 per cent. But two regiments had exceptionally high officer casualties, the *61e Ligne* 81 per cent and the *3e Ligne* 68 per cent; no regiment can continue to fulfil its tasks with losses of such severity.

Next comes the *Garde*. The *Jeune Garde* had fought entirely at Plancenoit, and the *Tirailleurs* had losses of 28 per cent and the *Voltigeurs* 30 per cent. The *Moyenne Garde* fought only against Wellington: its *Grenadiers à Pied* suffered equally with the *Chasseurs à Pied*, they all lost 62 per cent of their officers. Only the *Vieille Garde* remained at the end of the day: it had intervened successfully at Plancenoit and still later it gave proof of its determination and devotion. Its *Grenadiers à Pied* suffered 36 per cent officer losses and the *Chasseurs à Pied* 'only' 26 per cent: the latter a ratio that is slightly above the casualty rate for the British Guards Division.

These are terrible figures. They suggest that even if Wellington had lost the battle the French army would have been so desperately short of leaders that its ability to continue a campaign against any half decent military force would have been in question. Foy's reflection comes to mind: 'He [Napoleon] played for the highest stake but he played it against an ace. The action of the 16th cost him many men; four or five actions like that *would have sufficed to destroy his army*; he had to gain an overwhelming success.'[36] Provided the Allied high command in Germany did not waver, the Russian masses would soon be leading the other Allies into France, and the one good French army had been used up.

The hard figures demonstrate that the leaders showed unbelievable gallantry. What of the rank and file? Sir Charles Oman (rightly, I think) remarked that while the officers resisted or were shot down or made desperate efforts to get away and re-group, the rank and file surrendered freely when cut off. He thought that the officers in many cases may have suffered 'much heavier casualties than their normal one-to twenty percentage [to the rank and file]' in leading them in the great attacks but that after dark it was the ordinary soldier who surrendered, so that the general average of losses may have been restored with nightfall. Using a factor of 1:20 for Waterloo, Sir Charles concluded that the French casualties amounted to around 37,000 men, which meant an average loss of nearly 50 per cent: 'This would allow for the 1,405 officers whom we know to have been killed and wounded, for 28,100 rank and file killed and wounded, and for 7,500 unwounded prisoners, of whom I should guess that not more than 100 were officers.' He made no estimate for, nor comment on, the missing-presumed-dead, possibly because it would be difficult to separate them from disappeared–fled. Digby Smith provides an alternative estimate: 25,000 killed and wounded, 7,000 prisoners, 10,000 missing.[37]

Casualties are a good measure for the scale and intensity of fighting, but of course they are affected by the intentions of the opposing commanders in opting for the defensive or offensive, where hedges, walls and buildings, perhaps the lie of the ground, can assist the defence and shelter troops from the worst of short-range musketry, more distant cannon-fire, and the terrifying approaching surge of cavalry. These factors certainly helped the defenders of Wellington's bastions, Hougoumont, La Haye Sainte, and the men at Papelotte and Frischermont. Likewise they helped Lobau's men in their defence of Plancenoit. But mention of Plancenoit reminds us that once the enemy columns had closed upon the village and the Prussian artillery had to reduce its fire to avoid bombarding its own men, then the hand-to-hand fighting spares no one, defender or attacker. If the Prussian advance on Plancenoit took a heavier ratio of casualties initially when compared with the defence, Lobau's units and their reinforcements must have suffered equally in the later stages.

Napoleon as the attacker at Mont St Jean could not afford sophisticated and complex manoeuvres if he was to reach Brussels that night. He had only some nine hours of daylight to play with. But he ignored Reille's wise warning that Wellington knew exactly how to conceal and shelter infantry. The Emperor's initial plan was brutal and simple, while massed artillery destroyed the enemy centre Reille would take or neutralise Hougoumont; then d'Erlon would frontally assault the ridge, regardless of infantry casualties. It only just failed. Wellington's tactical dispositions reduced the casualties the Grand Battery expected to inflict; and his order that his relatively few guns should not waste ammunition on an artillery duel but should concentrate on the massed infantry, was wise. D'Erlon's assault proved costly, and it just failed, albeit that Picton's infantry and Uxbridge's cavalry took heavy losses in overturning that assault. Thus far it had been the French who must have suffered the heavier casualties and the hours of daylight were passing. But thereafter the toll became less unequal. Ney's cavalry charges were savagely rent by Wellington's guns, but the Allied infantry were forced into squares, and were for long hours shredded and pulverised by Napoleon's artillery, and so while hedges and buildings like La Haye Sainte and Hougoumont gave a degree of cover, the fighting along the Mont St Jean ridge had to be in exposed conditions that gave little advantage to the defence. It was indeed 'a very near run thing'.

Once Blücher was at Wavre and was prepared to support Wellington at Mont St Jean, Napoleon's chances of victory were greatly diminished. Once Napoleon had reason to think that Blücher could be at Wavre he should have adapted his plans. Even at the moment when Bülow was first seen he might have saved something. Instead he doubled his stake. And so between 50,000 and 60,000 men fell in consequence.

There, then, is the balance in blood and suffering that produced the Allied victory of 18 June 1815 at Mont St Jean and Plancenoit. But when we examine the figures we see that France's last army destroyed itself on the slopes of Mont St Jean, where its numbers engaged and its loss ratio were substantially greater than on the eastern flank at Plancenoit. Moreover, in trying to destroy Wellington, it incurred losses nearing 50 per cent, whereas it inflicted on him only about 25 per cent, and this with opposing forces that were not vastly different in size, and indeed where the greatest differential was in the amount of artillery, where the French had a decided superiority.

Chapter 46
The Aftermath of Battle
The Prussians and Grouchy, 19–20 June

I

WELLINGTON'S ARMY AFTER ITS LONG BATTERING had reached the limits of its strength by the time it had halted south of La Belle Alliance, and the Duke gladly let the Prussians come up and take on the pursuit. So for the present it is with the Prussians that we shall remain on 19 June, first seeing how Blücher and Gneisenau reported the great victory to the royal court and to their own families. But there still remained undecided the struggle between Grouchy and Thielemann, neither of whom was aware of the outcome at Mont St Jean, and that we shall examine fairly briefly. Next we will see what progress the main body of troops made down the roads towards France on the 19th, before seeing how Grouchy extricated himself from danger and successfully retired into France on the 20th.

II

Blücher wasted no time; once at Genappe he sent a very short note to the King's adviser Knesebeck at royal headquarters:

> The most splendid of battles has been fought, the most glorious victory won. Only details remain to be undertaken. I think Bonaparte is so shattered that it is very probably the end. La Belle Alliance! 19th, early morning.
>
> I cannot write more, for I tremble in every limb, the exertion has been too great. BLÜCHER, 19th, 2 a.m.[1]

Later that day he penned a reassuring letter to his young wife:

> The enemy's numerical superiority obliged me to give way on the 17th, but on the 18th, in conjunction with my friend Wellington, I at once put an end to Napoleon's dancing. His army is completely routed, and the whole of his

> artillery, baggage, caissons, and equipages are in my hands; the insignia of all the various orders he had worn are just brought me, having been found in his carriage, in a casket. I had two horses killed under me yesterday. It will soon be over with Bonaparte.[2]

Gneisenau, of course, spent the night leading the chase after Napoleon and the remnants of the French army. Having snatched some sleep, he wrote to his wife this day from Gosselies:

> My last letter reported on the accident we had suffered; this one brings news of one of the greatest victories ever won. After our misfortune the day before yesterday, where, due to unfortunate circumstances only three corps were present – the fourth of our army was absent, and the Duke of Wellington could not come to us – we faced the entire military force of Bonaparte and were subjected to its heavy attack; the troops, officers and soldiers, struggled for possession of two villages and finally retreated to Wavre, where we learned that the enemy, heady with victory, was now leading his entire force against the army of the Duke of Wellington. To leave him to fight alone was a certain prediction of defeat. We wanted revenge and therefore decided to come to the Duke's aid.
>
> Yesterday morning we set our columns in motion to attack the right flank of the enemy from the rear. We approached him with stealth, gained a small wood in his rear and remained quite quietly there.
>
> The battle against the Duke of Wellington had already lasted several hours with heavy fighting; the English had held their position with great courage, but when the enemy threw more and more forces against them and Wellington's position became more difficult and doubtful, we suddenly broke out of the woods and fired on the enemy's rear. He now had to turn his forces against us, the battle continued to rage, while we brought more and more forces into the battle and pushed steadily forward, until at the end the enemy's retreat turned into a complete rout . . .
>
> A lot of valuable time was lost through unrealistic plans for the campaign, allowing the enemy to assemble all his strength against us. We have successfully fought the battle and now want to end the war alone, without the help of other armies, which will only cross the Rhine at the end of June.[3]

Gneisenau was in a hurry, possibly still tired, and his summary had to leave out a great deal, but still the narrative is clear enough. The main surprise is to find no mention at all of the truly significant decision not to be diverted from the main objective by Thielemann's plight; that was possibly the high command's most praiseworthy decision during the battle of the 18th.

It was disingenuous still to pretend that at Ligny the Prussians had faced Napoleon's 'entire' army. The condemnation of Schwarzenberg for wasting valuable time was perhaps understandable, but the insistence that only the soldiers who fought the battles should determine the war's conclusion was a first sign of what would become a serious argument with the Allied sovereigns all through the summer, and even involve Wellington.

In recent years a series of criticisms have been levelled against Wellington's account of these June days, criticisms that would have seemed less one-sided if the accusers had examined his ally's accounts with anything like the same intensity.[4] A prosecuting counsel reading these letters could easily point to omissions and little exaggerations, but to what purpose? The Duke's Waterloo Despatch, penned between 4 a.m. and mid-morning on 19 June, is not a perfect account of everything that passed (as many British officers complained afterwards), but I think that in point of detail, coherence, avoidance of complaint, and praise of an ally, it does not suffer when compared with what the Prussian high command wrote on 19 June.

III

The collapse of the French army had meant that nobody at La Belle Alliance gave any thought to Grouchy's circumstances. Grouchy for his part took the night-time silence to mean that all had gone well. At 11.30 p.m. he wrote to Vandamme and Exelmans. He had decided to demonstrate at Wavre from the right bank of the Dyle, while striking hard by a left hook. He had at last realised that crossing to the left (west) bank of the river was the surest way of keeping between Napoleon and any Prussian threat, but this realisation came a day too late. His orders to Vandamme were as follows:

> Will you please go at once with your corps to Limal, leaving in front of Wavre only those troops essential for holding the part of the Wavre position that we occupy. At daybreak we shall attack the troops facing me and we shall, I hope, succeed in joining the Emperor, as he has ordered us to do. It is said that he has beaten the English, but I have no more news from him, and I am in the greatest embarrassment till I can give him ours. I place under your orders the entire Corps of General Gérard. I call on you in the name of *la patrie*, my dear General, to carry out the present order. I see no other way of getting out of the difficult position in which we find ourselves; and the safety of the army depends on it. I await you.
>
> P.S. Prisoners taken here report that Blücher and Bülow are in front of us. I doubt it very much.[5]

Vandamme did not obey. He retained most of his force in the Wavre–Bierges sector, and detached only Hulot's *14e Division* to join Grouchy. In fact this was sufficient, but that could be no real excuse for his disobedience and, to make that disobedience worse, he was entirely ignorant of the true situation at Limale.

Meanwhile, during the night of 18/19 June, nobody at Prussian headquarters thought to inform Thielemann of the victory. Acting on his own initiative he sent an officer to gather news of the fighting in the Lasne valley, and the man returned with the information that the French seemed to have been routed. It was not until dawn that headquarters sent a messenger to Wavre with the news of Napoleon's defeat, and telling Thielemann that Pirch's II Corps would strike south-east to take Grouchy in his rear.

Probably unknown to Thielemann, the Prussian position at Limale, guarding the left bank of the Dyle, had been greatly weakened. He was also unaware that this was the point at which Grouchy's left hook would strike next. On 18 June III Corp's 9th Brigade (Borcke), placed at Limale, had trailed off westwards to St-Lambert, where it spent the night awaiting in vain further orders from army headquarters. Ledebur's little detachment had also left the Limale sector to march west to re-join IV Corps and by dawn was close to it. (It is unclear who authorised these movements.) That left only Stengel's detachment to watch the crossing, although about 1½ miles downstream was Stülpnagel's 12th Brigade, posted at Bierges. So the Prussian position was seriously at risk. Then at dawn on the 19th Stengel's little force marched away to Borcke's camp at St-Lambert and reported that Grouchy's French were across the Dyle and marching straight for St-Lambert. These forces, Borcke, Ledebur and Stengel, together amounted to about 12 battalions, 7 squadrons, and more than one battery: well over 7,500 men. All they did was to stand on the defensive. Yet no French appeared. Had these St-Lambert troops made a move towards Thielemann, or even a feint, they might have caused a check or a little confusion to the plans of the French as they moved down the Dyle's west bank to attack Bierges. Instead, they stayed paralysed at St-Lambert, useless in the new Prussian battle.[6] Nor is that all. To anticipate my account of events later that day, had this force moved forward even slowly it might have been in a position later to endanger or at least embarrass Grouchy's troops when they broke off the fight with Thielemann and retreated towards Namur – and a harassing pursuit might have had an effect out of all proportion to the numbers involved.

Meanwhile, basing himself on his own emissary's information of a victory at Plancenoit/Mont St Jean, Thielemann in early morning concluded that Grouchy must also have heard the news and would therefore be in full

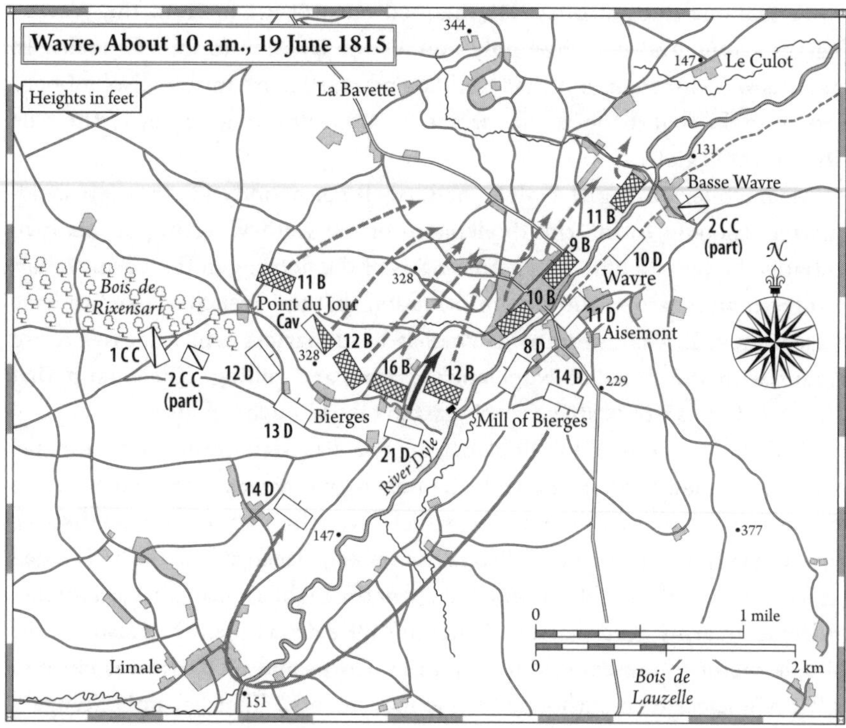

retreat. Consequently he launched a dawn attack on the French outposts. But Grouchy was still unaware of the true situation and his troops were still in the positions they had rested in overnight.

Thus Thielemann's dawn attack on a supposedly retreating French force, fell on troops rested and still confident, who beat off the attackers. Then, having beaten them off, the French launched their own attack. The Prussians had lost the upstream river line the previous night; now they were pushed back from the vicinity of Limale to a line running from the Dyle at Bierges to the woods that extended to Rixensart (and on to the Lasne stream). Bierges formed the centre of the Prussian defences that went from Rixensart right round to Wavre, and it was at a right-angle in the long line. As Grouchy's left wing pressed forward from Limale against the Prussian right wing, and Vandamme menaced the Prussian left wing from the eastern suburbs of Wavre, Teste's *21e Division* attacked and took Bierges in the centre. That loss was fatal to Thielemann's position. The Prussian right wing and centre fell back, wheeling on the left wing. Zeppelin evacuated the town he had held so successfully the day before. Thielemann ordered a short retirement north-eastwards and downstream in the general direction of Louvain, halting at St-Agathe-Rode, 5 miles down the Dyle. But by this time Grouchy had at last heard of Napoleon's disaster and the attack slackened and then stopped.[7]

From the moment that Grouchy received the news of Napoleon's defeat, he underwent a change. He had always been personally brave (he had been wounded twenty-three times) and had proved a good leader of large forces when under the Emperor's eye. He had swiftly crushed the royalist trouble in the Rhône valley that spring. But in this campaign his dealings with Napoleon and with his own subordinate (or rather, insubordinate) generals had been uneasy, and his own actions either too precipitate or too indolent. Recognising the catastrophe that threatened France he now became a *thinking* general, so that one has to ask yet again whether Napoleon's handling of him had been the real problem. His actions from this point till the end of June were of a totally different order from those of the past three days.

Grouchy called his senior officers together to discuss the new situation. On the evening of 18 June, ignorant of what was happening at Mont St Jean, he had not yet broken Thielemann's defence, and his subordinates had proved unhelpful and even disobedient to orders. By mid-morning on the 19th he had driven Thielemann back north-east towards Louvain, but casualties on both sides had been about equal, around 2,500 in the two days' fighting and the Prussians were not totally *hors de combat* and might still play a supporting role if further fighting were to develop. Now Grouchy suddenly found that Napoleon had been smashed, so that any further advance on his part could find Wellington on one flank, Thielemann on the other, and possibly Blücher to his rear. In any case his men had been stretched by fighting and it was unlikely that his 28,000 men could all cover the 15 miles in a dash upon Brussels before nightfall, even if the enemy did not move. Thus, as an independent commander, Grouchy was probably right in deciding to pull back to France the last cohort between the Allies and the French capital and link with whatever forces might be reassembling there.

Vandamme, however, so lethargic and so impatient by turns, so wild and so mutinous, proposed that they should indeed march on Brussels, release any French prisoners found there, and then turn away to return to north-western France by Enghien, Ath and Valenciennes or Lille. It might indeed have resulted in a critical situation in Brussels, perhaps even its fall, and it might have checked momentarily the immediate invasion of France, but it would have risked the total destruction of Grouchy's force as the Allied armies swung back. Hyde Kelly's judgement here seems reasonable:

> Of what use would such a movement have been, even had it been *successfully* carried out? To march boldly completely round the rear of the allied armies, liberate a few prisoners, and then march off in the opposite direction, would

> have been to waste the only formed body left of all Napoleon's army. And what would Thielemann do in the meantime? There was now no hope of *winning over* Brussels or the Dutch–Belgians, otherwise there would have been some weight in Vandamme's extraordinary proposal. But Grouchy counselled otherwise. He knew that he already ran the risk of being attacked in flank, most probably in rear, by a portion of Blücher's army, while Thielemann would certainly advance again as soon as the retreat began.[8]

In other words, Vandamme's recommendation was for a suicide mission. Curiously, the Duke of Wellington later thought Brussels might indeed have fallen, although all the evidence of the day suggests that he was not so worried at the time; the point is discussed in the appendix to this chapter.

Grouchy determined to pull back at once to Namur the only formed body left of all Napoleon's army and then bring his contingent to the support of whatever remnant remained of the *Armée du Nord*. The retirement was led by Exelmans's cavalry, followed by the guns, and next by the wounded. Starting from north of Wavre, this body had got as far as Namur by late afternoon. Next *4e Corps* began to move back across the Dyle at Limale, while Vandamme's *3e Corps* passed back through Wavre and continued on Sart-à-Walhain, the two corps reaching Temploux, 3 miles short of Namur, by 10–11 p.m. The rearguard under Pajol halted for the night somewhat further north. The success of this 30-mile withdrawal across country and by small roads was remarkable. Only Pajol's rearguard was seen by the Prussians, and neither of the two Prussian commanders involved in the pursuit, Thielemann and Pirch I, pushed their troops very hard. Thielemann may have been tired and perhaps slightly cautious after his morning's misreading of the situation, but for Pirch I there could not really be any such excuse.

IV

Overnight on 18/19 June the main Prussian army camped on the Waterloo battlefield. Ziethen's I Corps, save for the detachment taken by Gneisenau, rested around La Belle Alliance and the nearby La Maison du Roi. Bülow's IV Corps had camped above Plancenoit, with II Corps close by. The day had been strenuous for all three corps, but as the casualty figures had shown, the amount of fighting had been relatively minor for I and II Corps; IV Corps had borne the brunt. Fresh orders were issued from Gosselies after dawn on the 19th, and during the morning the troops marched once more. The direction given to I and IV Corps for 19 June was towards Charleroi and the Sambre bridges. For II Corps there was a slightly different plan: while a section of it should march for the area of Anderlues near Fontaine l'Evêque west of Charleroi, the major part under Pirch should strike south-east to take Grouchy in rear, and thus complete the destruction of the *Armée du Nord*.[9] Undoubtedly the troops were tired after so much marching since 15 June, but this could not be allowed to count in the balance against the enormous consequence of capturing the last French contingent in Belgium and northern France.

Ziethen's force moved south and reached the crossroads of Quatre Bras at 3 in the afternoon, a march of a little under 10 miles. There it received orders to continue, so as to reach the Sambre bridge at Marchienne by nightfall, a further 18 miles. IV Corps was at Mellet, 2 miles south of Frasnes, by 3 p.m.

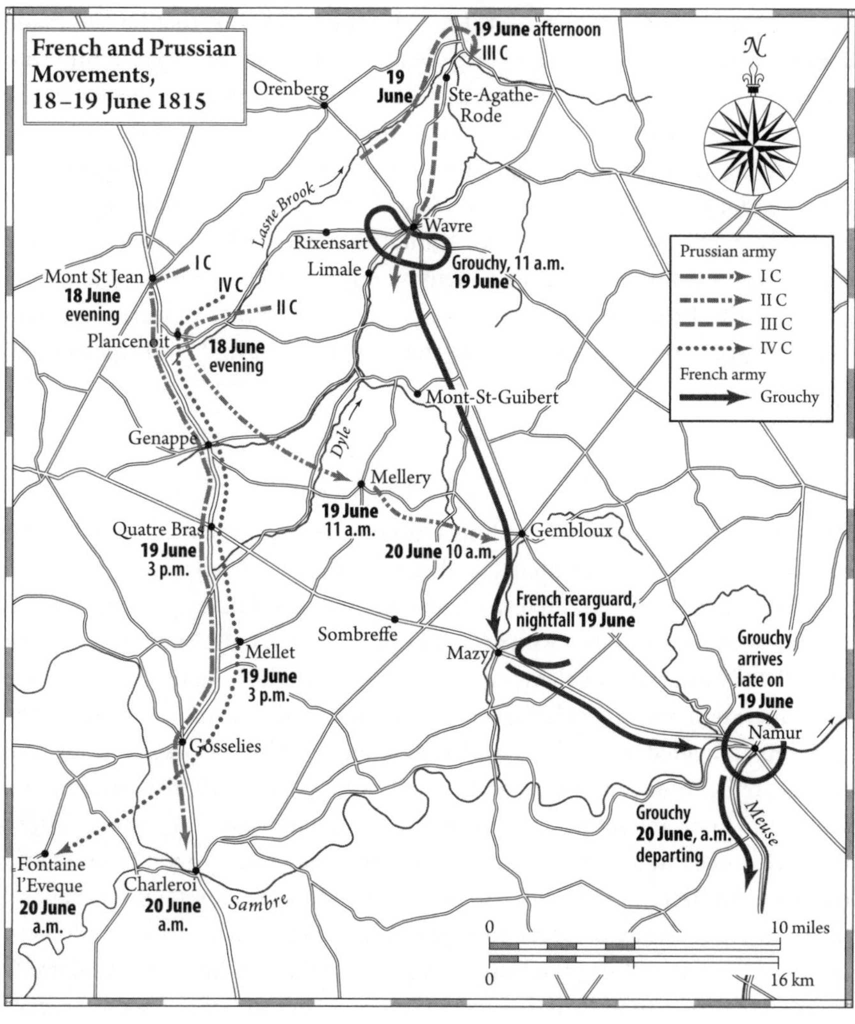

and continued south-west to Fontaine. Thus early on 20 June two Prussian corps and part of a third were close to the Sambre. By Blücher's orders – and in accordance with the terms agreed on 27 May (Chapter 13, Section IV) – they were to establish contact with Mons to obtain from Wellington's sector supplies of bread and other provisions.

As for the force chasing Grouchy, by 11 a.m. on the 19th Pirch had reached Mellery, about 8 miles from Plancenoit and 6 short of Gembloux. At this moment Grouchy's army was still well to the north of Gembloux and in real danger. But Pirch seems to have lacked resolution and clarity of thought. His scouts did not trace anything on the roads until the French rearguard moved past. His evening report of the day's events was muddled and unimpressive, for he claimed that Grouchy's expected withdrawal had not materialised as yet, that Mont-St-Guibert was still held by the Prussians, that he had made contact with Borcke's detached brigade and that the latter had told him that Thielemann had been defeated 'at Limale the day before yesterday [17 June]' and was falling back on Brussels, and that he [Pirch] intended to wait upon Grouchy's next movements. Once he knew what Grouchy was doing, said he, then he would act decisively. This was a thoroughly inadequate report and a glaring exposure of Pirch's own limitations. He had let Grouchy escape clean away.[10] As we shall see, Grouchy's continued liberty of action had its effect on the Prussian advance into France and resulted in a strong intact French force arriving to assist in the defence of Paris: that is the measure of Pirch's failure.

V

By mid-morning on Tuesday 20 June Grouchy's force was collected in Namur on the confluence of the Meuse and the Sambre. The retirement had been upset by yet another of Vandamme's unexpected acts. His corps was intended to cover the retreat of the wounded and of *4e Corps*, but Vandamme betook himself to Namur without leaving any orders to his subordinates. His divisions took their own routes and left the wounded and *4e Corps* unprotected. As the columns struggled back, elements from Thielemann's III Corps came up and a series of scuffles took place; then some units from Pirch also arrived and joined the fight, incurring 1,200 casualties in the process. The French fought them off and escaped into Namur. In the past it had been a great fortress-city but in recent times its defences had been allowed to deteriorate: it was beyond the capacity of Grouchy's force to hold it, and they would have to abandon the city to the enemy. It is something of a commentary on how the inhabitants recalled the sojourn of Prussian army Headquarters and of II Corps in recent

Wellington in 1814, aged 45, by Sir Thomas Lawrence. On meeting the Duke again after he had been in the Peninsula for five years Castlereagh noted, 'He does not show the effect of his campaigns as much as I expected in his countenance.'

Below: Lord Fitzroy Somerset: Wellington's courteous and able military secretary was of enormous value in smoothing the Duke's relations with the army.

Below right: Lord Hill: utterly trustworthy, Wellington told him, 'I have every disposition to approve of everything you do.'

Genappe: the narrow street and bridge significantly affected the fighting during Wellington's retreat on 17 June and again in the French rout after Waterloo.

The Household Brigade at Waterloo: the early afternoon charge against the French heavy cavalry was led by Uxbridge. La Haye Sainte can be seen in the background, as Wellington watches.

Closing the gates at Hougoumont by Robert Gibb. The desperate French assault under Sous-Lieut. Legros is checked by Lt.-Col. Macdonell, and other officers and men of the Coldstream Guards.

La Haye Sainte: Richard Knötel's fine depiction of Major Baring and the 2nd Light Battalion, KGL, defending the farm gate against men of Quiot's *1re Division*, urged on by a mounted officer.

Waterloo: 'Hard pounding, this, gentlemen', in Wellington's words: *cuirassiers* versus squares, mid-afternoon: a vivid impression painted almost sixty years after the battle by Félix Philippoteaux (1815–1884).

Plancenoit: a contemporary illustration of the hand-to-hand fighting between the French and Prussians, close to the church.

General Count Gneisenau: a staff officer of intellect and strong opinions who, as Chief of Staff, chafed at not being a line commander; his personal leadership in the night pursuit after Waterloo was unstinting.

General Mouton, created Comte Lobau for his endeavours at Aspern-Essling in 1809, one of the doughtiest of Napoleon's generals on 18 June 1815, at Plancenoit.

J. M. W. Turner's 1818 watercolour: 'There is nothing more mournful than a battle won, except a battle lost.' A ghostly La Haye Sainte in mid-foreground and the Belle Alliance ridge in the distance, harshly dominated by wreckage and death.

The night pursuit. The Prussians rode hard to the Genappe bottleneck where French discipline finally collapsed; they continued to hunt down the fugitives until dawn.

Napoleon comes aboard HMS *Bellerophon*. As the Prussian and royalist net closed upon Rochefort, Napoleon placed himself in British hands as the safer option. *Bellerophon* had been at Trafalgar and by chance was the scene of the final surrender. Napoleon's party included several wives and children; all were well treated.

months, that although the inhabitants realised that the French must abandon them, nevertheless they actively supplied the French troops with necessities. Teste's *21e Division* was given the task of maintaining the defence while the rest of the little army retired south into the valley of the upper Meuse towards Dinant.

Teste mounted a showy defence aimed at confusing the Prussians, who for their part were not ready to launch a frontal assault on the defences. Streets and bridges were barricaded and filled with inflammables, and as darkness fell Teste set them alight and withdrew from the town, knowing that these street encumbrances would keep the Prussians from a swift pursuit. By the morning of the 21st he had re-joined Grouchy and the entire force entered France, and turned towards Philippeville and the road south. They were not pursued.[11]

*

Appendix: An Attack on Brussels by Grouchy?

On 18 December 1816, the Duke told some dinner guests at his house near Cambrai that the greatest danger to Brussels was on 19 June 1815 'when it was uncertain which way Grouchy's corps had gone, that they might have fallen back on Brussels which was quite unprotected and made them all prisoners. The Duke added he should have escaped himself upon horseback.'[12]

This would seem to give more significance to Vandamme's proposal on 19 June 1815 for a dash at Brussels. Yet there are the considerations that Grouchy must have turned over, as set out in Section III above: his perception of the Allied dispositions on three sides, the tiredness of his men, the hour at which discussion took place (mid-to-late morning) and the distance to Brussels; all these must have made such a dash unwise and unjustifiable that day, and impossible thereafter.

Earlier in June Wellington had a reasonably strong force in garrison across Belgium, with the British 5th and elements of the British 6th Divisions guarding the capital. Moreover, there was Tindal's Netherlands Reserve Army gradually forming as a further support (for these British formations and Tindal's force see Volume 1, Chapter 17, Appendix 1). Once the invasion of France should begin then the safety of Brussels was guaranteed, but of course events led instead to the invasion of Belgium. After Picton's force left Brussels on 16 June there remained only the 2/81st Foot (around 500 strong), some 960 municipal guards, a 'carabinier' squadron, and Tindal's force, to man the city ramparts and maintain control. Exactly how strong the ramparts were is unclear. Pictures show the Hal gate as very strong, but though the ramparts on the south-east quadrant did still exist, the walkway was a fashionable promenade and the moat was dry.[13] A determined assault by 28,000 men might have overwhelmed the defenders.

That would appear to give extra point to the Duke's remarks to his guests at Cambrai, eighteen months later, and yet it seems quite impossible to credit them. That he was amusing the ladies with a little spice, and talking in private without thought that Mrs Lloyd (and many later, like Lord Mahon) was breaching society's rules of privacy in conversation and registering his (too often) loose recollections, seems to me quite likely. For what is the extant record of 19 June 1815 in Brussels?

Wellington did not issue one single order that day for the defence of the capital. On the contrary, on that day he issued a movement order for the army at Mont St Jean to advance to Nivelles starting at 5 a.m. on the 20th, and Bernard of Saxe-Weimar wrote to his father that day that he received this order on the 19th. Wellington had written to Lady Frances Wedderburn Webster at 3 a.m. on Sunday 18th that her family should be ready to flee Brussels at a moment's notice as Brussels might be uncovered; at 8.30 a.m. on the 19th he wrote to her that they could 'remain in Bruxelles in perfect security ... [the French] are in complete confusion'.[14] During the morning of 19 June Mr Creevey, that pertinacious Whig MP and someone deeply concerned for his wife and family who were still in Brussels, went to see the Duke, just returned to his Brussels residence. The Duke had finished drafting his Despatch that was now being copied by clerks. He was free to talk. During all their long conversation Wellington made no reference to any potential threat and seemed convinced that the French were utterly undone. Creevey stated:

> Before I left him I asked whether he thought the French would be able to take the field again, and he thought entirely not, giving as his reason that every corps of France, but one [Grouchy], had been in the battle, and that the whole army had gone off in such perfect rout and confusion he thought it quite impossible for them to give battle again before the Allies reached Paris.[15]

We may note that Wellington did not overlook Grouchy's detached force when talking with Creevey, and indeed among the insertions he had just made to the Despatch was, in paragraph 19, the reference to 'the 3d Corps' being detached to watch Blücher on 18 June. That corps was about 17,000 strong, but in fact other formations also went to Grouchy to give him 30,000 men, so that Wellington on 18 and 19 June 1815 seriously under-estimated Grouchy's fighting power. From all this positive evidence and the silences as to a defence of the Belgian capital I can only conclude that Wellington on 19 June rightly thought Grouchy's isolated '17,000' would fall back to protect France and would not attack Brussels.

Eighteen months later he was playing up to Mrs Lloyd's curiosity and perhaps even pulling his guests' legs.

Chapter 47

After the Battle

Wellington and his Army, 19–20 June

I

THE BATTLEFIELD HAD BEEN a scene of bravery and carnage all the afternoon and evening of Sunday. Overnight it was a place of agony and horror. There were some 52,000 men dead, dying, and wounded, and untold thousands of dead and mutilated cavalry and artillery horses, crowded into a swathe of land two miles long and a little over one mile broad.[1] Those still living had been on short commons since the 17th, had been soaked and half-frozen overnight, had fought in overcast heat, many with little water or food,[2] all day on the 18th, and now were in a desperate state. The late arrival of the Prussians had the fortunate effect of making Napoleon's defeat all the more catastrophic, but its less fortunate consequence was that it added enormously to the casualties suffered by Wellington's forces as they waited for the promised intervention. And consequentially the Prussians' delayed arrival meant that the French took additional losses at Mont St Jean, men for whom the collapse of the *Armée du Nord* meant medical abandonment.

The crisis had come in mid-evening, and by the time La Belle Alliance had been taken dusk was already drawing on, so that it was too late for proper search and recovery to be undertaken that night. Mercifully the night was dry, but still it was rendered horrible by the cries and groans of the wounded, and made even worse by the human jackals who roamed the field seeking plunder and who did not hesitate to murder their own countrymen in search of money, watches, or anything of value, even down to gold lace. This gave others all the more reason to search for friends and to protect them, even if they could bring no alleviation for their sufferings.

The French medical service had gone, swept away in the rout; any care of their wounded must fall upon the victorious armies. It is difficult to find out what was the situation of Prussian medical services. Two of their four corps had suffered heavy casualties on 16 June, but how many injured men stayed with the army is not clear, and large numbers of wounded must have been left on the field and become the responsibility of the French. Prussian casualties on 18 June at Papelotte and Smohain were slight, and those at Plancenoit ought not to have exceeded the capacity of the surgeons and bearers of II and IV Corps. But as the Prussian forces were now taking the road to the Sambre it is likely that they would have taken with them some and perhaps many of their medical staff. One British soldier noted that there were Prussian wounded among the thousands of casualties sent to Brussels. Indeed, Brussels was soon filled to overflowing with wounded, and in consequence the British lightly wounded were moved by barge to Antwerp; others were taken to Bruges and Ostend, and the Prussians went to Louvain.[3]

Thus it was upon the British and Netherlands forces that care of the British, German, Dutch, Belgian, Prussian and French wounded initially depended from La Belle Alliance even as far as Waterloo, but the dressing stations set up just behind the line were overwhelmed by the scale of the problem and by darkness. The regiments themselves were short of officers: some were now commanded by subalterns. The staff had been affected as badly: the Military Secretary was wounded; the Adjutant-General and his deputy were wounded, and six of their twenty-one subordinates were casualties; the DQMG De Lancey was mortally wounded, and nine of his twenty-seven subordinates were casualties. Many line commanders were dead or wounded. The instant and immediate strain on the organisation was immense.

When war came to Belgian soil the Brussels authorities called for bedding, sheets and blankets for the military hospital established there on 17 June – Wellington's hospital organisation had originally been set up in preparation for the invasion of France. It seems that a field hospital had been established at Nivelles and so could serve as a forward dressing station to which at least some of the wounded of Quatre Bras would have gone. Presumably they were evacuated to Brussels during the retreat on the 17th.[4] On the 18th many of the wounded were gathered inside the fighting squares – as Gronow remarked, the inside of a square resembled a hospital – or at dressing posts immediately behind the crest, or in nearby buildings, the main field hospital being at Mont St Jean farm. Those who could be transported were loaded onto wagons, but the evidence is clear that disorder and panic disgraced the medical evacuation in too many instances. For those who could not be moved there were available to treat them, according to Mark Adkin's estimates, about 300 qualified surgeons with Wellington's army.[5] They now had to treat over 50,000 casualties. The supply of medical men for the army had been by fits and starts, with comparatively inexperienced civilians being recruited when shortages appeared among army surgeons: Deputy Inspector Hume recorded an egregious junior proffering foolish suggestions when the advisability of amputating Uxbridge's leg was being debated. Luckily for Uxbridge the senior men made the decision and ignored the junior surgeon That was a nobleman and senior commander's case: what must it have been like for Tommy Atkins when no seniors were about?

Surgeons found that their scalpels and saws were blunted by non-stop use, several of them wrote of working day and night for up to three days, and medical men from London hastened across the Channel to assist (and study). The letters of the brilliant and influential Charles Bell of the Middlesex Hospital, who took leave to come over, serve, and make case notes, are perhaps the most notable instance.

The evidence of British and other residents of Brussels and various towns in Belgium is unanimous on the great and loving exertions made by the Belgian people to care for the wounded. The accounts of Thomas Creevey (and his step-daughter Miss Ord), Miss Charlotte Waldie, Madame D'Arblay (the former Miss Fanny Burney), and others, continue to make a deep impression on re-reading even 200 years later, and, if this was a social history and not a study of international policy and high command, there would be a full chapter relating their accounts; as it is, I hope the reader will understand if I recommend instead the eight pages on the Brussels effort in Antony Brett-James's anthology. That moving story of loving care makes a striking and agreeable contrast to the fear and disarray of the previous two days among the inhabitants and visitors in Brussels, two days so brilliantly pictured by Thackeray a generation later in *Vanity Fair*, when the ingenious Becky Sharp (wife of that puzzled dragoon Rawdon Crawley) thought that if Napoleon took Brussels she might drop her dragoon and catch someone who could make her *une duchesse* and *une maréchale*.[6]

II

Wellington had turned in to sleep around midnight, having given his bed to the dying Alexander Gordon. But the army still had to be administered and De Lancey's deputy, Colonel Broke, came at 3.30 a.m. in order to receive the day's directions. The surgeon Hume, who had just seen Gordon die, woke Wellington to tell him of the death and of Broke's arrival:

> He had as usual taken off all his clothes, but had not washed himself, and as I entered the room, he sat up in his bed, his face covered with the dust and sweat of the previous day, and extended his hand to me, which I took and held in mine, whilst I told him of Gordon's death, and of such of the

> casualties as had come to my knowledge. He was much affected. I felt the tears dropping fast upon my hand, and looking towards him, saw them chasing one another in furrows over his dusty cheeks. He brushed them suddenly away with his left hand, and said to me in a voice tremulous with emotion, 'Well, thank God, I don't know what it is to lose a battle; but certainly nothing can be more painful than to gain one with the loss of so many of one's friends.'[7]

Directions were given to Broke, and then Wellington sat to write his report to the government in London. This was of the utmost urgency, because he had had no time to write anything in the past three days, and there was the vital political and financial need to confirm to Whitehall and the City that Napoleon had been defeated.

That is not to say that Wellington had left the government without news. The Duke of Richmond had written to Bathurst early on 18 June: 'The Duke of Wellington had desired Apsley [Bathurst's eldest son and Richmond's nephew], if he wrote, to tell you he has not time to write on account of the business of the 16th and yesterday. It is shortly as follows', and then Richmond gave a fairly full narrative of events, the names of some casualties, concluding with a remark that he himself personally doubted Napoleon's intention to attack Mont St Jean and that 'I am just going over to look at the position.'[8] This summary, at third-hand, contained a number of inaccuracies but at least gave the government some notice of the way matters were going.

The Duke's Despatch came to be seen by many in later years as a definitive statement of events, and Wellington himself sometimes fell into this error. It was of course no such thing. It was an instant and coherent recollection of a mass of detail concerning the past three days, all the more impressive because the battle had ended only a few hours earlier and that during the campaign he had slept for no more than ten hours in the past ninety-six. For obvious reasons it had to be sent instantly, since so much turned on it, and indeed it was being read to the Prince Regent in St James's Square exactly seventy-two hours after the final advance had gone across the valley.[9] The draft shows that choosing an opening set of words required some thought and re-casting, for the first paragraph contained a very large number of corrections and changes of phrase, but he was soon settled in his approach to the matter and his subsequent paragraphs were generally very free from additions and corrections. He must have begun writing by 4 a.m.; we know that he made the 10-mile ride and reached Brussels before 8.30 a.m.; and there is a clear break in the draft after the sixteenth paragraph, after which a different pen was used and fresh news was recorded from the Prussians, all indicating the resumption of composition in Brussels. Thus the first thousand words were penned before about 6–6.30 a.m. and should be judged accordingly.

Once in his Brussels quarters Wellington wrote eight letters,[10] as well as completing the second half of his Despatch. The first letter was timed 8.30 a.m. and was to Lady Frances Webster, in whom he was particularly interested, to reassure her and her parents that they need not flee to Antwerp:

> My dear Lady Frances, Lord Mountnorris may remain in Bruxelles in perfect security. I yesterday, after a most severe and bloody contest, gained a complete victory, and pursued the French till after dark. They are in complete confusion; and I have, I believe, 150 pieces of cannon; and Blücher, who continued the pursuit all night, my soldiers being tired to death, sent me word this morning that he had got 60 more.
>
> My loss is immense. Lord Uxbridge, Lord FitzRoy Somerset, General Cooke, General Barnes, and Colonel Berkeley are wounded: Colonel De Lancey, Canning, Gordon, General Picton killed. The finger of providence was upon me, and I escaped unhurt.
>
> Believe me, etc, WELLINGTON.

There followed a short note to his brother, who sat in the Cabinet:

> My dear William, You'll see the account of our Desperate Battle and victory over Boney!! It was the most desperate business I ever was in; I never took so much trouble about any battle; & never was so near being beat.
>
> Our loss is immense, particularly in that best of all Instruments British Infantry. I never saw the Infantry behave so well. I am going immediately. Can we be reinforced in Cavalry or Infantry or both?
>
> We must have Lord Combermere as Lord Uxbridge has lost his leg. He was wounded when talking to me during the last attack, almost by the last shot.
>
> Ever yours most affectionately W.

All the while fresh reports were coming in, itemising battalion by battalion the casualties and the troops' immediate needs. While the clerks were fair-copying the finished Despatch Wellington wrote a personal letter to Bathurst on his immediate needs:

> My dear Lord, I am come in to arrange some matters, and start immediately [to return to the army for the advance]. Can you reinforce us in good British infantry particularly, and cavalry? You'll see how we are reduced. Some of the battalions have not 100 men. We must have Lord Combermere also, if he will come. Believe me, etc, WELLINGTON.

Late in the day he sent Bathurst an official letter concerning an urgent problem, the daunting scale of which must have severely tested the army's organisation in any circumstances, and more particularly now in its reduced state: the holding, feeding, and disposal of an enormous number of prisoners:

> My Lord, I have to inform your Lordship, in addition to my despatch of this morning, that we have already got here 5000 prisoners, taken in the action of yesterday, and that there are above 2000 more coming in tomorrow. There will probably be many more. Amongst the prisoners are the Comte de Lobau, who commanded the 6th corps, and General Cambrone [*sic*] who commanded a division of the Guards. I propose to send the whole to England, by Ostend. I have the honor to be, etc.

There was a short formal letter to the Duke of York as Commander-in-Chief with a separate copy of the Despatch. Some captured eagles had been sent to Brussels, although it is not clear whether the Duke actually saw them. The Despatch was finished and signed, and doubtless the copy for the Duke of York also, and then a senior ADC was selected to carry them. Colonel Fremantle was the most senior ADC, but had already carried despatches for Vitoria and in any case, with his immediate juniors Colonels Canning and Gordon dead, he could not be spared. So the privilege went to the next senior ADC, Major Percy, younger son of an earl. Percy collected the Despatch and some letters, took the captured eagles, and immediately started for the coast.

Likewise Wellington in his capacity as commander of the Netherlands army wrote a letter in French to King Willem. Wellington trusted that Dutch officers had, as requested, already briefed Willem on the victory, he indicated that the wounded Prince of Orange was progressing, and promised to send his despatch to the king tomorrow: it was at that moment being translated into Dutch from the draft.

The Corsican representative of the Tsar, Pozzo di Borgo, had been asked by Wellington to go at once to Ghent and inform Louis XVIII of the victory; perhaps in choosing Alexander's envoy for the task Wellington was binding the Tsar's retinue and perhaps the Tsar himself more closely with the Bourbon cause. In any case, from a study of the published *Wellington Despatches* it seems that although Wellington did on occasion visit the King, his correspondence usually was with the group round Louis: Sir Charles Stuart, the duc de Berri, Feltre, or Blacas.

While clerks were making copies of the finished Despatch, Wellington wrote two letters of commiseration: to the Duke of Beaufort concerning the wound that Beaufort's brother FitzRoy Somerset had suffered, and to the Earl of Aberdeen on the loss of his brother Alexander Gordon. Both letters dwelt on his liking and affection for the two men, and on his own grief and desolation that made the victory of no immediate consolation. The sentiments were direct and warm, and the words chosen gave glimpses of the inner man that were seldom seen. In commiserating with the families' grief and worry he admitted that 'the losses I have sustained have quite broke me down, and I have no feeling for the advantages we have acquired'. In this desolation one recalls that image of exhaustion and shock of the silent victor after Assaye sitting on the ground all night with his head bowed. It was not often that he let slip the mask.

These expressions of sorrow do Wellington great credit. But … there seems to have been no note or message of any kind for the one person who, with her two small sons, had the greatest claims of all for reassurance and for news – the Duchess of Wellington.

As we have seen already in the appendix to the previous chapter, there is an account of Wellington in his Brussels rooms at mid-morning on 19 June, penned by Thomas Creevey, MP. Creevey had gone to gaze at the house and was seen by Wellington from a window and beckoned up:

> The first thing I did, of course, was to put out my hand and congratulate him upon his victory. He made a variety of observations in his short, natural, blunt way, but with the greatest gravity all the time, and without the least approach to anything like triumph or joy. 'It has been a damned serious business,' he said, 'Blücher and I have lost 30,000 men. It has been a damned nice thing – the nearest run thing you ever saw in your life. Blücher lost 14,000 on Friday night, and got so damnably licked I could not find him on Saturday morning; so I was obliged to fall back to keep up my communications with him.' Then, as he walked about, he praised greatly those Guards who kept the farm (meaning Hougoumont) against the repeated attacks of the French; and then he praised all our troops, uttering repeated expressions of astonishment at our men's courage. He repeated so often its being so nice a thing – so nearly run a thing, that I asked him if the French had fought better than he had ever seen them do before. 'No', he said, 'they have always fought the same since I first saw them at Vimeira [*sic*].' Then he said: 'By God! I don't think it would have done if I had not been there' … before I left him, I asked whether he thought the French would be able to take the field again; and he said he thought certainly not, giving as his reason that every corps of France, but one, had been in the battle, and that the whole army had gone off in such perfect rout and confusion he thought it quite impossible for them to give battle again before the Allies reached Paris.[11]

III

There are no other papers or descriptions to show how the Duke spent his day, but he must have held meetings with such of his staff as remained: dealing with handling of sick and wounded, rations, pending courts martial, holding of prisoners of war, re-munitioning, movement orders, and a multitude of administrative matters that previously had been agreed with officers such as the Duke of Brunswick or De Lancey who had subsequently been struck down, that now had to be explained again to their successors or – given the carnage – even to their successors' successors.

Apart from the few words exchanged with Blücher in the dusk of 18 June, and a message sent by the Prussians in the morning, the Duke had only the broadest indication of what his ally would now do. That their two armies would form separate wings and co-operate in the invasion of France had been agreed as far back as a month before (see Volume 1, Chapter 13, for the terms agreed on 27 May), and from the circumstances of the fighting on 18 June the Prussians would necessarily lead the pursuit, marching through the day of Monday the 19th, while the Anglo-Allied army stood stationary and re-grouped. But Wellington's army would begin advancing on Tuesday 20 June, even though its first march would not be long.

It is perhaps worth repeating the essence of the agreement of 27 May, since there has been some confusion and claims that there was 'a race' between the allies. Assuming that the enemy's main army was shattered, the advance into France should be as rapid as possible, since a short war would lighten the sufferings of the French population. Paris was the agreed objective, but it was over 150 miles from the frontier. Thus the armies once inside France would need large supplies of food and fodder for the march, as well as ammunition and bridging equipment. The Prussians were short of food and short of cash to buy any. They needed their ally to supply ammunition (for instance, from the depot at Mons) and they lacked bridging material and pontoons, as well as heavy siege equipment. Even in defeat Napoleon could still prove dangerous, so that it was advisable that the two armies should not be further apart than the needs of supply and feeding made necessary. To maintain the freedom to advance, each wing would have to mask, blockade, or lay siege to, one or more of the frontier fortresses. Those were the main points agreed just over three weeks earlier.

Thus a long punitive campaign, or 'living off the country', had been ruled out, and it was expected that the Prussians once inside France would adopt the same system as the British: that is to say, issuing coupons for supplies, with the supplier later receiving cash from Bourbon officials in settlement for the coupons. This would have the double advantage of feeding the troops regularly and without recourse to violent seizure, and tying the peasants to the royalist cause by making them reliant on a Bourbon paymaster. The earlier caution was no longer so appropriate since the victory of 18 June had been so great that even Napoleon was unlikely to be able to find troops to stay in the field, and the one slight complication – Grouchy's force – ought not to remain long as a danger since on the night of 18/19 June Blücher had ordered Pirch's corps to cut off Grouchy's retreat to the Sambre, and there was every reason to expect that the latter would be trapped before he could enter France. French remnants might reassemble eastwards in the vicinity of Laon, but should present no paralysing threat, and if the Allies aimed for the uppermost stretch of the Sambre and then crossed the watershed into the upper valley of the River Oise as it turned south towards the Seine and the region of Paris, they would find good and fertile marching country, with their left (eastern) flank guarded by the Oise for much of the way.

On 19 June Blücher had (as agreed) immediately ordered his commissariat to draw bread and other supplies from Wellington's depots at Mons. For the task of position or even siege warfare, not only did Wellington possess twelve 18-pounders, assembled just as Waterloo was fought, but a whole battering train had been despatched from England in twenty-four vessels during the second half of May. Almost at once this siege train was asked for by the Prussians, and made available to them.[12] Given the arrangements agreed for supply of food and forage (and the reasoning upon which the arrangements were predicated), what was not foreseen was the reckless and systematic devastation wreaked by the Prussians in their advance, something that deeply shocked every British soldier who wrote of what he found along the road. For supplies were seized, the population terrified, houses and grounds looted and wrecked, burial lots defaced, anything fine or beautiful torn or broken, and mindless destruction wreaked, down to smashing the smallest window-pane and looking-glass. It certainly made a rapid advance much easier, not having to bother with agreements over getting food from French suppliers; but it left a permanent distinguishing mark on the record of the Prussian Army and the Prussian commanders and commissary officers who permitted and encouraged all this.

IV

Wellington spent 20 June at Nivelles, handling a variety of topics, including correspondence with Whitehall on miscellaneous problems such as the failure of the Portuguese to provide troops; he also had to deal with Ghent, urging the court of Louis XVIII to begin the journey back to France and advising how to canton the royalist troops along the way. He advised on a dispute between the Belgians and the Bourbons on supplying arms to the royalists. He gave instructions for the handling of French wounded, arranged the new command structure for the Brunswick contingent following the death of their Duke and the wounding of his successor. He received as a gift from the Saxon king the command of his '17,000 loyal troops' and consequently had to decide where to station them: he decided that somewhere out of the way was best, like Antwerp – but that in turn involved him in a negotiation with King Willem. The longest document was, however, his General Order to the army. Prince Blücher had issued a short triumphal victory proclamation to his army on the 19th.[13] Wellington's composition was of a more admonitory nature.

In many ways this General Order was of a type that veterans of the Duke's campaigns had come to expect: perfect clarity on what he expected his army to do, some short cool words of thanks to the army, a longer and hotter criticism and denunciation of observed faults, plus clear administrative instructions for the march.[14] The opening paragraph was striking, addressed as it was to 'the troops of the nations' at present under Wellington's command, for it set out the high rationale of the entire campaign with absolute clarity, and it imposed on the different national contingents a duty of fair dealing and restraint once in France. They were ordered: 'to recollect that their respective Sovereigns are the Allies of His Majesty the King of France, and that France ought, therefore, to be treated as a friendly country'.

The Duke then succinctly returned his thanks for the army's conduct on the 18th and promised 'to report his sense of their conduct in the terms which it deserves to their several sovereigns' (a remark that may of course be read in more than one way). That said, three paragraphs then followed on observed misconduct and unauthorised absence. There were also very clear and precise instructions on care for the wounded lying in Brussels when the army should march into France.[15] On the march all requisitions should be paid for, no extortion should be employed, and if and when foreign contingents needed supplies from other than British sources they should purchase them against proper documentation and would be held accountable for all supplies whether from British or French sources.

At the practical level such an instruction, and the detailed (and time-consuming) procedures for purchase on agreed terms and the concomitant paper-work, of itself indicated that the advance was intended to be measured, orderly, and leading to minimal disruption. It was not to be a wild dash into France. The army would, as far as possible, be properly fed, kept fit, and thus all the more capable of meeting and overcoming any sudden enemy attack.

But on the higher level, conceptually it was in close accordance with the Declaration of 13 March and the Treaty of 25 March in deeming Napoleon the real enemy and the King and his people the victims of an illegal usurpation. It no longer counted or could serve as an excuse for future bad conduct that, in the past, Holland and Belgium, and German states like Brunswick, Nassau and Hanover, had suffered under French domination. Their sovereigns had formally forgiven that by the recent treaty, and so therefore should their subjects.

This rule the Duke strenuously endeavoured to maintain with British, KGL, Hanoverian, Brunswick, Nassau and Netherlands forces. That was why he was so infuriated when Netherlands troops and others marauded on the march south. The strength of his language to the Netherlands general responsible was extreme, and the wretched man must have withered under the rebukes. In principle the same considerations applied to the proper conduct of those other Germans marching under the banner of Frederick William III, a signatory of both Declaration and Treaty, and although Wellington kept silent for the most part, his occasional comments at the time show how deeply he deplored Prussian behaviour to the civilian population. Twenty years later he gave his forthright opinion on Prussian indiscipline in 1815 to a House of Lords committee, an opinion that provoked a storm in Prussia when it was published; but if some of his recollections by then were marred by exaggeration, the kernel of his remarks was undoubtedly true.[16]

In Ghent the cannonade of Ligny and Quatre Bras had been heard on 16 June, but for atmospheric reasons the sound of gunfire seemed less violent on the 18th. At 10 a.m. on Monday 19 June Louis XVIII was told of the victory, and a crowd gathered in front of his residence and he came to the window and waved. He then composed a letter of congratulations and thanks to the Duke, hoping that his brave troops would soon march beside those of Wellington., and sending his brother Artois to express his views personally. Wellington on 20 June wrote several letters to urge that the Bourbon forces should march south via Grammont to Mons, and that the King should re-enter France as soon as possible to rally loyalists and re-establish his rule. He despatched Colonel Robert Torrens to him to repeat the advice. The duc de Feltre was at the king's side, whereas (perhaps fortunately) Talleyrand, whose views were for delay, was still dawdling on the road from Vienna. Thus Wellington's views came to predominate in these first days.[17]

Exactly thirty hours after it had halted on the battlefield, Wellington's army began its march on Paris. It moved at 5 a.m. on 20 June, and on this first day marched a gentle 10 miles (about two-thirds of the distance covered by the Prussians on 20 June), halting in the evening with the cavalry among the villages along the River Haine and towards Binche, and with light scouts close to Maubeuge. The Duke's headquarters remained for this day at Nivelles, midway between Brussels and his leading troops, that of the Prussians was at Merbes-le Château on the Sambre, halfway between Binche and Maubeuge. So at evening the two allies' headquarters were no more than about 18 miles apart.[18] The next day the Duke's army would enter France.

The Duke's order had defined what the position of France and the French was by international treaty. Developments in Paris were, however, taking a slightly different turn.

Chapter 48

France and the Problem of Napoleon

Return to Paris, the Abdication, the Danger

I

NAPOLEON HAD BEEN ON HIS FEET since dawn on Sunday 18 June, had lived through a day of increasing strain, and had been forced to flee on horseback all night. He had passed through Charleroi at 5 a.m. on the 19th and reached the French town of Philippeville four hours later, a distance of over 33 miles from La Belle Alliance. Those who speak of Napoleon's poor health affecting his faculties and performance during the campaign should also remember this remarkable eleven-hour ride by a stout man aged almost forty-six, who had just passed through four days of constant pressure and fairly constant activity. At Philippeville he issued fresh directions to the little circle gathering round him, Bertrand, Drouot, and then Maret and Soult as they arrived. These directions were for the commanders of such units as might re-form after the rout. A message was sent to Grouchy enjoining his retreat on Laon. The commanders of the northern military districts were told to hold firm among the frontier fortresses. Orders went to other outlying forces: Rapp in Alsace, the large force in the Belfort region, and Lamarque in the Vendée were to march and join him at Paris.[1]

Then the Emperor dictated a confidential note to Joseph in Paris, admitting the dire facts, with a second much less discouraging letter to be shown to the ministerial council recounting the campaign and minimising the disaster as much as possible. His confidential note spoke of rallying 150,000 men of the army, plus 100,000 national guards and 50,000 from depot battalions. He would use high-bred horses to pull cannon. He would call for a *levée en masse* in the loyal provinces. He would

> give Paris and France time for them to do their duty ... Everything can still come right. Let me know the effect this horrible affray [*échauffourée*] has produced in the Chamber. I believe that the deputies will see their duty in

> these great circumstances, and join with me in saving France. Prepare them so that they support me with dignity. Courage, firmness![2]

Then he sat down to compose a most remarkable *Bulletin* for publication. This was completed and dated 'Laon, 20 June', but as Napoleon arrived there only at 7 p.m. on the 20th, and as it was well over 2,000 words long, much of it may have been thought through and composed while on his journey. At first he outdistanced the terrible news, and was received with cheers by crowds at Rocroi. But by the time he reached Laon the news was already spreading, and when he halted and changed his carriage horses, people looked at him in silent astonishment, and when a few cheered him he raised his hat in salute. He raced on to Paris, by which time the army that had stood at La Belle Alliance amounted to 2,600 men at Philippeville and another 6,000 at Avesnes. To have stayed with the army, as his brothers suggested, would have been of little use. In 1814 he had abandoned Paris, with dire consequences; this time he would hold it and restore his position.

II

The *Moniteur* of Monday, 19 June, had published Soult's report to War Minister Davout on the victory at Ligny, and that of the 20th gave further details from a staff officer with the army: 'it is said that the enemy has lost 50,000 men; the Prussians are in total disarray, and we shall have nothing to say about them for some time. As to the English we shall see what will become of them today; the Emperor is there.'[3] But Paris was filling with rumours on 20 June, and during the late evening the gist of what Napoleon had told Joseph spread through political circles. Houssaye blamed for this leakage the man whom he consistently presents as the arch-villain – Fouché; that may be so, but he also admitted that during an evening party the minister and great patriot Carnot let slip the alarming news.

Joseph left a note of what happened elsewhere on the night of the 20th: 'In the night a large number of members of the Chamber of Deputies met in M. de La Fayette's house where they fixed on the way, not to save the nation and the Emperor, but to drop the Emperor to save the nation . . .'[4]

Joseph's words go to the heart of the problem: was the interest of France the same as the interest of the Emperor? Talleyrand had successfully protected France from savage retribution in 1814 by making the distinction. The leaders of the Chamber could not avoid it. They suspected, and rightly suspected, that Napoleon was intent on further war despite losing his last army in catastrophic defeat.

The appearance the next day of Napoleon's Laon account in the *Moniteur* left nothing still to doubt. Napoleon himself reached the Elysée Palace in Paris at 8 a.m. on 21 June, took a bath, then spoke to his ministerial council. He told his ministers of how he could meet and surmount the crisis: 'To save the nation what I need is to be given a great power, a temporary dictatorship. In the public interest I could seize this power, but it would be more useful and national if it were given me by the Chambers.' This was received with a significant silence: ministers were divided between those like Davout who approved these views, and Fouché who opposed them. Napoleon mentioned the word abdication only to deride the idea. The army drew its strength from his name; once he had abdicated all would collapse, whatever the Chamber might decree. 'They do not wish to see that I am merely the pretext [*sic*] for a war, and that it is France that is the object . . . I am part of what the enemy attacks; and thus I am part of what France must defend.' To give up Napoleon would be for France to recognise its own defeat.[5]

In another part of Paris men of different views were taking steps to protect France as far as they could. Many in the Chamber were willing to follow La Fayette's lead. To them he proposed five resolutions. They were carried without great argument: the independence of France was in danger; the Chamber should sit in permanence and any attempt to dissolve it would be treason; the army and national guard were worthy of the nation; the Parisian national guard should be strengthened and should protect the capital and the Chamber; the ministers of war, foreign affairs, interior and police should at once report to the Assembly.[6] The resolutions were sent to 'the other branches of representative authority', meaning the Chamber of Peers and Napoleon, but making him a branch only, and emphasising the Lower Chamber's status.

Napoleon was furious, exclaiming, 'I should have dismissed those gentry before I left Paris – they will ruin France.' He sent a message back to the president of the Lower Chamber stating that he was putting in place fresh measures for national defence, and wish to concert with them on national safety. 'I have formed a committee comprising the Minister of Foreign Affairs [the moderate Caulaincourt], Comte Carnot, and the duc d'Otrante [Fouché, Duke of Otranto], to renew and follow negotiations with foreign powers to establish their true intentions and to bring an end to the war if that is compatible with the nation's honour and independence.' But in vain he sent his ministers led by his brother Lucien (the former president of the Chamber at the coup of *18 Brumaire* that brought Napoleon to power in 1799) with this message.[7] If he had expected difficulty with the Lower House he was right, but the defection of the usually complaisant peers shook him.

He sent brother Lucien to make a second appeal. But when Lucien spoke of France's inconstancy in dropping Napoleon, La Fayette retorted that 'France's constancy towards him in the sands of Egypt and the deserts of Russia had cost her the blood of three million Frenchmen.' That retort was decisive.

Napoleon veered between dissolving the Chamber and abdicating. He half-thought of appealing to the mob, but his deepest lifelong instinct was hatred of mobs and their destruction of 'order', and so he declared that he could never be 'a king of the *Jacquerie*'. Finally on 22 June he gave way to the more moderate of his advisers, and dictated an act of abdication:

> In commencing the war to uphold national independence I called for the united efforts and willpower of all in authority: in that I placed my hopes of success. Circumstances have turned otherwise. I offer myself as a sacrifice to the hatred of France's enemies. May they be sincere in their declarations of seeking nothing but my person. Let all of you unite for the nation's independence and safety.
>
> [A postscript was added:] I proclaim my son under the name Napoleon II, Emperor of the French. [Five words eventually deleted are shown here in italics:] *Princes Joseph and Lucien and* the present ministers will form a provisional government. My interest in my son leads me to invite the Chamber immediately to organise a regency by an act of law.[8]

Fouché read the abdication to the Lower Chamber, Carnot read it to the Peers. A five-man provisional government was voted, incidentally totally ignoring the rules of the imperial constitution and thus the automatic accession of Napoleon II. The Lower Chamber nominated three ministers: Carnot, Fouché and the moderate General Grenier; the Peers chose Caulaincourt and the ex-regicide Quinette. The next day Fouché voted for Carnot as leader, Carnot voted for Fouché: Grenier, Caulaincourt and Quinette inclined to Fouché. On 23 June the Chamber debated whether to recognise Napoleon II, and although Houssaye strongly suggests that the outcome was pure chicanery, the account of the speeches tends to suggest a genuine puzzlement and an attempt to satisfy as many parties as possible so as to present a united front to the foreigner. Two resolutions were passed: that the Chamber declared Napoleon II as Emperor by the abdication of his father and by the imperial constitution; and that the newly established provisional government assured the nation's liberty and quiet, and enjoyed the entire confidence of the people. Such ostensibly was the imperial form. In reality whatever power still remained rested in the new and strange combination that took over the duty of saving something from the defeat, under the most astute of French politicians.

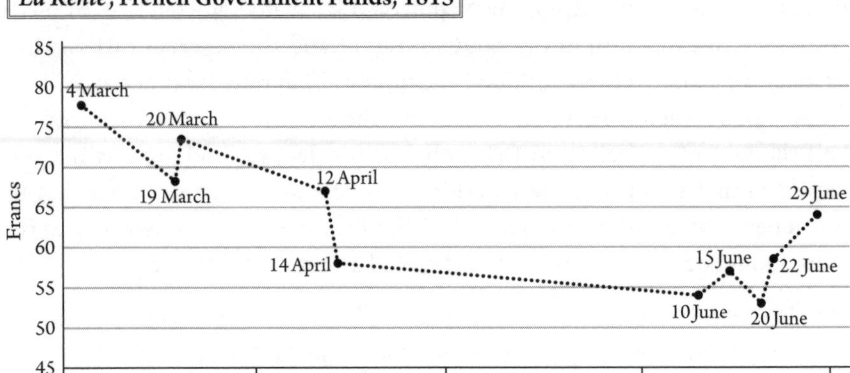

The men of business in Paris had watched the past week and had registered their hopes and fears in the movement of *La Rente* (the Funds). On 15 June the *Rente* stood at 57 francs. On 20 June it had fallen by 4 francs, but on the next day as news of the defeat was confirmed and the debates developed in the Chamber it rose to 55. On 22 June 1815 it rose another 4.50 to 59.50, on the prospect of an early peace.[9]

III

It is perhaps impossible for anyone but a Frenchman, and even then only Frenchmen whose memories go back to the stresses and revolts that came out of the Indo-China and Algerian conflicts or even the defeat of 1940, to understand the difficulties that the new provisional government faced. French society was deeply divided by ideology and by region: royalists, Bonapartists, republicans watched each other with distrust and even detestation, as the massacres in Marseilles on 25–26 June were to demonstrate. The north and west and the south were generally against Napoleon, the centre and east – the lands that had seen the invasion of 1814 – were for him; but within these regions many simply wanted peace, an end to conscription, and lower taxes. How to control and manage these discontents and divisions was a frightening enough problem in itself. Then there was the need to find some accommodation with the Allies, after the most shattering and decisive defeat, and that in turn added to the social tensions, for it necessarily raised the question of who, if anyone, should take the throne of France. As Fouché was to say, the new provisional government sat on no bed of roses.[10]

On 23 June that able and unscrupulous man drew up his first ideas on a negotiation for peace, and a delegation list. The ideas were plainly optimal as a first step in negotiation: integrity of French territory; no imposition of the Bourbons on France through foreign demand; recognition of Napoleon II; safety and inviolability of Napoleon I in his retirement. The delegates were of several minds, not all being hardened Bonapartists. They left Paris on 24 June. On this day Soult, in accordance with Davout's orders, called on the Prussians to agree to an armistice: this was rejected the next day. Napoleon was already considering his future safety. He asked the new authorities that two men-o'war should be provisioned at Rochefort for a voyage to America. On 26 June the ministers authorised the provision of these vessels and for an escort to guard him while in France, but they refused authority for the vessels to sail unless and until a safe-conduct had been given by the Allies. However, on this same day the team of negotiators at Laon warned the government that according to discussions with Blücher's suite it was Napoleon's person that was sought: 'It is our duty to warn that we believe that his escape before negotiations are complete will be seen as bad faith on our part, and that could in essence compromise the safety of France.'

On hearing this, Fouché immediately said to the ministerial meeting that it was necessary to halt Napoleon's departure; and none of the twenty present at that meeting (which included Carnot, Caulaincourt and Davout) disagreed. Houssaye saw this as a cunning move by Fouché to ensnare the Emperor, and yet the dilemma was real: it was desirable to see Napoleon removed far from Paris, even as far as the United States, unable to raise new armies; but was it wise to permit him to escape if the consequence was that France had to pay an additional penalty for his adventure?[11]

As to the escape to America, there were in any case two problems over which the new French government had no control. The British naval blockade made the project so hazardous that a safe-conduct pass was needed. The safe-conduct request was addressed by the government to the Allied commander most opposed to Napoleon's execution, only to receive a reply that it was a matter for the combined Allied governments to decide upon. Marshal Davout, as part of the provisional government, had already gone to see Napoleon at the Elysée on 24 June and told him of the need to leave the capital: 'the meeting was cold and the close even more so', said Davout. The ex-Emperor left Paris for Josephine's old home of Malmaison on the 25th. There, on the two following days, guarded by a military detachment that was not only for his protection but for his surveillance, he renewed his request for the two ships. By this time the attitudes of the victors were becoming clearer, and the danger of Napoleon falling into the hands of the rapidly advancing Prussians much greater. On the evening of 28 June, Fouché, concerned at the intransigent attitude of the victors as regards Napoleon, wrote that 'actual circumstances raised fears for Napoleon's safety', and thus he ordered that the safe-conduct stipulation no longer applied, the vessels could sail at any time, and Napoleon should leave at once so as to avoid risk of capture.[12]

At this point Napoleon suddenly changed his mind, and rumours of a new plan immediately circulated. Marshal Davout wrote at 2 a.m. on 29 June that rumours were current that Napoleon intended going to the fortified heights of Montmartre: if that happened Masséna and the national guard should take action to stop him. And indeed Napoleon did make a final appeal:

> France need not submit to a handful of Prussians . . . The situation of France, the wishes of patriots, the cries of soldiers, clamour for my presence to save the country. I ask for the command, not as Emperor, but as a general whose name and reputation can yet have a great influence on the fate of the nation. I promise on the faith of a soldier, citizen and Frenchman to leave for America, so as to fulfil my destiny, on the day that I have beaten the enemy.

It may have been sincere, but it contained echoes of the appeal from the rock of Elba just a few months earlier, and by now the Allies were in France in overwhelming strength. Unsurprisingly the government rejected this appeal and wrote to warn him to leave at once as 'the Prussians are marching on Versailles'. Napoleon left for Rochefort around 5 p.m. on 29 June.[13]

IV

The idea of a distinction, as between Napoleon and France, did not prove acceptable to an older generation of French historians. Partly this may be because of anger that, for whatever reason, foreigners had brought a French king back to Paris with a Bourbon flag, after France's Revolutionary and Imperial *tricolor* had proudly flown over many of those foreigners' capitals in The Hague, Madrid, Rome, Vienna, Berlin, Moscow. But also it must be in part the singularly unpleasant fact that the safety of France depended to a considerable extent not on a saintly heroine like Jeanne d'Arc, but on a most unprincipled and unsavoury character, the former pupil of the *Oratoriens*, ex-school-teacher, ex-regicide, a most feared police minister, and possibly the most powerful of Napoleon's ministers during the Hundred Days, Joseph Fouché, Duke of Otranto.

The role of Fouché was critical to the future of France, but it is impossible to be certain of the extent of his plans. Clearly his own survival came first, but there is no doubt that he sought to limit the damage to France itself. For a long time he had not regarded France and Napoleon as synonymous: perhaps that is why Houssaye hated him so much. Moreover he had already seen that in the longer term, despite any early victories, Napoleon must fail in this new endeavour. According to Chancellor Pasquier, on 3 May 1815 Fouché had remarked that Napoleon 'will be obliged to leave for the army before the month end. Once he has left we shall be masters of the ground. I wish him to win one or two battles, but he will lose the third; and then our role will commence. Believe me, we shall bring about a good dénouement.'[14] Now a crushing defeat had come. Peace and the avoidance of dismemberment were the two national objectives, and to those objectives Napoleon was an encumbrance that had to be disavowed. Whether Napoleon II was desirable seemed doubtful, although from Fouché's contacts with Metternich a regency over the Franco-Austrian child *might* be negotiable; the duc d'Orléans was a possible and acceptable choice for moderate monarchists and had been seen by many inside France and beyond as preferable to the old line;[15] a republic was unlikely to please the Allied sovereigns; and there was always Louis XVIII, with whom Fouché had maintained contact. As with Talleyrand in 1814, so for Fouché in this year, all lay in the art of the possible.

Houssaye denied the distinction between France and Napoleon, and adopted without qualification Napoleon's view of who was responsible for war and thus for France's current woes; in a neat inversion of the reality he wrote: 'The good sense of the public understood that if the Emperor was the cause of *or the pretext for* the war, he was in no way its promoter. *It was Europe that had willed and made inevitable* this war, so feared and execrated [my italics].'[16]

This thesis that Napoleon and France were one and the same, and that those who disputed this were in some way false to France, led to some strange contortions. Henri Welschinger, writing in 1893, went so far as to claim that when Louis XVIII and Talleyrand stated in the Cambrai proclamation (28 June 1815) that it was the treason of March 1815 that had 'called foreigners to the heart of France', they should not have blamed *Ney* for treason, *but Talleyrand, for it was he who had called them in* – since once Napoleon had returned to France Talleyrand recognised that foreign assistance was necessary to save the King. Thus he and not Ney was the real traitor![17]

The indefatigable if violent enthusiast Frédéric Masson was equally vehement on the treason of Napoleon's critics after Waterloo. Since for Masson it was a *sine qua non* that only Napoleon could save France, he described La Fayette's intervention on 21 June as,

> a coup d'état against the national sovereignty, an insurrection against legal authority, a crime of *lèse-patrie,* the most cowardly and foolish of aggressions against the sole man who could yet save the nation [*sic*]: this was the work of one who in the annals of his sad life registered three memorable dates: 5 October 1789, when he betrayed the king; 20 August 1792, when he went over to the enemy; 21 June 1815, when he dragged down the Emperor.[18]

After such warnings, and after the disappearance of 'the sole man who could yet save the nation', what could France expect from the vengeful and victorious Allies? Could any Frenchman undertake the task with any hope of success? Could any foreign statesman? Was France doomed to destruction? That must be the subject of a later chapter.

Chapter 49
The Allied Advance
And the Return of King Louis

I

THE TWO ALLIES HAD TO ENSURE their victory would end the Napoleonic regime for ever. Their basic plan for the invasion of France had been agreed in the exchange of views between Blücher and Wellington on 27 May, and so there was little need for discussion on the evening of 18 June. They would advance as rapidly as possible, but separately, partly for reasons of supply, but would still remain close to each other as surety against any sudden attack by the French. Also they would have to detach parts of their armies to the reduction of some of the French frontier fortresses that otherwise would menace their supply lines. In addition Blücher had a personal objective: to kill Napoleon. That objective Wellington did not share and indeed he was totally opposed to killing Boney; instead he was more concerned to ensure a smooth restoration of Louis XVIII. These differences – though in many ways to be expected by those familiar with the histories of coalition warfare – make for the main interest of these days, but the differences were more of degree, or over method, than about the great objective: freeing Europe from the menace of Napoleon's restless genius.

Waterloo was rightly termed by Wellington a battle between giants, and such a contest demands extended treatment, but nobody can seriously claim for the days that followed an equivalent number of pages; the combats and sieges took place between opponents of very different morale and power, so that long extracts from daily orders about routes through villages where no resistance was expected to be (or was) encountered, would be boring. Even when there was fighting occasionally, the tale of these skirmishes and escalades is so minor in the context of a world-shaking campaign that the episodes belong rather to regimental history than to this account of Great Powers at war. And so neither the brief British siege of Cambrai nor the Prusso-French clashes at Villers-Cotterêts will receive more than a passing mention.

Wellington was intent on rallying to the cause of Louis XVIII the provinces through which they advanced, and he wished the King to keep relatively close to the army so that the French monarch could immediately enter and raise the *fleurs-de-lys* over the captured or surrendered towns. This double desire for a conciliated friendly country under the flag of the legitimist monarchy made for a disciplined, measured advance. However, Blücher was daily becoming aware that the world at large saw Waterloo as Wellington's victory – King Frederick William's first letter to Wellington plainly said so, and it was only several days later (and doubtless upon indignant advice) that the monarch wrote of it being an Anglo-Prussian victory[1] – and just as Blücher had hoped that Ligny would be the victory establishing Prussian dominance in the peace settlement, so now he was anxious to be the first to reach Paris. Yet to speak of 'a race' between the two armies would be to misstate the situation, for that implies a willed contest between the two commanders, whereas Wellington was neither inclined to compete nor had any intention of doing so, given that his system was for an organised, steady attainment of objectives. And although Blücher was determined to spearhead the advance, his army could not afford to act as an independent self-contained force. On 19 June Blücher actually appealed for Wellington's army to take full advantage of the victory by an early movement, something that runs counter to a suggestion that he wished to *steal a march* on the English. He also had a practical reason for asking Wellington to move closer, for he pleaded for mortar and howitzer ammunition, and a million rounds of musket-ball, as well as *food* from Mons.[2]

The state of the Duke's army on 19 June was far worse than that of the Prussians and it was to the Allies' joint advantage that the Prussians should maintain pressure on any residual French forces in their path, backed as Blücher was by Wellington's force. The 'race', if such a word has to be used, was to stop the remnants of the French field army joining the garrison of Paris or joining Napoleon.

The Prussians, like most Continental armies, were notorious for 'over-marching' their troops and it was to be expected that they would achieve a longer daily mileage. What had not been expected was that the policy of 'frightfulness', *Schrecklichkeit,* would be enjoined and enthusiastically carried out. The evidence of many British diarists and letter writers shows how shocked they were at the scenes of wanton devastation created by the advancing Prussians, and as so often Cavalié Mercer is one of the best. His description of a vandalised memorial to a French lady, the trees cut down, the monument defaced, was soon followed by his account of a village where simple houses had been wrecked, doors and windows and furniture smashed, bed linen torn up, and later again a country house vandalised, 'pier-glasses of immense size shivered to atoms', the walls 'defaced and smeared with every species of filth'. Was it surprising that the French found the British so very preferable?[3]

II

By the evening of 20 June the Prussians had marched some 14 miles and were at Beaumont and Maubeuge, while Wellington was quartered about 12 miles further north with his leading troops between the Haine villages and Mons. The Prussians summoned Maubeuge to surrender, but the Bonapartist governor refused, and the Prussians were thus faced with a dual problem, since they had only field and no siege artillery, and, if they marched on, their line of communication might be attacked. Their solution was to leave a detachment masking Maubeuge and to continue the next day towards Avesnes and Landrecies, two fortresses about 15–20 miles further south.

Gneisenau repeated on 21 June the Prussian need for Wellington's siege artillery. On this day the Prussian high command was debating whether to turn away east towards Laon, or to continue the joint south-westerly movement. Significantly, Gneisenau was firmly of opinion that moving in parallel with Wellington's march to Cambrai was better. The knowledge that the Duke's army and its abundant matériel were not too far away remained an important consideration.[4]

At this point a lucky shot transformed the Prussian supply situation and reduced their dependence on Wellington for munitions replenishment. Both the fortresses of Avesnes and Landrecies had refused the Prussian summonses – and rightly, for the fortresses of the north were well stocked, even if the garrisons were not of the highest quality. A desultory bombardment of Avesnes in the night of 21/22 June had a fortunate outcome, one shell hitting a powder magazine; the resultant explosion and widespread damage to civilian, but not military, installations, led to a panic surrender. Thus some forty-seven cannon and their ammunition stocks, and a million rounds of musket-ball (indicating how strongly held the fortress was), all fell into Prussian hands, and suddenly rendered them rather less dependent on Wellington.

Nonetheless, the fall of Avesnes did not lead to a general collapse of the other Bonapartist strongholds in the north, for Maubeuge held out until 12 July, and Landrecies until 21 July, while the little frontier fort of Rocroi resisted until 18 August, two months after Waterloo. In other words, the so-called Prussian 'siege war' resembled rather an investment and blockade than an active operation.

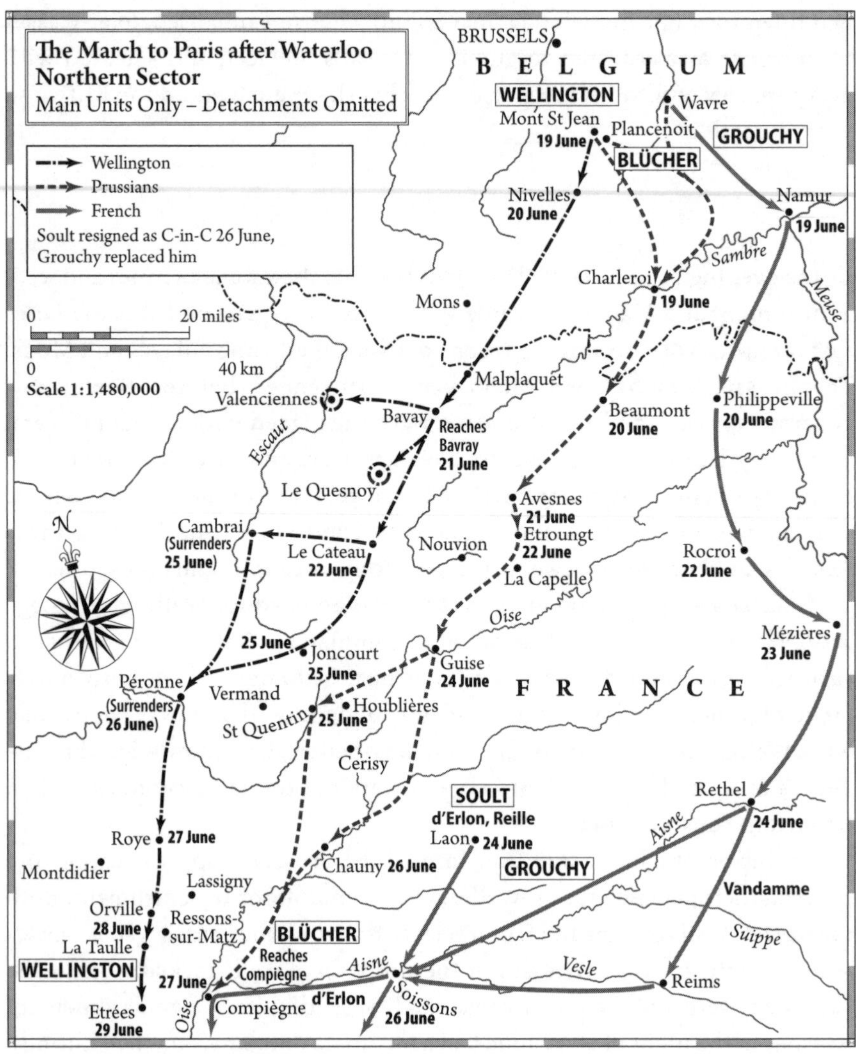

On 21 June 1815 Wellington's army entered France through the woods and meadows of the old (1709) battlefield of Malplaquet, an advance of about 24 miles. Wellington's forces moved west to the glacis of the great stronghold of Valenciennes and south to the small fortress of Le Quesnoy. Both were invested with a blockading and siege force under the young Prince Frederik of Orange: Valenciennes was one of the strongest places of the north and held out, but Le Quesnoy surrendered on 29 June. The Allied front therefore stretched across about 25 miles, from the River Scheldt or Escaut at Valenciennes, past Le Quesnoy, to the great forest of Mormal and beyond the forest eastwards, past the Sambre at Landrecies to Avesnes on

the River Helpe. Three days after the great battle the Allies were only a little more than a day's march from Cambrai and Guise, and Cambrai was the last great fortress in the defensive chain, while Guise, which stands on the River Oise where it turns south for the River Seine, opens the way into the region of Paris.[5]

On Thursday 22 June the Prussian I and IV Corps pushed south of Avesnes towards Nouvion (on the headwaters of the Sambre) and La Capelle. These marches were of only 5–6 miles. The III Corps by now was at Beaumont, 25 miles to the rear. For his part Wellington issued a proclamation to the French from his headquarters at Malplaquet, assuring them that the war was against Napoleon and not the French people, that his orders to his army were in this sense, and that the population should in their turn co-operate in providing supplies in return for official receipts. At the same time he wrote to Feltre expressing relief that the King had decided to enter France as soon as possible, for reports increasingly confirmed the disintegration of the French army. His headquarters that day moved to Le Cateau (a distance of 20 miles). During this period, according to Mercer, the weather had been showery and drizzly, and continued so to the 25th, on which day Frazer noted that rain was falling 'in torrents'.

The next day, 23 June, saw the Prussian I and IV Corps resting, while III Corps marched to Avesnes, thus bringing their field army into closer proximity. By this date a new command structure was operating for Blücher's rear areas. Pirch had been replaced as II Corps commander, ostensibly on grounds of 'deafness', but more probably for lack of energy, and the able Kleist had been replaced as commander of the North German Federal Army Corps; both formations now came under the command of the King's cousin, Prince August of Prussia, who was to be responsible for all the Prussian sieges.

On 23 June Wellington sent Colville's division to Cambrai to summon the town and citadel to surrender. Cambrai was 25 miles south-west of Bavay and well upstream of Valenciennes on the Escaut; its fall would cut off entirely Valenciennes and Le Quesnoy, but its defences were naturally strong and, if properly maintained, could be difficult to master. Wellington, however, trusted to pro-Bourbon sentiment to weaken the resistance. He was pleased at the progress he was making, 'not letting the grass grow', and confident that even if Napoleon could gather the remains of his army, plus Grouchy's force, and Rapp from Alsace and Lamarque from the Vendée, 'he can make no head against us'.[6] On this day Wellington and Müffling rode from Le Cateau to Catillon on the Sambre, where Blücher had his headquarters. The meeting was useful in defining the next steps to be taken. The Prussians had sent scouts eastwards to establish whether and where any French troops might be assembling, for reports were that Soult was gathering the remnants at the outcrop of high ground that is Laon. It was agreed that Laon could be left aside and Paris maintained as the objective. Both armies would continue south-west, with the River Oise as their eastern protection, also that, as the Prussians were lacking in sufficient bridging equipment, British pontoons should be provided for any crossings of the Oise, and that the British siege train should be made available for all sieges, whether in the British western or the Prussian eastern zones.[7]

Wellington had, however, a more immediate preoccupation that affected the movement south that his army might otherwise have taken. This was the possible need to support Colville if the defenders of Cambrai proved offensively minded, and in consequence the bulk of the Duke's forces were halted down the western side of the forest of Mormal. But Colville found the not inconsiderable defences somewhat run down and so he prepared escalading attacks on three different points. He boldly launched two of them, thereby securing the town's surrender on the evening of 24 June at a cost of only thirty-seven casualties. The citadel itself capitulated on the evening of the 25th.[8]

Louis XVIII had reached Le Cateau on 24 June while the British were attacking Cambrai, 12 miles to the west. The Prussians on 24 June had, by a long march of 16 miles, approached Guise on the upper Oise, with other troops moving shorter distances to between Guise and Nouvion. The next day, the seventh after the great battle, the Prussians by a further march neared St Quentin, on the upper Somme and a few miles west of the Oise, with I Corps even going beyond that town. Whereas Mont St Jean is 190 miles from Paris the fine basilica of St Quentin is only a hundred miles from Notre-Dame. And it was on the 25th that Louis issued from Le Cateau a proclamation to the French people, a message that we shall examine later.

June 26th saw British troops occupying the citadel of Cambrai, and on the evening of this day the outworks of Péronne, 20 miles further south, fell to Wellington's assault. For their part the Prussians reached roughly a line between the great arsenal of La Fère and Noyon, about 12 miles south of St Quentin. By 11 a.m. the next day (27 June, the date that on 6 June Schwarzenberg had chosen for the opening of the general advance) Wellington's headquarters were at Vermand, just west of St Quentin, while Louis entered Cambrai in state. But the main events of this day took place in Blücher's zone. On 24 June Blücher had received the first peace feelers from the French by a letter requesting the suspension of hostilities and a safe-conduct pass for Napoleon to leave France. All was summarily dismissed. In reply the Prussian high command laid down very stiff terms: the surrender of all French frontier fortresses between the rivers Sambre and Saar, the surrender of Laon, La Fère and Soissons[9] and all territory north of the Marne, the surrender of Paris and the fortress of Vincennes, the return of looted art treasures, payment of a war reparation, and the surrender of Napoleon.[10] Whether the Prussians thought that the French would even consider such demands is not clear; perhaps they hoped such terms would ensure that the war would continue.

III

It is time to turn to Wellington and his two main problems: the condition of his army and the restoration of Louis. The Prussians were fully aware that Wellington's army was falling behind, so much so that Müffling had to urge him to longer marches so as to keep up. According to Müffling's recollections, Wellington replied:

> Do not press me on this point, for I tell you, it won't do. If you were better acquainted with the English Army, its composition and habits, you would say the same. I cannot separate from my tents and my supplies. My troops must be well kept and well supplied in camp, if order and discipline are to be maintained. It is better that I should arrive two days later in Paris, than that discipline should be relaxed.[11]

Indeed by this time the Duke was becoming severely exercised by outbreaks of indiscipline, theft and looting in the contingents attached to the British army, and by poor staff-work in general. He himself was badly overstretched. Any satisfaction at gaining the victory had always been mixed with anguish at the cost, and although on the 22nd Frazer had found him 'in high glee', the mood had not lasted. His red box containing his papers had been lost on the battlefield after the orderly who carried it was shot dead, and then the ADC who snatched it up, Canning, was killed and his horse ran wild. Only on the 29th did Wellington get back some of the papers, found by artillerymen and sent forwards.[12] In the meantime he had to rely on his memory, and not only had he to handle the normal correspondence with Whitehall, but there were a number of administrative matters concerning Willem of the Netherlands and other diplomatic problems with the often fractious Bourbon court, where the *ultras* led by Artois invariably pestered the intelligent but lazy king with appallingly bad advice. There was the additional burden of army administration placed upon the Duke by the loss of Barnes and the casualties in the AG's department in general, and of De Lancey, and Fitzroy Somerset.

A tone of irritation is already audible in his remarks to Bathurst on 23 June about junior commissariat officers and their failings. Bathurst's son Apsley wrote privately to his father on 25 June to explain Wellington's troubles and to excuse some strong remarks about the commissariat, telling his father:

> I fear you will be much annoyed at the last letter the Duke wrote to you; he had given me the substance on the morning and I had hoped he had then vented himself. The fact is, he has lost in one battle his Adjutant and Quarter Master general and secretary so the whole business comes upon him. He is however particularly good humoured to me ...[13]

However, if polite to the minister's son, Wellington was by now at a pitch of irritation that produced some extraordinary outbursts of unmeasured criticism. On 25 June the hapless Colonel Wood, whose role as commander of the Duke's artillery had been somewhat circumscribed by Wellington's reliance on more tried and trusted subordinates such as Frazer, was given instructions for basic duties that were detailed to the point of insult. From what Wellington wrote it would seem that for the past week he had been unable to learn from the artillery/ordnance arm what ammunition the army could call upon and from where, and this at a time when the Prussians were clamouring for artillery support.

But the irritation was not confined to artillery matters, but to the condition of the army in general. For, on this 25 June, Wellington wrote to Bathurst in terms that are difficult to reconcile with many of his earlier remarks and the generally favourable turn of events. His description of his army and the prospects were so dreadful that it was as though Wellington could no longer see plainly, that he was in the grip of a mood of utter pessimism or exhaustion. To Müffling he had expressed himself in terms that were cogent and well-reasoned: his army needed a degree of care and cossetting after its exertions and losses if it was to maintain its fighting edge. But to Bathurst he sent an account that seems badly unbalanced and with confusing opinions, the opening remarks at variance with the closing ones, and the biting and unqualified criticism in striking contrast with the measured if brief praises of a few days before. Even if Apsley shows that Wellington was still capable of presenting a calmer side, the Duke's letter to Bathurst does mark the lowest point in his performance in this campaign.

> I hope we are going on well, and that what we are doing will bring matters to the earliest and best conclusion, as we are in a very bad way.
>
> We have not one quarter of the ammunition which we ought to have on account of the deficiency of our drivers and carriages; and really I believe

> that, with the exception of my old Spanish infantry, I have got not only the worst troops, but the worst equipped army, with the worst staff, that was ever brought together.
>
> [*In the original, but omitted from the printed text:* The commanding officer of the Artillery] knows no more of his business than a child, and I am obliged to do it for him – and after all I cannot get him to do what I order him. Some of the regiments (the new ones I mean) are reduced to nothing; but I must keep them as regiments, to the great inconvenience of the service, at great expense; or I must send them home, and part with the few British soldiers I have.
>
> I never was so disgusted with any concern as I am with this; and I only hope that I am going the right way to bring it to an early conclusion in some way or other.[14]

The complaint about artillery drivers and carriages, and about Wood, is an early sign of that later criticism of the Royal Artillery that became notorious and was still resented by the regiment's historian Duncan half a century later. Whether these criticisms of post-Waterloo performance were justified it is now impossible to say, but that they were addressed to the Secretary of State for War, who had no authority for the artillery or its drivers (belonging as they did to the Master-General of the Ordnance) does seem odd. That Wellington really was severely troubled by transport problems (for which he blamed 'stragglers and vagabonds of every description') was shown in the AG's instruction of 27 June to General Adam in Brussels, an instruction that represents the Duke's opinions and decisions very clearly; but what was said there shows that by the 27th the views expressed were wise, thoughtful and moderate, particularly so over the care of wounded, about which Wellington personally wrote several sensible letters.[15]

What that letter to Bathurst inadvertently tells us is how important was FitzRoy Somerset to the Duke, for it is unlikely that if the Military Secretary had been present any of this outburst would have reached paper. Writing of a much later period, J. H. Stocqueler remarked that Wellington's cold abruptness, irritability, and withering rebukes when commanding at the Horse Guards, were made endurable by Somerset's courtesy, gentleness and helpfulness, even when conveying the Duke's refusals;[16] and this I believe explains much about the immediate period after Waterloo when Somerset was away sick. There is a second point, one somewhat more speculative but arising from my reading of the correspondence of late June: on the day after the letter to Bathurst, Wellington replied to Schwarzenberg, whose incoming letter had said that nobody else could have earned 'so much glory':

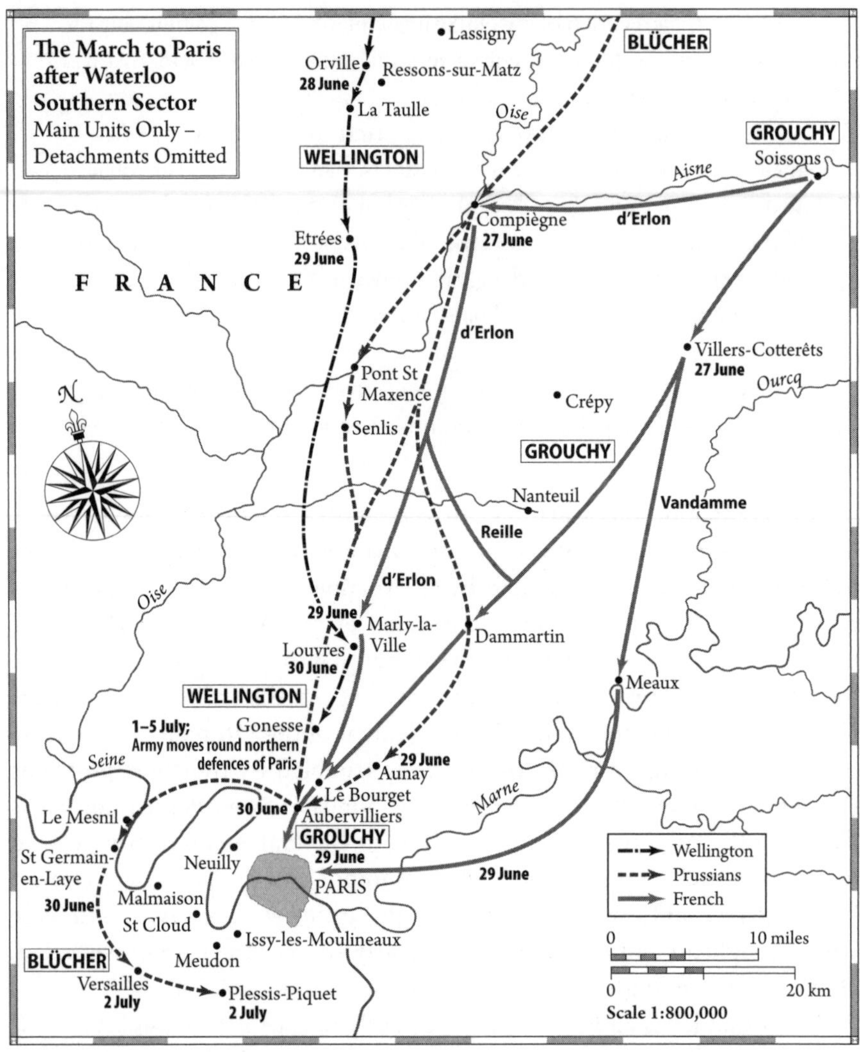

> Our battle on the 18th was one of giants; and our success has been complete, as you see. May God favour me sufficiently that I should never again have another, for I am desolated by the loss of my old friends and comrades.[17]

There were times, as I have said, when the cost of his victory, added to the difficulties of the moment, reduced him to something close to despair – and 25 and 26 June were such times.

In these circumstances it is pleasant to note that by 27 or 28 June a calmer mood was beginning to emerge, with Wellington being 'much obliged' to Bathurst for the reinforcements now promised: 'the greatest object is to have old infantry. The others are better than foreign troops; but they are nothing in comparison with the Spanish infantry.' And that the bitter black mood was passing seems confirmed by his unprecedented suggestion to the Commander-in-Chief on 28 June that a special medal should be awarded to the NCOs and soldiers who had taken part in Waterloo, as 'if that battle should settle our concerns, they will well deserve it'.[18]

Even the best regulated of campaigns will have their rough edges and unfairnesses, and the losses suffered by Wellington meant, as we have seen, that his army was far from perfectly organised, while the Prussians were avowedly living from hand to mouth. Whatever might be said about moving through 'a friendly country' and treating the populace with consideration, the reality was somewhat different. Thus on 27 June Wellington wrote a blistering letter to a senior Netherlands commander (with copy to King Willem), listing in minute detail the breakdown in their march discipline, their refusal to operate at the times ordered, their pillaging and thievery (even from the Duke's own quarters), blaming the Netherlands' arrangements 'as they are dying of hunger while the other troops of the army have abundant supplies', naming individual officers in these charges, and ending by saying 'I do not wish to command such officers. I have been a soldier long enough to know that pillagers and those who encourage them are worthless in front of an enemy, and I don't want them.' (Interestingly, he went out of his way to praise the Netherlands artillery, in a letter to Bathurst dated 28 June.[19]) That same 27 June he issued a General Order on the 'scandalous' habit of straggling.

No doubt the Duke was correct in his details, despite the protests of the older Netherlands historians, but whatever the defects of the Netherlands commissariat service, the situation in the British army was not altogether perfect. It does rather look as though the Netherlands regimental officers and staff were principally at fault, not setting good examples and permitting or aiding the excesses, but quite where the final responsibility for such misbehaviour lay – in habits gained in past campaigns in other armies, in poor training, in the demoralising effects of near starvation – it is not easy to say.[20]

Another problem concerned the populace of St Quentin, a town abandoned by the French forces before the Prussians reached it on 24 June. By 26 June a delegation from the town had appealed to King Louis for help, since the Prussians had taken 'enormous quantities of supplies, and apparently demanded a payment in addition of 600,000 in cash': Feltre wrote in confidence to Wellington asking him to intervene. The Duke answered that the King had a Prussian minister at his court to whom he should appeal, since 'there is no occasion for my getting into a dispute with [Blücher] on this or any other subject'.[21] This was a situation where no one could win. Louis was the rightful king, but one without any power over the Allied armies; the Prussian minister had little influence with the Prussian high command (as Wellington must surely have known); Wellington alone had any influence, but it was not unlimited and had to be saved for greater matters. It was indeed a case of 'rough edges'. This story of St Quentin's troubles leads us to deal with Louis the Well Beloved's return to France as king.

IV

The Duke of Wellington had recommended Louis's immediate return to France, and the King had left Ghent on 21 June. At Le Cateau on 24 June the King issued a short proclamation promising to re-establish the constitution, to repair the evils of revolt and war, to reward the good and use the law to punish the guilty. The wording showed how strong the *ultras'* views still were, despite Louis's own wish for moderation. Talleyrand, who had dawdled his way from Vienna until news of the *outcome* of Waterloo reached him, had arrived at Ghent only as Louis was leaving. He hastened after his sovereign (as Wellington had privately urged him to do) and by the time the court had established itself in the citadel of Cambrai, Talleyrand was once more exerting his old influence against Artois and his wild adherents. Talleyrand disliked the Le Cateau proclamation and worked hard to replace it with a more moderate one, the Cambrai Proclamation of 28 June. Essentially, the latter, appearing just four days after that issued at Le Cateau, did two things: it strengthened the commitment to the 1814 Charter and in very explicit terms, and it reduced the scope of the punishment that the earlier document had threatened. Now, a clear distinction was drawn between those who had actively promoted Napoleon's cause, and those who had 'strayed' in merely continuing to serve under the usurper.[22] Even Houssaye believed that his *bête noire* Talleyrand might have preferred a blanket amnesty had that been feasible politically, but for him to claim as a historian in the 1890s that the Cambrai distinction offered to the angry royalists 'an abundant harvest of vengeance' is to ignore both the reduction in the numbers threatened with vengeance, as well as the bloody outcomes of almost all failed *coups d'état.*[23] In the result, the royal ordinance of 24 July 1815 named eighteen individuals for arrest and trial for treasons committed before 23 March or for rebellion, and thirty-eight others for further investigation or exile: fifty-six names from such an extraordinary occurrence as the Hundred Days does not seem excessively vengeful (see Chapter 51).

Fouché had not been slow to put out feelers for royal forgiveness, and Talleyrand recognised that Fouché held so critical a position in the diplomatic game that he would have to be accommodated, perhaps even given office under the new *Restauration*: it was understandable that Louis should cry 'Never!' at such a hint, but Talleyrand was too experienced not to see reality – and after all, *never* is not a diplomatic concept.

Proclamations are fine things in themselves, and that from Cambrai was better by far than the one issued from Le Cateau. At the least, they promised an end to war and war taxation, a return to normal agricultural and commercial habits, and real guarantees of a constitutional and moderate government, with many faults and follies discreetly forgotten. In the several provinces where royalism was strong they may have been seen as too moderate, but, in the many where the Bourbons were not liked, they offered safeguards and consolations. They gave indications for France's future, but for the present all action depended on the Allied military chiefs and their sovereigns.

V

In the aftermath of defeat the French army had fallen back on a number of northern towns.[24] By 22 June about 15,000 soldiers were with Soult at Laon, with another 12,000 soon to join them. The *Garde* infantry was grouped under Morand, the *Garde* cavalry under Lefebvre-Desnouettes, while Reille combined the *6e Corps* with his own *2e*, and d'Erlon continued with the *1er Corps*. The cavalry commanders sought to collect their scattered men. But these were names and cadres rather than effective forces, and Soult as acting C-in-C had no illusions. On 23 June he received news from Davout of Napoleon's abdication, and this, when announced to the troops, caused further dismay. So, on 26 June, Soult resigned his command on grounds of ill-health. Davout then nominated Grouchy to replace him. The latter had marched south from Rocroi (22 June) to Mézières and then Rethel on the middle Aisne (24 June); there he split his force, sending Vandamme, with the remains of *3e* and *4e Corps*, south to Reims and the Marne country, while he himself turned west towards the Prussians and marched along the Aisne valley to Soissons. At this moment he became commander of some 50,000 men, for the troops at Laon had already retreated there. And Soissons lay just 20 miles east of Compiègne, where the Aisne meets the Oise.

Now a last attempt was made by French forces to turn back the tide. As the Prussians moved down to Compiègne, so at the same moment a force under d'Erlon sought to reach that town and hold it and the bridge over the Oise. The Prussians were almost worn out with the endless marching: a soldier reported that on halting, one officer's horse lay down without waking its rider who was asleep in the saddle.[25] Such exhaustion must have been a warning that exertions on the scale of 15–18 June were now beyond the strength of the army, and that if the French found again their old *élan* then matters might be serious.[26]

Grouchy's instructions to d'Erlon were to march west, defend the line of the Oise, destroy the bridges, hold Compiègne and Senlis (respectively 50 and 30 miles from Paris) and generally do everything to resist the Allied advance. Vandamme was also to assist in the operations. There was a possibility – to put it no more strongly – that the Allies had outrun their supplies, had worn themselves down with over-marching, and could be vulnerable to a sudden sharp attack: one thinks of what a Rommel would have done in such circumstances. Grouchy seems to have surmised this possibility, but he had d'Erlon and Vandamme as subordinates and both men failed him: d'Erlon was timid and swiftly discouraged, and Vandamme ignored repeated and perfectly clear orders and went his own way. The Prussians had tottered into Compiègne only half an hour before d'Erlon reached the place; a more positively minded commander might have contested their hold, but d'Erlon simply withdrew and counselled a general retreat. Grouchy's hand was forced, and the retreat was put in train accordingly. Henceforth there would be minor skirmishes and clashes between the Prussians and the French, at Villers-Cotterêts, Nanteuil and other little villages in the area beyond the Retz forest south of Soissons, but French morale had collapsed, and small encounters too often led to large panics, with guns abandoned and frequently between 500 and 1,000 prisoners taken by the Prussians. No significant effort to stand and fight could be expected until Grouchy's men reached Paris.[27]

Truly – as that excellent divisional commander Foy had implied – there was something very rotten in the spirit and cohesiveness of the leaders of the old *Armée du Nord,* from Soult right down to the surviving corps commanders.

VI

So the Prussians crossed the Oise and then turned for the north-east quadrant of Paris. One of the lessons borne in upon the Prussian high command was that, through over-marching, their forces had become dangerously dispersed. On 28 June they resumed their march, but in more compact form. By the evening of 28 June, just ten days after Waterloo, their troops were close to Paris, between Senlis and La Ferté-Milon on the River Ourcq, with outposts at le Bourget and Stains, le Plessis Belleville and Dammartin (that is to say in a radius of 5–10 miles from today's Charles De Gaulle airport), and with Blücher's quarters at Senlis, just over 30 miles from Notre-Dame. Wellington was some 20 miles further north-west of him at Orville, between Montdidier and Ressons-sur-Matz. With Grouchy falling back south-eastwards the direct road to Paris was wide open.

Chapter 50
The Fall of Paris
And Napoleon's Surrender

I

WHILE GROUCHY AND HIS REMNANTS were falling back before the Allied advance, the politicians in Paris were continually putting out feelers to the enemy commanders. From Blücher they had received an early rebuff so total and so menacing[1] that they recognised that their best hope of salvation lay with Wellington, although their initial approach to him had been no more successful in result: he deemed the French first approach 'a trick'. The substance of his answer was that an unconditional acceptance of Louis XVIII as monarch and an utter rejection of all Bonapartist pretensions were required before any cease-fire could be considered. Bonaparte and the army had invaded the Netherlands on 15 June, and until both were rendered utterly powerless there could be no peace. The only comfort was that though his reply was discouraging, it was polite in a frigid way.[2]

The British government had always favoured the Bourbon restoration, and had encouraged Louis XVIII's rights in framing the text of the Treaty of 25 March. It had nevertheless recognised that several sovereigns (notably Alexander) preferred other solutions, and so it refused to make Louis's rights a sine qua non of British policy.[3] But the sheer scale of Wellington's success on 18 June greatly assisted Louis in the eyes of all the sovereigns, and Talleyrand's skill while at Vienna had further promoted the cause of pure legitimism: the letters sent to Wellington by the sovereigns and men like Metternich in the week after Waterloo indicated that the Bourbons were now recognised as the inevitable choice. Louis could with some show of justice point to the 25 March Treaty so as to mitigate the hostility of the Allies towards his country; but when the provisional government, ostensibly working in the name of little Napoleon II (detained, however, in Vienna by his loving grandfather) advanced similar arguments – that France and Napoleon I were quite separate, and with the usurper's abdication in favour of his son there was no reason for a continuation of military operations – then the Allies understandably chose to disagree with them.

But the great victory also meant that an early answer had to be considered to the question of the relationship between Bonaparte and the French. The assembled powers at Vienna had singled out Napoleon as the disturber of the peace as early as 13 March, before he had gained control of France. Once he was in control, did that alter the situation of France and its people? Again the assembled powers debated the matter and on 12 May the eight great and eight minor powers concluded unanimously that the people had not chosen him as ruler, and were not responsible for his ruling again. He alone was the enemy. In principle, therefore, the 12 May declaration imposed on Wellington's army and the Prussian Army of the Lower Rhine certain obligations regarding an innocent France and its people.[4]

Wellington, fortunately for him, was fully aware of and in agreement with the views of his government; Blücher was aware of and in disagreement with those of King Frederick William III and Frederick William's alter ego the Tsar. But while the Prussian high command could not totally ignore the sovereigns' views, they sought to do so by using another argument. The only way in which the Prussian army could wreak vengeance on its French opponents to the degree that Blücher and Gneisenau desired, was if the French held out militarily, thus obliging the Prussians to waste the country and carry Paris by storm. Then the Prussian army could march through Paris as outright victors and wipe away all recollections of past defeats. But unfortunately the Prussians could not achieve this on their own: their casualties would be too great. Their dream required Wellington's participation in order for it fully to come about.

Hence the tensions arose between the two Allies in the last days of operations, since the Duke's General Order of 20 June and his Malplaquet Proclamation of 22 June left no doubt as to the official British attitude that France and the French should be considered an ally and friends.[5]

But while it had been declared that Napoleon was an outlaw who should be brought to public justice, the ways in which this could be achieved were unclear. The British Prime Minister had raised the question in a long discussion paper on 1 April: what if Bonaparte could not be totally defeated and held on to part of France, what means of pressure might there be in that case to make France co-operate, or what if Bonaparte was totally defeated and then escaped to America (with possibility of return)? The answers to these questions were difficult at that time, and could not really be given.[6] Now answers were urgently necessary.

The Prussian view was clearly stated by Gneisenau. The powers had declared Bonaparte an outlaw, and therefore he could be executed. As the British had scruples about this, let him be delivered over to the Prussians so as to avenge the Prussian blood spilt on 16 and 18 June. His execution would be in the dry moat of Vincennes fortress on the spot where the duc d'Enghien had been murdered by firing-squad in 1804.

> Ought we not to consider ourselves the tools of that Providence which has given us such a victory for the ends of eternal justice? Does not the death of the duc d'Enghien call for such a vengeance? Shall we not draw upon ourselves the reproaches of the people of Prussia, Russia, Spain and Portugal, if we leave unperformed the duty that devolves on us?[7]

Wellington held firmly to the Treaty of 25 March, by which Napoleon was to be placed in a situation where he could no longer disturb the peace of the world, something that was not necessarily the same as killing him. He thought the final decision was for the sovereigns in concert. In the meantime all that he was prepared to do was to prevent Bonaparte's escape from eventual public and international justice. So when the French provisional government sent General Tromelin to ask him on 28 June for a passport for Napoleon to sail for America, his reply was a simple negative. His other comments were tersely direct, both as to Blücher and the French appeals:

> I have answered that I have no authority. The Prussians think the Jacobins wish to give him over to me, believing that I will save his life. [Blücher] wishes to kill him, but I have told him that I shall remonstrate, and shall insist upon his being disposed by common accord. I have likewise said, that as a private friend, I advised him to have nothing to do with so foul a transaction; that he and I had acted too distinguished parts in these transactions to become executioners; and that I was determined that if the Sovereigns wish to put him to death they should appoint an executioner which should not be me.
>
> [Blücher] said nothing positive, excepting that [Fouché] was working for the King. He said they wished for securities, and that [Fouché] was anxious to communicate with me personally, if possible, or through a third person. I answered I would see him when he liked . . .[8]

This letter merits reading a second time, for there are still misconceptions floating that Wellington wished to kill Bonaparte or that he was working to bring him as a prisoner to Britain. We see that nothing could be further from the truth.[9] As to spiriting him to Britain, the reader should examine the Prime Minister's letter to the Foreign Secretary of 7 July 1815, discussing what would happen when all the sovereigns met in Paris:

> By that time we shall be able to form some judgment of the probable fate of Bonaparte. If he sails from either Rochefort or Cherbourg we have a good chance of laying hold of him. If we take him, we shall keep him on board ship till the opinion of the Allies has been taken. The most easy course would be to deliver him up to the King of France, who might try him as a rebel; but then we must be quite certain that he would be tried in such a manner as to have no chance of escape. Indeed, nothing could really be necessary but the identification of his person. I have had some conversation with the civilians [civil lawyers], and they are of opinion that this would be in all respects the least objectionable course [*sic*]. We should have a right to consider him as a French prisoner, and, as such, to give him up to the French government. They think likewise that the King of France would have a clear right to consider him as a rebel, and to deal with him accordingly.[10]

In other words, as the whole matter is far from nice we hope the other Allies will take him off our hands; and we hope in particular that the French will accept the poisoned chalice of dealing with him (something that, of course, the French government had been seeking desperately to avoid doing[11]). This of course would soon be upset and wrecked by the Emperor not being captured at sea as the British half-expected. Instead he surrendered while still on land, claiming prior British governmental approval of the terms that he proffered to the naval captain.

It cannot be said that Britain, any more than the other powers, was clear and consistent throughout: at first there was a feeling that Bonaparte was a trophy of victory, and like flags and cannon should be brought home in triumph as reward for over twenty years of war; but first visionary clamours were soon replaced by hard practical questions, and the evident complications soon brought about a recognition that taking responsibility for his person and his fate was almost certain to lead to trouble and aggravation. Lord Liverpool wavered from initially vengeful thoughts to a hope to avoid lodging Napoleon Bonaparte in the British Isles, or incurring the odium of trying him. Everyone was at the mercy of events and shifting opinions, of which that from Wellington on 28 June seems eminently moderate and balanced.

II

Fouché and his colleagues had less than a week in which to negotiate a most difficult series of tasks: ensuring the safety and integrity of French territory, an avoidance of a battle for and possible sacking of Paris, avoidance of financial and other penalties arising from Napoleon's usurpation, the legitimising of a new regime to govern the country, and (if possible) avoiding any involvement in and responsibility for arresting, trying and punishing Napoleon. And of course their own personal safety was much in their minds and calculations.

Although the French were acutely aware of the pressure from the armies of Blücher and Wellington, they also recognised that up to 450,000 men beyond the Rhine under Schwarzenberg's overall command would soon be deep inside eastern France and also marching on Paris.[12] Memories of 1814 and especially '*les cosaques*' were horrible. So despite the fact that Schwarzenberg's armies played no part in the defeat of Napoleon, they did in some degree help in bringing about an early conclusion to the fighting.

The different contingents under the sovereigns and the Austrian commander-in-chief were, from north to south, the Württemberg and Bavarian armies (sometimes termed 3rd and 4th Corps by the supreme commander Schwarzenberg), both under the Bavarian Marshal Prince Wrede, and relatively close to Germersheim on the Rhine and not far from the (then) French city of Landau; the Russian army was still marching through Germany, but would soon be close to them in reserve; further south on the Rhine stood the Austrian and minor states' forces (1st and 2nd Corps), which were close to Basle and the Swiss frontier; and yet other forces were in rear, destined to handle any siege operations behind the advancing fronts. Most of these exerted no great physical effect, and only the Bavarian army under Wrede need concern us, for Wellington and Blücher expected him to be marching with them to Paris by the beginning of July, adding force to their own pressure upon the capital. But that expectation proved over-optimistic.

Wrede's army was ready to cross the Rhine by 19 June and within the week it had taken Saarbrücken some 40 miles to the west, although it failed to take the fortress of Bitche in northern Alsace. It then advanced on Nancy, capital of Lorraine, and reached there by 27 June, thus isolating the French forces under Rapp in Alsace. It then turned west and had reached Châlons-sur-Marne (now 'en-Champagne') by 3 July (one day later than Blücher and Wellington expected[13]), but that town was all of 120 miles from Paris. A week later, long after the capitulation of Paris had been agreed, Wrede's headquarters were still 45 miles from Paris, at La Ferté-sous-Jouarre. All that can be said for Wrede's army was that expectation of its intervention did increase the despair of the French negotiators – and that is something of importance. The French negotiators always knew that even if their troops could hold in check the Anglo-Prussian forces, overwhelming numbers (many of them Russian) were closing on Paris from the east. Hence it was wisest to settle on whatever terms the two armies coming from the north insisted upon.

III

But France was not totally without soldiers, nor was Paris totally defenceless. The Allies had originally hoped that the French forces in northern France would not re-group, and would not endeavour to dispute seriously the road to Paris. When it was clear that Grouchy had got back from Belgium it was still hoped that the Prussians would cut him off from Paris. They failed to do so. Consequently it was necessary to assess what the Paris garrison and the field army that had fallen back from Namur and Laon and then subsequently reassembled, might be capable of doing, once behind the fortifications of Paris, and under the leadership of such a tough general as Davout.

Paris was a walled city, with the Seine dividing it into a large northern sector on the right bank, and a smaller southern sector on the left bank.[14] Outside its walls and on the right bank lay in clockwise direction from the west, the Bois de Boulogne and the suburban villages: Batignolles, Montmartre on its steep height, La Villette, Belleville on another hill, and Bercy. Further out from these villages were the towns of St Denis in the north and Aubervilliers in the north-east and the great fortress and prison of Vincennes to the east. Out west beyond the Bois, were Neuilly, the steep Mont Valérien, and the residences and palaces of Malmaison and St Cloud, with yet further west St Germain-en-Laye and Versailles. Many of the places to the west were either close to or on the Seine as it made its many loops, and there were numerous bridges of wood or stone. East of Paris the Marne flows into the upper Seine and one of its northern tributaries is the Ourcq, from which a canal had been dug, carrying water due west to La Villette, then into Paris, but with a spur running past the north-east quadrant of the Paris defences to the outlying fortifications of St Denis, where it joined the lower Seine at one of its downstream loops. So much for the northern sector. To the south of the Seine and close to the walls there were (again clockwise) the villages of Ivry, Montrouge, Vanvres and Issy.

Considerable work had been undertaken on the northern semi-circle of defences; St Denis was fortified, likewise the hills of Montmartre and Belleville; the ground between Vincennes and the city had been worked on; the Ourcq canal had been filled with water and its south bank strengthened with breastworks. This combination of a strong St Denis, two fortified hills and the defensible canal line made the sector formidable. It was the southern defences that were still neglected and left relatively weak. The city's garrison was a mixture of mature troops, drafts from depots, Parisian National Guards and various contingents from the countryside, and in numerical terms was not insignificant: over 78,000 troops and 600 cannon. The northern sector

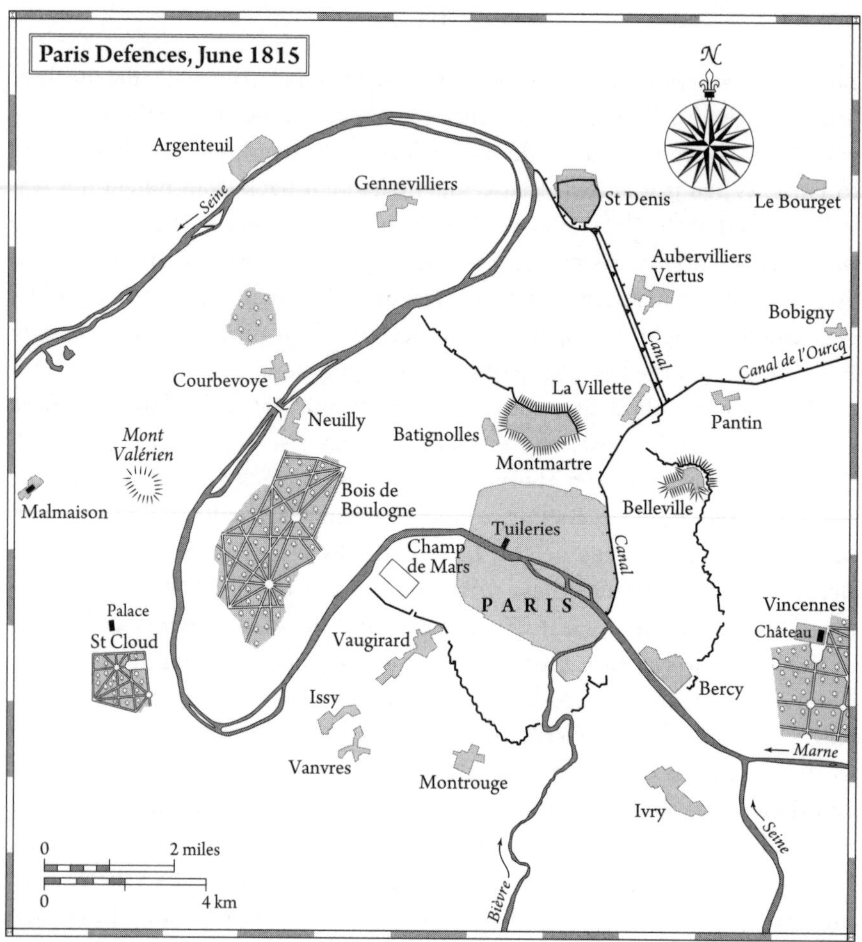

amounted to about 30,000 infantry (including nearly 6,000 of the *Garde*), 9,000 cavalry (3,400 *Garde*), and almost 2,600 artillerymen, while on the southern stood about 18,000 infantry, 5,000 cavalry and 2,600 artillerymen. National Guards totalled about 7,500 men.[15] The sector commanders included Drouot, Reille, d'Erlon, Vandamme, and the cavalry leaders Lefebvre-Desnouettes, Kellermann, Pajol, Exelmans and Milhaud, all very experienced men who, even if shaken by recent defeat, ought to be capable of maintaining a static battle behind fixed defences. A state of siege was declared on 28 June. Davout, the greatest and most respected of the living marshals, placed himself close to the northern sector, at La Villette; he entrusted Vandamme with the left bank sector.

Yet Davout scarcely hoped he could beat off for long a Prussian or an Anglo-Prussian assault. Despite the encouraging words used by this resolute soldier to buoy confidence, within days he was badly worried by food shortages inside the city.[16] He can have had no illusions about what an unsuccessful defence would mean for Paris and, moreover, even if he beat off a first attack, Schwarzenberg's masses must seal the city's doom. Negotiations had to be concluded as early as possible. In fact, the French authorities had on 27 June authorised Fouché and Davout to seek an armistice on the following express conditions:

> Your armistice must be purely military and contain *no political matters*.[17]

Indeed, on 28 June Davout formally repeated to Fouché his own recommendations of the day before, that in view of 'the state of affairs and of the troops' he thought 'there is no time to lose' and that Louis XVIII 'must' be asked to enter the capital as king before foreign troops got there, and this for the sake of France, not for the Bourbon dynasty.[18]

IV

As we saw earlier, the first delegation selected by the new provisional government had encountered a harsh rebuff from the Prussians round Blücher on 24 June. The amazingly arrogant instructions drawn up by the new foreign minister, Bignon, a confirmed Bonapartist, included demands that the Allies should not restore the Bourbons, should recognise Napoleon II and grant the father his safety and inviolability. Fouché and some of the delegation were by now very sceptical of Bonapartism, and recognised that a more modest set of proposals was not simply desirable but essential; yet Bignon continued to represent Napoleon II's rights at least until 4 July. Thus the French leaders remained divided. Meanwhile the foreign armies had got two days nearer to Paris.[19]

Fouché sought to open lines to the Bourbon court through Wellington's headquarters, and, since the Prussians were so hostile, tried to induce Wellington to help in an appeal to the sovereigns in Heidelberg. As with so much to do with Fouché, a great deal of mystery remains on exactly what he did and what he intended, and the degree to which others were his collaborators – or dupes. But it does appear that Wellington refused to be drawn into these schemes. He pointed out that he and Blücher were in full agreement in refusing to consider a cease-fire or a halt, had no authority to discuss Napoleon's departure from France or his future situation, or to argue what should happen to those who had assisted the usurper, or to consider anything other than a Bourbon restoration. All that he would do was forward a letter from Bignon to Castlereagh. In consequence it was not until 28 June, by which time the Allied advance had progressed further, that the French developed some outline proposals that had any likelihood of serving for substantive discussion.[20] Wellington was now hopeful that he might be at Paris by 1 July and that a conclusion could be attained without more fighting, and he used the evident intransigence of Blücher to bring more pressure on the French. It was not, indeed, quite a case of 'Spenlow and Jorkins' in *David Copperfield,* for unlike Jorkins, the Prussian commander was far from pacific and quiescent, but when Wellington claimed that he had to take account of Blücher's attitude (which was known and feared) before agreeing to anything, its effect told, and had the additional virtue of being true.

It was on 29 June that the first real attempt took place to define differences and seek a resolution to them. The French provisional government's delegation came to Wellington's headquarters to inform him of Napoleon's believed departure from Paris, failing which (they said) they were ready to take him and hand him over to either the Prince Regent or the Austrian Emperor. Wellington insisted that his place of captivity and fate would to be for all the Allies to decide, but that if the French really did intend to hand him over they should do so by giving him directly to Blücher or himself. As to terms for a peace, he 'had no authority to talk upon the subject, even from my own Government, much less from the Allies', but gave his private view that only Louis's restoration could bring peace, and that it would be wiser not to haggle with Louis for conditions, but restore him before it could be said that they had done it by Allied direction. He refused to accept that a cease-fire should be called while Napoleon II was termed ruler, and he rejected thoughts of other candidates for the throne. The Cambrai proclamation then arrived, signed by the King and counter-signed by Talleyrand. Wellington passed it to the delegates, who objected to the following paragraphs: exclusion of some persons from the King's presence, the intention to punish some who had plotted to bring Bonaparte back, and the calling back of the old legislatures. Wellington consequently wrote to Talleyrand apropos these objections, and showed his draft to the delegates. (In the result, the letter had no effect on the royalists' stance.)[21]

Nothing had been agreed. Consequently Wellington visited Blücher and both men accepted that operations should continue while Napoleon was in France and not in their hands. This decision was notified to the French by letter.

Blücher by now had issued orders for a cavalry raid to be made on the western approaches to Paris, but more particularly for the raiders to attack Malmaison and capture Napoleon. As we know, Napoleon had left Malmaison very early on the 29th, but the raiding party could start only that afternoon, taking a long and circuitous route well out from sight, round the north-western quadrant, resting for the night of 29/30 east of St Germain-en-Laye. To reach Malmaison some 3 miles further east, they would have to cross a loop of the Seine at Chatou, but the bridge there had been destroyed and all boats removed from the river. On learning that Napoleon had gone, they turned west and took the bridge at St Germain-en-Laye. That was a definite advantage, but, with several bridges on the lower Seine unusable, any operations from the west would have to depend on the arrival of Prussian and British pontoons and bridging equipment.

By nightfall on 29 June, the Prussian army was close to the north-east quadrant of the main defences. Blücher's quarters were at Gonesse (11 miles from Notre-Dame), Bülow's IV Corps was close to St Denis and the Ourcq canal, with I Corps moving from Dammartin (just over 20 miles from Paris) towards the eastern stretch of the canal, while III Corps occupied Dammartin. Wellington's army was a stage further north, between Pont St Maxence on the Oise, and Senlis, Clermont and Gournay, thus between 30 and 60 miles from Paris.

Up to this point the old Field Marshal seems to have been confident of his ability to attack and take Paris, but on this day he received a long report from Bülow, who had spent the 28th inspecting the French positions. St Denis and the canal were greater obstacles than had been expected. Blücher still dreamt of taking Paris by outright conquest and issued orders for probing attacks in the Aubervilliers sector, but at the same time sent more cavalry west towards St Germain to cut the roads from Paris and the south and west. Bülow and Ziethen did make attempts to carry out the attacks, but any successes gained by IV and I Corps were soon offset by French counter-attacks and by systematic artillery fire from the defences, and the easy successes of recent days seemed no longer to be possible. In consequence Blücher decided to leave this sector to Wellington, and move his I and III Corps by a great side-march round to the western and south-western side of Paris, to be followed by IV Corps – but only once the Duke had taken over. He hoped that burning campfires would conceal his departure, but in fact the movement of troops was seen from the northerly salient of St Denis. For some days the Prussian army would lie dispersed, forming two widely separated segments some 30 miles apart.

Wellington had likewise proposed that Paris should be menaced from the west as well as north, and argued that his army could cut a corner by continuing south-west down the Oise to the vicinity of St Germain-en-Laye, leaving the Prussians where they were, on the north-east quadrant. Judged according to its advantages, Wellington's advance would not be seen by the enemy and made good sense militarily. But Gneisenau simply replied on the afternoon of 30 June that although such a plan would rest the Prussian troops, it would entail too great a separation between the armies, and grant time to the enemy – Gneisenau estimated this disadvantage as four days (*'vier Tage'*) – and judged that his own soldiers were lighter on their feet (*'leichter bewegen'*), and as Prussian march orders had already been implemented, Wellington should not continue to the western quadrant but come towards Aubervilliers. There is no indication of what Wellington thought of this reply; but he fell in with the Prussian demands.[22] The efforts demanded of the two Prussian corps, a westward march of over 30 miles in a day, led to dreadful straggling, and total exhaustion by the time they bivouacked on 1 July; the march had thus rendered a significant part of the Prussian army incapable of instant action. And since the Prussian move had been observed (something Wellington's plan would have avoided), so the French at St Denis did strike out: the garrison there set upon IV Corps and a serious clash took place that ended only with nightfall. The next day (1 July) the struggle broke out again at Aubervilliers, but without advantage to either side. By that evening Wellington's troops were arriving to move into position, and after that IV Corps could march west to join Blücher at St Germain.

Also on 1 July the French cavalry trounced the Prussian hussars who had sought Napoleon at Malmaison and had taken Versailles. Exelmans's cavalry and a detachment of infantry made a surprise march westwards and dashed at the Prussians, camped in Versailles. The combat initially swung back and forth, but the two regiments of Brandenburg and Pomeranian hussars were badly cut up, and broke. Sohr, the Prussian local commander, was captured. Although it is impossible to establish total Prussian losses (and the cease-fire coming immediately after this setback complicated matters as between 'wounded' and 'prisoners') the French claimed 437 hussar prisoners, and each Prussian regiment admitted losing respectively 278 and 324 horses killed wounded and missing. Blücher was furious at this little defeat, and it did show that even now the French army was not utterly negligible.[23]

These military operations were the drum-beats to which the negotiations proceeded. Davout and Fouché had agreed by 27 June that Louis XVIII had to be accepted as monarch and that a capitulation was essential. On 30 June Davout had informed both Allied headquarters that Napoleon had left Paris and that there should be no further refusal of a cease-fire. 'I formally request an immediate halt to all hostilities, and that we draw up an armistice in awaiting the decision of the Congress.' He also pointed out that on the Savoyard front an armistice had been signed between the Austrians and the

French, but both Allied generals dismissed that as of no significance in the case of Paris.[24]

Blücher utterly rejected Davout's letter and stated his intention of taking Paris, either by storm (with all its consequences) or by surrender; the latter, he maintained, would be for the good of its citizens, since without a firm military hand on the city the mob would loot everything. The tone was menacing, and there were frightening hints in the wording. Wellington simply insisted that he had already made clear to the negotiators that the French army had to leave the city as a prerequisite for a cease-fire. Davout ignored the Prussian letter, but turned to Wellington and on 1 July simply asked what terms Wellington would grant.[25]

V

There had been some problems in passing messengers through the opposing lines, so that delays were adding to the concerns of those anxious for an early settlement, and in addition Wellington was finding Blücher's headquarters unwilling to treat with the French and disinclined to respond to his own enquiries. Müffling on 1 July had set out Wellington's view of matters, but there had been no reply from Blücher. Müffling was in a hurry and had dashed down comments on a whole range of items of news, and once again was not entirely clear in his expressions, but even so his letter was not really difficult to understand, so that the lack of response must have been deliberate.[26] Thus, on 2 July, Wellington was still unable to conclude the discussions, although certain that the French would accept his proposed terms, and so he addressed a long letter to Blücher, now quartered at Versailles, setting out what he considered the current military prospects to be, the costs involved in a fresh attack, the advisability of awaiting Wrede's imminent arrival, which would put the matter beyond any doubt, and the essential terms upon which he himself would insist. The letter and the marginal comments of Gneisenau are given in full in Appendix 1 to this chapter.

As we have seen, the Prussians had by their own choice abandoned all attacks on the strongly defended northern sector in favour of the less well prepared southern arc, leaving to Wellington's army the problem of an attack from the north. This prospect Wellington declined, preferring instead an attack from the north-west. That however, required crossing the loops of the Seine in two places and fighting through the woods and undergrowth of the Bois de Boulogne, tasks that bridging experts and infantrymen know to be easier to speak of than to perform. Wellington was not prepared to sacrifice perhaps 10,000 men for this, when within a few days a simple blockade of the city and the arrival of Wrede (and the sovereigns) would necessarily lead to a surrender. His four conditions were: to stand on the ground currently held; to have the French army out of Paris and beyond the River Loire; Paris to be in the care of its (bourgeois) National Guard until the Allies' friend King Louis should finally arrange matters; and strict terms to be fixed for the duration and termination of an armistice, thus enabling the Allies to resume if the French failed to perform their duties.

The four conditions were the natural outcome of reflection and humanity, appealing to the calmer part of Blücher's personality, and couched in terms of a discussion between two men of sound sense. The Duke felt certain that the French would accept them at once. Everything that the Allies had fought for would be secured by Louis's return as agreed by the French provisional government, the military – French and Allied – would have no part to play in the government of Paris and France since that was a matter for the sovereigns and their friend Louis. But – by these terms there would be no conquest of, or victory march across, Paris.

There was something more: and this placed the Prussian high command in a serious dilemma. Wellington deemed these terms so self-evidently reasonable that on them an armistice 'can be made, and on which alone I will consent to make it'. Of course he did not say that he would not continue a military co-operation with the Prussians if they rejected an armistice; if they went ahead with their major plans, he would 'be guided' by the response he received. But the Prussians had to ask themselves if that phrase meant that his army would merely demonstrate to distract the French? For everything that Gneisenau calculated upon was based on full use of the massive superiority of the '105,000 men' of the combined armies against '60,000' enemy: for the Prussians to act with lesser numbers (despite claims of not fearing an inferiority of numbers) was indeed problematical, especially as the degree to which Wellington's pontoons and hawser bridges and ammunition supplies were needed by the Prussians increased his influence. A refusal to agree to terms, and an attack on the southern arc that resulted in a check or some costly setback – even perhaps a success that resulted in a sacking of the city – would leave Blücher and Gneisenau isolated, having to explain why they had disagreed with Wellington (and Metternich, and Alexander, and possibly even with Alexander's disciple Frederick William) over the bloodshed and fate of a Paris already pretty willing to surrender peacefully.

The Duke's letter received no immediate answer. Ostensibly that was because Blücher had gone to bed and could not be disturbed: or so at least said Gneisenau's somewhat obsequious and temporising reply.[27] But the Prince was up and active, and – desperate not to halt matters now on the verge of conquest – was urgently arranging the final attack on Paris from the south-west. Gneisenau took Wellington's letter and annotated it not merely with protests but also with anger. His views were that the 60,000 opposition was too weak to count against the 105,000 Allies; Prussians in inferior numbers had everywhere shown how it was possible to overcome the French resistance (a point he had already actually made to Wellington in the earlier temporising letter); Wellington's list of complications over a Seine crossing in face of the enemy and the Bois attack were, though undeniable, over-stated – and he would be helped by coordinated attacks made at the same moment from the south-west and north-east (this opinion would have been more convincing if Prussian operational performance at rivers, and in managing timely and coordinated assistance, had not been so poor between 15 and 18 June); losses were regrettable, but when the honour of the Prussian and Allied armies was concerned, victory now was more important, and an armistice without Paris actually in the armies' hands would dishonour the army. It was the Allied forces and not the King of France who should make the arrangements for governance, especially as Louis was not a faithful ally of Prussia. Nor was Wellington's reliance on the good sense of the sovereigns really enough to ensure that Bonaparte never returned, a comment that rather implies Gneisenau still thought the danger could end only with the usurper's death.[28]

What should one make of these comments? Wellington was stressing the least favourable case, but his army had certainly suffered very heavily already and he had mixed views on its present efficiency. He had also been left facing the strongest defences. Some of Gneisenau's military opinions may have been no more than an attempt to see the better possibilities. Yet there is something in the remarks that jars. In fact, Gneisenau at this time was deeply depressed. He had written to Prince Hardenberg on 30 June in the following terms: he had been repeatedly promised and repeatedly denied senior command appointments ever since returning to Prussia from Britain in 1813. He had served as Blücher's chief of staff as a national duty but to no personal benefit(!). Bülow meanwhile had been promoted, was famous, and had the highest class of Iron Cross and the order of the Black Eagle, while Gneisenau received only the Red Eagle. All the corps commanders were younger than himself (of these five, four were in fact older and only one, Kleist, was younger) and some of them by their conduct on campaign had not deserved their promotion or reputation. 'I am placed at the rear, and I do not complain.' He was back at his old duty, 'although the ingratitude of my commander in Berlin has filled my heart with bitterness'. He was on a reduced salary and was little known by the troops. 'Despite my gay spirit and inner sense of duty, despite all my capacity for resignation I must nonetheless curse and execrate such a fate and I am tempted to make my complaints public.'[29]

But the comments scribbled on Wellington's letter were not merely due to over-tiredness, irritation, or whatever. They indicated the deeply frustrated views of the leader of one very powerful section within the Prussian Army, and they were harbingers of future trouble. To anyone pondering these views, they gave warning that unless the political establishment mastered the Army's 'political' ambitions, Prussian civil life might suffer and Prussia's relations with the wider world might depend on the Army's view of its own honour, its rights and its unchallengability. Within two generations such views could be held in check only by a politician as strong, far-sighted and astute as Bismarck; even by August 1815 some in Frederick William's immediate entourage were expressing alarm at these tendencies and linking them to Gneisenau's name.[30]

VI

On 3 July the Prussians duly attacked the south-west quadrant of the defences of Paris between Issy and Vaugirard and Montrouge. A detachment went north behind St Cloud and past Mont Valérien, and engaged in an indecisive skirmish near Neuilly. Davout had gone to command in the Montrouge sector and the forces under him counter-attacked the Prussians so that control of Issy was disputed for some hours. By evening the French were withdrawing to the city walls, but the combats of this day had been of more diplomatic than military significance. For the Prussians the day was a last day of campaigning against the *Armée du Nord* or its remnants, and a day of attack in which Wellington's forces had played almost no part (other than in support at Neuilly and at Argenteuil where, according to Robert Torrens, Wellington was 'throwing a bridge across the Seine'). For the French it allowed time for yet another call for a cease-fire to be sent early in the morning, while the city remained safe under the control of Fouché and Davout. It was addressed specifically to the Prussians, and at some time in the first half of the day Blücher replied from Versailles, some 6 miles from the front, that he would go to the palace of St Cloud, meet Wellington there, and also a French accredited delegation. The palace was one of Napoleon's favourites, high above the left bank of the Seine where its most southerly loop finishes, and not far beyond the western end of the Bois, and it was there that the French delegation arrived at 3 p.m., bearing a carefully phrased draft for an armistice and capitulation.

The meeting was influenced by everyone's recognition that continued fighting would entail considerable bloodshed. The Prussians and the British certainly enjoyed military preponderance, and knew that this advantage would increase with the approach of the armies now pressing forward from the Rhine. The French were running short of supplies, but they gained from the fact that they had prepared, and skilfully prepared, the draft text that served as the basis for negotiation. The two allies were certain that they were handling a purely military local matter – for there were other allies to consider, and neither Austria, nor Bavaria, nor Russia were represented, while Louis, who had no army in the field, was not even mentioned.

Davout, as we saw earlier, had been told by the French commissioners that 'your armistice must be purely military and contain no political matters'. He had told the Allied commanders on 30 June that the ceasefire he sought for the safety of Paris was to be reviewed and finally decided by the Congress. However, although he drafted several clauses including, it seems, Article XII, he did not conduct the negotiations.[31] They were handled by Bignon for the provisional government, Guilleminot for the army, and Bondy for the city of Paris.[32] Led by Bignon, the negotiators successfully presented arguments that seemed to relate to the military handover of Paris, very much in line with Bignon's own insistence at the start of July that the negotiators should 'distinguish the political question of the form of government for France from the actual question of an armistice' and that 'the general interest of France and the Powers themselves is to precipitate nothing and to not come to any definitive agreement' as to *who* should govern France.[33] This was a vital consideration at the time. For Louis's Cambrai proclamation had mentioned punishment for treason, and thus it was important in these negotiations not to accept any Bourbon right to the throne. If Louis did not regain the throne the Cambrai terms would be without effect. (Long after Louis had recovered the throne, Bignon admitted that in the situation of July 1815, 'prudence demanded precautions against vengeance' from the parties around Louis, meaning the menace contained in the Cambrai proclamation.) Hence Bignon continued to argue for the accession of Napoleon II. Indeed on 4 July, the day after he and the others had signed the military convention, Bignon was still trying to promote the child's claims

The three French delegates went to St Cloud on 3 July and met Müffling for Blücher, and Felton Hervey for Wellington. Ernouf, Bignon's son-in-law and inheritor of his papers, states that Blücher, Gneisenau and Nostitz were present and that Wellington came some thirty minutes later. The agreement, however, was signed only by the three French delegates and by Müffling and Hervey. '*La suspension d'armes*', as both Davout and Bignon separately termed it[34] – was then counter-signed in Paris by Davout, and then by Blücher and Wellington at their headquarters. The Duke wrote to Bathurst on 4 July that, 'Officers accordingly met on both sides at St Cloud . . . the military convention was agreed to last night, and which has been ratified by Marshal Prince Blücher and me and by the Prince d'Eckmuhl [Davout] on the part of the French army.'[35]

The draft contained twenty articles, most of which were agreed fairly easily. The armistice was made outside ('*sous*') the walls of Paris and applied to the military on both sides: to the two Allied armies of Blücher and Wellington and the French army in Paris, and would be binding on them until the conclusion of a peace unless a formal ten-day notice of breaking off should be issued (Articles I and XIV). The French army would totally evacuate the city within three days and retire beyond the Loire with all its material within one week, but the wounded and their attendants would remain under the protection of the Allies, as would soldiers' families if they wished to stay in Paris. Individual *arrondissements* were specified for surrender between 4 and 6 July, but internal security was left to the National Guard. The Allies would permit supplies into the city. The convention 'was common to all Allied armies, subject to ratification by the Powers whose armies they are' (Article XVI). Interpretation of the convention would favour the French army and the city of Paris, and its implementation would be supervised by a commission named 'by the respective parties' to the convention.

Some proposed articles created discussion. The French proposed that the government and national authorities should be respected and that the Allies should not involve themselves in the internal affairs of France, a nationwide concept extending far beyond the surrender of Paris. This the Allies would not consider. By Article X, the Allied commanders would ensure that the present authorities would be respected *for so long as they should exist* (this italicised stipulation was due to Wellington's demand) so that the amended text thus left open the future government of Paris. In the result, the implementing supervisory commission comprised three French soldiers: Grundler (who had defended the Pont de Neuilly on 29 June), Corbineau (who served under Napoleon in the June campaign before returning to defend Paris, and who – significantly – was dismissed by the Bourbons at the end of July), and a certain 'Cuirreau' (for whom no details seem to exist: Robert Torrens proffered the name 'Trumeau, former ambassador to America' and according to the *Dictionnaire Napoléon*, in that case he must have meant Turreau de Garambouville). Their term of office was ended when the provisional government ceased to exist (that happened on 8 July) and when the incoming government informed the Allies of this under Article X.[36]

Thus far it is plain from Article I and the implementation of Article X that it was the armies of Blücher and Wellington and of Davout – and not *King Louis's* government – that were involved in the capitulation and its initial implementation.

Article XI stated that public property, except that relating to war, would be left to French administration (the exception was insisted on by the Prussians). Unsurprisingly, when the Prussians later wanted to destroy public property after occupying the city, a French protest was made at this infringement of what Blücher himself had endorsed.

The French had sought a guarantee that all artistic treasures, museums and libraries in Paris should be left to the French: Blücher was vehemently opposed to this, and Wellington insisted that, although Britain had no demands, the Continental sovereigns he served had claims for restitution of items seized – members of the British Cabinet used the word 'pillaged' – during the wars. The point was of some importance, for had the Parisian request been granted it could have been used as precedent for France retaining treasures gained in war and stored both in Paris and elsewhere. Later Bignon disputed what had been agreed.[37] He argued that it was only because Wellington could not speak for the other sovereigns that 'he was obliged to ask for the clause to be omitted, without its object being compromised by this omission'. Consequently (he claimed) the French negotiators took his words to be 'just as inviolable [*aussi sacrées*] as a special engagement' and as virtually admitting the French wishes 'as covered by Article XI'. We have Castlereagh's own statement of 24 July that 'Wellington, I know, doubts very strongly the prudence of this measure [removal of works of art from French possession]', and that he told the French on 3 July that all they could hope for was the Allied sovereigns' benevolence. (That referral to the sovereigns was because it was not a military but a political matter.) From this it will be seen that Bignon was not altogether wrong in his view of the Duke's personal views, but went far too far in claiming that it was some form of tacit engagement. Bignon's skill at developing a remark beyond its true bounds is visible here.[38]

Under Article XII, drafted as we have seen by Davout, 'Persons and private property shall be equally respected. The inhabitants, and in general all the individuals who are in the capital, shall continue to enjoy their rights and liberties, without being in any manner subject to any inquiry or punishment in consequence of any office they may at present hold or may have held, or in consequence of their political conduct or opinions.' This French draft was read by the Allies as local and military, and Bignon and his colleagues claimed that it 'passed without the least discussion', something that Hervey corroborated six months later.[39]

However, it is here that Bignon, in his subsequent arguments, contradicts his own contemporary insistence on the military and non-political nature of the convention. For very soon after, this article was developed by the French into the political claim that 'all France could count on the guarantee in this article' and that it was binding on King Louis. Their argument went as follows: the two commanders had accepted the stipulations of this article 'in the same way' as the French, and had seen the stipulations as binding on the Allied sovereigns when they in turn should sign it. Because Louis was in alliance with those sovereigns, so 'the stipulations were above all on the King'. Such a claim runs flat counter to Hervey's recollection that the stipulation 'bound' Wellington and Blücher and 'those under their command ... but no other person ... I do not see how it can bear any other meaning.' Unlike Bignon, he did not know that Davout had been instructed by Bignon that the armistice must contain no political matters, nor that the negotiating brief had been framed in similar terms (by Bignon himself), but historians can all see that Hervey's interpretation was the true one. The next French argument – that had the article been rejected, then Davout would doubtless have broken off negotiation and fighting would probably have resumed, and that because the negotiation did not break down, so the Allies must be judged to have accepted the political interpretation – goes altogether beyond the bounds of sense.

Having gained agreement to the text, the French then nearly wrecked it by the next draft article: that between this date and the evacuation of France by the Allies, all persons wishing to leave France should be granted passports by the Allied generals and given all guarantees for their beings and their properties. This was flatly rejected as going far beyond the local situation and as a political matter, but, luckily for the French, it did not turn attention back to the previous article.

Such were the terms for the capitulation and safety of Paris. Wellington the very next day issued a General Order to his army informing them of 'a military convention ... with the Commander-in-Chief of the French army in Paris'. Likewise he told his government that: 'This convention decides all the military questions of this moment existing here, and touches nothing political.'[40]

Bignon was then sent to the Duke on 4 July to 'try to detach Wellington from Louis XVIII and get him to agree to support the group [*combinaison*] of Napoleon II ... or at least to obtain certain political guarantees independent of the amnesty granted by Article XII': the retention of the *tricolor* and the survival of the Lower Chamber. The attempt was a total failure.[41] Perhaps the most significant aspect of this *démarche* is that it still sought to promote

Napoleon II's cause *subsequent to* the 3 July convention and to *prevent* Louis's return. It runs flat counter to Bignon's thesis that the convention was made with Louis XVIII.

Moreover, there is the instance of Ney's actions on hearing of the convention. As early as 21 June he had received from Fouché passports in various names so as to flee the country. Yet Ney did not flee. He stayed on in Paris, though accused of treason by some Bonapartists and knowing how treasonable his actions on 14 March 1815 were regarded by the royalists. By 1 July his military colleagues and friends in authority in Paris were aware of the Cambrai proclamation and its threats against traitors. Still he stayed on, since Paris was held by the French army. On 5 July the *Moniteur* published the surrender convention, and that same day Ney abandoned Paris in an endeavour to reach the frontier and escape – an indication of how little he and his friends thought him covered politically by Article XII.[42]

The British government was uneasy over some of the terms of the surrender, and Bathurst instantly replied to Wellington's letter:

> Your Grace will receive a separate despatch on the subject of the 12th Article of the Convention. I do not think that it can be construed by anyone in the way in which the apprehension of some induce them to construe it, as binding the King [of France] to an act of unqualified indemnity towards the greatest traitors. We are all so convinced that some examples must be made, that many will not allow themselves to judge of the 12th Article but in the way which would preclude the King from any such exercise of his authority; and it may be as well that we should take the earliest opportunity of stating and placing on record our understanding of the Article, in case any persons in France should attempt to give this construction to it.

This the British government formally did, in an official despatch to Wellington, also dated 7 July, stating its views in the most explicit and emphatic terms and concluding that the British government 'deems the 12th Article to be binding only on the conduct of the British and Prussian commanders and the commanders of such of the Allies as may become parties to the present Convention by their ratification of it'. To this Wellington replied on the 13th that 'the convention binds nobody excepting the parties to it, viz, the French army on one side and the Allied armies under Marshal Prince Blücher and myself on the other; and the 12th Article cannot be considered, and never was intended, to bind any other persons or authorities whatsoever, unless they should become parties to the convention.'[43]

Wellington had already had to complain to Fouché of false and misleading public statements made by the French negotiators and the provisional government at various times, at Laon and at Allied headquarters, and had sent documentary proof to back his complaints. Moreover, Lt.-Colonel Torrens and a small party under his orders had been sent into Paris under flag of truce, to supervise with Davout's staff the process of handover. They were attacked by furious French soldiers, a British major was desperately wounded and then plundered, a dragoon killed, and Davout's ADC was powerless to protect them. Torrens eventually escaped, and Wellington the next day threatened to attack Paris unless satisfaction was given.[44] Grovelling apologies were duly provided, though the French army by then had left Paris. But it was a bad augury. Wellington's nature, seldom less than reserved and critical, now turned to a chilly disdain when dealing with such people, whom he characterised as, due to the effects of the French Revolution, 'resorting to falsehood, either to give a color to, or palliate their adoption or abandonment of any line of policy; and that they think that, provided the falsehood answers the purpose of the moment, it is fully justified'.[45]

Henceforth he sought to limit his exposure to French domestic politics. He held to his view of the 3 July convention and would not discuss it in relation to the authority of the restored government (which of course had not signed the document), and so it befell that when Ney's fate at the hands of the French government was in question and some French people turned to him for help, he refused to intervene in that domestic tragedy.

VII

The two main Allied demands had been for the surrender of Napoleon by the provisional government and the removal from Paris of the French army: by the end of June both allies recognised that the government no longer held Napoleon and that he had escaped from Malmaison towards the coast, so that this subject was no longer treatable in the convention. By this convention they did secure the immediate removal of the French army from the centre of power by about a hundred miles. On nearly all the other topics Wellington's views seem to have prevailed: avoiding all long-term questions of government and ensuring that Louis should be restored unconditionally (save for his Cambrai promises), recognising that the cease-fire was made outside and not inside the walls of Paris, leaving internal security to the bourgeois National Guard, but permitting Allied military entry to the different parts of the city according to a strict timetable and under properly regulated conditions. Any Prussian triumphal march through the city would take place not on the day of capitulation by act of conquest, but some days later under the peaceful conditions 'commonly agreed' by all sides.

Ratification came on Tuesday 4 July, and then Wellington at his quarters at Gonesse, north-east of Paris, and Blücher at Versailles, had to concert the measures agreed. Blücher sent strong detachments south to watch the French army as it began its march to the Loire, while Wellington's troops took over St Denis, St Ouen, Clichy and Neuilly. On 5 July Wellington moved to Neuilly and his men took over the commanding height of Montmartre, so that the entire northern sector's defences were in his hands. The next day saw some Prussian movements as well. Blücher himself left Versailles and installed himself at St Cloud, and each ally took control of the gates (*barrières*) of Paris, Wellington those on the right bank of the Seine and the Prussians those on the left. A letter of this date from Gneisenau to Müffling conceded with some bitterness that they would not move their headquarters to Paris, would not argue about 'the entry into Paris' or wish 'to give the Parisians the spectacle of a formal entry'.[46] On Friday 7 July, just nineteen days after Waterloo and three days after the convention was agreed, the two Allied armies entered Paris itself.

This culminating step had required some careful preparation. On 4 July Wellington proposed that a single Allied commandant should be appointed to administer the cease-fire in the city, and he recommended Müffling ('there is no person who, in his situation, has done more to forward the objects of the operations'), a suggestion pleasing to Blücher. On the same day he advised Fouché that as a result of the convention it would be best for the two chambers and the government to dissolve themselves and ask Louis to accept that they had acted in the best interest of France while stating their wishes for the future. Wellington added that the terms of the Cambrai proclamation and his own discussions with the King led him to believe that all would be well.

He had then asked Müffling to raise certain concerns about quartering inside the city. His own troops would be encamped in the Bois de Boulogne and the Champs Elysées, and fed from British depots, and therefore without prejudice to the supplies of the city, but if Blücher insisted on his troops living among the population and being fed by them, the payment scales of the Prussian Army would mean that people would be supplying it at a loss. To avoid discontent that would redound against Louis and peaceful relations generally, he suggested that the Prussians should draw upon the Duke's depots with the costs debited to the restored government. Blücher took this very badly, as an insult to his army, remarked that the army had been denied its rights over occupying Paris in the spring of 1814 (ignoring that it had been a decision by the three sovereign autocrats), that the French had treated Prussian towns in a similar way in the past, and that he intended to demonstrate the achievements of Prussia by a short victory march.[47]

Wellington had had so much his own way in major matters that he was at pains to conciliate the old Field Marshal. He suggested Müffling for commandant of the Anglo-Allied and Prussian garrison. Gneisenau made this a grievance, saying that the Prussians had (unilaterally it would seem} promised the post to Ziethen, but that they would accept Müffling so as not to annoy the Duke. Wellington sought Blücher's advice on the overlooked problem of the fortress of Vincennes (not covered by the convention, and a potential threat to Paris), and the matter was treated by a round-table discussion with the officer commanding the fortress, who duly handed it over to King Louis.

Thus it came about that the shabby red coats of the British army and those of its various contingents became a familiar sight in the Bois de Boulogne and in the streets of Paris. An observer of the formal entry to Paris saw Wellington 'five minutes before he mounted, he was standing in his stable yard giving directions to his coachman, with his handkerchief over his head instead of a hat,' and wearing 'his usual blue riding dress'. Later, when a lady in a carriage waved to him 'he jumped his horse over a drain to speak to her'. It sounds all very like an Irish country fair. Far different was the entry of Admiral Sir Sidney Smith, the hero of Acre in 1799, who followed in a carriage, his uniform covered in all his decorations. Perhaps the Parisians thought he was the real Wellington?[48]

The Duke did not further oppose a Prussian march through the city. But he did protest at certain other proposals, such as a forced levy of 100,000,000 francs (approximately £4 million) intended to be imposed on the people of Paris; as the sovereigns would arrive within days and as such matters should be by common accord, he advised delaying any unilateral action, and he also advised against implementing reported plans to blow up the Pont de Iéna until the sovereigns could decide it or until they could discuss the matter. In fact a discussion between Blücher and Gneisenau and Castlereagh and Wellington on 9 July brought about no meeting of minds on either the levy or the bridge, leaving matters unresolved when the three sovereigns entered Paris the next day.

The settlement of so many problems, large and small, would take much of the summer and early autumn, and will be dealt with in the next chapter. For now we must turn from Paris to follow Napoleon's final days in France.

VIII

Napoleon at Malmaison had sent Flahaut on 28 June to request the release of the two frigates for his departure, even without safe-conduct. He said farewell that evening to his mother, Joseph, his uncle Cardinal Fesch, Marie Walewska, and others. By the next dawn he knew the frigates were at his disposal, and by nightfall he was at Rambouillet. He had reached Poitiers by the evening of 30 June, and, though he could not know this, once south of the Loire he would have cover from the army once it had left Paris. After an almost uninterrupted journey of thirty-eight hours he arrived at Niort on 1 July, being joined there by brother Joseph, his ADC General Gourgaud, and General Lallemand (a leader of the premature Bonapartist Northern Conspiracy early in March). He continued to Rochefort, arriving at 8 a.m. on 3 July, only to find that there were always in view two or three British frigates and one or two ships of the line. His little group by now also comprised General Savary (duc de Rovigo), General Bertrand and his wife, the ADC Count Montholon and his wife and children, and Comte Las Cases a civilian of the Household, with his son. On 5 July the baggage and effects were put into the French frigates *Saale* and *Méduse* in readiness to sail. With the news of the capitulation of Paris, extra guards were set to protect the Emperor from raids and capture such as had so nearly happened at Malmaison, the unit being under the command of the provisional government's nominee, General Beker (under whose name Napoleon had travelled from Malmaison).[49] On the evening of the 8th the party boarded the *Saale,* moored off the Île d'Aix, but the winds made any departure impossible, so on the afternoon of the 9th Napoleon arranged to send envoys to the officer commanding HMS *Bellerophon,* 74 guns, lying a little way offshore watching the movements of shipping in Rochefort.[50]

Over the past few weeks the Royal Navy had established Rear-Admiral Hotham in the old 74 *Superb,* at Quiberon, with a number of brigs, corvettes and frigates, backed by another ship of the line (the *Bellerophon*), this screen to watch from Brest down to Arcachon, south of Bordeaux, some 330 miles of coast with many harbours, islets, and shallow inshore channels. The Navy relied upon royalist reports from shore to discover the whereabouts of the fugitive Emperor and what his plans might be. Of necessity the ships were dispersed, since only when they had firm information and some idea of the strength of the force that Napoleon could take to sea, would they be able to concentrate at the decisive point. And that would take some time.[51]

The Admiralty's orders were clear insofar as they went, but they were, of course, posited on a state of war existing, and on Napoleon seeking to escape. He was to be intercepted and taken into careful custody, removed from French waters and taken to the waters outside a British port. Napoleon would thus become a prisoner of war. It was implicit in the orders' wording that the Admiralty expected a flight, pursuit and *capture,* but also that no harm was to be done to the fugitives. But the orders did not cover the eventuality of a Napoleon, still on shore in freedom, *negotiating* a possible surrender to the Royal Navy. The actual outcome was not foreseen, and no guidance was available to the naval officers on station, thus placing them in a very delicate and awkward position. For it led to an officer below flag rank handling as best he could, in an unforeseen situation of most delicate negotiation, the demands of the ablest ruler in Europe and his team of highly experienced officials.

Admiralty orders to the C-in-C Channel Fleet, Admiral Lord Keith, were explicit:

> If they should be so fortunate as to intercept Bonaparte, the captain of HM ship should transfer him and his family to HM ship and there keeping him in careful custody should return to the nearest port of England with all possible expedition.[52]

Orders in conformity were received by Captain Maitland of the *Bellerophon* on 6 July. He was an officer with long experience of the Bay of Biscay. Hotham added:

> I depend on your using the best means that can be adopted to intercept the fugitive, on whose captivity the repose of Europe appears to depend. If he should be taken, he is to be brought to me in this bay, as I have orders for his disposal; he is to be removed from the ship in which he may be found to one of His Majesty's ships.

By 6 July Hotham had reports of Napoleon coming to Rochefort, and wrote to Maitland that he was to 'use your best endeavours to prevent him making his escape in either of the frigates'. The next day he sent a second message: that Lord Keith, had reported that a French government request for a passport for Napoleon had been received in London on 30 June, and 'answered in the negative'. On 8 July Hotham ordered Maitland:

> to make the strictest search of any vessel you may fall in with; and if you should be so fortunate as to intercept him, you are to transfer him and his family to the ship you command, and, there keeping him in careful custody, return to the nearest port in England, going into Torbay in preference to Plymouth, with all possible expedition; and upon your arrival you are not to permit any communication whatever with the shore, except as herein after directed; and you will be held responsible for keeping the whole transaction a profound secret, until you receive their Lordships' further orders.[53]

On 30 June Maitland received a message from Bordeaux that Napoleon intended to escape to America from that city. Maitland considered Rochefort

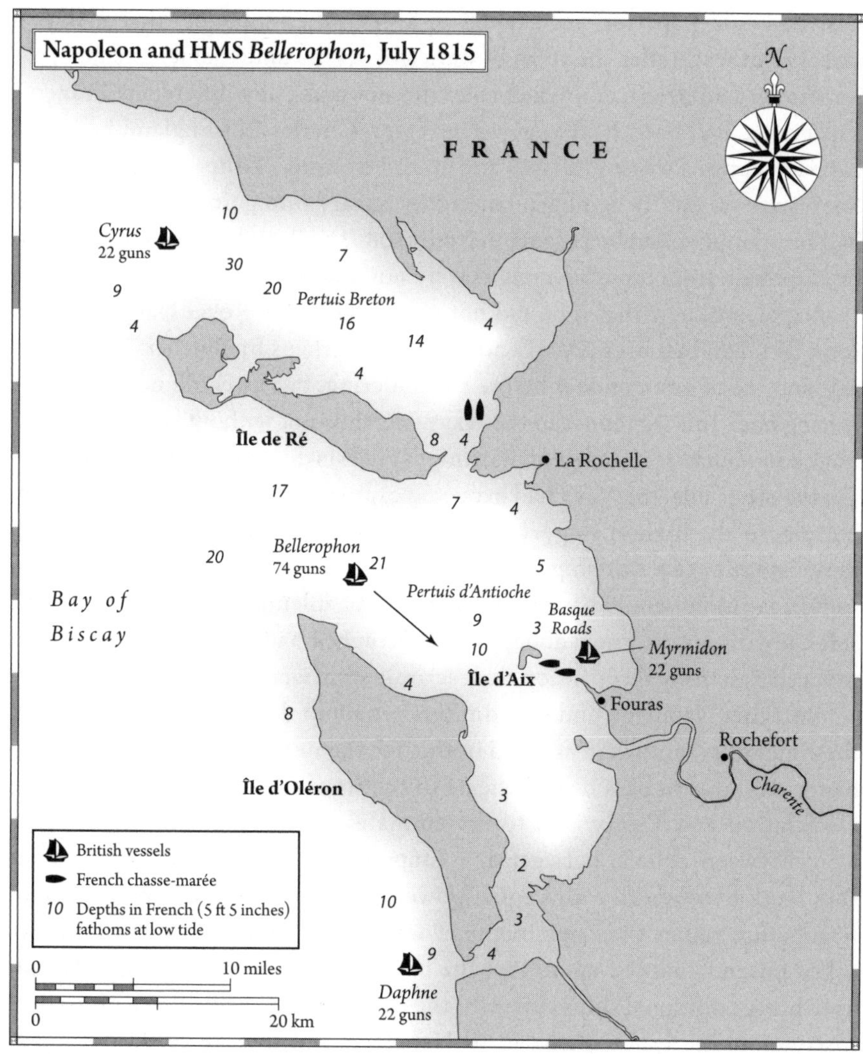

the more likely embarkation point, and kept *Bellerophon* there, although sending two smaller vessels south to Bordeaux and Arcachon. By 7 July he was sure that Napoleon was planning to sail from the nearby Île d'Aix via one of its several channels, but Hotham's force was now so dispersed that Maitland had no second vessel with him and could watch only one channel, a situation not improved until the frigate HMS *Falmouth* joined him on 10 July, with another frigate promised as soon as possible.

Napoleon and his adherents knew from the 13 March Declaration and the 25 March Treaty that the powers considered themselves at war with him and held him an outlaw. War had certainly followed, and after Waterloo the best he could hope for was asylum in a neutral country or surrender as a prisoner of war under the rules of war. This seems undeniable. The fact that he was (or had been) a crowned ruler did not make any difference: François I of France had been held a prisoner of war, Charles I of England had been beheaded after a war and a trial, and so had Louis XVI after a state trial. The Spanish royal family had been tricked by Savary into going to Bayonne and had been imprisoned by Napoleon from 1808. The Pope had been imprisoned by Napoleon from 1809. Sovereigns were not immune.

Napoleon knew that if he did not surrender to the Royal Navy, he could soon be taken by Louis XVIII's adherents or perhaps by Blücher. He wanted a guarantee of safe-conduct before surrendering, but he could not be sure of getting one. This surrender to the Navy was thus not without risk, and he did not know (but as an intelligent man might guess) what their instructions were. On the other side, the Navy had expected capture at sea and not a negotiation, but placed the highest importance on holding him without conditions and removing him to a British port. Yet as Napoleon was beyond reach on shore, some conditions would have to be agreed. This dilemma meant that for both sides any discussions held aboard the *Bellerophon* had to be crystal clear and reduced to writing if confusion and recrimination were not to follow.

But what Napoleon and his admirers set about doing at St Helena and in their memoirs (and were assisted in this for the next two centuries by many historians) was to pass over the facts of the words and their meaning in the Declaration and Treaty, and to disseminate a thesis that the negotiations were between equals, between the Emperor and the Prince Regent; that they were between free and equal powers who were in 'tacit conditions' of negotiation rather than opponents at war; that free asylum in Britain was asked for and counted upon; that the naval captain used delaying tactics so as to bring additional ships closer for the capture; that the British Admiralty's instructions were not disclosed to Napoleon and that he could not guess what was secretly intended, but relied upon additional verbal undertakings of a British naval captain as amending the written terms that this officer had presented to his emissaries. When it is added that the successive emissaries, first the Court chamberlain Las Cases with Savary (an ex-minister of police), and then Las Cases with General Lallemand, were the naïve dupes of a British sea captain, then the thesis is complete.

The thesis is not tenable because it starts from a wrong premise, ignoring the wider context. And I find many of the arguments self-serving and not a reasonable presentation of what happened. There were reticences and equivocations in the talks, but they arose on both sides; and the matter of who duped whom can be presented in a very different fashion, even on the evidence of the persons present. For those interested, all this is discussed in my Appendix 2 to this chapter.

In summary: on 10 July Savary and Las Cases went on board *Bellerophon* to see what possibility of negotiation there was. They 'flew a kite', but the results of their discussions with Captain Maitland were not encouraging. They drew him into conversation and he seemed to say something important (possibly he, too, 'flew a kite') but they declined to discuss it and they brought back to Napoleon a very negative and discouraging letter from Maitland, warning that as a state of war existed he would stop any ships that sailed from France. Meanwhile the Bourbon flag was being raised along the coast and the naval blockade was tightening: Napoleon's liberty of action was being reduced day by day. The naval officers of the *Saale* and *Méduse* proposed a break-out, one vessel being sacrificed in action to let the other escape with the Emperor, but Napoleon declined this. Plans for a seaward escape were investigated by Joseph and by Bertrand. Joseph advocated running the blockade in an American vessel; Bertrand looked at using two shallow-draught coastal craft or *chasse-marées*, *Elise* and *Deux-Amis*, in conjunction with a Danish vessel.[54]

Bertrand's project was approved and the baggage was loaded, but at the last minute Napoleon finally came to the view that the plan was impracticable. He told his entourage that he would not sail in the tiny boats or Danish vessel. This could only mean that if he was not to fall into the hands of royalists and Prussians, then he had to ask the British to accept him, and indeed at the time that Napoleon said this to his entourage, Bertrand noticed on the table a draft letter addressed to the Prince Regent and already amended by the Emperor. Napoleon's decision had been taken. The Grand Marshal later wrote that Napoleon sought his opinion on whether he would be 'left in liberty' if he went to Britain; his reply was that the Emperor 'was deluding himself' in such a hope, given 'what had passed since leaving Elba'. This decision and this warning should be recalled when we come to Las Cases's pretensions and timings.[55]

So by 13 July Napoleon recognised that he had no alternative to surrendering to Maitland. It was on *this day* that he finally signed his appeal to the Prince Regent, and it stressed the idea of living as a guest of the British and drew a comparison with a famous event in Athenian history. It could cite nothing of diplomatic value, it hoped for oblivion for past deeds, it relied on total forgiveness. The letter read:

> Your Royal Highness, Exposed to the factions that divide my country and to the enmity of the greatest Powers of Europe, I have terminated my political career, and I come like Themistocles, to sit at the hearth of the

> British people. I put myself under the protection of their laws, which I claim from Your Royal Highness, as the most powerful, the most constant, and the most generous of my enemies.
>
> Rochefort, 13 July 1815 NAPOLEON.[56]

This skilfully composed piece expunged a great deal of recent history, overlooked the current state of war (despite Maitland's 10 July letter having drawn his attention to the state of war existing), and implied that Napoleon was done with all these past tribulations and was coming in peace and retirement. The Athenian Themistocles in his eventual exile had found asylum among his former enemies the Persians, and Napoleon unilaterally claimed the same rights. The Prince and the British government were parties to the Declaration and the Treaty; Napoleon ignored that. There was not one scrap of paper from the Prince or the British authorities to suggest any hope or wish on their side to open a correspondence: yet Las Cases was to pretend later when speaking to Admiral Lord Keith that *simply by writing his letter of appeal* Napoleon had 'necessarily created tacit conditions', as if unsolicited letters laid obligations on their recipients.[57]

The letter having been signed by Napoleon, the next day, 14 July, Las Cases and Lallemand went to the *Bellerophon* to settle the final arrangements for his surrender. Las Cases was very pleased with the results of his negotiating skills and reassured Napoleon as to his reception. For his part, Maitland immediately wrote to the Admiralty that Las Cases and Lallemand had that morning proposed that Napoleon should be received on board, throwing himself on the Regent's generosity:

> Conceiving myself authorised by their Lordships' secret order, I have acceded to the proposal, and he is to embark on board this ship tomorrow morning. That no misunderstanding might arise, I have explicitly and clearly explained to the Count Las Cases, that I have no authority whatever to grant terms of any sort; but that all I can do is to convey him and his suite to England, to be received in such manner as His Royal Highness may deem expedient.[58]

It is significant, in the light of Las Cases's and Maitland's very different interpretations of what passed, that Maitland's words of that very day are clear. It is also significant that Lallemand actually *advised the Emperor not to go* as he and Las Cases had not obtained any formal guarantee, and that the British captain was not the British government.

There was a third meeting. Later on the 14th Las Cases and Gourgaud came aboard *Bellerophon*; the latter holding the 13 July letter to the Regent, which was copied by Maitland before Gourgaud crossed to HMS *Slaney* and departed for England with the appeal to the Regent. Gourgaud, too, was unhappy at Las Cases's over-confident attitude: on 3 July Las Cases had been certain that Napoleon would reign again and that the Bourbons would not be accepted in France, and Gourgaud noted his 'delight' at the way his negotiations had gone with the British sailors on the 14th.[59]

At dawn on Saturday, 15 July 1815, dressed as a colonel of the *Chasseurs de la Garde,* Napoleon stepped onto the brig *Epervier* and was taken to the *Bellerophon.* Just after this Admiral Hotham arrived, saw Maitland's correspondence, approved it, and then interviewed Napoleon.

Hotham noted that at that time Napoleon 'appeared extremely anxious to learn how I thought he would be disposed of, but equally confident in the generosity of the Prince Regent and the English nation,'[60] an anxious enquiry that was in line with Maitland's letter and Lallemand's warning. The anxiety does not look as though Napoleon was certain that a naval captain off the Île d'Aix had plenary powers. Nevertheless, as Maitland's narrative makes abundantly clear, throughout the voyage to Torbay Napoleon freely conversed with the naval officers and with his suite about life among the British in a most relaxed fashion.

Clearly Napoleon felt that he had made a better choice by putting himself in the hands of the Royal Navy than staying to take his chance in France. The idea of a welcome in Britain had for some time lain deep in the Emperor's mind. Montholon wrote as follows:

> It is true that, since La Malmaison the Emperor was convinced that a magnificent reception awaited him in England and that the scale of the popular ovation would match the level of esteem that the Emperor gave to the English people in asking for their hospitality. While staying at La Malmaison he had said to Queen Hortense [whom he never saw again after 29 June]: 'Hand myself to Austria, never; it holds my wife and son. Hand myself to Russia would be to give myself to a man. Give myself to England, will be to give myself to a people.[61]

Yet he had no assurances to go upon, and seems to have painted a mental picture of what he wished might happen.

In giving his letter to Gourgaud on 14 July and adding some details to be delivered orally to the Prince in London, Napoleon spoke to his ADC of his personal wishes: if it was not inconvenient to issue passports for the United States that was where he would prefer to go, but he disliked the thought of going to any colony. Failing America, he would prefer England. He would call himself Colonel Muiron (after an ADC, killed in 1796) and if he had to stay in England he would like to live as incognito as possible in a country house ten or twelve leagues from London, and the house should be sufficiently large to accommodate all his suite. He would like to stay away from London, as doubtless the British government would likewise desire. If ministers wished to attach British commissioners to him, they should take care that the arrangement did not have an air of captivity about it.[62]

Given the history of the past twenty-two years, was it reasonable for Napoleon to harbour such dreams? And on what basis? Largely it would seem on the claims of the self-promoting meddler Las Cases that his skills in negotiation had teased out a promise from a naval captain. And yet Napoleon had always been a cynical realist, dismissive of fine phrases. He had never had faith in promises, and he not infrequently ignored even written agreements. He knew what the Allies had decreed in March. He must have remembered how Savary's trickery had fooled the Spanish royal family into crossing into France, there to be detained during Napoleon's pleasure. He can scarcely have forgotten how he himself bullied and maltreated the Pope. Now he was seeking the sort of consideration in his misfortunes that he had denied others. Would he – did he deserve to – succeed?

Meanwhile, to Plymouth went the *Slaney* with the letter, and to Torbay went the *Bellerophon* with its strange cargo. The answer would not be long in coming.

*

Appendix 1: Wellington's Letter of 2 July 1815, and Gneisenau's Comments

This appendix gives Wellington's letter of 2 July to Blücher, as printed in Gurwood's edition of the Despatches, 526/184, with Gneisenau's marginal comments as printed in Delbrück's *Gneisenau*, iv, pp. 556–61. My thanks go to my friend Dr Gregory Pedlow for his careful translation of the original German. To simplify reading, I use italics for Gneisenau's comments, and inset them.

***

Gonesse, 2 July 1815.

Mein lieber Fürst, I requested General Müffling to write to your Highness yesterday, upon the subject of the propositions which had been made to me by the French Commissioners for a suspension of hostilities, upon which I have not yet had a positive answer from your Highness.

It appears to me that, with the force which you and I have under our command at present, the attack of Paris is a matter of great risk. I am convinced it cannot be made from this side with any hope of success.

Both armies [i.e. together] are 105,000 men strong, and the two commanders would show little confidence in their valorous armies if they did not want to conquer the enemy's troops numbering about 60,000 men. The Prussian attacks of yesterday demonstrate this sufficiently, as does today's battle.

The army under my command must then cross the Seine twice, and get into the Bois de Boulogne before the attack can be made; and even then if we should succeed the loss would be very severe.

It is true that Wellington's army must cross the Seine twice in order to operate from the side of the Neuilly bridge. But because they have equipment for 6 bridges and the enemy cannot act strongly there while he is being held here by us, crossing the Seine twice must not pose any difficulties. If the enemy wished to occupy the Boulogne Forest strongly, he would have to use more troops for this than he can spare. An attack on the Neuilly bridge on the left bank of the Seine and through the Boulogne Forest on the right bank of this river will cut off the defenders of the Neuilly bridge and probably cause disorder in the enemy's defensive efforts if we attack the troops on the south side of Paris and this is done in conjunction with an attack on St Denis.

We must incur a severe loss, if it is necessary, in any case. But in this case it is not necessary.

If it is ever advisable not to be concerned about the possibility of losses, then now, when our honour is at stake and when we can strike fear into the French nation.

By the delay of a few days we shall have here the army under Marshal Prince Wrede,

A delay of several days gives the time to recover his nerve, to consolidate his defensive efforts, to raise the morale of his troops, and we will then shed more blood later than an immediate attack would cost. Why wait for the uncertain arrival of other Allied troops?

and the Allied Sovereigns with it, who will decide upon the measures to be adopted, and success will then be certain with a comparatively trifling loss; or, if we choose it, we can settle all our matters now by agreeing to the proposed armistice.

For me a ceasefire in which Paris is not handed over to us reflects badly on the honour of our armies.

The terms on which I think this armistice can be made and on which alone I will consent to make it, are these:

First, that we shall remain in the positions we now occupy.

Why not take advantage of our situation?

Secondly, that the French army shall retire from Paris across the Loire.

We can accept this.

Thirdly, that Paris shall be given over to the care of the National Guard till the King shall order otherwise.

Paris must be given to us.

Fourthly, the time to be fixed for notice to break off the armistice.

A ceasefire that does not need to be cancelled can only be concluded in Paris.

By adopting this measure, we provide for the quiet restoration of His Majesty to his throne; which is that result of the war which the Sovereigns of all of us have always considered the most beneficial for us all, and the most likely to lead to permanent peace in Europe.

The goal towards which all monarchs must strive, who take the best interests of their people to heart, is a situation in which we no longer must always fear being forced into war with a restless neighbour. Any other kind of peace is in itself a betrayal and suicidal. Who can guarantee that Bonaparte – who is fleeing to America – does not return in one or two years and cause new convulsions? It is easy for England to be satisfied simply with the restoration of the Bourbons. Its islands are safe from any attack.

It is true we shall not have the vain triumph

It is not vain triumph, rather the duty of a commander to protect the honour of his troops. Only such sentiments bring victory.

of entering Paris at the head of our victorious troops; but, as I have already explained to your Highness, I doubt our having the means at present of succeeding in an attack upon Paris; and, if we are to wait till the arrival of Marshal Prince Wrede to make the attack, I think we shall find the Sovereigns disposed, as they were last year,

It was bad enough for us that in the previous year we did not make better use of the rights of the victor.

to spare the capital of their ally,

Louis XVIII cannot be considered a true ally of Prussia when he recently concluded an alliance against us.

and either not to enter the town at all,

That is certainly not their intention.

or enter it under an armistice, such as it is in your power and mine to sign this day.

I earnestly urge your Highness, then, to consider the reasoning which I have submitted to you on this occasion; and to let me have your decision whether you will agree to any armistice or not; and, if you will, I beg you to name a person to treat in your name with the French Commissioners. If you will not, my conduct will be guided by your decision.

I have the honour, etc WELLINGTON.

Appendix 2: Comte Las Cases and Captain Maitland

10 July 1815

As stated above, on 10 July 1815 Napoleon sent two emissaries to Captain Maitland of HMS *Bellerophon* in order to find out as much as possible as to his naval dispositions and about what British intentions were if the Emperor should surrender to him. One was his man of action, the ruthless General Savary, the feared ex-Minister of Police, notorious for his part in d'Enghien's execution in the moat of Vincennes and the entrapment of the Spanish royal family in 1808; the other was Las Cases, former marquis under the *ancien régime*, later one of Napoleon's chamberlains and a master of requests at the Council of State, who was enjoying the Emperor's increasing favour by his various services, and who had the advantage of understanding and speaking English, having lived and worked in England for a number of years. It was decided that Las Cases should conceal this and pretend to speak only French, as this would place the British at the disadvantage of using a foreign language, while enabling Las Cases to eavesdrop on remarks made by the British among themselves. Las Cases himself admitted in his book that Napoleon's situation was virtually hopeless, for he says that 'the political situation was such as to free me from all scruple'. He adds that when the British asked the emissaries if they could speak English, Las Cases left it to Savary to say 'no'. So the discussions began in the shadow of a falsehood – to be justified only as a negotiating tactic.[63]

But even as a negotiating tactic it had its own disadvantage. For it inevitably meant that the French needed to be careful that Maitland's limitations in French were recognised and allowed for by them. Otherwise, when reporting to their master, there was a risk of misinterpreting things the captain had said. Maitland's remark that he had 'considerable difficulty in expressing myself in French' seems very likely to be true, and has not, so far as I know, been challenged.[64] Bearing in mind Napoleon's parlous situation, it was infinitely more important *to obtain the most clear and perfect understanding of what the Captain meant* (since so much turned upon it), than to risk a misunderstanding through tricks of language. The point is fundamental to the whole business. It would have been better for everyone, including Napoleon, if Las Cases had conducted matters in English, to make sure that there was no mistake on either side. It would also have been good practice to insist that whatever was said, or thought to be agreed, was put down in writing at once and signed by both parties.

I do not think that Houssaye accepted this fundamental point, or allowed for it in his narrative, for he noted the French concealment of their knowledge of English so as to gain advantage, and praised the skill of the envoys in drawing out the sea-dog Maitland by leading questions in long gentlemanly conversations into which the captain could not refuse to join without impoliteness. This resulted in Houssaye admiring the cleverness and indeed over-cleverness of Las Cases's astute decision, accepting his concealment, but failing to see the basic point that clarity and certainty were necessary above everything else.[65] Of course in criticising Houssaye's presentation we need to remember that the official *Correspondance de Napoléon* misled him into believing that the famous surrender letter was written only after the final *Bellerophon* discussions had ended on 14 July. If that mistake excuses his approach, the fact that he was mistaken also weakens his case.

The emissaries carried an official letter from Bertrand dated 9 July. It confirmed that the Emperor had abdicated, wished to live in the USA, and was on board one of the two French frigates. It claimed that the British government had promised a passport for this journey, and asked if Maitland had any information on the passport (the enquiry was not a sincere one but a manoeuvre, since Napoleon, Bertrand and the emissaries already knew the passport had been refused: they were fishing). Bertrand's letter asked 'whether you think that the British government intends to place any impediment to our journeying to the USA'.

This letter received a formal written answer from Maitland. He noted the first statement, and the question of the passport and the enquiry about any impediments to sailing. He ignored the passport matter (although he knew one had been refused), but stated plainly: 'I cannot say what the intentions of my government may be, but the two countries being at present in a state of war it is impossible for me to permit any ship of war to put to sea from the port of Rochefort.' There can surely be no doubt as to what this meant.[66]

Maitland's formal reply also dealt with a purely verbal enquiry, 'a proposal' from the emissaries: if Napoleon sailed on a merchant vessel, would he be allowed to pass? The answer was that, 'it is out of my power – without the sanction of my commanding officer Sir Henry Hotham, who is at present in Quiberon Bay, and to whom I have forwarded your despatch – to allow any vessel under whatever flag she may be, to pass with a personage of such consequence.' Again, that was absolutely clear. But the significance of this does *not* reside in the extension of the ban from naval to merchant ships. It resides elsewhere, in that it addressed directly a *verbal* request with an absolute and clear *written* refusal. In other words the full extent of the exchange, as Maitland saw it, was in explicitly answering in writing the questions in the letter of enquiry *and the one proposal* made verbally. From 10 July onward the British position was clear.

Meanwhile HMS *Falmouth* (Captain Knight) had come alongside with letters from Hotham, and French newspapers.[67] Maitland passed the newspapers to the Frenchmen while he dealt with the letters. Maitland says that there were several hours of general conversation on all sorts of matters. This became utterly trying for the Captain. In writing to Hotham on this day, 10 July, he ended, 'excuse the confusion of this letter as the two Frenchmen are constantly addressing me with new proposals, which all tend to the same thing'.[68]

It is from this point onwards that British and French accounts begin to differ. Let us take first Maitland's version.

Maitland described himself as returning to the subject of a safe-conduct, and asking a hypothetical question: Even if the British government were to issue a safe-conduct to America, what certainty was there that Napoleon would not return? Savary made a bland reply that he would never return, even if asked to.

It was then that Maitland made an unfortunate remark, and something of a non sequitur: 'If that is the case why not ask an asylum in England?', only to be told that there were many reasons against it.[69] How shall we treat Maitland's remark? I think at best, a blunder or indiscretion; remembering that his instructions were to get the enemy supreme commander aboard and brought to a British port, it was probably a 'kite' flown intentionally, another card in this poker game. If so, the two emissaries played down any interest in the remark and did not seek to obtain any further clarification of exactly what Maitland meant, or could propose.

The French emissaries told the story thus:

According to Las Cases:

> We spoke of his [Napoleon's] passage in a neutral vessel; the reply was that all neutral vessels would be strictly inspected [*visité*], and perhaps even taken to English ports, but it was suggested to us to go to England, and was affirmed that we need fear no bad treatment whatever.'

It comes to this: the Royal Navy refused to let Napoleon go to the USA in a neutral vessel; it would be stopped and searched and the vessel might be forced to go to Britain – which sounds like an arrest. But they could be invited to Britain without fear. That is very much how Maitland described the matter, and so did Savary (as we shall see next).

Savary in his memoirs represented Maitland saying:

> 'I do not think that our government will let him go to America'. We replied to M. Maitland: 'Where then should he go?' He replied, 'I cannot tell, but I

> am almost certain of what I now say. What objection would he have to go to England? In that way he would cut short [*trancherait*] all difficulties.' M. de Las Cases replied that we had no mission to treat on this question ...[70]

Savary was an unpleasant and unscrupulous man, but he was not a preening meddler like Las Cases. His account has three points of interest.

First, that the conversation had reverted to the text (or what would become the text) of the letter refusing passage to the USA that Maitland wrote later on 10 July; Las Cases's version is less precise and more fanciful (neutrals in English ports).

Secondly, it was the *emissaries* who *then asked a leading question*, designed to draw Maitland out. Whereas Maitland recalled that it was he who volunteered the remark, Savary stated that they drew it from him ('Where then ...') but the answer that they heard was in terms that clearly disclosed a degree of uncertainty ('I cannot tell, but I am almost certain ...')

Thirdly, Savary stated that 'Las Cases replied that we had no mission to treat on this question.' In his account Las Cases is silent on whether or not he made any reply, which – since it went to the heart of his August 1815 accusation of Maitland's duplicity and double-dealing – is very odd. But that is not the main point. The main point is that in a matter of vital importance to Napoleon neither emissary made any attempt to find out anything more or to develop a possible opening.

For if Maitland's passing remark really had been seen at that time as of such vital importance, why was there no conversational follow up or verbal enquiry (as there was about a merchant vessel), or an attempt to obtain something in writing from Maitland before he concluded his formal reply? Maitland's remark was not raised with him by anyone during their contacts in the following days, so that it formed no part of the discussions as noted down by the two sides in their books. Indeed Maitland made the point very fairly when he wrote in his narrative: 'How could a stronger proof be adduced that no stipulations were agreed to respecting the reception of Buonaparte in England than the fact of their not being reduced to writing? which would certainly have been the case had any favourable terms been demanded on the part of Monsieur Las Cases and agreed by me.'[71]

Savary did indeed make a defence of this, and it is a most revealing one:

> It has been said that there was no convention written at Rochefort; that is true, but it matters little, for capitulations and written conventions are only used when it is a question of handing over a place of war, or to regulate the fate of a body of troops. The Emperor was nothing more than an individual, and one would have felt it an insult to those from whom one received

> hospitality, to stipulate anything. It is generosity that rules in such cases, and honour that carries them out. Moreover, for stipulating a written convention M. Maitland would have needed to have a power [*un pouvoir*], and he had only the approval of his admiral . . .[72]

Much of that – the excuse about the impossibility of extending written terms from standard cases to the fate of the Emperor because he was 'only an individual', the rigmarole about insulting hospitality – is transparent nonsense, but then suddenly there is the confession that the emissaries knew Maitland lacked the necessary authority, '*un pouvoir*', a document giving him power to make a written guarantee of asylum. Maitland was known to have no power.

11–13 July 1815

Time was running out for Napoleon. More and more Bourbon flags rose along the coast. An escape by sea was decided upon, only to be abandoned on Napoleon's own orders. Bertrand recounts that the Emperor had dreams of living at ease in Britain, and that he told him of the impossibility of this. Flahaut warned him that authority did not reside in *Bellerophon* but in the British Cabinet,[73] and the latter would use its power, backed by parliament, to override whatever personal inclinations the Prince Regent might have; Flahaut even offered to seek out the Tsar and ask for his generosity in granting asylum. But that quest would have taken days, and Napoleon no longer had time in hand. So, despite these warnings, on 13 July Napoleon gambled on a personal appeal to the Prince Regent. Hence his letter from Rochefort on 13 July. The letter renders false Las Cases's claim that it was only after the emissaries reported back following their visit to Maitland on the 14th that Napoleon dictated and signed his appeal 'from the Île d'Aix, 14 July 1815'.

14 July 1815

Given that the emissaries knew that Maitland's 10 July comment was lacking any *pouvoir* it is not surprising that when final terms were fixed on 14 July and in the presence of witnesses, there was not the least reference to that 10 July remark. What we do find, however, is that Las Cases later claimed that Maitland said that, although he had not yet received anything from England, 'according to his private opinion and those of several other captains present serving with him, there was no doubt that Napoleon would find in England all the respect and treatment he had the right to expect' and that the generosity and liberality of opinion of the people of England was greater than the sovereign powers. To this, Las Cases says he replied that, 'I would tell the Emperor of the Captain's offer [*sic*] and his entire conversation [*sic*].' Yet when Las Cases asked again about 'safe conduct passes to America', he claims that Maitland replied that 'it should be well understood that he did not guarantee that they would be accorded'. That is Las Cases's own version, not of the 10 July exchange but of the 14 July meeting: the British would welcome him – presumably with a pass – in England (why?) although they would probably not issue a pass to sail to the USA. Las Cases cannot have asked himself the obvious question: if a pass would probably be refused for America, why should it be granted for England? What are we supposed to make of that? All that flies in the face of Maitland's own report of 14 July, written immediately after the discussion with Las Cases; and the Count's claims were formally denied in three depositions of 8 August by Maitland and two other naval officers present. So what support from French colleagues did Las Cases obtain for his claims?[74]

Lallemand was an experienced soldier who may therefore have understood the British sailor better than did the civilian Las Cases. Upon returning from the 14 July meeting he answered Napoleon's enquiry about the solidity of Maitland's undertakings with Las Cases, with these words: 'I have confidence in him [Maitland], but none in the British government. They will make Captain Maitland despite himself the instrument of a perfidy and they will disavow him if necessary.'[75] If General Lallemand thought Maitland had made encouraging remarks, he also warned on 14 July that there was nothing bankable to rely upon. Maitland's words to Las Cases and Lallemand were deemed honest by the soldier, but the naval captain lacked a *pouvoir* (to use Savary's expression). There was no written undertaking from the British government. There was nothing that Napoleon could shield himself with. In his keenness to show off his skills and win his master's approval, Las Cases had built a house of cards upon nothing. Lallemand tried to make everyone see sense.

It is undoubtedly the case that the Allies were very anxious to capture Napoleon and not let him escape to do more damage. The instructions to Maitland were emphatic about this, as French historians have always been at pains to point out. Some infer that this meant that Maitland therefore would not scruple to use any means, fair or foul, to catch such a prize as Napoleon. But that is to ignore the Bourbon and Prussian net closing on the Emperor. All that I think that can be concluded is that Maitland threw out a suggestion to come aboard (as he was encouraged to do by Hotham's instructions), but that it was ignored, and did not feature in subsequent discussions. Only in

August was it recollected by Las Cases, who felt himself largely responsible for the mess he had negotiated his Emperor into, and was anxious to shift the blame for his own incompetence.

From 15 July onwards

Just prior to embarkation, said Montholon, Napoleon spoke to General Beker, who by order of the provisional government at this moment commanded his escort, dissuading Beker from accompanying him to the *Bellerophon*, because 'it will be said that you handed me to England'. That at least suggests some uncertainty over what the British intended, for it could scarcely apply if he were going to safety and liberty.[76]

Montholon was writing long after the event, but relying on his own notes and the memoirs of some of his companions, and his book the *History of the Captivity at St Helena* was published in 1846, twenty years after Maitland had published his narrative. So far as I can see, he made no reference to Maitland's book, which is a pity; but as he nowhere challenged anything in it – and Maitland in 1826 cited Montholon's remarks as notable evidence in his own defence – it seems that he found nothing seriously wrong in it.

With hindsight, Maitland acknowledged that it was a serious error of judgement not to put all his discussion of 10 July with Las Cases into writing and obtain a signature. But he did not realise this until 6 August, a week after the British government had conveyed its decision to Napoleon. On 6 August Las Cases told Maitland that he, Maitland, had assured him that the Emperor would have been allowed to reside in Britain. Maitland repudiated this at once, but added 'you questioned me frequently as to my private opinions; and as I was quite ignorant on the subject, I could only say I had no reason to believe he would be ill received.'[77] On the next day Las Cases asked to see the Admiral and Maitland sent him to Lord Keith. Keith heard him out and then asked Maitland for a written report on the matter.[78]

Maitland's report of 8 August[79] was very detailed, but dealt almost entirely with events of the day of 14 July when final discussions were taking place as to Napoleon's reception on board. His submission was backed by witness statements from two other naval captains present on the day. All stated that no promise of asylum was mentioned on 14 July or formed any part of the discussions, so far as British recollections went. The report also noted that Keith was a witness when Maitland publicly rejected Las Cases's 6 August allegations to the latter's face. Maitland also cited Montholon as saying to him apropos the allegation, 'Oh, Las Cases is disappointed in his expectations; and as he has negotiated the affair, he attributes the Emperor's situation to himself; but I can assure you that he [Napoleon] feels convinced you have acted like a man of honour throughout.'[80]

There are three comments necessary on this 8 August report. The first is that Maitland did not deal with the events of 10 July. That was a pity. But if anything material had been omitted on the 14th that had been discussed and agreed on the 10th, it would have been picked up and argued over by one side or the other. Nothing of the kind seems to have taken place. Secondly, Keith did not accept Las Cases's accusation, and accepted Maitland's report. Thirdly, while Montholon did not mention in his 1846 book any remarks made to Maitland, he did not dispute what the latter had written in his report, published in 1826; indeed he appears to have thought Las Cases the culprit. Maitland, in fact, is presented by Montholon as an honourable and courteous host to a most strange assortment of people, caught in the difficulty of awaiting orders as to what to do once they arrived in England.[81]

It has been averred that the British government ensured that Maitland 'received his knighthood for this high act of double-dealing'.[82] What he actually received was a CB, the lowest rank of the Bath and one given in 1815 to dozens of naval captains and army colonels at the war's end. He had to wait until 1830, when promotion to rear-admiral brought him a knighthood: fifteen years surely does make a difference and exposes that careless sneer. It may be that the authorities did not think he had handled matters off the Île d'Aix and on the voyage home altogether to their liking. But could he have done otherwise? That he was dealing with the most famous man in the world must have affected matters, since whoever took Napoleon, and the circumstances surrounding his capture and treatment, would become a matter of intense interest and scrutiny throughout Europe.

Napoleon had plenty of friends ready and willing to cry foul, not least among the British Whigs: and there was the instance of Lord Keith being chased from ship to ship by lawyers acting for British friends of Napoleon, who sought to secure Napoleon's release while in British waters.[83] Everything that Maitland did would become the subject of enquiry, and from his account of the next few weeks he was plainly conscious of the very difficult task he had to perform and was at pains to ensure all went well. Knowledge of being held accountable is a great encouragement for plain dealing. This point is not always conceded.

There also remains the matter of Las Cases. He had prided himself on being '*débarrassé de tout scrupule*' in handling the affair, which does not exactly help his case when a few weeks later he accused Maitland of duplicity. Montholon apparently thought that he had made a mess of things, and so did Gourgaud, who found Las Cases prone to over-play his hand, and who recorded day by day Maitland's growing embarrassment at the non-receipt of orders at Torbay and by news that seemed less and less favourable to Napoleon. The captain was left in limbo, and yet had to see the French party all the time. He seems to have treated them politely, fairly and openly, and to have left Gourgaud in no doubt of his good faith. I find Gourgaud's *Journal inédit* convincing of Maitland's innocence and Las Cases's misunderstanding of the true purposes of diplomacy and negotiation.[84]

For these reasons I find it difficult to accept Houssaye's attack on Maitland's frankness and honesty.[85] Houssaye was mistaken over the date of the surrender letter and so thought it followed the 14 July negotiation. But he played down the 'state of war' and how that complicated matters. He ignored that neither the Allied sovereigns nor the British Cabinet had come to any decision on exactly what to do, by 10 July. He presented Savary and Las Cases as skilled negotiators, drawing out the British naval officer, listening for chance remarks and gaining advantage thereby. But he then presented a contradictory view of them all: two trusting French lambs going to the slaughter, dupes of this same man, two diplomats who were so incompetent that they could not even turn a chance comment into a proper undertaking, puppets in the hands of a double-dealing mastermind: 'What would their thoughts have been if they could have seen through his mask and penetrated his thoughts! . . . in Maitland's mouth, full of lies and perfidy, asylum meant captivity.'[86] After all, who admitted to being *débarrassé de tout scrupule*? Houssaye did not highlight the uncertainty and fear that affected the little group around Napoleon after the emissaries' return on 10 July with Maitland's unequivocal letter, nor did he accept that the letter was a clear and complete reply to all the points in a written enquiry and also to a verbal proposition (or rather, *the* verbal proposition): which was precisely why there was so much depression. Nor did he face up to the implications of Maitland's question about why, if Las Cases was so definite in his claim, nothing was asked for or put in writing. It is scarcely how one should handle evidence.

Doubtless agreement will never be reached on this sad and sorry matter, but such are my own conclusions.

Chapter 51
The Settlement of 1815

I

TSAR ALEXANDER AND HIS FRIEND Frederick William of Prussia reached Paris on 10 July, the day after Louis XVIII had entered it, and with their arrival the worst fears of the denizens of Paris were over: the vengeful military cliques were no longer beyond control.[1] The sovereigns mingled and talked with Metternich, Castlereagh and Wellington, with Pozzo, and the restored French King's ministers. There were parades as the armies arrived and camped in and around the capital. Talleyrand and Fouché combined ('vice leaning on the arm of crime', in Chateaubriand's famous phrase) to secure a peaceful transition of power within the country and good relations with the friendlier Allies: seeing them arm-in-arm together Pozzo understandably wondered 'what those two lambs were saying to each other'. But it was not long before the populace of Paris came to resent the foreign presence and to forget what had caused it, and it was soon apparent that the Bourbon monarchy was by no means as popular as it had been on the morrow of the Cambrai proclamation. In the meantime there was still some unfinished military business to conclude, the fate of Napoleon to be decided, France had to agree (or argue) over the sort of internal governance there should be under the second Restoration, and the settlement between royalist France and Europe awaited negotiation. We shall look briefly at each of these topics in turn.

II

In Digby Smith's magnificent *Napoleonic Wars Data Book*, subsequent to the combats of Wavre and Namur there are listed forty skirmishes, clashes, blockades and sieges in France between 20 June and 24 September 1815. This list is not complete, for certainly Wellington's captures of Cambrai and Péronne have been omitted, but if we add these to the total we find that while well over twenty of the affairs involved either his or the Prussian army, no less than a further ten occurred on the Piedmontese and Jura front, and almost as many on the central Rhine front.[2] The words employed define the scale of these affairs: *skirmish* and *clash* are frequent, *blockade* nearly equally so, and the sieges partake more of *blockade* than *assault*. In many cases casualties are given as *slight*, although Hausbergen in Alsace cost the French 500 casualties and over 1,700 prisoners, against some 900 Allies; the capture of Grenoble cost about 200 Allied casualties; and the minor disaster at Versailles (Chapter 50, Section IV, above) cost the Prussians two regiments of fine cavalry.

Yet an English-language history must be careful not to ignore the military contributions to victory of the other Allies. The various components of Schwarzenberg's host crossed the Rhine between 22 and 25 June, and they ceased their advance only with the restoration of King Louis early in July, by which time they had reached Châlons-sur-Marne, Nancy, Chalon-sur-Saône and even La Ferté-sous-Jouarre. Nice capitulated on 9 July and Lyons on the 11th. Some of these troops were retained for the Army of Occupation, but most returned home to heroes' welcomes; but the Russians, who had reached the Rhine on 25 June, continued to Paris in mid-July.

Many of the blockades of fortresses went with tacit agreements as to quiet living, and the sieges were minor matters, for the forts in France were without resource and resembled cut flowers out of water – doomed to wither and die of their own accord; to waste lives taking them was unnecessary. The French commanders of the garrisons were under no illusions; sooner or later they would be starved out, and there was no possibility of a rescue – there were Bourbon flags all around. Let honour be satisfied and reasonable terms agreed and there would be no resistance *à outrance*. Thus to compare the garrison of, say, Rocroi, with the defenders of Plancenoit on 18 June would be ridiculous, just as to trumpet the capture of Rocroi would be almost an insult to the brave captors of Plancenoit. The so-called Siege War was all 'flat beer'.

Taking the northern forts was the responsibility of Prince Frederik of the Netherlands on one hand, and of Prince August of Prussia on the other. Wellington was greatly impressed by the young Dutch lad of seventeen (who in later life, although never monarch, was to prove a main pillar of the state), and praised him to the British Cabinet for his 'intelligence and spirit' in handling the various blockades and sieges.[3]

For his part, Prince August of Prussia was seriously hampered in conducting sieges, due to the insufficiency of Prussian equipment. To conduct his sieges he was obliged to turn to Wellington for assistance, for against defended fortress walls a siege without a siege train to do the work is scarcely a siege at all. His letter of appeal of 3 July explained that with only field-guns, some howitzers and twenty-five siege pieces he could do very little, and therefore requested that the large British train be given him. Wellington agreed on the 5th and instructed Lieutenant-Colonel Sir A. Dickson to support him with the British siege equipment.[4] The Prince then increased his demands as to guns, extra ammunition and men, and Dickson obliged him in this, but maintained a supervisory role, since British soldiers were thus being used by the Prussians. This British participation is not always remembered, but it played an absolutely essential part in what is sometimes inflated into the Prussian 'Fortress War'.

The corollary to this assistance was that it rested upon a clear agreement as to policy and objectives. By early August 1815 Prince August and his superiors were extending their ambitions and their demands. Now 150 pieces were deemed necessary for the attack on such places as Givet. But all arrangements about which forts were to be besieged had hitherto been decided between the Allies together, and the places now identified by the Prince were new targets. In consequence Wellington refused to let Prince August use the British train for those sieges that had not been agreed upon.[5] It is certainly true that some of the minor forts still refused to haul down the *tricolor*, but they had dwindling supplies, and little effect on the surrounding regions. The cut flowers could be left to wither.

In the days up to the formal cessation of all hostilities on 20 September, the forts actively besieged by the Prussians surrendered as follows: Maubeuge, on its fifth day, 12 July; Landrecies on its third day, 21 July; Mariembourg on its second day, 28 July; Philippeville on its second day, 8 August; Rocroi on its second day, 16 August; the garrisons of the outlying forts of Charlemont (Givet and Mont d'Hours) were withdrawn by agreement on 8 September and moved into the central fort, which was still awaiting siege when the war ended officially.[6]

III

The letter Napoleon had addressed to the Prince Regent had been handed to Gourgaud to take to England in Captain Sartorius's HMS *Slaney*. On reaching Plymouth on the evening of 22 July Gourgaud was detained on board the ship, since there were the strictest orders that none of the ex-Emperor's party should be allowed ashore or have any communication with it; and as he insisted that he alone should hand the letter to the Regent, it remained aboard with him. When the *Bellerophon* arrived the dilemma was explained to Napoleon, who told Maitland to take the letter and give it to Admiral Lord Keith, commanding the Channel fleet. This Maitland did on 27 July. Keith passed it to the First Lord of the Admiralty, who gave it to Lord Bathurst on 29 July. The letter to the Regent was without any practical effect.

It was on 21 July that the British Cabinet received the news of Napoleon's surrender and began reviewing the options of placing him in Gibraltar, Malta, the Cape of Good Hope or St Helena. The Admiralty at once recommended the last named place as 'particularly healthy' and difficult of access, and this was confirmed by a former governor of the island in a memorandum of 29 July. The London daily papers by 24 July were openly remarking that St Helena was the ultimate choice, and this news filtered through to the captives on the *Bellerophon* and created growing unease. On 30 July, the day after he had received Napoleon's letter to the Regent, Lord Bathurst was drafting instructions for the guidance of Admiral Cockburn, who was to command the expedition to take Napoleon to St Helena.

The naval officers meanwhile found themselves without instructions, and it was not until 31 July that Sir Henry Bunbury, Under-Secretary for War and Colonies, and Admiral Lord Keith from Plymouth, went together to see Napoleon with the government's official instructions. He protested against the decisions, claimed that he had come freely to England and wished to live there in quiet, that he would have to be removed by force, that he would die. He then studied the official notification and wrote a formal protest addressed to Lord Keith.

Keith in a note on the interview, wrote, 'He immediately took up the papers from the table and said with animation, "How so; St Helena?" to which I observed, "Sir, it is surely preferable to being confined in a smaller space in England, or being sent to France, or perhaps to Russia." "Russia! *Dieu garde!*" was his reply. I then withdrew.'[7]

From one point of view the famous Protest that Napoleon wrote on 4 August aboard the *Bellerophon* was and is – self-evidently right. That view was and is held by those who consider Napoleon the victim of the campaign, as someone trapped into the war of 1815 against his will, a peaceful democrat and admirer of all things British, an independent power who freely went on board as a guest of Britain – in short, those who accept the thesis of the Protest as it stands. This is what it said:

> I here solemnly protest, in the face of Heaven and of men, against the violence done to me, and against the violation of my most sacred rights, in disposing by force of my person and my liberty. I came freely aboard the 'Bellerophon'; I am in no way a prisoner, I am the guest of England.

I came on board at the Captain's own instigation, who said he had the orders of the Government to receive me and my suite, and conduct me to England, if that should be agreeable to me. I presented myself in good faith to place myself under the protection of the laws of England. Once seated aboard the 'Bellerophon' I was on the hearth of the British people.

If the Government, in giving orders to the Captain of the 'Bellerophon' to receive me as well as my suite, intended only to lay a snare for me, it has forfeited its honour and sullied its flag. If this act should be consummated, it will be in vain that the English will speak to Europe of their loyalty, of their laws, and of their liberty. The faith of Britain will be found lost in the hospitality of the 'Bellerophon'.

I appeal to History; she will say that an enemy who made war for twenty years against the English people, came freely in his misfortune to seek an asylum under their laws. What more striking proof could he give of his esteem and his confidence? But how did they respond in England to such magnanimity? They feigned to stretch forth the hand of hospitality to this enemy, and when he delivered himself in good faith, they immolated him.

[signed] NAPOLEON aboard the 'Bellerophon', 4 August 1815.

But there were and are those who see Napoleon Bonaparte in 1815 in a very different way, who consider him as having brought yet again nothing but unrest and war to a Europe that he had persistently trampled across for so many years. He was not a victim – or if he was, it was because of his own actions and the fall of the dice of war. His arguments were self-serving, specious, and not to be believed or accepted. They were the inventions of a man without means of escape, and they did not match what had been said or done by him prior to 18 June.

Many of the Bonapartist adherents and historians refused to face this truth, and wrote as though it should have been a negotiation between equals, as it had been at Dresden in 1813. But that was not the case now. Understandably they tended to emphasise all the better sides of the great man, his lawgiving, his passion for order, his great engineering and industrial schemes, and to see him as the bringer of light to an unenlightened Europe. So they implied that Napoleon had a right to expect especially favourable terms. But there was another side – and I do not speak here of the military achievements that, to some who are dazzled by the tales of Marbot and the pictures of Vernet and Meissonier, are simply to be gloried in. His conduct in his days of power had shown him over many years dismissive of anyone's rights, and capable of inhuman acts and behaviour. This was the man who without any justice sent the Jacobins to Guiana in 1800, who let Frotté be killed despite a safe-conduct pass, who was responsible for d'Enghien's murder, who had Palm shot for publishing a protest, who had tricked and kidnapped the Spanish royal family in 1808, the man who imprisoned, isolated and lied to the Pope, the man who had proved so difficult and inconstant an ally, so false a friend, so ruthless an enemy.

The conclusion that Lord Rosebery drew in his sympathetic study of 'The Last Phase' seems entirely just: Napoleon's dream of domesticating himself in England was impossible.

> Washington, a born country gentleman, could step down from the highest office and resume rural pursuits with dignity and satisfaction. But Napoleon in such guise would have deceived no one, least of all himself. His shepherds would have been suspected of intrigue, his bailiff would have been treated as a diplomatist, his oil-cake would have been probed for despatches. And in the midst of the byre would have been Napoleon, with some Poppleton in attendance, suspected of meditating, and no doubt meditating, very different things.
>
> It must indeed be conceded that it was not possible for him to live in England. There, to say the least, he would have been the figurehead of faction both in England and abroad. Napoleon in the Tower of London would have been an anachronism – and, even there, an unexploded shell. He would have been under the very eye of France ... he would have been a cause of unrest and agitation in England; he would have enjoyed in his prison the sympathy of Whigs like Sussex or Holland, and the enthusiasm of Radicals like Hobhouse ... It would have become at last impossible to keep him in and impossible to let him out. And all these drawbacks would have been multiplied a hundred-fold had he been allowed to be comparatively at large under supervision; even had the Confederate Powers agreed to such an arrangement, which, after the experience of Elba, we may be sure was out of the question. On the Continent outside France and Italy, he could have lived under custody of some kind ... There was no risk of his escaping from the affectionate solicitude of his father-in-law, or the vindictive vigilance of Prussia, or the outraged territory of Russia.[8]

Even the historian whose work has been for a century the foremost French account of 1815, a convinced devotee of the Emperor, gave the fundamental reason why Napoleon had to be imprisoned. I have quoted him at the end of my Chapter 3. Houssaye gave several secondary reasons for the return from Elba, but ended by identifying the fundamental one, the man's own *character*: 'The prime cause was that [he] was called Napoleon and that he was forty-five years old.' That was written of the Napoleon of

January 1815. In what way had his essential character changed by the late summer?

On 7 August Napoleon's little party, watched by Keith aboard HMS *Tonnant* at sea off Start Point, transferred from HMS *Bellerophon* to HMS *Northumberland*, and came under the command of Sir George Cockburn. *Northumberland* departed south for St Helena, where the party arrived on 17 October.[9]

If the British government's main decision was right – and by a convention signed on 2 August, the Four Powers agreed to regard Napoleon as their common prisoner, so that all four were consenting parties to the arrangement[10] – in smaller matters the decisions were too often unnecessary, too bureaucratic, or merely irritating to very little positive end. The island was healthy and was secure (not unimportant points, when all is said); it was roughly the size of Jersey, and Napoleon was granted open space in which to roam. That space amounted to about six square miles, about half as much again as the Duke of Marlborough's Oxfordshire estate at Blenheim; and indeed if Napoleon should accept the presence of a British officer he was free to go all over the island during daylight hours. Of course it was not as agreeable as Jersey or the Isle of Wight, but it was not small like Lundy, or St Kilda; nor was it Fenestrelle or the Château d'If. Life might have been tolerable.

But the Allied commissioners were of little use and no help, and the choice of Hudson Lowe as governor was unhappy. Lowe's fussiness and maladroit interpretation of his duties played into the hands of those whose aim was to create trouble and magnify any injustices. He must have been haunted by the memory of Neil Campbell and the deceit on Elba, and feared to find himself subjected to the same sort of snide sarcasm and comment as that unfortunate man never fully escaped after February 1815. But to call upon the officers of the 20th Foot to refuse to accept a copy of Coxe's *Life of Marlborough* because its donor inscribed himself as Emperor, showed Lowe at his pettifogging worst – but his 'worst' still was mere *pettifogging* and it was of course useful to the other side, and it suited their policy even if it did not suit them. In 1828 a prominent member of the imperial group at St Helena, Montholon, told one of Lowe's officers, Basil Jackson, that the policy of Longwood (the house where Napoleon was held) was to denigrate Sir Hudson and the system, admitting 'that an angel from Heaven as Governor could not have pleased them [at Longwood]'. That is why H. A. L. Fisher wrote early in the twentieth century, 'It was part of the policy of Longwood to court martyrdom and advertise woes.'[11] Even at best it would never have been a pleasant or amiable time, and it was, for one reason or another, very seldom so. The small isolated group of French officers, courtiers, and wives, clustered round Napoleon at Longwood, wore each other down, and made hatreds and disputes all the worse.[12]

The story from then on belongs to the Napoleonic Myth rather than to the Hundred Days and Waterloo.

IV

The Allied views on a new settlement for France were discordant and difficult to reconcile. British wealth and prestige and Russian imperial power probably proved the decisive factors.

The final act of the Congress of Vienna had been signed at the beginning of June 1815, when operations against Napoleon had not yet begun. The France as recognised by that act was essentially the France as defined by the first Peace of Paris of May 1814, a country not to be so weakened as to endanger its internal cohesion yet not so strong as to adversely affect its neighbours, a France with the frontiers of 1792, with additional lands that (like Avignon or Mulhouse) had formerly been foreign enclaves in France, and with a small residual colonial empire. But by the time the *final act* was being signed in Vienna, Stein and Hardenberg for Prussia and Metternich for Austria were already debating whether the strong western frontier of Germany created in 1814 was indeed strong enough: French Flanders, Alsace and Lorraine might be added to one or other of the German powers.

For its part, the French army under Davout honoured its undertakings as set down in the 3 July convention, went south of the Loire, and disbanded on 16 July. France now had no organised military force of its own and the Allies no longer had to worry about that. The deputies of the Lower Chamber, having received the letter of resignation from the provisional ministry, found that their meeting hall, the Palais Bourbon, was now under the protection of the National Guard, which ordered them to disperse (8 July). This they did, issuing a statement about what had just taken place. Parisians of all sorts and persuasions, with an insouciance that never ceases to amaze, then ran up the *fleurs-de-lys* and brought out their white cockades. Louis returned to a capital that seemingly was disposed to accept him back, and in the better *quartiers* was even cheered as he approached the Tuileries. But inside the courtyard the Prussian garrison ignored his arrival, and went about their domestic tasks. Prussia had not forgiven the French.

Thus, on 22 July, Hardenberg tabled proposals for the cession of the French northern fortresses and for the transfer of Alsace, parts of French Jura and of Savoy to the neighbouring powers. Prussia should gain back for

Germany most of the eastern lands that *Le Roi Soleil* had conquered in the seventeenth century. In this Hardenberg was fully supported by the militant group in the Prussian high command now stationed in France. Metternich played with the idea but his distrust of Prussia and his preoccupation with gains in Italy determined his final and adverse views. Castlereagh was concerned for the imbalance that the cessions could create in western Europe, and Wellington warned that a country so strong in population as France would never accede for long to such drastic amputation. It would make a war of *revanche* almost inevitable. The British arguments had a certain force, and if a peace settlement ought not to be poisoned by the seeds of future war, their arguments deserve praise. But the decisive factor was that Tsar Alexander refused to contemplate any major changes to the 1814 treaty.

How matters worked out belongs more to the history of Europe in the post-Napoleonic era than to the campaign of Waterloo, and a short summary must therefore suffice.

Russia's brilliant diplomat, the Corsican-born Pozzo di Borgo, had been attached to Wellington's headquarters, and soon came to admire the Duke and his manner of reasoning. It is not surprising, therefore, that he should find British views more acceptable than Prussian ones, or that he should find that 'Gneisenau's head is in the clouds', their headquarters 'almost drunk' with victory and incapable of viewing the future with any sense. These views were shared by Metternich, who so often held positions very different from those of the Russians.

In small matters a four-power group in Paris was able to arrange from week to week the administrative issues arising, but the major problems stemmed mainly from Prussian demands, and caused a great deal of difficulty for the other powers. The Pont de Iéna was not blown up, but that was not due to Wellington stationing a British sentry upon it. The sentry's life was only saved through Prussian incompetence with explosive charges.

The Allied troops were all-powerful, but their leaders were not united. The ministers of the four powers met constantly, but as time passed the Prussian position became more isolated, and once Alexander made his position plain their demands became almost impossible to maintain. Wellington was usually present at these sessions. A man unknown to foreign statesmen before May 1814, the great impression the Duke had made on them then, at Paris and Vienna, and his prestige after Waterloo gave him a position that in some ways was unique. He did not abuse it. In conference his views were clear, concise and to the point, but they were expressed mainly and most fully to his colleague and friend Castlereagh, who led for Britain.

Wellington disliked and distrusted Hardenberg's proposals for France, preferring a much more moderate settlement, with minimal land cessions. The future of France, the Allies, and the Allied Army of Occupation, were discussed by him in an official despatch to the Foreign Secretary (dated merely August 1815, but probably the 11th) and in a long and reasoned semi-official letter of 11 August. He countered one after another of the Prussian claims. The powers had given Louis the status of ally, and he could hardly be treated as an enemy without creating general resentment in France; he was included in the guarantee of the 25 March treaty and his country had to be granted that benefit; many in northern France had been well disposed to the king's return: 'it would be ridiculous to suppose that the Allies would have been in possession of Paris in a fortnight after one battle fought, if the French people in general had not been favourably disposed to the cause which the Allies were supposed to favour'. He accepted that the peace of May 1814 had left France too strong, but a great territorial cession forced upon France now would unite its people against the settlement and that could foment among them demands for a war to recover the lost territories; fear of such a possibility would oblige the powers to remain on a war footing and to disappoint hopes of much-needed peace and retrenchment for years to come. For the genuine peace and tranquillity of the world only minimal cessions ought to demanded and an occupation of the northern zone for only a few years. Of course the Allies should not entirely drop their guard or fritter their time and means, but should look to their own long-term security. But for that a war footing was not necessary. And even if this general peace lasted for only a term of years, it would allow time for the Allies to benefit from a peace dividend, and for France meanwhile to learn the advantages of moderate and stable government that could lead it away from adventurism.[13]

Castlereagh was equally prescient, and in a letter to Lord Liverpool of 17 August, in surveying the various Allied demands and the position of the restored government, he concurred with the Prime Minister that British interests were 'much more identified with those of Austria and Prussia ... than with those of Russia' but that Russia had come 'publicly to adopt all the principles of the Allied powers'; also Russia was closer to British views than to those of Austria and Prussia on not ruining France by excessive war indemnities. As to taking French territory, a sentiment that he admitted was fully understandable among Germans who had suffered so much, 'it is one thing to wish the thing done, and another to maintain it when done'. And so he insisted that 'it is not our business to collect trophies, but to try if we can bring back the world to peaceful habits. I do not believe this to be compatible with any attempt now materially and permanently to affect the territorial character of France, as settled by the Peace of Paris [of 1814].' Nor did he give up hope 'that France, even in her existing dimensions, may not be found a useful rather than a dangerous member of the European system'.[14]

By now Pozzo was greatly concerned by the Prussian attitude. He had noted Gneisenau's extreme irritation over the ceasefire proposals at the beginning of July, and judged that it would make a generally acceptable settlement all the more difficult to achieve. He had advised his master that the Prussian government should give Blücher not mere indications but direct orders to conform. (Alexander was independently coming to similar conclusions.) Soon Pozzo considered that Prussia was fomenting excesses inside France and creating resentment in order to justify stronger frontiers for Germany, and that Alsace and Lorraine were in reality a ploy, to be exchanged for the absorption into Prussia of the states of Hesse and Hanover that stood on either side of the route between Brandenburg and Rhenish Prussia. He warned the Tsar of 'a military conspiracy' taking control of Prussian policy and drew a startling picture of its eventual outcome. From the Prussian king's ADC Knesebeck he learned that the court feared the ambition and attitudes of Gneisenau and Grolman, their 'bad form of Germanism, blind hatred of France', and Gneisenau's wish to keep a large army in the Rhineland under his own command.[15]

And indeed the growing ill-temper among the Prussians was evident. Blücher's political and diplomatic skills were rudimentary and he was clearly ill-suited to the new situation. He resented his lack of influence when compared with such limited soldiers as Schwarzenberg and Wrede, who were quite skilful diplomatically, however. And Gneisenau was not slow to point out to him Wellington's increasing prominence. Blücher decided to leave St Cloud for the more distant and secluded Rambouillet, from where Hardinge reported on 26 July that certain movement orders issued by the high command had been countermanded by the King, leading Blücher to express an intention to resign. This placed Frederick William in a difficult position: the King was poorly regarded at home and Blücher's reasons for resigning would carry great weight with the Army and the nation. The monarch asked him not to resign until peace had been negotiated, but to leave the negotiations to Gneisenau. The *Feldmarschall* then went off to Caen in Normandy. But Gneisenau had less prestige than his old master and his views, stiff and narrow, were scarcely likely to convince the other Allies. Moreover Castlereagh noted that while most of the Allies were profiting from the British subsidy that would last until 1 April 1816 (or a peace treaty, if sooner) while paying, feeding and clothing their forces at French expense, the Prussians had brought into the Netherlands an entire army corps of

40,000 men, and fed it from local Netherlands resources until it marched on into France. Two hundred thousand Prussians were now in France and drawing rations.[16]

And here we must listen to Gneisenau for a final time in this history. On 17 August 1815 – the very day Castlereagh was setting out his views to the British Prime Minister on how to bring back the world to peaceful habits – Gneisenau opened his heart to his friend Arndt. He noted that Russia in the current negotiations tended to protect France from loss of territory. This, he thought, was quite understandable as its policy was that Prussia and Austria should have concerns over safety in western Europe, and France could assist Russia there as ally. But when Britain sought the integrity of French territory, that should be recognised as a desire 'to nurture war on the Continent and keep Germany dependent on England'. And Britain in opposing other powers making conquests was helping itself to the Ionian isles. Prussia was not demanding conquests, merely that France's neighbours be strengthened against 'this turbulent people, thirsting for revenge, and greedy'. Thus far Gneisenau was making a case that some might think at least arguable, though *ex parte*; but when we place it beside what Liverpool and Castlereagh were actually advocating we see how hopelessly inadequate Gneisenau's political conceptions were. However, he went further. He began to level accusations that were not simply viciously one-sided but that he must have known were not true – given what he had been told by Müffling and Wussow on 15 and 16 June, by the officer who encountered Gordon, by Massow and Wucherer all on the 17th, by his own recognition that Wellington had undertaken to fight at Mont St Jean on the express condition that *'zwei Korps geben wollen'*, and much else that he had himself said and written at the time.

> Wellington is the worst. He who without our help would have been destroyed, who did not keep his promises to be ready on the 16th [June], whom we – not thinking of the defeat we had suffered because of him [*sic*] – hastened like knights to help on the 18th; whom we led to Paris, because without us he would not have come so quickly, who was spared a second battle by our quick pursuit, because we forced the enemy to disintegrate and no Briton has had to fight since the 18th. These many services are repaid by this man with the most despicable ingratitude.[17]

Such bile was demeaning, perhaps despicable, and unfortunately it was Gneisenau.

Whether Alexander had to speak to Frederick William on the problems within the Prussian army we do not know. But Gneisenau was first awarded the Black Eagle he so coveted and moved to the Rhineland, then swiftly posted to the distant VIII Corps command in eastern Prussia, from which he resigned not long after, ostensibly on grounds of health. Blücher was idolised throughout Prussia, and loaded with honours, but he was ageing and tired; he rested for a while in Normandy but soon returned to his wife and estates to spend his final years in quiet. Clearly there was 'a military party', but if there really was 'a military conspiracy' it failed on this occasion to affect Prussian policy.

Before we deal with the political settlement, it may be as well to run a little ahead here, to round off the Allied military arrangements for the Occupation. By the autumn the strength and composition of the 150,000-man Army of Occupation had been agreed between the powers, and their respective stations in France. Wellington was to be Commander-in-Chief. Müffling gave up the governorship of Paris to serve as Prussian representative at headquarters under the Duke. Once the formal treaty of peace was signed in November 1815 the contingents moved to their future quarters; the Austrians along the Alsatian stretch of the Rhine, the Württembergers and Bavarians from Wissembourg to Bitche in Lorraine, the Prussians from there to Sedan and Mézières, the Russians in the Ardennes and in the towns west to Maubeuge and Landrecies, and such of Wellington's former contingents as were to remain in France held from there westward to the coast, with Wellington's headquarters at Cambrai.[18] Beyond a demilitarised zone, Paris was swiftly handed back to the royal army. In 1817 the Army of Occupation was reduced by 30,000 men and in 1818 it was repatriated. It was all very efficiently and very wisely arranged. Not all armies of occupation have been so lucky since.

In 1818 during an Allied sovereigns' visit to their armies (where the King of Prussia was accompanied by Knesebeck, Boyen and Müffling – but not by Gneisenau) a new Prussian field marshal was appointed alongside Blücher. This was Wellington.[19] The old wild hussar had greatly aged and died the next year; there was a pause, and finally in 1825 Gneisenau, too, was granted that rank; he died in 1831, guarding the frontier with Russia's province of Poland. The Austrian Schwarzenberg had died in 1820, and the Bavarian Wrede in 1838, by which time Wellington's career had taken him to the top of British politics, and thereby from being an idol he had become a detested figure to many Britons. But wheels continue to turn, he went each day to do the day's work in his austere and solitary way; and in his final silvery years the country placed him in a position only just below that of Queen Victoria and above all her other subjects.[20]

V

There is a footnote to the story of the armies after Waterloo that deserves brief mention. The British public opened a Waterloo Subscription for the widows, orphans and relatives of those killed, wounded and disabled, a 'British' fund being for the Duke's army and a 'Foreign' fund intended for Blücher's and other Allied contingents. By early 1816 it was estimated that a sum of around £500,000 had been raised through appeals to individuals, and from church and parish collections. To put this voluntary contribution in perspective, that voluntary gift equated to about 4 per cent of the total income tax levied and was of course additional to the compulsory levy. Most of the subscription was for the British fund, but nearly 10 per cent was given for Foreign relief. More money came from other sources, particularly the community in India which raised over £20,000. When the subscription was wound up in 1817 and its committee needed to decide on the use of the surplus still in its hands, the Duke was applied to. He remarked that the British sufferers had been relieved more generously than a strict *per capita* calculation would have allowed, and that Continental writers were complaining of the selfishness of the British people. To remove any ground for complaint, the entire surplus (£136,492 1*s* 11*d*) should be made over to foreign sufferers (excluding KGL, who were treated as British) for distribution to the casualties in proportion to the figures in the official returns.[21]

VI

Meanwhile, the good intentions of Louis XVIII and his renewed Charter were under threat. He had accepted that it would be wise to retain the great educational and banking institutions established under the Empire, and the Legion of Honour and the Napoleonic nobility, even if he refused to permit the supporters of the Hundred Days to enjoy full parliamentary rights. But during the late summer the interior of France saw the most savage outbursts of hatred and vengeance between those of opposing political, social, and religious views, an outburst that went down in history as 'The White Terror', a savagery against Bonapartists, Republicans, and Protestants, that spread across the south from Lyons to Toulon, to Marseilles, Avignon, Montpellier, Toulouse during a month of massacre. Such cruelty and destruction had not been seen in France since the September massacres of 1792, perhaps since St Bartholomew's Day in 1572, or would be seen again until the Paris Commune of 1871. Judged against this terrible outbreak of mass blood-letting, the royal ordinance of 24 July that Louis XVIII issued, naming those who should not benefit from the amnesty promised at Cambrai, was so tiny a list as to be almost invisible. The list could hardly have been shorter, given what these men (and not a few others) had done. Eighteen generals and officers were declared guilty of treason against Louis XVIII before 23 March 1815 and of armed rebellion. They included Ney, La Bédoyère, the two Lallemand brothers, Lavalette, d'Erlon, Lefebvre-Desnouettes, Bertrand, Drouot, Cambronne, Savary, Clausel, and six others. We know that the new government connived at Ney's escape by providing him with a false passport: they had no wish to find themselves trying him. But they had to show firmness in public, to please their extremists. Marshal Gouvion St Cyr had taken no part in the Hundred Days and was appointed War Minister on 8 July, but on 31 July he wrote to Macdonald, Davout's successor commanding the army, that those on the first list should be executed.[22] Of the second list of thirty-eight who were to be examined for further judgement or exile, the most prominent names were those of Soult, Carnot, Allix, Exelmans, Vandamme, Lobau, Lamarque, Piré, Marbot, Maret (Bassano), and the ADCs (whom we saw in the messages muddle at Ligny) Dejean and Forbin-Janson.[23]

Talleyrand sarcastically remarked that Fouché had been thorough enough, for he had taken care not to omit from the list even one of his own friends. Pasquier tells a story that sheds a curious light on this matter: he says that Fouché produced an enormous list to ensure that everyone would condemn it as excessive, so that the eventual list was very short. Pasquier also noted that, except for Lavalette, all of those mentioned were at the time 'far from the reach of justice and some were absolutely beyond its reach'.[24] All who wished for passports had received them and even money, often from Fouché himself, and there was no haste in the visits and searches for the wanted men. La Bédoyère indeed returned to Paris, despite warnings, was recognised on the coach, was arrested, tried and condemned. He was shot on 19 August. Ney was advised to leave the country, did nothing, and was eventually arrested and tried, and found guilty of treason. This was unsurprising, given Ney's behaviour in the spring, and given the terms of the Cambrai proclamation. Attempts were made to stretch the meaning of the 3 July military convention for the surrender of Paris by the French army to extend to matters that concerned only the internal governance of France. They were unavailing.

National elections had been held in the second half of August, and the results gave the royalists and ultras even more power. The moderate Louis had hoped for a moderate Chamber; he was saddled with one that he termed '*introuvable*'. For the next few months the royalists were beyond control and beyond reason, inflicting deep wounds on the social fabric. Fouché feared a civil war, and leaked his views to the world, for which breach of protocol Talleyrand promptly secured his dismissal: Louis had never wanted Fouché as a minister, and he sent him out of the country as ambassador to Saxony.

But Talleyrand had no intention of remaining as the minister saddled with responsibility for the terms of peace, and he was aware of the particular difficulty arising from Allied demands for the return of the looted art treasures to their former owners. This matter aroused the utmost fury among the French, yet it had to be settled on Allied terms. The Allies were agreed on that matter, but were bitterly divided over territorial questions and the war indemnity. The full story of the multiple exchanges of views, the angry denunciations, and the lamentations over restitution, land cession, and finance, is not an elevating one, and may be left to one side. It matters only that they were eventually concluded.

In the result the French were unable to stop the Allies taking back the art treasures in September, although their seizure by French armies had been forgiven on the earlier occasion. Had the Hundred Days not occurred, the treasures would have stayed in France's possession by the settlement of May 1814. It was not the Allies who had brought about a changed situation, but the restitution took place in the face of total French opposition.

The negotiations over territorial changes were conducted by the French with great pertinacity. By now the French ministry was no longer under Talleyrand. His attitude had become one of total opposition to all the Allied proposals, and he resigned as chief minister on 22 September. His stance had been deliberate and his resignation absolved him from any blame in the peace that would have to be signed. His successor, the duc de Richelieu, had been long absent from France, an *émigré* who had served his close friend the Tsar for the past quarter-century as governor of Odessa. When asked about his suitability, Talleyrand replied, 'He is the Frenchman who knows most about the Crimea.' It was true; he was almost unknown to the French, which was certainly a difficulty – but he had one great advantage. Whereas the venal and immoral Talleyrand was detested by the Tsar, Richelieu's character was fine, and he was admired by Alexander, who was thus perhaps more amenable to argument than one would have expected. That mysterious element of personal chemistry proved of great value for France – since it fell to Richelieu to agree the final terms and to sign the second Peace of Paris on 20 November 1815.

VII

The northern frontier of France was pushed south a few miles in the area east of Condé, but for some 15 miles in the zone south of Charleroi so that the little towns of Beaumont, Philippeville, Mariembourg, and Chimay, that had featured so prominently at the start of Napoleon's last campaign, passed to the King of the Netherlands. Givet, however, remained French, though with less land on either flank. Saarlouis and Saarbrücken became German, as did Landau. In the Jura, Fort Joux was ceded to the Swiss, and the neutral zone first established in 1814 immediately south of Lac Leman was maintained as neutral (the Chablais and the valley west of Mont Blanc). The King of Piedmont/Sardinia was allowed to add the western sector of Savoy (Annecy, Lac du Bourget, Chambéry) to his existing Savoyard possessions. In total, Napoleon's final adventure cost France no more than '395 square leagues' (say 2,470 square miles) of territory.[25] The French fort of Huningen on the Rhine near Basle was to be razed. There should be a military occupation of the frontier zones of northern France for a minimum three and a maximum five years by a force not exceeding 150,000 men. A war indemnity of 700 million francs would be paid by instalments over five years, and the costs of the army of occupation for three years was to be at the charge of the French government. A committee of ministers of the four powers should sit in Paris and receive daily reports from Louis's government on the situation inside France.[26]

Such were the penalties inflicted on a suffering France by the powers of Europe. France was once more back to the frontier of 1790, but with the enclaves retained, and still larger than the France of 1789. It might easily have been much worse. Yet for at least a generation after Waterloo many Frenchmen dreamt of overturning this peace and restoring France to a more prominent place in Europe. Perhaps that was understandable. But a France neither too weak nor too strong was better for it, and for Europe, than the Napoleonic dream. Since 1792 France had effected great changes to European frontiers, accumulated vast quantities of looted treasures, and had been paid enormous war indemnities by the defeated, all as the result of conquest and imposed peace treaties. The measures had been draconian, and unmindful of the views of the defeated.

There was a second treaty signed in Paris on 20 November 1815, and it was between the four Allied powers. It renewed the treaties of Chaumont of 1814 and of 25 March 1815, and it set up a system of regular and periodic European congresses to preserve the peace and protect the settlement of 1815. It was complicated by the Tsar's surprise announcement in September of a

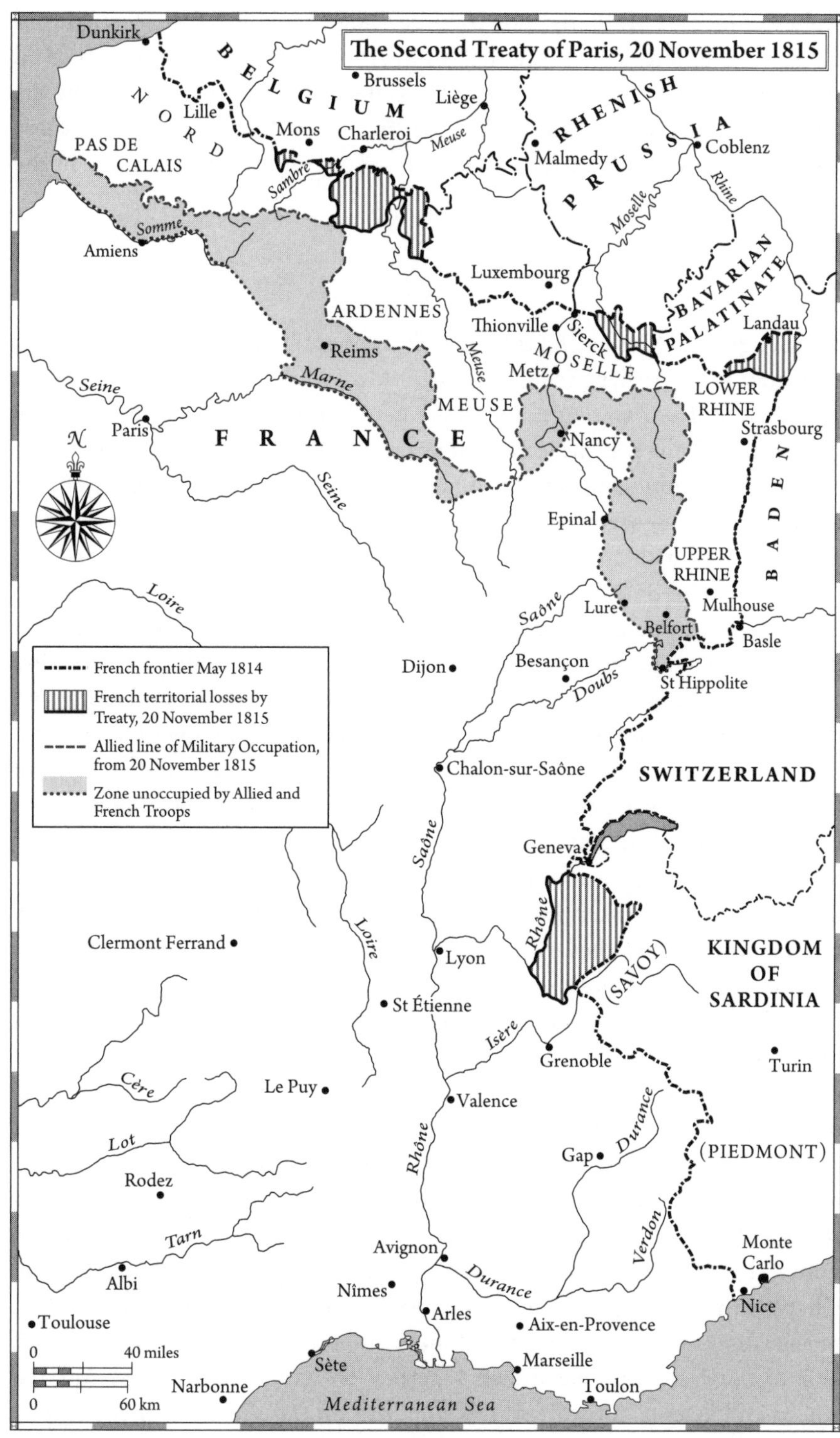
The Second Treaty of Paris, 20 November 1815
Dunkirk
BELGIUM
Brussels
Liège
NORD
Lille
Mons
Charleroi
PAS DE CALAIS
Sambre
Meuse
RHENISH PRUSSIA
Malmedy
Coblenz
Rhine
Moselle
Somme
Amiens
Luxembourg
BAVARIAN PALATINATE
ARDENNES
Thionville
Sierck
Landau
Reims
MOSELLE
Metz
Marne
Meuse
LOWER RHINE
Seine
Paris
MEUSE
FRANCE
Nancy
Strasbourg
Seine
Epinal
BADEN
UPPER RHINE
Loire
Saône
Lure
Mulhouse
Belfort
Basle
Dijon
Besançon
Doubs
St Hippolite
French frontier May 1814
French territorial losses by Treaty, 20 November 1815
Allied line of Military Occupation, from 20 November 1815
Zone unoccupied by Allied and French Troops
Chalon-sur-Saône
SWITZERLAND
Saône
Geneva
Loire
Rhône
Clermont Ferrand
Lyon
(SAVOY)
KINGDOM OF SARDINIA
St Étienne
Isère
Grenoble
Turin
Cère
Le Puy
Valence
Lot
Rhône
Gap
Durance
(PIEDMONT)
Rodez
Tarn
Verdon
Avignon
Monte Carlo
Albi
Durance
Nîmes
Nice
Arles
Toulouse
Aix-en-Provence
0
40 miles
Sète
Marseille
0
60 km
Narbonne
Toulon
Mediterranean Sea

Holy Alliance of brotherly monarchs seeking the good of their peoples in 'a universal union', something that all his royal colleagues secretly disliked and that ran flat counter to the state system that had emerged from the settlements of 1814 and 1815.[27] Reconciling (or failing to reconcile) these contradictory stage directions was to preoccupy European statesmen in the next act of the continent's story.

VIII

The Congress of Vienna and the Paris Treaties of 1814 and 1815 established for a generation, or perhaps even two generations, what their participants called 'a just equilibrium' so that no one state could destroy the European balance of power. In doing this the leaders of 1815 minimised or ignored certain forces that the Revolution and Napoleon had stimulated; so that viewed from, say, the year 1900, they seemed working against the tide of history.[28] But they were not concerned with creating a Europe suitable for their great-grandchildren; they were intent on effacing the damage that they considered had been done to the European fabric by a quarter century of aggressive war by the most populous and cohesive nation in Europe: they sought safety for themselves and their children against any Napoleonic resurgence. They could remember the world of the *ancien régime*, and they had seen the subsequent bloodbath. But their children had been born into a world of new ideas and changes in society that saw new pathways opening: of new sciences and techniques, the music of Beethoven and the poetry of Byron, the Romantic movement.[29] So the foundations were shifting from under the statesmen of 1815, and yet, despite several mistakes and misjudgements, some quite serious, to a very considerable degree they succeeded in averting and postponing for half a century any general European war.

And for a time, but with diminishing success, for seven years the system of 1815 was preserved as the 'Congress System', designed to settle all matters of importance for the European world by regular conference of the great powers and their satellites. That presupposed a community of interests, but the kernel of the system was the Tsar's mystical concept of a 'Holy Alliance' in which no one but him believed. The strains soon showed, but until at least 1818 the differences were containable. A welcome was extended to Bourbon France, by 1818 free of the Allied army of occupation and admitted at Aix-la-Chapelle to the Congress system. But by 1820 Metternich's repressive policies, serious discontent in Germany, and the murder in France of the duc de Berri, heir to the Dauphin, had drawn together 'the three autocracies', Austria, Russia and Prussia, into all-out reaction; Britain was driven to oppose them.

Castlereagh, the animator of the alliance in 1814, set out his opposition in his great state paper of May 1820; and he was supported by France at the Troppau Congress of 1820. The split grew. By the time of the next Congress, at Verona in 1822, where Wellington represented Britain, the 'Congress system' was doomed. Despite the occasional Congress – Paris in 1856, Berlin in 1878 – the old balance of power thenceforth had to serve for guidance. How did Europe and post-Napoleonic France rub along in such circumstances?

In the east and north-east Russia established itself more firmly in Finland and Poland, and Sweden finally ceased to be a factor in European politics. As the Swedish factor disappeared, so the future of the once aggressive but now somnolent Ottoman Empire in the south-east, for centuries so terrifying to its Christian neighbours, became a matter of growing if veiled contention. Its decline and possible extinction created tensions between Russia, Austria, France and Britain; disputes over the lands of the Balkans, the straits into the Mediterranean, the Christian communities, all would lead to crisis and conflict as the century wore on.

In central and western Europe the Holy Roman Empire or First Reich was not resurrected, despite the Pope's plea. And although Austria, in token of past history, was left president of the new Germanic Confederation, its main concerns were with lands outside Germany. Germany was now under the influence of a much-enlarged Prussia. The once great Saxony, so important to the Reformation, had sunk into insignificance; and the two principal counter-balances to Prussia were Hanover, in which Britain took only passing interest, and Bavaria, whose friendship towards France and dislike of Prussia were not quite sufficient to impede the march to ascendancy of the frugal, hard-working, and disciplined Prussians. Though Austria still got much of its way in Germany until around 1850, Prussia could not be stopped, and with the Seven Weeks' War of 1866 Prussia expelled the Habsburgs from German affairs. Within five years the kingdoms and principalities in Germany had accepted Prussian dominance in the new German Empire or Second Reich.

The sprawling assemblage of polyglot tribes that belonged to the Austrian Empire gradually woke to a sense of 'nationality'. A 'dynastic' policy' could offer no solution to this. The problem that Metternich and his successors faced was identified by the poet Grillparzer (b. 1791): 'It is the curse of our proud dynasty / To move half-heartedly, stop half-way and / Adopt half-measures hesitatingly'. Thus Prussia drove them from Germany. Austria dominated Italy, either directly as in the north, or through dynastic arrangements in the centre and south; but the House of Savoy, ruling Savoy, Piedmont, Sardinia and Genoa, and newly strengthened so as to bar France from Italy, was henceforth more intent on a challenge eastwards, to displace Austria in Lombardy and the Po valley. Austria-Hungary (as it became after 1848, with the Hungarian partner never happily in tandem with Habsburg Austria) would not give way without a fight, indeed several fights. When it was finally ejected from Venetia in 1866 as a side effect of its defeat by Prussia, it not only left a malformed Italy to the cares of the House of Savoy, but it redirected its own energies to the Balkans where sectional dreams were incompatible with either Habsburg dynastic ambitions, Hungarian supremacism, or Russian interests.

The Dutch–Belgian enforced union quickly failed, and broke apart after only fifteen years. The resultant armed struggle between them might have led to general war, for Prussia and France both interfered in the struggle and hampered the negotiations towards a settlement (indeed they both actively worked against the actual 1839 Belgian settlement until 1867 and even later), while Britain desperately sought to keep the Great Powers out of the cockpit of Europe and away from the coast facing Britain. There would remain a shadow from these Belgian events, as long and dark, perhaps, as that from Russian and Austrian rivalries over the nationalist Balkans and feuding Slav peoples.

Could Bourbon France – if helped by their southern cousins the Borbons in Naples and Sicily and in Spain – be deemed no longer capable of upsetting the European balance?

A resurgent France was not totally dissuaded from foreign adventures. The impossible Borbon monarchy of Spain was at war with the impossible Cortes, and while no power could accept that a Russian army should march there to restore order, most of them, save for Britain, agreed that a French Bourbon army should go in. Just ten years after Napoleon's armies had been driven out, this Bourbon army, quite amazingly, was acclaimed everywhere, down to distant Cadiz. Four years later a French army was involved in the Morea where Greeks were fighting against Turkish rule, while Codrington's British fleet dominated the sea. Perhaps it was just as well that France was soon to embark on its Algerian adventure – led by that same Bourmont who played such strange games in March, and June, and November in 1815 – an Algerian conquest that for several generations kept France well employed. The fall of the Bourbons in 1830 and the coming of the Orléans dynasty under Louis Philippe, brought to prominence once more names like Marmont, Benjamin Constant, La Fayette, and then Soult, in a last manifestation of old times. France, despite some scruples by Louis Philippe, actively worked to maintain a hold over Borbon Spain, and indeed considered France's rights over the future of the Spanish monarchy so special that they were to have distant consequences in 1870. Moreover it was under Orléanist ministers like the fiery little Thiers that relations between the powers and France worsened so much that war with Britain or with Prussia seemed possible as the 1830s ended.[30]

Yet despite Louis Philippe's skill in tranquilising France, Bonapartism was not dead, and when Queen Hortense's son Louis Napoleon, grandson of Josephine and nephew of the great Emperor, came to power in the 1848 revolution, Europe had cause to ask, what next? The Second Empire, an ominous title, quickly followed, but it was a mere pallid shadow of the First. And the mystery of the stagnant French birth-rate in a Europe where population growth was extraordinarily rapid by historical standards, was robbing France of its old pre-eminence. The Second Empire did involve, sooner or later, a French army at war in the Crimea against Russia, at war in northern Italy against Austria, at war in Mexico against Mexicans, but all these were limited wars, designed in part to please French domestic opinion. Sometimes the plan worked because the enemy was not prepared to fight *à outrance*; sometimes not, for Napoleon III often blanched at the bloody cost of adventures resulting from his own decisions. Thus when it came to changing the European balance, or stopping others from changing it, the Bonapartism of the mid-century could not match the realism and determination of Bismarck and the quality and skills of Krupp and the Elder Moltke. The lesson of 1870 was decisive. The Europe of the 1815 settlements had gone for ever, just as Bonapartism soon went for ever. The age of *Weltpolitik* and imperialism, based upon technology, steel, chemicals, smokeless powder, telegraph, mass communication, burgeoning birth-rates, was opening and would lead to 1914.

That is what, in the long term, would befall Europe. But we must not get ahead of ourselves. The 1815 settlement did, as Wellington had hoped, give Europe a general peace for another forty years, until new developments and new forces brought about change in the mid-nineteenth century. Even after that, only in the twentieth century did the strains lead to a world war. It was not a bad achievement.

So let us come back to the problems that peacemakers faced in the summer and autumn of 1815. The best short evaluation known to me of the settlement at the end of the Napoleonic wars was by that fine historian of the Dutch people who, mindful of his small nation's fate within the great Napoleonic Empire was yet an admirer of French civilisation and the gifts French historians brought to their subject. Writing in the much darker 1940s and after far more terrible wars, Pieter Geyl concluded:

> When one considers what France had brought upon the world for nearly a generation, and once again [in 1815] after her first defeat, it must be agreed that she was treated very gently and that the allies did indeed stick to their distinction between France and the disturber of the peace to whom she had entrusted herself.[31]

Chapter 52

Retrospect

I

THE ERA OF FRENCH DOMINANCE over western and central Europe that began with Cardinal Richelieu, and was the motif of Louis XIV's reign, reached its brief apogee under the impulsion of Napoleon's restless genius. But Napoleon would not content himself with the Low Countries, Switzerland, Germany and Italy, Portugal and the less amenable Spain. He sought to browbeat Russia. He also sought the subjugation of Britain and the destruction of its empire, and his policy of economic warfare against the island kingdom led by degrees to covert resistance and defiance of his economic policy all across Europe and to outright war with Russia. Nor was that all. His intentions towards the Ottoman Empire and Persia and India were no secret: there would be no end to the path of conquest.

Hence, for all these reasons, the great European coalition of sovereigns and peoples turned against France after the Russian disaster of 1812. But the coalition's leaders might well have been content with a negotiated peace in 1813 that left France in possession of its 'natural frontiers', if only Napoleon had been ready to treat. Instead, he conceded too little and too late and always – as the Allies eventually knew from intercepts – with an intention to disregard signed undertakings, should success return to his cause.

So in 1814 the problem was what to do with a defeated Napoleon. If he was not to be imprisoned, then he must be left too weak to cause further trouble, and the Tsar's offer of the sovereignty of Elba (or other islands in the Mediterranean) seemed to meet that requirement.

The victorious Allies were reasonably gentle with France,[1] but they soon fell out over the settlement of Europe and seemed irretrievably divided amongst themselves, almost to the point of war. The crisis of December 1814 passed, but if Talleyrand was right in seeing that the once solid anti-French coalition had split, so Napoleon was equally aware of what that could mean for his own secret hopes. To the Allies, the one cloud in the sky now seemed to be over Italy alone, where the traditional dynastic rivalries of Bourbon and Habsburg were active again. Those rivalries impinged on and threatened King Joachim Murat of Naples, husband to one of Napoleon's sisters. That should in itself have alerted the powers to the danger of leaving Murat's brother-in-law in Elba, but only Talleyrand seems to have urged and looked to his removal. The other powers treated Napoleon as politically dead, and judged the failure of France to honour its obligations to Napoleon under the Treaty of Fontainebleau as a real but minor nuisance, but one concerning France alone. This blindness to the danger of Napoleon at Elba is extraordinary.

Let it be granted that the Austrian insistence that Napoleon should never be reunited with his wife and child was a terrible action. And let us grant that the government of the restored Bourbon Louis XVIII made a series of disastrous mistakes that unsettled large numbers of Frenchmen, and that the French people who in the spring of 1814 had wished only for peace, were dismissive of the peace by that same autumn. It is true that the dishonouring of the Fontainebleau treaty gave Napoleon legitimate cause for protest, and so helped him claim that he was now free to protect his former rights. Yet the fundamental fact was that Napoleon by character and attainments was too great to be content with less than the throne of France.

In escaping Elba Napoleon claimed to be responding to calls from the French people and that he had 'come among you to reclaim my rights, which are also yours ... To you alone and to the brave army, I dedicate and will always dedicate the glory of everything I do.' But the reality was, as he found, that beyond the immediate circle of enthusiastic Bonapartists, there was visible an apathetic country. Foreign war and the re-imposition of the hated conscription were no part of any popular programme. Napoleon recognised this apathy, for as he said on reaching the Tuileries, 'they have let me come, as they let those people go'. Moreover, where apathy was not apparent there could be seen and heard some dangerous old Jacobinical sentiments: a cry for Revolutionary change, threatening internal stability.

But whereas *Le Grand Empire* could and did summarily suppress opposition, the returned Emperor had to negotiate his way among the distrustful factions, to present himself by the Acte Additionnel as a reformed constitutional ruler reliant on the people, and to temporise with leaders who were in reality dubious or hostile to his intentions and fearful of what renewed war would bring upon France.

Napoleon knew that several provinces were either in outright revolt or ready to rise against him, and he was conscious that Paris in 1815 was less surely under his control. His diplomatic *démarches* towards the Alliance failed, and he faced war again. He still hoped that a great victory in the field would enable him at home 'to send those gentry packing' and he turned his titanic efforts through the spring and early summer of 1815 to driving forward the armaments programme and the raising of new armies. But he had for years driven France very hard, and France was so disillusioned and drained that it could be driven little further.

So, provided the Allied sovereigns kept their nerve and held to the belief that the greatest threat to their countries lay in Napoleon's continuance in power, then in the long run they would attain what their 13 March Declaration and subsequent Treaty of 25 March had laid down as essential. They would remove 'the enemy and disturber of the peace of the world' and contain French power. Weight of numbers must tell in the end, and in the meantime, against generals of the calibre of Wellington and Blücher, any French success would come at a crippling cost.

II

Of course, the question arises: would the Allied sovereigns really have kept their nerve and held to their belief, if the Allied defeat at Ligny had been followed by a second defeat at Waterloo? Might they have sought to cut their losses and seek a compromise with the victorious Napoleon?

Here everyone must make his own judgement, but I believe neither the British government nor Tsar Alexander would have broken off the struggle. The mood of Parliament as it had developed through the spring and summer indicated a deep determination 'to finish the job', and although the shock of the hero Duke being defeated in battle would have been great, the experience of the past quarter century showed that with British maritime supremacy beyond challenge, with the continued return from America of the old Peninsular regiments, Britain could continue the fight, and finance the coalition. Napoleon's hope that a single great French victory over Wellington would break the City and the banking system and overthrow Lord Liverpool's government, seems altogether too sanguine. The dogged determination of the gentry and the blinkered insularity of the lower orders would, I think, have stimulated an early version of the Dunkirk spirit of 1940, rather than a wish to give in.

But a Wellingtonian defeat, even if made less humiliating by a subsequent victory, would have reduced very considerably the prestige and influence of Britain's ministers and generals in the peace talks and treaties.[2] The continued payment of subsidies to the Allies would not have offset this.

As to Alexander of Russia, he had promoted himself as the one outstanding person in the contest with Napoleon and in deciding on the future of France. He and Napoleon had shared out Europe in 1807, but after the experience and sufferings of 1812 he was no longer willing to recognise Napoleon's status among monarchs. In April 1814 Alexander been dissuaded from pursuing his first line of thoughts on France, but he had been responsible for placing Napoleon on Elba. Now he would be much harder to dissuade. With his hundreds of thousands of troops pressing forward across the Rhine, he would complete what had been only partly done in March 1814. He would accept neither Napoleon, nor Francis of Austria as controlling the Continent's destinies (he could ignore Frederick William of Prussia in this context), and with Britain chastened by a Wellingtonian defeat, he could indeed become the arbiter of Europe. What actually passed after victory at Waterloo in the summer and autumn of 1815 when Alexander had to *share* the laurels, surely makes good such a hypothesis.

What the map of Europe might then have looked like, how France would have fared, must remain questions to which no answer can be given.

III

Thus we come back to the brutal arithmetic of massed armies, backed by large financial subsidies. Sheer weight of numbers would ultimately tell. Napoleon could field one army, full of fiercely loyal veterans, but it was the last army of the Empire and far from well equipped; moreover, as the July situation in Paris was to show, the pay of the troops was three months in arrears – the treasury was empty. The army was a wasting asset, and there was nothing behind. That is why Fouché's remark was so apposite in summing up the extraordinary gamble of the Hundred Days. It went to the very heart of the matter. On 3 May 1815 he told Pasquier that Napoleon:

> will be obliged to leave for the army before the month end. Once he has left we shall be masters of the ground. I wish him to win one or two battles, but he will lose the third; and then our role will commence. Believe me, we shall bring about a good dénouement.[3]

It would require French leaders of extraordinary realism, whose judgement had not been overwhelmed by the Emperor's sheer brilliance into dreaming his dream, if a successful case was to be made for France as a nation worthy of continuing in a high place among the states of Europe. And so, in the strange nature of things, two of Napoleon's least trustworthy servants or former servants, Fouché and Talleyrand, men of deceit and unsavoury character but of singular judgement, came to play their great parts in saving France from savage punishment. Talleyrand in Vienna and Fouché in Paris set out in their equivocal ways, and largely succeeded, in turning away wrath from their country.

IV

The options that Napoleon set out in his memoir of 1815 indicate fairly clearly that whether he stood on the defensive or chose to attack, the chances of ultimate success were poor. A pure defensive would surrender all advantage to the Allies, and the assembly of additional French forces during the summer would be hampered by inadequate production of weapons and equipment, and by the growing dearth of funds. As for an all-out French offensive, if the Allies kept their heads, remained in contact with each other and played for time, they could hope to ride the blows that Napoleon could strike, and, having worn his numbers down, could swing the action against him decisively, while further Allied contingents threatened his flank. What Napoleon does not seem to have considered was a repetition of his campaign of early 1814, striking at any Allied advance and attacking operationally while remaining on the strategic defensive: the option that Wellington thought he should have pursued. But none of the choices open to Napoleon could overcome the disadvantage of disparity of scale between the two sides' front-line forces, nor the inequality of the opposing sides' reserves.

The prospects for the campaign were therefore unpromising for Napoleon, whichever option he took. But he might improve his chances if he was granted time enough and could thereby snatch the initiative, conceal his intentions as to the sector for attack, and concentrate suddenly on the decisive point. It is worth repeating for one last time what this could mean. General Sir David Fraser has summarised what losing the initiative can entail:

> To await the enemy's attack, to place troops in a purely reactive situation, to surrender the initiative is always to face a difficult task. It can lead to defeat – even defeat by numerically smaller forces, provided they are well trained and led with zest and energy.[4]

But there are limits, even so. Striking first could gain a day, perhaps two, while the defenders gradually reacted; Napoleon might indeed, in Fouché's words, 'win one or two battles', but if the enemy was not so badly defeated that he could not recover, if Napoleon could not in that time advance far enough to gain the key to the defence (Brussels certainly, but also Antwerp) and ensure the permanent separation of the Allies, he might well 'lose the third battle', in the grim knowledge that he would find too few fresh trained troops with which to continue.

Blücher and Wellington were impatient to advance into France. It was Schwarzenberg's Supreme Headquarters at Heidelberg that imposed delay upon delay, even until the day of 10 June 1815. It is entirely possible that a joint Anglo-Prussian advance from Belgium, aiming at two not greatly separated objectives on the road to the Aisne, could have begun at the start of June, and placed Napoleon 'in a purely reactive situation, surrendering the initiative, facing a difficult task that could lead to defeat against superior numbers' if the enemy was led with 'zest and energy', to adapt Sir David Fraser.

Let me repeat this fundamental point. The sovereigns and Schwarzenberg were the men who, in the result, let Napoleon take the initiative. Otherwise the initiative would have lain with Blücher and Wellington. Any decisive battle would have taken place eighty to a hundred miles inside France.

The 'ifs' of history can with caution be allowed a place in debate, but they should not supplant historical facts. And the facts were that Napoleon did snatch the initiative, and despite clear warnings Blücher and Wellington were surprised. So, in reflecting on the campaign it is best to begin with the French and only then turn to review the successes and setbacks of the Allies.

V

The concentration of the *Armée du Nord* did not go smoothly, and a whole day was lost due to some extraordinarily muddled orders, and the first day was therefore not on 14 June.[5] And yet still the Allies were not ready. June 15th, the actual first day, went passably well for the French, but the *Armée*'s slips and delays cannot be ascribed purely to the inherent 'frictions' of war: the troops played their parts better than did the senior officers. Disastrous orders seriously upset the arrangements for a three-pronged advance, and made the central force dreadfully unwieldy. D'Erlon on the left wing was unenterprising, and Reille perhaps too unwilling to take chances at the bridges over the Sambre. In the centre Vandamme showed deplorable mulishness, while on the right Bourmont played so foul a trick that the morale of that over-marched wing must have been badly affected. It was the cavalryman Grouchy, caught out by Soult's failure to issue timely orders, who nonetheless did what was called for, as did his cavalry subordinates.

It is hard to see why Napoleon judged that Soult would make a good chief of staff. Nothing in his earlier career marked him out for this, gifted strategist though he was. Moreover, after his plottings and his long misrule in Spain, and his role as a Bourbon war minister, the army distrusted him.

However, the Emperor chose to ignore these defects, or maybe judged that there was insufficient time to replace him – if indeed he thought there was anyone better. But then Napoleon surely should have brought him up short and kept him on a tight leash. This did not happen. Perhaps Napoleon's staccato abruptness and switches of thought made interpreting his words difficult. But Soult neither buckled to nor improved; he proved himself just as incompetent when intense fighting made vital clear thinking, efficient drafting, and expedition in despatch of orders. Leaving aside the terrible muddles over orders on 16 and 18 June, treated at length in chapters 20 to 45, there are two smaller but still significant instances from the quiet day of 17 June: first, Soult had forgotten to keep Ney informed of events at Ligny, and in a misdated letter had to start with some evasive excuses before dressing down his old enemy Ney for mistakes at Quatre Bras; secondly, he gave orders for troop movements that Davout could not understand so that the latter had to despatch an officer to put matters right.[6]

Intending that there should be two semi-independent wings, with himself controlling the central reserve, Napoleon needed utterly reliable commanders, but instead of Davout or Suchet, he selected the relatively untried Grouchy for one wing. Davout and Suchet, both excellent practitioners of battle, were marooned in Paris and Lyons. Might not Grouchy have been a sensible choice for the south where he had won recent fame, with Suchet then coming to command one of the wings of the *Armée du Nord*? Davout would be invaluable *if* Paris came under threat, but that would be the result of a *defeat*, and Davout with the *Armée* might give that lift and determination that could bring *victory*. Which task should have priority?

The name Grouchy immediately brings us to a central problem for the *Armée*. The choice and control of the highest posts lay with the Emperor himself. True, he no longer had the array of talented officers of past years. Too many were dead or refused to rejoin him in 1815, but those who did rally to him, thereby placing their necks in peril, were not put in the best posts or actively disliked each other. Grouchy was his choice. Grouchy did well on the first and second days, and yet after 16 June Napoleon sent him off on a distant mission without clear and consistent and timely orders. Moreover, from the very beginning Grouchy's subordinates, the capable but mutinously minded Vandamme and the ambitious Gérard, were chafing at being commanded by him, and Napoleon did nothing to knock heads together and ensure that the marshal was strictly to be obeyed.

And then there was Ney.

Despite the Emperor's fine promises at Auxerre, Ney was dumped outside the charmed circle for the next two months, even left in rustication; and the call when it belatedly came was not directly from Napoleon, but through Davout. When Ney reached the front in the afternoon of 15 June he received only the most sketchy of orders, and to this day argument has continued on whether or not he was told to take Quatre Bras that first evening. He had no staff to hand, and formations that appeared to be his to command were suddenly removed or reserved outside his control. His mind on 16 June was plainly in turmoil and his own plans and actions suffered thereby. Lethargy and over-confidence followed one upon the other, and although he was picked out for condemnation by Napoleonic myth, it may be that changes of plan at imperial headquarters, Soult's inactivity, d'Erlon's spinelessness and the caution that Reille (and Ney himself) had learned in Spain when facing Wellington, all contributed to the wasted morning of 16 June. For victory was within grasp at that moment. But the late afternoon snatched diversion of d'Erlon by imperial headquarters would have incensed even a man more balanced than Ney. Blind fury that afternoon and then Ney's renewed inaction on the morning of the 17th should have been warning signs that stress was eating away at the marshal, already suffering a degree of moral confusion since his fatal switch of allegiance in March. This was not the former tough Ney, paladin of *Le Grand Empire*, and Napoleon would have been wise to watch and supervise his angry and directionless old comrade as they prepared for Waterloo, not to leave him so much to his own devices.

Much – perhaps rather too much – has been said about Napoleon's state of health in 1815. Twenty years' hard campaigning, constant travel, disease, all these would take a toll of any man, and Napoleon was not immune. The still limited knowledge among the medical profession and its primitive remedies could not be relied upon to conquer bodily weakness. But his general stamina can be judged by the number of hours he was awake, journeying, and in military command, from the evening of 11 June when he was about to leave Paris to the evening of 16 June when he went to bed after Ligny; and again from the morning of Waterloo to the same hour the next day, by which time he had fought a desperate battle and then ridden in flight overnight a distance of 33 miles in eleven hours.[7] His correspondence also shows the same remarkable intellectual energy and ferment of ideas as in earlier years, but we do know from various witnesses that moods of lethargy, even of apathy, descended on him so plainly that they were evident to all. It may be that this was why Ney was not better counselled and controlled, and why Grouchy was left unguided for so many precious hours. But who shall say?

VI

The problem facing Napoleon was fourfold. He had to win a campaign in the north: (i) against enemies twice his numbers, (ii) against generals who did not fear him and who possessed the confidence of their own men, (iii) within a time-scale of less than a week, because of the probable speed of Anglo-Prussian combination in Belgium and also Allied movement from the middle Rhine, and (iv) over daily distances that were exhausting even without the stress of fighting. Only through a total mutual confidence and clear understanding between Napoleon (supported by Soult's staffwork), Ney and Grouchy could the plan have a chance of succeeding. The weaknesses in command and control, and in communications, of the French army threw an additional burden on its splendid and loyal troops. In working for a master who could contemplate calmly 'losing a million men', the rank and file were set a timetable that demanded too many miles to be marched every successive day, in blazing summer heat and then downpours, and without provision of food and fodder. They were expected to serve officers many of whom they had come to distrust. And when things were going very badly they were told blatant lies; in such circumstances, without mutual confidence and with trust lost, '*Nous sommes trahis*' and '*Sauve qui peut*' could swiftly replace '*Vive l'Empereur!*'

The Emperor's plan began well enough on 15 June, but he painted a false picture for himself on the 16th of what the '40,000' Prussians might do north of Fleurus. So he let time slip. The discovery of something of the truth as to Blücher's strength and intentions led to a recasting of French plans and an afternoon battle of attrition at Ligny that had too few hours of daylight to offer overwhelming victory. Quatre Bras might meanwhile have been a morning's victory. Ney bore much responsibility here, for Napoleon's orders for the day were generally plain enough and the long-term objective crystal clear. But by the time of the crux of Ligny–Quatre Bras the morning's errors and omissions were too many to be put right satisfactorily, as Foy recognised. Numbers, time, and distance were facts that no imaginings could change. The expectations of imperial headquarters of what Ney might achieve against the Prussian wing were no longer realistic, while the d'Erlon fiasco made plain that by afternoon French numbers were insufficient on either one or the other front to ensure overwhelming victory. Moreover, when the 'unidentified force' appeared, roughly from the direction from which d'Erlon was expected, the standstill imposed on the main battle by Napoleon is hard to explain: investigation of the mystery force seems to have been far too belated. And so Ligny ended with dusk falling, not on an overwhelming success but on a victory on points. In such circumstances a hot pursuit at the earliest possible hour at or before dawn should have been insisted upon, and yet, amazingly, what occurred was a repetition on the 17th of the previous dawn's delays.

The day of 17 June is therefore mainly interesting for the several orders by Soult and Bertrand directing Grouchy in his pursuit, and for the dispersal of force that resulted. It cannot be said that Grouchy performed his tasks with any great skill, but then neither did Ney south of Quatre Bras. The Emperor let time slip, and when later his energy resumed, time was just not sufficient to make up for Ney's inactivity. So another day went by without decision. As to Grouchy, there is such a difference between his performance, on the one hand, while following – or trying to comprehend – Napoleon's orders in the period 17–18 June, and on the other, during the days afterwards when he was free to form his own judgements and decisions, that it raises an intriguing question – that must ever remain unanswered.

VII

Napoleon's plan for the day of 18 June was good and came tantalisingly near to succeeding at several moments. The intention to start at 5 a.m. or 9 a.m. would have granted sufficient time for a decision well before dusk, but that was hampered by three difficulties: the scattered and hungry state of the French army, the difficulty in manhandling the artillery into position, and Napoleon's inability to sense how Wellington had deployed his troops. The first problem was resolved by mid-morning, the second by late morning, but even the planned 11 a.m. start was postponed by the need for further reconnaissance, leading to a last minute recasting of Reille's and d'Erlon's respective roles. Napoleon was intent on using his superiority in artillery and a large part of his available line infantry to achieve breakthrough in the centre. He was fully prepared to fight a murderous pinning-down infantry action on the left at Hougoumont in order to draw Wellington's reserves away from the vital point. In this he succeeded. He never called off the attack (nor did he ever try to explain it away) even though it consumed troops to an extent that he must have regretted later that day. Yet (like Wellington) he paid too little attention to La Haye Sainte farm on the forward slope, behind which lay his objective 'the village of Mont St Jean where are the crossroads'. The farm was a bastion that could and should have been blasted to pieces by his guns, yet was left virtually untouched.

The Grand Battery instead concentrated on the defenders along the crest, and it seemed that d'Erlon's massed infantry force would march itself over the defenders and achieve Napoleon's order to take the crossroads. Major breakthrough, preparatory to victory, was in sight by 2.30 p.m., until

Uxbridge's great cavalry charge and Picton's infantry overset d'Erlon's force and tumbled it into ruin. Now everything had to be thought out afresh.

One intriguing question remains about this phase, for it highlights an early moment when the Allied combined intention began to affect the battle. Had Lobau been kept behind d'Erlon's attack on the northern ridge, might d'Erlon's attack have succeeded, or at least might Lobau have checked the overset? Could Napoleon have discounted the slow Prussian approach from the east and have won the Mont St Jean crest now, in the full afternoon? The Prussian approach from the east was remarkably slow, but in turning Lobau eastwards to face it, the force that Lobau commanded was, in that general's own words, insufficient. We see, therefore, that circumstances demanded more manpower than Napoleon would, or perhaps could, release: there were too few men for too great a concept.

It was Napoleon who released the various formations to Ney for the next phase, the cavalry charges, and he left to Ney the tactical handling of this force. The great Napoleonic heavy cavalry charges of previous campaigns had broken enemy nerve and discipline and so had produced victory. Now the panacea was tried again. But Wellington's infantry did not lose cohesion and Allied artillery proved highly effective against the mounted mass, which failed to break the squares and suffered heavily as it rode round and back down again. But the charges forced Wellington's infantry to wait formed up in squares, and while awaiting the horsemen the squares were torn at by French artillery fire. The French cavalry were steadily shredded, but so were Wellington's squares. How long would attrition take?

French infantry were either too few or too tentative in the attacks on La Haye Sainte, for that key to the centre was taken only at 6 p.m. But intense Prussian pressure was now felt at Plancenoit and Napoleon had to give close attention to that eastern flank; a part of his cherished *Garde* reserve was already engaged there. Again one may ask whether the Emperor should not have called off his attacks before this complication hobbled his freedom to act. He knew Grouchy was too far distant that morning to come to the main army before evening, and he must have realised (even if his memoirs do not admit it) that the message sent at 1 p.m. calling Grouchy back, could not be acted upon by the distant marshal much before nightfall. Could Napoleon have pulled back in mid-afternoon, regrouped and chosen to fight another day? Or would that have roused his enemies in Paris? Did he see disengagement as no longer possible? Or was he merely gambling desperately with the lives of his last army in the face of growing odds?

Napoleon refused for far too long to give Ney the final reserve, most of his precious *Garde*, and left him with no guidance on its employment. It was all too late. And when the *Garde* fell back and the army shuddered and wavered, the lie deliberately circulated that Grouchy was arriving, merely added to the despair once the trick was seen for what it was.

In the French story of 18 June it is the middle-rank commanders, men like Foy, Bauduin, and Cubières, and the nearly forgotten junior commanders and the nameless rank and file, that deserve most honour, men who sacrificed themselves all afternoon in that inferno of fire. Of those who led them at corps and wing level few seem to merit great praise, and some of the bravest tarnished their lustre by quarrels and acts of disobedience, the reverse of Nelson's 'band of brothers': the uninspired Reille, d'Erlon, and Grouchy, and the troublesome and bickering Vandamme and Gérard. Of all the higher commanders, only Lobau and, in his own way, Ney stand out for their intrepid endeavours. How much better it would have been for Ney to have died on the battlefield, in his rightful place of glory. How much better, too, had Napoleon died there close by him.

It was a catastrophic defeat. But such were the French losses in the day that even had Napoleon won on the Mont St Jean slopes that evening of 18 June, his army would have been too shattered to reap much benefit the next day, with the Prussians now on hand and at least part of Wellington's right wing still in being. Brussels was still a long way off, and who could now hope for 'Antwerp by the 21st', the true measure of success?

VIII

So we turn to the Allies. Napoleon's memoirs insisted on the serious limitations in generalship of the Prussian and Anglo-Allied commanders, and the poor record of Wellington for co-operation in an alliance. To emphasise this, in special 'observations' on the campaign he elaborated a list of nine Allied 'mistakes' so gross that French victory became a certainty. The reader has therefore no clue by which to explain the Emperor's total disaster. Such an utterly disastrous outcome can only mean that the premises are false, that it is myth-making, or propaganda.[8]

Neither Blücher nor Wellington was afraid of fighting the Emperor, and although Wellington had never yet fought him, his skills in thrashing every French marshal he had encountered had instilled in all Napoleon's generals a deep sense of their own inferiority, and that should have induced rather more thought than it did in Napoleon's mind. As we saw, the opening of battle on 18 June was delayed in some part because Napoleon only slowly established what the Duke's position was: proof that Reille's warning was not incorrect. And as a battlefield tactician and leader of troops Wellington once again showed himself remarkably capable. Blücher had indeed been defeated by Napoleon in the past, but 'that old devil' was always ready to fight again without delay. If, as we saw at Ligny, his tactical skills did not match his courage or his ability to inspire his troops, these *moral* qualities ensured that Napoleon did not gain the overwhelming victory so necessary to his cause.

Clemenceau's tart observation during the First World War, 'My opinion of Napoleon has sunk since the start of this war: he only had to fight against allies,' could certainly be applied to the year 1815. The interminable delays imposed by the discussions and doubts at Heidelberg and the effect that this had on the two high commands in Belgium need to be remembered in judging Anglo-Allied and Prussian performance. I have already given my reasons why a single high command in Belgium might have caused more trouble than benefit. How unhelpfully Gneisenau might have treated Wellington if the latter had been subordinate to Blücher, and how complainingly or discontentedly Gneisenau would have performed his role if subordinate to Wellington, are questions requiring very little imagination to answer. A duality of command was better, but it did place an extremely high premium on mutual consideration, trust, and efficiency in liaison.

And both Allied generals knew that they had to combine in order to bring the maximum force to bear. That is indeed what they planned, and we have the evidence of the Tirlemont meeting of 3 May and later discussions to prove it. Even Gneisenau's dismissive opinion of Wellington's army: 'If we do not stand arm-in-arm with this army it will be completely useless,' does imply combination. In the result, that is what they achieved, albeit with delays and lapses of communication that complicated their responses. The lapses in communication were unfortunate, but were inherently more likely when no supreme command existed to coordinate, let alone seek to control, two independent powers whose contingents relied on divergent lines of communication. (No such disadvantage could apply to the *Armée du Nord* of course, and yet that army's failures in coordination and communication may be deemed at least as serious as those of the Allies.) Wellington's good sense and patience were remarkable as Gneisenau gradually and hesitantly was brought to consent to a combined strategy: it cannot have been easy for either of them but it was brought about.

Napoleon was not alone in having his attention distracted by domestic discontents and problems. How were the Allies to manage a quarter of a million British, Dutch, minor-German and Prussian troops camped for months on end in Belgium? Certain contingents' civic relations with their hosts, their feeding and the payment for supplies, their actions and their complaints form a sad chapter in the story of the campaign. The phrase 'give and take' acquired almost a new meaning in these months, and the narrowness of view and strength of ill-feeling took up the time and energies of men who had many more important worries to contend with. The Duke's best efforts seem to have had little ameliorating effect. The breakdown of relations between the Dutch and the Prussians was almost total by the end of the waiting period, and violence was in prospect by mid-June that might have complicated matters at the worst possible moment.

Had that been an isolated case it would have been bad enough, but the ill-judged Prussian plans for taking over the Saxon army added to the complications and led to a Saxon mutiny at a dangerous moment. A revolt that forces a commander-in-chief to flee implies bad management somewhere, and at a time early in May when it was feared that Napoleon might attack Belgium, a sizeable part of the Prussian army was caught up in containing the revolt. The support available to Wellington on 4 May judged against the promises at the Tirlemont meeting could have been both smaller and slower than the Duke was led to expect.

Napoleon phrased the commentary in the memoirs as though the Allies planned to stay on the defensive. They intended no such thing, but on the contrary were preparing for an offensive into France along separate lines of advance, by routes relatively close together in Wellington's suggestion, and widely separated in Gneisenau's. Of necessity their armies meanwhile were spread for reasons of subsistence. They would be the ones who would choose where to strike, and Napoleon would be the one to wonder where the blow might fall. And in fact, although Wellington had warned the Prussian ambassador in early June that Napoleon was strengthening daily, once working in combination the two Allies did prove that they were too strong for him. Yet there was an unjustified sense of superiority, plainly visible in the repeated statements of Blücher and Gneisenau and Wellington that the initiative lay with the Allies, that any danger was 'fast disappearing', and that 'we are too strong' for Napoleon. They failed to account for 'the unlikely' and they paid for it. They were not short of warnings, and if some of these seemed to contradict each other yet a trend soon became clear and was accurately reported.[9]

IX

By June the Prussians had resolved their Saxon embarrassments and were confidently looking forward to battle. The Duke's army was receiving successive reinforcements from the German states and of British troops returning from America, but only a week before the opening of the campaign Gneisenau judged the value of Wellington's forces as 'completely useless' unless upheld by Prussian support, remarks that foresee combination but show that he saw the Prussian role as predominant. The Duke shared this idea of combination, considering that Blücher and he himself together were 'too strong' for Napoleon. But their dispositions were not similar, and in the Prussian case unwise.

The dispositions of Wellington's army were so arranged that the enemy would need at least one day's march before closing with it, and that would allow time for the defence to concentrate at the threatened point. That was why the Duke was able to say to van Reede on 15 June regarding any enemy attack that he would remain at Brussels and generally wait until the French movements became evident before himself moving. The dispositions of the Prussians, equally dispersed, did not grant to their leaders a similar allowance of time, for they had made themselves extremely vulnerable by keeping the lengthy cordon of I Corps troops too close against the frontier. Battle there would be joined at once, and very far forward, under circumstances unfavourable to that corps, while assistance from the three other Prussian corps would take a full day (or more) to come up.

In these circumstances the situation was more risky for the Prussians than for Wellington, and it behoved Prussian headquarters to maintain the closest possible contact and liaison with their own distant and rearward formations and also with Wellington, and to ensure that information and instructions were of the utmost clarity. Their record during the two days 14 and 15 June must be judged as anywhere between inadequate and lamentable. The messages to Bülow were so unclear as to prove actually dangerous. Contact with their liaison in Brussels, Müffling, was minimal – nothing on the night of 14/15 June and one factual report on the 15th that merely enquired 'what' Wellington would do, and 'when', and this at a time when every effort should have been made to explain Prussian needs and intentions. By contrast, Müffling undoubtedly worked for a good understanding between the two headquarters.

The front-line commander Ziethen seems to have been somewhat confused in his thinking and actions on 15 June, and if his decision to evacuate Binche was excusable, that to abandon Gosselies and the *chaussée* to Quatre Bras and Brussels was little short of disastrous. He chose to create a gap in the Allied line and then enlarged it by his eastward withdrawal. Without any warning it exposed the tiny Netherlands garrison south of Quatre Bras, and it even gave Gneisenau overnight alarms as he foresaw French troops curling unchecked behind his western flank.

The brief reports that Wellington had received thus far did not prepare him for the sudden midnight news received from Constant Rebecque that

Quatre Bras was in danger and the road to Brussels wide open. Everything had to be re-thought. Winand Aerts long ago showed that Saxe-Weimar's and Perponcher's initiative in these hours at Quatre Bras was that rightly expected of front-line commanders, and that the praises of Netherlands historians for the Prince of Orange and their dispraise of Wellington in this were misjudged. But could Wellington make up for lost time? There was no longer any prospect of major clashes not occurring before 17 June, and all would depend on the marching powers of the troops, timed against the hour when the French thrust would begin afresh the next morning, the 16th. But no Prussian messages came, so that the Duke was isolated in an information vacuum right up until he met Blücher at Brye at 1 p.m. on the 16th, as his Frasnes letter showed.

X

When the double battle of Quatre Bras–Ligny did begin, it showed the Allies still not wholly at one, though the efforts of each helped ease the plight of its ally on the other field. Wellington was fortunate in the successive last-minute arrivals of Picton, Brunswick, Alten and Cooke, each just when his cause seemed critical. His tactical eye and the confidence which he inspired in his troops certainly helped sustain the defence, and by the end of the day it was he who dominated the field. But it is doubtful if he could have held his own if d'Erlon's force had been at Ney's disposal in mid-afternoon. Müffling played his part well in sending to Blücher reports on the progress of the fight, though the Prussians, once Hardinge was wounded and *hors de combat*, were less efficient in sending their accounts to Quatre Bras, so that even at 10 at night Wellington's staff believed that the Prussians had won a victory. Only at around 7 a.m. on the 17th did Wellington learn the grim truth.

Had Ligny been fought as planned, it might indeed have been a drawn battle or a Prussian victory. The original long-chosen position was on high ground well back from the Ligne brook, with space for cavalry to charge French infantry emerging across the brook; only on the 16th did the dispositions change, with a high proportion of the army pushed forward into holding the villages on the brook, and creating a kink in the battle-line between the western and eastern sectors. Napoleon was able to inflict much more significant damage to the Prussians than he could have in the first position, and the nature of the fighting down in the villages consumed forces very rapidly. Blücher's interventions used up his reserves somewhat prematurely and his use of cavalry was not as successful as it might otherwise have been. In personal leadership his warrior instincts helped sustain his young troops, but not all his subordinate commanders performed so well at critical moments: Jürgass, for instance, dithered. Nor was the staff-work distinguished. Gneisenau seemed unduly pessimistic at times, overbearing at others, and when the battle ended in darkness and with Blücher missing and perhaps dead, the army went to the rear more or less by itself, and such direction as was given to it was due not to the Chief of Staff but to the admirable General Grolman.

Wellington at Quatre Bras, left in ignorance of his isolated position, might therefore have been in serious danger had Napoleon and Ney combined early on the 17th. The subsequent British retirement is mainly interesting for an early display of Uxbridge's penchant for rash cavalry tactics. Meanwhile, learning of the Prussian retreat, Wellington again proposed joint action the next day subject to additional support, an offer and request to which Gneisenau agreed. Indeed it was vital for Gneisenau that the remnants of the Prussian army should close upon Wellington, for the alternative was to find the Prussian remnants a prey to Napoleon in the middle of Belgium, far from Wellington and even further from the Rhine. Good reporting by their outposts, the reappearance of the battered Blücher, and the arrival of other Prussian formations restored a measure of calm at headquarters. And yet it was none of these that amounted to perhaps the most significant episode of the whole day. For it was the French discovery of the wandering Prussian Horse Battery Nr. 14, lost way to the east of Ligny field, that misled the French high command in its deductions on the direction of Prussian flight. The French right wing was sent to chase a will-o'-the-wisp.

XI

In considering Wellington's army at Waterloo, the most striking points are the Duke's belief in an attack on his western flank and his under-estimate of La Haye Sainte. His reasons for such a massive force in the west have not always been appreciated: for he under-estimated the contingent that Napoleon had detached to Grouchy, and therefore did not realise that Napoleon lacked sufficient force for a major turning movement. Hence he judged that the Emperor had kept in hand some 16,000 more men than he really had, quite sufficient to strike on the western flank. For this reason he posted a strong detachment at Hal and within the miniature redoubt in the triangle round Merbe Braine above Hougoumont. He placed his most reliable commander, Hill, on that flank.

If he over-insured on the west, he under-insured at La Haye Sainte. It was sheltered from the west, but would be a key point in any attack straight up the Brussels *chaussée*. What one half the preparatory effort expended on Hougoumont could have made of that little farm is obvious from the brave and prolonged defence of La Haye Sainte in its natural state. It is possible, of course, that La Haye Sainte would have been annihilated by an hour's concentrated bombardment by the Grand Battery, and that no such bombardment took place is one of the mysteries of Waterloo, but if the farm had not been blown to pieces but had survived, then with additional defences it might have held out till nightfall. As it was, it fell only at 6 p.m. after dislocating the French plan all the afternoon.

The oversight about the farm led to that terrible moment when it seemed that d'Erlon's advance and the sweeps made along the slope by French cavalry would win the battle within minutes. Napoleon's central thrust was entirely well judged in this respect. Wellington was powerless to affect matters. He was saved by the independent actions of Uxbridge and Picton, acting entirely on their own initiatives. Under their leadership Edward Somerset, William Ponsonby, Kempt and Pack altered the face of battle – also within minutes. Uxbridge, it is true, having taken his fine decision, then forgot that his role was to control the formations and not join in a steeple-chase, and so the British cavalry was let loose to gallop wild and suffer the consequences of such rashness. But at least one crisis was surmounted.

From this moment the battle settled into plain attrition, and here the skill with which the Duke handled his squares and his reserves was exemplary, and continued so until the end. As was said earlier, the tactical formations that stymied the French cavalry charges were vulnerable to French artillery, and there was no help for it, but the condition of the ground over which the French had to attack was becoming dreadful, and that was an advantage to the defence. The grasp by subordinate commanders of what the Duke required and would wish them to do was also quite excellent: Colin Halkett, John Colborne, Hussey Vivian come to mind, though, alas, not the Prince of Orange. Meanwhile the grim slogging match in the Lasne valley reached its climax, and the sheer weight of Prussian numbers bore down Napoleon's defences on his right flank. Then came the final crisis with the *Garde* on the slopes of Mont St Jean, a crisis overcome by the perfect interaction of the defence, by leaders and led. The Napoleonic threat was shattered. The Allies had won.

The further Prussian contribution was to ensure that victory, when eventually it came, was one of annihilation. Blücher shines at his brightest in his 17th/18th overnight answer to Wellington that he would bring not two corps but his whole army to the battle – and the doubting note that Gneisenau made Nostitz add to the message does nothing to detract from Blücher's glory.

Yet a distinction has to be made. Blücher would not place his army alongside Wellington's line; he would determine victory by an independent movement of his whole army aimed at Napoleon's right rear. Napoleon should be trapped between two grindstones, each of separate power, and indeed, if the Prussian grindstone had pulverised the French an hour earlier than it did, the title and fame of the battle might have been differently named and celebrated. That it did not do so in time must in part be ascribed to the extraordinarily inept Prussian staff-work in organising the various corps' movements. Paths crossing, distant formations taking precedence over formations closer to the battlefield, were complications that seriously delayed the approach march: had someone wished to apply a brake to the advance he could scarcely have done better. Then to insist on a halt under cover of the Bois de Paris although the enemy was plainly fully engaged in battering an Ally who needed and expected your support is to add to the uneasiness, for had not Müffling been sending reports and requests for just that intervention? When Ziethen did move there were still problems and misunderstandings: once again the name Grolman shines for intelligence and decision. Nor did Bülow fall short in determination, and against a tough and courageous defence mustered by the French under Lobau, the Prussian achievement at Plancenoit is the more to be praised. Once committed, Gneisenau, too, rose to the challenge. The response to Thielemann, fighting Grouchy at Wavre, that nothing mattered judged against victory here, went to the heart of the matter. Thus the grindstones did their work.

XII

The aftermath showed divisions between the Allies because their policies and motivations were so different. It is indisputable that Wellington's perceptions were more moderate than Blücher's and Gneisenau's. Can it be doubted that his were also more sound? A hundred and twenty-nine years later, in 1944, Hitler asked 'Is Paris burning?' and his question has gone down as the acme of stupid barbarity. Did the lesser but still savage punishments that the Prussians imposed on their march on Paris in 1815 or that they tried to impose on Paris after its submission, really redound to their credit among the concert of powers? By the time that the Prussians demanded Alsace-Lorraine later that summer their stock had fallen consequentially with all those who mattered. Their other demands received short shrift from their allies. The attitude of their high command had brought about their own disappointments. Even inside Prussian ruling circles the demands of men like Gneisenau were causing concern. The impressionable Tsar Alexander decided to favour

France, possibly because of his friendship with the duc de Richelieu, possibly because his envoy Pozzo was deeply influenced by Wellington. Austria had no wish to overset the 1814 balance between states, provided it could dominate Italy – and it distrusted Prussia. France, despite the domestic fury caused by the restitution of art treasures looted by French armies, was gently treated and so *revanche*, though often popular, never became the settled policy of post-Napoleonic France. Waterloo had put a term to that insatiable bloody adventure.

XIII

In the era of Thomas Carlyle history was the story of Heroes. By contrast, the Marxist interpretation of history at its best disclosed the great economic and social factors that brought about change, but at its worst reduced matters simply to 'man is what he eats', and by insisting on historical inevitability reduced the influence of human beings in the long process. In the history of 1815 we have seen the power of brute force, weight of numbers and financial and economic strength when deployed against Napoleonic France. But it would be idle to pretend that individuals in high position did not affect the outcome. Let us close by looking at the great leaders of the three states primarily involved in the short campaign, and whose roles were vital to the outcome.

In Blücher Prussia possessed a warrior who never accepted defeat, who was always anxious to renew battle and secure victory, even against great odds. He had been a hell-rake, was still a gambler, was sometimes quite unhinged (as his friend Boyen admitted), was ageing and in physical and mental decline. He needed support and guidance in strategy and the many small things that result from that – and it certainly must be said that Gneisenau knew these smaller things, all useful and necessary to mounting a campaign. But Blücher knew one big thing. The flame that burned in him was seen by all, and he loved and was loved by his men. For him they would always 'go the extra mile' even if it meant the mile to death in avenging Napoleon's 1806 humiliation of Prussia. The battle of Ligny might not have been lost if the Prussians, with their numerical superiority had not changed their plan, but in the event it would have been lost hours earlier than was the case had Blücher's courage and dash not lifted spirits. No one but Blücher could have driven his men forward so insistently on the morning of 18 June. There shines through him a simple and heart-warming belief that he and his friend Wellington would always work together, that no individual factor between them or their countries mattered so much as the utter and final defeat of Napoleon. He was a good ally.

The old *Feldmarschall* could not formulate a campaign plan, and so for that he was reliant upon his staff; nor did he possess a political sense, so that in the weeks after Waterloo his passions and demands generally were ignored or overborne. But in many ways he had an engaging natural shrewdness that could judge between good sense and folly. Here is one almost perfect example: as Paris capitulated, Blücher installed himself in the beautiful Palace of St Cloud, with its splendid views across the Seine and the Bois de Boulogne, with Paris beyond. Metternich went to see him and found the old soldier living like a hussar and wreathed in smoke, an uncouth ambiance very different from the time not so many years past when the elegant Metternich waited on Napoleon there. In writing to his daughter on 13 July, Metternich lamented the barrack-room atmosphere that pervaded everything, but he added this: 'In crossing the grand gallery the old Marshal said this to me, "That man must have been a regular fool to have all this and go running after Moscow!"'[10]

Against the clear simplicity of Blücher we must contrast the trained staff officer who had been appointed to make good any deficiencies in Blücher's military education. Count Gneisenau could be charming and warm on occasion, but his military contemporaries found him difficult, sometimes rough, temperamental, and subject to swings between over-confidence and timidity. Triumphalist when the enemy was on the run, he became prey to his own worst imaginings when matters were going badly. Müffling, who seems to have disliked Gneisenau as much as the latter disliked him, claimed that from the first Gneisenau believed Wellington duplicitous; and certainly he was quick to differ from the Duke in many secondary matters, as we have seen in the early chapters. Coupled with Gneisenau's tendency to ignore Müffling (possibly because he got on so well with the Duke) and to leave him uninformed at key moments, this distrustful reserve greatly complicated the problem of co-operation between the armies.

Some of the worries that Blücher and Gneisenau had to endure on 15 June and the next day sprang directly from their own communication failures with Bülow and Wellington. To these were added by dawn on the 17th the need to explain a major defeat. Unfortunately, Gneisenau, a man prone to see enemies, dark deeds and threats whether he looked at Brussels or (as we saw) even at Berlin, was by now mulling over recent events and beginning to create a narrative in which Wellingtonian 'duplicity' was the cause of all Prussian misfortune.

This idea Gneisenau was to elaborate, and so successfully that it became a significant theme of later Prussian historiography. The facts show otherwise. And by contrast to Gneisenau's *ex parte* denunciations, it is noticeable that the Duke, so blisteringly critical of shortcomings in his own armies, patiently put up with much annoyance from the Prussians before the campaign started, and never once during it blamed them for any failures of commission or omission. Their reporting was lamentably poor, the unannounced abandonment of Gosselies a scandal, and these Prussian failures placed him in serious jeopardy. At the shocking dénouement during the Richmond Ball Wellington claimed that Boney had 'humbugged' him; in truth he had been humbugged by the Prussians. He breathed not one word of complaint, he was concerned only to save matters. Less than ninety hours later his Waterloo Despatch was notably generous in passing over their shortcomings and praising their contribution. Clear, bleak, and chilly the Duke may generally have been in his views and opinions, but these are admirable virtues when contrasted with the smoky, carping and sulphurous outbursts of the self-pitying Gneisenau.

We have seen how Wellington pulled together his polyglot contingents, fed them and so mixed them that weak units were always buttressed by more reliable ones. It was not exactly making bricks without straw, but it was a difficult enough task nonetheless. The army performed perhaps better than even he expected in the days of operations. There is no doubt that throughout the spring and early summer he had far too much to do personally, and that he may not have had time enough to sit still and ponder. A ministerial colleague with whom he was in sympathy (or possibly his former chief and friend, the Duke of Richmond) might have lightened the diplomatic burden somewhat if placed in Brussels with clear and agreed terms of reference. How clear Wellington's political perception usually was can be judged by his dealings for the surrender of Paris and the settlement of France.

One strange matter is why Wellington kept to his original view of Napoleon's plans, for he remained throughout concerned for his western flank, and later the Hal position, whereas Napoleon had a record of striking at the junctions between Allied armies and seeking to defeat them in detail. It was, in my opinion, one of the four serious operational mistakes made by the Duke in this campaign. The second was not to issue precautionary orders on 14 June, which could have lessened the assembly delays and enabled marching to start sooner once the news came a little after 5 p.m. on 15 June. The third was his failure to pay enough attention to La Haye Sainte, to make it as strong as possible. And the fourth mistake was his failure to foresee the dangerous crisis in the centre as d'Erlon advanced. Two of these were mistakes in battle, but when I reflect upon the incessant changes and chances that the fighting threw up, all calling for rapid reconsideration and swift decision, I am amazed at how well he rose to the challenge. Those errors granted, Wellington at Mont St Jean seems to have been generally at his best, and insofar as man can bear such burdens to have borne them extraordinarily well. In such circumstances it is not the oversight about La Haye Sainte that should surprise, but the fact that oversights were so few. From all parts of his army came testimony that if any one man won the battle of Waterloo that man was the Duke of Wellington.

Wellington as a British general can be compared only with Marlborough, and after seventy years of study I am still divided as to which stands the higher.[11] Wellington's young manhood began just as the *ancien régime* ended and a Revolutionary age began. He retained an eighteenth-century, pre-Revolutionary view of society, of constitutions, and of the desirability of the old status quo. He was, as he said, a *nimmuk-wallah* who had eaten his sovereign's salt and was in lifelong allegiance to the Crown. Twice, despite his deep conservatism, his grim realism enabled him to conquer personal aversion and bring about massive but peaceful political change to avert threat of revolution, and this in the teeth of the objections of many traditionalists who were otherwise his natural supporters: as Prime Minister over Catholic Emancipation in 1829 and as counsellor to Peel over the repeal of the Corn Laws in 1846. He stood above and apart from his contemporaries, and they came to see him in his spartan aloof old age as a symbol of an heroic past, as that sharp observer Greville famously recorded.[12] In all his sentiments and ideas Wellington stands as the antithesis of that restless and colossal genius and disturber of the world's peace, Napoleon Bonaparte.

For Napoleon was far more multi-sided. He could deploy a charm that Wellington neither possessed nor sought to possess. It is revealing that so tough an officer as the elderly Admiral Lord Keith, a taciturn unsusceptible Scot, could say after first meeting with the fallen Emperor, 'Damn the fellow! If he had obtained an interview with His Royal Highness [the Prince Regent], in half an hour they would have been the best friends in Europe!' Whether the charm was more than a weapon is open to doubt. Napoleon was a demonic worker and innovator once in power, self-sufficient, with an eye on all aspects of society, a lawgiver and a tyrant, a man who offered careers open to talent but who imposed a crushing monotheism on his subjects (as witness the Napoleonic creed in the church).

In the Waterloo campaign he took on too great a task for the means available, and he painted for himself too many pictures. His choices for main command and senior staff were poor, and his orders and decisions repeatedly fell short of satisfactory. Given the need for unremitting energy if the timetable was to lead to the two Allied armies going down to destruction, there were delays and lost hours while Napoleon chatted politics with his generals. Yet in this campaign he faced, almost for the first time, two Allied leaders in combination who did not fear him. The challenge that he faced required his clearest thinking and incessant energy. But this was not the Napoleon of the high Empire, and sadly the brave men of 1815 whom he called upon to realise his dream served him better than he served them.

There was a darker side to Napoleon that seems almost to come from an Italy of an earlier century. He could be coldly cruel, indifferent to promises and engagements, an unsafe friend and an unsettling ally. He was also a born conspirator,[13] an agitator, a man quick to profit from the instability arising from the French Revolution, an inspirer of *coups*. The name spans an age of history, for good – and ill. Indeed it might have been better for the quiet happiness of France if this ardent friend of Augustin Robespierre had disappeared from history with the fall of the Robespierres, Maximilien and Augustin.[14] But then where would French glory have been?

So the path stretched from Toulon through Arcola and Rivoli, to Egypt, and Germany, and Spain, and Russia ('to have all this and go running after Moscow!'), past Leipzig, to Elba, and thence to Waterloo and St Helena, leaving millions dead in his wake.[15] That was the tale. What of the epitaph? It was written by a Frenchman, an acute observer from the next generation, Alexis de Tocqueville. He identified with perfect precision the one great gift that was denied to Napoleon, the lack of which eventually rendered impotent all the others. He characterised the Emperor thus: 'He was as great as a man can be without virtue.'[16]

Twenty years of measureless ambition, of energy unharnessed to virtue. It could not be left to race away yet again. It had to be stopped. That was why Waterloo had to be fought and won.

Envoi

AND SO I CONCLUDE THIS STUDY of a great conflict, of brave soldiers and outstanding commanders. It has demanded such hours as I could spare from a far more important duty, and doubtless suffers in consequence. But I can say and do no more.

In 1891 Lord Rosebery prefaced his *Pitt*, a part of the series 'Twelve English Statesmen', with a short but heartfelt note that read:

> This little book has been written under many disadvantages but with a sincere desire to ascertain the truth. My chief happiness in completing it would have been to give it to my wife; it can now only be inscribed to her memory.

MERIEL
who so believed in this project
till her death on 25 July 2014.

NOTES AND APPENDICES

Notes

Abbreviations and Conventions Used

BD	*British Diplomacy, 1813–15*, ed. Webster
BL	British Library
BMP	'On Waterloo, Clausewitz, Wellington and the Campaign of 1815', in Clausewitz, C. von, *The Campaign of 1815*, ed. Bassford, Moran & Pedlow
CHBFP	*The Cambridge History of British Foreign Policy.*
CMH	*The Cambridge Modern History*
CTS	*Consolidated Treaty Series, 1648–1918*, which see
DBTS	De Bas & T'Serclaes de Wommersom, *La Campagne de 1815*
Dict. Nap.	*Dictionnaire Napoléon*, ed. J. Tulard
HMC	Publications of private archives by the Historical Manuscripts Commission, issued periodically from 1870 to the present, e.g. Lord Bathurst's papers [then] at Cirencester House, published by HMSO in 1923 as HMC *Bathurst* (vol. 76)
JFDAM	*Jahrbücher für die deutsche Armee und Marine*
JSAHR	*Journal of the Society for Army Historical Research*
LW	*Letters from the Battle of Waterloo* (ed. Glover)
NA	The National Archives, Kew (formerly Public Records Office – PRO)
RA	Royal Archives at Windsor Castle
USJ	*United Service Journal*, sometimes appearing as *USM* (*United Service Magazine*)
WA	*Waterloo Archive* (ed. Glover)
WL	*Waterloo Letters* (ed. Siborne)
WD	*Wellington Despatches, 1799–1818*, ed. Col. J. Gurwood. Gurwood's original edn., 1834–8, ran to twelve vols. of which the last dealt with the 1815 campaign. In 1845–7 he reissued it in eight vols., the eighth covering 1815, and this was reprinted unchanged in an edition of 1852. Continually to source a document such as Wellington's advice to the Prince of Orange on 11 May 1815 as '*WD*, xii, 375, or *WD*, viii, 78' would be tedious so I use a shortened form: *WD*, 375/78. Where I use Gurwood for earlier periods, I refer to the first edn. of 1834–8.
WSD	*Wellington Supplementary Despatches*, ed. 2nd Duke of Wellington (1857–73)

CHAPTER 31: The Allies

1. Winterfeldt, falling in with some French sharpshooters near Thyle, was severely wounded and left for dead, but was found later by some Nassauers to whom he spoke, saying that 'he was charged with a message' for Müffling. The latter learned this only after 9 p.m. on the 16th 'when it was already dark' and still 'remained ignorant' of the message itself. Presumably, therefore, Winterfeldt travelled without escort, with nothing in writing, and was too badly wounded or too cautious to tell the (German-speaking) Nassauers what the information was: Ollech, *Geschichte*, p. 138, and Müffling, *Memoirs*, pp. 238–9.
2. See the fuller reports in vol. 1, chap. 29, sec. X.
3. Report of Captain v. Scriba of the Bremen battalion in *Belle-Alliance*, no. 12: 17 June losses at p. 37. The brigade casualty figure is from no. 19, p. 51. These were the only casualties the Hanoverian force – infantry, artillery, and cavalry (Cumberland Hussars) – suffered on 17 June. Also in *WA*, ii, nos. 2 and 29.
4. For the patrol, see *WL*, nos. 71 and 75. Gordon was killed the next day, and Grey left no account. Wellington in his 1842 memorandum (*WSD*, x, p. 527) mis-recollected the event, thinking that Gordon met Ziethen himself at Sombreffe: Ollech (p. 179) adopted this version. But as Lettow-Vorbeck pointed out (*Napoleons Untergang*, p. 360), I Corps had moved north during the night towards Wavre, with II Corps remaining to cover the retreat, and that it would have been Sohr's 2nd Brigade of Jürgass's II Corps Reserve Cavalry that Gordon found. Ziethen had no reason to remain at Tilly. Ollech said Gordon met Wellington again at 7.30, Lettow-Vorbeck said around 8 a.m.
5. Müffling, *Memoirs*, p. 240. Müffling's account in his *History* (written 1815, published 1816) says that the first intelligence of the Prussian 'retreat' was received, 'accidentally', on the 17th (p. 13, Eng. version).
6. Somerset's account, in Owen, p. 10; Müffling, *Memoirs*, p. 239, without specifying the ADC's name, which is supplied by Lettow-Vorbeck, p. 360.
7. Colonel Sir A. S. Frazer, writing from Quatre Bras at 9.30 a.m.: 'An officer has just come from Blücher to the Duke', *Letters*, p. 542.
8. The Gneisenau statement of 17 June 1815 is in Lettow-Vorbeck, quoted at p. 527. It is worth noting that in his *History*, written in 1815, Müffling also said it was 'two corps' that were wanted (p. 16, Eng. edn.). He muddled matters later, telling the German historian General Hofmann in the 1840s, that Wellington replied: 'Yesterday in no way changed my intentions for a joint offensive. I will retire to my camp [*Lager*] at Mont St Jean, and if I am supported there by one [*einem*] Prussian corps, then I will fight a defensive battle there. If I cannot receive this support and Napoleon leads against me everything he has, then I cannot accept battle but must retreat to Brussels': Hofmann in Lettow-Vorbeck, pp. 360–1. Hofmann's words 'must retreat to Brussels' [*müsste auf* [*sic*] *Brüssel zurückgehen*] as given by Lettow-Vorbeck, have been misread by Peter Hofschröer, who in citing Lettow-Vorbeck, transforms them to mean something quite different: that without the requested support Wellington 'would abandon [*sic*] Brussels and fall back to Antwerp and the River Scheldt': *1815*, ii, pp. 24–5.

9. Sir G. Bowles, undated memorandum in *Letters of the 1st Earl of Malmesbury*, ii, pp. 446–7; [James Hope], *Letters from Portugal, Spain and France, by a British Officer* (1819), pp. 236–8; Constant Rebecque, quoted in De Bas, *Prins Frederik*, iii, II, p. 621; Lord Vivian in *WL*, no. 71.
10. Frazer, 18 June, 3 a.m., in *Letters*, p. 545; Clark Kennedy, *WL*, no. 34; Jackson, *USM*, June 1834, p. 163 fn., and *USM*, Sept. 1847, p. 11; Sgt. Doring, in *WA*, vol. ii, no. 47.
11. *WD*, 475/144. These orders are given more fully in the 1852 edition than in the first edition of 1838, being taken from a copy made by de Lacy Evans, 'copied from the Duke's writing. Saw the Duke write them while seated on the ground.' Siborne, *History*, p. 158 (1848 edition) had to rely on the first edition of *WD*, and the order printed there was the one addressed specifically to Lord Hill, and did not itemise formations outside his command. Peter Hofschröer, *1815*, ii, p. 25, gives the order to Hill, but not the 1852 edition's fuller orders.
12. Somerset, in Owen, pp. 10–11.
13. See vol. 1, chap. 28, sec. VIII.
14. Nostitz, 'Tagebuch', *Kr. Einzel.*, Heft 6, pp. 32–3; for Napoleon's praise, see Campbell, *Napoleon at Fontainebleau and Elba*, p. 220 (21 April 1814).
15. Aerts, *Opérations*, pp. 190–1.
16. Lettow-Vorbeck, p. 368. He placed an editorial exclamation mark after the sentence about St Trond.
17. The Thielemann reply and Bülow's next message may be read in Lettow-Vorbeck, p. 369. The suggested routes are not of significance today.
18. For the letters, see vol. 1, chap. 21, sec. IX.
19. The report is some 1,400 words long. The tiny extracts from two of its paragraphs given in Hofschröer, *1815*, i, pp. 350–1, amount to only a hundred words and so give a somewhat inadequate impression of the report's contents and tone.
20. See vol. 1, chap. 21, sec. VI for Gneisenau's 15 June noon letter about giving battle on the 16th; chap. 26: sec. II for the time on the 16th when it was known that IV Corps could not arrive; sec. VI for Ropes's 'We are asked to believe'; App. 1, for Pflugk-Harttung's belief that significant Wellingtonian assistance was not really desired until very late in the day, as it was intended to be a Prussian victory.
21. According to Müffling's recollections: *see* vol. 1, chap. 26, App. 2.
22. *Agricola*, chap. 27 (trans. H. Mattingley, Penguin Classics): *'Inquissima haec bellorum condicio est, prospera omnes sibi indiant, adversa uni imputantur.'* It was given new familiarity by President Kennedy after the Bay of Pigs fiasco in 1961.
23. All Gneisenau's old concepts of early April 1815 resurfaced in this new report. Brussels was mentioned only in terms of Wellington's views. Gneisenau himself did not allude to the city, for all his attention was eastwards towards Germany. The commandants of Luxembourg and Jülich had been sent instructions. Kleist in Luxembourg would defend Cologne. For 'the enemy might take Liège in order to go up the Rhine', thus menacing the Allied armies gathering in Germany. The Argonne zone in Lorraine needed watching (one of the despised Müffling's pet theories).

24. Gneisenau is here referring to Bourmont, who had come over to the Prussians early on the morning of the 15th but cannot have known of Napoleon's intentions for Ney and a semi-independent left wing. Who Napoleon's aide was I have not discovered.
25. Colonel Sir A. S. Frazer wrote at 9.15 a.m. on 18 June: 'The Russians will reach Metz in six days, so says General von Müffling, the Prussian general officer with the Duke. The Austrians are expected to reach Metz at the same time. Admitting this, Bonaparte cannot afford to remain long in our front. He must take care that the Russians and the Austrians do not get into his rear', *Letters*, p. 546. The difference between the optimism of Müffling (and Frazer, it would seem) and the view of the precarious Argonne expressed by Gneisenau is striking.
26. K. Griewank, *Gneisenau: Ein Leben in Briefen*, p. 322. We may note how in this most private of letters Gneisenau stressed the need for the various Prussian detachments to stay close to the Anglo-Allied army, recognising that, caught isolated in eastern Belgium and still far from the Rhine, the Prussians would have risked annihilation. But it seems to me that at the necessary moment Grolman had been much more decisive in the matter of moving on Wavre and parallel to Wellington's line of communications than had Gneisenau. I refer the reader to my comments on this in vol. 1, chap. 28, at the close of sec. VIII.

CHAPTER 32: Napoleon

1. My first sentence is based on Napoleon's own remark in the letter to Ney early on 17 June. I give the letter in full later in my main text, but the key admission is: 'If Comte d'Erlon had carried out the movement on St Amand that the Emperor ordered, the Prussian army would have been totally destroyed.' The message to Joseph is in Grouchy, *Mémoires*, iv, p. 169.
2. See Bertrand's comment about Napoleon's overnight working routine to Admiral Sir Pulteney Malcolm's wife at St Helena: her letter, 25 July 1816, in Kerry, p. 194. See also Appendix 4, esp. sec. VII onwards.
3. See Napoleon's memoir 'The Campaign of 1815', in *Corr. de Nap.*, xxxi, p. 207 in the 4to edition (1869); p. 172 in the 8vo edition (1870); Jomini in his *Précis Politique et Militaire de la Campagne de 1815* (Paris, 1839), p. 154, fn. It was mentioned by Ropes, p. 205 fn., and Houssaye, *Waterloo*, Book II, chap. 4, sec. I, p. 218 fn., Eng. trans., p. 125 fn. (this volume was the only one of his four dealing with the Waterloo campaign to be translated into English). Bailly de Monthyon (1776–1850) had served on the staff under Murat and Berthier and for Napoleon himself, although Davout thought him untrustworthy. It is difficult to believe that if given this task he would not have reported back to Napoleon on this occasion, but there is no report, and he seems never to have referred to this mission.
4. Houssaye's comment in II, 4, I, p. 218 fn.; Eng. trans., pp. 125–6 fn. – I have not checked the pamphlets in question, and take his comment on trust. Grouchy, *Mémoires*, iv, p. 43.
5. For these reports or messages from Pajol and Exelmans see Houssaye, II, chap. 4, sec. II, p. 224 fn.; Eng. trans. 129 fn.

6. Elchingen, *Documents Inédits*, p. 45. Also in Siborne, *History*, App. 27.
7. Aerts, *Opérations*, p. 168. What was the well-trained chief of staff of III Corps thinking about, leaving these *Uhlans* unrecalled?
8. That only six guns of the battery were captured was because two howitzers had been sent in a different direction overnight: Lettow-Vorbeck, p. 379, fn. 3.
9. This *first* Bertrand order has not (I believe) ever been printed in full, but Houssaye gives the essence of it from a copy found in the War Archives: II, 4, II, p. 229; Eng. trans., p. 131. Domon's *3e Division de Cavalerie* (in Vandamme's *3e Corps*) and Milhaud's two *cuirassier* divisions (*13e* Watier and *14e* Delort) of *4e Corps de Cavalerie* would be needed with the main army.
10. Subervie's *5e Division de Cavalerie* had been taken from Pajol on the 16th (Houssaye, II, 5, II, p. 256 fn.; Eng. trans., p. 146 fn), so possibly it may have been intended to replace it with Maurin's *7e Division de Cavalerie* (hitherto in Gérard's *4e Corps*). It is not at all clear whether Maurin would henceforth report to Gérard or to Pajol. There are always disadvantages in implying and not stating things in cases like this, and it is another example of how puzzling such instructions could be. Is it surprising that at critical moments various officers became confused?
11. Bertrand's *second* order is given in French in Ropes, p. 358, from E. Pascallet, '*Notice Biogr sur Ml Grouchy*' (1842); Ropes gave an English translation, p. 209. The version eventually printed in Grouchy's *Mémoires*, iv, p. 50 is somewhat different from Pascallet, but corresponds with the text in Houssaye. The *Mémoires* version (but not Houssaye) claims that it was written from 'Ligny, 17 June, towards 3 p.m.', whereas Napoleon had left the windmill around noon. The key paragraph in the *Mémoires* version (and Houssaye) reads: 'It is important to penetrate what Blücher and Wellington intend and if they plan to join their armies to cover Brussels and Liège, in seeking the fate of a new battle. In all circumstances keep your two infantry corps together within one league's extent, with several different paths of retreat.' Until 1842 Grouchy repeatedly insisted that he never received *any* written orders from Napoleon on 17 June. Some writers debate what the verbal orders were, as Houssaye does at some length, but whatever may – or may not – have been said was rendered obsolete by what Bertrand wrote only very shortly after Grouchy had left the Emperor.
12. Important instructions about pursuit and enemy intentions are mixed with secondary matters. Even on secondary points, 'communication by the paved road' is separated from the 'cavalry detachments on it' by minor matters about 'occupying Namur from Charlemont'. A clean instruction checked and revised from the dictated scribble should not have taken much longer to issue and would have set out the matter in a better order.
13. Compare the order with this passage in Napoleon's memoirs on the instructions to Grouchy: 'He was recommended to pursue the Prussian army at sword-point to stop it rallying, and he received the positive order to keep always between the Charleroi–Brussels highway and Marshal Blücher, so as always to be in communication and able to reunite with the army. It was probable that Marshal Blücher would retire upon Wavre, and Grouchy should get there at the same time as him. If the enemy continued

to march on Brussels and passed the night protected by Soignies forest, he should be followed to the forest outskirts; if he retired on the Meuse to cover his communications with Germany, he should be watched by the advance guard of General Pajol, and Wavre occupied with Exelmans's cavalry and the infantry of *3e* and *4e Corps*, so as to be in touch with headquarters' (pp. 212–13; p. 176).

14. These points were made by the military historian Hereford George (1838–1910) in *EHR*, xv (1900), p. 811–16, and by Fortescue, x, pp. 330–1.
15. See note 10 concerning Subervie's *5e Division de Cavalerie*, 1,200 men and 6 guns, being with Lobau's force. It has therefore been deducted from the totals given here.
16. Pétiet, *Souvenirs*, p. 202.
17. *Docs inéds*, p. 44. Surprisingly, it is addressed to 'the Marshal Prince of the Moskova, *4e Corps*, at Gosselies': what was Soult thinking of? Also in Siborne, *History*, app. 28.

CHAPTER 33: Napoleon Pursues Wellington

1. Napoleon, 'The Campaign of 1815', *Corr. de Nap.*, xxxi, p. 213; p. 177. Another instance of confusion over uniforms leading to 'friendly fire'.
2. See Napoleon's memoirs for the *vivandière* (pp. 213–14; 177) and for the meeting with Ney mentioned later (p. 214;177). Colonel W. H. James doubted the story of the *vivandière* on the grounds that such women were not attached to the British army (*Campaign of 1815*, p. 188, fn), but there would be no point in inventing her seizure, even if her function was not correctly recorded. Moreover, Sergeant Doring of the Orange-Nassau Nr. 28 remarked during the retreat of 17 June that the Scottish regiments had a great 'wagon train with the camp followers', and the woman may well have been one of these who had become separated, and captured: *WA*, vol. ii, no. 47, p. 165.
3. For the meeting between Napoleon and d'Erlon, see the statements of Foy and d'Erlon noted under the date of 17 June in vol. 1, chap. 30, sec. VII.
4. Mercer, *Journal*, chap. 12, at p. 146 in the 1927 Soldiers' Tales edition; Taylor in *WL*, no. 75. Foy's comment, *Vie Militaire*, p. 273. One recalls Napoleon's remark about Junot, in Portugal, 'I do not accept that, on the pretext of lack of supplies his march should have been put back by a day: that reason is good only for men who do not want to do anything: 20,000 men can live anywhere, even in a desert': *Corr. de Nap.*, no. 13,327 (*Corr. Gén.*, no. 16,706), 5 Nov. 1807. This may work on occasion and for a short time. But as a system, if it saves money it is expensive in lives and damages discipline.
5. Napoleon's Memoirs, p. 214; p. 177.
6. For the thought of attacking, see Vivian; the change of mind, see Taylor; for Arthur Hill, see Ingleby: all in *WL*, nos. 71, 75, 81 respectively. Although it is less authoritative, O'Grady (whom I quote later – see fn. 14 below) remarked of a little charge or counter-charge between pickets made by an officer of the 7th later in this day that 'the Duke of Wellington sent to stop him', C. R. B. Barrett, *The 7th (Queen's Own) Hussars* (1914), i, p. 378.
7. The RHA troops under Uxbridge seem to have been allocated somewhat chaotically, according to Lipscombe, *Wellington's Guns*, pp. 363–4.

8. Mercer, pp. 146–7. His account of the rearguard is really the one justification for Chartier's scene. But note this, also: Mercer watched Whinyate's rocket troop in action later that day, and one rocket turned back and narrowly missed Mercer: 'it actually put me in more danger than *all the fire of the enemy* throughout the day' (p. 153, my italics). Uxbridge's confusion between Prussian and French uniforms luckily had no bad consequences, but again it indicates why there were several 'friendly fire' incidents during the campaign.
9. Mercer, p. 148. I cite him here because of his proximity to Lord Uxbridge, but other descriptions, some very good, are in Taylor, Tomkinson, Napoleon, Pétiet, Gourgaud, Mauduit. All stress the severity and duration of the storm, and the unceasing rain, that made secondary roads dreadful.
10. Mercer, p. 148.
11. Lieutenant John Vandeleur, a relative of the general, in a letter home, dated 23 June 1815: *Letters of Colonel John Vandeleur, 1810–46*, privately printed, 1894, p. 161.
12. Vivian, *WL*, no. 71: 'Lord Anglesey, who remained [after Wellington left], told me we were to retire, and that Vandeleur's brigade would support mine, and he then left me.' In other correspondence with Vivian, Vandeleur explained what his orders had been, but their recollections seemed to differ (*ibid.*, no. 52). Tomkinson, *Diary*, p. 284 for Peninsular practice; Bacon, 10th Hussars, *Letters from the Battle of Waterloo*, no. 62, item 4, for standard practice and Vandeleur's 'stupidity', which he thought habitual. Mercer also found Vandeleur difficult.
13. Ingleby, *WL*, no. 81. The farrier would no doubt not take many minutes to shoe the horse, but the entire 6-pounder gun team would be stationary for that time, and a *really determined attack* might well have entailed the capture of this gun.
14. Lt. O'Grady wrote to his father, 31 July 1815, and made a statement dated 10 April 1837. The former is in Barrett, *7th Hussars*, i, p. 373 onwards, the part of the letter dealing with Waterloo begins on p. 392; all repr. in *WA*, iii, no. 54. The statement dated 10 April 1837, printed by Barrett, i, p. 379 is not in *WA*, iii.
15. Uxbridge had been Colonel of the 7th Hussars since 1801 and retained the colonelcy for over forty years: he was totally devoted to it and its glory. The Colonel of the 23rd Light Dragoons in 1815 was Major-General Sir George Anson, and the Colonel of the 1st Life Guards was General the Earl of Harrington.
16. Having seen the failure of the sabre-bearing 7th Hussars when pitted against long lances, the sabre-armed 23rd Light Dragoons exhibited 'lack of enthusiasm' when Uxbridge ordered them to advance. It seems reasonable to judge that light cavalry ought not to have been used in such a combat. Uxbridge himself, writing as a hussar colonel to the officers of his own regiment on 28 June 1815 admitted that his order to attack the *lanciers* in such a flankless position was to ask a great deal, that although it 'failed' and the 7th were 'repulsed' in consequence, yet he renewed the attack, which failed again 'from the same cause'; it required the heavies, the Life Guards, to succeed (quoted in full in Barrett, i, p. 384). This account is not flattering to his generalship. Uxbridge's imperfect performance of his duties as an overall cavalry commander on this occasion may have counted when Trip of the Netherlands heavy cavalry refused to obey him on 18 June.

17. Gourgaud, *Campaign of 1815*, Eng. version, p. 82: 'the enemy was closely pursued at the sword's point'. In the more vivid French version,'*l'ennemi fut poussé l'épée dans les reins*' ('pursued, sword in the kidneys').
18. See the full account in Oman, *Hist. Peninsular War*, vol. iv, p. 140 onwards.
19. Very few accounts mention the transport on the road on 17 June, and only one (so far as I know) mentions that 'the side of the highway was filled with overturned ammunition carts, demolished guns or guns jammed into each other; and on the road were ambulances carrying the wounded and an endless wagon train' (Doring of the Orange-Nassau Nr. 28, in *WA*, vol. ii, no. 47). It is hard to see why the main army's undisturbed retreat should have created havoc on the roadside, but where gun-carriages had collapsed they would indeed have to be pushed aside. Possibly some of this roadside lumber dated from vehicle breakdown during the advance south on the previous day, as Wellington had issued in the morning of the 16th 'very particular orders to see that the roads were kept clear of baggage, and every thing likely to impede the movements of the troops' (Kincaid's remark, quoted in my chap. 24). Having as he said read Brialmont & Gleig's book of 1858, Sir George Scovell wrote memories of the campaign. He badly mixed up the sequence of events on 13 and 15 June, as was remarked in chap. 22, n. 18 (on p. 659); for the detail of his muddle see my article in *War in History*, vi (1), 1999, p. 110 and fn. But in general terms his memory of the scenes of confusion on the road early on 18 June fits with other evidence of blocked and abandoned vehicles, how Wellington told him to clear the way using dragoons, and how he got Lambert's infantry to clear them as fuel for their cooking: *WA*, iii, No 1.
20. For Chartier, see this chapter's n. 8 above. There are tiny indications in Napoleon's account of the whole advance that they were chasing and close to only the fraction of a fraction. He claimed that there were 'two' British batteries at the Quatre Bras position, and the pursuing troops were opposed by only 'a few pieces of cannon': Memoirs, p. 214; pp. 177–8. In essence that seems correct.
21. The figure for the 17 June loss was 238 all units and all arms, *WD*, 485/151. This gave 108 British casualties and 121 Hanoverian. The 108 'British' looks as though it approximates to Siborne's 114 'British and KGL' (Siborne, App. 29). The Hanoverian 1st Brigade's casualty return for 17 June amounted to 121 (*Belle-Alliance*, no. 19, p. 51; also *WA*, ii, no. 2): that was due to the pre-dawn flare up. Napoleon thought that on following the high road 'it was easy to see how great the English loss had been, even though they had already buried most of their dead' (Memoirs, p. 215; p. 178), but he gave no indicative estimates.
22. Colonel Baron J.-B.-J. Sourd (1775–1849) is justly famous for his bravery. In fighting the Life Guards his head received two sabre cuts, his left shoulder one, and his right arm three. His arm was then amputated by Larrey in the town. During this operation Sourd dictated a letter to Napoleon, refusing his nomination as general as 'the rank of colonel is everything to me'. Then he rose and went forward to re-join his beloved regiment, continuing to command it at Waterloo: Houssaye, pp. 263–4; Eng. trans., p. 150; and *Dict. Nap.*, ii, p. 782.
23. The account of the army's retreat from Quatre Bras to Mont St Jean and the clash at

Genappe in Hofschröer, *1815*, ii, pp. 28–30, is extremely disappointing. Of his 1,100 words, about 350 are given over to an extract (from Pflugk-Harttung, *Belle-Alliance*) concerning the relatively peaceful movement of the Hanoverian Bremen battalion. The one sentence on the Genappe combat is misleading to the point of plain inaccuracy: 'the Allied cavalry were able to cross the narrow bridge at Genappe before the pursuing French caught up with them. There was a brief combat, in which Uxbridge, leading his [*sic*] 1st Life Guards, was able to hold off the French 1er [*sic*] Line Lancers who were closely pursuing the 7th Hussars'.

24. Uxbridge in *WL*, no. 4; Banner's memorandum makes some fairly clear allusions to Uxbridge's role as regimental Colonel of the 7th Hussars, *ibid.*, no. 47; O'Grady on Dörnberg's opinion, *ibid.*, no. 65; Tomkinson, *Diary*, pp. 285–6.
25. It is unfortunate that just over six months from this time Wellington insisted that he 'did not leave the ground at Quatre Bras with the cavalry till nearly 5 in the evening' and so the retirement of the baggage columns, ordered at 6 a.m., should have been managed with order and safety, but that the baggage retirement was badly handled and hence some baggage was captured by the French: *WSD*, xi, p. 266, 2 Jan 1816. He was plainly 'out' in his timing. Coming from such a source, it would have been difficult for the Board of Claims to challenge his statement that was made to dispute certain claims from the men involved. In a separate outburst to Lord Mulgrave he was similarly scathing about the Royal Artillery at Waterloo, 'one of those sweeping indictments … [that seems] too hasty to be accurate': Fortescue, x, p. 414; also Colonel Hime's useful analysis of the Duke's denunciation, for which see his *History of the Royal Artillery, 1815–1853*, app. D and Lipscombe's chap. 24.
26. The first instruction is in *WD*, 1852 edn., viii, p. 144 and in the appendix volume of *WSD*, xiv, p. 559; the second is in both editions of *WD*, 476/144, and *WSD*, xiv, 559. Torrens, in his letter of 1 Oct. 1815, said that he was personally chosen as messenger by Wellington himself because of his expert knowledge of the country, and with instructions to avoid all risk of capture; that he set off at 11 p.m., went on a round trip of 60 miles via Brussels, and delivered the messages 'before break of day'. He had not been to bed since the 14th and had little to eat since, and fell asleep at full gallop: 'A Waterloo Letter', pp. 841–2.
27. See the accounts collected in Antony Brett-James's anthology, *The Hundred Days* (1964), pp. 95–105; the Royal Dragoon in *JSAHR*, xxxiv (1956), pp. 20–1; Kincaid, *Adventures*, pp. 326 and 335, or in the 1927 reprint, 243, 250; Tupper Carey's Reminiscences in *Cornhill Magazine*, June 1899, esp. at pp. 727–8.
28. For the later stages of the French advance, see Houssaye, II, 5, III, pp. 264–5; Eng. trans. pp. 150–1, and Napoleon's memoirs p. 214/p. 178 for the artillery firing to get the British to disclose: he thought they replied with 50–60 guns. Rudyard of Lloyd's battery, *WL*, no. 98, speaking of his and Cleeves's batteries, says that they fired because the French infantry had come too close; but by his description they were no closer than la Belle Alliance, which is well over 2 miles from Mont St Jean. Cleeves, writing of the morning of the 18th, says that the Duke was insistent on not engaging in counter-battery work but only against infantry on the move, and conserving ammunition: Pflugk-Harttung, *Belle-*

Alliance, no. 63, p. 177, and *WA*, ii, no. 16. FitzRoy Somerset recorded that the guns fired about 7 in the evening, that 'the Duke was very angry, not wishing to provoke hostilities, and ordered the firing to cease. The French fired from a few guns and about eight o'clock drew off', Owen, p. 11.

29. Houssaye, II, chap. 5, sec. IV, p. 267; Eng. trans., p. 152 (my italics). The consequences were slightly different for the defenders, for it was not they who had to set the ball rolling, and delay gave them the advantage. For readers in English there are excellent collections of translated French accounts of this night in Andrew Field's fine *Waterloo, the French Perspective* (2012), chapter 3. It is indispensable reading alongside Houssaye, and is broader in its treatment of the great battle than its subtitle might suggest.
30. *WL*, no. 71, p. 152. Vivian did not entirely endorse Ponsonby's claim, but he let it go for what it was worth.
31. *WL*, no. 34.
32. The Duke's Waterloo Despatch termed De Lancey's reported death 'a serious loss to His Majesty's Service and to me at this moment'. But see also his opinion of 1812 which is pleasant but not totally complimentary: my vol. 1, chap. 25, sec. V.
33. The two extracts that I quote from Somerset's account are in Owen, pp. 10–11.
34. Constant's journal, in De Bas, *Prins Frederik*, iii, II, p. 621 and again p. 634. This was written only days after the event, and the identification of the site is quite clear. There is some slight corroboration in Basil Jackson's recollection of 1877, published in 1903: he said that he was sent from Quatre Bras to Mont St Jean to assist De Lancey, but that the latter asked him to help sort out the confusion in the street of Genappe as 'I shall not want you at Waterloo.' But this is the 83-year-old Jackson of 1877, not the Jackson of his prime in the 1830s and 40s, and is long after the event; by itself it is not the strongest evidence.
35. *Letters of Colonel Sir A. S. Frazer*, p. 544.
36. Clinton to Lynedoch, 23 June 1815, in G. Glover, *Waterloo: The Defeat of Napoleon's Imperial Guard*, p. 105.
37. Oldfield's MS has often been used by the older historians and accepted as inherently sound, e.g. by Whitworth Porter's *History of the Corps of Royal Engineers*, vol. i (1889), and by Sir C. W. Robinson in his *Wellington's Campaigns*. It has now been published in G. Glover, *WA*, vol. vi, no. 90. Oldfield's colleague Lieutenant John Sperling, RE, independently confirmed that he heard Wellington's orders as to Braine l'Alleud 'which was to form a protection on the right of our intended [*sic*] position': letter dated 20 June 1815, quoted in Porter, i, p. 378 from the *Letters of an Officer* of 1872, and now reprinted as no. 93 in *WA*, vol. vi, just after Oldfield.
38. The map and its strange story were mentioned by Scott in *Paul's Letters* (1816), p. 124, and printed in C. D. Yonge's *Life of Wellington* (1860), vol. i, opp p. 565, and reprinted in Colonel David Miller's *Lady De Lancey at Waterloo* (2000), p. 61. My friend David Miller deals extensively with the battle-site controversy, pp. 60–5, although I personally differ from his conclusions.
39. Burgoyne's statement in G. Wrottesley (ed.), *The Life of F. M. Sir J. F. Burgoyne* (1873), i, p. 329. He added, 'Two companies of Sappers and 3000 men might, on the night of the

17th ... have thrown up such a line as would have afforded great cover to our infantry and guns.'

40. The fact that the Prussians on the day decided to make their main thrust against Plancenoit, close to La Belle Alliance, does not affect the considerations of Wellington and Gneisenau on the 17th.

CHAPTER 34: Grouchy and the Prussians

1. Much of this section on the orders and times is drawn from Houssaye, *1815, Waterloo*, Book II, chap. 4. However, my conclusions from the data are somewhat different from his.
2. See chap. 32, sec. III for the two Bertrand orders. Houssaye records the statement of Colonel Baudus that Grouchy met Soult just after receiving the first Bertrand order removing three cavalry divisions. After Grouchy left, Soult deplored that so large a force should be employed against the shaken Prussians (he thought one small infantry corps and Pajol and Exelmans would suffice) when the main army was going to encounter Wellington. But as Houssaye adds, Soult made no complaint of the direction of search enjoined on Grouchy (II, 4, V, p. 240; Eng. trans., p. 137).
3. Houssaye, II, 4, V, p. 242; Eng. trans., p. 138, says that the vanguard of *3e Corps* broke camp at noon but still did not reach le Point du Jour until 3 p.m., a distance of about 4 miles.
4. There is an interesting passage in Clausewitz, *On War*, that touches on this, book 4, chap. 12, some 400 words long: 'Normally both sides ... call a halt'.
5. Grouchy to Exelmans, Gembloux, 7 p.m.: 'I am arriving here with the corps of Vandamme and Gérard': Houssaye, p. 244 fn.; Eng. trans. p. 139 fn. Of course nobody thought that this meant that both corps arrived at the same time, but it does fix where Grouchy was at that hour.
6. Pollio, pp. 338–9, for this version, copied from the minute in the *Archives de Guerre*. In most respects the archival version resembles very closely the text first published in 1830 by General Gérard. Pollio placed the archival version beside the one Grouchy published in 1843, which, said Pollio, 'agrees perfectly with the archival version in all minor matters, but *omits or alters* the expressions that would confirm the Emperor in thinking that *Blücher's intervention* on 18 June was impossible' (my emphasis). Ropes, pp. 358–9 also preferred the Gérard version. I set out the main differences in the texts in Appendix 1 to this chapter.
7. For these orders see Houssaye, II, 4, V, p. 250; Eng. trans., p. 142.
8. The second Bertrand letter seems to me to follow perfectly the sharp succession of thoughts that Napoleon rapped out, allowing no time for reading over and revision before despatch. The letter clearly shows at the moment of dictation Napoleon's *uncertainty* of where the Prussians might go, whereas the memoirs written at St Helena pretend quite *otherwise*. Speaking of the night of the 15th they claim such success that henceforth the Emperor could defeat each ally in detail: that 'to avoid this misfortune, the greatest of all, they could do no other than cede ground and unite at Brussels or further beyond'; and

later, that having been defeated at Ligny, 'Blücher would probably retreat on Wavre': 'The Campaign of 1815', *Corr. de Nap.*, pp. 203/168 and 212/176.

9. Ropes may possibly have gone slightly astray in summarising Napoleon's intentions in the second Bertrand letter. On p. 211 he wrote that Napoleon gave Grouchy no instructions on what to do if he encountered the Prussians – 'it was left to him to determine for himself. It might be that he could hinder the accomplishment of their design most effectually by attacking them; it might be that his best course would be to rejoin the main army as soon as he could, or to manoeuvre so as to act in conjunction with it.' It is true that what Grouchy was to do if the Prussians massed and stood firm was not stated. He was certainly to 'pursue' them in their flight, but Napoleon also wrote 'in all circumstances keep your two infantry corps together within one league's extent, and every night hold a good military position, with several different paths of retreat'. Surely that reads as a caution against engaging in battle and keeping lines of escape open. After all, what he wanted was for Grouchy 'to penetrate the enemy's intentions' while keeping them on the run. But perhaps this difference between Ropes and myself comes simply to this: the instructions should have been clearer.
10. Clausewitz points to the imprecise orders issued so late by imperial headquarters, with the belief that the Meuse and the east was the Prussian objective, all leading Grouchy to neglect the Dyle in favour of Gembloux. He suggests that if a detachment had gone to Mont-St-Guibert it would have kept some real contact with the main army, but that French doctrine was against too much dispersion. However, once Grouchy by 10 p.m. on 17 June had learned that Blücher had turned towards Wavre, 'his innermost thoughts should have been that this could only be happening in order to regain contact with Wellington, for one does not leave one's natural line of retreat without reason … [He] should have taken the shortest route possible from Gembloux towards the Dyle, thus via Mont-St-Guibert in order to drive away the Prussian corps that might be in this area or to take up a position himself along the left bank if it was still unoccupied and thus hold the corps at Wavre in check' (*Campaign*, chap. 50, pp. 179–80 BMP). That seems entirely fair. Instead I note that Grouchy continued to order his force's 'fragmentation' in several directions. I can see no reason for this, other than that Napoleon had so emphasised the eastern thesis in the second Bertrand letter, and so often hectored his generals when they came up with suggestions that did not fit his conceptions, that it was Grouchy's attempt to propitiate him.
11. Lettow-Vorbeck, p. 374; Hofschröer, *1815*, ii, p. 38.
12. Bülow's 10 p.m. report to Blücher is in Lettow Vorbeck, p. 375 fn., and the orders to IV Corps' brigades are in Pflugk-Harttung, 'Von Wavre bis Belle-Alliance', p. 418. Both are in Hofschröer, *1815*, ii, pp. 40–1.
13. The Gröben reports are best read in Lettow-Vorbeck, Anlage 12, pp. 529–30. Ollech's version is less exact. English versions are in Hofschröer, *1815*, ii, pp. 33–8.
14. We have seen these Prussian opinions and fears stated in earlier chapters, though few historians seem to have paid much if any attention to them. Lützow, who was captured at Ligny, may have been flattering Napoleon or may have been saying no more than

what he really felt: 'the Prussian army was lost and Blücher had for a second time *put in danger the Prussian monarchy*' (my emphasis). On 17 June these considerations became of acute significance. So far as I can tell only one other writer has presented the dilemma of 17 June in explicit terms: Barry Van Danzig in his penetrating study, *Who Won Waterloo?* (2007), chap. 7.

15. Hofschröer, *1815*, ii, p. 25, quoting Hofmann. Nostitz seems to have made no reference to all this.
16. Stanhope's *Conversations*, 26 October 1837, p. 110. Blücher spent the night of 16/17 at Mellery and was so battered that he was carried from there on the 17th, but by the time he had rested at Wavre (night 17/18) he was active enough once more. Hence I think Hardinge's recollection fits with Wavre, 17/18 June. Stanhope had spent the day of 26 Oct. 1837 in hunting, dining, and late evening conversation, and the conversation ranged very widely, so that the record runs to about a thousand words. The recollection reads authentically and catches the tone very well, but it is a recollection, written only after getting back to the privacy of his room; and Hardinge never saw the result. It is worth noting that Lettow-Vorbeck, who generally avoided reminiscences and accounts written long after the event, did treat this relation of Hardinge's as genuine and truthful. While accepting that the date might be inaccurate, Lettow-Vorbeck, thought that the evidence of an internal dispute among the high command was valid: *Napoleons Untergang*, p. 398, fn.
17. Colonel (Maj.-Gen. Sir) J. F. Maurice, in *United Service Magazine*, July 1890, at p. 355, the fourth of his articles on Waterloo.
18. Quoted in Leggiere, *Blücher*, p. 403.
19. Lettow-Vorbeck, p. 365. He could not trace the Müffling letter, but its terms can be guessed from Blücher's reply.
20. Lettow-Vorbeck, p. 376: the Ledebur detachment from IV Corps was to stay at Mont-St-Guibert to cover the route from Sombreffe to Wavre.
21. Book II, chap. 4, sec. III, p. 233 (Eng. trans. p. 133). Alessandro Barbero grants it the honour of a full chapter heading, *The Battle*, chapter 3.
22. A. Pfister, *Aus Dem Lager der Verbündeten, 1814 und 1815* (1897), p. 371.
23. The Dutch version of the Despatch is printed in full in F. De Bas, *Prins Frederik*, iii, II, p. 1213 onwards.

CHAPTER 35: Wellington and the Battleground

1. The three letters are in *WD*, 476–8/145–6.
2. *WSD*, x, p. 501. Lady Frances was the fourth daughter of the Irish peer and rake Lord Mountnorris, by his second wife (married 1783). Shortly after marrying his first wife he had run off with Mrs Grace Elliott, the famous 'Dolly the tall'; the paternity of a daughter Dolly bore ten years later was claimed by the Prince of Wales and three other gentlemen: she later became the mistress of the *égalité* duc d'Orléans: *DNB*, Elliott, G. D. Lady Frances's upbringing may thus have been unfortunate, her mother was rumoured to like

wine too much, and the girl was married off in 1810, almost out of the schoolroom, to Byron's friend James Wedderburn Webster. He treated her very badly, and she and Byron had an unconsummated *affaire* in 1813. She and her husband were in Brussels early in 1815, but he returned to England leaving her with her parents, and nearly seven months pregnant. During the spring and summer she flirted conspicuously with Wellington, and followed him to Paris, where she gave birth shortly after. Several military diarists (Digby Mackworth and others) commented on their activities in Brussels. In 1816 there was a successful libel case (*Webster* v. *Baldwin*) against a paper that had published allegations of adultery with Wellington. In later years the Websters separated, and in the 1821 she had something of an *affaire* with Lord Petersham. She died in 1837. The index volume to Marchand's edition of *Byron's Letters and Journals* (12 vols, 1973–82) has many entries about her and her buffoon of a husband, and as Byron is supreme among letter writers his remarks are always a delight.

3. There are many descriptions of the battlefield as well as maps: among the most useful seem Siborne, Shaw Kennedy and Fortescue among the older historians, Mark Adkin and Barry Van Danzig recently. Craan's and Siborne's maps are very useful, and the modern 1:20,000 map of the Belgian IGN is the best accompaniment to a walk over the ground. Since the topography has been explained in detail by innumerable historians, and life is short, footnoting anew each and every feature would serve little purpose.
4. I say 'had', because of the massive excavations of soil taken for the construction of that blight on the battlefield, the Lion Mound (visitors to Ramillies and Malplaquet can still find their sites mercifully undisturbed). At least the excavators did not touch the ground around the monument to Colonel Sir Alexander Gordon, and thus we can judge the original level of the ground as being about 12 feet higher than today.
5. One should also note three streams, not so much for their intrinsic importance as for the effect of rain in making their levels rise and affecting their banks and the nearby ground: the Hain that flowed due north through Braine l'Alleud; the Smohain brook that rose close to Papelotte and flowed east; and the Lasne stream that rose near Rossomme and Plancenoit, and flowed north-east to Chapelle-St-Lambert and towards Wavre.
6. Having been at the commemorations in Ypres on 11 November 1998, I made a visit to the riding school at Papelotte farm on the 13th, driving a hired car. Taking the crest road and descending into a sunken lane rather like the ones in Devon, after crossing the stream, the hired car – perhaps happier on the Flanders levels – found the steep climb to the farm almost too much for it until I went into bottom gear.
7. Until well into the twentieth century crop varieties grew much taller than those used in modern farming.
8. The subsidiary ridge (with *Chemin de Braine l'Alleud* marked on it) is very clearly shown in Craan's beautiful map of 1816: BL Map room, 31885 (1), and often reprinted. It can also be seen in the less fine map in Shaw Kennedy's *Notes on the Battle of Waterloo* (at the end of the 1865 edition, but moved to before p. 1 in the 2003 Spellmount reprint).
9. See the colour illustration from 1816 in *WA*, vol. iii, illustration 8. The famous surgeon of the Middlesex Hospital, Charles Bell (1774–1842, FRS, FRSE, knighted 1831), after a

stint in the Brussels hospitals, took a short break and visited the field on 6 July 1815, and climbed the first 25 feet of the construction, which he estimated at 60 feet overall: see the valuable *Letters of Sir Charles Bell with his Brother* (1870), this visit being at pp. 232–8. My old friend Jacques Logie always insisted that Napoleon did not climb it, but as it stood there I suspect some staff officers were sent up with telescopes.

10. For further details and indeed for Wellington's artillery's performance throughout the battle, see Lipscombe, *Wellington's Guns*, chap. 23. For the initial artillery deployment west of the Charleroi road, see Siborne, *History*, p. 219; Shaw Kennedy, *Notes*, para. 48, p. 72; Adkin, p. 274; and the artillery section in *WL*. Hime in app. D to his *Hist. of the RA, 1815–1853*, points out that Wellington certainly intended to have a reserve of artillery comprising Ross, Beane and Sandham, but that the intensity of the fighting obliged their almost immediate deployment. The Duke had forgotten this deployment by the time he wrote to Mulgrave on 21 Dec. 1815 concerning the failings of the artillery.
11. Until the morning of 18 June the Prince of Orange, at his own request, had commanded all Netherlands cavalry. Uxbridge had no authority over them. On this morning Orange asked that their command should be transferred to Uxbridge (*WL*, no. 3), and it may be this late change that stopped Trip's and de Ghigny's and van Merlen's brigades being deployed separately.
12. George Cathcart's letter of 1835, *WL*, no. 15.
13. Bylandt's 1st Brigade was placed on the forward slope by the Prince of Orange at about 9 a.m., but the 2nd Netherlands Divisional commander, Perponcher, pulled it back into cover behind the hedge, certainly before Napoleon's Grand Battery opened a murderous fire on the slope. Kempt and Pack gave ground to allow Bylandt back. For these moves and the local action during the day see my detailed article 'Bylandt's Brigade' in *British Army Review*, no. 129, Spring 2002, with an enlargement of Craan's map and casualty figures. It looks as though later writers have accepted my conclusions. Perponcher spent the early part of the battle with Bylandt, had two horses killed under him during the charge and retreat of Ponsonby's Union Brigade, and only at 6 p.m. went across to Saxe-Weimar's 2nd Brigade at Papelotte: see the divisional report in Boulger, at p. 62.
14. Ian Fletcher, *Galloping at Everything* (1999), p. 225.
15. The special consideration shown to Uxbridge is visible in the pencil note sent to him by Wellington in the middle stages of Waterloo: it is an order but couched as a suggestion: see chap. 42, sec. V.
16. Uxbridge later lamented his failure of control over his reserve line in the Waterloo charges, and recognised that this had previously happened at Sahagun (the name that H. T. Siborne misread as 'Irtragau') when he had neglected management of his reserve line and so could not take full advantage of his first line's success: *WL*, no. 5. For his extra authority at Waterloo and lack of any orders from Wellington: *ibid.*, no. 3.
17. Constant noted in his journal that around 10 a.m. the Prince, who was with Alten's 3rd British Division (of the Prince's I Corps), told him that Wellington had ordered Chassé (3rd Netherlands Division, I Corps) to report to Hill, Perponcher (2nd Netherlands Division, I Corps) to Picton, all the cavalry to Uxbridge so that the Prince commanded

directly no Netherlands troops; however he was generally in charge of the 'left centre'. Constant also noted that the Duke would concern himself directly with 'the troops of the right, the Guards Division [officially part of the Prince's corps] and the Brunswickers'. As Wellington was concerned principally for his right, and had removed the Guards from Orange's command, he had done everything he could to limit the Prince's activities without breaching diplomatic relations. The Orange/Alten relationship was still to create problems, however. *Constant's Journal*, in Logie, *Mélanges*, p. 143.

18. 'The Campaign of 1815', *Corr. de Nap.*, xxxi, p. 218/181 and p. 219/182. Napoleon's whole calculation on the day was that there was *no* second enemy army beyond the forest (see chap. 36, sec. II) and that he could smash the only one, south of the forest, that day. So the caveat was without much value, except to imply that without a second enemy army to fear, 'a French army' could cross the forest. But by the same token that implies that Wellington's men could have retreated through the forest. Napoleon did not admit that groups of fighting men could retreat through the woodland while firing from behind trees to hamper pursuit, and that they could do this more easily than the now tired advancing troops could follow, and by following risk ambush.
19. Frazer, letters timed 18 June, 3 a.m. and 9.15 a.m., *Letters*, pp. 544–5.
20. *WL*, no. 81.
21. Baron A. H. Jomini, *Précis de la Campagne de 1815* (Paris, 1839), p. 195; examined in more detail in his *Art of War* (trans. 1862, Greenhill reprint 1992), chap. 4, art. xxx, p. 183.
22. W. Napier's letters of 1832 to the 'Bath Journal' in his *Life*, by H. A. Bruce, (1864), vol. i, pp. 389–94.
23. F. De Bas, *Prins Frederik*, iii, II, p. 795 from a MS in Apsley House. Sir H. Maxwell quoted the document in his *Life of Wellington* (1900), ii, p. 48, with slight variations. Littleton had married a daughter of Marquess Wellesley in 1812; he became Lord Hatherton in 1835. His diaries ran from 1817 to March 1825, and from Jan. 1828 to 1862, so this must be a separate memorandum. As to what was recorded, there are two points of interest: (i) The Duke's comment that he was not deceived in relying on the Prussians contrasts agreeably with Gneisenau's endless complaints about Wellington; nor did Wellington complain of their slow advance that caused his army so many extra casualties. (ii) The Duke was clear as to his *next* step, if defeated: joining with Hill, moving to his 'right', and 'towards' the coast, while the Prussians still distracted Napoleon. But that was as far as his plans went, and it was typical of his empiricism. He did not say 'to Ostend', and nor did he say 'to Antwerp' which was not to his right but was *behind* and *beyond* an 'uncovered Brussels'. I have heard it asserted that his plan was to retire 'on Antwerp' but I know of not one jot of evidence for that claim, and do not believe that the Duke's mind worked like that (*cf.* his 11 May remarks to Orange).
24. Few historians have remarked on the significance of this passage. Maxwell did in passing (ii, p. 46) and so more clearly has Philip Haythornthwaite in *Waterloo Men* (1999), p. 39 and footnotes.
25. Journal, in G. Glover, *Eyewitness to the Peninsular War and the Battle of Waterloo* (2010), Stanhope's letters and journals, 1803–25, at p. 180. This passage had previously been quoted

by Colonel Maurice in his Waterloo articles, *USM*, Sept. 1890, p. 539, and by Fortescue, *History*, x, p. 347. Josephina Grassini (1773–1850) was an Italian contralto, brought to Paris by Bonaparte after Marengo; she sang in London in 1804–6, then returned to Paris and the French court till her voice became impaired. She returned to Italy in 1817. She was reportedly a mistress of Napoleon, and Greville later said that Wellington was 'very fond' of her.

26. See DBTS, ii, pp. 64–5, for these bridges and their importance.
27. The Hal concept is discussed by B. Van Danzig, *Who Won Waterloo?*, pp. 62–3.
28. For the western reconnaissance by night, see 'The Campaign of 1815', *Corr. de Nap.*, xxxi, p. 216; p. 179. But see n. 29 below.
29. Las Cases, *Mémorial*, 4–5 Dec. 1815, i, p. 277 in Dunan's edition. He went on to say that Grouchy went missing, Ney was visibly confused, beside himself with remorse for Fontainebleau (March 1814) and Lons-le-Saulnier (March 1815), d'Erlon proved to be useless, and nobody was himself. Note that in 'The Campaign of 1815', *Corr. de Nap.*, xxxi, p. 216; p. 179, Napoleon claimed that he decided to attack the 'enemy left' or eastern flank because it was weaker, would drive Wellington away from the Prussians, and was where Grouchy was expected to join him.
30. Gourgaud, *Campaign of 1815*, Eng. version 1818, pp. 124–5; the French original (pp. 104–5), published only later in the year, is identical. By contrast, the memoirs state that before he gave the signal to open battle Napoleon 'perceived in the direction of St-Lambert a cloud which seemed to be of troops', that confirmation came in fifteen minutes, and shortly after that he decided to switch Lobau to oppose the Prussians. There is no mention of the Nivelles road idea. *Corr. de Nap.*, xxxi, pp. 227–9/188–90.
31. Walter Scott heard Wellington make a significant remark apropos this, at Paris in August 1815. Someone said (incorrectly, as we now know) that there had been no rear entrance at La Haye Sainte, nor any made before the battle began. Wellington replied '*I* ought to have thought of it, but my mind could not embrace every thing at once': Scott felt that Wellington 'considered it as his duty to superintend and direct even the most minute details of that complicated action' and therefore that the Duke thought this apology was necessary. Scott's *Paul's Letters to his Kinsfolk*, pp. 165–6.
32. Lettow-Vorbeck, p. 404, had the notion that on 6 June a council of war (*Kriegsrat*) recommended field-works and suchlike but that Wellington objected to putting infantry and artillery behind walls which could interfere with their freedom of movement. But he cited no source for this. As Wellington did not hold with councils of war, and as there is the sapper Sperling's evidence that Wellington had intended that Braine l'Alleud should be strengthened by entrenchments – but that this was neglected (*WA*, vi, no. 93, at p. 221), for these reasons I have not put Lettow's claim into my text.
33. The question is always about the loss of Wellington, with Blücher and Napoleon as constants. But let us posit that instead it was Napoleon who for some reason was struck down or killed. How would the French army have coped with that? The conclusion of Lt.-Colonel René Tournès, 'Le GQG de Napoléon Ier', *Revue de Paris*, 1 May 1921, pp. 134–58, based on a close study of the 1813 spring campaign, was that under Berthier the staff

were simple executants of the Emperor's orders, and the *major-général* himself neither sought to, nor did, initiate *anything*. 'In the imperial headquarters the dominant factor and one that cannot be over-stated was the importance of the Emperor's role; beside that central character of the supreme commander everything else in the picture is flat.' And Soult was less efficient than Berthier and was widely distrusted by the army.

34. When Müffling expressed concern that Hougoumont might prove 'untenable', Wellington dismissed the thought by saying simply, 'I have thrown Macdonell into it': Müffling, *Memoirs*, p. 243.
35. W. Tomkinson, *The Diary of a Cavalry Officer*, p. 286.
36. Wellington to Bathurst, 30 Oct. 1814, HMC *Bathurst*, pp. 302–3.
37. Unsigned article, 'Waterloo and the Waterloo Model', *USJ*, June 1839, pp. 201–5, at p. 204.
38. This characterisation extended beyond the British forces for, as my friend Maj.-Gen. Melvin has reminded me, it applied to others, 'including the Hanoverian Landwehr (much neglected in most British descriptions)'.
39. Clearly Wellington's absence from the scene in the 1820s and later would also have affected British politics, but that is not my concern here.

CHAPTER 36: Napoleon Plans his Battle

1. The existence of the evening directive for battle the next morning is proved by two sources: (1) Soult's reference to it in his orders just after dawn on the 18th; (2) Colonel Trefcon (of Bachelu's divisional staff), who says that they stood to arms at first light in conformity with Reille's order to march at 5 a.m., but that it was countermanded just as they moved, so that cleaning and cooking could take place: Field, *Waterloo*, p. 46.
2. Napoleon's memoirs repeatedly state that at this moment he was already convinced that Blücher was moving towards or was at Wavre, that at 11 p.m. on 17 June he had received a despatch from Grouchy saying exactly that, so that it was 'probable' that Wellington and Blücher would combine in front of Brussels: *Corr. de Nap.*, xxxi, pp. 217–8/180–1. That is not what the record shows.
3. *Memoirs*, pp. 219–20/182 on the twelve hours needed. Andrew Field quotes the valet Marchand as saying that Drouot of the *Garde* gave Napoleon a similar opinion but without specifying how many hours: Field, p. 45. The 9 o'clock opinion is in *Corr. de Nap.*, xxxi, p. 221/183.
4. Elchingen, *Docs. Inéd.*, p. 52.
5. Divisional report, Boulger, p. 59.
6. Field, p. 48.
7. The proclamation announced the restored Empire's first annexation: 'The ephemeral successes of my enemies detached you momentarily from my Empire. In my exile on a rock in the sea I heard your cries of distress. The God of battles has decided the fate of your beautiful provinces. Napoleon is in your midst; you are worthy of being French. Rise in your masses, join my invincible phalanxes to exterminate the remains of these barbarians who are your enemies and mine; they flee with rage and despair in their

hearts': DBTS, ii, p. 28. Laeken was just north of Brussels. The Rhine frontier meant that those Dutch, Belgians and Germans living on the left bank would become French subjects. Who next?

8. Foy, *Vie Militaire*, p. 277 (18 June), and p. 278 (23 June). I discuss the additions in Appendix 1 to this chapter.
9. Napoleon's way with his subordinates, high or low, was all too often to ignore, snub, and rebuke whatever opinion they might advance, or whatever question or clarification they might seek. One of his junior secretaries, Fleury de Chaboulon, wrote (i, p. 176 in Cornet's edition) that certain events happened so fast that Napoleon had scarcely time to react or receive any advice, to which the Emperor replied in the margin with contempt, 'The Emperor regarded his secretary as a machine to which he did not speak [? converse].' This may explain why Soult was so unsure and obsequious as Chief of Staff.
10. There had been a significant instance around Salamanca in November 1812 when Soult's worries about Wellington led to the latter's army escaping unscathed. The united French armies of the South, Centre and of Portugal amounted to some 90,000 men, a massive 20,000 more than Wellington's. Soult's positive advice had been accepted by King Joseph, but in the event his manoeuvres were feeble. The weather was bad but, in Oman's view, Soult was haunted by memories of Albuera and by Marmont's recent overset: 'After Albuera he had a wholesome dread of attacking a British army in position, if it could be avoided, and preferred to manoeuvre it from its chosen ground, even if he thereby sacrificed the possibility of a great victory and secured only an illusory advantage' (*Pen. War*, vi, pp. 120–40, the quotation being at p. 140). And now, Mont St Jean.
11. Houssaye, *1815, Waterloo*, Book III, chap. 2, sec. III, pp. 311–12 and notes; Eng. trans., p. 178 and notes. A further proof of Wellington's moral ascendancy over the French commanders in Spain is Marshal Jourdan's telling appraisal of the very able Suchet, that on the battlefield 'he only had to combat Spanish armies': *Mémoires*, p. 366. Jourdan was never dazzled by the Napoleonic mystique and as King Joseph's military adviser his assessments of the realities in the Peninsular war were shrewd.
12. Oman's *History of the Peninsular War* is full of instances, too many to number.
13. Grouchy, *Mémoires*, iv, p. 175.
14. 'A French chief commissary told me afterwards that during the action [of the 18th] casks of brandy were brought on to the ground, the heads knocked out, and the men about to attack were allowed to help themselves ... I can positively assert that during the time I was with the [British] troops, both in the Peninsula and Waterloo, no spirits were issued previous to any action, but only in the evening when all was over': Commissary Tupper Carey, *Cornhill*, p. 729. But the French that dawn were badly off for food, and were soaked: brandy was all the more essential in consequence.
15. *Corr. de Nap.*, no. 22,061, at the start of the section on Waterloo.
16. Gourgaud, *Campaign of 1815*, pp. 92 and 95.
17. 'The Campaign of 1815', *Corr. de Nap.*, xxxi, pp. 224/185; 226/187; 229–30/190–1.
18. Coppens & Courcelle, *Papelotte*, p. 13, col b. This entire section on the *6e Corps* conundrum owes a great deal to their researches and copious quotations.

19. Field, pp. 54–6, gives several eye-witness accounts, all supporting Napoleon's claim that there was wild enthusiasm among the ranks.
20. Shaw Kennedy spoke of a deployment 'highly interesting, and, as a sight, majestic and beautiful' (*Notes*, para. 51, p. 74); F. M. Sir William Gomm wrote of this passage, that the sight 'was indeed a magnificent spectacle, never to be obliterated from or darkened on the memory of any one who witnessed it' (holograph comment, bound into Lady Gomm's copy of Shaw Kennedy's *Notes* at p. 74, now owned by the London Library). Kincaid likewise wrote of this 'grand and imposing' spectacle, from 'the *rub-a-dub* of drums and the *tantarara* of trumpets, in addition to their increasing shouts, it looked at first as if they had some hopes of scaring us off the ground; for it was a singular contrast to the stern silence reigning on our side' (pp. 333–4; 1929, pp. 248–9).
21. Field, pp. 56–60 for details from Pétiet, Foy and Fée about the table, map and stones; and regarding the observers Baudus and the equerry Jardin Ainé (this last published only in English in 1911, not in French) who thought the Emperor was apathetic or depressed.
22. The speed with which ground can dry is surprising. Third Ypres (31 July–11 November 1917) was notorious for dreadful weather. The appalling August rainfall was the worst for that month in thirty years, with rain on twenty-eight days, and this continued into the first week of September, with 5 and 6 September suffering heavy downpours, added to which the ground was made worse by the shellfire. Yet the soldier and novelist Henry Williamson testified that shells *skidded on the hard ground* at the Menin road ridge battle on 26 September: see P. H. Liddle (ed.), *Passchendaele in Perspective* (1997), chapter 10, 'The Flanders Battleground and the Weather in 1917'.
23. The Provost-Marshal of the *Armée du Nord*, Radet, wrote on 16 June complaining, 'There has been nothing but ravaging, pillaging, as much in farms as in military depots. They even go to the length of stealing military horses, though securely tethered by picket. There are scuffles, and fires are deliberately started. The authority of *gendarmerie* officers and even of *Garde* officers is ignored.' He asked to be allowed to resign. The next day he wrote of the breakdown of discipline in the *Garde*, men of which ransacked houses and smashed chests, cupboards and counters: Pollio, p. 43.
24. Houssaye, Book III, chap. 2, IV, p. 322; Eng. trans., p. 185. Napoleon's figures, using 'estimates of the best informed officers', of 90,000 Anglo-Allied to 62,000 French, can be noted but left to one side (*Corr. de Nap.*, xxxi, p. 221/183). Siborne, *Hist.*, 3rd edn., pp. 230–1 and 388, and appendices: his figures would appear to include Lambert's brigade but to exclude at this time in the morning Chassé's division (12 battalions); I have always found useful Fortescue's rule of thumb of a one-eighth addition for bandsmen and officers. Adkin, *Waterloo Companion*, pp. 37, 51. The figures in Digby Smith's magnificent *Napoleonic Wars Data Book*, pp. 538–48 are too many and too complex to summarise here. Haythornthwaite's appendices in *Waterloo Armies* appear very close to Digby Smith's, and are my prime source.
25 Possibly the most arithmetically faulty return was that for 'The French Armies in Spain, Oct. 15, 1812', copied from the French War Archives and printed in Oman, vol. vi, app. 2. The many small mistakes do not materially affect the story, however.

26. For Frazer's work, see his *Letters*, p. 551. There is a great deal of information about the arrival and assembling of the 18-pounder heavy batteries in Captain Ilbert's long series of letters, in G. Glover (ed.), *WA*, vol. iii. The gun teams, unable to bring up their guns, nevertheless worked at providing small arms ammunition to the army on 18 June.
27. I put this at its simplest. I am still uncertain how much Napoleon knew of Wellington's real dispositions. Did he know of the interlocking defensive system at Merbe Braine–Hougoumont that would have so complicated a western thrust by the Nivelles road? Did he then know that the infantry on the eastern wing of Wellington's army comprised mainly Netherlands and Nassau troops? (There is somewhere among French sources a reference to Prussians holding that part of the line: that report may have resulted from a confusion over uniforms.) Had he received reports of the broken nature of the ground near Papelotte and of the problem of the stream there, which could impede the movement of artillery? There was little time to find out all this on Sunday morning.
28. *Corr. de Nap.*, no. 22,060. In his memoirs, however, Napoleon indicated that d'Erlon should send two divisions against La Haye Sainte and two against the eastern hamlet of 'La Haye', thus attacking the centre *and* turning Wellington's eastern flank, which would then be rolled up. His reasons for preferring the eastern flank were (1) it would drive Wellington from the Prussians 'if [*sic*] they had planned to unite', (2) the eastern flank was weakest, (3) Grouchy was expected on this side. Thus his memoirs were less specific as to a central attack and he more or less stated that he intended an eastern assault ('The Campaign of 1815', *Corr. de Nap.*, xxxi, p. 226/187). I do not find Barbero's chap. 19 altogether clear or convincing on Napoleon's attack order.
29. Napoleon's 11 a.m. order states 'twenty-four' 12-pounders, but each of the three corps had only six. This is further discussed in chap. 38, n. 4. Or maybe 'twenty-four' was an error on Napoleon's or his staff's part and should read 'eighteen'. Adkin concludes (pp. 286, 296) that eighteen 12-pounders formed the nucleus of the Grand Battery, to which was added forty-two 6-pounders and twenty howitzers, to give a total of eighty pieces. However, he thinks all the *Garde* pieces were 6-pounders or howitzers, whereas the *Garde* reserve had available eighteen 12-pounders (Adkin, p. 55) from which six might easily have been spared. But neither at the time, nor since, have the authorities' calculations all agreed.
30. Marbot, *Mémoires*, iii, in the section 'Letters on Waterloo': Marbot's letter of 1830 to a member of Grouchy's family (p. 376).
31. Thus Houssaye, III, 3, II, p. 334 (Eng. trans., p. 191) from the original in the War Archives. He remarked that copies have a number of different times marked on them, but he considered 6 a.m. as best, since its remarks fit Soult's 1 p.m. reply, whereas they would not fit with what Soult wrote at 10 a.m.
32. Grouard, p. 155.
33. Elchingen, *Docs. Inéd.*, p. 54, Ney's amendment, together with the original order.
34. 'The Campaign of 1815', *Corr. de Nap.*, xxxi, pp. 226–7/188.
35. Gourgaud, *Campaign of 1815*, Eng. version, p. 92.
36. On 26 June 1815 Ney wrote a letter to Fouché, Duke of Otranto (by then the head of government), dealing with the campaign. It is about 2,000 words long, and almost 40 per

cent deals with the day of 18 June. But the period of battle before 7 p.m. is covered very summarily, in some 70 words, and says only that 'the battle began at 1 p.m.', and nothing about any orders: the letter is in *Booth's Battle of Waterloo*, 11th edn. (1852, sometimes called the George Jones edition, from his illustrations), pp. 385–9. Reille's remarks are in Elchingen, *Docs. Inéd.*, p. 61.

37. A. du Casse, *Méms et Corr. du Roi Jérome et de la Reine Catherine*, vol. vii (Paris, 1866), pp. 89 and 83.
38. In writing to Ney early on 16 June Napoleon said that the capture of Brussels would isolate Wellington from *western* Belgium, which meant that the Duke must be *east* of the city and therefore not far from Blücher; Napoleon nevertheless insisted that Blücher was isolated and too weak to stand and fight. His remarks about corps commanders reporting to Ney when the Emperor was not present, and the limited use of Lefebvre-Desnouette's and Kellermann's cavalry had also complicated the action on 16 June (see vol. 1, chap. 27–30).
39. Coignet, *Notebooks* ('Soldiers Tales' series, 1928), p. 278; Riddock's unpublished letter in the Siborne MSS in the BL, quoted by Uffindell & Corum, in their excellent *On the Fields of Glory* (1996) in a note on pp. 155–6; Bacon's letter (undated but 1844 or later), in G. Glover (ed.), *LW*, no. 62, at p. 103. Also, in March 1814, as d'Erlon retreated from Vic-de-Bigorre, 'an English staff officer, Captain Light, did indeed gallop from end to end of one such rearguard, feigning to be wounded, and counted the battalions as he rode; but this was an expedient that could only be employed once': Fortescue, *History of the British Army*, x, p. 25.
40. As previously mentioned, in Foy, *Vie Militaire*, pp. 277, 278.
41. Gourgaud, *Campaign of 1815*, Eng. version, p. 86; 'The Campaign of 1815', *Corr. de Nap.*, xxxi, p. 218/181.
42. Zenowicz, *Waterloo, déposition sur les quatre jours de la campagne de 1815* (Paris, 1848), pp. 28–30. This was a second or perhaps revised edition of a pamphlet he had issued in 1820. The 1820 edition was bought in by someone and apparently suppressed. He had been attacked in various publications, e.g. in the 1830s, and replied in this new edition. I owe sight of it to my friend Philippe de Callataÿ, who has a copy in his magnificent library on Waterloo.
43. DBTS, iii, p. 575, from the original in the French War Archives.

CHAPTER 37: Battle Commences

1. General Sir James Shaw Kennedy, *Notes on the Battle of Waterloo* (1865), para. 8, p. 54. The French historian Houssaye noted that he was 'the best informed and most judicious of the English historians' and 'of all those who have written of the battle, none has seen it more clearly. His opinion therefore carries great weight' (p. 382 and fn./Eng. trans. p. 218); the Belgian Aerts said much the same. As to the intervals of inactivity, Sergeant Robertson of the 92nd somewhat clumsily remarked that after the failure of d'Erlon's great attack, 'we were not troubled for a long time nor did we fire any for two hours': *With Napoleon at Waterloo*, p. 161.

2. There has been some controversy on who fired first, and at exactly what time. I rely on Ensign Wedgwood (3rd Guards), letter of 19 June 1815: 'the action commenced at about ½ past 11 by our artillery, which was drawn up about 20 yards before the first line,' and his battalion commander, Lt.-Colonel Home, who said that the 'English' fired first and timed it 'exactly ½ past 11': *WA*, i, nos. 38 and 37. The battery commander Andrew Cleeves claimed the honour (*ibid.*, ii, no. 16). Houssaye, III, 3, I, p. 328 (Eng. trans., p. 187) claims that a divisional battery of Reille's corps began, and the British immediately replied; for timing he accepts the various statements in *WL*: 11.35 a.m. The controversy is not of great importance.
3. So said Lord Saltoun, *LW*, no. 96.
4. Due to casualties at Quatre Bras the light companies of the Coldstream and 3rd Guards formed in effect a large single company.
5. Some writers described the thick cloud of skirmishers as making 'the first' attack, with the line infantry assault being 'the second', but this seems altogether too 'structured' in the circumstances of the day. I put them together, since it seems inherently unlikely that the skirmishers could do more than suppress defensive fire from prepared positions during the time that the line troops simultaneously moved up for the major assault.
6. The Hanoverians were withdrawn to the main force on the ridge. The Nassauers remained. For these developments see the Nassau commander Captain Büsgen's 'Relation' in *Belle-Alliance*, no. 75 and *WA*, ii, no. 43. Büsgen had his command post in the château, and his narrative gives principal credit for the repulse of the attack to Macdonell's 'English Guards'.
7. Captain Robinaux, *2e Ligne*, in Field, p. 70.
8. Given Napoleon's habit of direct command when on the battlefield (witness his letter to Ney on the morning of 16 June, about corps commanders obeying Ney at Quatre Bras unless Napoleon was present, when they would 'obey my orders directly'), he may not have passed orders via Ney, but it seems difficult to believe that he could bypass Reille, since Jerome would need coordinated support from his fellow divisional commanders and only Reille could ensure that. Indeed, unless he could call upon Reille's support, it was not impossible that this most light-weight of the rather unimpressive Bonaparte brothers could bring obloquy on the family name.
9. Major Lebeau, *1re Ligne*, in Field, p. 70.
10. Foy, *Vie Militaire*, p. 280. The point is made quite emphatically by Andrew Field. Since Foy's *2e Brigade* and Bachelu's entire *5e Division* could be deployed in a main infantry attack on the ridge at 5–6 p.m. this supports Field's argument over their non-engagement at Hougoumont. Uffindell & Corum also indicate this, I think: pp. 161, 180.
11. As previously mentioned, on 10 June the duc de Feltre in Ghent had sent Wellington a detailed tabulation of the French army by corps and provinces, obtained from an agent in the Paris war ministry; for Vandamme the official figure was 15,000 men, but Feltre thought it was more likely to be 10,000: *WSD*, x, p. 449. In fact the official morning state of 10 June at Chimay gave Vandamme just over 15,000 infantry, 1,000 cavalry and 38 guns.
12. Mark Adkin set down the effort at Hougoumont over the whole day as absorbing only

2,600 Allied troops against 12,500 French (p. 341), but this is without allowing for Allied troops that had been tied to the summit behind it so as to support the defence, and he includes both brigades of Foy. By contrast Barry Van Danzig, on the basis of a large-scale war game, includes in the Duke's supporting force: Chassé's 3rd Netherlands Division, Dörnberg's and the Brunswickers' cavalry 'and the Cumberland Hussars', and allocates 'at least five British batteries' to it. He estimates that 'Reille pinned down 25,000 infantry, 4,000 cavalry and over 60 Allied guns', whereas Napoleon did not allocate additional formations to back up Reille, so that the Emperor had significantly increased his uncommitted advantage in percentage terms (pp. 128–9).

CHAPTER 38: The Second Act

1. If, as De Salle maintains, 'Souvenirs' in *Revue de Paris*, p. 428, the hauling forward of heavy 12-pounders was to be halted to range, aim, fire and resume movement, then the advance up the Mont St Jean slope must have been even slower.
2. My hunch is that Napoleon was more intent on destruction from a forward position than concerned about casualties to his artillery. Wellington's quiescence would have encouraged him in this. Of course, one thinks of cavalry impulsiveness, of Uxbridge's at Genappe and Waterloo, and forty years later of the Light Brigade at Balaclava. But at this stage there was no sudden crisis and the Duke was to hand. Wellington was not usually inclined to let his cavalry loose on such forays. And the experience of both the Union Brigade charge and that of British artillery under Ney's cavalry attacks in the afternoon show that material damage was difficult to inflict in a mere foray.
3. Adkin, *The Waterloo Companion*, is of enormous help to everyone studying the battle, and his section on the Grand Battery, pp. 294–301 is a principal source for this part of my account. Alessandro Barbero, *The Battle*, chapter 26, by contrast tends to the other view of the placement of the Grand Battery. Three more recent works differ about the Grand Battery, its composition and placement. Nick Lipscombe (*Wellington's Guns*, p. 372) places it 'about 500 yards' south of the Allied road along the crest. Andrew Field's *Waterloo, the French Perspective*, chap. 6, tends to the Adkin position, contrary to Gareth Glover, *Waterloo Myth and Reality*, esp. pp. 124–7. All these are matters of debate, but I find Adkin, Lipscombe and Field the more convincing.
4. Napoleon at 11 a.m. ordered the deployment of 'twenty-four 12-pounders', though he itemised only eighteen (*Corr. de Nap.*, no. 22,060). At St Helena he recalled it as a total of ten batteries to fire at the crossroads, including 'three batteries of 12-pounders' ('The Campaign of 1815', *Corr. de Nap.*, xxxi, 226/187). Adkin concludes that there were eighteen 12-pounders, forty-two 6-pounders, twenty howitzers. Field's *Waterloo, the French Perspective*, chapter 6, examines in detail French and other accounts and recollections, points to the discrepancies in calculations of gun numbers, and thus itemises 62 pieces but seems to tend towards a higher figure. Glover, *Waterloo Myth and Reality*, esp. pp. 124–7, argues that there was not one massed Grand Battery and the gun-line was not so far forward, and that the force comprised a total of sixty-two pieces (forty-six, mainly

6-pounder, cannon and sixteen howitzers). But he seems to have overlooked Napoleon's order about 'twenty-four 12-pounders'. See also note 8 below.

5. De Salle, 'Souvenirs' in *Revue de Paris*, pp. 426–8. 'Half way on the slope that we occupied' must mean the Belle Alliance slope, and he says that the bombardment was intended 'to astonish and shake the enemy morale'. But as this must have been at extreme range it is difficult to see how his batteries came under 'a very intense fire', including, he says, howitzer shells (i.e. short-range). He was ordered to examine a position further forward, and he claims that without orders a subordinate had moved the 12-pounder batteries just as the Union Brigade began its charge. The whole account is thus confusing, for there is no indication that the Grand Battery was installed so late or was still in movement when the charge came. That the Grand Battery was well forward seems attested by Ingilby (of Gardiner's RHA Battery on Wellington's extreme eastern wing, some 2,600 yards from the Charleroi road). He came under 'accurate' fire from a gun on the eastern or nearer end of the Grand Battery's high position, which must therefore have been well within 1,400 yards of him (*WL*, no. 82). This at least is some indication of the Grand Battery's lateral length.
6. 'The Campaign of 1815', *Corr. de Nap.*, xxxi, p. 227/188.
7. I have taken this from the original found by Houssaye and published in facsimile in the 46th and later editions of his book (p. 566).
8. It is questionable to argue that the Grand Battery needed strong infantry cover and thus would not be on the ridge that Mark Adkin has selected. That seems to be Gareth Glover's objection, but he does not mention Napoleonic 'grand battery' use at Friedland, Wagram and Lützen. Andrew Field does allude to Sénarmont's achievement at Friedland, where, *unsupported*, he advanced his 36 pieces upon the Russian batteries, opened massed fire at 400 yards then closed to under 150, blew away the Russian batteries and destroyed their troops. Nor was a forward deployment unknown in World War 2. In this context may I be forgiven for remembering a kinsman, Brigadier Charles Armitage, who, in 1941 in the Western Desert, won an MC and two bars within a year for his leadership of his battery: 'If you found yourself in front of Charles, you knew that you were behind enemy lines' (obit., *The Times*, 16 March 1998).
9. I have heard it said that Baring's men were armed with muskets. It may be so, but none of the accounts known to me of the defence of La Haye Sainte suggests that muskets were in use in this battalion. Baring's own account of 1816 (*LW*, no. 163) neither mentions nor implies it, and the editorial note of 1831 at his account's first publication in the *Hanoverian Military Journal* repeats that 'the battalion were armed with rifles and therefore could not make use of the ordinary infantry ammunition' (*LW*, p. 246 fn). In 1835 Baring provided Siborne with the 1831 published account without referring to or challenging this editorial comment. Given his frequent emphasis on the ammunition re-supply problem leading to the loss of the farm, one might have expected some comment on the complication of two types of shot if the defenders relied upon muskets as well.
10. As Field, the best and most recent historian of the French at Waterloo, points out (p. 85), 'most accounts state that a brigade of cuirassiers was allocated from Watier's 13th Cavalry

Division, either that of Dubois or of Travers; however, there is disagreement as to which one it was.' Field argues from the account given by Levavasseur (an ADC to Ney) that squadrons from the brigades of both Dubois and Travers were employed as a composite force under another ADC, Crabbé; and I am happy to follow him in this otherwise insoluble question.

11. There is a first-hand account by Captain Jacobi of this battalion in *WA*, ii, no. 39, which I have followed here; Jacobi's own footnote, on p. 229 (n. 297) gives further important details. Ian Fletcher, *Galloping at Everything*, p. 242 and especially his long note 10 reviewing the various accounts by Evelyn Wood, Chandler and Hamilton-Williams, is also useful. Adkin (p. 368) is wrong in saying that Klencke was killed; Jacobi reported that he survived, though wounded.
12. Sir Andrew Barnard's letter of 23 June 1815 was discovered and published by Mark Urban, *Rifles* (2003), p. 272, emphasis in the original. The letter may also be read in *WA*, vi, no. 84, and Van Danzig, *Who Won Waterloo?*, pp. 155–61. I fear my friend Gareth Glover may not have recognised quite how mortifying was this unsteadiness in an elite battalion. He writes: 'Much has been made of this statement recently in an attempt to damage the reputation of the Rifles', and argues that there were 'raw recruits' with 'every regiment containing men who go to the rear if given the chance' (*WA*, vi, p. 194 fn.). But surely the 95th was not just any ordinary regiment. Moreover his comment rather minimises the hard fact that the experienced Barnard actually wrote about 'men he little expected to go to the rear'.
13. Accounts such as Uffindell & Corum; Coppens & Courcelle, *Chemin d'Ohain*; D. Brown in *Age of Napoleon*, no. 25; André Dellevoet, in the US journal *Napoleon*, no. 16; Haythornthwaite, *Waterloo Men*; Adkin; Van Danzig; Field; all these have demolished the very unfair account produced by William Siborne, though it is only fair to add that many of his correspondents led him to his conclusions (see *WL*). De Bas & T'Serclaes de Wommersom went to the other extreme from Siborne. See also my own investigation in the *British Army Review* no. 129, Spring 2002.
14. Since I do not particularise in my text, the units were: Kempt, 8th Brigade: 1/28th, 1/32nd, 1/79th, 1/95th. Pack, 9th Brigade: 3/1st, 1/42nd, 2/44th, 1/92nd. Bylandt, 1st Brigade of 2nd Netherlands Division: 27/Jager, 7e Ligne, National Militia Battalions, 5, 7, 8.
15. *WL*, no. 102 (Major Rogers). The sergeant who did this was following standard practice, stopping the gun from being used by the enemy foot soldiers. This is the only occasion when spiking was noted on this day. Generally speaking, when the French *cavalry* swept through the gun-line, Allied artillerymen left their guns unworkable (by removing a wheel) and unspiked, and thus usable again when the cavalry withdrew.
16. Pollio is one of the few commentators who mention this (p. 424), but I note that recently Van Danzig also raises the point (pp. 175–6).
17. Scheltens of 7e Ligne in Coppens & Courcelle, *Chemin d'Ohain* (1999) p. 33; Hope of 92nd in David Brown in *Age of Napoleon*, no. 25 (1998), pp. 33–4; Gore of 30th in Haythornthwaite, *Waterloo Men*, p. 55.

18. Sergeant Robertson of the 92nd confirms that the French had got beyond the southern hedge: 'General Pack ordered us to advance and line the hedge to oppose the advance of the column. But when we got to the side of the hedge we found the French were there as soon as we': *With Napoleon at Waterloo*, p. 160.
19. I do not say that the British were breaking, but the calls of Pack and Picton indicate how desperate was the position all along Picton's front. This needs to be remembered when picking out for criticism Bylandt's brigade for its wavering and falling back. Clausewitz here has an interesting comment. We have noted how Wellington shredded Orange's command as far as possible and broke up Perponcher's division between separate sectors. Clausewitz, in referring to the way that Wellington mixed unreliable units among stronger ones, and specifically referring to 'unreliable Belgian' units, remarks that if an entire Belgian division (and not merely one brigade) had held this part of the front and had given way, 'the gap would possibly have become too large': *Campaign*, chap. 49, pp. 178–9, BMP.
20. See the differing accounts in Fletcher, p. 244 onwards and Field, p. 116 onwards.
21. Until this time the French attacks on the buildings of Papelotte, La Haye, Smohain and Frischermont had been relatively easily repulsed, but this attack seems to have thrust the Nassauers out of Papelotte, though DBTS are somewhat reluctant to admit this. Their account (ii, p. 162) is very short and colourless, while Hofschröer (*1815*, ii, pp. 77–8) quotes *Belle-Alliance* accounts but adds very little.
22. Mauduit, ii, pp. 310–11. Interestingly, on 10 May 1815 Clinton had made the same complaint about Uxbridge's cavalry being ordered about without reference to the infantry commander with whom they were working: *Clinton Corr.*, ii, p. 35.
23. Why were these terrible guns not spiked? There may be two reasons. First, Ingilby of the RHA (on the eastern wing of the line) thought that as the guns were in British hands for about a quarter of an hour and were left unspiked, the cavalry could not have been 'furnished with spikes [or] acquainted with their use' (*WL*, no. 82). Secondly, I hazard the suggestion that in the charge it was simpler and safer to stay in the saddle, keep moving and ride down and sabre the gunners, rather than to halt, dismount, hand one's horse to someone (or risk it galloping off), and stand by a gun for as long as it took to disable it; or to think that such a task might have been left to a second line – but in the event there was no second line.
24. General L. Bro, *Mémoires* (Paris, 1914), p. 149, said that one of his *4e Lanciers* NCOs named Orban '*tué d'un coup de lance le général Ponsonby*'; so does Mauduit, *Derniers Jours* (Paris, 1854), p. 299. Sergeant John Dickson of the Greys said that he found Ponsonby's lanced body still in its cloak: *With Napoleon at Waterloo,* p. 146; the nature of the weapon was confirmed by Tomkinson, p. 302. De Lacy Evans, Ponsonby's ADC, said that the general and others tried to get 'round the left of the French Lancers . . . all these fell into the hands of the enemy' (*WL*, no. 31). Although various Scots Greys claimed that Ponsonby was shot through the head or breast during the initial charge or at the moment of apparent victory (*WA*, i, nos. 12, 13, 15), I think their claims unconvincing.

25. Vandeleur, in *WL*, no. 51.
26. Fortescue, x, pp. 366–7.
27. Letter, 8 Nov. 1839, in *WL*, no. 5. See chap. 35, n. 16.
28. The first sentence of Wellington's memorandum to cavalry brigade commanders of the Army of Occupation in France reads: 'It is so desirable that a reserve should be kept in all cases in which the cavalry is employed to charge, that it appears to be a matter of necessity; and the officers and troops should be accustomed to form and conduct this reserve in exercise.' He set out its purpose: 'to improve and complete the success of the charge; secondly, to protect the retreat of troops retiring, supposing those who charge are unsuccessful, or possibly to acquire success after their failure': quoted in Fletcher, *Galloping at Everything*, p. 28. Ian Fletcher goes on to discuss very helpfully these tactical and command weaknesses on his next page.
29. The 7th Marquess of Anglesey, *One Leg*, p. 135, from a note made by his ancestor, preserved in the Plas Newydd papers. One of Wellington's closest colleagues from Indian days, Colonel Sir Colin Campbell, now commandant at the Duke's headquarters, wrote to another former 'Indian' Sir Henry Torrens at the Horse Guards on 19 June that 'Lord Uxbridge is by no means satisfied with them [many of the cavalry regiments]': *WA*, iv, no. 2. And if Uxbridge was not, was Wellington likely to be?
30. Grouchy, *Mémoires*, iv, p. 176.
31. Grouchy, *Mémoires*, iv, p. 177. In his *Bulletin* account of Waterloo Napoleon suggested that this order was designed to create a defensive *bloc* past which the army could march in retreat. That is possible, but my impression is that his comment was only an afterthought, and that the order was intended to bring forward man-power for the next phase of operations, as no suggestion was made of erecting any defences at Quatre Bras.
32. Jacobi, in *WA*, ii, no. 39 and its footnote number 297.
33. *LW*, no. 137.
34. In fact Wellington was indeed close to the 1st Light KGL at the time, as we shall see.
35. The report of the 8th Line KGL tells of the brigade's deployment, but without indicating who ordered it: *Belle-Alliance*, no. 38, also in J. Franklin (ed.), *Waterloo: Hanoverian Corr.* (see Brinckmann), p. 78.
36. Heise, 1840 and 1842, in *LW*, nos. 153, 156; the quotation is from the second letter.
37. Shaw Kennedy, *Notes*, para. 92, p. 98.
38. *WSD*, x, p. 534; see also pp. 543 and 559.
39. C. Hibbert (ed.), *The Wheatley Diary* (1964), pp. 64–6. The diary was put into finished form before May 1817. Although Wheatley did not describe the Lüneburg affair, his remark is significant. Hibbert's commentary on the Ompteda affair (pp. 68–9) does mention Alten being involved to some extent, but places the principal responsibility on the Prince and his ADC.
40. Frazer, letter of 9 a.m., 20 June 1815, *Letters*, p. 554. Plainly a case of 'too many cooks'. Frazer did as much as possible to sort out the ammunition problem; the ammunition orders may have been part of the instructions to leave Alten and go to the crossroads, but that is surmise.

41. For this contretemps and its outcome, see Glover, *Myth and Reality*, p. 219, and Scovell's recollection of the affair, *WA*, iii, no. 1.
42. Jacobi, in *WA*, ii, no. 39 and its n. 300.

CHAPTER 39: The Third Act

1. 'The Campaign of 1815', *Corr. de Nap.*, xxxi, p. 231/192. Clausewitz acutely observed that 'Bonaparte has always spoken only of Bülow, as if the rest of the Prussians were incapable of further action after the battle of Ligny. But this was a foolish assumption' (*Campaign*, chap. 48, p. 170 in BMP). But it was not so much a foolish *assumption* as a deliberate attempt to mislead his readers and conceal his own fundamental errors of appreciation, as Clausewitz's entire chapter makes plain.
2. The 2/3rd Guards light company was already with Macdonell; Douglas Mercer had just brought in two companies; one of the battalion's ten companies remained with the colours on the ridge.
3. Pte. Matthew Clay, 3rd Guards, *Narrative* (undated, 2006 repr.), p. 27.
4. Facsimiles appear in numerous works, and a recent one is in Paget & Saunders, *Hougoumont* (1992), p. 55. I have modernised the capitalisation
5. There are references to this from both sides: Colonel Woodford (1838) in *WL*, no. 115; Ensign Wedgwood's letter of 19 June 1815, *WA*, i, no. 38; Büsgen's 'Relation', *Belle-Alliance*, no. 75, mentions seven intruders being taken prisoner; Clay mentions the capture of one intruder who lived – the drummer-boy (p. 27); Gareth Glover indicates a fifth Allied witness, Ensign Standen: *Myth and Reality*, p. 121. Additionally, Andrew Field, p. 127, notes that Battalion-Commander Sarrand, *3e Ligne, 6e Division*, speaks of 'breaking open a small door on the side of the building'. Glover, *Myth*, p. 121, surmises that there may have been a third break-in.
6. Colonel Trefcon, quoted in Field, p. 128.
7. The cart is mentioned in *WL*, no. 9 (Seymour's letter of 1842: he claims he found it on the 'crest', indicated where he thought it was needed and that the driver promptly and gallantly went straight down the hill). Various authorities offer a name, Brewer or Brewster: *The Waterloo Medal Roll* (1992), p. 75, taken from the muster rolls, registers him as Private Joseph Brewer.
8. Among writers of the twenty-first century, Adkin, Paget and Saunders, Van Danzig all come to different figures. All totals are guesswork to some degree.
9. *WA*, i, no. 35: the wording and grammar are confused, and I have taken them exactly as printed. In view of the complicated seniority, I list these officers according to the March 1815 *Army List*. Hepburn became full colonel on 4 June 1814 and stood 194th among the 284 colonels; Woodford, 4 June 1814 (276th). In these circumstances Hepburn was of the same day's promotion as, but eighty-four places senior to, Woodford, which places a question-mark against Woodford's claim. Among lt.-colonels, Macdonell dated from 7 Sept. 1809 (105th among 828 of that rank); Saltoun, 25 Dec 1813 (620th); Home, 15 March 1814 (649th).

10. Andrew Field's chapter 13 is the fullest treatment of this second French assault on La Haye Sainte; I think that he would not disagree with my conclusions on the wastefulness of the attack and Ney's culpability. Major Baring's account in *LW*, no. 163, and Rifleman Lindau's reminiscences in *WA*, ii, no. 25 tell the story of the defence.
11. Du Casse, *Mémoires du Jérome*, vii, p. 23.
12. Milhaud's strength on 10 June: Watier (brigades of Dubois and Travers), *1er, 4e, 7e, 12e cuirassiers*, 11 squadrons, 1,200 men; Delort (Farine and Vial), *5e, 10e, 6e, 9e cuirassiers*, 13 squadrons, 1,600 men. Also 12 guns.
13. This episode draws upon Houssaye, III, 4, I, pp. 355–6 (Eng. trans., p. 203) and Andrew Field, pp. 138–9, for the Ney–Delort–Milhaud exchange. I do not accept Napoleon's version in Gourgaud or his memoir: see 'The Campaign of 1815', *Corr. de Nap.*, xxxi, p. 234/194 for the claim that Guyot engaged his force of cavalry without the Emperor's agreement. Houssaye and Field note an uncorroborated anecdote over why Lefebvre-Desnouettes acted (as he undoubtedly did), which is that Milhaud in riding to the attack met Lefebvre-Desnouettes and said, 'I am going to charge – support me,' and Lefebvre-Desnouettes mistook this as an order from Napoleon himself. It is certainly one explanation, and has the advantage of exonerating Napoleon and Ney from any blame. My own opinion is somewhat divergent. Jerome's letter to his wife is in his *Mémoires*, vii, pp. 12–26, at p. 23, and gives his understanding of the Emperor's views. Field, p. 147 gives Guyot's letter of 4 July 1820 to Drouot. In *Victoires, Conquêtes, etc, des français, 1792–1815*, xxiv (Paris, 1821), p. 217 fn., the compilers printed Guyot's denial of the statement in Napoleon's memoirs.
14. Houssaye, II, 4, I, p. 358; Eng. trans., p. 204.
15. This significant point about the highly visible and comparatively lengthy movement of more than 4,000 horsemen from one side of the road to the other – and Napoleon not querying or countermanding it – is admirably made by Van Danzig, p. 193.
16. Observations on Rogniat's book: *Corr. de Nap.*, xxxi, p. 474 fn./398. Rogniat was arguing that cavalry attacks on unshaken infantry risked setbacks that could react on the cohesion of one's own army. Napoleon remarked that Milhaud's '4 p.m.' cavalry charge was made 'a little too soon, but once made, had to be supported' and hence, although vexed, he sent Kellermann to assist Milhaud. While Milhaud was thus attacking, 'Napoleon was occupied in repulsing Bülow, whose shot was already [*sic*] hitting the road at Belle Alliance.'
17. *Corr. de Nap.*, xxxi, p. 233/193–4.
18. Jac Weller, *Wellington at Waterloo* (1967), Part Two, chap. V, 'Cavalry Attacks on Infantry Squares' is particularly useful in this matter.
19. Lambert's 10th Brigade: 1/4th, 1/27th, 2/40th, 1/81st, total 2,550 r/f. The 6th Division's other brigade, Best's 4th Hanoverian, had been with Picton's division throughout. Their divisional commander, Lowry Cole, was still in England, getting married.
20. Field, pp. 144–5.
21. *Corr. de Nap.*, xxxi, 233/194. For Kellermann's exact position, '*en arrière sur la gauche*', see Napoleon in xxxi, 474 fn./398. One of Kellermann's subordinates, Lhéritier (*11e Division*

de Cavalerie) told Vivian years later that the artillery fire had so punished the cavalry as they waited for orders that they successfully 'demanded to be led against the enemy' (Vivian's letter, *USJ*, July 1833, p. 312). This adds to the complexity of the evidence.

CHAPTER 40: In Another Part of Brabant

1. The instructions to Bülow are in Lettow-Vorbeck, pp. 376–7; also in English in Hofschröer, *1815*, ii, p. 41. It is noteworthy that the Prussian high command now was as anxious to retain their independence while assisting Wellington as they had been for him to form virtually a part of their army in the discussions at Brye on the 16th. I find their present wish quite understandable, but it does suggest that Gneisenau had been somewhat arbitrary in his demands upon Wellington on the earlier occasion.
2. Ollech, p. 188.
3. For this meeting see Ollech, pp. 188–9; it is not mentioned in Hofschröer, *1815*, ii.
4. Ollech, p. 189 and Lettow-Vorbeck, p. 397 for the letter. Hofschröer, *1815*, ii, states merely: 'Blücher also dictated a note to the Duke later that morning stating that, ill though he might be, he would ride at the head of his men to attack the right flank of the French immediately his troops were in a position to do so' (p. 42). The letter said rather more than that.
5. This singular postscript is in Ollech, p. 189 and Lettow-Vorbeck, p. 397 but not in Hofschröer, *1815*, ii.
6. Müffling, *Memoirs*, pp. 124–6.
7. Van Danzig (p. 235) reads the message as a cautious concern that 'if Wellington had been thrown back [in battle] then the Prussian army would be in an impossible position'. But that was a risk that Blücher had already *recognised and accepted* when sending his midnight message. He confirmed that acceptance in the morning. Gneisenau's postscript, however, was not about an adverse result of a battle but about Wellington standing to fight. That was a quite different matter.
8. Lamarque was suppressing the Vendée in 1815, but thereafter was in exile in Belgium until 1820; his comments are in Charras, ii, pp. 119–20 fn. H. B. George's comments are in *EHR*, xv, 1900, pp. 814–16. Although George took orders, he was a noted climber and Alpinist, an Oxford don, and a well-regarded military historian. He was reviewing O'Connor Morris's *The Campaign of 1815*, and his comments on Morris, Thiers, and other matters, merit reading even today.
9. For the various times quoted in this account of the march of the Prussian army I rely on Hofschröer, *1815*, ii, chap. 3, itself based on regimental and other accounts, and also on the careful account in Aerts, *Opérations*, chap. 4.
10. A battery of 12-pounders marched in the advance guard, and duly got bogged down on upward slopes, adding to delays. Consequently it was ordered to bring up the rear with the rest of the artillery. Whether it had been wise to place it in front seems open to doubt.
11. Hofschröer, *1815*, ii, pp. 57–8. There is a very illuminating map of the crossing march-routes in Pollio, p. 474, from which my own map is taken. An initial march of just 2 miles

would have moved I Corps right out of the way of the other two corps and have avoided all the delay at the crossing point. Van Danzig, who bases himself on the distances and times given by Hofschröer, produces two coloured maps of his own (pp. 232–3) showing the routes actually taken and an alternative set of routes that could have avoided most of these blockages. He judges that British historians like Siborne have been 'too kind' to the Prussians over this part of their performance. Van Danzig has calculated the speed of movement on each stage of IV Corps' march: from Dion to Wavre (120 mins: 6 km, or 50 metres per minute), from Wavre to St-Lambert (150 mins: 8.5 km, 56 metres per minute) and from there to the Bois de Paris (90 mins: 5 km, 55 metres per minute). Thus he thinks that the difficulties claimed for the Lasne defile are exaggerated (pp. 234–5).

12. Report of IV Corps, DBTS, iii, Note 31, D1, in German, p. 522, and French, p. 523.
13. Müffling, *History* (Eng. version, 1816), pp. 17–18 for the three cases, and the next steps. See also his *Memoirs*, pp. 241–2 with its confirmation that Wellington fell in with his proposals. Hofschröer, *1815*, ii, p. 95 for the *MWB* of 1907. Adkin, p. 380, places the Müffling–Bülow meeting towards 2 p.m. but this surely would render pointless the discussion of the various options. Neither in the Waterloo Despatch (see paras 19 and 28) nor in his querulous 1842 Memorandum (*WSD*, x, at pp. 528–9) did Wellington remark on the Prussian delay, though his casualty bill was all the higher because of it.
14. Müffling, *History*, p. 19; Bülow's report, already cited, at p. 524 and 525; Thurn und Taxis and other details in Hofschröer, *1815*, ii, pp. 95–8, who nevertheless judges that: 'At the beginning of the battle, Wellington was fully aware of the situation of the Prussian Army, and of the time at which he could expect to start to receive effective support'; Constant's journal: Logie, *Mélanges*, p. 147.
15. Felton Hervey's letter, *Nineteenth Century*, March 1893, p. 433. Ingilby, of Gardiner's troop RHA, *WL*, no. 82. Taylor of the 10th Hussars had in the morning been close to Papelotte. He met a Prussian officer with a patrol, who informed him that Bülow with his corps was within three-quarters of a league and advancing (*ibid.*, no. 75). Fremantle, ADC to the Duke, gives the time when the Duke heard the news (*ibid.*, no. 11).
16. For these orders see Houssaye, II, 4, V, p. 250; Eng. trans., p. 142.
17. Grouchy, *Mémoires*, iv, p. 71. The three long reports that he enclosed run to about 500 words. Grouchy in his letter accurately summarised them. The third report from a well-disposed retired veteran, received around 10 a.m. read: 'The injured are going to Liège via Beauwale, Jodoigne and Tirlemont. The troops still available and those who did not partake in the battle of Fleurus are moving on Wavre, some on Tirlemont. The bulk is camped on the la Chyse plain close to the Namur–Louvain road. The la Chyse plain is two and a half leagues from Wavre on the right, close to Goddechins. This last piece of information is definite [*positif*]. It is there that they seem to want to mass. They say that they held the battlefield [at Ligny] and only retired in order to renew battle after reuniting, which they say has been agreed between Blücher and Wellington': Houssaye, from the original in the War Archives (Book III, chap. I, sec. II, p. 291 fn.; Eng. trans., p. 398, fn. 31)
18. Houssaye's footnote for this strong statement quotes Grouchy's report to Napoleon of 19 June. That report says: 'Having been informed by Your Majesty, when I left Ligny,

that you were marching on the English to fight them, if they should wish to stand [*s'ils voulaient tenir*] on this side of the forest of Soignies'. That is all. I find this statement slightly less cogent a proof than Houssaye obviously did. At that time on 17 June Napoleon was confident of catching and destroying Wellington at Quatre Bras. It was not until 10 a.m. on 18 June that Soult penned the next information, 'At this moment His Majesty is about to attack the English army which has taken position at Waterloo, close to the Forest of Soignies.' Moreover Soult then approved Grouchy's 'move on Wavre', thereby 'pushing before you' any Prussians 'found in that direction'. This is hardly a clear call to march to Mont St Jean or La Belle Alliance.

19. Houssaye, III, 1, II, p. 285 onwards (Eng. trans., p. 164 onwards, though with some idiosyncrasies of translation).
20. Grouard, pp. 180–2.

CHAPTER 41: First Signs of the Prussian Advance

1. Houssaye (Book III, chap. 3, sec. II, p. 336; Eng. trans., p. 192) considered that the mention in the captured letter of 'a corps' without any reference to the rest of the Prussian army, misled Napoleon into thinking that the bulk of the Prussian army would remain stationary at Wavre, so that Grouchy could neutralise it or instead might pursue Bülow. But I believe that the tone of the postscript does not support Houssaye's view.
2. Both these officers are quoted by Andrew Field in his *Waterloo,* chap. 14. They seem to me to run together the events they witnessed, for Combes-Brassard recalled a *simultaneous* Prussian advance from St-Lambert and Ohain, and Janin that they were at once faced with *two* columns of 10,000 men *each,* whereas the advance from Ohain came later and IV Corps' initial attacks were much smaller in size. Houssaye maintained that the former's recollections were stuffed with errors or doubtful claims (*La Garde Meurt,* p. 14), but this claim that they originally faced north and only later were ordered east seems quite true.
3. Field, p. 135.
4. Blücher seems to have had no doubts, but his ADC Nostitz was possibly not alone in fearing that the French might defer a Mont St Jean attack and switch their main effort to the Lasne valley; Gneisenau, however, was satisfied that the attack was so heavily committed against Wellington's centre that a major switch was very unlikely.
5. Marbot, *Mémoires,* Paris (1898, new edition 1946), iii, p. 376. H. B. George suggested that this account was a typical instance of Marbot romancing, and even at best was 'out' by two to three hours (*EHR,* xv, p. 814).
6. Marbot, iii, p. 375.
7. Those who consider the Hal/Tubize detachment a serious fault may add this to the list of Wellingtonian errors. The full list is drawn up in Napoleon's chapter 'Observations' in his memoirs, which gives a multiplicity of reasons why Wellington had to lose the battle.
8. In the letter that he wrote at 11 a.m. Grouchy said that he was at Sart-à-Walhain, but the researches of Aerts seem definitely to fix him at Walhain (otherwise called Walhain St Paul or Walhain sur Nil), a mile to the west.

9. This and the previous paragraph rely upon Houssaye's vivid description, based upon a wide array of first-hand sources, Book III, chap. 1, sec. III, pp. 293–7; Eng. trans., pp. 167–70. Of course all the participants' comments were self-justificatory *ex post facto*, but there is a reasonable measure of agreement on the drift if not the exact words of the discussion. Houssaye's very evident bias and introduction of hindsight does not invalidate his summary of the exchanges.
10. Clausewitz, *Campaign of 1815*, chap. 50, pp. 180–1 BMP.
11. Grouard, *Critique*, pp. 193–4, with my emphasis added. Charras concluded that 'on reaching these places [Frischermont or Plancenoit] Grouchy's column could not but have been enveloped in the catastrophe': ii, p. 124. I find unconvincing the claim by A. F. Becke that 'had Gérard intervened at Plancenoit by 7 p.m. victory might have declared for Napoleon' (1936 edition, p. 251), especially as it is not really supported by any clear argumentation.
12. About which DBTS discourses at perhaps undue length (ii, pp. 62–73).
13. Wellington at a dinner in Paris in the late summer of 1815 was heard to say, 'It is very easy to fight a battle when it's over. How could Grouchy come to his assistance? He had a superior army in his front, which it was necessary to keep in check': James Stanhope's journal in Glover, *Eyewitness*, p. 181.
14. Of those marshals still active and Bonapartist in 1815, I can think of only Davout and Suchet who might have made a difference; but Napoleon obliged Davout to stay in Paris, and was wasting Suchet's abilities at Lyons, facing the Alps.
15. Yet again, Grouchy's evidence is of little help, for he nowhere refers to receiving the '10 a.m.' letter; and when he does say that he duly received the '1.30 p.m.' letter and postscript he times that variously, at 5 p.m. (at iv, p. 42) and at 7 p.m. (iv, p. 82). It is anyone's guess if the 5 p.m. receipt was really of the 10 a.m. letter.
16. Clausewitz, *Campaign*, chap. 50, is highly critical of Grouchy's failure to see that his proper course was to envelop the Prussians by the left bank of the Dyle, by which he would also be closer to the main French army. For details of the bridges in 1815, see Aerts, *Opérations*, p. 229 fn.
17. Aerts, *Opérations*, p. 278. His entire chap. VI is an excellent and helpful account of the combats at Wavre and Limale. Hofschröer, *1815*, ii, chap. 11, has some interesting unit accounts on the Prussian side. Houssaye's Book III, chap. 7 is a full account from a French perspective. Clausewitz's short chapter 50 (pp. 179–82, BMP) is full of insights, but one would never guess from it that as Thielemann's chief of staff he was directly involved in the battle. Hyde Kelly's *The Battle of Wavre* (1905) adds very little, though its coloured map is helpful.
18. Zeppelin's little force from 9th Brigade was later reinforced by a battalion from 11th Brigade: I/4th Kurmark Landwehr: he was fighting with young battalions, two of them merely Landwehr.
19. The opening sentence of Grouchy's report to the Emperor, written at Dinant on 20 June 1815 reads: 'Sire, it was towards 7 in the evening of 18 June when I received the Duke of Dalmatia's letter, which prescribed me to march on St-Lambert and attack General

Bülow': DBTS, iii, p. 575, from the French War Archives. This suggests that the courier took some five hours to trace him, which seems unduly long, and there must be a suspicion that he made the arrival appear late so as to excuse his belated march west. On the other hand, if he had wanted to shift the blame to a *scapegoat* to explain away any delay, Vandamme's disobedience and involvement in Wavre would have given a perfect excuse, and Grouchy *did not take it.* As so often with Grouchy, even when his case seems good, there remains a niggling doubt as to his strict veracity. Moreover he descended to chicanery over the wording of Soult's 1 p.m. letter, as I explained in chap. 38, app. 1.

20. As the story of previous days had shown, there was something very amiss with the 'human chemistry' between Grouchy, Vandamme, Gérard and some other less senior officers. Jealousy, insolence, disrespect on one side, and on the other an inability to lift and bind together those whose duty was to obey, together these weaknesses made co-operation almost impossible. There had been something of a similar breakdown in the relations of Marshals Tallard and Marsin and the Bavarian Elector in the days before Blenheim in 1704, as Tallard bitterly complained after the defeat.
21. Aerts, *Opérations*, p. 286. All four were young battalions and the Kurmark men were Landwehr. A short account of their movements is in Hofschröer, *1815*, ii, p. 162.
22. Stengel's force comprised the three battalions of the 19th Infantry Regiment, two squadrons of the 6th Uhlans and one of 1st Westphalian Landwehr.
23. Houssaye, p. 457: '*La route de Mont St Jean était ouverte; mais depuis longtemps on n'entendait plus le canon de l'empereur*'. I find this short sentence of lost endeavour among the most moving in his entire book.

CHAPTER 42: The Fourth Act

1. Foy, letter of 23 June 1815, *Vie Militaire*, p. 283.
2. Foy, and Bachelu's chief staff officer, are quoted in Uffindell & Corum, pp. 181–2. It is puzzling that one of Foy's ADCs should write later, 'Bachelu and Foy, formed in squares' and moved off to the attack (*ibid.*, p. 181). I think the 23 June 1815 evidence of Foy must be the more trustworthy recollection: after all, he issued the order. The ADC added that Bachelu's square 'collapsed into a triangle', so I wonder if he confused his memories with the triangle formation that, late in the day, one square of the *Vieille Garde* did indeed adopt in its last extremity.
3. On this disputed matter, see the appendix to this chapter.
4. Adkin, pp. 366–78 is very helpful in understanding the course of the struggle for La Haye Sainte and has excellent photographs and maps; his pp. 415–16 are particularly cogent and valuable on the ammunition question.
5. Shaw Kennedy, *Notes*, para. 118, pp. 122–3.
6. Letter to Siborne, 12 March 1835, in *LW*, no. 163.
7. If La Haye Sainte was to perform the same function as Hougoumont it was the duty of the high command to ensure that it was generously stocked with ammunition. But Baring as the commander on the spot should have made the point very forcibly when

posted to the farm, for it was on a forward slope and re-supply would be problematical. It seems that his superiors in 3rd Division ignored his repeated requests in the afternoon, and thought that additional men would suffice (bringing whatever remained in their pouches). Henegan, who was in charge of the Field Train, stated in his memoirs that he was responsible for supplying all units with small arms and artillery ammunition, that he did it successfully, but that by late in the day he had issued the last available rifle ammunition needed by the three battalions of the 95th (Henegan, ii, p. 321 fn.; he does not mention musket ammunition). That was also the calibre needed by Baring, and of course Baring was in a much more exposed and forward position than the 95th, and more difficult to supply. The entire question of stocks of ammunition at 11 a.m., their rate of consumption, and the stocks at 7.45 p.m. in all three armies, would make an interesting study.

8. When some of the KGL initially placed in the orchard were driven back by the French, rather than try to crowd into the gateways of the building they fled back 'to the squares behind us', i.e. on the crest, and so ceased to form part of the garrison for the rest of the day (*WA*, vol. v, no. 14, 19 July 1815). Gareth Glover has further remarked that some casualties may have occurred later in the day and after the loss of the farm. He also highlights the often forgotten fact that Baring was referring only to his own battalion and at nightfall when the fighting was over. He also warns that some and perhaps many reappeared the next day. His note on the subject in *Myth and Reality*, p. 162 is most useful.
9. Book III, chap. 4, sec. IV, p. 374; Eng. trans., p. 213. Houssaye does not mention in this list of cavalry casualties that of the two corps commanders one was wounded and the other unhorsed. For detailed officer casualties see the appendix to chap. 39, with a further estimate for the other ranks losses. And remember also the fate of the horses!
10. De Salle, *Souvenirs*, p. 429; Heymès in *Docs inéds*, p. 18: '*Où voulez-vous que j'en prenne? Voulez-vous que j'en fasse?*' Nobody is quite certain when these words were spoken, other than that they were uttered in late afternoon or early evening: Kennedy timed them as 6 p.m. (*Notes*, para. 130, p. 138).
11. Kincaid, p. 342 (1830), or p. 255 (1929); Fortescue, *History*, x, p. 396. It is a remarkable tribute to the badness of French shooting or to the skill of British surgeons or to sheer Irish buoyancy, that only 83 other ranks were killed, while of the 344 wounded, only 34 died of wounds, and as many as 236 had re-joined the regiment by April 1816 (*WD*, xii, p. 486 and *WSD*, xiv, p. 633).
12. Captain Dansey, *WL*, no. 87.
13. Alten's post-battle report is far from clear in its description of the incident; it also lavishes praise on Orange's courage and Klencke's conduct. The report of the 5th Line KGL emphasizes Ompteda's concern and his formation of the battalion in square, only to be forced into line by the Prince's direct order: *Belle-Alliance*, Nrs 5 and 36, and *WA*, ii, nos. 24 and 26. The verbal exchanges and casualties are as given in the Ompteda memorial volume, *A Hanoverian-English Officer* (1892), compiled by his great-nephew, pp. 311–12.
14. Kincaid, p. 342 (1830), or p. 255 (1929). Keppel, Lawrence and Leeke are in Brett-James, *Hundred Days*, pp. 147, 133, 131–2 respectively.

15. Ellesmere, *Personal Reminiscences*, p. 179. For less hopeful views, see Mercer's account of Colonel Gould, RA, who having thought the position 'rather desperate' before the cavalry attacks, thought 'all was over' when the horsemen first swept round the squares: *Journal* ('Soldiers' Tales' series, 1927), pp. 167–8.
16. [Walter Scott], *Paul's Letters to his Kinsfolk* (1816), p. 167, and the phrase about the 'hard pounding' on the same page. Major Macready's Journals, *USM*, August 1852, p. 527: part of this in a slightly different order of wording was previously in *USM*, March 1845, p. 395. Gronow, *Reminiscences*, p. 96 (1862), p. 65 (1964).
17. Mercer, *Journal*, p. 168, in the 1927 'Soldiers' Tales' series. It is good to see this clear recognition of the morale of these Netherlands infantry. Mercer initially thought them Frenchmen from their blue tunics, but luckily the truth was quickly perceived. Some of the 3/14th thought the same (*WA*, i, at p. 172).
18. Shaw Kennedy, *Notes*, paras 122–4, pp. 126–9. If Napoleon 'did not exert that activity and personal energy in superintending and conforming to the progress of the action, which he ought to have done', surely that applied – if at all – to the earlier hours of the battle rather than this stage. He was now most actively committed to repulsing the Prussians while still scrutinising Ney's progress. It was not energy that was wanting, but men.
19. *WL*, no. 8.
20. Müffling, *Memoirs*, p. 245 and his long footnote. Vandeleur, who on 17 June had been somewhat difficult with Vivian on acting together on their own initiative, is more likely to have expressed such views than Vivian – as we shall soon see.
21. The more I consider this terrible afternoon and its critical moments, the more convinced do I become that the westward movement of Vivian's brigade was determined by the gap in the centre and not by the sighting of Prussian troops in the distance. The sighting was a mere bonus. Wellington's pencil note to Uxbridge (see sec. V) is telling in this respect. In other terms, it was Ney's success at La Haye Sainte and not knowledge of a Prussian approach march against the French that led to the decision to weaken the eastern wing or leave unsupported Saxe-Weimar's Nassauers, and instead to move and shore up the shaken squares in the centre. Difficult as it is to fix absolute times to events, I think both the chronology and a recognition of which danger was 'mortal' and which was 'short of catastrophic', give support to this view. But of course it does reduce somewhat the Prussian contribution to events, and advocates of that view may not agree.
22. Müffling, *Memoirs*, p. 247 and his long footnote of 1846 after reading Vivian's remarks in Siborne. (The 1997 *Introduction* to the *Memoirs* says nothing on this not unimportant point.) In his 1815 version (*History*, p. 32) Müffling merely said that a message was sent to the Prussian I Corps to march to Papelotte and 'it was settled that as soon as that corps appeared on the rise between Papelotte and Ohain, the cavalry brigades of Vandeleur and Vivian should move off to reinforce the centre'. Who 'settled' the matter was not stated.
23. Vivian in *WL*, no. 70 (for the extract to his wife), and *WA*, iv, nos. 22, 21, 23. In referring to Vandeleur, Vivian used not his first name (John) but his second, Ormsby. It is good to see that Vivian's very important letter to Siborne (vol. iv, no. 23) is now published; its

absence from the invaluable *Letters from the Battle of Waterloo* was one of the few editorial decisions that could be faulted. That decision had been made on the general basis that where *other* letters by a writer had already appeared in *WL,* no further letters of his should be given.

24. *WL*, nos. 7 and 9, dated 1835 and 1842 respectively. Despite the late dates the accuracy of their recollections of their chief sending an order cannot really be doubted.
25. Maxwell, ii, p. 75 fn., and Anglesey, *One Leg*, p. 364. Passing reference has been made to this note in chap. 35, sec. V, fn. 14.
26. *WL*, no. 6. Anglesey added his discontent 'with a Colonel commanding a young regiment of Hanoverian Hussars'. There has never been any real doubt about the feeble conduct of the Cumberland Hussars, whose colonel was subsequently tried by court-martial and disgraced.
27. The 12 June muster lists, the casualties and the officer casualties by name are in DBTS, iii, schedules commencing on pp. 100, 201, 214. There are discrepancies of course: two regiments (4th and 5th Light Dragoons) have differing officer figures in separate tables, p. 201 and 214; and there may be other differences.
28. Boulger's defence of the Netherlands cavalry suffers from his treatment of the category 'killed *plus* missing' as all 'killed': *The Belgians at Waterloo,* pp. 30–1. The matter had previously been debated between Sir H. Maxwell and Charles Oman in *The Nineteenth Century,* vol. 48, September 1900, pp. 407–22, and October 1900, pp. 629–38. Maxwell's good feeling for the Prussian, other German and Netherlands allies, was marred by occasional carelessness; Oman replied about the Netherlanders, giving Maxwell a perhaps over-zealous drubbing.
29. Oman relied on a ratio of killed to wounded of approx 1:3.5, so that when a killed plus missing figure exceeded the wounded category – as in certain of these cases – he worked backwards from the wounded figure to identify dead from disappeared: thus his system would have yielded figures for the men of the 1st Carabiniers of 66 wounded (as given), 19 dead (66 divided by 3.5) and 6 missing (25 k + m less 19).
30. Trip's undated report is in DBTS, iii, p. 402 onwards, and in English in Boulger, pp. 65–6. His later report of 1823 adds nothing (DBTS, iii, p. 409). He gives no statement of strengths or casualties. The Cavalry Division report of Oct. 1815 is totally uninformative, merely saying that the brigades all acted independently (DBTS, iii, p. 422, Boulger, p. 67).
31. For the information in this and the previous paragraph see Captain Morbotter's letter to van Löben Sels, 21 July 1841, *Waterloo: Netherlands Corresp.*, ed. Franklin, vol. i, pp. 161–2.
32. Boulger, p. 65.
33. *WL*, no. 9. W. H. James, in a long footnote (pp. 247–50) judges that Lord Edward's remark was about Ghigny's 1st Light Brigade near the Charleroi road; Trip had certainly been sent during the afternoon towards Hougoumont, as Gawler testifies: maybe he was still there, but De Bas's map in *Prins Frederik*, after p. 1416, puts Trip well down the reverse slope, *due north of the modern Lion mound.*
34. *WL*, no. 124: Adkin (p. 223) remarks that the carabinier regiments had 'Roman' helmets with wool on the crests, and plumes. Shaw Kennedy, *Notes*, para. 115. See also Lautour's

passing comment in *WL*, no. 49, on the Netherlands cavalry failing to deploy to counter-attack during Ney's onsets.

35. F. Snappers, 'The Netherlands Heavy Cavalry's Refusal to Attack', in *Mars et Victoria* (Netherlands), xxxv, 2001: an English translation was kindly given to me by the late Marquess of Anglesey.
36. De Bas, *Prins Frederik*, iii (2), pp. 729–30.
37. If the Prince had said to the 2nd Carabiniers after the charge, 'you have done enough at present' instead of 'you have done enough today' it would have been wiser.
38. The 7th Marquess of Anglesey, *One Leg*, p. 36. The youth wrote, 'I have so far gained ground in French that I know how ill I speak it; which, I think, is being very much improved' (p. 31).
39. This is the conclusion of Adkin.
40. Moore Smith, *Life of Colborne*, p. 126; Oman, *Wellington's Army*, p. 151 and p. 47 (slightly adapted).
41. Stanhope's note, summer 1815, in Glover, *Eyewitness*, p. 179.

CHAPTER 43: The Prussian Intervention

1. I have quoted Bülow's own report in chap. 40, sec. IV: 'notwithstanding that the 13th and 14th Brigades had not yet crossed the Lasne defile, the Field Marshal ordered that those troops available should attack immediately, to give breathing space to the English army': DBTS, iii, p. 524 onwards. There is no doubt who forced the pace.
2. The course of events in this sector of the battlefield is not always very clear. Houssaye treats the fighting in more general terms than for the Mont St Jean struggle. Adkin is clear but fairly brief; his splendid maps are all the more useful in consequence. Field is useful for eye-witness accounts from the French side and quotes very fully the notable narrative of General Pelet (originally published by Vicomte d'Avout in the magazine *Carnet de la Sabretache* in 1905). Aerts, as usual, is impartial and does not let the detail mask the principal happenings. Coppens & Courcelle, *Papelotte*, in the 'Carnets de la Campagne' series, provide some little-known quotations from eye-witnesses, with a challenging analysis of events that questions many assumptions. Lettow-Vorbeck is only moderately useful. Hofschröer gives many Prussian unit battle reports. I have relied on them all to varying degrees for the sections on Plancenoit.
3. Hofschröer, *1815*, ii, p. 117: 'This symbolic union of German soldier with German soldier marked the beginning of the end of the battle for Napoleon.'
4. Houssaye, III, 4, III, p. 370; Eng. trans., p. 211. Later, in the course of blaming the Emperor's subordinates for ruining the Emperor's plan, he blames Lobau (III, 8, IV, Eng. trans. p. 291), for not taking the trouble to choose a sensible place for his initial stand, relying on Napoleon's somewhat dubious claim that he ordered Lobau to support the light cavalry by 'going towards St-Lambert, to choose a good intermediate position where 10,000 men could stop 30,000' (*Corr. de Nap.*, xxxi, p. 229, 4to; 190, 8vo). Houssaye accuses him of not making the effort, and says that slopes above the bridge at Lasne were the right

place. Doubtless if Lobau had been ordered to march earlier, and if the light cavalry had been east of the Bois de Paris, that might have been the case. But as it was, the position by Hannotelet was the best he could reach in the time if he was to keep La Belle Alliance beyond cannon range and free of trouble.

5. Writing in 1908 Aerts noted that Plancenoit village in its dell was invisible from the top of the Lion Mound (140 feet above the surrounding ground), except for the spire of the mid-nineteenth century church (*Opérations*, p. 243, and again p. 252 fn., confirming Siborne's statement in *History*, p. 326). What could be seen from the Mont St Jean crossroads through the dense smoke was obviously much less. Sir A. S. Frazer, who had been on the ridge all day on 18 June wrote an account of the battle, two days later: 'I may seem to have forgotten the Prussians in this battle. I saw none; but I believe that on our left they did advance ... it was not visible from any point where the Duke was till dusk, when we had swept the enemy from the plain in our front': *Letters*, p. 561.
6. It is this colonel's death that establishes where Bellair's brigade was in the fighting, a position that would otherwise have to be guessed.
7. So says the 18th Regiment's battle report, quoted in Hofschröer, *1815*, ii, p. 119. Not only does this indicate the intensity of the initial encounters, but also the risk that Blücher was prepared to run, since replenishment ammunition had to come from other units; the munitions supplies generally must have been miles back down the muddy tracks.
8. Aerts quotes a gazetteer of 1815 that assessed the village at some 500 inhabitants. They fled their homes when the French army loomed up on the night of 17/18 June. Aerts gives a good description of the village houses and alleys. The church was rebuilt in 1857 with a much taller spire: on 18 June it was filled with wounded and dying. As so often when describing north European terrain in terms of fighting, it is difficult to convey how slight and gentle are the slopes, and French terms such as '*ravin*' for a fairly small gully, may give an English-language reader far too sheer an impression – as at St Amand on 16 June 1815, or on many a fairly featureless field of action in 1914–18, where a hollow of only a few feet can make an enormous difference.
9. Ollech, p. 196 gives the famous message thus: '*er solle dem Feinde nach Kräften jeden Schritt vorwärts streitig machen, den der grösste Verlust des Korps würde durch den Sieg über Napoleon gelangte*'. Note the unlimited concept, not a local success, but the entire destruction of Napoleon: the concept that I have outlined in the opening paragraphs of this chapter. I see that, unlike Ollech, DBTS, ii, p. 225 add the comment that the message was '*de la part du commandant en chef*', but whether that is from sight of some document or memoir or is their own deduction they do not say.
10. This, it may be objected, is a British view on how a Prussian chief of staff and commander interacted, and under-values the role of Gneisenau vis-à-vis Blücher. May I therefore quote perhaps the greatest German commander and staff officer of the twentieth century, Field Marshal von Manstein (1887–1973): 'For a commander, understanding, knowledge and experience are essential prerequisites. *Deficiencies in these qualities can to some extent* be made good by a chief of staff, provided the commander is willing to follow his advice. More importantly, the commander must possess *character* and a *human soul.*

These qualities alone bring him the resolution to withstand the inevitable crises in war. In addition to professional ability, they provide the basis for *daring decisions* in difficult situations. Finally, the confidence of troops that the commander leads is based primarily on the steadfastness of his character': quoted in Mungo Melvin, *Manstein: Hitler's Greatest General* (London, 2010), p. 94, emphasis added.

11. Quoted in Brett-James, *Hundred Days*, pp. 148–50.
12. Müffling, *Memoirs*, pp. 248–9. Nothing of any of this appeared in his 1815 *History*.
13. Aerts, *Opérations*, p. 254.
14. See Seymour and Fremantle in *WL*, nos. 9 and 11. There is a further claim, by the then Major William Staveley of the Royal Staff Corps in a letter dated four days after the battle: 'Blucher sent word at one o'clock that he would attack in half an hour. At four Lord Wellington sent me to him to see what he was about and tell him how well we were getting on. I rode all along our line at full gallop and after crossing the country about two miles to our left found him. He told me to tell Lord Wellington that he would attack as soon as he could form his men, which would probably be in an hour or less, but he did not come up with the enemy until they were fairly driven from the field. He was, however, of great use in pursuing . . .': quoted in *JSAHR*, vol. 14 (1935), at p. 162. We have already noted in chap. 42, sec. IV Gronow's later recollection of Wellington saying somewhat after 4 p.m. that, 'The battle is mine; and if the Prussians arrive soon, there will be an end of the war'; so that it is interesting to find Staveley on 22 June independently using the words 'how well we were getting on' at that point in the afternoon. Constant's perception of the Duke's disquiet (chap. 40, sec. IV) seems to qualify this, but it was the *continued non-appearance* of the Prussians rather than the present state of his own front that caused this.
15. Undated note, *WL*, no. 73.
16. Reiche's account, quoted in Hofschröer, *1815*, ii, p. 127. Outlines of the clash are also in the 2nd Netherlands Division report, in DBTS, iii, p. 343, and Boulger, p. 63. Further details from the Nassauers are in Pflugk-Harttung, *Belle-Alliance*, Nrs 85 and 86 (now also in *WA*, v, nos. 26 and 27). For the problem in general see Uffindell's 'Friendly Fire'.
17. *WL*, no. 11. This positioning is confirmed by the report of one of the Prussian battery commanders, Captain Borowsky, in Hofschröer, *1815*, ii, p. 127.
18. Aerts, *Opérations*, p. 258. He timed this as 7.30 p.m. See also note 3 above.
19. Quoted in Coppens & Courcelle, *Papelotte*, p. 14, col a.
20. I Corps strengths and casualty figures come from Delbrück, *Gneisenau*, iv, p. 682 and Siborne, *History*, App. 46; for a breakdown by arms of the forces actually engaged, Aerts, *Opérations*, p. 255, fn. The casualties in other units of the corps were Silesian sharpshooters, 29; 1st Westphalian Landwehr, 13; cavalry, 13; artillery, 11.
21. Oman, 'French Losses', *EHR*, 19, p. 684.
22. Ziethen's autobiography (sometimes called his *Journal*) of 1839 awarded himself the main credit for victory. General Lettow-Vorbeck showed in his article 'Die Zietenische Tagebuch' in the *Jahrbücher für die deutsche Armee und Marine* of 1903, pp. 436–9, that while the semi-official war diary (*Tagebuch*) was acceptable, Ziethen's autobiography,

published by Dietrich Hafner in a Leipzig monthly journal *Militärisches* of 1896, was a tissue of inaccuracies, and that virtually everything in the following extract was wrong. The passage in question dealing with Waterloo, termed by Hafner a 'characteristic episode' (p. 327), reads at *Militärisches,* p. 328: 'I received no orders on 18 June before 10 a.m. ... I knew where the English were located and I deduced that I Corps had to take the open position between the right wing of General von Bülow and the left of the Scots. At 11 a.m. on my own initiative [here Lettow-Vorbeck threw in his own exclamation mark] I issued the orders, took up the direction of march, and was rewarded by arriving in time to save the Scots. Bonaparte thought I was Grouchy; 96 guns proved him wrong [Ziethen's corps establishment was 96 guns, but on this day he fielded only 12]. The Old Guard advanced against me in masses, musket in hand [*Die alte Garde avancierte in Masse, das Gewehr in Arm, gegen mich*]; they came up to 200 paces in front of the guns: canister shook them. The Brandenburg Dragoon Regiment then slashed its way in to the French Old Guard and forced them into a hasty retreat': all this is discussed in Dr G. Pedlow's article, 'Back to the Sources', *First Empire,* no. 82, pp. 30–6, May/June 2005, from which (p. 31) I take his translation. As to relying on anything from Ziethen's *Journal,* the only good advice is *caveat emptor.* And that is a pity, because what Ziethen actually did this day was praiseworthy enough in itself.

CHAPTER 44: The Fifth Act

1. To recapitulate the infantry strengths and availabilities: Lobau, having seen one division (Teste) sent to Grouchy, retained the following regiments of the *Ligne*: *5e, 11e* (3 battalions), *27e, 84e,* making 9 battalions. *Jeune Garde*: *tirailleurs,* 4 battalions; *voltigeurs,* 4 battalions. There remained with Napoleon seven battalions of the *Moyenne Garde*: *grenadiers,* 3; *chasseurs,* 4; and eight of the *Vieille Garde*: *grenadiers,* 4; *chasseurs,* 4.
2. It is so well known to French readers that they will have it at their fingertips; Andrew Field has printed an English translation on pages 177–82 of his recent *Waterloo, the French Perspective.* My own work is more concerned with certain aspects of command in a four months' European crisis, rather than a tactical analysis or a collection of personal recollections of an extraordinary day, and I must hope that this reference to that invaluable book will be enough.
3. Petit, 'Account of the Waterloo Campaign', *EHR,* 18, p. 324.
4. Grouchy's 32,000 men ought to be with them by the next day at latest, and *7e Division,* though much weakened by Ligny, would be rested and had been called forward to Quatre Bras. Lack of both munitions and fresh horses might have been the greatest worry.
5. '*Es war ½ 8 Uhr* [a half hour before 8 o'clock], *und noch standt die Schlacht*': official Prussian report of 20 June 1815, signed by Gneisenau, DBTS, iii, p. 486; their French version is on p. 487 (also in *WSD,* x, p. 505): '*A 7 heures et demie l'issue de la bataille était encore incertaine.*'
6. Tomkinson of the 16th Light Dragoons saw some unsteady Netherlanders to his front: 'the Duke rode up and encouraged them. He said to us: "*That is right, that is right; keep them up.*" Childers then brought up his squadron, and by placing it in their rear they

continued steady. The Duke rode away again immediately. Had this one battalion run away at that moment, the consequence might have been fatal': Tomkinson's *Diary*, p. 309.

7. *The Dynasts*, Part 3, Scene VII, at the start of a most interesting sequence of imagined exchanges of words between Wellington and his colleagues.
8. Constant's *Journal*, on the night of the battle; and the letter to William Wellesley Pole, 19 June 1815, in 'Some Letters of Wellington', ed. Sir Charles Webster, *Camden Miscellany*, 3rd Series, vol. 79 (1948), letter 31, p. 35. My emphasis in both quotations.
9. The *cuirassier* was seen by a number of eye-witnesses as well as by Colborne and his men: Frazer in particular (*Letters*, 20 June, p. 552). The narrative of the 52nd's role in the climax of the battle is from Colborne's own account of 1847–8, published in his *Life* by G. C. Moore Smith (1903), App. 2, and also given in *LW*, no. 122, with small differences of wording in a few places. Unfortunately *Letters* attributes this no. 122 to John Cross, who is the undoubted author of Letter 120 of 1843, which he signed himself; it is worth noting that item 121 of 1843 was not in Cross's handwriting, but was a copy made by a clerk, who wrote the name Cross as author although the 'signature' was actually in the clerk's hand and not Cross's. But the unsigned no. 122, also in the same clerk's hand, was certainly by Colborne (as Moore Smith stated) and not by Cross: for whereas in no. 120 Cross writes that he revisited the battlefield 'in the summer of 1818', in no. 122 (written – by Colborne – when Siborne was preparing his *History*) it states that 'the writer has never been on the ground since [the battle]'.
10. The editor of *LW* originally footnoted this comment as indicating that the wounded would be an encumbrance to be abandoned in any retreat, a point I contested with him as an inference only, and as suggesting dereliction of duty in a commanding officer. For Colborne said nothing about any 'retreat' at all; and I note that Macready of the 30th vouched for Wellington saying to Colin Halkett, 'there must not be even a *symptom* of retreat' (*USM*, March 1845, p. 402 fn.). There was a simple explanation given by Colborne's son, who found him a few days before his death weeping in memory of his injured soldier servant, to whom he had said 'lie quietly, the battle will be over in half an hour, when you will be carried to the rear and all will be well' (Moore Smith, p. 376), which surely settles the matter. Gareth Glover magnanimously accepted the main point: *First Empire*, nos. 95, 96 and 98, July 2007 to Feb 2008.
11. Sergeant Robertson of the 92nd remarks that 'a volley of rockets' and a musket volley turned d'Erlon's men back: *With Napoleon at Waterloo*, p. 164. But was this rocket salvo the one recorded earlier above La Haye Sainte (chap. 42, sec. III) or a fresh occasion?
12. Martin of the *45e Ligne*, quoted in Field, p. 194.
13. Reille, in Elchingen, *Docs. Inéd., p. 62*.
14. Kincaid, 1830 p. 343, 1929 p. 255. I once heard Gen.l Sir Anthony Farrar-Hockley remark about undergoing water torture as a prisoner during the Korean War: each time he survived the repeated drowning experience, he told himself to hold on 'one more time!' and after the next choking, still 'one more time'! His torturers were the first to give up.
15. Among those historians who favoured 'column' were Siborne, Charras, Chesney, Ropes, Houssaye (*La Garde meurt*), Pollio, James, Fortescue, Weller, Chandler, Logie, and Van

Danzig; Oman in his chapter in the *CMH* favoured the 'hollow square', as did Houssaye (*1815, Waterloo*), De Bas and T'Serclaes de Wommersom, and more recently Hamilton-Williams, Adkin, and Field. The Prussians Ollech and Lettow-Vorbeck, conscious of the difficulties, mentioned column in a general way, but were disinclined to go into any detail, the latter referring to Charras as a guide. Others simply duck the issue.

16. Macready was insistent that French skirmishers were not involved: *USM*, March 1845, p. 399. He is supported by a quotation in Field, p. 191: a *Chasseur* officer thought success would have come (in part) 'if we had engaged the enemy first with some skirmishers'. Yet I note that Siborne wrote of the *Garde* advance that 'a swarm of skirmishers opened a sharp and teasing fire among the British gunners', p. 340: perhaps they stopped at the advance (gun) position having silenced the destructive guns, leaving the infantry to go over an apparently empty crest? As to the number of *Garde* artillery batteries deployed among the *Garde* infantry, accounts differ: Ropes speaks of two, Adkin of one. As the horse batteries each had four 6-pounders and there were five separate attacking formations, two pieces between each formation would suggest two batteries, and I note that Field (p. 189) quotes Pontécoulant of the *Garde* artillery deploying 'two batteries of horse artillery'.

Mercer recalled 'a [French] battery' appearing from nowhere and opening destructive fire on him, until a battery of 'Belgic Horse Artillery' drove off the French (*WL*, No. 89). But the only Belgic guns were van der Smissen/Kramer's, at least 500 yards or more to his east, and no non-British/KGL companies were nearby, so this remains a mystery. Moreover, Duchand's French horse artillery were an integral part of the Garde advance, not an isolated force. As Sharpin (Bolton's company, 200 yards east of Mercer) thought that the *Garde*'s tall bonnets only became visible over the corn when 'within forty to fifty yards of our guns' (*WL*, No. 97), and as Duchand's guns could not be much forward of the infantry columns, this seems to me to indicate that at so close a range Duchand's fire was to suppress and destroy all opposition whether from musketry or cannon rather than to engage in an artillery duel as such. Unquestionably Colin Halkett's infantry were sorely smitten by cannon-fire. The point, however, is a minor one.

17. There is no consensus on why this second wave was kept apart from the first: the matter is discussed in Field, p. 188, who contrasts the remark of Napoleon that the *Vieille Garde* should have gone forward with the *Moyenne*, but arrived too late for some reason (yet as Field remarks, they were together when Napoleon's order to leave the high ground was issued), as against Mauduit who said that the need was so urgent that the *Moyenne* had to be used at once, before the *Vieille* could arrive (which is what Gourgaud half suggests in his *Campaign of 1815*). But Napoleon was always niggardly in spending his *Vieille Garde*, and I think may well have intended to use and perhaps expend his first wave in breaking-in, and using his second (less expensively) for the break-out.

18. *Belle-Alliance*, nos. 71 (regt) and 73 (Kruse); *WA*, ii, no. 29 and v, no. 31. Kruse maintained that he faced the *Garde*, but this seems unlikely. The regiment says the two-battalion attack had no effect ('*keine Folge hatte*'). On the other hand, in Hofschröer, *1815*, ii, the Nassau attack is cited (together with the Osnabrück Landwehr in Hugh Halkett's

brigade), as playing 'a major part in the achievement' of defeating the *Garde* attack: pp. 135–7.

19. There are admissions of a panic and brief flight by some in the brigade, a movement that was stopped only with some difficulty. This might be understood either as giving way before the *Garde* on this portion of the front (who were stopped by the savagery of cannon shot), or as a freak of mass psychology in tired and confused men – like the widening ripple spreading later among the French of '*Sauve qui peut*'. It may have been a mistake to order a slight retirement to a hedge, since once a retirement starts it may continue of itself, or be due to one tired and exhausted battalion becoming entangled in another during a change of position (it was said that 'turn right' was mistaken for 'turn right about' making the muddle that confused everyone). Nobody likes revealing such mishaps but Macready did let us see something (see for instance, *USM*, Aug 1852, p. 528).
20. DBTS, ii, p. 267 onwards, especially pp. 271 and 275; I have taken their quotation of the divisional narrative from Boulger's translation, on his p. 46.
21. Macready, *USM*, March 1845, p. 401. Thus Detmers's men passed after this British battalion's final casualties had been suffered and just before they piled arms. DBTS, ii, p. 267 onwards, quoted at length from Macready's account pp. 400–1, but, significantly, they omitted this 'chakos' remark. It is notable that the generously minded Hill wrote merely of Chassé's infantry's 'steady conduct' when 'supporting' Adam, but singled out for praise, and rightly so, van de Smissen's 'Belgian battery' for its 'well directed fire' (20 June, *WSD*, x, p. 544).
22. Crabbé, in Field, p. 201: that the force on stopping 'formed into square' surely must mean that the previous formation as they advanced was a different one.
23. Sir H. Clinton's formal report to Lord Hill, 19 June 1815: in praising the three battalions of Adam's brigade (and forwarding to Hill Adam's own report), Clinton stated that while he himself gave orders to advance to Hugh Halkett's and the KGL brigades, the repulse of the *Garde* 'afforded the opportunity to become ourselves the attacking body, so judiciously taken advantage of by Major-General C. [*sic*, read F.] Adam's Brigade *under your lordship's immediate direction*' [emphasis added]. It could be argued that this relates only to the advance immediately after the *Garde's* repulse, but I think it may apply equally to the moment of crisis. The full report is in G. Glover, *Waterloo: The Defeat of Napoleon's Imperial Guard*, p. 170. Hill's misfortune with his horse is noted by Horace Churchill, in his 28 June 1815 letter to his father.
24. Gomm's comment of 1867 is in his *Letters and Journals*, p. 372. My account of Colborne's action is taken mainly from G. C. Moore Smith's *Life of John Colborne, Field-Marshal Lord Seaton*, App. II, a series of accounts written or dictated by Sir John in his later years; letters nos. 120–2 in *LW*; and the accounts in *WL* (Colborne, Gawler), Siborne, James, Fortescue, Adkin, Glover's *Waterloo: The Defeat of Napoleon's Imperial Guard*, etc. The achievement gets only the briefest three-line mention in Hofschröer, *1815*, ii, and Colborne's name is not mentioned in the text or the index.
25. Revd W. Leeke, *History of Lord Seaton's Regiment at Waterloo*, i, p. 45. I think this is a safe observation. Ensign Leeke was an eye-witness, but his anger at praise given to the Guards

for the repulse instead of to the 52nd (whom he claimed had done the deed alone) nearly approached monomania. He even ignored Colborne's repeated statements that the left flanking company wheeled back, and insisted on his own very different version. For all the larger matters I prefer to rely on Colborne or, failing him, Gawler, in preference to Leeke: to me Leeke's little 1871 *Supplementary* third volume is, like the productions of some other enthusiastic literary clergymen, a matter for despair. Sir William Gomm in notes of 1868, subjected Leeke's arguments to a very critical review and reduced his enormous claims to their proper scale (Gomm's *Letters and Journals*, p. 369 onwards).

26. Captain Powell of the 1st Guards, *WL*, no. 109.
27. Colborne was acutely aware of the risks of an open flank, William Stewart having sent him forward in line at Albuera in 1811, where he was cut up by French cavalry, losing 1,250 men out of 1,650 (Oman, *Peninsular War*, iv, pp. 383–4). That he took the risk again at Waterloo shows both his moral courage and the depth of the crisis. To turn from line to square once horsemen were seen was wise, but it entailed stopping: and this consideration, too, is relevant to the *Garde*'s formation in its approach march and its response in 'facing outwards' to meet the 52nd's attack.
28. 'The Osnabrück Landwehr Battalion, part of Hugh Halkett's brigade, joined this attack. Napoleon's invincibles broke': Hofschröer, *1815*, ii, p. 137. Certainly this battalion caught up, and performed well later in the pursuit, but as Adam's brigade launched the attack and was already proceeding across the battlefield, I think that the facts indicate that these two sentences quoted above are in the wrong sequence.
29. Sir John Byng of the Guards put the pause between the *Garde*'s retirement and the general advance as 'ten or twelve minutes', and Gawler of the 52nd even at 'a full quarter of an hour': *WL*, nos. 113 and 124. See Siborne, *History*, at p. 361; once Siborne realised that there had been this pause, he recognised that the position of the Prussians on his model at that time was too far forward. It was for that reason that he drew them back from his original placement: see also Hofschröer's *Wellington's Smallest Victory*. The matter was painstakingly investigated and confirmed by my friend Gary Cousins in 'Left Wing History (7)', *First Empire*, no. 85, Dec 2005, pp. 18–28.
30. Sgt. D. Robertson, in *With Napoleon at Waterloo*, pp. 151–66, at p. 163.
31. Ney's letter to Fouché, head of the provisional government, 26 June 1815: *Booth's Waterloo*, 11th edition, at p. 387. Barry Van Danzig has overlooked this testimony when arguing that 'Here is Grouchy' is a fabrication by those exiled on St Helena. Field, who quotes Levavasseur and Mauduit, writes with his customary shrewdness, pp. 203–4.
32. Frazer, 9 a.m., 20 June, *Letters*, p. 553; MS account (of 1816), Murray papers, National Library of Scotland, Adv MS 46.9.19, unsigned, but marked by Murray as by De Lacy Evans.
33. '*A moi, Chasseurs! Sauvons l'aigle ou mourons autour d'elle*': Haythornthwaite, *Waterloo Armies*, p. 106; Pelet's call is also recorded in Stawitzky's *History of the 25th Regiment* (Coblenz, 1857), quoted in Hofschröer, *1815*, ii, p. 145. Houssaye is very brief and not particularly helpful on the final phase at Plancenoit, so that (once again) Field's chapter 18 is to be preferred.

34. Excluding *Vieille Garde*, the officer casualties were *Jeune Garde*, 5 k, 29 w; Lobau, 22 k, 102 w; Domon, 1 k, 10 w; Subervie, 2 k, 26 w; total 31 k, 167 w: Oman, *EHR*, xix, pp. 686–7.
35. Hofschröer, *1815*, ii, p. 145.
36. Pflugk-Harttung's conclusion reads more fully: 'The main problem for the Prussians was their lack of success at Plancenoit. Here and not at Smouhain was the decisive point. Because the enemy *Garde* battalions unswervingly held this village until Wellington's line had achieved the final victory, they also kept the Prussians from gaining the laurels of the day ... If Bülow had captured Plancenoit an hour earlier, he would have achieved the decisive results in the flank and rear, which Wellington now won at the front': 'Das I Korps Zieten bei Belle-Alliance und Wavre', in *Jahrbücher für die deutsche Armee und Marine*, Jan.–June 1905, p. 239, two final paragraphs.
37. Preface, p. 9: Ardant du Picq was Paddy's favourite military book, with Oman's *Peninsular War* coming second. The first part of Ardant du Picq's work originally appeared in the *Bulletin de la Réunion des Officiers* in 1868; the second part was left unfinished and appeared posthumously. The complete book was published in Paris in 1903, and was translated into English in 1921 as *Battle Studies*. A French reprint came out in Paris in 1942.
38. *Etudes*, Part Two, chap. 1, sec. V; p. 137 in the 1942 edition. My translation.
39. Oman took French official casualty statistics for those battles where both officer and other rank figures were given: Talavera, Bussaco, Barrosa, the Pyrenees, Nivelle, Bayonne and St Pierre (Albuera, Salamanca and Vittoria were never properly listed), and established that there was on average one officer to 23 other rank casualties. He took a ratio of 1:20 as reasonable for Waterloo, where the army was especially heavily officered.
40. Adkin, p. 404, based upon Scott Bowden's *Armies at Waterloo*.
41. Major G. Gawler of the 52nd, 'The Crisis', *USJ*, July 1833, p. 305.
42. Petit, Pelet, Guillemin, Franquin and Prax, all of the *Garde*, plus Crabbé and Levavasseur, have been usefully presented by Andrew Field, pp. 196–203 and 256–9, and my use of their evidence draws on those pages. As I have said elsewhere his book is a mine of extremely valuable information based on the most extensive research.
43. Petit, *EHR*, xviii, p. 325.
44. Adkin, p. 420, argues that Petit's remarks are conclusive as to the formation adopted. Field, p. 191, also relies on Petit's views to a considerable extent (while also citing many other Frenchmen), but does recognise that he was back near La Belle Alliance with his *1er Grenadiers* right to the end of the day, and therefore not in a position to see what was happening in the smoke a mile away. Because the *Garde* stood in square as a defensive backstop behind Plancenoit does not of itself mean that it stayed in square when attacking the distant Mont St Jean ridge, especially as those on the ridge who were close to hand and in a position to see were sure that it marched in column.
45. *Victoires et Conquêtes des Français*, vol. xxiv (1821), pp. 220–1.
46. See Napoleon to Bertrand, Paris, 27 March 1813, about forming *squares* three ranks deep to repulse cavalry attacks; the infantry *colonne d'attaque* should advance with the division at the head of each column using bayonets, the first two ranks of the leading platoons opening fire while the column deploys under cover of this fire: *Corr. de Nap.*,

no. 19,775 and now in *Corr. Gén.*, no. 33,475. He had previously emphasised the need to practise forming *bataillon carré* to resist cavalry, and training in *colonne d'attaque*, in letters to Davout and Ney, 2 and 3 March 1813 (*CdN*, 19,638 and 19,714; *CG*, 32,933 and 33,213).

47. Bertrand, *Cahiers*, i (1951), p. 290: Napoleon's actual words were: '*Si vous attaquez en colonne, vous n'avez pas de feux. A Waterloo, la Garde n'a pas eu le temps de se déployer, n'a pas fait de feux, ce qui a occasionné la déroute.*' This seems to establish that two years after the battle Napoleon thought they advanced in column.
48. Gourgaud, *Journal inédit*, ii, p. 370, and *Campaign of 1815*, English version (1818), pp. 106–8. Ney's letter of 26 June to Fouché said 'four regiments' (not battalions) of the *Moyenne Garde* were given him by the Emperor for the attack, and that later, 'four squares' of the *Vieille* were protecting the retreat.
49. Both these are in Houssaye's little booklet, *La Garde meurt et ne se rendre pas* (1907), pp. 27 and 30. He found them sincere, but the first full of basic mistakes and the other unreliable. He himself seemed now to favour the *colonne d'attaque* theory (p. 5), having in 1898 plumped for the square: *1815, Waterloo*, Book III, chap. 5, sec. II, p. 392 (Eng. trans., p. 225).
50. This is the formation suggested by James, Fortescue and Chandler. Diagrammatic examples are given in a number of works: see for instance Haythornthwaite, *Waterloo Armies*, pp. 118–19.
51. This, it seems to me, would apply also if there were *only two squares*, which is why the square's proponents argue for *five*: but that is almost by definition to admit that there might be *five* columns. Five separate formations there almost definitely were.
52. Speaking in general terms, Napoleon's view was that a battalion in line, with ranks two-deep, had a frontage of '40 *toises*' or 85 yards, but if supported by a battalion in square on each flank for protection against cavalry, would have a frontage of '80 *toises*' or 170 yards: Bertrand's notes of 1820, *Cahiers*, ii, p. 440. Of course, if moving in line it would already be deployed to fire. But Napoleon had earlier (1817) claimed that the *Garde* had not deployed. Taking the frontage on the ridge as 440 yards or 206 *toises*, I do not see how 'five squares' could squeeze in.
53. An officer of the 5th British Brigade [Macready] in *USM*, March 1845, pp. 396–7, citing the evidence of Craan's plan published in 1816, and several officers: Howard, Rogers, an unidentified officer, all of his regiment the 30th, and his own journal. It may be objected that all are from one battalion that was unsteady at the crisis and that they were colouring their accounts, but the unsteadiness does not affect their testimony as to the French formation. In any case, Colborne of the 52nd, some distance to the west, speaks of columns (*LW*, no. 122), and there are many others, like Powell of the 1st Guards, who say the same. In all the British testimony I have come across only one passing reference to 'squares', Major Blair of the 91st, attached to Adam's staff: 'after the repulse of the squares of the Old Guard...' (*WL*, no. 121).
54. This point was well made by Major Gordon Corrigan, who in 1992 took a platoon of his Gurkhas up the slope. To replicate the conditions of Waterloo he had them semi-

blindfolded. They all veered under the gravitational pull of the slope: Corrigan, p. 326, and his note 7 on p. 373. Dr Pedlow of NATO has noted the same experience when taking parties of officers on the battlefield walk.

CHAPTER 45: The Victory

1. Tomkinson, p. 313: his italics.
2. Siborne, *History*, edn. 3 of 1848, p. 363. On reading the Revd Gleig's *The Story of Waterloo*, of 1847, a smooth version taken from Siborne's second edition, Arbuthnot remarked to his son, 'the concluding part of it and the end of battle is ill done, I think. The Duke told me that after ordering the advance, he halted the army for a short time, in order they should all be up in rank. This Gleig does not mention' (letter, 3 Dec 1847, *Arbuthnot Corr.*, p. 246).
3. There are two versions of this story. Houssaye's version (p. 405, Eng. trans. p. 232) is that Cambronne refused to surrender, shouted '*Merde!*', and 'seconds later a bullet full in the face knocked him down bleeding and unconscious'. He cites Cambronne's own statement at his first interrogation (29 Jan. 1816) that he was 'wounded and left for dead on 18 June', and Petit's remark that he saw him fall wounded from his horse (see *EHR*, 17, pp. 325–6), and contrasts these with Halkett's version. Halkett wrote (*WL*, no. 130) that Cambronne and two officers were trying to animate their men, were abandoned by them, and as Halkett was about to cut Cambronne down the latter surrendered. Then Halkett's horse momentarily fell and his prisoner tried to slip away, whereupon Halkett caught him by the aiguillette and delivered him over to be taken to the Duke. Eels of the 3/95th was sure that he saw Halkett ride forward and take a French officer prisoner (*WL*, no. 129). Recently Peter Hofschröer has produced further evidence for Halkett's version, quoting several Osnabrück soldiers' accounts, all of which independently agree (*1815*, ii, pp. 146–8). Cambronne had been hit in the head and in other places, but was still active enough to lead men, to try to escape, and proved as a walking prisoner fit enough to be marched some distance across the battlefield to Wellington. The story that he was found unconscious, was 'stripped as naked as John the Baptist, and robbed of everything' (Brunschvicq, p. 157) is therefore inaccurate in at least some respects. See also Adkin, p. 418, on the controversy of what Cambronne shouted.
4. Houssaye, Book III, chap. 5, sec. IV, p. 403; Eng. trans., p. 231: the story apparently came from one of d'Erlon's ADCs who served him in the 1830s.
5. Houssaye, Book III, chap. 5, sec. IV, p. 403; Eng. trans., p. 231. Durutte's division performed well enough by the standards of the other divisions, and the derogatory statements that Napoleon made against it in his 1820 memoirs are scandalously unfair.
6. Capturing the gun-line deprives an army of a weapon (and its munitions) that is irreplaceable in the short term. Men can usually be found from somewhere, but not field-guns and shells. The one major exception that comes to mind is after the great German offensive of March 1918, when Winston Churchill's Ministry of Munitions made good British losses in miraculously short time. As Colonel Michael Crawshaw wrote in his brilliant analysis of industry, technology and command in his chapter in *Haig, a Reappraisal* (1999): 'when

equipment losses are immediately made good with new and shiny replacements, with the assurance that there is more where that came from, tails lift' (p. 169).

7. Müffling, *History*, p. 35; de Sales, *LW*, no. 1. Had the Prussians reached the great *chaussée* first, then this contretemps could not have happened: it would also have given some semblance of authenticity to claims that Prussia gained the victory.
8. DBTS, iii, pp. 534–7 in German and French. Constant made this marginal comment about the first sentence: 'Error: the Duke was in person already between Rossomme farm and Plancenoit when he ordered me to tell General Bülow that it was us he was cannonading and not the enemy. Lord Wellington's leading troops were already further in advance than he was' (p. 536 fn.). Perhaps that explains why La Belle Alliance was not really a suitable name for the place of victory.
9. The incident is recounted by Gawler of the 52nd in his 'The Crisis and the Close of the Action at Waterloo', *USJ*, July 1833, pp. 299–310, at p. 305. It is a further confirmation that Wellington's army had advanced some 2 miles when Plancenoit was still being disputed.
10. This misfortune would not have surprised or displeased Talleyrand, who had nothing but contempt for Maret, and famously remarked, 'There is no man more stupid than M. Maret, except the Duc de Bassano.'
11. Houssaye, and Ney's letter to Fouché, 26 June. Field's chapters 20–25 are full of quotations by witnesses from both sides. Napoleon's direct order is reported by the battalion commander, Guillemin (Field, p. 209). I cannot establish with certainty why Ney did not stay with it but went his own way: I believe that he simply would not give up the fight. This belief seems to be supported by Pelet, who, retreating from Plancenoit, found Ney with 'a handful of men', left him and continued on his way, then found 'a great crowd' which turned out to be the *Garde*, and marched off with them (Field, pp. 214–15).
12. Castlereagh at the Foreign Office, to Canning, 22 June 1815, *Castlereagh Corr.*, vol. x (3rd Series, vol. 2) (1853), p. 383 – I have reversed the order of phrasing. Wellington had been slightly touched by a spent bullet at Salamanca in 1812, and more severely bruised in the thigh and temporarily lamed, again by a spent bullet, at Orthez in 1814. Given his active habits in campaigning and in battle he was amazingly lucky.
13. As recounted by Thomas Sydenham, one of the Duke's set, in a letter from Paris, 15 July 1815: Owen, *Waterloo Papers*, p. 35.
14. The Richmonds and their relations were prominent this day. The Duke was a full general, but without war experience and so refused to wear uniform so as not to outrank any possible successor if Wellington should be wounded. His eldest son Lord March was an ADC to Orange, and Lord William Pitt Lennox by having lost an eye in an accident was no longer an active subaltern. Richmond's sister's sons were Lord Apsley and Ensign Seymour Bathurst. See Lord W. P. Lennox and Colonel Miller in *WL*, nos. 17 and 46; and Lt.-Colonel Cowell Stepney's *Leaves from a Diary* (1854), p. 168.
15. Rossomme farm was about 1,000 yards south of La Belle Alliance, with La Maison du Roi about 500 yards further and Le Caillou farm yet another 700 yards to the south. Caillou wood nowadays is about half a mile west of the road. Genappe is 3 miles further on from Le Caillou.

16. DBTS, iii, pp. 484–93, in German and French, and with Constant's marginal comment.
17. Wellington to Mr Mudford, 8 June 1816, *WSD*, x, pp. 508–9. Hofschröer puts the meeting at Genappe, and rightly terms Gneisenau's claim for La Belle Alliance 'a rather romantic invention': Hofschröer, *1815*, ii, p. 151.
18. *With Napoleon at Waterloo*, p. 164. Being without water all day, they drew it from the farm well to drink. It was not until morning that they saw the well was full of bodies, but 'we never felt any bad effects' from having drunk it. For the Prussians playing 'God save the King', see General Maitland in *WL*, no. 105.
19. For the pursuit overnight Siborne is sound, Houssaye's treatment is vivid and sweeping, while Field and Hofschröer provide extensive quotations from individuals and units; but in some ways Aerts's *Opérations* is perhaps the most useful.
20. With a slight resemblance to Napoleon and being smartly dressed, the Prussians seized him, then stripped him of almost everything. An unnamed Prussian general prepared to have him shot, until he was rescued in time by a more senior officer, Bülow, who took him to Blücher. Larrey had once treated a wound in Blücher's son. The old man set him free, gave him some supper and twelve gold Fredericks: Dible, *Napoleon's Surgeon*, pp. 240–1. There were not many Prussian generals at Genappe that night.
21. Wellington's words, in *The Diary of Frances, Lady Shelley, 1787–1817*, ed. R. Edgcombe (1912), p. 102.
22. The Emperor's first account is in *Corr. de Nap.*, no. 22,061; Constant's marginalia were gathered by DBTS, iii, p. 551 onwards.
23. Ney to Fouché, 26 June 1815: *Booth*, at p. 387.
24. Nollet, *Drouot*, p. 159.
25. Du Casse, *Jérome*, vii, p. 24.
26. *Souvenirs of de Salle*, pp. 430–1.
27. *Sir Douglas Haig's Despatches*, edited by J. H. Boraston (1919), Despatch of 21 March 1919, para. 10, p. 320: my italics.
28. Other figures can be found in Siborne, *Hist.*, p. 386 and apps. 36–40, and for the Netherlanders, p. 387 (campaign) and p. 102 (Quatre Bras only); also Adkin, p. 73, for a short summary; Digby Smith gives extensive tables of casualty figures, pp. 541–8. Unfortunately the official Netherlands casualty figures in DBTS are not allocated to the different days (except for officers, who are given by name, day, and category) and moreover the missing are bundled together with those killed, as 'k plus m' as distinct from 'wounded': see DBTS, iii (1908), tables on pp. 200–19. Oman in his somewhat polemical *Nineteenth Century* article (Oct. 1900) makes a stab at breaking down some but not all Netherlands unit figures to establish a large number of '*disparus*' as fleeing. I have adopted Siborne's estimate that the Netherlands Army's 'other ranks' campaign casualties (15–18 June) were 446 killed, 1,936 wounded and 1,612 missing, that casualties at Quatre Bras were about a thousand, and so 3,000 were casualties at Waterloo: I have split these in my table fairly arbitrarily pro rata to his campaign casualties.
29. AG's return, *WSD*, xiv, p. 633; British/KGL foot and horse artillery officers (5 k, 27 w) from Duncan, ii, pp. 432–3.

30. *Waterloo Roll Call* for officers. A. S. Frazer's letter to Colonel Robe, 19 June 1815, is not in Sabine's edition of his letters, but is printed in *JSAHR*, vol. 42 (1964) at p. 113. Wood's return is in Duncan, *Hist. of RA*, ii, pp. 432–3. The RHA casualties amounted to 17 officers, 9 sergeants and 145 men (31 men killed); the RA Foot casualties to 8 officers, 4 sergeants and 82 men (19 men killed), and the KGL to 7, 2, and 58 (10 men killed). Taking the artillery's opening states of 'men' as printed in Siborne, App. VI, this would give a casualty rate for the RHA of 10.4%, of about 3.5% for foot batteries present (Siborne's 'men' figure included the three 18-pdr batteries that were not in the battle, although some assisted with ammunition supplies), and for KGL artillery, about 11%. Casualties among horses came to RHA 309, RA 126, KGL 94, totalling 529.
31. Two of Kielmansegge's six battalions stand out: Verden's 39 per cent losses and the unfortunate Lüneburg's 36 per cent.
32. These figures are confirmed from the Brunswick Colonel Olfermann's statement of 19 June 1815 in *WA*, v, no. 36. Elsewhere 50 are given as missing, in addition.
33. These are my best estimates from DBTS, after breaking out the 15–16 June figures, but there are still gaps and unresolved questions. The Nassau Inf. Regt. Nr. 1 casualties are in *Belle-Alliance*, no. 78.
34. Delbrück, iv, pp. 679–82; Siborne, *History*, App. 46; Oman, *EHR*, xix, tables on pp. 686–7, with revision for the *Garde*, xxi, pp. 132–5. Note, however, that one or two of Oman's summary totals and their consequential percentages (in xix, p. 691) are erroneous. Adkin, pp. 389–90 comes to a somewhat different estimate for the French killed and wounded, 4,500. Hofschröer gives no casualty figures.
35. Writing of these two incidents in the great Uxbridge charge, Oman commented: 'while the rank and file yielded, the officers resisted and were cut down ... 64 officers out of 85 present were killed or wounded, though the number of unwounded rank and file taken was very large indeed': *EHR*, xix, p. 690.
36. Foy, 23 June 1815, *Vie Militaire*, p. 278, my emphasis.
37. Oman, *EHR*, xix, p. 690. One or two of his individual details may need amendment, but the argument holds good. Digby Smith, *Napoleonic Wars Data Book*, p. 539.

CHAPTER 46: The Aftermath of Battle

1. Blücher's letter as repeated by Metternich in a letter to his daughter, 24 June, enclosing 'a literal copy' of what the old man had written; he must have seen it at Prussian royal headquarters: Metternich, *Mémoires*, ii, no. 198, p. 518 (Eng. trans., ii, p. 604).
2. Brett-James, *The Hundred Days*, p. 184.
3. Gneisenau to his wife, Gosselies, 19 June: Griewank, *Gneisenau*, p. 323.
4. P. Hofschröer, 'Wellington: the Genesis of his Waterloo Myths', *Napoleonic Scholarship*, vol. i, no. 2, 1998; 'Did Wellington Deceive his Allies', *War in History*, v (2), 1998, with a debate with myself through three further issues to vii (4) 2000. His central argument of ducal duplicity was initially praised and accepted by some, though others like Mr Carey and Mr Gingerich (*First Empire*, nos. 43 and 44 of 1998–9) showed up flaws in

his arguments, and this culminated with Dr G. Pedlow's devastating critique, 'Back to the Sources', *First Empire*, no. 82, 2005. Huw J. Davies, *Wellington's Wars* (2012), a study of generally high standard, seems suddenly to lack grasp and insight in the short chapter on 1815, and makes too many errors of fact to be judged satisfactory. Davies goes so far as to term the Duke's despatch 'infamous' (p. 246).

5. Aerts, *Opérations*, p. 287.
6. The point is especially well made by Aerts, *Opérations*, at the end of his chap. 6.
7. Clausewitz, who was Thielemann's chief of staff, says relatively little about the battle of Wavre in his *Campaign*, but this may be because he was writing a strategical study rather than a tactical one.
8. Hyde Kelly, *The Battle of Wavre*, p. 134, emphasis added.
9. These orders to I, II and IV Corps were issued from Gosselies on the morning of 19 June: Hofschröer, *1815*, ii, p. 184. They must presumably have been written after 3 a.m. and not received for some time.
10. Most of Pirch's report is printed in Hofschröer, *1815*, ii, p. 186, but omits the name 'Limale' that appears in Lettow-Vorbeck's version, pp. 462–3. I do not accept Hofschröer's view of II Corps' failure on 19 June (p. 185) 'After their night march a period of rest was due and was taken. Thus one cannot attach any blame to these Prussians for having let Grouchy slip.' The order was plain, and the objective clear; one further effort could destroy the last free element of Napoleon's army. That really would have been a true German victory. As to being tired, Grouchy's force was equally tired and had done more fighting on 18 and 19 June than II Corps. It had also made – and was still to make – many long marches.
11. Anyone wanting a minutely detailed account of the movements of Grouchy and the Prussians on 19–21 June and one that is easily comprehended, should turn to Aerts, *Opérations*, chap. 7. There are slighter narratives in Siborne's chap. 17, Hyde Kelly's chapter 8 and Houssaye's Book III, chap. 7, Sections III and IV. Prussian orders and various unit reports down to company level are given in the relevant parts of Hofschröer, *1815*, ii, chaps. 11 and 13.
12. Diary of Mrs Louisa Lloyd, Nat. Lib. of Wales, Aston Hall Deeds, no. 5,196, kindly brought to my attention by Colonel David Miller.
13. See Fleishman & Aerts, *Bruxelles pendant la bataille de Waterloo*, pp. 20–1, 37, 118, and the picture of the Hal gate opposite p. 128.
14. See *WSD*, x, pp. 501, 531, 533, 538 for these statements.
15. *Creevey Papers*, i, pp. 237–8, recorded in these terms in 1822, but taken from a letter that Creevey immediately wrote to a close friend, that was carried 'by the same courier who carried Wellington's despatch'. Creevey's editor pointed out (i, p. 236, fn.) that an independent account of 1836 by Lady Salisbury corroborates Creevey's version of the meeting in many ways.

CHAPTER 47: After the Battle

1. To bring home the scale of disaster, take a map of some familiar rural place, lay over it a sheet of paper with a window cut to the battlefield dimensions, and judge what the human and animal casualties, guns and wrecked material must have looked like.
2. Tupper Carey, a commissary with 2nd Division, noted that three days' meat and biscuit had been issued early on 16 June, but believed that much had been eaten 'improvidently'. He recalled the dislocation of 'baggage, tents, and provisions' during the movements of 16 and 17 June, of camp followers pillaging and wrecking wagons, and of misdirected supply convoys. On 18 June no spirits were available for distribution to the soaked troops before the battle or to the exhausted men after the battle's end, and 'it was altogether impracticable to obtain supplies'; he returned to Brussels and his first convoy started early on the 19th but reached the division only as darkness fell. Nevertheless Carey insisted that 'it is not the case ... that the troops were without food on the 18th': see his reminiscences in *Cornhill Magazine*, June 1899, pp. 724–38.
3. For this detail see *WA*, vol. iii, p. 217.
4. For the proclamation establishing 'the large general hospital of the Allied army' in the city on 17 June, see Brett-James, *The Hundred Days*, p. 196. I regret that I have mislaid the reference to the Nivelles field hospital. Since writing this, I see that storekeeper Robinson told Clinton in August 1815 that during the evacuation of Nivelles on the 17th many wagons and stores were lost to the enemy due to the rapidity of the French advance: Gareth Glover, *WA*, vol. vi, no. 95. Whether the French were concerned to handle the Allied wounded is at least open to doubt; they had enough difficulty looking after themselves.
5. Commissary Tupper Carey noted that on the 18th the medical officers collected and treated the wounded at Waterloo and at Mont St Jean farm: 'Reminiscences', in *Cornhill*, pp. 734–5. See Adkin, pp. 312–24 for medical services; Haythornthwaite gives the following figures for the entire British army at the battle: 47 regimental surgeons, 94 assistants, 21 medical staff officers, 4 surgeons and 13 assistants, and 1 apothecary; there were 45 British wounded 16–18 June for each British medical officer: *Waterloo Men*, p. 103.
6. A mass of detail can be found in *Letters of [Sir] Charles Bell* (1870); *The Creevey Papers*, vol. i; Mrs C. A. Eaton (Miss Charlotte Waldie in 1815) *The Days of Battle* (edn. of 1853 of her original narrative); the sections on medical services and civilian reports in Gareth Glover's *WA* series, vols i, iii, iv and v; Brett-James, *The Hundred Days*, pp. 170–85 for eye-witness accounts of the battlefield situation, and pp. 196–203 for the care of wounded in Brussels and elsewhere.
7. Quoted in Lord William Pitt Lennox, *Fifty Years' Biographical Reminiscences* (1863), i, p. 249.
8. Richmond in Brussels, to Bathurst, 18 June, HMC *Bathurst*, p. 356; original in B. Lib, Loan 57, vol. 9, f. 1000. As a matter of interest I give the full HMC letter in my appendix concerning Wellington's Despatch. Tupper Carey recalled seeing on the 18th the Duke of Richmond's carriage lying upset by the roadside through the forest (p. 732).
9. Mrs Edmund Boehm was giving a reception at her house in the square and Major Percy was directed to it by civil servants at the War Office; Percy dashed in with flags and

despatch. 'Ministers and all wept in triumph among the bottles and glasses. The Regent fell into a sort of womanish hysteric,' and the poor lady never ceased to lament that her soirée was ruined by the news, her supper left untouched. See the account in Brett-James, *The Hundred Days*, pp. 190–2. The house is now owned by the East India & Sports Club, next door to the London Library.

10. Four in *WD*, 488–9/152–4, three in *WSD*, x, p. 531, one in the *Camden Miscellany* ('Some Letters', edited by Webster, Letter no. 31).
11. See chap. 46, n. 10, above.
12. Partial details of the battering train are given in *WSD*, x, p. 463, including Colonel Chapman's 'Enclosure', which in fact is Enclosure no. 2 (I do not repeat that enclosure here). Enclosure no. 1 was omitted from *WSD*, but through the diligence of Karen Robson of the Hartley Library, Southampton, has now been found and catalogued, WP.1/467/30. The guns and ammunition listed in Enclosure no. 1 include, *iron guns*: sixty 24-pounders, eighteen 18-pounders, nine 12-pounders, nine 68-pounder carronades, twenty-one 6-inch mortars, fifteen 8-inch mortars; *brass guns*: eighteen 5½-inch mortars, twelve 8-inch howitzers; over 100,000 rounds of ammunition for all these guns, over 4,000 barrels of powder, 120 wagons, 132 carts, etc., etc. No wonder the Prussians were anxious to borrow the siege train.
13. The proclamation is given by Delbrück, *Gneisenau*, iv, p. 523, and is mentioned in passing by Siborne, *History*, p. 420, but it is not referred to by Hofschröer so far as I can see.
14. The first and second paragraphs of the General Order are printed in *WD*, xii, 493, and in Siborne, *History*, p. 423; the other paragraphs, possibly from a slightly different copy, are in *WD*, viii, 156, and also in *WSD*, x, p. 538. The admonition as to good behaviour in France would be repeated in somewhat different terms a century later, when Lord Kitchener had a notice pasted into each BEF soldier's pay book in August 1914: on that occasion K. warned of the temptations of French wine and women, dangers that clearly did not worry the Duke to the same degree.
15. On 26 June £6,000 was authorised to be disbursed as might be necessary to wounded officers and men in Brussels, through an officer nominated from each regiment, *WD*, 510–11/170.
16. Wellington's crisp and plain-spoken evidence to the Royal Commission on Military Punishments, 20 February 1836, was in response to questions 5,796–5,883; a few extracts of his less contentious remarks were printed in an appendix to *WD*, 1852 edition, volume viii, but with the remarks on the Prussians deleted. The key answers were to Q. 5,830–2. Grolman and Müffling published some sharp and even vitriolic replies in *MWB*, no. 21 of 1836, pp. 90–102.
17. For the situation in Ghent, 16–20 June, see a MS journal quoted in *Librairie Clavreuil (Teissèdre)* catalogue no. 388 (2014), item 1,329; Louis' letter, *WSD*, xiv, p. 560 (*WD*, 1852, viii, 152); Wellington's letters to Feltre and Berri, *WD*, 492/157–8.
18. The two headquarters were roughly as far apart as Ziethen's HQ had been from Blücher's army headquarters on 14 June.

CHAPTER 48: France and the Problem of Napoleon

1. These orders stripped the outlying provinces of their cover, something that his original dispositions had refused to consider. It is a further proof that the dispersion of forces all round France was unwise. Though the Vendée revolt certainly had to be stopped by force, the addition to the *Armée du Nord* of Rapp's men from Alsace would have made a difference in early June.
2. Quoted fully in Charras, ii, p. 131.
3. The successive *Moniteur* reports on Ligny are in Houssaye, *Seconde Abdication*, p. 6, fn. 3. I find this fourth and final volume of Houssaye's work on 1814–15 is the least satisfactory; information can be found there in abundance, but the standpoint is so partisan that the interpretation of events is that of an extreme advocate. Nevertheless I draw upon his first 200 pages of narrative for details, even where I differ from his reading of them.
4. Joseph's note is in Masson, *Napoléon et sa Famille*, xi, p. 332. Masson had the habit, infuriating to his contemporaries and all later generations, of not citing his sources; but his research was always thorough, even though his opinions often went to the far side of extreme. Several of the documents quoted in this chapter (such as La Fayette's resolution and Napoleon's abdication) can be found in an English translation in Siborne's *History*, chap. 18.
5. Houssaye, *Seconde Abdication*, pp. 21–2.
6. Houssaye, *Seconde Abdication*, p. 28, from the *Moniteur* of 22 June.
7. This letter is not given by Houssaye, but appears in De Bas, *Prins Frederik*, iii (2), p. 831. It shows that Napoleon was already prepared to involve Fouché in some sort of peace process, even if the nomination and the process were not sincerely meant, and that Fouché was not acting *entirely* on his own.
8. Houssaye, *Seconde Abdication*, pp. 61–2. It is strange that Napoleon initially ignored the succession until warned by his advisers that he might be thought to be leaving open the door to a Bourbon restoration. Later he was advised to delete the mention of his two brothers, and this he did. These details suggest how far the disaster of Waterloo had affected his normal clarity of mind.
9. Houssaye, *Seconde Abdication*, p. 6 and p. 81.
10. Historical parallels are never exact, and yet I see in this crisis of late June 1815 dim outlines of the dilemmas of the France of June 1940. To fight to the end, or to save something from the wreck by compromise, in a society that in the previous decade had been fractured by internal stresses, and haunted by a sense that its earlier victories had been snatched from it: those were the questions that faced France's greatest living general, Marshal Pétain, and the men round him. The junior general and ex-minister De Gaulle – and the late Georges Clemenceau's right-hand man, Georges Mandel – saw Pétain's solution as wrong. And fortunately, in the result, the Free French cause eventually prevailed. But it might have failed in that generation without foreign allies. And since parallels are inexact, so are their solutions in different epochs. If the defiant vision of De Gaulle was right in 1940 and Pétain's appeasing one was wrong, nevertheless Fouché's was right for France in 1815 and Napoleon's was wrong.

11. Houssaye, *Seconde Abdication*, p. 116, for the armistice proposal, and p. 206 for the team's warning and the ministerial decision.
12. Houssaye, *Seconde Abdication*, p. 219.
13. Houssaye, *Seconde Abdication*, p. 218 fn., for Davout's urgent note, pp. 222–3 for the final appeal, p. 226 for the reply. Fouché remarked (pp. 224–6) when the appeal was delivered by the head of the Emperor's escort: 'Is he making fools of us? We can't accept the proposal; all hope for a negotiated settlement would be lost. It is most urgent that he should leave immediately for Rochefort, where he will be safer than here' and also 'Do you think that we are on a bed of roses? We can't make any changes to the dispositions we have entered into.' Houssaye terms Fouché's attitude to the appeal 'defiant and almost one of hatred', but I suspect that *exasperation* and *concern* for Napoleon's life would be more correct. After all, at this late stage what real choice did the government have?
14. Pasquier's *Mémoires*, iii, p. 195.
15. The Bourbon King Louis XIII [d. 1643] had established a cadet branch of Orléans for his younger son; so that Louis XVIII and Louis-Philippe of Orléans were cousins of the sixth generation. In theory the Spanish *Borbon* kings (*les Blancs d'Espagne*), descended from a grandson of Louis XIV, should have taken precedence over Orléans, but the eternal separation of the French and Spanish thrones was registered in eighteenth-century treaties and was reaffirmed in 1815.
16. Houssaye, *Seconde Abdication*, p. 2: in essence this was Napoleon's own *ex parte* defence: the Europeans were thus the guilty criminals, punishing an innocent man.
17. Welschinger, *Ney*, pp. 93–4. In justification of this sophistry whereby cause and effect are turned on their heads, Welschinger quoted Talleyrand's letter of 12 March: 'it is sad that France cannot pass over this [the Tsar's offer of troops], an offer that one cannot positively refuse' and added that (the exiled) Louis wrote on 10 April that his cause was weakening so much that: 'the Allied armies should enter France as soon as possible'. But all this arose primarily from Napoleon's invasion, reinforced as it was by Ney's change of sides: Louis and Talleyrand were merely reacting to a swelling rebellion in which Ney played a conspicuous part.
18. Masson xi, p. 335. The description of La Fayette, incidentally, is worth checking against the facts (e.g. of 1792, when the undoubtedly ruthless and probably sanguinary authorities having deposed the King, menacingly decreed La Fayette's dismissal from his military posts, as a result of which he understandably fled the country). What did Masson think the national sovereignty consisted of, and what was *18 Brumaire* if not an insurrection against legal authority?

CHAPTER 49: The Allied Advance

1. Frederick William's enthusiastic letter to Wellington of 24 June makes no allusion to any Prussian part in the victory; that of 26 June, upon information received from Blücher, speaks of '*les armées Anglaises et Prussiennes combinées*': *WSD*, x, pp. 570 and 590.
2. See Wellington to Bathurst, 19 June, *WSD*, x, p. 531; to Dumouriez, 20 June, *WD*, 1852 edn.,

p. 155, and to Feltre, 22 June, *WD*, 495/159; Blücher to Müffling, 19 June, in Hofschröer, *1815*, ii, p. 187.

3. Mercer, *Journal*, chaps. 16 and 17: pp. 224, 231–2, 242 in the 1927 edition.
4. See Gneisenau to Müffling, 21 June, in Hofschröer, *1815*, ii, p. 198.
5. For those conversant with Marlborough's war and the war of 1914–18, the names of the towns and villages all across this part of France have enormous resonance. The victory of Marlborough and Eugene at Malplaquet on 11 September 1709 was in everyone's minds as Wellington's army passed through it; Le Quesnoy had an even earlier fame, as the place where in 1346 the English first encountered cannon; that little town was the scene of a brilliant escalade of its sheer walls by the BEF in 1918. The night affair at Landrecies and the full-scale battle at Le Cateau were of course significant events for the British I and II Corps during the Retreat from Mons. St Quentin, Péronne, Ressons-sur-Matz: the list of names is endless.
6. To Uxbridge, 23 June, *WD*, 499/162.
7. Hofschröer, *1815*, ii, p. 202, citing Voss (the successor to the late Lettow-Vorbeck as official historian), *Napoleons Untergang*, 1906, ii, p. 24. Somewhat oddly, given his rivalry theory, Hofschröer thinks that the Duke 'now perceived the danger of the Prussians getting to Paris first' (p. 201) and sought to exert some restraining influence at this meeting, but then says that in consequence 'Wellington's forces did not make any significant movement the next day and the Prussians gained more ground in the race to Paris' (p. 203). The rivalry seems to feature more prominently in his own mind than in that of Wellington.
8. For the capture of Cambrai and its citadel, see *WD*, 497/161 to 506/166 and *WSD*, x, pp. 567, 569, 576. The casualties (incorrectly printed in *WD* 1838) were 1 officer and 7 o/r killed, and 3 officers and 26 o/r wounded (*WD*, 1852, p. 165).
9. The Bonapartist garrison commander at Laon wrote on 26 June 1815 that his 2,000 men showed 'a bad spirit' and were saying openly that they 'would not fight': quoted by Arthur Chuquet, in *Feuilles d'Histoire*, vol. 3 (Jan.–June 1910), p. 82.
10. Ollech, pp. 299–300.
11. Müffling, *Memoirs*, p. 251. Although this passage is quoted by Hofschröer he does not appear to realise that (1) the Prussian remonstrance through Müffling showed that they were worried about getting too far ahead, and (2) the final sentence of the Duke's reply goes clearly against any theory of the Duke worrying about an Anglo-Prussian 'race'.
12. See Frazer, *Letters*, 24 and 29 June, pp. 572 and 582.
13. Brit. Lib. Loan 57/vol. 9, f. 1007; omitted from HMC *Bathurst*.
14. To Bathurst, 25 June 1815, *WD*, 509/168: by 'Spanish infantry' Wellington of course always meant the British regiments that had served under him in the Peninsula. Lipscombe, pp. 389–90, quotes Wood as writing four days after the battle that his career was over, 'having received the most severe reprimand before the whole staff and servants' for not collecting all the French artillery, a task performed by Frazer. There is abundant evidence in *Wellington's Guns* that the Duke had very little patience with a number of his artillery officers, and also disliked their inclination to deal directly with the Ordnance

department for pensions and rewards without going through the commander of the forces. This was now coupled with the strain of working without a staff, but it is shocking to read of the public way that this rebuke was delivered.

15. The notorious letter of 21 December 1815 from Wellington to Lord Mulgrave, MGO ('to tell you the truth I was not very well pleased with the artillery at the battle of Waterloo', is in *WSD*, xiv, p. 618, and is the subject of Appendix A of Duncan's *History* vol. ii of 1873 and Hime's *History* (1908), app. D. The discussion of the Duke's 'Mulgrave letter' and its justification or otherwise is handled with care and balance in Lipscombe's chap. 24. For the instruction from AG to Adam, 27 June, see *WD*, 1852, p. 174; *WSD*, xiv, p. 563; the various letters from Wellington about care for and payment due to the sick, etc., are in *WD*, 510–11/170.
16. On this matter of FitzRoy Somerset, see J. H. Stocqueler, *A Personal History of the Horse Guards, 1752–1872* (1873), pp. 140–3.
17. Schwarzenberg, in *WSD*, x, p. 552; Wellington's reply in *WD*, 510/169: in his reply the Duke also referred gracefully to his collaborator Blücher, whom Schwarzenberg had not included in his praise.
18. *WD*, 518/172. Bathurst in two letters of 24 June had written of about 7,000 British infantry and 800 cavalry being sent, with more to follow, and including three regiments of 'old infantry' from Ireland (*WSD*, x, pp. 571–2). For the Waterloo medal, see *WD*, 520/178: the caution as to some further fighting is interesting.
19. *WD*, 517/176: he was reporting on the capture of Péronne. In this praise he was not alone of course, for the Netherlands batteries on 16 and 18 June were widely applauded for their steadfastness.
20. The letter of 27 June, *WD*, 513/172; the General Order of the same date, *WSD*, xiv, p. 563. De Bas, *Prins Frederik*, iii (2) pp. 1236–8, gives some details of the difficulties the Netherlands troops faced over supplies.
21. Feltre to Wellington 26 June, *WSD*, x, p. 596; Wellington to Charles Stuart, 28 June, *WD*, 516/175: Wellington had also been irritated by something the King had quibbled over concerning the occupation of Péronne, so he was in a more than usually prickly mood.
22. In discussions with the French provisional government's delegation Wellington found some disquiet over three short passages in the royalist Cambrai proclamation, and advised Talleyrand to modify them as a necessary sacrifice for peace. It does not seem that any changes were made, however: Wellington to Talleyrand, 29 June, *WSD*, xiv, pp. 564–6.
23. The texts of the two successive proclamations are in *WSD*, x, pp. 580 and 615; an English version of that of 28 June is in Siborne, App. 49. See also Houssaye, *Seconde Abdication*, pp. 143–7. The radical J. C. Hobhouse, though anti-Tory and pro-Napoleon, saw in the lists of the proscribed, 'nothing unusual … nor, it may be said, unjust; want of success in enterprises of this nature has always been so rewarded'. After Ney's execution he also said that Ney should have pleaded guilty 'and accepted the fate reserved in all times for unsuccessful patriots' (*Substance of Letters*, ii, p. 209 and fn.). The French post-*Libération* state trials of 1944–6 also come to mind.

24. This account of the French in retreat relies largely but not exclusively upon various passages in Houssaye's *Seconde Abdication* and Hyde Kelly's *Wavre*, and the latter's clear and useful map of Grouchy's retreat from Namur to Paris. For the Prussian advance, a short impartial account is in Clausewitz's *Campaign of 1815*, chap. 55; even shorter daily summaries for all the armies can be found in Siborne's chap. 18.
25. This incident, in the 29th Infantry Regiment of I Corps, is recorded in Hofschröer, *1815*, ii, pp. 223–4.
26. An instance of what might have been can be seen in Kellermann's night attack late on 27 June from Crépy, launching his remaining heavy cavalry on the tired Prussian units camped at Senlis, some 12 miles to the west, covering the Oise crossings. The Prussians put up very little resistance, and fled along the road towards Pont St Maxence, 6 miles away. Had d'Erlon's infantry been in strength and led with determination, they might have followed up this temporary success. It might have made a difference. I recall the tough New Zealand veteran Sir Howard Kippenberger's verdict in 1952 on his nation's commanders in Crete, 1941: 'they answered all questions pessimistically, saw all dangers, real or imagined, or possible; none made any efforts to dictate or control events; they were utterly without offensive spirit; and invariably in each case they adopted a course that made victory impossible' (*JSAHR*, vol. 72, 1994, p. 254). See for the French side on this night attack, Houssaye, *Seconde Abdication*, p. 117 and its detailed note; for the German, Hofschröer, *1815*, ii, p. 230.
27. Extremely detailed accounts of these skirmishes and minor operations can be found in Hofschröer, *1815*, ii, chap. 16, based upon regimental and other works.

CHAPTER 50: The Fall of Paris

1. Blücher wrote to wife from Châtillon-sur-Sambre on 23 June, 'If the Parisians do not kill the tyrant before I get to Paris, then I will kill the Parisians – they are a terrible people': Leggiere, *Blücher*, p. 421.
2. Wellington to the French Commissioners, 26 June, 10 p.m., *WD*, 512/170.
3. See Castlereagh, 9 April 1815, and especially the enclosure, *WSD*, x, pp. 44–5.
4. The full text of the 12 May Declaration is in *WSD*, x, pp. 339–44: the states signing were Austria (Metternich), France (Talleyrand), Britain (Clancarty, Cathcart, Stewart), Prussia (Hardenberg, Humboldt), Russia (Rassumovsky, Stackelberg, Nesselrode), Portugal, Spain, Sweden; they were joined by Bavaria, Denmark, Hanover, Low Countries, Sardinia, Saxony, Two Sicilies, Württemberg.
5. See chap. 49, sec. II.
6. Lord Liverpool's memorandum and lists of questions of 1 April 1815, *WSD*, x, pp. 35–7, with remarks by other Cabinet members printed in the following pages.
7. See Gneisenau's letters to Müffling, 27–9 June 1815, in Müffling, *Memoirs*, pp. 272–5 (nos. 1–4): the quotation is from Letter 4. The strength of his argument lay in the reference to the kidnapping from a neutral foreign country, summary trial and instant execution of Enghien, an act that even in his final days Napoleon defended as justified by *raison d'état*.

The two weaknesses were (1) that the 13 March Declaration had not actually specified 'death' as the penalty but merely 'public justice', and (2) that Gneisenau arrogated to the commanders of the Prussian Army of the Lower Rhine rights and final powers that really belonged to the collective sovereigns and which had not been delegated to the army commanders. Gneisenau might have replied that the Prussian Army represented the state, but that argument, of course, raises other issues.

8. Wellington to Sir Charles Stuart, 28 June 1815, *WD*, 516/175.
9. Two instances of these misconceptions may be given. Daniel Moran, an acknowledged expert on Clausewitz, wrote in his commentary for *The Campaign of 1815* (BMP, p. 244) that 'Wellington and Blücher would have been perfectly satisfied to see Napoleon hung from a gibbet,' a statement that runs flat counter to Wellington's letter of 28 June (*WD*, 516/175). Peter Hofschröer wrote that Tromelin's unsuccessful visit 'did not stop him [Wellington] beginning to make arrangements for the handing over of Bonaparte to Britain': Hofschröer, *1815*, ii, p. 222. To substantiate this he relied upon *WD*, xii, pp. 512–16, and *WSD*, x, pp. 583–97, which is most strange, for nothing in any of those pages even hints at the handing over of Bonaparte to Britain, as Wellington always insisted that decisions on Napoleon were reserved to the judgement of all the Allies.
10. Liverpool to Castlereagh, 7 July 1815, *WSD*, x, p. 677.
11. When Decrès, as Minister of Marine issued 'top secret orders' to the two frigate captains to take an incognito Napoleon to America, he ordered that if they encountered superior British naval opposition, then the frigate on which Napoleon was *not* aboard should 'sacrifice itself' so as to let the other escape, as 'the Chambers and the government have placed Napoleon's person under the safeguard of French loyalty': *WSD*, xiv, p. 570.
12. This section relies mainly on Siborne's 'Supplement' in his *History*, p. 511 onwards, and passing references in *Wellington's Despatches* during the week of negotiations.
13. See Wellington to Bathurst, 2 July 1815, *WD*, 532/188.
14. The best map known to me of Paris and its defences in 1815 is in Couderc de St Chamant, but there is a clear one also at the back of Voss (Lettow-Vorbeck's successor), vol. ii. Many of these villages (though not the towns) are today within the circuit of 1840 walls, now boulevards named after the marshals.
15. A tabulation in the French war archives was printed by Charras, ii, Notes, pp. 219–22; this was used by Voss, pp. 86–7, and slightly corrected (Voss noted that 1,939 men had been withdrawn from Aubervilliers and should not be in the table). Voss is followed by Hofschröer, *1815*, ii, see table on pp. 242–3.
16. Davout on the various shortages, to the Government Commission, 2 July, *Davout Corr.*, no. 1776, iv, p. 583.
17. My emphasis. Fouché produced an instruction for Davout which the French Commissioners examined and then added: '*Votre armistice doit être purement militaire, et qu'il ne doit contenir aucune question politique*': *WSD*, x, pp. 611–12, at end. The editor of Davout's *Correspondance* (iv, p. 579) gave the substance of Fouché's letter, but omitted any mention of the Commission's additional instruction. This omission is of consequence in judging certain French arguments over Ney's trial.

18. *Davout Corr.*, no. 1770, iv, p. 578, 28 June. This view of the state of his troops and his urgent recommendation, together with his 2 July warning (no. 1776) of serious shortages in supplies inside Paris, reduces belief in his December 1815 recollection that he had full trust in a strong defence. Méneval in old age recounted a strange story at second hand: that Gneisenau tried to persuade the military governor of Paris to keep out the Bourbons by proclaiming a Prussian prince as king, but that the governor 'preferred Louis XVIII to a Prussian yoke'. But as he named General Maison as that governor, a man who had been governor from June 1814 to 20 March 1815, had then fled to Ghent, and was not restored to his post until 8 July (well after the surrender), the tale had little value: see his *Méms*, iii, p. 535, and Six, ii, pp. 141–2 for Maison's career.
19. I have relentlessly abbreviated the story of these days, and most of the intricate, confusing and often contradictory details asserted by different participants. I recount only the main stages and the outcomes reached. There is consequentially no mention here of the agents and intermediaries Otto's, Gaillard's, Macirone's or Marshall's activities. Houssaye's final volume, Davout's *Correspondance*, Bignon's papers in Ernouf's *La Dernière Capitulation*, and the sequence of documents in *Wellington's Despatches* and *Supplementary Despatches* between 22 June and 3 July provide sufficient detail in any case, while Delbrück, *Gneisenau*, vol. iv, has a long series of letters between Blücher, Gneisenau and Müffling. Voss, *Napoleons Untergang*, vol. ii, has a few additional letters.
20. The five commissioners sent to handle these discussions represented a wide variety of opinion. La Besnardière was a Councillor of State from 1813 onwards, a long-time subordinate of Talleyrand, with whom he served at Vienna in 1814–15. Valence had served in the army from Valmy up to the defence of France in 1814, had been of the Orléanist group, but upheld the claims of Napoleon II. Boissy d'Anglas had a distinguished career under the Empire, voted for Napoleon's abdication in 1814, but rallied to him in 1815, only to vote against Napoleon II after the second abdication. Andréossy was a soldier (and was with Bonaparte in Egypt) and ambassador of wide experience (London, Vienna, Constantinople). Flaugergues, a lawyer who held posts under the Empire, voted for the first abdication, and was a moderate deputy in the Chamber during the Hundred Days. Whatever their views on domestic politics, all were well suited to present to foreigners the most acceptable face of France in its present crisis.
21. Wellington's very clear report of the discussions, alas too long to quote here, is dated 2 July, and may be read in *WD*, 532/188. The French record of the discussions, dated 30 June, gives a very similar account: Ernouf, *Dernière Capitulation*, p. 62. Welschinger remarks that the Duke's notification to Talleyrand of the delegates' objections to parts of the Cambrai proclamation 'cannot have been taken very seriously, for it was totally disregarded' (*Ney*, p. 93). His remark does indicate that Wellington was not all-powerful at the court, nor could he formally deal in its name.
22. What the Prussians were about to do was to repeat on a larger scale Marmont's sideways move at Salamanca under the eye of the enemy, trusting that there was no French general capable of seizing his chance. The exchange of views between Müffling (for Wellington) and Gneisenau is in Voss, ii, pp. 99–100, and in an English translation, Hofschröer, *1815*,

ii, pp. 250–1. As the latter says, Wellington's plan was better militarily but Gneisenau was determined to reduce the Duke's part in the final stages of the campaign.

23. Full accounts are in Ollech, pp. 383–7; Houssaye, *Seconde Abdication*, pp. 261–66; Voss, ii, pp. 108–111; and Hofschröer, *1815*, ii, pp. 258–60.
24. The developments can be followed in these letters: Davout, 26 and 27 June (this last to Fouché, with the latter's reply), in *WSD*, x, pp. 587, 611; Davout, 30 June to the Allied Cs-in-C, in *Davout Corr.*, no. 1774, iv, p. 581 (*'on s'occupe d'un armistice en attendant la décision du congrès'*).
25. Blücher's reply to Davout, 1 July, in Voss, p. 138 ,and Hofschröer, *1815*, ii, p. 269; Wellington's reply, 1 July, *WD*, 524/181; Fouché (Otranto), 1 July, *WSD*, x, p. 641; and Davout, 1 July, *Davout Corr.*, no. 1775, iv, p. 582 and also *WSD*, x, p. 546.
26. Müffling to Gneisenau, 1 July, in Voss, ii, p. 119, and Hofschröer, *1815*, ii, p. 270.
27. Gneisenau to Wellington, Versailles, 2 July, *WSD*, x, p. 651, in French.
28. This accusation referred to Louis's government having signed the 3 January 1815 treaty with Austria and Britain, combating Prussian demands over Saxony – but by extension such reasoning must also have applied to Britain, and where then did such reasoning lead? It also ignored the later declarations of March 1815 in support of Louis that Prussia had agreed to.
29. Delbrück, *Gneisenau*, iv, pp. 545–8. It is usually said that 'the ingratitude of my commander' refers to Blücher, but my friend Dr Gregory Pedlow argues that the words 'in Berlin' are hardly appropriate to Blücher's location on 30 June, and may perhaps refer less directly and more circumspectly to the monarch in his capital (though the King was at this moment on the Rhine). Either way, it shows considerable animus against whichever superior is meant. Blücher would write to his wife from Meudon, 4 July: 'Paris is mine … the city will surrender to me. I owe everything to the indescribable bravery of my troops, their unparalleled perseverance, and my iron will': quoted in Leggiere, *Blücher*, p. 424. Where is Gneisenau in all this?
30. Wellington's long letter in English, dated 2 July, is in *WD*, 526/184; a German translation of it, with Gneisenau's annotations, are given by Delbrück, *Gneisenau*, iv, pp. 556–61, and both are given in Appendix 1 to this chapter. Marginalia seldom show their authors to advantage, and these certainly did not, but they are models of reasonability when compared to a later set from the same school of Prussian thought: Kaiser Wilhelm II's marginal scribbles on state papers. As I have previously said, the belief that the Army owned the state, and that its honour stood above everything, culminated in Ludendorff dictating to his own Kaiser.
31. At Ney's trial Davout told the court that he himself added to the draft convention 'everything relative to demarcation of the military line; I added the articles relating to the safety of persons and properties'; if these guarantees were refused he would break off discussions and continue the fight: Welschinger, *Ney*, p. 281. Since the court would not permit any debate on Article XII there must be a natural suspicion that it feared disclosure of how far that article might stretch. Davout's words at the trial could mean either that he was concerned with his primary military duty of insuring against the

genuine danger that the Prussians might sack the city of Paris, an immediate prospect given Blücher's words; or it could mean that, looking beyond his immediate duty, he was negotiating for all France. Of itself his phrase remains neutral, but we need to remember that he had been formally instructed to limit negotiations to things military and avoid all political matters.

32. Bignon was one of Napoleon's most experienced diplomats and was currently acting as foreign minister. Guilleminot had long service in the army, had served Jerome at Waterloo and was now on Davout's staff. Bondy was one of the most prominent administrators under the Empire, and handled as well as anyone could the troubles between Napoleon and the Church, being a man of skill and intelligence. It was a very strong team.
33. Ernouf, *Dernière Capitulation*, pp. 69–70, a long document by Bignon, who ends by saying that Wellington and the sovereigns will see the unwisdom of 'making France submit by violence to a government that the great majority of the population does not want'. By limiting discussion to military matters, any admission of the Cambrai proclamation's validity could be avoided, and of course if the Bourbons should not be restored the proclamation would be null.
34. Davout in counter-signing the convention, and Bignon in writing to French diplomats at Heidelberg on 4 July (Ernouf, p. 200). The French army's disciplined retirement from Paris was due in part to Davout's ascendancy, but also to Fouché's obtaining from the banker Lafitte a Frs. 2 million loan by which to settle the three months' arrears of army pay: Hall, *Bourbon Rest.*, p. 124.
35. The Convention is given in full in French in *WD*, 542/193, and in an English version in Siborne, *History*, p. 506. Ernouf prints the draft and amendments, pp. 101–5. There is a commentary (with the rejected or amended articles) in Houssaye, *Seconde Abdication*, pp. 296–300. The commentary is perhaps a little one-sided. For Wellington's official letter to Bathurst, 4 July, enclosing the convention: *WD*, 541/196.
36. The supervisory commission appears in *WSD*, xi, p. 22 (the personal details come from G. Six); the dissolution of the government on 8 July, *ibid.*, p. 16; and the appointment of a Bourbon government on 9 July, *ibid.*, p. 21.
37. Bignon's accounts of the 3 July discussions, and his statement on the art treasures clause, can be read in his son-in-law Ernouf's book, pp. 109 (Art. XI), 112–15 (Art. XII), 130–2 (treasures).
38. Ernouf, pp. 130–2; Castlereagh to Liverpool, 24 July 1815, *WSD*, xi, p. 54.
39. Colonel Sir Felton Hervey to Lord Bathurst, Paris, 14 Jan 1816, *WSD*, xiv, p. 628; where Hervey's recollections are mentioned elsewhere in this section, they are from this letter.
40. Wellington, G.O. to Army, 4 July, *WD*, 545/196; to Bathurst, 4 July, *WD*, 541/196. It is notable that the draft for a 'capitulation' was amended to 'convention' by Fouché for domestic reasons, and the change was allowed by the Allies. On 7 July the British Prime Minister stated to Castlereagh that 'I am glad that Paris has been taken by a military Convention, rather than by a capitulation to the King, as it will leave us more unfettered as to the conditions on which peace is to be restored': *Cas. Corr.*, x, p. 415.
41. Ernouf, pp. 118–19.

42. Fouché issued a passport in the name of 'Ney', and a second in the name of 'Neubourg', businessman travelling to Lausanne. After explaining his actions during the campaign at the session of 22 June in the *Pairs*, Ney – having there been accused of treason against Napoleon by La Bédoyère – remarked: 'I spoke in support of my country. Don't I know that, if Louis XVIII should return, I shall be shot?' Despite that, a third passport for an ex-soldier called 'Felize', travelling to New Orléans, was issued after the Second Restoration under the signatures of, *inter alia*, Decazes (Prefect of Parisian Police from 7 July) and Talleyrand (Foreign Minister from 7 July): Welschinger, *Ney*, pp. 72, 75, 80 fn.
43. Bathurst to Wellington, 7 July, *WSD*, x, p. 670, and his formal despatch of the same date, *WSD*, x, p. 670, the latter also in *WD* (1852), viii, 206; Wellington, 13 July, *WD*, 557/206.
44. For full details, see Robert Torrens's letter, 1 Oct 1815, 'A Waterloo Letter', pp. 846–7. Major Staveley, who was with Colonel Torrens, gives a vivid account of their troubles inside Paris at the hands of furious French soldiery in a letter of 7 July 1815: *JSAHR*, vol. 14 (1935), p. 162.
45. Wellington to Bathurst, 8 July 1815, *WD*, 549/201. He had been especially disgusted by the provisional government's letter to the two *chambres* of 7 July. In it the five ministers stated that 'until now' they had been led to believe that the Allies were not unanimous about who should reign in France, and that the delegates had brought back this same assurance. Only 'yesterday' (6 July) had the Allied generals disclosed to Fouché that the sovereigns had determined to restore Louis XVIII, who would arrive almost at once; foreign troops surrounded the Tuileries where the government was based; since their deliberations were no longer free, they had to disperse (full text in Lamartine, *Hist. Restaur.*, vol. 5, book 29, sec 29, p. 142). Fouché was actually somewhat relieved by the arrival of the Prussians as there remained a risk of violence in Paris; he also concealed in this letter that he was at that moment one of Louis's ministers. As to the disclosure of 'yesterday', Ernouf, (*Dernière Capitulation*, p. 68) admitted, on the basis of documents, that the provisional government knew from the delegates by 1 July [*sic*] of the categorical demand of the Allies for the restoration of Louis XVIII.
46. Letter printed in Müffling, *Memoirs*, p. 275 (no. 4), misdated to 15 July, but plainly from its contents an immediate reply to Wellington's of the 5th.
47. For Wellington's recommendation about Müffling and the advice to Fouché, see *WD*, 540, 545, 546/197–8; for the Müffling–Blücher exchange over Prussian plans for Paris, see Voss, ii, p. 142, followed by Hofschröer, *1815*, ii, p. 276.
48. These details come from letters in John Colville, *Portrait of a General*, p. 211.
49. Gourgaud confirms that Napoleon used Beker's name as a cover: see Gourgaud's private diary of the flight to the sea, published in 1899: *Journal inédit 1815–1818*, vol. ii, app. 32, pp. 551–60, at p. 558. Beker's name is variously spelt, but I have followed G. Six who drew upon government records.
50. The most unvarnished French account of these days on the coast is to be found in Gourgaud, *Journal inédit*, vol. i, pp. 27–43; Montholon also left an account in his *Hist. de la Captivité*, but it is of late date (1846), though apparently based on contemporary notes. Bertrand's 'Avant-Propos' of 1842 to *Guerre d'Orient* is short but valuable and is

given in note 55 below. Savary's account in his memoirs (1828) is short but in places very illuminating. Marchand's memoirs contain a short description that is unclear on some points as to advice proffered. Las Cases in his famous and propagandist *Le Mémorial de Ste-Hélène* (I have used the integral and critical edition by Marcel Dunan, Paris, 1951) has statements that seem at odds with each other, has silences and some discrepancies when judged against other accounts; but he is making a case in self-exculpation. Lallemand left a short account (published in 1949) containing an important point. Houssaye's version in his *Seconde Abdication* is dramatic: Las Cases is absolved by describing him and Savary as dupes of a cleverer schemer. British accounts include those of Captain Maitland, in his *The Surrender of Napoleon*, Admiral Lord Keith's in Kerry's *The First Napoleon*, Part VIII, and *The Keith Papers*, vol. iii, and various reports and papers in Rose's *Napoleonic Studies*, chap. XII.

51. The list of Hotham's twelve ships and their dispositions on 6 July 1815 is given in the *Keith Papers*, iii, p. 349. They were spaced from Quiberon to Arcachon.
52. Secretary of the Admiralty (Croker) to Keith, 1 July 1815, *The Keith Papers*, iii, p. 347.
53. Maitland, *Surrender*: Hotham's letters of 7 and 8 July, pp. 18–25.
54. Houssaye rightly concludes that the many accounts by eye-witnesses (and others) are confusing (*Seconde Abdication*, p. 387 fn.), so it is not certain whether the baggage finally went to a little chasse-marée or to the Danish vessel (as Bertrand insists). Bausset, who was not present and may not be reliable, suggests that the little boat would have sailed for the Danish vessel 'lying 40 leagues offshore' (*Méms*, iii, p. 274).
55. Bertrand's 'Avant-Propos' of 1842 to *Guerre d'Orient*, at pp. xxxiii–xxxiv. As it is little known and is written by the most faithful and honourable of Napoleon's servants, I give this extract of the central points. The baggage of Napoleon, Savary, Bertrand and Marchand had been placed on a Danish vessel. '*A trois heures du matin les partans devaient être avertis. L'Empereur changea d'avis. En nous rendant le lendemain matin chez lui, nous vîmes sur une table de salon un projet de lettre minuté de la main de l'Empereur, lettre par laquelle il annonçait au prince régent d'Angleterre son désir d'aller s'asseoir au foyer britannique. Bientôt l'Empereur entra et demanda l'avis de ceux qui étaient près de lui. Sa détermination était prise; le général Lallemant fut le seul qui la combattit … Jamais le général Bertrand n'a conseillé à l'Empereur de se rendre à l'Angleterre … l'Empereur … demandait au grand-maréchal s'il pensait que le gouvernement anglais le laisserait libre en Angleterre, celui-ci répondit que ce serait s'abuser que de se flatter d'un pareil espoir; qu'après les évènemens qui avaient suivi le retour de l'île d'Elbe, on ne lui laisserait pas la faculté de les recommencer. Le grand-maréchal, il est vrai, n'avait pas prévu Sainte-Hélène.*'
56. I reproduce the original letter dated 'Rochefort 13 Juillet 1815', now in the Royal Archives at Windsor (RA, GEO/MAIN/21730). The original letter was filed at Windsor under the year 1819 (due to the way the '5' was written) and thus escaped notice until 1914, when the King's librarian, John Fortescue, wrote to his publisher Sir Frederick Macmillan, 'We have made a great discovery among the papers here – Napoleon's letter of surrender to the Prince Regent in July 1815.' Fortescue wrote more fully of the discovery in his autobiography: see BL Add MSS 55,064, fol. 181 verso, letter from Windsor Castle, 24 Jan.

1914, and *Author and Curator* (1933), pp. 147–8. The letter has *'en but'*, *'des plus grandes'*, *'sur le foyer'* (the correct grammatical phrase would be *'au foyer'*) and a fully legible signature. Maitland copied the original letter in French and with a translation, printed in *Surrender*, and his copy is faithful. It is also in *WSD*, xi (1864), p. 31, taken from Maitland's copy, dated *'Rochefort, 13 Juillet'*. The version in *Corr. de Nap.* (1869), no. 22,066, is dated *'Île d'Aix, 14 juillet 1815'* and has *'en butte'*, *'au foyer'*, and omits *'plus grandes'*; Houssaye, *Seconde Rest.*, p. 393, follows this version. The original was thus penned before Las Cases and Lallemand met Maitland on 14 July, *and as Bertrand had indeed indicated* in his 'Avant-Propos'. Napoleon's letter was therefore *not written as a consequence* of the 14 July meeting, it was written as a consequence of the great decision he had reached on the 13th. This invalidates Las Cases's claim that it was because Maitland had made an offer on the 14th not long before noon, that further discussion took place thereafter with the Emperor, and only then (*'alors'*) did Napoleon write the letter (vol, i, pp. 27–8). Dunan in his 1951 edition of Las Cases says that the holograph letter was undated, and asks whether Maitland added a date 'so as to deny the effects of his overtures of the 14th' (vol. i, p. 28 fn. 3). I am unclear on what 'overtures' means, but his question can be seen to be totally irrelevant, for I note that André Castelot, *Napoléon*, vol. 2 (Paris, 1968), p. 832 correctly quotes the letter as 'Rochefort, 13 July'.

57. Las Cases, *Le Mémorial*, i, p. 59. This was on 6 or 7 August when he was accusing Maitland of making false promises.
58. Maitland to Admiralty, Basque Roads, 14 July 1815, published by the Admiralty Office, 25 July, and printed in [Booth's] *The Battle of Waterloo, by a Near Observer* (7th edn., 1815), p. 218. It is curious how French writers pay neither attention nor reference to this statement.
59. Gourgaud, *Journal inédit*, i, pp. 29–40, 3–14 July. Once aboard the *Bellerophon* Las Cases on 26 July still expressed no doubts and foresaw Napoleon II as a future monarch, and was full of praise for British liberty. He was now in the uniform of a French naval captain (having briefly been a cadet before the Revolution over twenty-five years earlier) and sporting the Legion of Honour just given him for his negotiating skills. When the crowds at Torbay came to gaze, Las Cases drew reassurance from the 'red button-holes' he saw among them: Gourgaud, pp. 26, 44, 47. It does suggest that he was something of a *fantaisist*.
60. Hotham to Croker of the Admiralty, quoted in Rose, *Studies*, p. 314.
61. Montholon, pp. 70–1.
62. Napoleon's ruminations are in Houssaye, *Seconde Abdication*, pp. 393–4. For Muiron, who died screening General Bonaparte with his own body at Arcola, and Napoleon's esteem for him, see the article in *Dict. Nap.*, ii, p. 356.
63. Las Cases, *Mémorial*, i, pp. 23–4, under rubric, 10 July. He is equivocal in his book and pretends that it was later on the *Northumberland* that he made progress in speaking English, but that is untrue. He understood English and spoke it extremely well, since from the time of the failed Quiberon expedition of 1795 in which he had taken part, until the Consulate permitted 'rallied' *émigrés* to return, he lived and worked in England: and as anyone knows who lived in a foreign country for a few years but has left it for some

time, fluency in the foreign tongue returns virtually at once. It was only the first of several untruths: later Maitland discovered Las Cases tricking him over a fairly minor matter, and although the captain gave him the benefit of the doubt at the time, he later found out that it had indeed been a lie (*Surrender of Napoleon*, p. 44).

64. Maitland, *Surrender of Napoleon*, p. 177. Maitland goes on to say that he was astonished when he belatedly discovered after three weeks together that Las Cases could speak English. At least one officer on the *Northumberland* seems to have thought Maitland had been taken advantage of in this matter: see the *Northumberland* letter, 22 August 1815, in *Surrender*, p. 178. There was a feeling that Maitland was too impressed with Napoleon and his entourage: see remarks on the over-high respect shown by the officers of the *Bellerophon*, written by the First Lord of the Admiralty, Lord Melville, to Lord Keith, in two letters dated 25 July, in Kerry, *The First Napoleon*, pp. 157–8.
65. Strangely enough the greatest of Napoleon's apologists, Frédéric Masson, took a softer line than Houssaye. In dealing with the 14 July discussions and the surrender letter that he believed was of that date, Masson wrote: 'Moreover Maitland was a naval officer and very brave. Doubtless there were officers under the British flag who by ignorance or superstition believed in British good faith and the nation's magnanimity, and there is nothing to show that Maitland was not in good faith': *Napoléon à Ste-Hélène*, Paris, 1912, p. 41.
66. For the texts of the exchange of letters, see *Surrender*, pp. 26 and 29.
67. Savary, *Mémoires*, viii, p. 221, who noted that Captain Knight lunched with them all and stayed on during the afternoon conversations. Also *Surrender*, p. 35, for the presence of Knight. It was unfortunate (and a gift for theorists of double-dealing) that Knight was apparently not asked for a witness statement later. It is just possible that as he was carrying despatches to Admiral Hotham he was then sent on another mission and was not available. But it is odd.
68. Maitland to Hotham, *Bellerophon*, 10 July 1815: *Keith Papers*, iii, pp. 351–2.
69. Maitland, *Surrender*, p. 33.
70. Las Cases, i, pp. 23–4, 10 July; Savary, viii, pp. 222–3.
71. Montholon, in his account of these days says nothing of the matter: *Hist. de la Captivité*, pp. 66–8; for Maitland's comment, see *Surrender*, p. 57.
72. Savary, viii, pp. 258–9. Generosity and honour – this from Savary, of the Vincennes murder and Bayonne infamy!
73. Lord Kerry, Flahaut's direct descendant, quotes his letter to Thiers of 1861: 'I told him not to expect any generosity from a responsible cabinet government ('*un gouvernement collectif et responsable*'): see the entire letter in Kerry, app. 14, pp. 317–19.
74. Las Cases, i, pp. 26–30, 14 July.
75. Quoted from Lallemand's report (printed in *French-American Review*, April 1949) in Marcel Dunan's 1951 edition of *Le Mémorial*, i, p. 27 fn. 3. Lallemand comes out well in this saga.
76. Montholon, p. 75. This point is also made by the French editors of Gourgaud's *Journal*, i, p. 39.

77. Maitland, *Surrender*, p. 176.
78. In addition to his claim that Maitland had given a promise, Las Cases again overplayed his hand when he told Keith that 'the Emperor's letter to the Prince of Wales had necessarily created tacit conditions' (i, p. 59).
79. Maitland, *Surrender*, appendix, pp. 231–40.
80. Maitland, *Surrender*, report at p. 238.
81. It was then discovered that some of the party had been proscribed as traitors to France by the ordinance of 24 July; Lallemand and Savary were particularly disturbed at the thought of being handed back. Maitland having accepted them on board, threatened to resign as dishonoured if they were sent back to France. *Surrender*, pp. 150–3. This redounds to his honour, but is seldom mentioned. None of them was handed over to the Bourbon authorities.
82. So at least says the writer of the short article on Maitland in *Dict. Nap.*, ii, p. 249; he clearly has never heard of the old *DNB*, which could have put him right.
83. See Keith's account of these tribulations, from 5 August onwards, in Kerry, from p. 168.
84. Las Cases, Montholon, Gourgaud, all vain and jealous men, came to hate each other, but we have to take note of what they put on record about the negotiation.
85. Houssaye's use of language is not particularly helpful. If one accepts that Maitland's closing towards shore to stop Napoleon's escape by sea may be presented as 'advancing on his prey to trap him' (p. 378 fn.), is it fair to say that Las Cases was '*un peu abusé*' (a little misled) by Maitland's words, when (a) it was Las Cases who by definitely misleading Maitland as to his lack of English obliged Maitland to speak in French, and (b) the words spoken conformed to what was given to him in writing (p. 389)? Dunan judged that Las Cases was 'concerned to tear the Emperor from his indecisions', but as he 'took his own desires for reality and the banal words of courtesy for formal engagements' (1951 edition of Las Cases, i, p. 27, fn. 2), he steered the Emperor from uncertainty to disaster; later Dunan spoke of his naïve belief in his own powers. So when Houssaye claims that 'Las Cases was Maitland's dupe and Maitland his own dupe' (p. 391), would it not be reasonable to protest that it was Napoleon who was duped by Las Cases and Las Cases was his own dupe? He was the worst sort of man for such a task, one who blinded himself and so added to his master's problems: both too clever by half and a fool.
86. *Seconde Abdication*, pp. 376–7.

CHAPTER 51: The Settlement of 1815

1. A fearful Paris still managed to display its drollery. A wag named Louis XVIII as '*deux fois neuf*': 'twice 9' and 'new for the second time'.
2. This is also to ignore the Austrian and British expeditions destined for the French Mediterranean ports. Admiral Lord Exmouth and Hudson Lowe began embarking at Genoa on 4 July. But the war was over before they could engage.
3. See, for instance, the close of the long report to Bathurst of 2 July, *WD*, 532/188.
4. See chap. 47, n. 12.

5. The letters of Prince August, Wellington and Dickson are in *WD*, 545–6/198, 557/207, 586/227, 626–7/256; *WSD*, x, pp. 654 and 668.
6. Data from Siborne, *History*, p. 520.
7. This comes mainly from Maitland's *Surrender*; Gourgaud's *Journal*; some items in HMC *Bathurst*; Kerry's *The First Napoleon*, Part VIII, Keith's letters and papers, July–August 1815: the Keith extract is on p. 165, and the Emperor's letter of protest on p. 166; in addition there is a further series of documents, including some from the above works, in *Keith Papers*, iii, pp. 328–409.
8. *Napoleon, the Last Phase* (1900), Introductory Chapter to the new edition of 1909. Captain Poppleton was the British orderly officer at Longwood House on St Helena, 1815–16. It may not be too fanciful to think of a later era, and ask what the Allies, including the French, would have said if, in November 1918, Kaiser Wilhelm had asked his dear cousin King George to let bygones be bygones, to permit him to live quietly and free from bother at Osborne House or Balmoral, let alone Dublin Castle.
9. The island comprises roughly 47 sq. miles/112 sq. km, with the area round Longwood standing at 1,700 feet; the summer temperatures at that altitude are roughly 60–75 °F and winter 45–60 °F, rainfall being 30–50 inches per annum. There is abundant pure spring water (*Encycl. Brit.*). Parts are rocky and bleak, but apart from its remoteness it is not a disagreeable place. Brunyee's *Napoleon's Britons* gives a good modern description.
10. The Lord Chancellor, Eldon, was deeply worried that this was 'an irregular third-party treaty' entered into without the approval of Parliament, and he was unwilling to affix the great seal until ministers had been given guarantees of indemnity from prosecution. Bathurst thought the bills of indemnity 'very good things, but not settling all points'. And in fact in 1816 Lord Holland in Parliament, in criticising the government's actions, raised precisely those points that Eldon had deployed in the secrecy of Cabinet: N. Thompson, *Lord Bathurst and the British Empire, 1762–1834* (1999), p. 103.
11. Basil Jackson, *Notes and Reminiscences of a Staff Officer*, [1877] pub. 1903, pp. 160–1; Fisher in *CMH*, ix, p. 760. Those who wish to study this melancholy topic in more detail should examine R. C. Seaton's 1903 study of Napoleon's relations with Lowe, and a useful modern account in Desmond Gregory's *Napoleon's Jailer* (1996), that takes account of French twentieth-century reconsiderations.
12. When in 1809 Pope Pius VII, already virtually Napoleon's prisoner in Rome, opposed the Emperor's instructions to the Church, he was abducted and held incommunicado. His secretary, Cardinal Pacca, was incarcerated for four years in Fenestrelle state prison, high in the Piedmontese Alps, his room with blackened smoky walls and a floor of dusty broken planks. Consequently when Napoleon complained of illegal detention in the harsh conditions of Longwood, Pacca unsympathetically remarked that it 'should be regarded as a fresh evidence of that Divine Providence that rules human vicissitudes and which, by a sort of *lex talonis*, strikes down and punishes the guilty here below' (quoted in M. D. Sibalis's chapter in *Napoleon and his Empire* [ed. Dwyer & Forrest], p. 109). Was this, in effect, the just riposte to Lord Eldon's worries and to Lord Holland's criticisms of the British ministry?

13. The two papers are in *WD*, 596 and 600. Sorel, generally no friend to British policy, nevertheless wrote of Wellington at this time that 'he showed himself as the politician and the rare head of an army who, as conqueror, held to the letter of his declarations before the battle and made it a point of honour to respect them' (*L'Europe et la Révolution*, viii, p. 458).
14. Castlereagh to Liverpool, 17 August 1815, *Cas. Corr.*, x, p. 484. That policy was denounced on the same day by Gneisenau as Britain nurturing war on the Continent, as we shall shortly see.
15. Pozzo, *Corr. Diplomatique*, vol. i, pp. 186–8, 189, 202–3 and fn., 211–19 (at p. 217), 219–20; various dates from July to October 1815. There are also many references to Wellington throughout Pozzo's 1815 despatches, favourable and sometimes laudatory.
16. Hardinge to Stewart, 26 July, *WSD*, xi, p. 62; Leggiere, *Blücher*, pp. 426–7; Castlereagh to Liverpool, 17 Aug. 1815, *Cas. Corr.*, x, p. 484. Prussian diplomatic isolation and Gneisenau's complaints had their effect on Blücher, who by September could write 'Wellington's conduct was not always good, for if we had supported him on the 18th as he had us on the 16th, Fouché could not have called him the saviour of France': Delbrück, *Gneisenau*, iv, p. 619; Hofschröer, *1815*, ii, 351.
17. '*Wenn aber England auf der Integrität des Französischen Gebiets besteht, so kann man in einer solchen Verkehrtheit nicht als das Bestreben erbicken, den Krieg auf den Kontinent zu nähren und Deutschland von sich abhängig zu machen . . . Am schlechtesten benimmt sich Wellington, er, der ohne uns zertrümmert worden wäre, der uns die Zusagen, zu unserer Hülfe am 16ten [Juni.] in Bereitschaftt zu sein, nicht gehalten hatte, dem wir, uneingedenk des durch seine Schuld erlittenen Unglücks, am 18ten ritterlich zu Hülfe gekommen sind; die wir ihn vor Paris geführt haben: der ohne uns wäre er nicht so schnell gekommen; die wir ihm durch unser schnelles Verfolgen eine zweiter Schlacht erspart haben: den wir haben den Feind aufgelöst und sein Britte hat seit der Schlacht am 18ten ein Gefecht bestanden. So viele Verdienste um ihn vergilt der Mann durch den schnödesten Undank.*' These extracts come from the letter, Gneisenau to Arndt, 17 August 1815, given in full in Delbrück, *Gneisenau*, iv, p. 605. The section denouncing Wellington was chosen as epigraph for Hofschröer's *1815: The German Victory*.
18. The 148,000 combatant troops comprised (to the nearest thousand): Austrians 29; Russians 32; Prussians 28; British 31; Bavarians 10; Saxons, Württembergers, Danes and Hanoverians, each between 4 and 5: *WSD*, xi, 419.
19. He had been made a Russian field marshal early in November 1818 at the Congress of Aix, and became next an Austrian and a Prussian field marshal later in the month.
20. I do not know of a better summary of how well-informed Victorians regarded Wellington when his death was announced, than the long and thoughtful assessment by Charles Greville in his *Memoirs* (ed. Strachey & Fulford, entry for 18 Sept. 1852, vol. vi, pp. 360–4).
21. The story is set out in *WSD*, xi, pp. 100, 238, 444, 577–8, 580, 731, 736. Whether any similar schemes were set up in other Allied countries or France I do not know. I hope so.
22. J. G. Gallaher, *Napoleon's Enfant Terrible, Vandamme*, p. 288. He adds that Davout had done everything possible to persuade those officers on the first list to disappear.
23. The proscription lists are in Pétiet, *Souvenirs Militaires*, pp. 251–4. Lavalette had seized the postal services and control of government communications on 20 March, before

Napoleon reached Paris, and issued statements encouraging support for him. After the second Restoration he was tried, sentenced to the guillotine but escaped from prison, having exchanged clothes with his wife during a visit. She was eventually released, but her mind became deranged. He was pardoned in 1822. Ney and La Bédoyère were tried, sentenced and shot. Cambronne was tried and acquitted, since he had gone to Elba in Napoleon's service and had never sworn allegiance to Louis XVIII; he later married the widow of a Scottish merchant.

24. Pasquier, *Mémoires*, vol. iii, p. 369. Pasquier (1767–1862) had just entered the new ministry. In his previous career he had been *inter alia* an ineffective police minister under the Empire, who failed to uncover the Malet conspiracy in 1812. During the Hundred Days he was unemployed and in retirement, but joined the Fouché–Talleyrand ministry in July 1815. In fact he served every head of state from Louis XVI to Napoleon III.
25. J. E. Mansion's *Harrap's French Dictionary* gives a French league as 4 km (or about 2.5 miles). For a rough comparison, the *Département* of Seine-Maritime covered 2,448 sq. miles and that of Somme 2,443 sq. miles. This amount of cession after a second decisive defeat is not really so devastating, especially since the enclaves were gains for France: far worse was to befall in 1871.
26. The protocol between the Allies and France, dated 2 October 1815, setting out the settlement terms agreed, can be read in [Booth's] *The Battle of Waterloo, by a Near Observer*, 7th edn., 1815, p. 260. The treaty of 20 Nov. 1815 is in *CTS*, vol. 65, p. 251 (Eng. version at p. 301). The indemnity was paid off in good time, and hence the Army of Occupation withdrew in 1818.
27. Castlereagh openly called it 'a piece of sublime mysticism and nonsense', but in 1815 Alexander was too powerful to be ignored and had to be allowed his way. Not until his state paper of May 1820 did Castlereagh state Britain's opposition to the Holy Alliance's doctrine of protective intervention in foreign states, and it was Canning who finally broke with it.
28. Against these criticisms should be set the impulsion that Britain forced upon the powers for the abolition of the slave trade, an impulsion strengthened by British wealth and the prestige Britain gained from Waterloo. Foreign Office records contain 229 volumes of correspondence on this between 1816 and 1837: *CHBFP*, ii, p. 5 fn.
29. One must avoid stereotyping 'eras', for Goethe, Herder, Jean Paul (Richter), and Schiller had long since created a ferment in German literature, as had *Lyrical Ballads* in the Britain of 1798, while the middle-aged Scott's *Waverley* (1814) and its successors were about to do the same for the novel and opera. Even Regency morals were changing: at Vienna in 1814 Beethoven's champion Count Rasumovski found he could not organise a recital on a Sunday because of British evangelical objections, a foretaste of things to come. But if we take those born between 1790 and 1799 and thus aged between sixteen and twenty-five in 1815, we can see the changing spirit of the times: Lamartine, Meyerbeer, Rossini, Shelley, Carlyle, Ranke, Keats, Donizetti, de Vigny, Heine, Schubert, Balzac, Pushkin, Mary Wollstonecraft Shelley: these would take their listeners and readers far from many conventions of their childhood.

30. Thiers's *revanchisme*, and his policy over the Ottoman Empire and Syria in 1839–40, nearly brought about a declaration of war against Britain, and his mutterings about war with Prussia led to the composition in Germany of *Die Wacht am Rhein*.
31. P. Geyl, *Napoleon, For and Against*, p. 156 (Perigrine edition, 1965). Yet old feelings die hard. In 2010 Thierry Lentz, writing of the 1815 settlement, finds that 'despite the principles of the Holy Alliance there was no Christian charity in the treatment inflicted on France': *Les Cent Jours*, p. 541.

CHAPTER 52: Retrospect

1. This was not recognised for the most part by the French historians of the Third Republic, perhaps understandably. With hindsight and from a very particular standpoint they saw the settlements of 1814 and 1815 as bringing militant Prussia ever closer to a hapless France, with 1870 and 1914 as inevitable consequences: hence in part their denunciations of Talleyrand and his policy. Certainly he was venal and cynical, but he had few cards to play against the victorious Allies and yet he played them *at the time* with extraordinary finesse. But the fifty years from 1815 saw unimaginable changes to the course of history and in fifty years the options, the forks in the road, were many. That is why, in looking back at these writers of the Third Republic I think de Waresquiel in a new century is right to warn his French readers of tunnel vision, of eyes 'so fixed on the Belgian frontier as though the relinquishment of Namur, Tournai and Charleroi was the cause of all French woes in 1914 and 1940', *Talleyrand* (2003), pp. 464–5.
2. One has only to think of the tepid or even hostile attitudes of many states towards abolishing the slave trade, as against the unremitting pressure for abolition from the Liverpool ministry in the peace negotiations of 1814 and again in 1815, to estimate how much more difficult it would have been to achieve if Britain's and Wellington's prestige had been compromised by major defeat.
3. Pasquier, *Mémoires*, iii, p. 195.
4. Gen. Sir D. Fraser, *And We Shall Shock Them: The British Army in the Second World War* (1983), p. 227. He was writing in the context of the Western Desert, Rommel, and the hapless and baffled state of the British under Ritchie (himself under Auchinleck).
5. For new information on this subject see Appendix 4, Bertrand's Letter of 10 June 1815.
6. For the first instance, misdated by Soult '15' June, see chap. 32, sec. II; for the second, note the understandably frustrated tone in Davout's 19 June reply to Soult's message of 17 June. The ever-efficient Davout complained: 'I should have liked you to have informed me of the places to which you have sent orders for the ten National Guard battalions of the 16th Military Division [the northern sector] to go to at Avesnes. Anyway, I shall send Gen. Solignac to go round and work out what is for the best . . .': *Davout Corr.*, no. 1759, vol. iv, p. 568.
7. This ride reduces the 'piles' excuse to its proper status. The 'ill health' protagonists for Napoleon never seem to extend their argument to account for 'wear and tear' in the cases of the ageing Blücher, or to that veteran of the tropics, Wellington.

8. *Corr. de Nap.*, xxxi, 248–59 (4to ed), pp. 205–14 (8vo).
9. Dörnberg's work in particular was of the highest quality, and merited more credence than it received in Brussels. Clinton of 2nd Division on seeing what Dörnberg's material pointed to, said on 14 June, 'Yes, now I believe it – but the Duke, who is always very well informed, does not believe it.'
10. Metternich to his daughter, Paris, 13 July 1815, letter no. 202 in his *Mémoires*, vol. ii, p. 523 (p. 612 in Eng. trans.).
11. Students of Wellington's own papers, of the memoirs both French and British, and of the *Histories*, may well agree with that redoubtable military historian C. T. Atkinson when, in reviewing Oman's *magnum opus* and judging Wellington's qualities and achievements, he pertinently asked: 'Had Arthur Wellesley perished at Vimeiro, as Moore did at Corunna, would the British Army have been treading on French soil ten days before Leipzig?': *Quarterly Review*, vol. 257, Oct. 1931, pp. 355–74, at end.
12. See chap. 51, n. 20.
13. The extraordinary way in which the young Jacobin officer Buonaparte fomented trouble in Ajaccio at Easter 1792, unsuccessfully tried to subvert the regular forces garrisoned there, fired on the townspeople and terrorised them, misrepresented what had happened and falsely gave out that he was acting under orders, is not often given much attention. The story is told in great detail by the Napoleonic scholar Arthur Chuquet in *La Jeunesse de Napoléon*, ii, pp. 264–92: 'carried away by ambition, this young man of [under] 23 will not draw back from anything'. The only English-language author known to me to give it sufficient prominence is Correlli Barnett in his interesting character study, *Bonaparte*, 'Prologue', pp. 11–14: Buonaparte's tactics, he concluded, 'could hardly be bettered by any modern political militant, least of all in the unhesitating assertion of the moral initiative by means of loading his opponents with the blame for conflict he himself had provoked'. See also Philip Dwyer, *Napoleon, the Path to Power*, pp. 85–92, who generally follows Chuquet.
14. A French cultural historian, A. L. Guérard, made an interesting point, arguing that the young Buonaparte 'was a Jacobin when it served his purpose; he was a friend of the Robespierre brothers in the same way as he was later a Mussulman in Egypt': *Reflections on the Napoleonic Legend*, p. 35.
15. Two of Louis XIV's most horrific acts of war were the burning of the Palatinate in 1674, and a second time and much more severely in 1689, the latter a war crime for which his contemporaries could never forgive him. Chaptal recounts a conversation with Napoleon in which the Emperor dealt with the 1689 devastation: 'the glory of this was not due to Louis XIV, it all belongs to Louvois and was the finest act of his life', Chaptal, *Mes Souvenirs*, pp. 304–5. Nothing can excuse such a remark.
16. Tocqueville, quoted in *CMH*, ix, p. 769. Napoleon's Scottish contemporary Walter Scott, in the concluding chapter to the final volume of his *Life of Napoleon*, made much the same point, that he was a very great man, but also a bad one: 'Arrived at the possession of supreme power, a height that dazzles and confounds so many, Napoleon seemed only to occupy the station for which he was born, to which his peculiar powers adapted him.' But

'he who was conscious of having forced his own way, had little to bind him in gratitude or kindness to those, who only made room for him because they durst not oppose him. His ambition was a modification of selfishness, sublime indeed in its effects and consequences, but yet, when strictly analysed, leaving little but egotism in the crucible': ix, pp. 312, 316. While the *Life* has been long out-dated, this chapter is still worth reading for it is full of Scott's humanity and good feeling.

Appendix 1

The Original Draft of Wellington's Waterloo Despatch *And Related Reports*

I

THE TEXT OF THE WATERLOO DESPATCH that follows has been taken with permission from the original document in the British Library, Add. MS 69,850. The Waterloo Despatch has of course been published in its *final* version in almost every history of the campaign, since that first printed in *The London Gazette Extraordinary,* No. XXXI, of 22 June 1815. The special interest of the draft lies in Wellington's deletions and insertions, showing how he marshalled his thoughts and the degree to which he received new information and realised changes to be necessary as he proceeded with his composition. I originally published the draft's text in *First Empire* No. 87, March/April 2006, and I remain grateful to the late David Watkins, the editor of that excellent and much regretted magazine, for encouraging my researches.

Wellington drafted his despatch in ink on foolscap paper, each page being divided vertically so as to leave a margin usually half-a-page wide for any additions, although most of the insertions were above the lines of text.

The Duke began drafting the despatch at Waterloo at around 4 a.m. on 19 June, just five or six hours after his meeting with Blücher at La Belle Alliance at the end of one of the most stressful days of his life. He broke off in order to ride to Brussels, where he was installed by 8.30 a.m. There is a change of pen after paragraph 16, and this may mark the moment when he broke off to ride to the capital. In that case he had written 1,140 words while at Waterloo out of the total 2,400 words. At 8.30 a.m. he wrote to Lady Frances Wedderburn Webster from his quarters in Brussels mentioning that he had taken 150 cannon and that he had heard from Blücher that morning that the latter had taken 60 more.[1] As this fresh information on the 60 cannon appears as part of the narrative of paragraph 19 and is not inserted as a later addition, it suggests that this paragraph was written at or after 8.30 a.m.

The paragraphs were not numbered by Wellington and the numbers now given are merely for ease of reference. I have marked the Duke's handwritten *additions* to his draft in *italic* type, and his deletions are shown ~~struck through~~; square brackets [ ] are used for editorial comments, including the supplied paragraph numbers, in the usual way. The capitalization conforms to the Duke's way, but his ampersands '&' have been replaced by the word 'and'. It can easily be seen that the changes were due to fresh information coming in, or from his quest for greater definition. The initial paragraph with its multiple changes of syntax (not changes of substance) suggests that the Duke was only slowly feeling his way towards his line of presentation, but thereafter his amendments were surprisingly few. They also indicate how quickly he noticed mistakes: for instance, in paragraph 30, where 'before Y' was deleted, Wellington, in saying that the eagles were to be brought to HRH the Prince Regent, momentarily forgot that he was not addressing the Prince Regent himself, but the Secretary of State, Lord Bathurst – but instantly recollected and altered his sentence.

The Duke was also the Netherlands Commander-in-Chief, and therefore had to send a despatch to King Willem I. Hence he made a few pencil marks on his draft indicating where a clerk should amend the Netherlands copy. I give details of these marks and instructions after printing the full text.

II

The document is endorsed thus as a docket:

> ~~Waterloo~~ Bruxelles June 19th 1815
> To   No 23
> Lord Bathurst
> Report of the Operations
> Battle of Waterloo

On the reverse of the docket Wellington has written part of paragraph 29, starting with the phrase 'found myself in a situation' through to 'have succeeded'.

> [In the left hand margin:] The Earl Bathurst, Waterloo, June ~~2~~ 19, 1815

> [1] My Lord, Buonaparte having collected the 1st, 2d, 3d, 4th, and 6th Corps of the French Army, and the *Imperial* Guards, *and nearly all the Cavalry,* on the ~~frontier~~ *Sambre and* between that river and the Meuse, between the 10th

and 14th of the Month, advanced ~~at daylight~~ on the 15th and attacked [two illegible words struck out] the Prussian Posts at Thuin and Lobez on the Sambre, at day-light in the morning.

[2] I did not hear of these events till in the evening of the 15th, and I immediately ordered the troops to prepare to march, and afterwards to march to their left, as soon as I had Intelligence from other quarters to prove that the enemy's movement upon Charleroy was the real attack.

[3] The Enemy drove the Prussian Posts from the Sambre on that day, and General Zieten who commanded the Corps that had been at Charleroy retired upon Fleurus, and marshall Prince Blucher concentrated the Prussian Army upon Sombref, holding the villages in front of his Position of St Amand and Ligny.

[4] The Enemy continued his March along the Road from Charleroy towards Bruxelles, and on the same evening the 15th attacked a Brigade of the Army of the Netherlands *under the Prince de Weimar and* posted at Frasne, and forced it back to the farmhouse on the same Road called les quatre bras.

[5] The Prince of Orange immediately reinforced this Brigade with another of the same division, under general Perponcher, and in the morning early regained part of the ground which had been lost so as to have command of the Communication leading from Nivelles and Bruxelles, with Marshall Blucher's position.

[6] In the mean time I had directed the whole Army to March upon les quatre bras, and the 5th division under Lt Gl Sir Thomas Picton, arrived at about half past two in the day, followed by the Corps of Troops under the Duke of Brunswick, and afterwards by the contingent of Nassau.

[7] At this time the Enemy commenced an attack upon Prince Blucher with his whole force excepting the 1st and 2d Corps and a Corps of Cavalry under General Kellerman, with which he attacked our Post at Les quatre bras.

[8] The Prussian army maintained their ~~post~~ *position* with their usual Gallantry and Perseverance, against a great disparity of Numbers, as the 4th Corps of their Army under General Bulow had not joined, and I was not able to assist them as I wished, as I was attacked myself, and the troops the cavalry in particular which had a long distance to march had not arrived.

[9] We maintained our Position also, and completely defeated and repulsed all the Enemy's attempts to get possession of it. The Enemy repeatedly attacked us with a large body of Infantry and Cavalry supported by a numerous and Powerful Artillery; ~~and when~~ he made several Charges with the Cavalry upon our Infantry but all were repulsed in the steadiest manner. In this affair HRH the Prince of Orange the Duke of Brunswick

and L Genl Sir Thomas Picton and MGenl Sir Kempt and Sir Dennis Pack ~~highly d~~ who were engaged from the commencement of the *Enemy's* attack highly distinguished themselves as well as Lt Genl Charles Baron Alten M General Sir C Halkett Lt General Cooke and M Generals Maitland and Byng as they successively arrived. The troops of the 5th Divn and *those* of the Brunswick corps were long and severely engaged, and conducted themselves with the utmost Gallantry. [Added in the margin:] *I must particularly mention the 28th, 42d, 79th, and 92d Regts, and the Battallion of Hanoverians.*

[10] Our loss was great as Your Lordship will perceive by the inclosed return; and I have particularly to regret H S Highness the Duke of Brunswick who fell fighting gallantly at the head of his Troops.

[11] Although Marshall Blucher had maintained his position at Sombref, he still found himself [an isolated letter here deleted] much weakened by the severity of the Contest in which he had been engaged, and as the 4th Corps had not arrived he determined to fall back *and concentrate his army* upon Wavre; and he marched in the night after the action was over.

[12] This movement of the Marshalls rendered necessary a corresponding one on my part; and I retired from the farm of quatre Bras *upon Genappe and thence upon Waterloo* the next morning the 17th at ten o'clock.

[13] The Enemy made no effort [illegible word deleted] to pursue Marshall Blucher. On the contrary a Patrole which I sent to Sombref in the morning found all quiet and the Enemy's Vedettes fell back as the Patrole advanced. Neither did he attempt to molest our March to the Rear although made in the middle of the day, excepting by following with a large body of Cavalry brought from [illegible word deleted] *his* right the Cavalry under the Earl of Uxbridge.

[14] This gave Lord Uxbridge an opportunity of charging them with the 1st Life Guards upon their debouché from the Village of Genappe upon which His Lordship has declared himself to be well satisfied with that Regt.

[15] The Position which I took up in front of Waterloo *crossed the high roads from Charleroy and Nivelle, and* had its right thrown back to a Ravine near Merbe Braine which was occupied and its left extended to a height above the hamlet of *Ter* la Haye which was likewise occupied. In front of the right *Centre* near the Nivelle Road we occupied the House and *Garden* of Hougoumont which covered the return of that flank; and in front of the left Centre we occupied the farm of La Haye Sainte. By our left we communicated with Marshall Prince Blucher at Wavre through Ohain; and the Marshall had promised me that in case we should be attacked he would support me with one or more Corps as might be necessary.

[16] The Enemy collected his Army *with the exception of the 3d Corps which had been sent to observe Marsh Blucher* on a range of heights in our front in the course of the night of the 17th and yesterday morning; and [word deleted] *at about ten o'clock* he commenced a furious attack upon our Post at Hougoumont. I had occupied that Post with a detachment from General *Byng's* Brigade of Guards which was in position in its rear, and it was for some time under the Command of Lt.-Col. Macdonel and afterwards of Col Home; and I am happy to add that it was maintained throughout the day with the utmost gallantry by these brave Troops notwithstanding the repeated efforts of large bodies of the Enemy to obtain possession of it.[2]

[17] This attack upon the right of our Centre was accompanied by a very heavy cannonade upon our whole line, which was [illegible word deleted] *destined to* support [illegible word deleted] the repeated attacks of Cavalry and Infantry occasionally mixed, but sometimes separate, which were made upon it. In one of these the Enemy carried the farm house of La Haye Sainte, as the [illegible word deleted] detachment of the lt Batn of the Legion which occupied it had expended all their ammunition, and the Enemy occupied the only communication there was with them.

[18] The Enemy repeatedly charged our Infantry with his Cavalry but these attacks were uniformly unsuccessful; and they afforded opportunities to our Cavalry to charge in one of which Lord E Somerset's Brigade consisting of the Life Guards [illegible word deleted] *Royal Horse Guards* and 1st Dragoon Guards highly distinguished themselves. [Added in the margin:] *as did that of M Genl Sir Wm Ponsonby having taken many Prisoners and an Eagle.*

[19] These attacks were repeated till about 7 in the evening, when the Enemy made a desperate effort with the Cavalry and Infantry, supported by the fire of artillery, [three illegible words deleted] *to force our left* Centre near the farm of La Haye Sainte, which after a severe contest was defeated; and having observed that the troops retired from this attack in great confusion, and that the March of General Bulow's Corps *by Frischermont* upon Plancenoit and la belle Alliance had begun to take effect, and as I could perceive the fire of his Cannon [added in the margin:] *and as Marshall Prince Blucher had joined in person, with a corps of his army to the left of our line by Ohain,* I determined to attack the Enemy, and immediately advanced the whole line of Infantry, supported by the Cavalry and Artillery. The attack succeeded in every [word deleted] point, the Enemy *was forced* from his positions on the heights and fled in the utmost confusion leaving behind him as far as I could judge 150 pieces with their Ammunition, which fell into our hands. I continued the pursuit until long after dark; and then discontinued it only

on account of the fatigue of our Troops, who had been engaged during 12 hours, and because I found myself on the same Road as Marshall Blucher, who assured me of his Intention to follow the Enemy throughout the night. He has sent me word this morning that he had taken 60 pieces of Cannon belonging to the Imperial Guard, and several Carriages, *Baggage* etc belonging to Buonaparte in Genappe.

[20] I propose to move this morning upon Nivelles and not to discontinue my operations.

[21] Your Lordship will observe that such a desperate action could not be fought and such advantages could not be gained without great loss, and I am sorry to add that ours has been immense. In Lt Genl Sir Thomas Picton H M has sustained the loss of an Officer who has frequently distinguished himself in his Service and he fell gloriously ~~in~~ leading his Division to a charge with Bayonets, by which one of the most serious attacks made by the Enemy on our Position was repulsed.[3] The Earl of Uxbridge after having successfully got through this arduous day received a wound *by almost the last shot fired* which will I am afraid deprive H M for some time of his Services.

[22] [Heavily crossed through:] ~~Those Officers who distinguished themselves the~~ *HRH* the Prince of Orange distinguished himself by his Gallantry and conduct till he received a Wound from a Musquet Ball through the Shoulder which obliged him to quit the field.

[23] It gives me the greatest satisfaction to assure Your Lordship that the Army never on any occasion conducted itself better. The Division *of Guards* under Lt Genl Cooke *who is severely wounded* M General Maitland and M Gl Byng set an example which was followed by all, and there is no Officer nor description of Troops that did not behave well.

[24] I must however particularly mention for HRH's approbation Lt General Sir H Clinton, M Genl Adam, Lt Genl Charles Baron Alten severely wounded, M General Sir Colin Halkett severely wounded, Col Ompteda Colonel Mitchell commanding a Brigade of the 4th Divn, M Generals Sir Kempt and Sir D Pack, M Genl Lambert, MGenl Lord E Somerset, M Genl Sir W Ponsonby, M Genl *Sir C* Grant and M Genl Sir H Vivian, M Genl Sir O Vandeleur M Genl Count Dornberg. I am also particularly indebted to General Lord Hill for his assistance and conduct upon this as upon all former occasions.

[25] The Artillery and Engineer departments were conducted much to my satisfaction by *Colonel* Sir George Wood and Col Smyth; and I have every reason to be satisfied with the conduct of the Adj General M Genl Barnes who was wounded; and of the QM Genl Colonel De Lancey who

was killed *by a Cannon Shot in the middle of the Action.* This officer is a serious loss to His Majesty's Service and to me at this moment. I was likewise much indebted to the Assistance of Lt.-Col. Lord Fitzroy Somerset who was severely wounded, and of the officers composing my personal Staff who have suffered severely in this action. Lt.-Col. the Honble Sir Alexr Gordon who has died of his Wounds was a most promising officer and is a severe loss to H M's service.

[26] General Kruse of the Nassau Service likewise conducted himself much to my satisfaction as did *General Trip commanding the Heavy Brigade of Cavalry and* General [4] comg a Brigade of Infantry of the King of the Netherlands.

[27] General Pozzo di Borgo General Baron Vincent *General Muffling* and General Alava were in the field during the action, and rendered me every assistance in their Power. Baron Vincent is wounded, but I hope not severely; and Genl Pozzo di Borgo received a Contusion.

[28] I should not do justice to my own feelings,[5] or to ~~the~~ *Marshall Blucher and the* Prussian Army, if I did not attribute the successful Result of this Arduous day to the cordial *and timely* assistance I received from them.

[29] The operation of General Bulow upon the Enemy's flank was a most decisive one; and even if I had not found myself in a situation to make the attack which produced the final result, it would have [three illegible words struck through] *forced the Enemy* to retire, if his attacks should have failed, and would have prevented him from taking advantage of them, if they should *unfortunately* have succeeded.

[30] I send[6] with this dispatch three eagles[7] taken by the Troops in this action which Major Percy will have the Honor of laying ~~before Y~~ at the feet of His Royal Highness.

[31] I beg leave to recommend him to Your Lordship's protection.

There were two postscripts:

> [32] Since writing the above I have received a Report that *Major Genl* Sir Wm Ponsonby [word over-written] is killed; and in announcing this Intelligence to Your Lordship I have to add the expression of my [word deleted] grief for the fate of an Officer who had already rendered very brilliant and important Services and was [word deleted] an ornament to his Profession.

The second P.S. is not among the draft papers and is first given in the *London Gazette* of 22 June:

> [33] I have not yet got the returns of killed and wounded but I enclose a list of Officers killed and wounded on the two days, as far as the same can be

made out without the returns; and I am very happy to add that Colonel De Lancey is not dead and that strong hopes of his recovery are entertained.

III

The Version for King Willem I of the Netherlands

This version was sent by Wellington from Nivelles on 21 June to the Prince of Orange for on-forwarding to the King. He asked the Prince to insert the name of the ADC selected for this honour, and the Prince chose Webster. The despatch was published in a special supplement to the *Nederlandsche Staats-courant* on Friday 23 June 1815, omitting paragraphs 24, 25 and 30–33, but with a final paragraph unique to the Dutch version, mentioning 7,000 prisoners taken, including Lobau and Cambronne.

As we saw, the Württemberg envoy at The Hague made a copy in German and sent it to his own monarch (see Appendix 2 to Chapter 34).

The Duke's pencil marginalia are in soft lead, sometimes smudged and generally very faint:

> [Para. 1] I have the honour of informing Your Majesty that Buonaparte.
>
> [Para. 4] [Beside 'Army of the Netherlands'] of Your Majesty.
>
> [Para. 6] [Between '5th' and 'Division'] British.
>
> [Para. 17] [Before the word 'Legion'] German.
>
> [Para. 18] [After 'Somerset's Brigade'] of British Cavalry.
>
> [Para. 19] [After '150 pieces'] of cannon [this clarification also appears in *The London Gazette*].
>
> [21] [Replace 'Lordship with] Majesty [after 'Picton' and again after 'deprive' insert] H B M [that is, His Britannic Majesty as distinct from the Netherlands monarch].
>
> [Para. 23] [Replace 'Lordship' with] Majesty.
>
> [Para. 24 onwards] Has a line drawn down through the text.

The English and Dutch versions were printed in parallel columns by Colonel F. De Bas in his *Prins Frederik der Nederlanden*, vol. iii, part II, p. 1213 onwards.

IV

The Duke of Richmond's Letter to Earl Bathurst, Brussels, 18 June 1815

From HMC *Bathurst Papers*, 1923, p. 356. Richmond was reporting on the morning of 18 June what Bathurst's son (Richmond's nephew) Lord Apsley – who lacked the time to write – had told him of events on the 16th and 17th, and there were probably some mistakes made in the repetition. I have therefore not made any notes or corrections to Richmond's third-hand account.

> The Duke of Wellington has desired Apsley, [three words inserted:] *if he wrote*, to tell you he has not time to write an account of the business of the 16th and yesterday. It is shortly as follows:
>
> On the 16th Buonaparte passed some of the outposts. How I can't tell you, but he was between the Prussian right and English left. He attacked the Prussians who stood very well for a considerable time. The division from hence (Picton's) started early and came up when the Prussians were giving way to a degree. The Brunswick troops were a short time in action before them. The Duke of Brunswick was killed at their head. These troops sustained a very severe attack, in which the 28th, the Royal, the 44th, 42nd, 79th, and 92nd lost a very great number; so did the 61st and 58th. They, however, beat the French completely. Our arty and cavalry could not arrive in time and the French lancers did much mischief. During the night of the 16th and 17th the arty and cavalry came up. The Duke intended to attack yesterday but to his great disappointment Blücher could not collect his force, which had been attacked at 9 o'clock on the night of the 16th by the French cavalry and in fact surprised. He has thought it necessary in consequence of this to retire to a strong position about eight miles from hence, where the Prussians have joined him, and if they will stand he is perfectly safe. Buonaparte did not venture to prevent the retreat and has not yet attacked. I doubt his doing so. His loss has been severe, as well as that of the Allies. I am just going over to look at the position, and if I have any news will write it on my return. We are all ready to start, but I trust it will not be necessary. Your sons and mine are well. Pack is wounded, I hear, but not badly. Poor Lord Hay is killed. The commanding officers of the 42nd and 92nd are killed (Macara and Cameron). I have not heard of anybody else that is particularly interesting.

Lord Apsley's Letter to his Father, Earl Bathurst, Brussels, 19 June 1815

From HMC *Bathurst Papers*, 1923, pp. 356–7, extract only. It can be seen that this letter is quite specific as to the attack by the *Garde* and the part played by the 1st Guards. It therefore contrasts with Wellington's paragraph 19, which is a non-specific overview of events and makes no reference to any Allied regiment, British Guards, British Line, or Netherlands line in the defeat of the *Garde*. Indeed that paragraph is mainly valuable as extolling the part played by the Prussians. From a comparison of Apsley's letter and what his father announced to the Lords on 23 June it seems almost certain that Bathurst was relaying to the House information additional to the *Despatch* that reached him from Ensign Seymour Bathurst of the 1st Guards via his elder son Apsley.[8]

> He [Napoleon] led the Imperial Guard in person. He was met by the 1st Guards, which threw them quite over. Seymour was in this affair.

Earl Bathurst in the House of Lords, 23 June 1815

From *Hansard*, 23 June 1815, vol 31, column 973.

> Towards the close of the day, Buonaparte himself, at the head of his guards, made a desperate charge upon the British guards, and the British guards instantly overthrew the French . . .

V

The Reports of the Allied Commissioners

At Waterloo the Duke was accompanied by the official representatives of the Allies, several of whom wrote to their own courts about the battle. Staying close to Wellington, they shared his risks and observed events from roughly the same position. Consequently, their reports act as a sort of 'control' on Wellington's own 2,400-word Despatch. I shall not print them in full, but give a summary of their main observations.

General Pozzo di Borgo, representing the Tsar, was slightly hurt during the fighting. His despatch was written in Brussels on 19 June, and totalled about 650 words in French. He gave a general description of the field and the course of events. He fixed the start at midday, mentioned the struggle for Hougoumont and Uxbridge's cavalry action, timed the French massed cavalry attacks as starting at about 4 p.m., and the crisis on the ridge coming at about 6 p.m., following which came Wellington's advance and the French '*déroute universelle*'. The Prussian advance against the French right wing coincided, he thought, with the Blücher–Wellington meeting at 8 p.m. A summary of senior casualties was given, and then a last-minute postscript added that innumerable prisoners, 300 cannon and Napoleon's equipage had been taken.[9]

General Hügel, representing the King of Württemberg, wrote from Brussels at noon on 19 June, using about 450 words in German. He timed the start of battle at 12.30 p.m. and the British cavalry charge and the capture of several eagles at 3 p.m. He noted the Prussian attack as made with extraordinary vehemence at 6 p.m. and that Napoleon opposed it with everything possible while Wellington attacked with all possible vigour. After a period of indecision the battle ended with victory, but with immense loss. The Prussians were in active pursuit. Senior casualties were briefly given. A postscript gave news of the capture of the equipage and 300 cannon.[10]

The Spanish General Alava was slightly hurt in the battle, and his report was completed in Brussels on 20 June and was over 2,800 words long in Spanish. It dealt with events from 16 June onwards, but said that he only reached the front on the 17th. He timed the start of battle at 11.30 a.m. on the 18th, reported one eagle captured by the British cavalry, timed the receipt of the news that the Prussians had reached St Lambert as about 5 p.m. He timed Napoleon's final attack on the ridge as 7 p.m., at which moment Blücher's fire was perceived and Wellington led the British Guards to the counter-attack. Some 150 cannon were taken from the enemy. Senior casualties were noted, and the fact of Wellington shedding tears. Alava went on to speculate at length on Napoleon's future. A postscript announced the capture of Lobau and Cambronne.[11]

General Müffling seems to have written no battle report to Prussian headquarters; this may be because he met Blücher at the end of the day and reported verbally. His next letter to Prussian headquarters was from Binche on the evening of 20 June and was concerned with organisational affairs, noting that because so many of Wellington's staff had been killed or wounded, the Duke was seriously stretched in administering his army.[12]

Other commissioners either did not report or their reports have not been traced. The Austrian Vincent was wounded in the battle and his first report was dated 26 June, and was concerned with post-battle matters only. If the Sardinian Comte de Salles made a report, he did not mention it in correspondence with Siborne in 1842. Whether van Reede made a report is uncertain, but the Prince of Orange's Chief of Staff, Constant Rebecque, wrote to the Netherlands king, for Willem I replied thanking him from The Hague on 20 June.[13]

The Prince of Orange wrote to his father from Brussels on 22 June and his 600-word letter was plainly based on his reading of Wellington's Dutch Despatch. His enumeration of Napoleon's forces on 18 June came straight from paragraph 1, even though this was the force on the 15th, and the Duke for the 18th had specifically deducted the French *3e Corps* (paragraph 16), which Orange left included. He followed the Duke's paragraphs 17 to 19, although with less clarity. He picked out General Chassé for special praise. From his separate letter to the Duke, dated 21 June, it is clear that his wound accounted for the lack of detail he was providing to his father, and in any case he knew that Willem had already received Wellington's own Despatch.[14]

Baron Alten's special report to the government of Hanover, dated 20 June, ran to some 1,150 words. After setting the general scene he was mainly concerned with the affairs of his own men. He timed the start of the battle at 1 p.m. and suggested that it was at 'the critical moment' of Napoleon's final attack on the ridge that Bülow and 30,000 Prussians attacked the French flank.

When one thinks that the commissioners were there to observe and – with the exceptions of Orange, Alten, and possibly Müffling later in the day – had no command responsibilities, their reports seem quite slight and lacking in detail by comparison with the Duke's Despatch. Indeed they seem to underplay the Prussian contribution. By contrast Wellington's paragraphs 28 and 29 go far beyond them in praise of the Prussians.

VI

There is one question that has always puzzled students of the campaign: how many eagles did Wellington send to London with Major Percy? Wellington definitely wrote 'three eagles' in his draft, and this was obviously his understanding at the moment of writing, at around 9–10 a.m. on 19 June. But the *Gazette* of 22 June states that there were 'two eagles'.

Part of the problem may be that original draft of the Despatch remained in Brussels, first for the clerk to produce the fair-hand official or London version and secondly for making the Dutch version (that second version does not mention the eagles at all, but has supplementary information on the numbers of prisoners), and stayed among the Duke's papers. All the changes made on the draft were in Wellington's own hand. In writing out the fair version the clerk may have been given amendments additional to those, and updated his version accordingly: we simply do not know. We do know that Wellington made one addition to the Despatch in time for it to be recorded with the draft, and that is the first postscript (paragraph 32). But the second postscript (paragraph 33) that was handed to Percy, *and duly appeared* in the *Gazette* of 22 June, was written so late that there was no time to take a file copy to place with the draft.

Once the fair version was finished and taken to the Duke to sign, it would then have been given to Major Percy, who left Brussels that same 19 June, together with the eagles. He reached Ostend, 72 miles from Brussels, at noon on the 20th; and Admiral Malcolm ordered the *Peruvian* to carry him across the Channel.[15] He had to cover another 72 miles to reach London in mid-evening of 21 June, where he handed the Despatch to Lord Bathurst and was taken by him to the Prince Regent, with the eagles. The government printers worked overnight and issued the *Gazette* the next morning.

This timetable suggests that Wellington had little time to reconsider or revise the Despatch before Percy left. Information was still coming in, but it was essential to get the news to London at top speed and Percy had to set off in haste. Reporting the downfall of Napoleon was far more urgent than polishing the phrases of the Despatch, although in dashing it off so quickly Wellington silently passed over and failed to do justice to several meritorious units.[16]

The Despatch, once sent, received no further consideration from him. The need to see to the problems of the army was his next task, and the scale was daunting. Wellington's Adjutant General, DQMG, Military Secretary and several ADCs, two of his three corps commanders, and three of his five British divisional commanders were wounded, dying, or dead. There were casualties by the thousand all requiring treatment. Fresh troops and ammunition were urgently needed. It was essential to keep the Bourbon royalists from doing something silly and stimulating opposition inside France.

Given the disorganised state of the army after this most destructive battle, we do not know whether Wellington was given the eagles or was merely told of them. We do know that Sergeant Ewart of the Scots Greys captured the eagle of the *45e Ligne* and that Captain Clark-Kennedy of the Royal Dragoons took that of the *105e Ligne* (though the name of Corporal Styles confused the issue). There was a story that Private Penfold of the Inniskillings took one but that it disappeared in Brussels. One of the Duke's AQMGs even claimed on 20 June that a private of the 42nd Foot was said to have captured one.[17] We do not know from whom Percy received the eagles. We do not know whether the Despatch was sealed, or carried unsealed (thus enabling Percy to read it). It is impossible that Percy should have lost an eagle on his journey, and as nobody has ever identified the French unit that lost the *third* eagle, it seems likely that he was handed only two. But between Percy's arrival and the *Gazette* publication someone made the change to the text of the Despatch – Bathurst intentionally or the printers unintentionally.

That is the best solution that I can find for the conundrum.

Notes to Appendix 1

1. *WSD*, x, p.531.
2. After this sentence Wellington changed to a new pen with finer strokes, and used it to the end of the Despatch. It probably marked his arrival at his Brussels residence.
3. The version published in Gurwood's *Despatches* follows the draft, not the *Gazette*. Here Gurwood has 'repulsed', but the *Gazette* for some reason has 'defeated'.
4. There is a gap here. De Bas in the Dutch version gives 'd'Aubremé' at this point, whereas the *Gazette* has 'Vanhope'. Was the name Vanhope dreamt up by the Duke at the last minute, or was it suggested by Percy when Bathurst read the Despatch and noted the gap?
5. The word 'own' is perfectly clear in the draft, and is so printed by Gurwood, but the *Gazette* omits it.
6. Paragraphs 30 and 31 are on the recto side of a half sheet of paper; the first P.S. (paragraph 32) is on the verso.
7. The *Gazette* has 'two eagles'.
8. I mention this as in 2005 an article by Nigel Sale in *J RUSI* accused Wellington of secretly priming Bathurst with false information about the overthrow of the *Garde* so as to deprive the 52nd Foot of any part in what Sale believed was its exclusive victory in that action. He claimed that the information was sent by Wellington, either in a letter that nobody ever saw, then or later; or by word of mouth through Major Percy (carrying the *Despatch*) – that was never hinted at by Percy or anyone else: in other words the argument seemed to rely for proof on the thesis that the best evidence for a surmise is where there is *no evidence*. It was claimed (*inter alia*) that the two British corps commanders were suborned from giving credit to the 52nd: that Uxbridge's step in the peerage to Marquess was Wellington's means of stopping Uxbridge's mouth, though why the cavalry commander should be at all involved in this purely infantry matter is nowhere explained, and Uxbridge's performance that day was surely worthy of his sovereign's recognition; Hill's barony was likewise adduced as a bribe – though it was granted in 1814. There followed an exchange in the *Journal*'s correspondence columns, where I pointed out (*J RUSI*, vol. 151 [3], June 2006, p. 8) that there was *a simple and extant documentary explanation* for Bathurst's statement, quoting the Apsley letter (with its source) and comparing it with the statement in the Lords and the 19th paragraph of the *Despatch*. Thus, against a surmise of conspiracy for which there was no evidence, I submitted long-published evidence for a straightforward explanation. The earlier claims reappeared essentially unchanged in 2015, and I note that Gareth Glover has demolished most of them in his book on the defeat of the *Garde*, app. 2.
9. In the original French, in *Belle-Alliance*, no. 123, p. 286.
10. In German, in *Belle-Alliance*, no. 122, p. 285.
11. In an English translation in C. Kelly, *A full and Circumstantial Account of the Memorable Battle of Waterloo* (1817, repr, 1818), p. 64.
12. Pflugk-Harttung, *Vorgeschichte*, app. IX, no. 24.

13. Willem to Constant, in De Bas, *Prins Frederik*, p. 765.
14. *WSD*, x, p. 551.
15. Sir Pulteney Malcolm's Journal, 20 June 1815, TNA, ADM.50/87. The sea passage could take 24 hours in calm weather. In Disraeli's *Coningsby* (1844), book 7, chap. 1, we find that light coaches on modern roads in daylight could do 'their ten miles in the hour'.
16. At a quick count, eighty to ninety words each are given to the three efforts at Hougoumont, La Haye Sainte with Uxbridge's charge, and Ney's great cavalry attacks, and about 150 altogether to the crisis and Bülow's appearance and the victorious counter-attack. The officers of Colborne's 1/52nd were outraged (though Colborne reproved them for this) and never really forgave the Duke for ignoring their devastating attack on the *Garde*'s flank, and many other regiments likewise felt unfairly neglected.
17. For a neat account of these questions see Ian Fletcher, *Galloping at Everything*, pp. 250–1. Also Felton Hervey AQMG, in *WA*, i, No. 2.

Appendix 2

Gneisenau's Report

The Operations of the Prussian Army of the Lower Rhine

The German original is in Delbrück, *Gneisenau*, iv, pp. 703–9; there is a French translation in *WSD*, x, pp. 502–6; this English version comes primarily from Booth's *Battle of Waterloo* (1817), ii, pp. 201–7, but corrected in places after comparison with the German text. Gneisenau's letter of 17 June recounting the battle of Ligny is given in the appendix to Chapter 31.

*

It was on 15 June that Napoleon, after having collected on the 14th five corps of his army, and the several corps of the Guard, between Maubeuge and Beaumont, commenced hostilities. The points of concentration of the four Prussian corps, were Fleurus, Namur, Ciney, and Hannut, the situation of which made it possible to unite the army at one of these points in 24 hours.

On the 15th, Napoleon advanced by Thuin, upon both banks [*beiden Seiten*] of the Sambre, against Charleroi. General Ziethen had collected I Corps near Fleurus, and had on that day a very warm action with the enemy who, having taken Charleroi, directed his march upon Fleurus. General Ziethen maintained himself in his position near that place.

Field Marshal Blücher intending to fight a great battle with the enemy as soon as possible, the three other corps of the Prussian army were consequently directed upon Sombreffe, 1½ [German] miles [about 6 British miles] from Fleurus, where II and III Corps were to arrive on the 15th, and IV Corps on the 16th. Lord Wellington had united his army between Ath and Nivelles on the 15th, which enabled him to assist Field Marshal Blücher, in case the battle should be fought on the 16th.[1]

Battle of 16 June at Ligny

The Prussian army was posted on the heights between Brie and Sombreffe, and beyond the latter place, and occupied with a large force the villages of St Amand and Ligny situated to its front. However, only three Corps had joined, the fourth, which was stationed between Liège and Hannut, had been delayed in its march by several circumstances and had not yet come up. Nevertheless Field Marshal Blücher resolved to give battle, Lord Wellington having already set in motion a strong detachment [*eine starke Abteilung*] of his army to support him, as well as all [*alle*] his reserve stationed in the environs of Brussels, and IV Corps of the Prussian army being also on the point of arriving.

At 3 p.m. the battle began. The enemy brought up over 130,000 men. The Prussian army was 80,000 strong. The village of St Amand was the first point attacked by the enemy, who carried it after a vigorous resistance. He then directed his efforts against Ligny. It is a large village, solidly built, situated on a rivulet of the same name. It was there that a contest began which may be considered as one of the most obstinate recorded in history. Villages have often been taken and retaken; but here the combat continued for five hours in the villages themselves, and the movements back and forth were confined to a very narrow space. Fresh troops continually came up on both sides. Each army had great masses of infantry behind the part of the village that it occupied, and these maintained the struggle, and were continually renewed by the reinforcements that they received from their rear, as well as from the heights on the right and left. Fire from very nearly two hundred cannon of both armies was directed against the village, which was on fire in several places at once. From time to time the combat extended along the whole line, the enemy having also directed numerous troops against III Corps; however, the main combat was near Ligny. Things seemed to take a favourable turn for the Prussian troops, a part of St Amand village having been retaken by a battalion commanded by the Field Marshal in person, as a result of which we had regained a height that had been abandoned after the loss of St Amand. Despite this the battle continued around Ligny with the same fury. The issue seemed to depend on the arrival of the English or on that of IV Corps of the Prussian army; in fact the arrival of the latter would have afforded the Field Marshal the means of making an immediate attack with the right wing, from which great success might be expected. But we received news that the detachment of the English army, intended for our support, was violently attacked by a corps of the French army, and that it was with great difficulty that it retained the position of Quatre Bras; and IV

Corps did not appear, so that we were forced to maintain the contest, alone, against an army greatly superior in numbers.

The evening was already much advanced, and the combat around Ligny continued with the same fury, and equal success on both sides. We pined in vain for the arrival of that much-needed help; the danger became more urgent by the hour. All our troops were engaged or had already been committed and there were no fresh units to hand. Suddenly an enemy infantry force which, under favour of dusk, had made a circuit round the village without being observed, simultaneously as some *cuirassier* regiments had forced a passage on the other side, took in the rear the main body of our army, which was posted behind the houses. This surprise on the part of the enemy was decisive, especially at the moment when our cavalry, also posted on a height behind the village, was repulsed by the enemy's cavalry in repeated attacks.

Our infantry, placed behind Ligny, though forced to retreat, did not let itself become discouraged, either by being surprised by the enemy in the dusk, a circumstance that in a man's mind exaggerates the dangers to which he finds himself exposed, or by the idea of being surrounded on all sides. Formed in mass, it coolly repulsed all the cavalry attacks and retreated to the heights in good order, whence it continued its retirement upon Tilly [*gegen Tilly*]. Because of the sudden irruption of the enemy's cavalry, several of our cannons, in their precipitate retreat, had taken directions that led them into defiles in which they necessarily fell into disorder; in this manner fifteen pieces fell into the hands of the enemy. At 4 [German] miles from the battlefield the army formed again; the enemy did not venture to pursue it. The village of Brie remained in our possession during the night, as well as Sombreffe, where General Thielemann had fought with III Corps, and whence at daybreak he began to retreat towards Gembloux, where IV Corps under General Bülow had at last [*eingetroffen*] arrived during the night. In the morning I and II Corps proceeded beyond the defile of Mont St Guibert. Our loss in killed and wounded was great; however, the enemy took from us no prisoners except some of our wounded.

The battle was lost, but not our honour. Our soldiers had fought with a bravery that equalled every expectation; their fortitude remained unshaken, because everyone retained confidence in his own strength. On this day Field Marshal Blücher had encountered the greatest dangers. A cavalry charge that he personally led, had failed. While that of the enemy was vigorously pursuing ours, a shot struck the Field Marshal's horse. The animal, far from being stopped by this bullet, began to gallop convulsively until it fell dead. The Field Marshal, stunned by the violent fall, lay entangled under his horse. The enemy's *cuirassiers*, following up their advantage, advanced; our last horseman had already passed by the Field Marshal, only an adjutant remained with him, having just dismounted to share his fate. The danger was great, but Heaven watched over us. Pursuing their charge, the enemy passed rapidly by the Field Marshal without seeing him; the next moment a second charge of our cavalry having repulsed them, they again passed him by with the same precipitation and without seeing him any more than they had done the first time. Then, with difficulty the Field Marshal was freed from under the dead horse, and he immediately mounted a dragoon horse.

On the evening of the 17th of June the Prussian army concentrated in the vicinity of Wavre. Napoleon put himself in motion against Lord Wellington upon the great road from Charleroi to Brussels. An English detachment maintained a severe contest with the enemy around Quatre Bras. Lord Wellington had taken a position on the road to Brussels, with his right wing resting on La Haye. From this position Lord Wellington wrote to the Field Marshal that he was willing to accept battle if the Field Marshal would support him with two corps [*zwei Armeekorps*]. The Field Marshal promised to come with his whole army, and further proposed that, if Napoleon should not attack, the Allies themselves with their whole united force should fall upon him the next day. This shows how little the battle of the 16th had damaged the Prussian army or reduced its morale. Thus was battle decided upon.

The Battle of the 18th

At daybreak the Prussian army began to move. IV and II Corps marched by St Lambert where they were to take position, covered by the forest near Frischermont, to take the enemy in rear when the moment should prove favourable. I Corps was to operate by Ohain, on the right flank of the enemy. III Corps was to follow slowly, in order to afford help in case of need.

The battle began about 10 a.m. The English army occupied the heights of Mont St Jean; the French were on the heights forward of Plancenoit: the former was about 80,000 strong, the enemy above 130,000. In a short while the battle became general all along the line. It seems that Napoleon designed to throw the left wing back upon the centre and thus to effect the separation of the English army from the Prussian, which he believed to be retreating upon Maastricht.

For this purpose he had placed the greatest part of his reserve in the centre, against his right wing, and upon this part he attacked the English with fury. The British army fought with a valour that is impossible to surpass.

The repeated charges of the Old Guard failed against the intrepidity of the Scottish regiments; and at every encounter the French cavalry was repulsed by the English cavalry. But the enemy's superior numbers were too great. Napoleon continually brought forward considerable masses against the English, and with whatever firmness they maintained themselves in their position, it was impossible that such heroic exertions should not have a limit.

It was 4.30 p.m. The excessive difficulties of the St Lambert defile had considerably delayed the march of the Prussian columns, so that only two brigades of IV Corps had arrived at the concealed position assigned to them. The decisive moment had come and there was not an instant to be lost. The Prussian generals did not suffer it to escape; they resolved immediately to begin the attack with such troops as they had at hand. And so General Bülow, with two brigades and a corps of cavalry, advanced rapidly upon the rear of the enemy's right wing. The enemy did not lose his presence of mind; he instantly turned his reserves against us, and a murderous struggle began. The combat remained long uncertain, while the battle with the English army still continued with the same violence.

Towards 6 p.m. we received news that General Thielemann, with III Corps, was attacked near Wavre by a very considerable corps of the enemy, and that they were already disputing the possession of the town. The Field Marshal, however, did not let himself be disturbed by this news; it was where he was, and nowhere else, that the affair would be decided. A combat maintained with tenacity and continually supported by fresh troops could alone secure victory, and if it were obtained here, any reverse sustained near Wavre was of little consequence. The columns, therefore, continued their movements.

It was 7.30 p.m. and still the issue of the battle was uncertain. The whole of IV Corps and a part of II under General Pirch had successively come up. The French troops fought with desperate fury; however some uncertainty was seen in their movements and it was observed that some pieces were retreating. At this moment, the first columns of General Ziethen's corps arrived at the points of attack near the village of Smouhen, on the enemy's right flank, and instantly charged. This moment marked the enemy's defeat. His right wing was broken in three places; he abandoned his positions; our troops rushed forward at the charge and attacked him on all sides, while, at the same time, the whole British line advanced.

Circumstances were entirely favourable to the Prussian army's attack. The terrain here rose in terraces, so that our artillery could freely open fire from the summit of a great many heights gradually rising one behind another, in between which the infantry could descend to the plain, formed in brigades and in the greatest order, while fresh units continually appeared out of the woods on the height behind us.

However, the enemy retained some means of retreat, until Plancenoit village, which was in his rear and which was defended by the Guard, was, after several bloody attacks, carried by storm. From that time the retreat became a rout, which soon spread through the entire French army [*Nun wurde aus dem Rückzuge eine Flucht, die bald das ganze französiche Heer ergriff*], and in its dreadful confusion swept away everything that tried to halt it, and soon assumed the appearance of a flight of an army of savages [*wilder*].

It was 9.30 p.m. The Field Marshal assembled all his senior officers and gave them orders to send every last man and horse in pursuit of the enemy. The head of the army accelerated its march. The French army, pursued without respite, became entirely disorganised. The *chaussée* resembled an immense shipwreck; it was covered by a vast quantity of cannon, powder wagons, carriages, baggage, arms, and debris of every kind. Those of the enemy who had sought to rest for a while and had not expected to be pursued so quickly, were chased from more than nine bivouacs. In some villages they tried to make a stand, but as soon as they heard the beating of our drums, or the trumpet's sound, they either fled or hid in the houses, where they were cut down or made prisoners. Moonlight greatly favoured the pursuit, and the entire march was but a continual chase through the houses and in the cornfields.

At Genappe the enemy had dug in with cannon and overturned ammunition wagons and carriages. As we approached, we heard a great noise in the town and the sound of carriages; at the entrance we were exposed to a brisk fire of musketry; we answered with some cannon shot, followed by a *Hurrah*, and in an instant the town was ours. It was here that, among many other equipages, Napoleon's carriage was taken. He had just abandoned it to mount on horseback, and in his hurry had forgotten in it his sword and hat. Thus matters went on until daybreak. About 40,000 men in the most complete disorder, the remains of the entire army, have saved themselves, retreating through Charleroi, some without arms, and taking with them only twenty-seven pieces out of all their numerous artillery.

At 3 o'clock Napoleon had sent from the battlefield a courier to Paris with the news that victory was no longer in doubt. A few hours later he no longer had an army. We have not yet any exact account of the enemy's loss; it is enough to know that two-thirds of the whole were killed, wounded, or prisoners; among the latter are Generals Mouton, Duhesme and Compans. Up to the present about 300 cannon and over 500 powder wagons are in our hands.

Few victories have been so complete, and there is certainly no example of an army, two days after losing a battle, engaging in such an action and so gloriously sustaining it. Honour to troops capable of so much firmness and valour.

In the middle of the position occupied by the French army and right on the summit stands a farm called La Belle Alliance. All the Prussian columns had been marching towards this farm, visible from all sides, where Napoleon stood during the battle, whence he sent his orders, where he flattered himself with hopes of victory, and where his ruin was decided. By happy chance it was there also that Marshal Blücher and Lord Wellington met in the dark and saluted each other as victors.

In commemoration of the alliance that now subsists between the English and Prussian nations, of the union of the two armies, and their reciprocal confidence, the Field Marshal desires that this battle should bear the name of La Belle Alliance.

Headquarters, Merbes le Château, 20 June 1815,

By order of Field-Marshal Prince Blücher, [signed]

GENERAL COUNT VON GNEISENAU

Note to Appendix 2

1. Note that both Booth and the French version ignore the date ('*den 15ten*') given for Wellington's concentration, and as to the assistance in battle they mistranslate the date, writing 'should be fought on the 15th', whereas the German has '*am 16ten*'.

Appendix 3

Napoleon's Accounts

1815 and 1820

Bulletin on Ligny, Quatre Bras and Waterloo, *Correspondance de Napoleon,* no. 22,061. The despatch, finished at Laon on 20 June, was published in the *Moniteur,* 21 June 1815.

The Battle of Ligny, Near Fleurus

On the morning of the 16th the army occupied the following positions: the left wing, commanded by Marshal Ney, duc d'Elchingen, comprising the *1er* and *2e Corps* of infantry and the *2e* of Cavalry, occupied the position of Frasnes. The right wing, commanded by Marshal Grouchy, comprising the *3e* and *4e Corps* of infantry and the *3e Corps* of cavalry, occupied the heights behind Fleurus. The Emperor's headquarters were at Charleroi, where was also the *Garde Impériale* and the *6e Corps.*

The left wing had orders to march on Quatre Bras and the right on Sombreffe. The Emperor went to Fleurus with his *Garde.* Marshal Grouchy's columns on marching past Fleurus perceived the enemy army commanded by Field Marshal Blücher occupying the plateau of Bussy mill, to the left of the village of Sombreffe, and with its cavalry spread out well in advance of the road to Namur; its right was at St Amand, holding most of this village with strong forces, with before it a hollow [*ravin,* i.e. the Ligne brook] that formed its position.

The Emperor examined the enemy forces and the positions, and decided to attack without delay. This necessitated a change of front, the right going forward and pivoting on Fleurus. General Vandamme marched on St Amand, General Gérard on Ligny, and Marshal Grouchy on Sombreffe. The third [i.e. of four, and numbered the *7e*] division of *2e Corps,* commanded by General Girard, marched in reserve behind General Vandamme's corps.

The *Garde* and the *cuirassiers* of General Milhaud were placed on the heights of Fleurus.

These dispositions were completed by 3 o'clock in the afternoon.

General Lefol's division, part of General Vandamme's corps, was the first to engage and took St Amand, from which it chased the enemy with the bayonet, and throughout the entire battle it held St Amand's church and cemetery. But this village, which is very extensive, was the scene of several combats during the evening; the whole corps of General Vandamme was engaged there, the enemy engaging considerable numbers against him. General Girard, placed in reserve behind General Vandamme's *Corps*, turned the village with his the right and fought with his habitual bravery. The respective forces were supported on each side by some sixty cannon. On the right General Gérard attacked the village of Ligny, which was taken and retaken several times. On the extreme right Marshal Grouchy and General Pajol fought at Sombreffe village. The enemy amounted to 80,000–90,000 men and a large number of guns.

At 7 p.m. we were masters of all the villages along the hollow [*ravin*] that covered the enemy position; but the enemy still held the plateau of Bussy mill with all his masses.

The Emperor went with his *Garde* to the village of Ligny; General Gérard launched General Pécheux with what remained of the reserve, for almost all the troops had been engaged in this village. Eight battalions of the *Garde* went in with the bayonet, behind them the four service squadrons, General Delort's *cuirassiers*, those of General Milhaud and the *Grenadiers à Cheval* of the *Garde*. The *Vieille Garde* made a bayonet attack on the enemy columns that were on the heights of Bussy, and in an instant covered the field of battle with dead. The service squadron attacked and broke a square, and the *cuirassiers* drove the enemy in all directions. At 7.30 p.m. we had [taken] forty cannon, many carriages, flags and prisoners, and the enemy sought safety in a headlong retreat. At 10 p.m. the battle was over and we found ourselves masters of the entire battlefield.

The partisan General Lützow was captured, and prisoners assured us that Field Marshal Blücher had been wounded. The elite of the Prussian army was destroyed in this battle, with its loss at least 15,000 men; ours were 3,000 killed or wounded.

On the left Marshal Ney had marched on Quatre Bras with a division that overthrew an English division it found there. But, attacked by the Prince of Orange with 25,000 men, partly English, partly Hanoverian in English pay, he fell back on his position of Frasnes. There combats multiplied, the enemy vainly trying to take the place. The duc d'Elchingen awaited the

1er Corps, but it only came at night, so he limited himself to guarding his position. The flag of the English 69th Foot fell into our hands when the *8e Cuirassiers* attacked its square. The Duke of Brunswick was killed and the Prince of Orange was wounded. We have been told that the enemy had many important personages and generals killed or wounded. We put the English loss at 4,000–5000 men; ours on that front were very considerable, amounting to 4,200 men killed or wounded. This combat ended with the night. Lord Wellington later evacuated Quatre Bras and went to Genappe.

On the morning of the 17th the Emperor went to Quatre Bras, whence he marched to attack the English army, which he pushed with the left wing and the reserve to the entrance to the forest of Soignies. The right wing went via Sombreffe in pursuit of Field Marshal Blücher who fell back on Wavre, where it seems he wished to establish himself.

At 10 p.m. the English army, its centre occupying Mont St Jean, positioned itself before the forest of Soignies; as it would have required three hours to mount an attack, we were obliged to put it off to the next day.

The Emperor's headquarters were established at the farm of Le Caillou, near Plancenoit. The rain fell in torrents. Thus on the day of the 16th the left, right and the reserve were all engaged across a distance of about two leagues.

The Battle of Mont Saint Jean

At nine in the morning, the rain having slackened somewhat, the *1er Corps* moved and placed itself with its left on the road to Brussels and opposite the village of Mont St Jean, which seemed to be the centre of the enemy position. The *2e Corps* had its right on the Brussels road, with its left on a small wood a cannon's distance from the English army. The *cuirassiers* stood in reserve behind, and the *Garde* in reserve on the heights. The *6e Corps* with the cavalry of General Domon, under the orders of Comte Lobau, was ordered to move behind our right, to oppose a Prussian corps that seemed to have escaped Marshal Grouchy and to intend to fall on our right flank, an intention that we learned from our own reports and from a letter of a Prussian general, carried by an orderly who was taken by our scouts. The troops were full of ardour.

We estimated the strength of the English army at 80,000 men, and thought the Prussian corps, which could be in action by the evening, 15,000 men. The enemy forces therefore were more than 90,000 men; we were less numerous.

At noon all preparations were complete and Prince Jerome, commanding a division of *2e Corps*, and on the extreme left, moved against the wood, part of which was held by the enemy. A cannonade began, the enemy supporting with thirty cannon the troops sent to hold the wood. We likewise deployed artillery. At 1 p.m. Prince Jerome was master of all the wood and the entire English army fell back behind a screen [*rideau*]. Comte d'Erlon then attacked the village of Mont St Jean, supporting his attack with eighty cannon, firing a terrible cannonade that made the English army suffer greatly, every shot hit the plateau. A brigade of the *1re Division* of Comte d'Erlon took Mont St Jean village; a second brigade was charged by a corps of English cavalry which inflicted heavy casualties. At the same moment an English cavalry division charged the battery of Comte d'Erlon by its right and upset several pieces, but General Milhaud's *cuirassiers* charged this division of which three regiments were broken and cut up.

It was 3 p.m. The Emperor sent the *Garde* onto the ground that *1er Corps* had originally held, that corps now being further forward. The Prussian division, as expected, began to engage the skirmishers of Comte Lobau, plunging its fire all along our right flank. It was advisable to await the outcome of this attack before doing anything elsewhere and consequently all the resources of the reserve were in readiness to assist Comte Lobau and to crush the Prussian corps when it should advance.

That done, the Emperor planned to develop an attack by Mont St Jean village, from which one hoped for a decisive success; but due to a moment of impatience so frequent in our military annals and which has often been so fatal for us, the reserve cavalry, seeing the English make a movement of retreat to shelter from our batteries, from which they had suffered so much, crowned [*couronna*] the heights of Mont St Jean and charged the infantry. This movement which, made at the right time and supported by reserves, would have decided the day, being made in isolation and before matters on the right had been concluded, became fatal. Having no means of countermanding it, [and] the enemy deploying large masses of infantry and cavalry, and the two *cuirassier* divisions being engaged, all our cavalry rushed at the same moment to support their comrades. There, for three hours, numerous charges took place which led to the breaking of several squares and [taking] six flags of the English infantry, an advantage not proportionate to the losses our cavalry suffered from the hail of fire and fusillades. It was impossible to use our infantry reserves until they should have repulsed the flank attack of the Prussian corps. That attack continually extended, and perpendicularly to our right flank. The Emperor sent General Duhesme and the *Jeune Garde* there with several reserve batteries. The enemy was contained, was pushed back and retreated, having exhausted his forces, so that we had nothing to fear. This was the moment indicated for an attack on the enemy's centre.

As things stood, the battle was won. We occupied all the positions that the enemy held at the start of the action; our cavalry having been employed too soon and badly we could no longer hope for a decisive success. But Marshal Grouchy, having learned of the movement of a Prussian corps, marched on the rear of that corps, thus assuring us of a striking success during the next day. After eight hours of firing and charges by infantry and cavalry, all the army saw with satisfaction that the battle was gained and the battlefield in our power.

Around 8.30 p.m. the four battalions of the *Moyenne Garde*, which had been sent to the plateau beyond Mont St Jean to support the *cuirassiers*, being irritated by the enemy cannon-fire, marched with the bayonet against the enemy to take his batteries. The day was ending; a charge on their flank by several English squadrons threw them into disorder; the fleeing men came back across the valley; the neighbouring regiments, seeing some troops belonging to the *Garde* in flight, thought they were the *Vieille Garde*, and gave way; cries of 'All is lost, the *Garde* has been repulsed!' were heard; some soldiers even say that malevolents stationed at various points cried '*Sauve qui peut!*' However that may be, a terrified panic spread all at once across the entire battlefield; men dashed in the greatest disorder on the line of communications; soldiers, gunners, caissons fought to reach it; the *Vieille Garde* that was in reserve was assailed and itself borne away.

In an instant the army was nothing but a confused mass, all arms were mixed up, it was impossible to re-form a corps. The enemy who saw this astonishing confusion, launched cavalry columns; the disorder grew, the confusion of night made it impossible to rally the troops and show them their error.

Thus a battle concluded, a day finished, the false measures put right, the greatest success assured for the next day, all was lost by a moment of panic terror. Even the service squadrons, drawn up beside the Emperor, were overthrown and disorganised by these tumultuous waves, and there was nothing to do but follow the torrent. The reserve *parcs*, the baggage that had not been sent beyond the Sambre and everything still on the battlefield remained in the enemy's power. There was no means of waiting for the troops of our right. That was the fate of the bravest army in the world, when disordered and when its organisation no longer exists.

The Emperor passed the Sambre at Charleroi at 5 a.m. on the 19th. Philippeville and Avesnes have been given as assembly points. Prince Jerome, General Morand and the other generals have already rallied a part of the army. Marshal Grouchy with the corps of the right is operating on the lower Sambre.

The enemy's loss must have been very great, to judge from the colours we have taken from him and by the retrograde movements he made. Ours cannot be calculated until the troops have rallied. Before the disorder broke out we had already suffered considerable losses, especially in our cavalry, so fatally and yet so bravely engaged. Despite these losses this valiant cavalry constantly guarded the position it had taken from the English, and only abandoned it when the tumult and disorder of the battlefield forced it to. In the middle of the night and with obstacles encumbering the road, it could not, however, maintain its organisation.

The artillery as usual covered itself with glory.

The carriages of the imperial staff stayed in their ordinary position, no retrograde movement being judged necessary. In the course of the night they fell into the hands of the enemy.

Such was the issue of the battle of Mont St Jean, glorious for the French armies and yet so fatal.

*

The End of the Battle of Waterloo: The Later Version

Having given Napoleon's earliest account of the battle, I print below an extract from his third version, first published in 1820 and included in the *Correspondance*, volume 31.[1] For the intermediate version, dictated to Gourgaud and published in 1818, the reader is referred to Gourgaud's *Campaign of 1815*, pp. 103–14 in the English-language edition. I have not included the 'Observations' that conclude the intermediate and final versions. My extract from 'The 1815 Campaign' begins at Chapter 6, Section X, that is to say, from about the point where the *Bulletin* had stated, 'As things stood, the battle was won':

As soon as Bülow's attack had been repulsed, the Emperor ordered General Drouot, who served as Aide Major-General of the *Garde*, to assemble all his *Garde* in front of La Belle Alliance farm, where he stood with eight battalions drawn up in two lines; the other eight having marched to the support of the *Jeune Garde* and to defend Plancenoit. However the cavalry, which continued to occupy the position on the plateau, thereby dominating the entire battlefield, having seen General Bülow's movement, but taking confidence from the reserves of the *Garde* that it saw placed to contain him, felt no disquiet and shouted cries of victory when it saw that force pushed back; it awaited only the arrival of the *Garde* infantry for victory to be decided; but it was astonished when it saw arriving the numerous columns of Marshal Blücher. Some regiments moved back, as the Emperor saw. It was of the utmost importance to restore the cavalry's confidence, and seeing that it needed another quarter of an hour to rally all the *Garde*, he placed himself at the head of four battalions and advanced on the left below La Haye Sainte, sending his ADCs to ride along the line to announce the arrival of Grouchy, and say that with a little constancy victory would come. General Reille united his entire corps on the left in front of the château of Goumont, and prepared his attack; it was important that the *Garde* should all be together in attacking, but the other eight battalions were still in rear. Dominated by events, seeing the cavalry out of countenance and that it required an infantry reserve to sustain it, he ordered General Friant to take four battalions of the *Moyenne Garde* in advance of the enemy's attack; the cavalry settled and marched forward with its customary intrepidity. The four battalions of the *Garde* threw back all whom they encountered; the charges of the cavalry spread terror in the English ranks. Ten minutes later the other *Garde* battalions arrived; the Emperor ranged them by brigades: two battalions in battle [order] and two in columns on the right and left, the 2nd brigade in echelons; this combined the advantage of the two orders. The sun had set. General Friant, wounded, passing at this moment, said that all was going well, that the enemy seemed to be forming a rearguard to cover his retreat, but that it would be entirely broken as soon as the rest of the *Garde* should come up. It needed a quarter of an hour! It was at this moment that Marshal Blücher arrived at La Haye and overthrew the French corps that defended it: it was the *4e Division* of *1er Corps*: it fell into rout and put up only a slight resistance. Although attacked by four times its own numbers, although it showed little resolution, and although it was sheltering [*crénelée*] among the houses, it was night and Marshal Blücher would not have time to force the village. It is there where it is said was heard the cry '*Sauve qui peut!*' The hole made, the line broken by the lack of vigour of the troops at La Haye, the cavalry swamped the battlefield; Bülow marched ahead. Comte Lobau put a good face upon it. The throng was such that a change of front had to be ordered to the *Garde*, that had been drawn up to go forward. This change of front was performed in a orderly fashion; the *Garde* faced about, the left on the side of La Haye Sainte, the front to the Prussians and the attack from La Haye; immediately after, each battalion formed square. The four service squadrons charged the Prussians. At this moment the English cavalry brigade that came from Ohain marched forward, and these 2,000 horsemen penetrated between General Reille and the *Garde*. The disorder became appalling across the entire battlefield; the Emperor had only time to throw himself inside the protection of one of the *Garde* squares. If the reserve division of cavalry under General Guyot had not been engaged without orders in support of the *cuirassiers* of Kellermann, it could have repulsed this charge, stopped the English cavalry penetrating the battlefield, [and] the *Garde à Pied* could have contained all the efforts of the enemy. General Bülow marched by his left, spreading over the whole battlefield. Night increased the disorder and worsened everything: had it been day and could the troops have seen the Emperor, they would have rallied. Nothing was possible in the obscurity. The *Garde* began to retreat. The enemy fire was already 400 *toises* [800 yards] from the rear, and the roads were cut. The Emperor, with his staff, remained for a long while with the *Garde* regiments on a mound, and four guns there fired into the valley: the last shot wounded the English general Uxbridge. Finally there was not a moment to lose, the Emperor could only retire across the fields: cavalry, infantry, artillery, all went pell-mell. The staff reached the little town of Genappe, where it was hoped to rally a rearguard, but the disorder was terrible and all efforts were in vain. It was 10 p.m. It being impossible to organise a defence, the Emperor placed his hopes in Girard's division, the third in the *2e Corps*, that he had left on Ligny battlefield, and to which he had sent orders to move to Quatre Bras to support the retreat.

Never had the French army fought better than on this day, displaying prodigies of valour; and the superiority of French troops, infantry, cavalry, artillery, over the enemy was such that, without the arrival of the I and II Prussian corps, a complete victory over the Anglo-Dutch army and General Bülow's corps would have been gained: that is to say one against two (62,000 men against 120,000).

The losses of the Anglo-Dutch army and of General Bülow in this battle were much higher than those of the French (and the French losses in the retreat were very considerable, for they lost 6,000 prisoners), which [French losses on the day] did not compensate for the allied losses on the four days, losses which they admit were 60,000 men: 11,300 English, 3,500 Hanoverians, 8,000 Belgians, Nassauers and Brunswickers, making a total 22,800 for the Anglo-Dutch; Prussians, 38,000; grand total 60,800 men. The French army's losses, even including those lost in the rout and as far as the gates of Paris, were 41,000 at most.

The *Garde Impériale* maintained its ancient reputation, but found itself engaged in unhappy circumstances; it was exposed to right and left and swamped by those fleeing and by the enemy as it entered the line, for if this *Garde* had been supported on its flanks it would have repulsed the united efforts of two enemy armies. For more than four hours 12,000 French cavalry were masters of part of the enemy position, fought against all the infantry and against 18,000 Anglo-Dutch cavalry, which were constantly thrown back in all their charges.

Houssaye remarked of the part that I have just quoted: '*Il y a quelque confusion et des inexactitudes dans les recits de Sainte Hélène*'.[2] There are indeed.

Notes to Appendix 3

1. In the Imperial quarto edition of 1869, xxxi, pp. 237–41; and in the Plon & Dumaine octavo edition of 1870, xxxi, pp. 197–200.
2. *1815, Waterloo,* Book III, chap. 5, sec. IV, p. 402 fn.; Eng. trans., n. 34 on p. 432, slightly differently worded.

Appendix 4

Bertrand's Letter of 10 June 1815

A New Piece in the Puzzle

I

In the first volume of my *Waterloo* I drew attention to Napoleon's abrupt style in command. He could take sudden snap decisions, could order re-organisations, could send away his chief of staff within days of the opening of the campaign, could issue orders, then suddenly change them. This could leave his subordinates puzzled and uncertain of how to resolve conflicting orders and even contradictions. I suggested that it was a material factor in the operations of the *Armée du Nord* in its final desperate campaign, when the short time-schedule, the adverse odds in manpower, the distances involved, and the quality of the enemy's leadership made prompt and crystal-clear orders absolutely vital.[1]

While my first volume was in the press a further instance was kindly brought to my attention by Mr Stephen M. Beckett, a newly discovered letter from a sale by Christie's in 2015. Until then we had relied upon Napoleon's Order of the Day of 10 June 1815, an order that I shall here term A. Now we also have a letter from Napoleon's Grand Marshal of the Palace General Bertrand, likewise dated 10 June 1815, written at Napoleon's behest. This letter, that I shall differentiate as letter B, in several respects conflicts with the Order of the Day.[2]

I referred to the 10 June Order of the Day in summary terms in my Volume 1, Chapter 19, Section V, and I contrasted it with Soult's own orders to the army that seemed seriously to misinterpret the Order of the Day in certain very material aspects. As my friend Philippe de Callataÿ has said, Soult's misinterpretation of a perfectly clear order seemed 'incredible and incomprehensible'. Letter B from Bertrand goes a long way to explain how the confusion arose. But to make the differences plain I shall now print in full, but in an English translation of my own, the texts both of the Order of the Day[3] and the Bertrand letter. I shall then draw some contrasts and comparisons,

and will conclude with a somewhat wider consideration of how orders and indeed general correspondence were handled at imperial headquarters.

II
A. The Order of the Day

Paris, 10 June: Order of the Day,

Positions of the Army on the 13th:

Headquarters and *Garde Impériale* at Avesnes;

Artillery and bridging-train before Avesnes on the glacis;

1er and *2e Reserve Corps de Cavalerie de la Réserve* at Beaumont, the *3e* and *4e* between Avesnes and Beaumont;

6e Corps at Beaumont. Its HQ behind [*derrière*]. If attaining Beaumont proves inconvenient it may stop halfway;

1er Corps at Pont-sur-Sambre [6 miles SW of Maubeuge]. This corps will move without passing Bavay. It will march by Le Quesnoy so keeping away from the enemy and its march-route concealed as long as possible. As one assumes that it should not take more than one day from Valenciennes, its march to arrive at the Sambre will not take place until the 13th;

2e Corps behind [*derrière*] Maubeuge in columns, on the route towards Thuin [*sic*], not passing the frontier; it must take care to be seen as little as possible;

3e Corps Philippeville;

Army of the Moselle [*4e Corps*], Mariembourg.

All communication along the frontier will stop. The soldiers will have four days' bread on their backs, a half-pound of rice, 50 cartridges. The batteries will be with the divisions, reserve batteries with their corps. The light cavalry of each corps will be in front of the corps. Each ambulance to its division. Each division will have on its auxiliary or military wagons eight days' bread, biscuits, and a troop of beasts for eight days.

[*signed*] Napoleon: for the Emperor, the Grand Marshal, Bertrand.

[*There was a postscript*]

No change should be made along the frontier. It must not be crossed at any point. Not a single cannon-shot must be fired. Nothing must be done that could alert the enemy. The present order will remain secret.

[*signed personally*] NAPOLEON.

B. The Bertrand Letter

Paris, 10 June 1815: To his Excellency the Chief of Staff,

Monsieur le Maréchal, The intention of the Emperor remains still to depart at 9 p.m. on Sunday the 11th, to be at Soissons at 4 in the morning, leaving at 9, to be at Laon at noon, and to leave in the evening so as to be at Avesnes at 2 a.m. on the 13th.

The Emperor's intention is that that general headquarters should travel to Avesnes on the 12th; that the *Garde Impériale* follows it on the 12th; that Avesnes should be vacated by *2e Corps* which will move behind Maubeuge; that you should bring Gen Erlon [*sic*] close to Maubeuge behind the Sambre and closed-up to *2e Corps*; and finally that likewise you arrange the forward movement [*déboucher*] of *6e Corps* which must be beyond [*avant*] Avesnes [18 miles west of Beaumont], behind the *2e*; that General Vandamme should be on the right; that he closes up and places himself between Beaumont and Avesnes [that is between 14 and 30 miles west of Philippeville] in such a way that the army shall be on the 12th:

2e Corps in the centre,
1er on the left,
3e on the right,
6e in rear,
Garde Impériale at Avesnes,
The mass of artillery and reserve, bridging-train in front [*en avant*] of Avesnes.

In the context of these dispositions the Emperor on the day of the 13th will see Generals Reille, d'Erlon, Vandamme, and will go forward on the 14th either by Maubeuge on Mons in the hope of attacking the English, or in marching by his right so as to follow the Prussians rapidly from Charleroy.

It is therefore necessary that the army corps [plural] should be placed so as to advance either by Maubeuge to attack Mons or towards the right.

I have the honour to send you the order of the day indicating the position of the army on the 13th; this order must be kept secret. I am sending it to Generals Reille, d'Erlon, Lobau, Vandamme, and I request that your Excellence should communicate it to Marshal Grouchy, to the commissary-in-chief and to the commander-in-chief of the artillery.

General Drouot has sent an order to the Marshal Duc de Treviso [Mortier] concerning the *Garde Impériale*.

The equipages of the Emperor's household are being ordered to move to Avesnes.

Will you please order that no cannon salvo shall be fired at Avesnes or Maubeuge, so that the enemy does not notice any movement. You may fire at Laon.

I remain, etc

Le grand maréchal, [signed] BERTRAND

III

The main differences between these documents are clear, both in dispositions and in style. If we plot the instructions on a map, we see at once that there is a great change of emphasis between the two documents.

The Order of the Day places a mass [*2e* and *1er Corps*] close to Maubeuge but with a directional indication north-eastwards towards 'Thuin', that is in the direction of Charleroi. This mass will be supported by the small *6e Corps* at Beaumont, south of Charleroi, and further east was to be *3e Corps* at Philippeville with the 'Army of the Moselle' (*4e Corps*) to its south at Mariembourg. The *Garde*, the artillery and bridging train remained with headquarters at Avesnes. Beaumont, Philippeville and Mariembourg are not well-suited positions for a main attack on Mons. But a force close to Thuin, Beaumont and Philippeville clearly menaces Charleroi and will have only a left flank looking towards Mons.

By contrast the Bertrand letter B pulls the weight of the army well to the west. As in the Order, the two-corps mass near Maubeuge remains there, but with *6e Corps* drawn west by 18 miles, about a day's march, to stand to the south of Maubeuge and near Beaufort, backed also at Avesnes by the *Garde*, artillery and so on. Vandamme's *3e Corps* is also drawn west by some 20 or more miles, and *well west* of Beaumont, yet is still deemed 'the right wing'. However, nothing is said about the rest of the proposed right wing or the cavalry. Indeed, as the letter states that it serves as covering note to the Order of the Day and as it requests Soult to forward the Order of the Day to Grouchy as commander of the cavalry, and to certain others, they would appear to be left confusingly in ignorance of the Emperor's revised dispositions as given by Bertrand's letter.

The indication from letter B is that on 10 June Napoleon was equally disposed to attack Wellington at Mons or Blücher at Charleroi, whereas the enclosed Order of the Day implied a main thrust at Charleroi. Some 24,500 infantry, 1,200 cavalry and 76 guns [*3e* and *6e Corps*] might need to move an extra (full day's) march depending on whether the 'western plan' was followed or not. Which instruction was to take precedence? Even if – perhaps even though[4] – Napoleon in his innermost thinking could have sensed

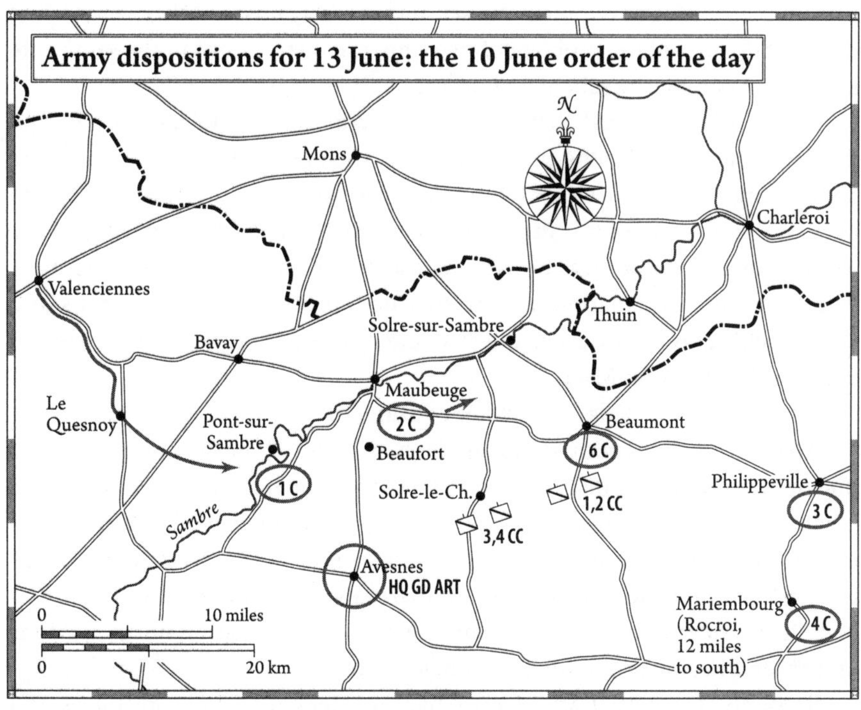
Army dispositions for 13 June: the 10 June order of the day
N
Mons
Charleroi
Valenciennes
Thuin
Solre-sur-Sambre
Bavay
Maubeuge
Le
Quesnoy
Pont-sur-
Sambre
2 C
Beaumont
Beaufort
6 C
1 C
Solre-le-Ch.
Philippeville
1,2 CC
3 C
Sambre
3,4 CC
Avesnes
HQ GD ART
Mariembourg
(Rocroi,
12 miles
to south)
4 C
0
10 miles
0
20 km

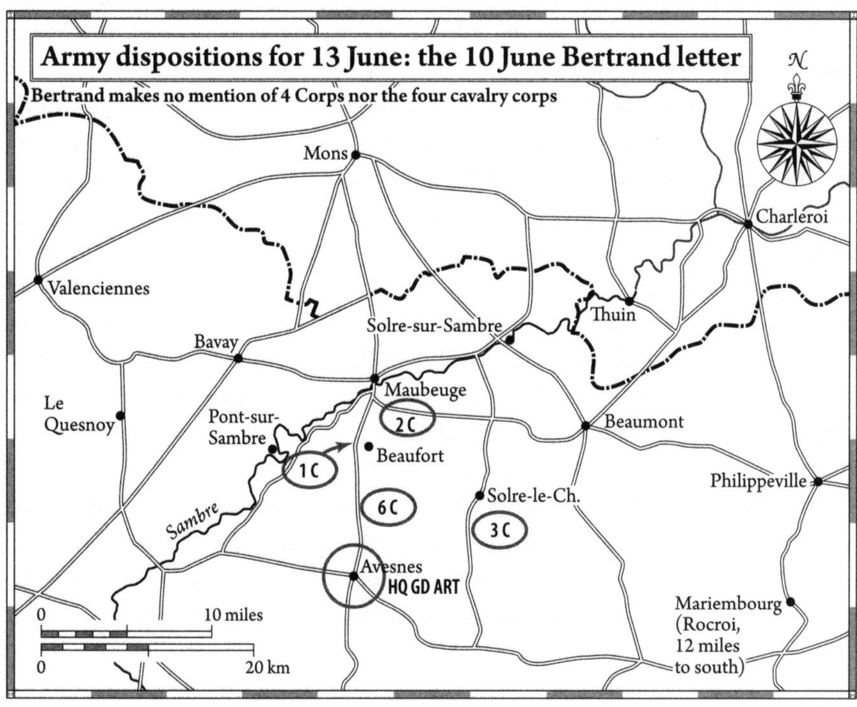
Army dispositions for 13 June: the 10 June Bertrand letter
Bertrand makes no mention of 4 Corps nor the four cavalry corps
N
Mons
Charleroi
Valenciennes
Thuin
Solre-sur-Sambre
Bavay
Maubeuge
Le
Quesnoy
Pont-sur-
Sambre
2 C
Beaumont
Beaufort
1 C
Philippeville
6 C
Solre-le-Ch.
3 C
Sambre
Avesnes
HQ GD ART
Mariembourg
(Rocroi,
12 miles
to south)
0
10 miles
0
20 km

certain reasons for developing one set of ideas as against another set, yet that does not dispose of the problem of two imperial instructions of the same date setting out conflicting movement orders.

Grouchy was ignored with respect for a plan for an attack on Mons, and yet surely he needed to be included in any such plan. We may say the same concerning Gérard's *4e Corps* ('Army of the Moselle'): that it was specified to be at Mariembourg for the attack on Charleroi, but was not mentioned in the Mons plan and Gérard was not among the commanders to be called to meet Napoleon. The explanation may be that he was still simply too far distant, still marching from Lorraine, and so could not be with the *Armée du Nord* in time for the attack on Mons.

But that in turn leads to a further consideration.

Apart from confirming that Napoleon intended from the outset to attack one or other of his enemies and not merely to manoeuvre between them (see Chapter 20, third paragraph), it indicates that although Wellington was ill-advised not to issue some warning order on 14 June he was wise in his remark to van Reede on the 15th that before marching he would wait until sure of Napoleon's intentions. His army could have been in position north of Mons and around Braine or Enghien in sufficient time.

Secondly, the actual attack on Charleroi, including both *4e Corps* and Grouchy's entire force of cavalry, was launched on 15 June with some 120,000 men and 350 guns under command. Reverting to the plans, if in the Mons case *4e Corps* was so far to the east as to be left out of account, Wellington would be attacked by fewer than 100,000 men and 300 guns, for Mons would have to be masked by a detachment[5] – and would *4e Corps* by itself at Mariembourg and Philippeville, even aided by the Reserve Cavalry, really have been sufficient to keep the Prussians in check? If Napoleon was well informed of Wellington's cantonments he could scarcely expect to reach the Duke's principal concentration line from Audenarde via Ath to Nivelles within 24 hours, and what of the Prussians meanwhile? Napoleon recognised Blücher's love of the headlong offensive whatever the risk. Would it be sensible to discount a Prussian march upon Nivelles, or perhaps more importantly upon Maubeuge and Mons and thus threatening Napoleon's line of communication within a couple of days?[6]

So what was to be done with Gérard's 15,500 infantry, 1,200 cavalry and 38 guns of *4e Corps*, and Grouchy's 12,100 cavalry and 48 guns? Nothing was said. Was it not dangerous at this late stage in the preparations to leave in confusion the intentions for no fewer than 55,500 men and 162 guns?

IV

The Order of the Day was short, staccato and imbued with the style of the Emperor, and while the Order was actually signed on the Emperor's behalf by the man at his side, the Grand Marshal of the Palace, the postscript was signed by Napoleon himself.

The Bertrand letter B was much smoother, more polite, elegantly scripted and without erasures or corrections (except for one word, '*les*' and the slip over the '*d*' in '*d'Erlon*'), and served as a gloss on the Order that it enclosed. It was written in the hand of one of Bertrand's usual staff, right down to and including '*Le grand maréchal*'; only the signature was by Bertrand.[7] Given the Emperor's rapid method of dictation the final version was clearly a fair copy of an initial draft by Bertrand.

Bertrand was a practical engineer officer and had commanded a corps in the later campaigns of the Empire. He was trusted and performed daily duties at the heart of the imperial establishment. He was no novice at war. Once Napoleon had ordered Soult away to the north on 7 June 1815, Bertrand was the officer in closest attendance on him, and would therefore have been the ideal man to take dictation on 10 June. In later years he said that he could on occasion induce the Emperor to change his mind when his reasoning was leading him astray. But here, on 10 June he signed the Order of the Day and then the covering letter despite plain inconsistencies and even contradictions between them. Either he did not notice them, or he left it to Soult to puzzle out the Emperor's ideas. He cannot have raised them with his master.[8]

V

There are two additional letters from Bertrand that shed some further light on his sense and his capacity when repeating orders: one dated 10 June and now made available by the anonymous purchaser from the Christie's sale, the other dated 11 June, first printed in 1913 by the Napoleonic scholar Arthur Chuquet.

On 10 June Bertrand again wrote from Paris to the Chief of Staff, who was then touring the northern provinces. To distinguish it from the letter previously quoted I shall term this letter C:

> *Monsieur le Maréchal,* Although I am sending an officer to Valenciennes [d'Erlon's *1er Corps* HQ], I require [*engage*] Your Excellency to send a duplicate of the order that will arrive sooner perhaps by the road from [or via? *route de*] Laon.[9] I pray Your Excellency to deliver to General Vandamme

> the order which I leave unsealed [*cachet volant*]. I remain, etc, *Le grand maréchal*, [signed] Bertrand.

Chuquet printed a Bertrand letter of 11 June, addressed to Reille of *2e Corps*:

> The Emperor's intention is that headquarters should go to Avesnes on the 12th; that the *Garde Impériale* should be there on the 12th; that your corps should vacate Avesnes and go behind Maubeuge, but that you personally remain so as to provide information as the Emperor is due to arrive at 2 a.m. on the 13th. It is very important that you place your corps behind Maubeuge so that the enemy perceives nothing. Forbid most strictly all communication.[10]

From letter C and Chuquet it is plain that Bertrand sent d'Erlon, if not the twelve copies of a message that Berthier was alleged always to have issued, at least two. More importantly, in all matters concerning Reille's corps he was completely faithful to the Order of the Day (and to its covering letter B). We see also that Reille as commander was informed only of what concerned him personally. Soult was to read Bertrand's instructions to Vandamme before sending them on. And it was not the orders to Reille but those to Vandamme where the mystery resides. Bertrand was totally accurate in relation to Reille's orders, but were his separate instructions to Vandamme *in conformity with the Order of the Day or with the 10 June covering letter B*, both of which stated unequivocally that they represented the Emperor's intentions?[11]

VI

What was Soult to do on reaching Avesnes on the 12th, and reading the Order of the Day and letter B – especially as Bertrand was meanwhile sending the Order directly to various subordinate commanders? Which document was the one to follow, which held priority? Soult was facing a virtual *fait accompli* by the time he opened the packet of papers and discovered the complications. This is how he treated matters in a series of instructions dated 12 June.[12]

Soult ordered Vandamme's *3e Corps* to march to Beaumont, and he also informed Napoleon of this. In other words he followed letter B and not the Order of the Day. To Gérard of *4e Corps* he wrote that, as they were behind schedule and would only reach Rocroi on 15 June although the Emperor wished to have 'the whole army on the Sambre' by the 14th with the intention possibly to attack on that day, so Gérard should aim at Beaumont because Vandamme should be forward of that place. Again that disposition corresponds largely with the Bertrand letter B and not the Order. The

6e Corps was no longer to be at Beaumont but to have its HQ at Beaufort, that is to say between Avesnes and Maubeuge, as Bertrand had required. As to Grouchy, Soult ordered him to move the *1er* and *2e Corps de Cavalerie* to Solre-sur-Sambre (whereas the Order of the Day had said Beaumont), the *3e* and *4e* to Solre-le-Château (which roughly corresponds to the Order of the Day's 'between Avesnes and Beaumont'). It would seem (though this is my personal opinion only) that he considered that letter B modified the Orders in A.

On reaching Imperial Headquarters on the 13th Napoleon disagreed with Soult's dispositions, as we saw in Chapter 19. Fresh orders were issued. 'Order, counter-order, disorder'.

It is all so very odd that it raises the wider question of how the Napoleonic headquarters habitually functioned, and while the subject goes far beyond the scope of my book, some consideration of it cannot be avoided here.

VII

When at the Tuileries the Emperor kept a room close by him for his Chief of Staff, though on campaign they were lodged further apart. In Napoleon's own private inner room or *cabinet* his secretary occupied one corner. As he himself said, he treated his relays of secretaries 'as a writing machine', working day and night to prepare his letters and orders, till they collapsed under the strain. Whole books have been dedicated to the subject – those of Méneval and Fain and in one sense the multi-volume *Correspondance* – but for my purpose, I shall limit myself to the views of three French authorities, beginning with the testimony of Baron Fain in the 1820s.[13]

Fain recorded that Napoleon kept beside him a set of bound booklets (*livrets*), each for a different topic, regularly updated fortnightly or monthly by the minister in question: war (comprising army, navy, foreign armies and navies, amounting to eighteen volumes in duodecimo and quarto), finance, merchandise prices and availabilities (corn being a special preoccupation). These *livrets* he studied incessantly ('the army states are the most agreeable literary works in all my library and the books that I read with the greatest pleasure when taking rest'), and they explain in part how he seemed always to be master of every subject. The most important of the war *livrets* was that of the army. It contained several series. A tabulation by regiment gave names of their senior officers, current strength, recruitment, depot situation, and a weekly schedule of its marches; another was by the Military Divisions into which the Empire was divided; another by brigades and divisions and army corps; another the lists of all generals; yet another the data on artillery and engineers. As these states had been drawn up by the War Minister and/or the Chief of Staff, it meant that all the high officials and the Emperor were cognisant of the same information.[14]

In a long passage on Napoleon's habits Fain remarked[15] that in taking down dictation at break-neck speed blanks had to be left simply to keep pace with the torrent of words; that in gathering up the papers that Napoleon threw down after dealing with them the secretary would scan them for clues as to names, places, figures, meaning, so as to improve and give proper accuracy to the dictated letter. Two hours' dictation meant a full day's secretarial work, and in writing out fair the documents emerging from the day's scribbles, it was not always possible to tidy those scribbles still to be copied from the previous day's work:

> There was no way of getting him to repeat anything … All his thought process would have been upset. One had to follow as best one could if one was not to be too overwhelmed by the phrases that fell pell-mell; the art was to leave blanks to keep up constantly with the train of thought. Later one went back over it once the rush had passed and the links between the ideas helped fill in the gaps; but it needed intelligence concerning the matter in question; it was indispensable for remedying misunderstandings, avoiding phrases bearing two different meanings, and for rendering clear the vague phrases. In this sense it could be said that the secretary was obliged to have as good a grasp of the day's affairs as did the Emperor himself.[16]
>
> When the Emperor did not want to write himself, either because the matter was not worth the trouble, or for reasons of not wishing to enter too directly into correspondence, he had the letter written in his secretary's name and often [*souvent*] he dictated the letter that opened with these sacramental words, 'The Emperor has charged me', etc.; and it also happened when matters pressed and the Emperor could not wait and so was unable to sign the letter, the secretary would write this at the bottom where Napoleon's signature should be, and sign it himself.

This seems to fit perfectly with Bertrand's letter B of 10 June 1815, in-filling some verbal gaps and using the Emperor's name. But Bertrand was an intelligent engineer, used to exact specifications and practical problems: how did he come to leave the discrepancies between the Order of the Day and the letter?

Perhaps here we need to look beyond the civilian Fain to another military man: at Berthier's practice down the years. Although in one way this takes us far from the Hundred Days' campaign, yet the findings do bear upon the puzzle of 10 June 1815.

VIII

Marshal Berthier holds a very high place as a chief of staff in the estimation of most Napoleonic military historians and I am not directly concerned with that estimation here. I seek only to examine *the conception and transmission of the intentions of the commander-in-chief.* And since there were so many campaigns I have selected the great spring campaigns of 1809 and 1813 as judged by two expert French military historians, General Bonnal in 1905 and Colonel Tournès in 1921.[17] That Berthier did not shine as a field commander is generally agreed, and it may be thought that Bonnal is too severe in his judgements on him. But his verdict on the conception and expression of Napoleon's intentions and how Berthier handled them is instructive.

Bonnal examined in the greatest detail the planning of the 1809 campaign. The Emperor had returned from Spain but was still in Paris, not wishing to raise Austrian suspicions. Meanwhile Berthier had been sent forward to Strasbourg as interim commander of the army prior to the outbreak of war with Austria. The 120,000 French together with allied contingents were dispersed across Bavaria, Davout's forces in the north, and Lefebvre's and Oudinot's along and south of the Danube; Masséna commanded close to the Rhine, and Lannes was returning from Spain. Napoleon despatched his strategic plans to Berthier on 30 March, and sent further thoughts on 1, 2 and 6 April; he reasoned that the Austrians would be ready by 30 March but that they had only two options: to begin operations either before 5 April, or on or after 15 April. His plans followed upon that hypothesis.

Berthier had implicitly trusted the Emperor's 30 March–6 April assessments, although the more perceptive and practical Davout at that time was trying to alert the interim commander to new developments. On 11 April Berthier left for the Danube on learning of the Austrian attack north-west from Austria (launched on the 10th, despite Napoleon's conviction that they would not strike between 5 and 15 April) and the next day heard from Davout that the Austrians had attacked south-west out of Bohemia (on the 9th). Napoleon in Paris learned on 10 April of Austrian moves and immediately sent to Strasbourg modified instructions, with a further amendment on the 12th. Delays in the semaphore telegraph to Strasbourg due to poor visibility, and Berthier's departure from there on 11 April, merely added to the Chief of Staff's problems. It is generally agreed that the Marshal's subsequent orders to the various formations in the field were confused, unfortunate, and 'lacking in grip' but uncertainty and control from over-far were at least in part to blame.[18]

Bonnal admitted that:

> One has to say that when Napoleon was fired by inspiration, and moreover was dictating with giddying speed, he expressed his thoughts too summarily and with many unspoken assumptions … Did Marshal Berthier have a lively enough intelligence to understand the spirit of instructions dictated in this manner? One may doubt it … The impetuosity of Napoleon's thought often led to mental leaps in his orders that could disconcert or baffle those of mediocre foresight or who were shallow thinkers.
>
> Napoleon intuitively saw solutions to fresh problems as they arose; he did not linger to spell out his motivation. He set them down as they came to his mind, without explanations, and without worrying whether Marshal Berthier had or had not the ability to understand them.
>
> In stipulating that Davout's corps should march to Ratisbon *in all eventualities* [*dans tous les événements*] the Emperor had in mind *a delay among the Austrians* [Bonnal's emphasis in both cases], and could not imagine that the expression '*dans tous les événements*' should be taken literally [*au pied de la lettre*] by the Chief of Staff, irrespective of what these eventualities should be.[19]
>
> Perhaps only Davout, Lannes and Masséna would have been capable of grasping his meaning and recognising in his messages what was impassioned exaggeration. Be that as it may, Napoleon made a psychological mistake in failing to subordinate his thought process to the need for the man who was to execute his orders to understand them. The authors who have written about these operations have taken an easy pleasure in launching gibes on Berthier's lack of skill but not one has dreamt of blaming Napoleon in this instance for the stupidities [*sottises*] committed by his lieutenant.[20]

Yet the Emperor and Berthier had worked closely side by side for *thirteen years*, since 1796.[21] Surely the Emperor by now should have suspected Berthier's limitations and taken some care to express himself suitably. If only the three best marshals were likely to grasp his nuanced meaning, does not that give weight to Bonnal's criticism of Napoleon for not guiding his unfortunate assistant more carefully with properly explained advice?

Colonel Tournès provided further information on the Emperor's methods. Writing of 1813 he described the overall headquarters structure in the field. It comprised a number of functions each reporting to Napoleon himself, but the two main branches were the 'Imperial Headquarters' and a civilian-run 'Administrative Headquarters'. The 'Imperial Headquarters' was itself divided into the 'Imperial Household', handling intelligence, mapping, and topography, backed by the personal secretariat or '*cabinet*' run in succession by Méneval and Fain. In attendance upon the Household were the personal ADCs and *ordonnance* officers of the Emperor. Within 'Imperial Headquarters' but quite separate from the Household was the Army Headquarters Staff, the latter under the command of Marshal Berthier during his lifetime.

How then did Napoleon receive his intelligence and issue his commands?

Colonel Tournès's findings may be summarised thus. The first rule at Imperial Headquarters was that the Commander-in-Chief personally took every decision. Each incoming report was shown to Berthier, who read it and then wrote at the top of the paper three or four lines summarising the information received; for matters touching organisation, he joined to it the original documents, leaving to the Emperor whether or not to examine the elements underlying Berthier's appreciation. The paper was sent to Napoleon, who read it in his *cabinet* and then dictated his decision to Fain, and the note, when checked and signed, was sent back to Berthier. Everything was reduced to writing.

The formulation of a decision had nothing to do with Berthier (though Fain may have had some slight influence as draftsman). He merely executed whatever orders his chief gave him; he never acted as counsellor, never on his own took the least decision about operations. Tournès came to a judgement of considerable significance (p. 154) about the limits to Berthier's role, and his words have a bearing on Bertrand and letter B. Berthier 'had only to amplify the instructions emerging from the *cabinet,* and ensure when sending on the orders that he had *retained the original terms used*' (my emphasis), to decide upon the number of different couriers for each message and the routes they were to take, and mark these on the documents.[22]

IX

It is time to return to 10 June 1815 after these diversions into other campaigns.

While Berthier's care in multiplying the number of ways by which the orders could reach the intended recipient is rightly famous, witnesses in the army staff of 1815 confirm that the practice under Soult fell short of that standard, though it must be recognised that money was in such short supply that Napoleon himself insisted on a much reduced establishment.

However, Soult's military gifts were vastly greater than Berthier's, and he did occasionally venture an opinion during the 1815 campaign. When this occurred, though, he was almost invariably ignored or snubbed, and his own personality defects made for difficult relations with his colleagues.

The Emperor still stood as sole and unique decision taker.[23] The silent and invariably polite Bertrand, familiar with Napoleon's methods, but less senior than Berthier and Soult, may simply have abandoned any hope of correcting the muddle on 10 June 1815.

The worst mistake on 10 June 1815 was not that of speculating on two quite different options only some ninety hours before the great attack should begin, although these fresh thoughts were likely to lead to confusion somewhere, if not everywhere. And to be sure, the options carried with them logistical and additional marching consequences, straining the troops just when they needed a little time to assemble and prepare. But the great mistake was to leave both options for execution, and not to withdraw one of them. Bertrand either failed to spot the problem or decided to leave it to Soult, and Soult was caught unawares and blundered. It was a bad start.

But it was Napoleon who had dictated both the Order of the Day and the Bertrand letter B. The Emperor ultimately was responsible for the confusion.

Notes to Appendix 4

1. See for instance, Volume 1, pp. 321, 325, 328, 343, 345, 360.
2. Mr Beckett saw a Christie's sale catalogue of June 2015, No. 10,414, in which a number of Napoleonic letters were pictured (item 19) displayed in fan-shape, the Bertrand material thus being partially covered. Mr Beckett contacted Mr Pierre de Wit who then partially transcribed the pictured letter in his www.waterloo-campaign.nl, *Preambles, Napoleon's Plans and Preparations, I*, under the date 10 June (NB, where I further cite Pierre's documents it is to this section of his website). They then generously passed their findings to me. Thanks to the assistance of Christie's and of Beattie, The Creative Communications Group, the anonymous purchaser has kindly sent to me full photocopies of all the documents. Hence the entire Bertrand letter can now be published.
3. The order can be read in the original French in Pierre de Wit's site, under the date 10 June. A German version of most of the document was printed by Lettow-Vorbeck in *Napoleons Untergang, 1815* (Berlin, 1904), vol. 1, p. 222, omitting the separate postscript.
4. Pierre de Wit, whose analysis is always acute, judges that the Vendée rising having collapsed by early June, Napoleon by 10 June was calculating on the return from there of the regular units for future action in the north. Thus he was consequently altering his objective from Charleroi to Mons and swinging *3e* and *6e Corps* westwards. But if it was coming, Lamarque's Vendée detached force did not arrive in time; indeed on 19 June most if not all of it was still thought to be in the Vendée: see chap. 48, sec. I, opening sentences.
5. On 7 June 1815 Wellington had formally warned governors of the fortified towns including Mons that to surrender the town to a French attack before a serious breach had been opened and an assault made on the breach, 'would be an act not merely of military

disobedience but of treason' (*WD*, xii [1838], p. 450 / viii [1852], p. 126). The French could scarcely hope to take Mons by escalade, and they could not risk by-passing the town and leaving its garrison unmasked, ready to strike at their backs.

6. These are merely my own hypothetical suggestions, but they surely must have been considered by Napoleon, however briefly. Perhaps that is why he reverted to the Charleroi plan.
7. This amanuensis was a frequent writer of Bertrand's military letters and his envelopes during the campaigns of 1813–14, as can be see from a comparison of this 10 June letter with the facsimiles reproduced in Bertrand's *Lettres à Fanny, 1808–1815* (Paris, 1979). Bertrand's own letters, also illustrated in the book, are in a very different hand. Writing to his wife on 17 July 1813, he notes 'a secretary is not without use and on campaign often saves me the bother of myself writing, or addressing envelopes, finding paper or wax. It is not necessary for a commanding officer, but useful': *Lettres*, p. 271.
8. Bertrand silently accepted rebuke and insult from Napoleon, even to the extent of hearing and recording remarks made in front of the entourage that his wife was a whore ('*catin*') and had sex in ditches with British officers (his *Cahiers de Ste-Hélène* [Paris, 1949], entries for 9 and 21 April 1821). But he was aware of Napoleon's capacity to go 'off course' and in old age he stated that when Napoleon's reasoning was at fault, he might reconsider and revise or totally rewrite an appreciation or order if he saw that the (well-informed and trusted) taker of dictation was uneasy at the result. (I have to say that neither Méneval nor Fain, the successive Intimate Secretaries, give that impression of Napoleon's malleability.) For several such instances of reconsideration see Bertrand, 'Avant-Propos' of 1842 to *Guerre d'Orient, Campagnes d'Egypte et de Syrie, 1798–1799 ... dictés par Napoléon à Ste-Hélène*, 2 vols (Paris, 1847), at i, pp. xi–xv: at one point there Bertrand notes, 'It sometimes happened that the first draft contained some key ideas that did not reappear in the second and that were difficult to insert because generally Napoleon's dictation was closely reasoned with the ideas linked together'. Did this occur on 10 June 1815?
9. Pierre de Wit shows that d'Erlon received this message by both routes: his acknowledgement at 9 a.m. on 12 June.
10. For this 10 June letter C, see my acknowledgement in note 2. For that of 11 June, see Arthur Chuquet (1853–1925), *Inédits Napoléoniens*, vol, 1 (Paris, 1913), no. 1,684, p. 457; I referred to this 11 June letter in my chap. 19, n. 43, in a different context: as showing how at that date Ney was not mentioned as joining the army so that Reille was expected to report directly to the Emperor. Mr de Wit prints two versions of the Chuquet document (one dated 10 June and the other 11th) and with textual variations due, perhaps, to differing habits of the copyists.
11. Neither of Vandamme's biographers, Du Casse (1870) and Gallaher (2008), makes any reference to this instruction as being among his papers.
12. All the following 12 June instructions are from Pierre de Wit's website.
13. Baron Fain (1778–1837), *Mémoires* (Paris, 1908), and particularly pp. 56–61. His Preface is dated October 1829.
14. Fain's chap. 8 is a guide to all this. See also Méneval, *Mémoires* iii, pp. 415–24. The practice

sometimes fell below the theory: Feltre was upbraided on 8 April 1812 when the latest *livret* for artillery was still that dated 1 February (in the nineteenth-century *Corr. de Nap.*, no. 18,637; in the new *Napoléon Bonaparte, Corr. Générale*, no. 30,415).

15. See note 13 above.
16. Fain remarked that the danger was that as spoken by the Corsican Napoleon the rivers 'Ebre' [Ebro] and 'Elbe' sounded the same, 'Smolensk' like 'Salamanque', the medical term 'hyssop' too like the north Italian fortress 'Osopo'.
17. General H. Bonnal (1844–1917), *La Manouevre de Landshut* (Paris, 1905). Lt.-Col. René Tournès, 'Le GQG de Napoléon Ier', *Revue de Paris*, 1 May 1921, pp. 134–58.
18. Bonnal, pp. 48, 57–74.
19. Bonnal, pp. 48 and 51. Bonnal's distinction is perhaps too fine; he meant here that Napoleon's words 'in all eventualities' should apply to French actions within and only within the context of a tardy Austrian concentration. If the Austrians did something else, then those 'eventualities' might not apply. However, I personally think that the fault lay with Napoleon, who should have made his meaning far clearer.
20. Bonnal, pp. 72–3.
21. One recalls the officer who sought promotion from Frederick the Great on the basis of service in many campaigns; Frederick pointed to another that had equally long service: 'But that mule is still a mule.'
22. Tournès, especially pp. 152–4.
23. In the 1815 campaign Pétiet of the French staff wrote of advice proffered on 17 June: 'word spread at headquarters that the Chief of Staff had represented to Napoleon the danger of reducing forces aimed at beating the English army; that the detachment for Grouchy was too large. But the Emperor, used to *the passive obedience of Berthier,* would not listen': *Souvenirs Militaires* (Paris, 1844), p. 202, my emphasis.

Orders of Battle

I have compiled orders of battle for the three contending armies, as they were assembled in early June before the start of operations. I have used mainly the works of Houssaye, 1898, Couderc, 1902, and De Bas and T'Serclaes de Wommersom (DBTS), 1908, for Napoleon's army; Lettow-Vorbeck, 1904, and DBTS for Blücher's army; Siborne, 1848, and DBTS for Wellington's army. None of them is without slips and uncertainties: Fortescue in 1920 remarked that Siborne's Waterloo order of battle 'seems from internal evidence to be imperfect', and various returns given in *WD* and *WSD* also show variations. Fortescue relied principally on Lt.-Colonel W. H. James's book on the campaign, 1908, which distilled the figures from the above and other sources. A recent and extensive set of orders of battle can be found in Adkin's *Waterloo Companion*, 2001, but even that has some small slips, e.g. the King's Dragoon Guards, and a misprint over Grouchy's strength at Wavre.

Given these disparities between good authorities, it would be foolish to pretend that my listings are without errors and omissions, and I submit them with due diffidence.

Orders of Battle 1

Anglo-Allied Army

Commander-in-Chief	***Field Marshal The Duke of Wellington***	
Military Secretary	*Lt.-Col. Lord F. Somerset*	
5 ADCs; 3 Extra ADCs,		
Adjutant-General	*Maj.-Gen. Sir E. Barnes*	
11 AAGs; 10 DAAGs		
Deputy QMG	*Col. Sir W. H. De Lancey*	
17 AQMGs; 12 DAQMGs		
Commandant, Headquarters	*Col. Sir C. Campbell*	
Commanding Artillery	*Col. Sir G. Wood*	
Commanding RHA	*Lt.-Col. Sir A. S. Fraser*	
Commanding Train	*Lt.-Col. Sir A. Dickson*	
I Corps	***Gen. The Prince of Orange***	25,233 men and 56 guns
1st Division	***Maj.-Gen. Cooke***	
1st British Brigade	*Maj.-Gen. Maitland*	
2/1st Guards		976
3/1st Guards		1,021
2nd British Brigade	*Maj.-Gen. Sir J. Byng*	
2/Coldstream Guards		1,003
2/Scots Guards		1,061
Artillery	*Lt.-Col. Adye*	
Capt. Sandham's British FB		5 x 9-pdr, 1 x 5.5 inch how.
Maj. Kuhlmann's HB, KGL		5 x 9-pdr, 1 x 5.5 inch how.

Note: strengths given for British, KGL, Hanoverian and Brunswick forces are derived from Siborne and are for rank and file only. Figures for the Netherlands forces are from DBTS and are for 'all ranks'. FB = Foot Battery; HB = Horse Battery; D = Dutch; B = Belgian.

3rd Division	**Lt.-Gen. Sir C. Alten**	
5th British Brigade	*Maj.-Gen. Sir Colin Halkett*	
2/30th Foot		615
33rd Foot		561
2/69th Foot		516
2/73rd Foot		562
2nd Brigade, KGL	*Col. von Ompteda*	
1/Light, KGL		423
2/Light, KGL		337
5/Line, KGL		379
8/Line, KGL		388
1st Hanoverian Brigade	*Maj.-Gen. Count Kielmansegge*	
Field Battalion Bremen		512
Field Battalion Verden		533
Field Battalion York		507
Field Battalion Lüneburg		595
Field Battalion Grubenhagen		621
Jäger Corps		321
Artillery	*Lt.-Col. Williamson*	
Maj. Lloyd's British FB		5 x 9-pdr, 1 x 5.5-inch how.
Capt. Cleeves's FB, KGL		5 x 9-pdr, 1 x 5.5-inch how.
2nd Netherlands Division	***Lt.-Gen. Perponcher***	
1st Brigade	*Maj.-Gen. van Bylandt*	
7/Line Regiment [B]		701
27/Jager Battalion [D]		809
5/National Militia Battalion [D]		482
7/National Militia Battalion [D]		675
8/National Militia Battalion [D]		566
2nd Brigade	*Col. von Goedecke [replaced 15 June by HSH Prince Bernard of Saxe-Weimar]*	
I, II, III Battalions/Nassau Infantry Regiment, Nr. 2		2,709
I, II Battalions/Regiment of Orange-Nassau Nr. 28		1,581
Nassau Jäger [Coy]		177
Artillery	*Maj. von Opstal*	
Capt. Byleveldt's HB		6 x 6-pdr, 2 x how.
Capt. Stevenart's FB		6 x 6-pdr, 2 x how.

3rd Netherlands Division	***Lt.-Gen. Chassé***	
1st Brigade	*Maj.-Gen. Detmers*	
2/Line Regiment [D]		471
35/Chasseur Battalion [B]		605
4/National Militia Battalion [D]		523
6/National Militia Battalion [D]		492
17/National Militia Battalion [D]		534
19/National Militia Battalion [D]		467
2nd Brigade	*Maj.-Gen. d'Aubremé*	
3/Line Regiment [B]		629
12/Line Regiment [D]		431
13/Line Regiment [D]		664
36/Chasseur Battalion [B]		633
3/National Militia Battalion [D]		592
10/National Militia Battalion [D]		632
Artillery	*Maj. van der Smissen*	
Capt. Kramer's HB		6 x 6-pdr, 2 x how.
Capt. Lux's FB		6 x 6-pdr, 2 x how.
II Corps	***Lt.-Gen. Lord Hill***	24,033 men, 40 guns
2nd Division	***Lt.-Gen. Sir H Clinton***	
3rd British Brigade	*Maj.-Gen. Adam*	
1/52nd Foot		1,038
1/71st Foot		810
2/95th Foot		585
3/95th Foot		188
1st Brigade, KGL	*Col. Du Plat*	
1/Line Battalion		411
2/Line Battalion		437
3/Line Battalion		494
4/Line Battalion		416
3rd Hanoverian Brigade	*Col. Hugh Halkett*	
Landwehr Battalions:		
Bremervörde		632
Osnabrück		612
Quackenbrück		588
Salzgitter		622

Artillery	*Lt.-Col. Gold*	
Capt. Bolton's British FB		5 x 9-pdr, 1 x 5.5-inch how.
Maj. Sympher's KGL HB		5 x 9-pdr, 1 x 5.5-inch how.
4th Division	**Lt.-Gen. Sir C. Colville**	
4th British Brigade	*Col. Mitchell*	
3/14th Foot		571
1/23rd Foot		647
51st Foot		549
6th British Brigade	*Maj.-Gen. Johnstone*	
2/35th Foot		570
1/54th Foot		541
2/59th Foot		461
1/91st Foot		824
6th Hanoverian Brigade	*Maj.-Gen. Sir J. Lyon*	
Field Battalion Lauenburg		553
Field Battalion Calenberg		634
Landwehr Battalion Nienburg		625
Landwehr Battalion Hoya		629
Landwehr Battalion Bentheim		608
Artillery	*Lt.-Col. Hawker*	
Maj. Brome's British FB		5 x 9-pdr, 1 x 5.5-inch how.
Capt. von Rettberg's Hanoverian FB		5 x 9-pdr, 1 x 5.5-inch how.
1st Netherlands Division	***Lt.-Gen. Stedman***	
1st Brigade	*Maj.-Gen. Hauw*	
4/Line Regiment [B]		548
6/Line Regiment [D]		431
16/Jaeger Battalion [D]		490
9/National Militia Battalion [D]		555
14/National Militia Battalion [D]		586
15/National Militia Battalion [D]		659
2nd Brigade	*Maj.-Gen. Eerens*	
1/Line Regiment [B]		682
18/Jaeger Battalion [D]		798
1/National Militia Battalion [D]		592
2/National Militia Battalion [D]		582
18/National Militia Battalion [D]		515

Artillery		
Capt. Wynand's FB		6 x 6-pdr, 2 x how.
Netherlands Indian Bde	*Lt.-Gen. Anthing*	
I, II/5th Regiment		1,486
Flankers (composite)		507
10/Jaeger		679
11/Jaeger		679
Capt. Reisz's FB		225 men, 6 x 6-pdr, 2 x how.
Sundry KGL Detachments		16

Reserve — 32,796 men, 64 guns

5th Division	**Lt.-Gen. Sir T. Picton**	
8th British Brigade	*Maj.-Gen. Sir J. Kempt*	
1/28th Foot		557
1/32nd Foot		662
1/79th Foot		703
1/95th Foot		549
9th British Brigade	*Maj.-Gen. Sir D. Pack*	
3/1st Foot		604
1/42nd Foot		526
2/44th Foot		455
1/92nd Foot		588
5th Hanoverian Brigade	*Col. von Vincke*	
Landwehr Battalions:		
Hameln		669
Gifhorn		617
Hildesheim		617
Peine		611
Artillery	*Maj. Heise*	
Maj. Rogers's British FB		5 x 9-pdr, 1 x 5.5-inch how.
Capt. Braun's Hanoverian FB		5 x 6-pdr, 1 x 5.5-inch how.

6th Division	**Lt.-Gen. Sir L. Cole**	
10th British Brigade	*Maj.-Gen. Sir J. Lambert*	
1/4th Foot		669
1/27th Foot		698
1/40th Foot		761
2/81st Foot		439
4th Hanoverian Brigade	*Col. Best*	
Landwehr Battalions:		
Verden		621
Lüneburg		624
Osterode		677
Münden		660
Artillery	*Lt.-Col. Brückmann*	
Maj. Unett's British FB		5 x 9-pdr, 1 x 5.5-inch how.
Capt. Sinclair's British FB		5 x 9-pdr, 1 x 5.5-inch how.
British Reserve Artillery	*Maj. Drummond*	
Lt.-Col. Sir H Ross's 'A' Troop, RHA		5 x 9-pdr, 1 x 5.5-inch how.
Maj. Beane's 'D' Troop, RHA		5 x 9-pdr, 1 x 5.5-inch how.
Maj. Morrison's FB*		5 x 9-pdr, 1 x 5.5-inch how.
Capt. Hutcheson's FB*		5 x 9-pdr, 1 x 5.5-inch how.
Capt. Ilbert's FB*		5 x 9-pdr, 1 x 5.5-inch how.

* Each in process of being re-equipped with 4 x 18-pdr, on 18 June.

7th Division	
7th British Brigade	
2/25th Foot	388
2/37th Foot	491
2/78th Foot	337
British Garrison Troops	
13/Veteran Battalion	683
1/Foreign Battalion	595
2/Garrison Battalion	739

Brunswick Corps	***The Duke of Brunswick****	
Advance Guard	*Maj. von Rauschenplatt*	
Advance Guard Battalion		672
Light Brigade	*Lt.-Col. von Bennigsen*	
Guard Battalion		672
1/Light Battalion		672
2/Light Battalion		672
3/Light Battalion		672
Line Brigade	*Lt.-Col. von Specht*	
1/Line Battalion		672
2/Line Battalion		672
3/Line Battalion		672
Artillery	*Maj. Mahn*	
Capt. Heinemann's HB		8 x 6-pdr
Maj. Moll's FB		8 x 6-pdr

* Col. Olfermann in command after the Duke's death at Quatre Bras.

Hanoverian Reserve Corps	***Lt.-Gen. von der Decken***	9,000
1st Brigade	*Lt.-Col. von Bennigsen*	
Field Battalion Hoya		
Landwehr Battalion Mölln		
Landwehr Battalion Bremerlehe		
2nd Brigade	*Lt.-Col. von Beaulieu*	
Landwehr Battalion Nordhem		
Landwehr Battalion Ahlefeldt		
Landwehr Battalion Springe		
3rd Brigade	*Lt.-Col. Bodecker*	
Landwehr Battalion Otterndorf		
Landwehr Battalion Zelle		
Landwehr Battalion Ratzeburg		
4th Brigade	*Lt.-Col. Wissel*	
Landwehr Battalion Hanover		
Landwehr Battalion Uelzen		
Landwehr Battalion Neustadt		
Landwehr Battalion Diepholz		

Nassau Contingent	***Gen von Kruse***	
I, II, III/Nassau Infantry Regiment Nr. 1		2,880

Cavalry	***Lt.-Gen. The Earl of Uxbridge***	14,482 men 44 guns
British and KGL		
1st [Household] Brigade	*Maj.-Gen. Lord Edward Somerset*	
1st Life Guards		228
2nd Life Guards		231
Royal Horse Guards [Blues]		237
1st [King's] Dragoon Guards		530
2nd [Union] Brigade	*Maj.-Gen. Sir W. Ponsonby*	
1st Royal Dragoons		394
2nd Dragoons [Scots Greys]		391
6th Inniskilling Dragoons		396
3rd Brigade	*Maj.-Gen. Sir W. Dörnberg*	
1st Light Dragoons, KGL		462
2nd Light Dragoons, KGL		419
23rd Light Dragoons		387
4th Brigade	*Maj.-Gen. Sir J. Vandeleur*	
11th Light Dragoons		390
12th Light Dragoons		388
16th Light Dragoons		393
5th Brigade	*Maj.-Gen. Sir C. Grant*	
2nd Hussars, KGL		564
7th Hussars		380
15th Hussars		392
6th Brigade	*Maj.-Gen. Sir H. Vivian*	
1st Hussars, KGL		493
10th Hussars		390
18th Hussars		396
7th Brigade	*Col. Sir F. von Arentsschildt*	
3rd Hussars, KGL		622
13th Light Dragoons		390
Royal Horse Artillery Troops attached to the Cavalry		
Maj. Bull's 'I' Troop		6 x 5.5-inch how.
Lt.-Col. Webber-Smith's 'F' Troop		5 x 6-pdr, 1 how.
Lt.-Col. Gardiner's 'E' Troop		5 x 6-pdr, 1 how.
Capt. Whinyates' 2nd Rocket Troop		1 rocket section, 5 x 6-pdr, 1 how.
Capt. Mercer's 'G' Troop		5 x 9-pdr, 1 how.
Capt. Ramsay's 'H' Troop		5 x 9-pdr, 1 how.

Hanoverian		
1st Brigade	*Col. von Estorff*	
Prince Regent's Hussars		596
Bremen & Verden Hussars		589
Cumberland Hussars		497
Brunswick Cavalry		
Hussar Regiment		690
Uhlans [one sqdn]		232

Netherlands*

Heavy Brigade	*Maj.-Gen. Trip*	
1st Carabiniers [D]		446
2nd Carabiniers [B]		399
3rd Carabiniers [D]		392
1st Light Brigade	*Maj.-Gen. de Ghigny*	
4th Light Dragoons [D]		647
8th Hussars [B]		439
2nd Light Brigade	*Maj.-Gen. van Merlen*	
5th Light Dragoons [B]		441
6th Hussars [D]		641
Horse Artillery		
Capt. Petter's half HB		3 x 6-pdr, 1 how.
Capt. Gey's half HB		3 x 6-pdr, 1 how.

* Under the Prince of Orange until a.m. 18 June, then relinquished to Lord Uxbridge.

Artillery Summary

British	7 FB of 6 guns each	42 guns	3,630 men
	3 FB of 4 guns each [18-pdr]	12 guns	
	8 HB of 6 guns each	48 guns	1,400 men
KGL	1 FB of 6 guns	6 guns	526 men
	2 HB of 6 guns each	12 guns	
Hanoverian	2 FB of 6 guns each	12 guns	465 men
Brunswick	1 FB of 8 guns	8 guns	510 men
	1 HB of 8 guns	8 guns	
Netherlands	4 FB of 8 guns each	32 guns	667 men
	3 HB of 8 guns each	24 guns	
Total		204 guns	8,166 men

Engineers, Sappers & Miners, Wagon Train, Staff Corps	1,240 men

Recapitulation

Infantry	82,062
Cavalry	14,482
Artillery	8,166
Engineers etc.	1,240
	105,950 and 204 guns

Note: Rank & File only; to include officers, sergeants, etc., Fortescue's rule was to add one-eighth.

Sources: Principally Siborne, *History* (3rd edn., 1848), Appendix VI. Note that the morning state for 2nd Anglo-Hanoverian Division (the main subject of Glover, *Waterloo, The Defeat of the Imperial Guard*, pp. 102–3) has slight differences, mainly in Du Plat's and Hugh Halkett's brigades.

Orders of Battle 2

Prussian Army of the Lower Rhine

Commander in Chief	***Field Marshal Prince Blücher***	
Officers attached to the C-in-C, 4		
QMG and Chief of Staff	*Lt.-Gen. Count von Gneisenau*	
Chief of the General Staff	*Maj.-Gen. von Grolman*	
Staff Officers, 15		
Adjutantur, 5; Volunteers, 17		
Commanding at Headquarters	*Maj. von Pflugk*	
Commanding Artillery	*General of Infantry Prince Augustus of Prussia*	
I Corps	***Lt.-Gen. von Ziethen II***	32,568 all ranks 88 guns
1st Brigade	***Maj.-Gen. von Steinmetz***	8,647
Brandenburg Infantry Regiment Nr. 2		
Infantry Regiment Nr. 24		
Westphalian Landwehr Infantry Regiment Nr. 1		
Westphalian Cavalry Regiment		
Foot Battery Nr. 7		6 x 6-pdr, 2 x 7-pdr how.
Horse Battery Nr. 7		6 x 6-pdr, 2 x 7-pdr how.

Notes: Note: each infantry regiment, Line and Landwehr, comprised a I and II Battalion of musketeers, with the III (Fusilier) Battalion composed of light infantry; each cavalry regiment, line and Landwehr, comprised four squadrons. Units such as pioneers, commissariat, medical, artillery train, have not been separately listed and appear only in the corps totals.

2nd Brigade,	***Maj.-Gen. von Pirch II***	7,666
West Prussian Infantry Regiment Nr. 1		
Berg Infantry Regiment Nr. 28		
Westphalian Landwehr Infantry Regiment Nr. 2		
Westphalian Landwehr Cavalry Regiment		
Foot Battery Nr. 3		6 x 6-pdr, 2 x 7-pdr how.
3rd Brigade	***Maj.-Gen. von Jagow***	6,853
West Prussian Infantry Regiment Nr. 2		
Berg Infantry Regiment Nr. 29		
Westphalian Landwehr Infantry Regiment Nr. 3		
Two companies Silesian Sharpshooters,		
Foot Battery Nr. 8		6 x 6-pdr, 2 x 7-pdr how.
4th Brigade	***Maj.-Gen. Henckel von Donnesmark***	4,721
Infantry Regiment Nr. 13 [stationed at Mainz]		
Infantry Regiment Nr. 12		
Westphalian Landwehr Infantry Regiment Nr. 4		
Foot Battery Nr. 15		6 x 6-pdr, 2 x 7-pdr how.
Reserve Cavalry	***Maj.-Gen. von Röder***	2,025
1st Brigade	*Maj.-Gen. von Treckow II*	
Brandenburg Dragoon Regiment		
West Prussian Dragoon Regiment Nr. 1		
Brandenburg Uhlan Regiment		
Horse Battery Nr. 2		6 x 6-pdr, 2 x 7-pdr how.
2nd Brigade	*Lt.-Col. von Lützow*	
Kurmärk Landwehr Cavalry Nr. 1		
Kurmärk Landwehr Cavalry Nr. 2		
Horse Battery Nr. 7 [det. to 1st Brigade of infantry]		6 x 6-pdr, 2 x 7-pdr how.
Reserve Artillery	***Lt.-Col. Lehmann***	1,019
Foot Battery Nr. 2		8 x 12-pdr
Foot Battery Nr. 6*		8 x 12-pdr
Foot Battery Nr. 1		8 x 6-pdr
Horse Battery Nr. 10		6 x 6-pdr, 2 x 7-pdr how.
Howitzer Battery Nr. 1		8 x 7-pdr how.

* Foot Battery Nr. 6 mobilised in Germany and joined I Corps on the evening of 15 June. Lettow-Vorbeck included this FB in his total of 304 guns whereas DBTS seem to have excluded it from their figure of 296 guns.

II Corps	***Maj.-Gen. von Pirch I***	33,048 all ranks 80 guns
5th Brigade	***Maj.-Gen. von Tippelskirch***	6,851
Pomeranian Infantry Regiment Nr. 1		
Infantry Regiment Nr. 25		
Westphalian Landwehr Infantry Regiment Nr. 5		
Company of Jäger		
Foot Battery Nr. 10,		6 x 6-pdr, 2 x 7-pdr how.
6th Brigade	***Maj.-Gen. von Krafft***	6,469
Kolberg Infantry Regiment		
Infantry Regiment Nr. 26		
Elbe Landwehr Infantry Regiment Nr. 1		
Foot Battery Nr. 5		6 x 6-pdr, 2 x 7-pdr how.
7th Brigade	***Maj.-Gen. von Brause***	6,224
Infantry Regiment Nr. 14		
Infantry Regiment Nr. 22		
Elbe Landwehr Infantry Regiment Nr. 2		
Foot Battery Nr. 34		6 x 6-pdr, 2 x 7-pdr how.
8th Brigade	***Maj.-Gen. von Bose***	6,292
Infantry Regiment Nr. 21		
Infantry Regiment Nr. 23		
Elbe Landwehr Infantry Regiment Nr. 3		
Foot Battery Nr. 12		6 x 6-pdr, 2 x 7-pdr how.
Reserve Cavalry	***Maj.-Gen. von Jürgass***	4,168
1st Brigade	*Col. von Thümen*	
Queen's Dragoon Regiment		
Neumärk Dragoon Regiment		
Silesian Uhlan Regiment		
Horse Battery Nr. 6		6 x 6-pdr, 2 x 7-pdr how.
2nd Brigade	*Lt.-Col. von Sohr*	
Brandenburg Hussar Regiment		
Pomeranian Hussar Regiment		
Hussar Regiment Nr. 11 [2 sqdns att. to 5th Bde, 2 to 6th Bde]		

3rd Brigade *Col. von der Schulenburg*

Kurmärk Landwehr Cavalry Regiment Nr. 4
Kurmärk Landwehr Cavalry Regiment Nr. 5
Elbe Landwehr Cavalry Regiment [2 sqdns att.to 7th Bde, 2 to 8th Bde]

Reserve Artillery*	***Maj. Lehmann***	1,454
Foot Battery Nr. 4		6 x 12-pdr, 2 x 10-pdr how.
Foot Battery Nr. 8		6 x 12-pdr, 2 x 10-pdr how.
Foot Battery Nr. 37		6 x 6-pdr, 2 x 7-pdr how.
Horse Battery Nr. 5		6 x 6-pdr, 2 x 7-pdr how.
Horse Battery Nr. 14		6 x 6-pdr, 2 x 7-pdr how.

* Excluding units that arrived too late for the battles.

III Corps *Lt.-Gen. von Thielemann* 25,318 all ranks 48 guns

9th Brigade	***Maj.-Gen. von Borcke***	6,946
Leib-Infantry Regiment		
Infantry Regiment Nr. 30		
Kurmärk Landwehr Infantry Regiment Nr. 1		
Kurmärk Landwehr Cavalry Regiment Nr. 3 [2 sqdns]		
Foot Battery Nr. 18		6 x 6-pdr, 2 x 7-pdr how.

10th Brigade	***Maj.-Gen. von Krauseneck***	4,223
Infantry Regiment Nr. 20 [at Mainz until late June]		
Infantry Regiment Nr. 27		
Kurmärk Landwehr Infantry Regiment Nr. 2		
Kurmärk Landwehr Cavalry Regiment Nr. 3 [2 sqdns]		
Foot Battery Nr. 35		6 x 6-pdr, 2 x 7-pdr how.

11th Brigade	***Maj.-Gen. von Rijssel***	3,789
Kurmärk Landwehr Infantry Regiment Nr. 3		
Kurmärk Landwehr Infantry Regiment Nr. 4		
Kurmärk Landwehr Cavalry Regiment Nr. 6 [two sqdns]		
Foot Battery Nr. 36 [arrived 15 June]		6 x 6-pdr, 2 x 7-pdr how.

12th Brigade *Maj.-Gen. von Lossau* 6,330

Infantry Regiment Nr. 31
Infantry Regiment Nr. 23
Kurmärk Landwehr Infantry Regiment Nr. 5
Kurmärk Landwehr Infantry Regiment Nr. 6
Kurmärk Landwehr Cavalry Regiment Nr. 6 [2 sqdns]
Foot Battery Nr. 24 [arrived 6 July 6 x 6-pdr, 2 x 7-pdr how.]

Reserve Cavalry *Maj.-Gen. von Hobe* 1,828

1st Brigade *Col. von der Marwitz*

Hussar Regiment Nr. 12
Hellwig Uhlan Regiment [3 sqdns, fourth joining after Ligny]
Uhlan Regiment Nr. 8

2nd Brigade *Col. Count von Lottum*

Dragoon Regiment Nr. 7
Hussar Regiment Nr. 9
Uhlan Regiment Nr. 5
Horse Battery Nr. 20 6 x 6-pdr, 2 x 7-pdr how.

Reserve Artillery* *Maj. von Grevenitz* 964

Foot Battery Nr. 7 6 x 12-pdr, 2 x 10-pdr how.
Horse Battery Nr. 18 6 x 6-pdr, 2 x 7-pdr how.
Horse Battery Nr. 19 6 x 6-pdr, 2 x 7-pdr how.

* Excluding units that arrived too late for the battles.

IV Corps *Gen. Count Bülow von Dennewitz*

32,239 all ranks, 88 guns

13th Brigade *Maj.-Gen. von Hake* 6,385

Silesian Infantry Regiment Nr. 1
Neumärk Landwehr Infantry Regiment Nr. 2
Neumärk Landwehr Infantry Regiment Nr. 3
Silesian Landwehr Cavalry Regiment Nr. 2 [2 sqdns]
Foot Battery Nr. 21 6 x 6-pdr, 2 x 7-pdr how.

14th Brigade *Maj.-Gen. von Rijssel* 6,953

Silesian Infantry Regiment Nr. 2
Pomeranian Landwehr Infantry Regiment Nr. 1
Pomeranian Landwehr Infantry Regiment Nr. 2
Silesian Landwehr Cavalry Regiment Nr. 2 [2 sqdns]
Foot Battery Nr. 13 6 x 6-pdr, 2 x 7-pdr how.

15th Brigade	*Maj.-Gen. von Losthin*	6,881
Infantry Regiment Nr. 18		
Silesian Landwehr Infantry Regiment Nr. 3		
Silesian Landwehr Infantry Regiment Nr. 4		
Silesian Landwehr Cavalry Regiment Nr. 3 [2 sqdns]		
Foot Battery Nr. 14		6 x 6-pdr, 2 x 7-pdr how.
16th Brigade	*Maj.-Gen. von Hiller*	6,162
Infantry Regiment Nr. 15		
Silesian Landwehr Infantry Regiment Nr. 1		
Silesian Landwehr Infantry Regiment Nr. 2		
Silesian Landwehr Cavalry Regiment Nr. 3 [2 sqdns]		
Foot Battery Nr. 2		6 x 6-pdr, 2 x 7-pdr how.
Reserve Cavalry	***Gen. of Cav. Prince William of Prussia***	3,081
1st Brigade	*Col. Count Schwerin*	
Silesian Hussar Regiment Nr. 2		
Hussar Regiment Nr. 10		
West Prussian Uhlan Regiment		
2nd Brigade	*Lt.-Col. von Watzdorff*	
Dragoon Regiment Nr. 8 [arrived late June]		
Hussar Regiment Nr. 8		
Horse Battery Nr. 12		6 x 6-pdr, 2 x 7-pdr how.
3rd Brigade	*Maj.-Gen. von Sydow*	
Neumärk Landwehr Cavalry Regiment Nr. 1		
Neumärk Landwehr Cavalry Regiment Nr. 2		
Pomeranian Landwehr Cavalry Regiment Nr. 1		
Pomeranian Landwehr Cavalry Regiment Nr. 2		
Silesian Landwehr Cavalry Regiment Nr. 1		
Reserve Artillery*	*Maj. von Bardeleben*	1,266
Foot Battery Nr. 3		6 x 12-pdr, 2 x 10-pdr how.
Foot Battery Nr. 5		6 x 12-pdr, 2 x 10-pdr how.
Foot Battery Nr. 13		6 x 12-pdr, 2 x 10-pdr how.
Foot Battery Nr. 11		6 x 6-pdr, 2 x 7-pdr how.
Horse Battery Nr. 11		6 x 6-pdr, 2 x 7-pdr how.

* Excluding units that arrived too late for the battles.

Recapitulation *from Lettow-Vorbeck*				
Corps	*Officers*	*Bandsmen*	*NCOs/men*	*Guns*
I	812	627	31,129*	88*
II	892	627	31,529	80
III	710	467	24,141	48
IV	858	508	30,873*	88
Total	3,272	2,229	117,672	304*

* DBTS state a total Army figure of 296 guns, reporting I Corps artillery as 80 guns by excluding FB Nr. 6. However, they retain the I Corps figure of 31,129 for NCOs/men, which would seem therefore to include the gun-crews though not the guns. They also give a IV Corps total for NCOs/men of 30,862. I mention this simply to show how difficult it is to reconcile different authorities.

Sources: Principally, Lettow-Vorbeck, *Napoleons Untergang*, Anlage 1; also DBTS, vol. iii, pp. 121–65.

Orders of Battle 3

French Army of the North

Commander-in-Chief	***The Emperor Napoleon***	
Personal ADCs		
Generals Duc de Plaisance, Comte Drouot, Comte Corbineau, Comte Flahaut, Comte Dejean, Baron Bernard, Comte La Bédoyère; Chief Orderly Officer, Col. Gourgaud		
Chief of Army Staff	***Marshal Jean de Dieu Soult, Duke of Dalmatia***	
Chief of the General Staff	***Lt.-Gen. Comte Bailly de Monthyon***	
Senior Staff Officers, 42		
Commanding Artillery	***Lt.-Gen. Ruty***	
Commanding Engineers	***Lt.-Gen. Baron Rogniat***	
Imperial Guard	***Lt.-Gen. Comte Drouot***	19,909 (inc. 3,795 Cav.), 96 guns
Vieille Garde		
1er Grenadiers à Pied	*Lt.-Gen. Friant*	32, 1,006
2e Grenadiers à Pied	*Lt.-Gen. Friant*	32, 1,063
1er Chasseurs à Pied	*Lt.-Gen. Morand*	36, 1,271
2e Chasseurs à Pied	*Lt.-Gen. Morand*	32, 1,131

Notes: the § symbol indicates an error in Houssaye's order of battle (Book I, chap. 2); a list of probable corrections is given at the end of my version. Unless otherwise noted, all infantry regiments are composed of two battalions and all cavalry regiments of four squadrons. Strengths are in the format 32 [officers], 1,006 [men] – see *1er Grenadiers à Pied* above for this example. Names of officers conform to G. Six's *Dictionnaire Biographique* in cases where they are differently spelt in other references.

Moyenne Garde		
3e Grenadiers à Pied	*Lt.-Gen. Roguet*	34, 1,146
4e Grenadiers à Pied [1 bn.]	*Lt.-Gen. Roguet*	25, 503
3e Chasseurs à Pied	*Lt.-Gen. Michel*	34, 1,028
4e Chasseurs à Pied	*Lt.-Gen. Michel*	30, 1,041
Jeune Garde		
3e Voltigeurs	*Lt.-Gen. Duhesme*	26, 1,083
3e Tirailleurs	*Lt.-Gen. Duhesme*	28, 960
1er Voltigeurs	*Lt.-Gen. Barrois*	31, 1,188
1er Tirailleurs	*Lt.-Gen. Barrois*	32, 935
***Vieille Garde* Cavalry**		
Light Cavalry	*Lt.-Gen. Lefebvre-Desnouettes*	
2e Chevaux Légers, Lanciers Rouges [5 sqdns]		47, 833
Chasseurs à Cheval [5 sqdns]		59, 1,138
Heavy Cavalry	*Lt.-Gen. Guyot*	
Grenadiers à Cheval		44, 792
Dragons de l'Imperatrice		51, 765
Gendarmerie d'Elite	*Gen Dautancourt*	4, 102
***Vieille Garde* Artillery**	*Lt.-Gen. Desvaux de St Maurice*	
Foot		28, 702
Horse		19, 380
Train		20, 904
Auxiliary Artillery		18, 484
Engineers		3, 109
Marines		3, 104

I Corps

Lt.-Gen. Comte Drouet d'Erlon 19,839 men (incl 1,506 Cav.), 46 guns

1ere Division	***Lt.-Gen. Allix, on detachment, replaced by Maj.-Gen. Quiot***	
1er Brigade	*Maj.-Gen. Quiot*	
54e Ligne		41, 921
55e Ligne		45, 1,103

2e Brigade	*Maj.-Gen. Bourgeois*	
28e Ligne		42, 856
105e Ligne		42, 941
Artillery & Train		
6e Artillery, 20e coy		4, 81
1er Train Sqdn, 5e coy		3, 103
2e Division	***Lt.-Gen. Donzelot***	
1er Brigade	*Maj.-Gen. Schmitz*	
13e Léger[§] [3 battalions]		61, 1,814
17e Ligne		42, 1,015
2e Brigade	*Maj.-Gen. Aulard*	
19e Ligne		43, 989
51e Ligne[§]		42, 1,126
Artillery & Train		
6e Artillery, 10e coy		3, 86
1er Train Sqdn, 9e coy		1, 95
3e Division	***Lt.-Gen. Marcognet***	
1er Brigade	*Maj.-Gen. Noguès*	
21e Ligne		42, 996
46e Ligne		43, 845
2e Brigade	*Maj.-Gen. Grenier*	
25e Ligne		40, 934
45e Ligne		43, 960
Artillery & Train		
6e Artillery, 19e coy		4, 81
1er Train Sqdn, 2e coy		2, 92
4e Division	***Lt.-Gen. Durutte***	
1er Brigade	*Maj.-Gen. Pégot*	
8e Ligne		40, 943
29e Ligne		40, 1,106
2e Brigade	*Maj.-Gen. Brue*	
85e Ligne		40, 591
95e Ligne		40, 1,060
Artillery & Train		
6e Artillery, 9e coy		3, 81
1er Train Sqdn, 3e coy		1, 92

1ere Division, Light Cav.	***Lt.-Gen. Jacquinot***	
1er Brigade	*Maj.-Gen. Bruno*	
7e Hussards		28, 411
3e Chasseurs		29, 336
2e Brigade	*Maj.-Gen. Gobrecht*	
3e Lanciers		27, 379
4e Lanciers		22, 274
Artillery & Train		
1ere Horse Artillery, 2e coy		3, 70
1er Train Sqdn, 4e coy		2, 83
Reserve Artillery		
6e Artillery, 11e coy		3, 84
1er Train Sqdn, 6e coy		1, 118
1er Regiment Engineers, 2e Batt, coys 1 to 5		21, 330

II Corps — *Lt.-Gen. Comte Reille* — 25,134 men (inc. 1,838 Cav.), 46 guns

5e Division	***Lt.-Gen. Bachelu***	
1er Brigade	*Maj.-Gen. Husson*	
2e Léger* [4 battalions, replacing 3e Ligne, 12 June]		94, 2,247
61e Ligne		41, 817
2e Brigade	*Maj.-Gen. Campy*	
72e Ligne		42, 953
108e Ligne [3 battalions]		61, 1,846
Artillery & Train		
6e Artillery, 18e coy		4, 86
1er Train Sqdn, 3e coy		2, 99

* I have here followed the Houssaye and DBTS orbats; but Adkin shows Husson's Brigade, retaining *3e* and *61e Ligne*; with *6e Div.*, Bauduin's Brigade, having *1er* and *2e Léger*.

6e Division	***Lt.-Gen. Prince Jerome***	
1er Brigade	*Maj.-Gen. Bauduin*	
1er Léger [3 battalions]		64, 1,824
3e Ligne* [4 battalions, and replacing 2e Léger, 12 June]		42, 1,101
2e Brigade	*Maj.-Gen. Soye*	
1er Ligne [3 battalions]		59, 1,736
2e Ligne [3 battalions]		65, 1,730

Artillery & Train		
2e Artillery, 2e coy		4, 92
1er Train Sqdn, 1ere coy		2, 102
7e Division	***Lt.-Gen. Girard***	
1er Brigade	*Maj.-Gen. Devilliers*	
11e Léger		42, 913
82e Ligne [1 battalion]		27, 550
2e Brigade	*Maj.-Gen. Piat*	
12e Léger [3 battalions]		51, 1,141
4e Ligne		44, 1,157
Artillery & Train		
2e Artillery, 3e coy		3, 74
1er Train Sqdn, 1ere coy		1, 58
2e Train Sqdn, 2e coy		1, 43
9e Division§	***Lt.-Gen. Foy***	
1er Brigade	*Maj.-Gen. Gauthier*	
92e Ligne		40, 1,028
93e Ligne [3 battalions]		41, 927
2e Brigade	*Maj.-Gen. Jamin*	
100e Ligne [3 battalions]		51, 1,067
4e Léger [3 battalions]		61, 1,573
Artillery & Train		
6e Artillery, 1ere coy		4, 84
1er Train Sqdn, 2e coy		2, 97
2e Division, Light Cavalry	***Lt.-Gen. Piré***	
1er Brigade	*Maj.-Gen. Huber*	
1er Chasseurs		40, 445
6e Chasseurs		34, 526
2e Brigade	*Maj.-Gen. Wathiez*	
5e Lanciers [3 sqdns]		25, 387
6e Lanciers		34, 347
Artillery & Train		
4e Horse Artillery, 2e coy		4, 76
1er Train Sqdn, 2e coy		2, 81

Reserve Artillery

2e Artillery, 7e coy	4, 96
1er Horse Artillery, 1ere coy	4, 68
1er Horse Artillery, 4e coy	3, 69
1er Train Sqdn, 2e coy	1, 79
1er Train Sqdn, 7e coy	2, 114
1er Train Sqdn, 10e coy	2, 67
1er Regiment Engineers, 1er Batt, coys 1 to 5	22, 409

III Corps — *Lt.-Gen. Comte Vandamme* — 17,429 men (inc. 1,017 Cav.), 38 guns

8e Division[§] — ***Lt.-Gen. Lefol***

1er Brigade — *Maj.-Gen. Billard*

15e Léger [3 battalions]	62, 1,676
23e Ligne [3 battalions]	62, 1,152

2e Brigade — *Maj.-Gen. Corsin*

37e Ligne [3 battalions]	59, 1,117
64e Ligne	40, 891

Artillery, Train, etc.

6e Artillery, 7e coy	4, 83
1er Train Sqdn, 1ere coy	2, 97
2e Regiment Engineers, 2e Batt, 2e coy	1, 15
Ambulances	11

10e Division — ***Lt.-Gen. Habert***

1er Brigade — *Maj.-Gen. Gengoult*

34e Ligne[§] [3 battalions]	55, 1,384
88e Ligne [3 battalions]	57, 1,265

2e Brigade — *Maj.-Gen. Dupeyroux*

22e Ligne [3 battalions]	55, 1,406
70e Ligne	45, 909
2e Régiment Etranger (Swiss) [1 battalion]	21, 386

Artillery, Train, etc.

2e Artillery, 18e coy	4, 89
5e Train Sqdn, 4e coy	2, 92
2e Engineers, 2e Bn, 2e coy	4, 81
Ambulances	8

11e Division	***Lt.-Gen. Berthezène***	
1er Brigade	*Maj.-Gen. Dufour*	
12e Ligne		41, 1,171
56e Ligne		42, 1,234
2e Brigade	*Maj.-Gen. Lagarde*	
33e Ligne		39, 1,097
86e Ligne		44, 870
Artillery, Train, etc.		
2e Artillery, 17e coy		4, 96
5e Train Sqdn, 5e coy		2, 94
2e Regiment Engineers, 2e Batt, 2e coy		2, 48
Ambulances		7
3e Division, Light Cavalry	***Lt.-Gen. Domon***	
1er Brigade	*Maj.-Gen. Dommanget*	
4e Chasseurs		31, 306
9e Chasseurs		25, 337
2e Brigade	*Maj.-Gen. Vinot*	
12e Chasseurs		29, 289
2e Horse Artillery, 4e coy		3, 74
5e Train Sqdn, 6e coy		3, 100
Reserve Artillery		
2e Artillery, 1ere coy		4, 95
2e Artillery, 19e coy		4, 97
5e Train Sqdn, 6e coy		2, 104

IV Corps or Army of the Moselle

Lt.-Gen. Comte Gérard 16,634 men (inc. 1,751 Cav.), 38 guns

12e Division	***Lt.-Gen. Pécheux***	
1er Brigade	*Maj.-Gen. Rome*	
30e Ligne [3 battalions]		34, 1,399
96e Ligne [3 battalions]		31, 1,387
2e Brigade	*Maj.-Gen. Schaeffer*	
63e Ligne [3 battalions]		53, 1,214
6e Léger [1 battalion]		20, 591

Artillery, Train, etc.		
5e Artillery, 2e coy		3, 98
2e Train Sqdn, 6e coy		2, 97
13e Division	***Lt.-Gen. Vichery***	
1er Brigade	*Maj.-Gen. Le Capitaine*	
59e Ligne		42, 1,015
76e Ligne		40, 1014
2e Brigade	*Maj.-Gen. Desprez*	
48e Ligne		43, 834
69e Ligne§		40, 1,077
Artillery, Train, etc.		
5e Artillery, 1ere coy		5, 97
2e Train Sqdn, 2e coy		3, 92
2e Regiment Engineers, 2e Batt, 5e coy		58
14e Division	***Lt.-Gen. Bourmont***	
1er Brigade	*Maj.-Gen. Hulot*	
9e Léger		43, 1,215
111e Ligne		43, 1,035
2e Brigade	*Maj.-Gen. Toussaint*	
44e Ligne		43, 934
50e Ligne		40, 874
Artillery, Train. etc.		
3e Horse Artillery, 3e coy		4, 80
2e Train Sqdn, 2e coy		2, 76
2e Regiment Engineers, 2e Batt, 3e coy		3, 74
7e Division, Light Cavalry	***Lt.-Gen. Maurin***	
1er Brigade	*Maj.-Gen. Vallin*	
6e Hussards [3 sqdns]		26, 387
2e Brigade	*Maj.-Gen. Berruyer*	
8e Chasseurs [3 sqdns]		30, 371
Reserve Cavalry		
1er Brigade	*Maj.-Gen. Cureley*	
6e Dragons [3 sqdns]		20, 211
11e Dragons		30, 340

2e Brigade	*Maj.-Gen. Gauthrin*	
15e Dragons [3 sqdns]		28, 308
16e Dragons		*unknown*
2e Horse Artillery		3, 75
2e Train Sqdn		2, 79
Reserve Artillery, Engineers		
5e Artillery, 3e, 4e, 5e, 11e coys		13, 386
1er Battn Pontoons, 4e coy		4, 63
2e Train Sqdn, 5e,7e, 8e, 9e coys		9, 383
2e Regiment Engineers, 4e coy		2, 69

VI Corps — *Lt.-Gen. Mouton, Comte de Lobau*

10,400 men, 38 guns

19e Division	***Lt.-Gen. Simmer***	
1er Brigade	*Maj.-Gen. de Bellair*	
5e Ligne		42, 910
11e Ligne [3 battalions]		61, 1,135
2e Brigade	*Maj.-Gen. Jamin*	
27e Ligne		39, 782
84e Ligne		45, 894
Artillery, Train, etc.		
8e Artillery, 1ere coy		3, 83
7e Train Sqdn, -e coy		3, 53
8e Train Sqdn, 4e coy		1, 37
3e Regiment Engineers, 1ere Battalion, 1ere coy		4, 91
3e Sqdn, 1ere coy Military Equipments		12
Auxiliaries of Oise, 3e coy Equipmts		2, 50
20e Division	***Lt.-Gen. Jeanin***	
1er Brigade	*Maj.-Gen. Bony*	
5e Léger		42, 834
10e Ligne		56, 1,375
2e Brigade	*Maj.-Gen. Tromelin*	
47e Ligne [detached to La Vendée]		[45, 1,008]
107e Ligne		44, 692

Artillery, Train, etc.		
8e Artillery, 2e coy		3, 88
8e Train Sqdn, 3e coy		2, 102
3e Regiment Engineers, 1ere Battalion, 2e coy [detached to Laon]		[3, 97]
3e Sqdn, 1ere coy Military Equipments		12
Auxiliaries of Aisne, 3e coy Equipmts		2, 50
21e Division	***Lt.-Gen. Teste***	
1er Brigade	*Maj.-Gen. Laffite*	
8e Léger		42, 896
40e Ligne [assembling in depot]		–
2e Brigade	*Maj.-Gen. Penne*	
65e Ligne [1 battalion]		22, 481
75e Ligne		42, 939
Artillery, Train, etc.		
8e Artillery, 3e coy		3, 91
6e Train Sqdn, 4e coy		2, 70
3e Regiment Engineers, 1ere Battalion, 3e coy		3, 98
3e Sqdn, 1ere coy Military Equipments		14
Auxiliaries of Aisne, 4e coy Equipmts		1, 13
Reserve Artillery		
8e Artillery, 4e coy		3, 92
8e Train Sqdn, 3e, 4e, 5e coys		2, 27

Reserve Cavalry — *Marshal Marquis de Grouchy*

I Cavalry Corps	***Lt.-Gen. Comte Pajol***	2,860 men, 12 guns
4e Cavalry Division	***Lt.-Gen. Pierre Soult***	
1er Brigade	*Maj.-Gen. St Laurent*	
1er Hussards		36, 489
4e Hussards		29, 346
2e Brigade	*Maj.-Gen. Amiel*	
5e Hussards		29, 399
1er Horse Artillery, 1ere coy		2, 70
1er Train Sqdn, 3e coy		1, 84

5e Cavalry Division	***Lt.-Gen. Subervie***	
1er Brigade	*Maj.-Gen. Colbert*	
1er Lanciers		40, 375
2e Lanciers		41, 379
2e Brigade	*Maj.-Gen. Merlin*	
11e Chasseurs		37, 336
1er Horse Artillery, 3e coy		2, 74
1er Train Sqdn, 4e coy		2, 89
II Cavalry Corps	***Lt.-Gen. Comte Exelmans***	3,750 men, 12 guns
9e Cavalry Division	***Lt.-Gen. Strolz***	
1er Brigade	*Maj.-Gen. Burthe*	
5e Dragons		41, 465
13e Dragons		35, 389
2e Brigade	*Maj.-Gen. Vincent*	
15e Dragons		34, 381
20e Dragons		31, 316
1er Horse Artillery, 4e coy		4, 55
1er Train Sqdn, 6e coy		1, 59
10e Cavalry Division	***Lt.-Gen. Chastel***	
1er Brigade	*Maj.-Gen. Bonnemains*	
4e Dragons		35, 530
12e Dragons		30, 510
2e Brigade	*Maj.-Gen. Berton*	
14e Dragons		34, 339
17e Dragons		39, 287
4e Horse Artillery, 4e coy		2, 60
2e Train Sqdn, 1ere coy		1, 72
III Cavalry Corps	***Lt.-Gen. Kellermann, Comte de Valmy***	3,814 men, 12 guns
11e Cavalry Division	***Lt.-Gen. Lhéritier***	
1er Brigade	*Maj.-Gen. Picquet*	
2e Dragons		40, 54
7e Dragons3		41, 475

2e Brigade	*Maj.-Gen. Guiton*[§]	
8e Cuirassiers [3 sqdns]		31, 421
11e Cuirassiers [2 sqdns]		21, 304
2e Horse Artillery, 3e coy		3, 75
2e Train Sqdn, 3e coy		2, 81
12e Cavalry Division	***Lt.-Gen. Roussel d'Hurbal***	
1er Brigade	*Maj.-Gen. Blancard*	
1er Carabiniers [3 sqdns]		30, 403
2e Carabiniers [3 sqdns]		29, 380
2e Brigade	*Maj.-Gen. Donop*	
2e Cuirassiers [2 sqdns]		21, 292
3e Cuirassiers		37, 427
2e Horse Artillery, 2e coy		3, 75
2e Train Sqdn, 4e coy		2, 78
IV Cavalry Corps	***Lt.-Gen. Comte Milhaud***	3,120 men, 12 guns
13e Cavalry Division	***Lt.-Gen. Watier de St Alphonse***	
1er Brigade	*Maj.-Gen. Dubois*	
1er Cuirassiers		41, 411
4e Cuirassiers [3 sqdns]		28, 278
2e Brigade	*Maj.-Gen. Travers*	
7e Cuirassiers [2 sqdns]		21, 151
12e Cuirassiers [2 sqdns]		22, 226
1er Horse Artillery, 5e coy		3, 75
1er Train Sqdn, 8e coy		2, 79
14e Cavalry Division	***Lt.-Gen. Delort***	
1er Brigade	*Maj.-Gen. Farine*	
5e Cuirassiers [3 sqdns]		34, 380
10e Cuirassiers [3 sqdns]		26, 309
2e Brigade	*Maj.-Gen. Vial*	
6e Cuirassiers		37, 474
9e Cuirassiers [3 sqdns]		32, 327
3e Horse Artillery, 4e coy		3, 70
1er Train Sqdn, –e coy		2, 89

Recapitulation

Staff	664
Infantry	88,702
Cavalry	22,231
Artillery	5,139
Train, Engineers etc	6,907
	123,033 and 346 guns

Note: officers included, staff total incomplete.

Suggested corrections to Houssaye's Orbat:

I Corps, 2e Division: 13e Regiment should be Léger, not Ligne; 51e should be Ligne, not Léger.

II Corps: Foy's Division was not the *8e* but the *9e*.

III Corps: Lefol's Division was not the 9e but the 8e. In the 10e Division [Habert], in the 1e Brigade the 34e Ligne was omitted in the English translated edition, though present in the French.

IV Corps, 13e Division: 60e Ligne should be 69e Ligne.

III Cavalry Corps, 11e Cavalry Division: 2e Brigade [Guiton] correctly has 8e and 11e Cuirassiers in both French and English editions but, on p. 332 of the English edition only, these two regiments again wrongly appear in II Cavalry Corps, 9e Cavalry Division, 2e Brigade.

Sources: Principally, Houssaye's *Waterloo*, Book 1, chap. 2; and DBTS, vol. iii, pp. 166–99.

Sources Consulted

Manuscript Sources

Wellington Papers	Hartley Library, University of Southampton
Admiralty Papers	National Archives, Kew: HMS *Partridge*: Captain's and Master's Logs (ship's log has not survived)
Bathurst Papers	British Library (formerly at Cirencester House)
Hill Papers	British Library
Louisa Lloyd's Diary	National Library of Wales
Lowe Papers	British Library
Macmillan & Co correspondence with Sir John Fortescue	British Library
Sir P. Malcolm's Journal	National Archives, Kew
Murray Papers (De Lacy Evans MS on Waterloo)	National Library of Scotland
Raglan Papers	Gwent Record Office
Royal Archives	Windsor Castle (Napoleon's letter to the Prince Regent, Rochefort, 13 July 1815)
Scovell memorandum	National Archives, Kew
Siborne Papers	British Library
Sir Charles Stuart's Despatches	National Archives, Kew

Printed Sources

Adkin, Mark, *The Waterloo Companion*, 2001

Aerts, Winand, *Waterloo: Opérations de l'Armée Prussienne du Bas-Rhin pendant la Campagne de Belgique en 1815*, Brussels, 1908

Albemarle, 6th Earl of, *Fifty Years of My Life*, 2 vols, 1876 (Ensign G. T. Keppel in 1815)

Anglesey, 7th Marquess of, *One Leg*, 1961

Annual Register

Arbuthnot, Charles, *Correspondence*, ed. A. Aspinall, Royal Historical Society/Camden Society, new series vol. 65, 1941

Arbuthnot, Mrs, *Journal, 1820–32*, ed. F. Bamford and the 7th Duke of Wellington, 2 vols, 1950

Ardant du Picq, Colonel C., *Etudes sur le Combat*, Paris, 1903 (first complete edition) reprinted 1942
Army List, The, edition dated 13 March 1815
Atkinson, C. T., 'An "Infamous Army"', *JSAHR*, vol. 32, 1954, pp. 48–53, and also Note 1,139 (by Colonel Martin)

Barbero, A., *The Battle: A new history of Waterloo*, 2003, Engl. trans., 2005
Barnett, Correlli, *Bonaparte*, 1978
Barrett, C. R. B., *The 7th (Queen's Own) Hussars*, vol. i, 1914 (1815 letter and 1837 statement of Lt. O'Grady)
Beamish, Major N. Ludlow, *History of the King's German Legion*, 2 vols, 1832–7
Bausset, L. F. J. de, *Mémoires sur l'Intérieur du Palais, 3 vols,* Paris, 1828–9
Becke, Major A. F., *Napoleon and Waterloo*, 2nd edition, 1936
Beckett (II), Stephen M., *Waterloo Betrayed*, Canton, Georgia, 2015
Belle-Alliance (Verbündetes Heer), ed. J. von Pflugk-Harttung, Berlin, 1915
Bernard, Colonel Henri, *Le Duc de Wellington et la Belgique,* Brussels, 1973, repr. 1983
Berthezène, General, *Souvenirs Militaires*, 2 vols, Paris, 1855
Bertrand, General (Comte Henri), *Cahiers de Ste-Hélène*, deciphered and ed. P. Fleuriot de Langle, Paris, 3 vols, 1949–59 (published out of sequence: vol. 3, 1821; vol. 1,1816–17; vol. 2, 1818–19)
Bertrand, General (Comte Henri), *Lettres à Fanny, 1808–1815*, ed. S. de la Vaissière-Orfila, Paris, 1979
———, 'Avant-Propos' of 1842 to *Guerre d'Orient, Campagnes d'Egypte et de Syrie, 1798–1799 ... dictés par Napoléon à Ste-Hélène*, Paris, 2 vols, 1847.
Bertrand, P., *Lettres Inédites de Talleyrand à Napoléon, 1800–1809*, Paris, 1889
Biddulph, Col. H., *The XIXth and their Times*, 1899 (eyewitness on Wellesley at Assaye)
Blok, P. J., *A History of the People of the Netherlands*, vol. v, Engl trans, New York, 1912
Bonnal, Gen. H., *La Manouevre de Landshut*, Paris, 1905
Bonnefonds, A., *Un Allié de Napoléon, Frédéric-Auguste* (of Saxony), Paris, 1902
Booth's Battle of Waterloo: first published by John Booth as *The Battle of Waterloo, by a Near Observer*: the seventh edition, dated 1815, has been republished for 2015 by Osprey Books. (The eleventh revised edition *illustrated by George Jones RA*, 1852, is often mistakenly referred to as written by Jones)
Boudon, J.-O., *Napoléon et la Dernière Campagne, Les Cent Jours 1815*, Paris, 2015
Boulger, Demetrius, *The Belgians at Waterloo*, 1901
Bourgeois, E., *Manuel Historique de Politique Etrangère*, vol. 2 (1789–1830), Paris, 9th edn., 1926
Bowles, Captain George: see Malmesbury
Brett-James, Antony, *The Hundred Days: Napoleon's last campaign from eye-witness accounts*, 1964
Brialmont A., *Histoire du Duc de Wellington*, Brussels and Paris, 3 vols, 1856–57; also as *History of the Life of Arthur, Duke of Wellington, from the French of M. Brialmont, with emendations and additions by the Revd G. R. Gleig*, 4 vols, 1858
British Diplomacy, 1813–1815, ed. C. K. Webster, 1920: BD (documents)
Bro, General Louis, *Mémoires*, Paris, 1914 (the French account of Sir W. Ponsonby's death)
Brotonne, L. de, *Dernières Lettres Inédites de Napoléon I*, 2 vols, Paris, 1898
Bruce, H. A., *The Life of General Sir William Napier*, 2 vols, 1864
Brunschvicg, Léon, *Cambronne, après les documents inédits*, Nantes, 1894
Brunyee, P. F., *Napoleon's Britons and the St Helena Decision*, 2009

Bunbury, Sir C. J. F., *Memoir and Literary Remains of Lt.-Gen.eral Sir H. E. Bunbury*, 1868

Burghersh, John, Lord (11th Earl of Westmorland, 1841), *Correspondence of Lord Burghersh, 1808–40*, ed. R. Weigall, 1912

———, *Memoir of the Operations of the Allied Armies, late 1813 and 1814* (in Germany and eastern France), 1822

Burghersh, Priscilla (*née* Wellesley), Lady, *The Letters of Lady Burghersh, 1813–1814*, ed. R. Weigall, 1893

Callataÿ, Philippe de, 'La Concentration de l'Armée française pour la campagne de Juin 1815', *Bulletin de la Soc. Royale Belge d'Etudes Napoléoniennes*, tome 51, 2007; Engl transl, *First Empire*, No. 102, Sept/Oct 2008, pp. 22–9.

Cambridge History of the British Empire, The, vol. ii, *1783–1870*, ed. Rose, Newton & Benians, 1940

Cambridge History of British Foreign Policy, The, vol. i, *1783–1815*, ed. Ward & Gooch, 1922 (*CHBFP*)

Cambridge Modern History, The, vol. ix *Napoleon*, ed. Ward, Prothero & Leathes, 1906 (*CMH*)

Camon, Colonel Hubert, *La Guerre Napoléonienne*, vol. 3, *Les Batailles*. Paris, 1910

Capel Letters 1814–17, The, ed. Marquess of Anglesey, 1955

Castlereagh Correspondence, ed. Lord Londonderry (the former Charles, the Lord Stewart of Vienna fame), vol. x, 1853

Campbell, Sir Neil, *Napoleon at Fontainebleau and Elba*, 1869

Carew, P., *Combat and Carnival*, 1954 (Taylor letters)

Carey, Neil, 'Quatre Bras and Ligny', *First Empire*, no.43, Nov./Dec. 1998, pp. 33–4

Castelot, André, *Napoléon*, 2 vols, Paris, 1968

Caulaincourt A.-A., Duc de Vicence, *Mémoires*, 3 vols, Paris, 1933

Cavalry Journal, 'Raids; Horsemastership and Long Distance Riding', in vol. 1, Jan 1906, pp. 33–45

Chandler, David, *The Campaigns of Napoleon*, 1967 (Part 17 contains the 1815 campaign; at the time it was written and perhaps still today the best short account)

———, *Waterloo, The Hundred Days*, 1980

Chaptal, Comte, *Mes Souvenirs sur Napoléon*, Paris, 1893

Charras, Lt-Colonel J. B. A., *Histoire de la Campagne de 1815, Waterloo*, 2 vols, Brussels, 1858

Chesney, Colonel Charles, *Waterloo Lectures*, 4th edn. of 1907, repr 1997 (1st edn., 1868)

Chuquet, Arthur, *La Jeunesse de Napoléon*, 3 vols, Paris, 1898 (vol. ii describes his role in the Ajaccio troubles of Easter 1792)

Chuquet, Arthur, see *Inédits Napoléoniens*, and *Ordres et Apostilles*

Churchill, Major (later Maj.-Gen.), Chatham Horace, 'Letter' of 28 June 1815, in H. A Bruce, i, p. 175 (*see* Bruce)

Clapham, (Sir) John H., *The Economic Development of France and Germany, 1815–1914*, 3rd edn., 1927

Clausewitz, C. von, *On War*, transl and ed. M. Howard & P. Paret, Princeton, 1992

———, *Historical & Political Writings*, ed. P. Paret & D. Moran, 1992

———, *The Campaign of 1812 in Russia*, Engl. trans (by Lord F. Egerton), 1843.

———, *The Campaign of 1815*, (in 'On Waterloo, Clausewitz, Wellington and the Campaign of 1815'), ed. Christopher Bassford, Daniel Moran & Gregory W. Pedlow (BMP), 2010

Clay, Matthew, 3rd Guards, *Narrative of Battles of Quatre Bras and Waterloo*, n/d , repr 2006, ed. G. Glover

Clayton, Tim, *Waterloo, Four Days that Changed Europe's Destiny*, 2014

Clinton, Lt.-General Sir H., *Correspondence of Sir H. Clinton in the Waterloo Campaign, 1814–18*, 2 vols, ed. G. Glover, 2015

Coignet, Captain J.-R., *The Notebooks of Captain Coignet*, 'Soldiers' Tales Series', 1929

Consolidated Treaty Series, 1648–1918, ed. C. Parry, vols 63 and 64 (1813–1815), New York, 1969 (*CTS*).

Constant Rebecque, Baron J. V. de, 'Journal', ed. J. Logie, in *Mélanges Historiques*, Soc. d'Etudes Hist. de Waterloo, Braine l'Alleud, 1970

Coppens, B. & Courcelle, P., *Les Carnets de la Campagne*, 5 vols, Brussels, 1999–2002

Corbett, Sir Julian, 'Napoleon and the British Navy after Trafalgar' (the Creighton Lecture, 1921), *Quarterly Review*, vol. 237, 1922, pp. 238–55

Corrigan, Major Gordon, *Wellington, a Military Life*, 2001

Cotton, Sgt.-Major E., *A Voice from Waterloo*, 5th edn., 1854

Couderc de St Chamant, Captain Henri, *Napoléon, ses dernières armées*, Paris, 1902

Cousins, Gary, 'A Belle Alliance', *First Empire*, No. 67, Nov/Dec 2002, pp. 4–7, 23–5.

———, 'A Message about Siborne and Clausewitz', *First Empire*, No. 70, May/June 2003, pp. 31–5

———, 'Wellington's Meeting with Blücher before Ligny', *First Empire*, No. 71, July/Aug 2003, pp. 28–33

———, 'Left Wing History', seven long articles in *First Empire*, Nos 76, commencing at p. 4; 77, p. 4; 78, p. 22; 79, p. 23; 80, p. 28; 84, p. 26; 85, p. 18 - from May/June 2004 to Nov/Dec 2005. (The final article on 'the pause' after the *Garde's* defeat demonstrates how Siborne eventually realised that he had placed the Prussians too far forward on his famous model.)

(Cowell Stepney, Lt.-Colonel S.) Anon., *Leaves from a Diary of an Officer of the Guards*, 1854

Craan, W. B., *Waterloo Map, 1817, with Historical Account in Elucidation, transl into English*, Napoleonic Archive, ND

Creevey Papers, The, ed. Sir H. Maxwell, 2 vols, 1903

De Bas, Colonel F., *Prins Frederik der Nederlanden*, vol. 3, part II, Schiedam, 1904

De Bas, Colonel F., and T'Serclaes de Wommersom, General J., *La Campagne de 1815*, 3 vols and a vol. of maps, Brussels, 1908 (DBTS)

Dalton, Charles, *The Waterloo Roll Call*, 2nd edn., 1904, repr. 1971

Davies, Huw J., *Wellington's Wars, the Making of a Military Genius*, Yale, 2012 (pp. 214–47 concern the 1815 campaign)

Davout, Marshal, *Correspondance 1801–15*, vol. iv (1813–15), ed. C. de Mazade, Paris, 1885 (see also Gallaher)

Delbrück, Hans, *Das Leben des Feldmarschalls Grafen Neithardt von Gneisenau*, vol. 4 (1814–15), Berlin, 1880 (continuation of the late G. Perz's biography, and sometimes listed under *Perz*)

Delhaize, Jules, & Aerts, Winand, *Etudes rélatives à la Campagne de Waterloo* (only the first volume was published), Brussels, 1915

Dellevoet, André, 'Cowards at Waterloo? Bijlandt's Brigade in 1815', in *Napoleon* (Berkeley, Calif.), No. 16, Summer 2000, pp. 18–36

De Salle, General Baron, 'Souvenirs', in *Revue de Paris*, 15 Jan 1895, pp. 407–37

Dible, J. H., *Napoleon's Surgeon* (Larrey), 1970

Dictionnaire Napoléon, ed. J. Tulard, 2nd edn., 2 vols, Paris, 1999 (*Dict Nap*)

Du Casse, A., *Le Général Vandamme*, vol. 2, Paris, 1870

Duncan, Captain Francis, *The History of the Royal Regiment of Artillery*, vol. 2, 1873; see also Hime

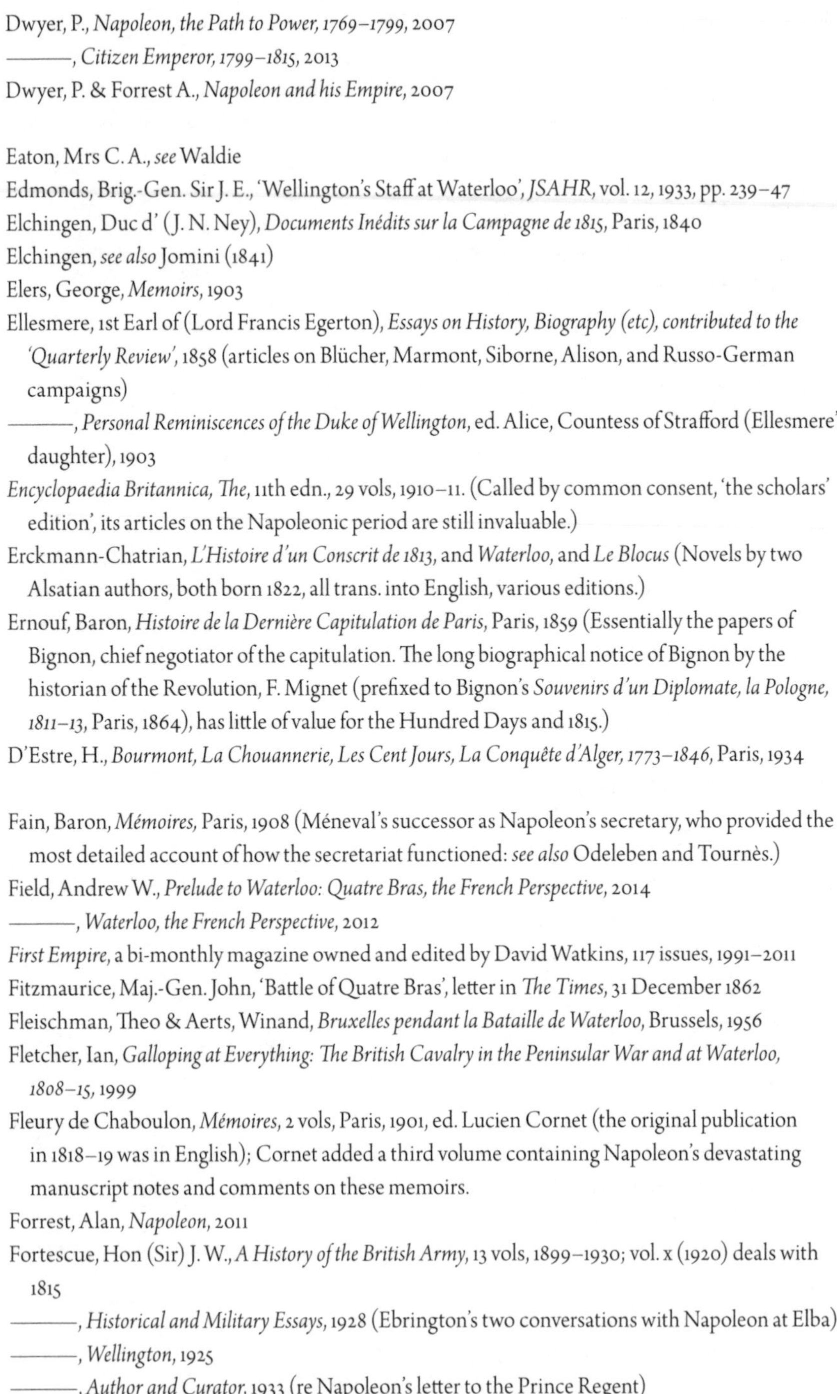

Dwyer, P., *Napoleon, the Path to Power, 1769–1799*, 2007

———, *Citizen Emperor, 1799–1815*, 2013

Dwyer, P. & Forrest A., *Napoleon and his Empire*, 2007

Eaton, Mrs C. A., *see* Waldie

Edmonds, Brig.-Gen. Sir J. E., 'Wellington's Staff at Waterloo', *JSAHR*, vol. 12, 1933, pp. 239–47

Elchingen, Duc d' (J. N. Ney), *Documents Inédits sur la Campagne de 1815*, Paris, 1840

Elchingen, *see also* Jomini (1841)

Elers, George, *Memoirs*, 1903

Ellesmere, 1st Earl of (Lord Francis Egerton), *Essays on History, Biography (etc), contributed to the 'Quarterly Review'*, 1858 (articles on Blücher, Marmont, Siborne, Alison, and Russo-German campaigns)

———, *Personal Reminiscences of the Duke of Wellington*, ed. Alice, Countess of Strafford (Ellesmere's daughter), 1903

Encyclopaedia Britannica, The, 11th edn., 29 vols, 1910–11. (Called by common consent, 'the scholars' edition', its articles on the Napoleonic period are still invaluable.)

Erckmann-Chatrian, *L'Histoire d'un Conscrit de 1813*, and *Waterloo*, and *Le Blocus* (Novels by two Alsatian authors, both born 1822, all trans. into English, various editions.)

Ernouf, Baron, *Histoire de la Dernière Capitulation de Paris*, Paris, 1859 (Essentially the papers of Bignon, chief negotiator of the capitulation. The long biographical notice of Bignon by the historian of the Revolution, F. Mignet (prefixed to Bignon's *Souvenirs d'un Diplomate, la Pologne, 1811–13*, Paris, 1864), has little of value for the Hundred Days and 1815.)

D'Estre, H., *Bourmont, La Chouannerie, Les Cent Jours, La Conquête d'Alger, 1773–1846*, Paris, 1934

Fain, Baron, *Mémoires*, Paris, 1908 (Méneval's successor as Napoleon's secretary, who provided the most detailed account of how the secretariat functioned: *see also* Odeleben and Tournès.)

Field, Andrew W., *Prelude to Waterloo: Quatre Bras, the French Perspective*, 2014

———, *Waterloo, the French Perspective*, 2012

First Empire, a bi-monthly magazine owned and edited by David Watkins, 117 issues, 1991–2011

Fitzmaurice, Maj.-Gen. John, 'Battle of Quatre Bras', letter in *The Times*, 31 December 1862

Fleischman, Theo & Aerts, Winand, *Bruxelles pendant la Bataille de Waterloo*, Brussels, 1956

Fletcher, Ian, *Galloping at Everything: The British Cavalry in the Peninsular War and at Waterloo, 1808–15*, 1999

Fleury de Chaboulon, *Mémoires*, 2 vols, Paris, 1901, ed. Lucien Cornet (the original publication in 1818–19 was in English); Cornet added a third volume containing Napoleon's devastating manuscript notes and comments on these memoirs.

Forrest, Alan, *Napoleon*, 2011

Fortescue, Hon (Sir) J. W., *A History of the British Army*, 13 vols, 1899–1930; vol. x (1920) deals with 1815

———, *Historical and Military Essays*, 1928 (Ebrington's two conversations with Napoleon at Elba)

———, *Wellington*, 1925

———, *Author and Curator*, 1933 (re Napoleon's letter to the Prince Regent)

Fouché, Joseph, Duc of Otranto, *Mémoires*, 2 vols, Paris, 1824 (based on some authentic papers, but with much posthumous editorial elaboration)

Fournier, August, *Der Congress von Châtillon*, Vienna, 1900 (despite the French surname he was Austrian by birth and nationality)

Fournier, August, *Napoleon I, a Biography*, Eng. trans. 2 vols, 1911 (from the German text, Vienna, 3 vols, 2nd edn., 1903–5)

Foy, General Maximilien, *La Vie Militaire du Général Foy*, by Girod de l'Ain, Paris, 1900

Franklin, J. (ed), *Waterloo: Hanoverian Correspondence*, vol. 1, 2010

———, *Waterloo: Netherlands Correspondence*, vol. 1, 2010.

Fraser, Gen. Sir David, *And We Shall Shock Them: The British Army in the Second World War*, 1983

Fraser, Sir W., *Words on Wellington*, 1889

Frazer, Sir Augustus Simon, *Letters of Colonel Sir A. S. Frazer*, ed. E. Sabine, 1859

Gallaher, John G., *The Iron Marshal, the Life of L. N. Davout*, 1976, repr. 2000

———, *Napoleon's Enfant Terrible, General Dominique Vandamme*, Norman, Oklahoma, 2008

Gawler, Major George, 'The Crisis & Close of the Action at Waterloo', *USJ*, July 1833, pp. 299–310

Gawler, Major George, 'Answer to Sir R. H. Vivian's Reply, *USJ*, Sept 1833, pp. 1–16

Germain, Pierre, *Drouet d'Erlon*, Paris, 1985

Geyl, Pieter, *Napoleon: For and Against*, 1948; Peregrine edition, 1966 (with a different pagination from the 1948 edition; the work of a great European historian on the Emperor; and a penetrating analysis of a century of French interpretations, e.g. of Houssaye, Masson, Thiers, Vandal.)

Gingerich, Jonathan, 'A Commentary on *1815, the Waterloo Campaign*', First Empire, no. 44, Jan./Feb. 1999, pp. 26–7

Girod de l'Ain, *see* Foy

Gleig, Revd G. R., (see also Brialmont)

———, *The Life of Arthur, 1st Duke of Wellington*, 1862 (a popular condensation of Brialmont–Gleig)

———, *Personal Reminiscences of the 1st Duke of Wellington*, 1903

———, *The Story of the Battle of Waterloo*, 1847 (see the adverse 'Remarks' by W. Siborne in his *History*, ed. 3, pp. ix–xxvii; and by Charles Arbuthnot)

Glover, Gareth, *Eyewitness to the Peninsular War and the Battle of Waterloo: The letters and journals of Colonel James Stanhope, 1803–25*, 2010

———, *Waterloo, Myth and Reality*, 2014

———, *Waterloo: The Defeat of Napoleon's Imperial Guard*, 2015

———, *see also* Clinton, Fremantle, *Letters from Waterloo*, Sperling, *Waterloo Archive*

Gneisenau, Count, *The Life and Campaigns of Marshal Prince Blücher*, Eng. trans. 1815 (in reality this ends with 1814; the translator adds notes of later events)

Gomm, Field Marshal Sir William Maynard, *Letters & Journals, 1799–1815*, ed. F. C. Carr-Gomm, 1881

Gordon, Sir Alexander, *At Wellington's Right Hand* (Gordon's letters), ed. Rory Muir, Army Records Soc., 2003

Gourgaud, General Baron G., *The Campaign of 1815*, 1818, repr 1982 (the French version has a different pagination)

———, *Ste-Hélène, Journal inédit de 1815 à 1818*, 2 vols, Paris, 1899

Granville, *The Letters of Harriet, Countess Granville, 1810–45*, 2 vols, 1894

Gregory, Desmond, *Napoleon's Jailer, Lt. Gen. Sir Hudson Lowe*, 1996

Greville, Charles C. F., *Memoirs*, ed. L. Strachey & R. Fulford, 8 vols, 1938 (vols 1 and 6 in particular)

Griewank, Karl, *Gneisenau: Ein Leben in Briefen*, Leipzig, 1939
Grouard, A. (writing as 'AG'), *La Critique de la Campagne de 1815* (Part 3 of 'Stratégie Napoléonienne'), Paris, 1904 (makes a reasoned case against Houssaye)
Gronow, Captain R., *Reminiscences*, 1862, reprinted with different pagination 1964
Grouchy, Marshal E. de, *Mémoires*, ed. A. de Grouchy, vols 3, 4, 5, Paris, 1873–4 (many useful documents but because of omissions and corruptions requires to be used with great care)
Guedalla, Philip, *The Hundred Days*, 1934, repr 1939
Guérard, Albert Leon, *Reflections on the Napoleonic Legend*, 1924 (A French humanist who settled in the USA aged 26 and stayed till his death in 1959; a refreshing treatment apparently never published in France.)

Hafner, Dietrich, 'Hans Carl Ernst Graf von Zieten', *Militärisches* (*Militärischen Rundschau*), Leipzig, 1896 (for extracts from Ziethen's unreliable 1839 autobiographical 'Aus dem leben' or reminiscences)
Hall, Major (Sir) John R., *The Bourbon Restoration*, 1909
Hamilton-Williams, D., *Waterloo, New Perspectives*, 1993
Hamley, Col. (later Gen Sir) E. B. Hamley, *The Operations of War*, 1866, 6th edn. 1913 as revised by Col. (Lt.-Gen. Sir) L. E. Kiggell (Hamley's criticisms of Thiers's account of Waterloo were silently adopted by Chesney in 1868 without acknowledgement.)
Harrison, David, *The Bridges of Medieval England: Transport and society, 400–1800*, 2004
Hayman, Peter, *Soult, Napoleon's Maligned Marshal*, 1990
Haythornthwaite, Philip, *The Armies of Wellington*, 1994, edition of 1998
———, *Waterloo Men, the Experience of Battle, 16–18 June 1815*, 1999
———, *The Waterloo Armies: men, organization, tactics*, 2007.
———, *Redcoats, the British Soldiers of the Napoleonic Wars*, 2012
Heeley, Edward, *Journal of the 1815 campaign*, ed. D. Chandler, *JSAHR*, vol. 64, 1986, pp. 94–117, 129–42 (Sir G. Scovell's servant)
Helfert, *Maria Louise*, Vienna, 1873 (Dresden, 1813, and Metternich's estimate of Napoleon)
Henderson, E. F., *Blücher and the Uprising of Prussia against Napoleon*, 1911
Henegan, Sir Richard D., *Seven Years' Campaigning in the Peninsula and the Netherlands, 1808–1815*, 2 vols, 1846
Hertslet, E., *The Map of Europe by Treaty*, 1875
Hervey, Sir Felton, Letter (undated, but 1817–19) in *The Nineteenth Century*, vol. 33, March 1893, pp. 430–5
Heymès, Colonel, *Relation* (1829), in Elchingen, *Documents Inédits*
Hill, Joanna, *Wellington's Right Hand: Rowland, Viscount Hill*, 2011
Hime, Col. H. W. L., *History of the Royal Regiment of Artillery, 1815–1853*, 1908; see also Duncan
HMC, Bathurst Papers, 1923
(Hobhouse, J. C.) Anon., *The Substance of Some Letters from Paris*, 2 vols, 1816
Hofschröer, Peter, *1815, the Waterloo Campaign*, 2 vols, 1998–9 (generally referred to as Hofschröer, *1815*, by vol. number)
Hofschröer, Peter, 'Did the Duke of Wellington Deceive his Prussian Allies in the 1815 Campaign?', *War in History*, vol. v (2), 1998, pp. 176–203. (see Hussey, *War in History*)
Hofschröer, Peter, 'Reply to John Hussey: at what time did Wellington *really* learn of Napoleon's

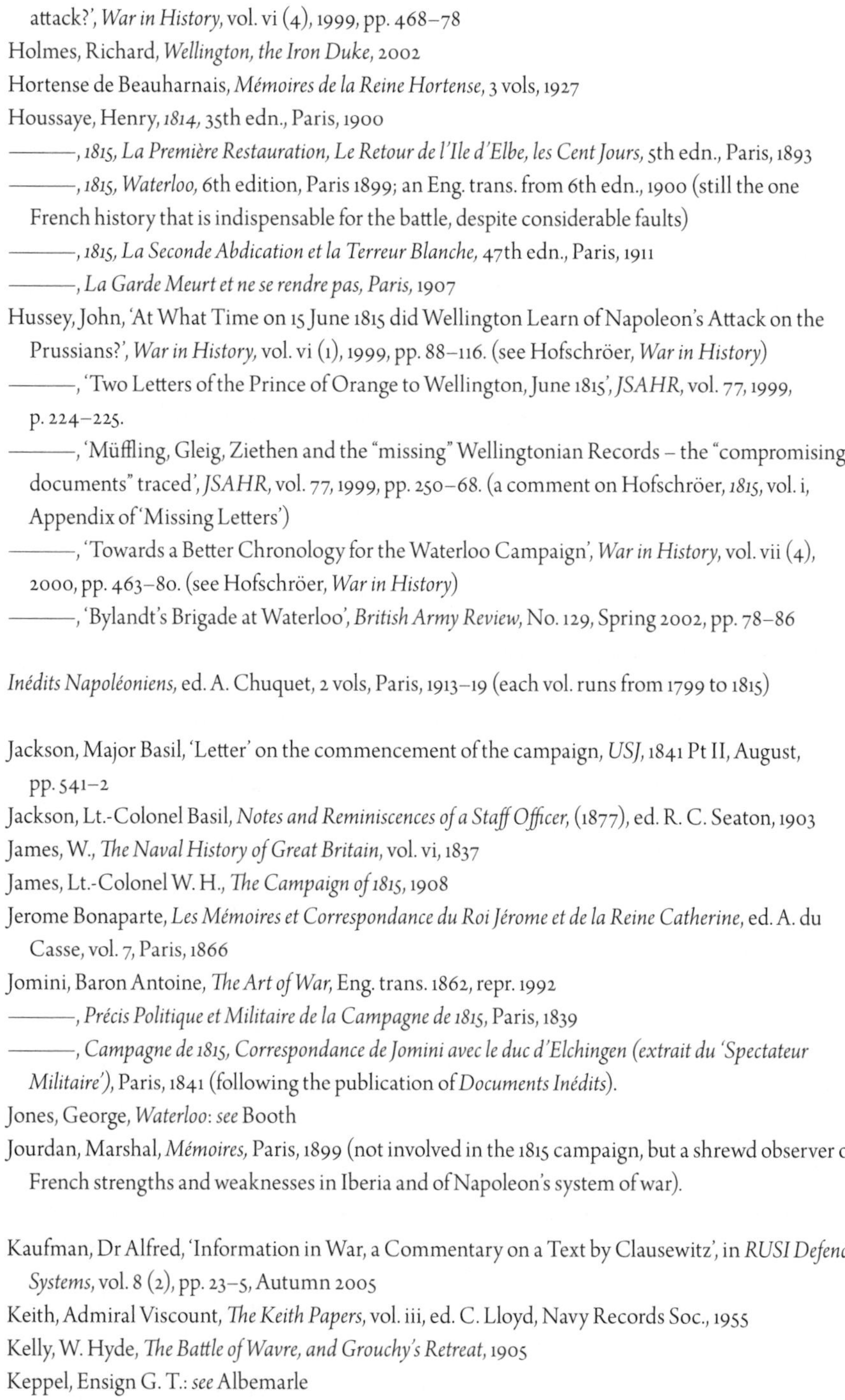

attack?', *War in History*, vol. vi (4), 1999, pp. 468–78

Holmes, Richard, *Wellington, the Iron Duke*, 2002

Hortense de Beauharnais, *Mémoires de la Reine Hortense*, 3 vols, 1927

Houssaye, Henry, *1814*, 35th edn., Paris, 1900

———, *1815, La Première Restauration, Le Retour de l'Ile d'Elbe, les Cent Jours*, 5th edn., Paris, 1893

———, *1815, Waterloo*, 6th edition, Paris 1899; an Eng. trans. from 6th edn., 1900 (still the one French history that is indispensable for the battle, despite considerable faults)

———, *1815, La Seconde Abdication et la Terreur Blanche*, 47th edn., Paris, 1911

———, *La Garde Meurt et ne se rendre pas, Paris*, 1907

Hussey, John, 'At What Time on 15 June 1815 did Wellington Learn of Napoleon's Attack on the Prussians?', *War in History*, vol. vi (1), 1999, pp. 88–116. (see Hofschröer, *War in History*)

———, 'Two Letters of the Prince of Orange to Wellington, June 1815', *JSAHR*, vol. 77, 1999, p. 224–225.

———, 'Müffling, Gleig, Ziethen and the "missing" Wellingtonian Records – the "compromising documents" traced', *JSAHR*, vol. 77, 1999, pp. 250–68. (a comment on Hofschröer, *1815*, vol. i, Appendix of 'Missing Letters')

———, 'Towards a Better Chronology for the Waterloo Campaign', *War in History*, vol. vii (4), 2000, pp. 463–80. (see Hofschröer, *War in History*)

———, 'Bylandt's Brigade at Waterloo', *British Army Review*, No. 129, Spring 2002, pp. 78–86

Inédits Napoléoniens, ed. A. Chuquet, 2 vols, Paris, 1913–19 (each vol. runs from 1799 to 1815)

Jackson, Major Basil, 'Letter' on the commencement of the campaign, *USJ*, 1841 Pt II, August, pp. 541–2

Jackson, Lt.-Colonel Basil, *Notes and Reminiscences of a Staff Officer*, (1877), ed. R. C. Seaton, 1903

James, W., *The Naval History of Great Britain*, vol. vi, 1837

James, Lt.-Colonel W. H., *The Campaign of 1815*, 1908

Jerome Bonaparte, *Les Mémoires et Correspondance du Roi Jérome et de la Reine Catherine*, ed. A. du Casse, vol. 7, Paris, 1866

Jomini, Baron Antoine, *The Art of War*, Eng. trans. 1862, repr. 1992

———, *Précis Politique et Militaire de la Campagne de 1815*, Paris, 1839

———, *Campagne de 1815, Correspondance de Jomini avec le duc d'Elchingen (extrait du 'Spectateur Militaire')*, Paris, 1841 (following the publication of *Documents Inédits*).

Jones, George, *Waterloo: see* Booth

Jourdan, Marshal, *Mémoires*, Paris, 1899 (not involved in the 1815 campaign, but a shrewd observer of French strengths and weaknesses in Iberia and of Napoleon's system of war).

Kaufman, Dr Alfred, 'Information in War, a Commentary on a Text by Clausewitz', in *RUSI Defence Systems*, vol. 8 (2), pp. 23–5, Autumn 2005

Keith, Admiral Viscount, *The Keith Papers*, vol. iii, ed. C. Lloyd, Navy Records Soc., 1955

Kelly, W. Hyde, *The Battle of Wavre, and Grouchy's Retreat*, 1905

Keppel, Ensign G. T.: *see* Albemarle

Kerry, Earl of (later 6th Marquess of Lansdowne), *The First Napoleon: some unpublished documents from the Bowood papers*, 1925 (the 4th Marquess married the daughter of General Flahaut – who himself had married the daughter of Adm. Viscount Keith – and on marriage inherited their papers)

Kincaid, Captain J., *Adventures in the Rifle Brigade,* 1830, repr. from 2nd edn. 1838, 'Soldiers' Tales Series', 1929

Knight, Roger, *The Pursuit of Victory: the Life and Achievement of Horatio Nelson,* 2005

Kurtz, Harold, *The Trial of Marshal Ney,* 1957

Lacour-Gayet, G., *Napoléon,* Paris, 1921

———, *Talleyrand,* 4 vols, Paris, 1928–34 (one of the best of the older biographies, using unpublished papers destroyed during World War II; *see also* Waresquiel)

Lamartine, A. de, *Histoire de la Restauration,* Paris, 8 vols, 1852 (vol. 5 deals with the period from 24 June 1815 to the summer White Terror)

Lanzac de Laborie, *La Domination française en Belgique: Directoire, Consulat, Empire,* 2 vols, Paris, 1895

Larpent, F. S., *The Private Journal of F. S. Larpent,* 3rd edn., 1854 (insights on Wellington in the Peninsula).

Las Cases, Comte de, *Le Mémorial de Sainte-Hélène* (fundamental to the success of the Myth when first published in 1823; I have used the critical annotated edition by Marcel Dunan, 2 vols, Paris, 1951)

Laws, L.-Colonel M. E. S., *Battery Records of the Royal Artillery, 1716–1859,* 1952

Lecestre, Léon, *Lettres Inédites de Napoléon I,* 2 vols, Paris, 1897

Leeke, Revd William, *The History of Lord Seaton's Regiment at Waterloo,* 2 vols, 1866, and Supplementary volume, 1871 (a work by a former ensign that insists on an extreme point of view to the extent that I believe it defeats its own object: literary clergymen with monomania can be pestilential. Lord Seaton's own views were much saner: *see* Moore Smith)

Leggiere, Michael V., *Blücher: Scourge of Napoleon,* Norman, Oklahoma, 2014

Lemoinne, John, *Wellington, from a French Point of View,* 1852 (the author, a contributor to *Le Journal des Débats,* translated into English his appreciation written originally for that paper)

Lenient, E., *La Solution des Enigmes de Waterloo,* Paris, 1915 (a stimulating if extreme critique of almost all historians of Waterloo)

Lennox, Lord William Pitt, *A Memoir of the 5th Duke of Richmond,* 1862

———, *Fifty Years' Biographical Reminiscences,* 2 vols, 1863

Lentz, Thierry, *Nouvelle Histoire du Premier Empire,* vol. iv, *Les Cent-Jours, 1815,* Paris, 2010

Letters from the Battle of Waterloo, ed. Gareth Glover, 2004 (LW – *see also Waterloo Archive* and *Waterloo Letters*)

Lettow-Vorbeck, General O. von, *Napoleons Untergang, 1815,* vol. 1, Berlin, 1904 (the General Staff historian for the War of Liberation continued his account into 1815, but although more careful than Ollech in his handling of documents he was a tired man whose treatment of the campaign is too slight; he died just as vol. 1 was published: Voss compiled the second and post Waterloo volume.)

———, 'Das Zietenische Tagebuch für den Feldzug von 1815', *JFDAM,* Berlin, Jan-Jun 1903, pp. 436–9. (a major critique of Ziethen's reminiscences: see Hafner and Pedlow)

———: *see also* Voss

Lettres inédites de Napoléon à Marie-Louise, 1810–1814, Paris, 1935 (see also *Marie-Louise*)

Levavasseur, Octave, *Souvenirs Militaires, 1802–1815,* Paris, 1914

Lever, Charles J., novelist, *The Confessions of Harry Lorrequer*, 1839, chap. 30 (Capt. Trevanion and the French chasseur Capt. Gendémar at the Café Philidor in Paris, 1815)

Lieven, Dominic, *Russia Against Napoleon*, 2009

Lipscombe, Nick, *Wellington's Guns*, 2013

Logie, J., 'Le Journal de Constant Rebecque', in *Mélanges Historiques sur Napoléon, Wellington, Waterloo* (Soc. d'Etudes Hist. de Waterloo, Braine l'Alleud, 1970)

———, *Waterloo, La Campagne de 1815*, Brussels, 2003

Longford, Elizabeth (Lady), *Wellington, The Years of the Sword*, 1969

Louis XVIII et les Cent Jours à Gand: *see* Romberg & Malet

Lyon, David, *The Sailing Navy List, (RN) 1688–1860*, 1993

Mackenzie, Norman, *The Escape from Elba*, 1982

Mackworth, Sir Digby, 'Waterloo Diary', *Army Quarterly*, vol. 35, Oct 1937, Jan 1938, pp. 123–31, 320–7

Madan, Spencer, *Spencer at Waterloo: the Letters of Spencer Madan, 1814–1816*, edited by B. Madan, 1970

Maitland, Rear Adm. Sir Frederick Lewis, *The Surrender of Napoleon*, 1904 (reprint of *Narrative of the Surrender of Buonaparte*, 1826)

Malmesbury, 1st Earl of, *Letters of the 1st Earl of Malmesbury, his family and friends*, 2 vols, 1870 (Letters of Captain, later General Sir, George Bowles)

Marchand, L. J. N., premier valet de chambre, *Mémoires*, 2 vols, Paris, 1952–55.

Marie-Louise à Napoléon, 1813–14, Paris, 1955 (the counter-part to his *Lettres inédites*)

Martin, Adm. of the Fleet Sir T. Byam, *Letters and Papers*, volume iii, Navy Records Soc., 1903

Martinien, A., *Tableaux des Officiers Tués et Blessés, 1805–1815*, Paris, 1899, repr. 1982 (extremely useful, but formulated by regiment and within that by day)

Masson, Frédéric, *Napoléon à Ste-Hélène*, Paris, 1912 (The most dedicated of all enthusiasts and the most extreme: Geyl's assessment of him seems fair.)

———, *Napoléon et sa Famille*, vol. xi (1815), Paris, 1914

Mauduit, Hippolyte de, *Les Dernières Jours de la Grande Armée*, 2 vols, Paris, 1847–8

Maurice, Colonel (later Maj.-General Sir) J. F., 'Waterloo', seven articles in *United Service Magazine*, New Series, vol. 1, April–Sept. 1890, pp. 61–81, 137–52, 257–63, 344–55, 533–50, and vol. 2, Oct 1890 and Jan 1891, pp. 73–9, 330–9

Maxwell, Sir Herbert, *The Life of Wellington*, 2 vols, 1900

———, 'Our Allies at Waterloo', *The Nineteenth Century*, vol. 48, Sept 1900, pp. 407–22 (*see also* Oman)

May, Captain E. S., 'A Prussian Gunner's Adventures in 1815' (Captain Reuter), *United Service Magazine*, (NS) vol. 4, Oct 1891, pp. 43–50

Méneval, Baron C. F. de, *Mémoires*, 3 vols, Paris, 1894 (Napoleon's secretary on their working methods)

Mercer, General Cavalié, *Journal of the Waterloo Campaign*, 1870, and in 'Soldiers' Tales Series', 1927.

Metternich, Prince, *Mémoires, Documents, et Ecrits divers*, vol. ii, Paris, 1880 (an English translation, *Memoirs, 1773–1815*, vol. ii, has different pagination)

Meulenaere, Philippe de, *Bibliographie Analytique des Témoinages Oculaires Imprimés de la Campagne de Waterloo*, Paris, 2004 (a massive annotated bibliography of everything published in French, English, Dutch and German)

Militär Wochenblatt, Berlin, from 1816 onwards, especially volumes 30, 31 and 36, 1846–1852 (the Prussian Army's weekly gazette, including articles by veterans of 1815)

Miller, Colonel David, *Lady De Lancey at Waterloo*, 2000

———, *The Duchess of Richmond's Ball*, 2005

———, 'In Support of Wellington's Army: the Royal Navy's Contribution to the Waterloo Campaign', *JSAHR*, vol. 86, 2008, pp. 286–96

Miot de Melito, Comte, *Mémoires*, 3 vols, Paris, 1858 (vol. i contains the remarkable interview with Bonaparte, 1797)

Mitchell, B. R. & Deane, P., *Abstract of British Historical Statistics*, 1962

Mitchell, Lt.-Col. (later Maj.-Gen.) J., *The Fall of Napoleon, an historical memoir*, 3 vols, 1845, (Book Four covers from Elba onwards, an interesting early study of foreign sources, yet Chesney in 1868 made no reference to it.)

Mittelacher, Martin, 'The Nassauers at Hougoumont', *JSAHR*, vol. 81, 2003, pp. 228–42

Mollien, Comte, *Mémoires d'un Ministre du Trésor Public*, 3 vols, Paris, 1898

Moltke the Elder, *Moltke on the Art of War, selected writings*, ed. D. J. Hughes, Presidio, USA, 1993

Montchenu, Marquis de, *La Captivité de Ste-Hélène, d'après les rapports inédits du*, ed. G. Firmin-Didot, Paris, 1894 (the French royalist observer at St Helena)

Montholon, General, *Histoire de la Captivité de Ste-Hélène*, 3 vols, Brussels, 1846 (vol. i deals with the *Bellerophon* episode)

Moore Smith, G. C., *The Life of John Colborne, F.-M. Lord Seaton*, 1903

Müffling, Baron C. von, *Memoirs*, 1997 (repr of 1853 Eng. trans. of *Aus meinem Leben*, Berlin, 1851)

Müffling (writing under the initials C. de M.), *History of the Campaign in 1815*, 1816, repr. 1983 (German language edition not pub. until 1817)

Muir, R., & Burnham R., & Muir, H., & McGuigan, R., *Inside Wellington's Peninsular Army, 1808–1814*, 2006 (a companion – but more than a companion – to Oman's *Wellington's Army*).

Muir, Rory, *Wellington*, 2 vols, Yale, 2013–15 (the period covered in my work is dealt with in the first hundred pages of the second volume).

Myatt, F., *Peninsular General: Sir Thomas Picton, 1758–1815*, 1980

Napoleon I, *Correspondance*, 32 vols (including the writings at St Helena in vols 29–32), Paris, 1858–70; vol. 27 covers 1814, and 28 covers 1815; vol. 31 contains Napoleon's memoir of the Campaign of 1815, published in Paris in 1820 under the title 'Mémoires pour servir à l'Histoire de France en 1815', unattributed but clearly the work of Napoleon. Page references to the *Correspondance* are given both to the 4to edition (1869) and the 8vo edition (1870). (See also Bretonne, Lecestre, *Inédits Napoléoniens, Ordres et Apostilles,* and *Lettres inédites*; the Fondation Napoléon's great new *Napoléon, Correspondance Générale* that began to appear in 2004 has now reached early 1813 with Tome xiii published in 2016, so there may be fresh discoveries to come for 1815.)

Napoléon, De la Guerre, ed. B. Colson, Paris, 2011 (a brilliant selection of the Emperor's words, formatted by sections as in Clausewitz's *On War*; perceptively reviewed by Prof. B. Heuser, *J. RUSI*, vol. 157 (2), 2012)

Naval Intelligence Division, *Geographical Handbook of Belgium*, B.R. 521, 1944

Navy List, The, edition corrected to 30 June 1815

Neue Deutsche Biographie, Munich, 1955-

New Cambridge Modern History, The, vol. ix, *War and Peace in an Age of Upheaval, 1793–1830*, ed. C. W. Crawley, 1965 (*NCMH*)

Noailles, M. de, *Le Comte Molé*, Paris, 1922

Nollet (Fabert), Jules, *Biographie du Général Drouot*, Paris, 1850

Nostitz, Count (ADC to Blücher in 1815), Memoir of his Career, in *Kriegsgeschichtliche-Einzelschriften*, Heft 5 and (more especially) 6, Berlin, 1885

Odeleben, Baron von, *The Campaign in Saxony in 1813*, Eng. trans., 2 vols, 1820 (This Saxon officer was attached to Napoleon's headquarters in 1813: vol. 1, chap. 2 contains a valuable appreciation of the Emperor's working habits.)

O'Grady, Lieut (later Lt.-Col). Standish: *see* Barrett

Oldfield, Major John, RE, Manuscript Account (now in *The Waterloo Archive*, vol. vi)

Ollech, General C. von, *Geschichte des Feldzuges von 1815*, Berlin, 1876 (still useful together with Lettow-Vorbeck)

Oman, (Sir) Charles, *History of the Peninsular War*, 7 vols, 1902–30 (this enduring masterpiece is full of insights on the men who were to serve in the 1815 campaign: Soult, Reille, Suchet, etc.)

———, *Wellington's Army*, 1912

———, 'The Dutch–Belgians at Waterloo', *The Nineteenth Century*, vol. 48, Oct 1900, pp. 629–38 (*see also* Maxwell)

———, 'French Losses in the Waterloo Campaign', *EHR*, vol. 19, 1904, pp. 681–93, and vol. 21, 1906, pp. 132–5

O'Meara, Barry, *A Voice from St Helena*, 2 vols, 1822

Ompteda Memoir, *A Hanoverian-English Officer a Hundred Years Ago*, assembled and ed. by L. von Ompteda, Eng. trans., 1892

Ordres et Apostilles de Napoléon, ed. A Chuquet, 4 vols, Paris, 1911–12 (each vol. runs from 1799 to 1815)

Paget, Julian & Saunders, Derek, *Hougoumont, the key to victory at Waterloo*, 1992

Pallain, G., *Correspondance inédite de Talleyrand and et Louis XVIII pendant le Congrès de Vienne*, Paris, 1881 (Eng. trans., in 2 vols, 1881)

Parkinson, Roger, *The Hussar General* (Blücher), 1975

Parliamentary Debates, ed. T. C. Hansard, 1815: vol. xxix (session of 8 Nov.–1 Dec. 1814), xxx (9 Feb.–28 April 1815), xxxi (2 May–12 July 1815)

Pasquier, E. D., *Mémoires du Chancelier Pasquier*, Paris, 6 vols, 1893–5: Part 1, vol. iii, deals with 1814–15

Pedlow, G. W., 'Back to the Sources: Gen. Zieten's Message to Wellington, 15 June 1815', *First Empire*, No. 82, May/June 2005, pp. 30–6 (The contrasting versions by Pflugk-Harttung and Hofschröer)

Pétiet, General A., *Souvenirs Militaires*, Paris, 1844

Petit, General J.-M., 'Account of the Waterloo Campaign', *EHR*, vol. 18, 1903, pp. 321–6

Petty, S., 'Wellington's General Orders, 1808–14', pp. 139–63 in Woolgar, vol. 1 (*which see*)

Pfister, A., Maj.-Gen., *Aus dem Lager der Verbündeten, 1814–1815*, Stuttgart, 1897 (An interesting Württemberg viewpoint, as distinct from a Prussian one; and with a crucial letter dated 15 June by General von Hügel.)

Pflugk-Harttung, J. von, *Vorgeschichte der Schlacht bei Belle-Alliance: Wellington*, Berlin, 1903 (The best and most closely reasoned Prussian account of the prelude to Waterloo, based upon detailed researches in the archives that resulted in all the Pflugk-Harttung articles listed below.)

———, 'Der Verhandlungen Wellingtons und Blüchers auf der Windmühle bei Brye', *Historisches Jahrbuch*, vol. xxiii, Munich, 1902, pp. 41–61

———, 'Die preussische Berichterstattung an Wellington vor der Schlacht bei Ligny', *Historisches Jahrbuch*, vol. xxiv, Munich, 1903, pp. 80–97

———, 'Zu Blüchers Brief an den König von Preussen vom 17 Juni 1815', *JFDAM*, Berlin, Jan.–Jun. 1904, pp. 219–21

———, 'Das I preussische Korps bei Belle-Alliance', *JFDAM*, Berlin, Jan.–Jun. 1905, pp. 143–68; 209–39

———, 'Archivalische Beiträge zur Geschichte des Feldzuges 1815, 16–24 Juni 1815', *JFDAM*, Berlin, Jul.–Dec. 1906, pp. 509–22, 608–24

———, 'Das I Korps Zieten bei Belle-Alliance und Wavre', *JFDAM*, Berlin, Jan.–Jun. 1908, pp. 196–209.

———, 'Von Wavre bis Belle-Alliance (18. Juni)', *JFDAM*, Berlin, Jan.–Jun. 1908, pp. 413–24; 500–12; 613–35 ('Von Wavre')

———, *Das Preussische Heer und die Norddeutschen Bundestruppen unter General von Kleist, 1815*, Gotha, 1911 (*Bundestruppen*)

Pollio, General A., *Waterloo (1815), avec de nouveaux documents*, Paris, 1908 (trans. of original Italian edn., Rome, 1906)

Porter, Maj.-General W., *History of the Corps of Royal Engineers*, vol. i, 1889

Pozzo di Borgo, *Correspondance diplomatique du Pozzo di Borgo avec Nesselrode, 1814–1818*, 2 vols, Paris, 1890

Pradt, Abbé de, *Histoire de l'Ambassade dans le Grande Duché de Varsovie en 1812*, 2nd edn., Paris, 1815

Reinhardt, Madame, *Une Femme de Diplomate*, letters trans. and ed. by her grand-daughter Baronne de Wimpffen for Soc. d'Hist. Contemporaine, Paris, 1900

Roberts, Andrew, *Napoleon and Wellington*, 2001

———, *Waterloo, Napoleon's Last Gamble*, 2005

Robinson, Maj.-General (Sir) C. W., 'Waterloo and the De Lancey Memorandum', *Journal of the RUSI*, vol. 54, May 1910, pp. 582–97. Also in *First Empire*, No. 84, Sept/Oct 2005, pp. 9–18.

Robinson, H. B., *Memoirs of Lt.-General Sir Thomas Picton, GCB*, 2 vols, 1836

Robinson, Mike, *The Battle of Quatre Bras, 1815*, 2008

Rodger, N. A. M., *The Command of the Ocean: A Naval History of Britain, 1649–1815*, 2004

Romberg, E. & Malet, A., eds, *Louis XVIII et les Cent Jours à Gand*, 2 vols, Soc. d'Hist. Contemporaine, Paris, 1898–1902

Ropes, John Codman, *The Campaign of Waterloo*, repr. 1995 from 1893 original edn

Rose, J. Holland, *Life of Napoleon I*, 2 vols, 1904

———, *Pitt and Napoleon*, 1912

———, *Napoleonic Studies*, 1904

———, *The Personality of Napoleon*, 1912, repr. 1929

———, 'Sir Hudson Lowe and the Beginnings of the Campaign of 1815', *EHR*, vol. xvi, 1901, pp. 517–27 (Rose, *EHR*).

———, 'The Health of Napoleon during the Waterloo Campaign', *Army Quarterly*, vol. 28, July 1934, pp. 260–6

Rosebery, Lord (5th Earl of), *Napoleon, the Last Phase* (1900), rev. ed. with new introductory chapter, 1909

———, *Pitt*, in the 'Twelve English Statesmen' series, 1891
Rumigny, General Comte, *Souvenirs, 1789–1860*, Paris, 1921
Russell, Earl, *The Early Correspondence of Lord John Russell, 1805–40*, vol. i, 1913 (visit to Elba)

Saager, Adolf, *Blüchers Briefe an seiner Frau*, Stuttgart, n.d.
Sale, Nigel, 'More Controversy from Waterloo' (the 52nd and the defeat of the *Garde*), *RUSI Journal*, vol. 150 (4), Aug 2005, pp. 66–71; with correspondence on the controversy in vols 150 (6), pp. 7–8 (N. Evans), 151 (2) of 2006, p. 10 (N. Sale), and 151 (3), p. 8 (J. Hussey).
Salle, General Baron de, *Souvenirs*, in *Revue de Paris*, 15 Jan 1895, pp. 407–37
Savary, J. M. R., Duc de Rovigo, *Mémoires*, vol. 8, Paris, 1828
Schroeder, Paul W., *The Transformation of European Politics, 1763–1848* (Oxford History of Modern Europe), 1994
Schuermans, Albert, *Itinéraire Générale de Napoleon 1er*, Paris, 1908
Schwarzenberg, Fürst Karl, *Feldmarschall Fürst Schwarzenberg, der Sieger von Leipzig*, Vienna, 1964
Scott, Sir Walter, *The Life of Napoleon Buonaparte*, 9 vols, 1827 (originally 'by the Author of "Waverley"'): vols viii and ix for 1815 and the aftermath
[Scott, Sir Walter], *Paul's Letters to his Kinsfolk*, 1815
Scovell, Lt.-Gen. Sir George, 'Memorandum on Waterloo' (undated, but as it quotes Brialmont–Gleig is post-1858), NA WO/37/12, reprinted in *Waterloo Archive*, vol. 3
Seaton, R. C., *Napoleon's Captivity in relation to Sir Hudson Lowe*, 1903 (in part a critique of Lord Rosebery's *Napoleon, the Last Phase*)
Ségur, General Comte de: *Histoire et Mémoires*, vol. vi, Paris, 1873
Shaw Kennedy, General Sir James, *Notes on the Battle of Waterloo*, 1865, repr. 2003
Shelley, Lady, *The Diary of Frances, Lady Shelley, 1787–1817*, ed. R. Edgcombe, 1912
Siborne, Captain W., *History of the Waterloo Campaign* (1995 repr. of *History of the War in France and Belgium in 1815*, 3rd edn., 1848)
Sidney, Revd E, *Life of Lord Hill*, 1845
Six, Georges, *Dictionnaire Biographique des Généraux et Amiraux Français, 1792–1815*, 2 vols, Paris, 1934
Smith, Digby, *The Napoleonic Wars Data Book*, 1998
Smith, Lt. Gen. Sir Harry, *Autobiography*, ed. G. C. Moore Smith, 2 vols, 1902
Snapper, Dr Frits, 'The Netherlands Heavy Cavalry Brigade's refusal to attack as ordered by Lord Uxbridge', an English translation from an article in *Mars et Historia* (The Hague), xxxv, Nr. 4, Oct.–Dec. 2001
Sorel, Albert, *L'Europe et la Révolution française*, 8 vols, Paris, 1885–1904 (the fourth volume reaches 1795, the final volume (1812–15) is slight, the year 1815 being given a hundred pages. Geyl rightly notes the final volume's weakness: 'his thesis has to be defended from beginning to end, against overwhelming odds in the shape of facts and probability'.)
Soult, Marshal, *Mémoire Justificatif*, Paris, 1815 (a 33-page pamphlet in Brit. Lib. volume, 'Tracts, France, 1815: 934.c.17(3)')
Sperling, Lieut, John, RE, *Letters from an Officer of the Corps of Engineers, 1813–16*, ed. G. Glover, 2011 – see also *Waterloo Archive*, vi
Stanhope, Philip, 5th Earl (previously Lord Mahon), *Conversations with the Duke of Wellington*, 1881, 'World Classics' edition, 1938
Starklof, R., *Das Leben des Herzog Bernhard von Saschen-Weimar*, vol. 1, Gotha, 1865

Stein, H. F. K., *Freiherr vom Stein, Briefe und Amtliche Schriften*, ed. Botzenhart & Hubatsch, vol. 5, Stuttgart, 1964
Stocqueler, J. H., *A Personal History of the Horse Guards, 1752–1872*, 1873
Strafford, Alice, Countess of, *Personal Reminiscences* – see Ellesmere
Sweetman, John, *Raglan, from the Peninsula to the Crimea*, 1993

Talleyrand, Prince de, *Mémoires*, ed. Duc de Broglie, 5 vols, Paris, 1891–2 (The published text was entirely from a copy in the hand of A. Bacourt, guaranteed authentic by Talleyrand's niece, both being executors. It was the subject of long debate in the *Revue Historique* of 1892, vol. 48, pp. 72–80, 299–316; vol. 49, pp. 69–99. Lacour-Gayet's *Talleyrand*, iv, chaps 4 and 28, using some rediscovered fragments of the original MSS, shows by comparison that the executors piously altered and extensively garbled significant passages in the *Mémoires*, i, pp. 125–36, 325–390.) For Talleyrand's authentic letters, see also P. Bertrand (1889) and G. Pallain (1881)
Temperley, Harold, *Life of Canning*, 1905
Thiers, Adolphe, *Histoire du Consulat et de l'Empire*, vol. 20, Paris, 1862
Thiry, Jean, *La Chute de Napoléon 1er*, 2 vols, Paris, 1938–9
Thompson, Neville, *Lord Bathurst and the British Empire, 1762–1834*, 1999
Thurn und Taxis, Prince, see item 3 in Pflugk-Harttung, J. von, 'Archivalische Beiträge', pp. 608–24
Tomkinson, Lt.-Col. W., *The Diary of a Cavalry Officer, 1809–15*, 1895, repr. 1999
Torrens, Lt.-Col. Robert, 'A Waterloo Letter' (1 Oct. 1815), *Monthly Review*, July 1914, vol. 63, pp. 834–49
Tournès, Lt.-Col. René, 'Le GQG de Napoléon 1er', *Revue de Paris*, 1 May 1921, pp. 134–58
Tulard, Jean, *Le Grand Empire, 1804–1815*, 2nd edn., Paris, 2009
Tupper Carey, Commissary-General, 'Reminiscences', *Cornhill Magazine*, vol. 6, New Series, June 1899, pp. 724–38

Uffindell, Andrew, *The Eagle's Last Triumph: Napoleon's Victory at Ligny, June 1815*, 1994
———, 'Friendly Fire at Waterloo', *British Army Review*, No 116, Aug 1997, pp. 65–77
Uffindell, Andrew, & Corum, Michael, *On the Fields of Glory: the battlefields of the 1815 campaign*, 1996
Unger, Lt.-Gen. W. von, *Blücher*, 2 vols, Berlin, 1908

Vandal, Albert, *L'Avènement de Bonaparte*, 2 vols, Paris, 1903-07
Vandeleur, John, *The Letters of Colonel John Vandeleur, 1810–1846*, privately printed 1894
Van Danzig, Barry, *Who Won Waterloo? The Trial of Captain Siborne*, 2006
Vick, Brian E., *The Congress of Vienna: Power and Politics after Napoleon*, 2014
Victoires, Conquêtes, etc., des français, 1792–1815, 28 vols, Paris, 1817–27; vol. xxiv (1821) deals with the Hundred Days
Vidal de la Blache, Captain, *L'Evacuation de l'Espagne, et l'invasion dans le Midi, 1813–1814*, 2 vols, Paris, 1914 (insights into relations between the French Peninsular generals)
Vivian, Hon. Claud, *Richard Hussey Vivian, a Memoir*, 1897
Vivian, Sir R. H. (later Lord), 'Reply to Gawler's Crisis at Waterloo', *USJ*, July 1833, pp. 310–24
———, '(Second) Reply to Major Gawler', *USJ*, Sept 1833, pp. 145–9
Voss, Major-General von, *Napoleons Untergang, 1815*, vol. 2, Berlin, 1906 (the concluding volume of Lettow-Vorbeck's work, left unfinished at his death in 1904)

Wagner, August, *Plane der Schlachten und Treffen, 1813, 1814, 1815*, 5 vols, Berlin, 1825: vol. 4 for 1815

Waldie, Charlotte Ann, *Narrative of a Residence in Belgium during the Campaign of 1815 . . . by an Englishwoman*, 1817; repr. 1853 with her married name Mrs Eaton, and entitled *Days of Battle*

Ward, S. G. P., *Wellington's Headquarters*, 1957

Waresquiel, E. de, *Talleyrand, le prince immobile*, Paris, 2003

Waterloo Archive, The, ed. Gareth Glover, 6 vols, 2010–14 (WA)

Waterloo Letters, ed. Major-General H. T. Siborne, 1891 (WL)

Waterloo Papers, 1815 and Beyond, ed. E. Owen, 1998

Webster, Sir Charles, ed., 'Some Letters of the Duke of Wellington to his Brother', *Camden Miscellany*, vol. 18, in Royal Historical Society/Camden Society, Third Series, vol. 79, 1948

Weil, M.-H., *Les Dessous du Congrès de Vienne*, 2 vols, Paris, 1917 (reports of the Austrian secret police on the Congress)

Weller, Jac, *Wellington at Waterloo*, 1967

Wellington, Commander, ed. Paddy Griffith, 1985 (essays by various military historians)

Wellington Despatches, 1799–1818, ed. Colonel J. Gurwood, 12 vols plus index vol., 1834–8 (also revised and re-issued in 8 vols, 1847, and again in 8 vols, 1852)

Wellington Supplementary Despatches, ed. 2nd Duke of Wellington, 14 vols, 1857–1873; vol. x covers 1815, and xiv has addenda for that year

Welschinger, H., *Le Maréchal Ney: 1815*, Paris, 2nd edn., 1893 (mainly concerned with Ney's political troubles, trial and execution)

Wheatley, E., *The Wheatley Diary*, ed. C. Hibbert, 1964

Wildman, Captain T., 'Letter on Waterloo, 19 June 1815', *The Listener*, vol. 51, 24 June 1954, pp. 1085–7, and now in *The Waterloo Archive*, vol. vi

Williams, Helen Maria, *Narrative of the Events in France from the landing of Napoleon Bonaparte till the Restoration of Louis XVIII*, 1815

de Wit, Pierre, 'Waterloo, 1815', a series of excellent studies with a massive collection of transcripts in different languages, regularly updated 2004–15, on his website www.waterloo-campaign.nl

With Napoleon at Waterloo, and papers of the late E. B. Low, ed. Mackenzie Macbride, 1911 (material by or about Hougoumont, the Scots Greys [J. Dickson], Sgt. Robertson, Life Guardsman Shaw, Napoleon's ADC [Jardin Ainé])

Wood, General (F. M.) Sir Evelyn, VC, *Cavalry in the Waterloo Campaign*, 1895

Woolgar, C. M., ed., *Wellington Studies*, 4 vols, 1996–2008

———, 'Wellington, His Papers and the Nineteenth Century revolution in Communication' inaugural lecture, 2009

Wrottesley, G., *The Life and Correspondence of F. M. Sir John Burgoyne*, vol. i, 1873

Yonge, C. D., *Life and Administration of the 2nd Earl of Liverpool*, vol. 2, 1868

Young, J. C., *A Memoir of Charles Mayne Young, tragedian*, 1871

Ziethen, General, see for his reminiscences: Hafner, Hussey (*JSAHR*, 1999), Lettow-Vorbeck (*JFDAM*, 1903), Pedlow; and more generally Pflugk-Harttung (*Vorgeschichte*, and *JFDAM*, 1905) and Maurice (*USM*, October 1890)

Index

Entries for Chapter 52, Retrospect, pages 366–89, are occasionally summaries of earlier entries. Titles, offices, and military ranks are those of 1815. Entries for senior officers, e.g. Picton of 5th Division, can also apply to their formations.